WORLD ENCYCLOPEDIA
OF
ANIMALS

WORLD ENCYCLOPEDIA
OF
ANIMALS

Elena Marcon & Manuel Mongini

Illustrations by Sergio, in association
with Lorenzo Orlandi

Greenwich House
New York

Acknowledgments

Photographs were kindly supplied by the following sources:
H. Chaumeton 22, 23t, 23, 97, 117t, 117, 120; B. Coleman 240, 319,
(R. Austing) 139, (J. & D. Bartlett) 173t, 177, (J. Burton) 262,
(R.I.M. Campbell) 293, (B.J. Coates) 241, (G. Cubitt) 272,
(A. Davis) 61, (Duscher) 216, (F. Erize) 285, (R. Gillmor) 180t,
(U. Hirsch) 180, (J. Markham) 151, (Oxford Scientific Films) 139,
(H. Reinhard) 330, (S. Trevor) 292t (J. Van Wormer) 303; Foto
Archivio B 10; IGDA (Donnini) 16, Giacomelli) 10t, (E.
Giovenzana) 20, (La Palude) 92, (C. Rives) 13, Jacana (Arthus-
Bertrand) 286t, (L. Chana) 292, (L.S. Dubois) 185, (Elliot) 168,
(A. Kerneis) 96, (J.M. Labat) 166, (B. Rebouleau) 173, (Robert)
220, (J. Robert) 319t, (R. Ross) 12, (Varin-Visage) 286, 302;
Oxford Scientific Films (G.I. Bernard) 60, (S. Dalton 70).

English language edition © 1984 by Orbis Publishing Limited

Translated by Richard Lister

© 1983 by Instituto Geografico De Agostini S.p.A Novara

First published in Great Britain by Orbis Publishing Limited,
London 1984

This 1987 edition published by Greenwich House, a division of
Arlington House, Inc., distributed by Crown Publishers Inc.,
225 Park Avenue South, New York, New York 10003

Printed and bound in Hong Kong by Dai Nippon

CONTENTS

The common names of animals can be found in the index.

INTRODUCTION

We share the Earth with well over one million different kinds of animals. They range in size from the microscopic Protozoa to the gigantic blue whale —the biggest animal there has ever been. Many of these creatures are conspicuous or familiar, but there are a whole host of animals of whose existence we are largely unaware, ranging from the remote deep sea starfish to the thoroughly obscure such as the parasitic worms in a snake's nostrils. Many animals are very tiny and will even fit inside a human red blood cell, where some of them do great damage and may cause the death of their host. The malarial parasite is one such creature whose effects are out of all proportion to its size, killing more people every year than all the poisonous snakes put together. Until recently much of human history has been moulded and diverted by interactions with the animals that cause disease, those that provide food from the land and sea, and those that offer the prospect of valuable products from pearls to ivory and honey. By contrast, some animals are rare, obscure and might easily become extinct in the near future with very little consequence. Yet they too, because of their vulnerability, are internationally known and the object of energetic crusading by conservationists.

Some animals alive today are almost identical to their ancestors that lived more than two hundred million years ago, yet others have evolved in the space of only a few thousand years. There are animals living almost everywhere, from steamy jungles and torrid deserts to our own backgardens. Some live on the permanent ice of the polar regions and mountain tops; others live in eternal darkness underground or at the bottom of the ocean subjected to unimaginable pressures from the water above. One species, our own, has emerged from among the rest to do all these things, and has even taken the first steps towards living in other worlds.

There is no doubt that our animal neighbours are of great diversity and interest, yet we cannot know them all. How should we make sense of the multitude and not muddle worms with wombats and waxwings in some huge jungle of animal life?

To achieve order and understanding, animals are given names and put into groups, just as with humans and out of the same need for tidiness and control. We each are assigned to a nation, depending on where we were born; we all belong to tribes or clans or some other social group and we all have a family name. Each of us belongs to a family that belongs to a larger group which in turn is part of something even larger; the bigger the group, the fewer things its members have in common. The same applies to animals. The animal kingdom is divided into some two dozen or more major groups called 'phyla' and these are the principal groupings used in this book. Phyla are subdivided into classes and these in turn are split into orders. Within reach of these are one or more families which group together closely related species. An individual animal species has a double-barrelled name consisting of the genus and species name, just like our family and given names.

The classification of animals thus follows a logical series of subdivisions into smaller and smaller groups, like the branches of a huge tree. This system was devised by the Swedish naturalist Linnaeus 300 years ago at a time when Latin was the language of scholarship. Consequently the scientific names of animals and the groups to which they belong are of Latin origin and thus a little unfamiliar to us these days. Even so, the names are not difficult to recognize and they do form a logical set of mental pigeon-holes among which the multitude of animals can be distributed to help us recognize them and understand their significance and place. This book follows that same orderly structure and aims to provide an illustrated guide to the spectacular assortment of animals that are our companions and partners on this planet.

However, animal groups are not all of equal size; three-quarters of all animals are insects, mostly beetles, and there are more moths in the world than mammals. This book does not attempt to allocate space in proportion to numbers, but instead gives the emphasis to such groups as mammals and birds because of their greater familiarity and the comparative ease with which many of them can be seen. This is why vertebrates, comprising only 5 per cent of the animal kingdom (and consisting mostly of fish), actually take up half of the book. Nevertheless, all animal groups are treated here and over one thousand species are illustrated in full colour too.

PROTOZOA

The Protozoa form that part of the animal kingdom containing the smallest of all animals. Their bodies, usually of microscopic dimensions and not therefore visible to the naked eye, are in fact made up of only a single cell capable of feeding and of reproducing itself. 20,000 fossil species are known, of which the oldest go back more than 500 million years. The 45,000 species living at the present day (the known species, that is) are found wherever water is present – in the sea, in fresh water and in the soil.

Most of the Protozoa are solitary species. There exist however many 'colonial' forms. All can be either mobile or sedentary. Movement is achieved by means of either cilia or flagella – hair-like or whip-like projections – or pseudopodia ('false feet'), which are temporary finger-like projections. They live on bacteria, on algae, on protozoa of smaller dimensions, or on particles of organic matter. Many are also parasitic. The most primitive forms are autotrophic, which means that, like plants, they are able to build up the food they need from chemicals. Indeed many of them contain small green bodies called chloroplasts, which, like plants, are able to carry out photosynthesis and manufacture food sugars from carbon dioxide and water in the presence of sunlight.

There are four kinds of Protozoa: Flagellata, Sarcodina, Sporozoa and Infusoria. Most have transparent, often jelly-like bodies, but some groups possess an elegant shell or covering ornamented with spines and delicate tracery patterns.

Flagellata. The most primitive of the Protozoa belong to the Flagellata, which, as their name implies, are provided with whip-like projections on their surface (flagella). They are divided, according to the type of nutrition, into plant flagellates (Phytomastigina) and animal flagellates (Zoomastigina). The first of these are provided with chlorophyll-bearing corpuscles (chloroplasts), and so are capable of photosynthesis, like plants; for this reason botanists consider most members of this group as algae and not as part of the animal kingdom at all. They include most of the species that lead a free and independent life and such common forms as *Euglena*, *Chlamydomonas*, *Volvox* and *Peranema*.

The animal flagellates are for the most part symbiotic (that is living in mutually beneficial association) with, or parasitic on, both invertebrates and vertebrates. Among the parasites on man are, for example, *Trypanosoma gambiense* and *T. rhodesiense* of the Protomastigina group, which, distributed throughout tropical Africa, are responsible for sleeping sickness.

Individuals of the Hypermastigina, such as *Joenia annectens* (illustrated), live symbiotically in the intestines of termites, (where they play a vital role in helping to digest the wood fragments and plant material on which the termites feed), while those of the Opalinida are usually parasites in the intestines of amphibians. The Choanoflagellata on the other hand are sedentary forms living in fresh water, either as solitary individuals or in colonies.

Sarcodina. The Sarcodina include those species which both move and capture their food by means of pseudopodia (temporary finger-like projections). The group known as Lobopodia includes all the amoebae, with their characteristic soft and tubular pseudopodia which, retracting and expanding, cause them continually to change shape ('amoeba' is derived from the Greek word 'to change'). Some amoebae support themselves, feeding on algae, bacteria and even smaller protozoa; others are parasitic on other animals. Among these is *Entamoeba histolytica*, which lives in the human intestine and is the cause of amoebic dysentery.

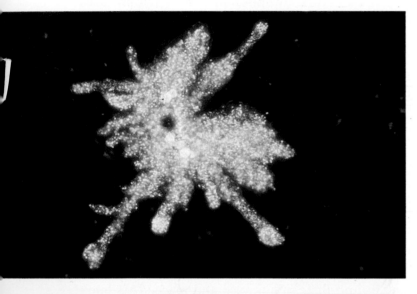

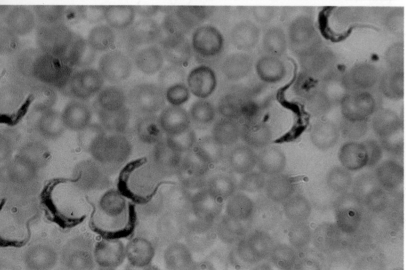

Above left Amoeba proteus, showing the finger-like pseudopodia.
Left Hook-shaped *Trypanosoma gambiense* among red blood cells.

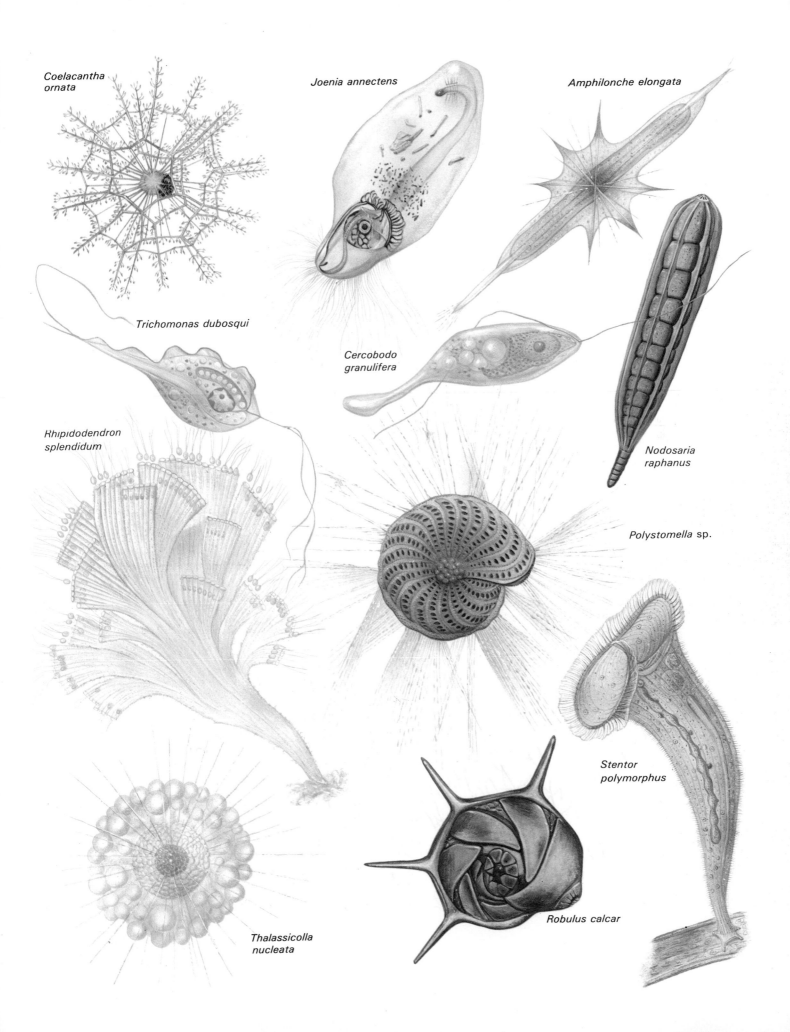

Coelacantha
ornata

Joenia annectens

Amphilonche elongata

Trichomonas dubosqui

Cercobodo
granulifera

Nodosaria
raphanus

Rhipidodendron
splendidum

Polystomella sp.

Stentor
polymorphus

Thalassicolla
nucleata

Robulus calcar

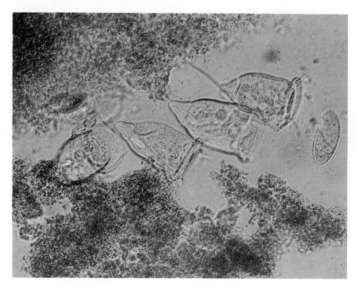

Several individuals of *Vorticella* sp., stalked ciliates.

Marine Protozoa include the Rhizopoda, which are distinguished by their root-like pseudopodia. They include the Foraminifera, which have a calcareous shell with numerous pores or perforations through which the very slender pseudopodia emerge. They mostly creep along the bottoms of the oceans, but some, including *Globigerina*, float on the surface, forming part of the abundant marine food known as plankton. After death these organisms sink to the ocean floor, and 20 to 40 per cent of the sea bed is composed of foraminiferous mud, which in some areas is principally composed of the remains of *Globigerina*. In the course of time these deposits consolidate to form limestone and chalk, which, when raised up by geological convulsions, are the material of limestone mountain ranges and chalk cliffs. Other species of Foraminifera (*see* p. 11), are of the genera *Nodosaria*, *Polystomella* and *Robulus*.

In the Actinopoda the pseudopodia, unlike those of the Rhizopoda, are stiffened by a bundle of fibres known as an axoneme. The Heliozoa, which form part of this group, live for the most part in fresh water. They have spherical bodies from which radiate the rigid pseudopodia like the rays of the sun – hence the group name 'Heliozoa' meaning 'sun animals'. They prey on other Protozoa and on the Rotifera, whose rings of waving cilia give them the appearance of minute rotating wheels.

The Radiolaria are marine Protozoa and are mostly planktonic, floating on or near the surface. Their skeletons, which are often very beautiful and complex in shape, mostly contain large amounts of silica, or occasionally other minerals such as strontium sulphate. About 5 per cent of the ocean floor is made up of radiolarian ooze. The species *Coelacantha ornata*, *Amphilonche elongata* and *Thassicolla nucleata* are illustrated on p. 11.

Sporozoa. The Sporozoa are made up of forms lacking cilia and flagella. All are parasitic. Among them are the Gregarinida, which are parasitic on invertebrates, living in the intestines of insects; Coccidia, which live in the intestines, liver and spleen of vertebrates and cause coccidiosis in domestic animals; and Haemosporidia, which are parasitic on the red blood cells of vertebrates and include *Plasmodium* which causes malaria.

Other Sporozoa are the Cnidosporidia, parasitic on worms, arthropods and fish, and Sarcosporidia, which flourish in the muscular tissues of some vertebrates.

Infusoria. The Infusoria, or Ciliophora, are the most highly evolved of the Protozoa and are distinguished by the possession of cilia, which may be present throughout their lives (Ciliata) or only in their early stages (Suctoria). The cilia are generally found in rows. *Paramecium* (or slipper animal) is often used in scientific research. The Heterotrichida are generally beautifully coloured, green, pink, blue or orange; they include the *Stentor* group (*Stentor polymorphus*) (*see* p. 11), some of which are large enough to be seen with the naked eye. Hypotrichida, with species living in both fresh and salt water, are among the most complex of the Protozoa, some containing, besides a supporting skeleton, highly developed digestive and muscular systems. The Oligotrichida include species which live symbiotically in the stomach of ruminants, such as cattle and sheep, helping to digest their food and thus playing an important role in their success. The Peritrichida include *Vorticella nebulifera*, which is common in both fresh and sea water and is provided with a peduncle or stalk by which it attaches itself to the substrate.

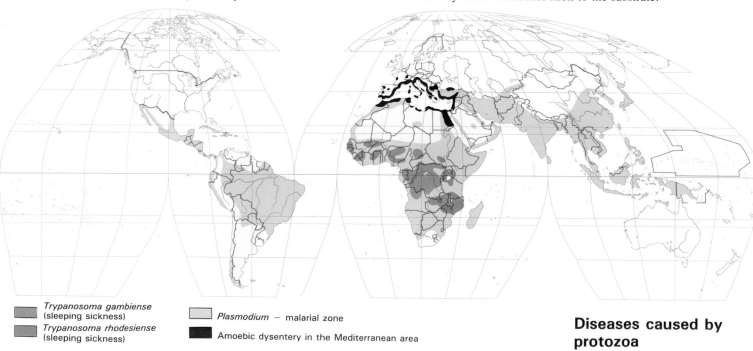

Trypanosoma gambiense (sleeping sickness)

Trypanosoma rhodesiense (sleeping sickness)

Plasmodium — malarial zone

Amoebic dysentery in the Mediterranean area

Diseases caused by protozoa

METAZOA

The Metazoa, many-celled animals, as opposed to the Protozoa, which are single-celled, include all animal organisms made up of two or more cells grouped together. They include, therefore, all animals except the Protozoa.

The activities of the cells are co-ordinated in such a manner as to guarantee the regular functioning of the organism as a whole. If the links between the various cells are destroyed it becomes impossible for life to continue. In the Metazoa the division of functions between different cells and structures becomes greater as they become more complex. Their dimensions may in some cases by microscopic but they are most often at least visible to the naked eye, ranging upwards to the positively gigantic.

Porifera

The Porifera, or sponges, are the simplest of the Metazoa. Although their cells function co-operatively as a single co-ordinated animal, they can also function as isolated cells. Sponges can be torn into pieces, yet still live and reconstitute themselves. Thus they are like colonies of Protozoans in many ways, yet, because their cells do not normally live as isolated units, but function in co-ordination with others like a single large animal, they are regarded as simple Metazoans. In the most primitive forms, which comprise the species of the smallest size, the body is radially symmetrical in the form of a sac; this encloses a central cavity which opens to the exterior through the osculum, a simple and relatively wide exit. The water penetrates into the sponge through small holes, which extend from the external surface to the internal one, and flows out by the osculum.

The flow of water is maintained by the movement of the flagella of the choanocytes, collared cells that coat the inner surface; food particles dispersed throughout the water are extracted as it passes through the sponge. The collared cells pass nutrients to wandering, amoeba-like cells that transport them to all parts of the sponge by crawling between other cells. The current of water also provides oxygen and removes wastes and carbon dioxide.

The body of the sponge is supported by skeletal spicules, minute splinter-like bodies in the gelatinous layer that separates the external epidermal layer from the internal layer of choanocytes. Most of the sponges have lost their ancestral symmetry; the body has become irregular and has been made more complicated by the bending inwards of the internal walls, with a consequent reduction in size of the central cavity. These changes have made possible a better flow of water through the body of the sponge and have enabled it to attain larger dimensions. Three kinds of sponges can be distinguished: Calcarea, Hexactinellida and Demospongiae.

Calcarea. Calcarea, or chalk sponges, are characterized by the presence of a skeleton of calcium carbonate. The most primitive sponges are of this kind and are mostly small, attaining less than 10 cm (4 in) in diameter. Exclusively marine, they inhabit for the most part shallow waters and include many that grow in rock pools and on seashells washed up on the shore.

Hexactinellida. Hexactinellida, or glass sponges, have silicaceous spicules that look like fine threads of glass and are often fused into a continuous network. Present in all the oceans, they live at depths varying from 100 m (330 ft) to 5000 m (3 miles). To this class belong, among others, the beautiful and delicate Venus flower basket (*Euplectella aspergillum*), with its characteristic net-like skeleton, and *Hyalonema sieboldi*, which is found in the seas surrounding Japan.

Demospongiae. Demospongiae, or horny sponges, have skeletons composed either of siliceous spicules or of fibres of a horny substance called spongin, and sometimes of both types together; they always live in colonies and are mostly marine.

Among various species belonging to this group are the ordinary bath-sponge (*Spongia officinalis*); Neptune's cup (*Poterion neptuni*), which can reach 2 m (over 6 ft) in diameter; and *Spongilla lacustris*, which lives in fresh water and is coloured green by the presence of algae which live on its body.

A sponge of the genus *Hemimycale.* Water enters through the numerous tiny pores and exits through the larger holes.

Coelenterata

The coelenterates, or Cnidaria – the polyps and jellyfish – are multicellular animals whose bodies have a radial or biradial symmetry and are in the form of a sac. The central cavity, which functions as an intestine, communicates with the exterior through a single aperture which serves for both the entry of food and the ejection of refuse. The coelenterates can appear in two different shapes: as polyps, fixed to the substrate, such as the common hydra of fresh waters, *Hydra vulgaris* and *H. viridis* (illustrated); and as medusae or jellyfish, capable of swimming freely. In both types the mouth is surrounded by a ring of tentacles provided with stinging cells, the cnidoblasts, used for defence and for obtaining food by paralysing suitable prey. Many coelenterates alternate between one form and another in their biological cycle. They can reproduce themselves either sexually or asexually, and often the two modes of reproduction are used alternately. The sexual mode produces a ciliate larva called a planula, which may settle and grow into a polyp; this later gives rise to more polyps or produces medusae which can reproduce sexually, forming more planulae.

Coelenterates were already existing in the Cambrian era (over 500 million years ago) and 9000 species are known, which live for the most part in the sea and above all in tropical seas. They are divided into Hydrozoa, Scyphozoa and Anthozoa.

Hydrozoa. The Hydrozoa, most of which alternate between the forms of jellyfish and polyps, are predominantly marine. Among them are the hydroids and the more showy Milleporina or millepore corals whose colonies, living in shallow tropical seas, contribute their minute calcareous skeletons to the formation of immense coral reefs. Reefs are created habitat for a multitude of other animals and plants which would otherwise have no protected place to live in on the open sandy coasts. Reefs also form whole islands (atolls). Siphonophores on the other hand, although also colonial hydroids, are inhabitants of the wide oceans, and are predatory creatures: the Portuguese man-of-war (*Physalia physalis*) of tropical seas has a bladder-like float, and *Velella* has a disc-shaped float with an upright sail to catch the winds. They drift in the surface waters, catching unwary fish in their tentacles. The poisons released by the stinging cells of these creatures are extremely powerful and can be fatal to humans. They are common on the coast of Florida and may be carried from there to the south coast of Britain by the Gulf Stream and south-westerly winds.

Scyphozoa. The Scyphozoa, commonly known as jellyfish or medusae, have a life-cycle in which the medusan stage predominates. They are found in all the seas, and their dimensions range from 2 cm (0.8 in) to 2 m (6½ ft) in diameter. In contrast to the medusae of the Hydrozoa, those of the Scyphozoa usually have brilliant colouring. The great Mediterranean jellyfish belong to this group, including *Rhizostoma pulmo* and *Pelagia noctiluca* (illustrated), the last characterized by its luminescence at night.

Anthozoa. The Anthozoa are all polyps and are divided into the Hexacorallia, whose tentacles number either six or a multiple of six, and the Octocorallia, which have eight tentacles. The sea anemones and the stony corals belong to the Hexacorallia. Sea anemones are usually solitary animals, attaching themselves to rocks by using their basal disc like a suction cup. They sometimes release themselves and move slowly to another place. Sea anemones may be classified into several groups, including the Actiniaria, or true sea anemones, of which *Bunodactis verrucosa* is illustrated here, and the Ceriantharia, of which *Cerianthus filiformis* is illustrated here. The corals commonly known as madrepores almost always live in colonies. An exception is the solitary Mediterranean madrepore (*Cariophyllia clava*, illustrated here). The colonial madrepores are the principal agents in the formation of the great coral reefs and atolls of the tropical seas, to which protozoans of the Foraminifera type also contribute. The coral reef is home to a great variety of marine life and, despite their small size, coral polyps can build huge structures.

The Octocorallia all live in colonies and include the true corals such as the red coral (*Corallium rubrum*), one of the Gorgonians, found in the Mediterranean and in the waters around Japan. Red coral has a calcareous skeleton, but other Gorgonians, known variously as the sea whips, sea feathers and sea fans (such as *Eunicella cavolinii*, illustrated here), have horny skeletons. Other corals of striking appearance are the blue corals (*Heliopora*) and the purple organ-pipe corals (*Tubipora*). One coral illustrated here is *Xenia* sp. The Pennatularia form soft colonies and are known as 'sea pens' because they look like big quill pens stuck in the sea bed (an example, *Pennatula phosphorea*, is illustrated here).

Ctenophora

The Ctenophora, or comb jellies, contain only about ninety species, mostly planktonic. They are carnivorous and are found in all the oceans both at the surface and at great depths. Similar to the jellyfish in having a gelatinous body, they differ from them in the absence of stinging cells, in the type of symmetry (their body is organized in quadrants) and in using for locomotion a set of eight vibrating 'comb plates' (bands of cilia running along the length of the body). They are known commonly as comb jellies. Most are transparent like glass, and globular in shape, but some are flattened, such as the Venus girdle (*Cestus veneris*), which is like a transparent ribbon more than 1 m (3¼ ft) long, and some are more or less oval, like *Beroë cucumis*, a predator of marine plankton.

Mesozoa

The Mesozoa form a small group of invertebrate marine parasites. Their position in the system of classification of animals is still uncertain; they are of so simple a structure that they come somewhere in between the unicellular Protozoa and the multicellular Metazoa. Some zoologists regard them as representing an evolutionary branch derived from an unknown form of Protozoon, while others believe them to be degenerate forms of flatworms and flukes. Their bodies are made up of twenty to thirty cells arranged in two layers; often the inner layer consists of a single cell which has no function other than reproduction. The function of the outer layer is digestion.

There are two kinds of Mesozoa, the Dicyemida and the Orthonectida. The Dicyemida live exclusively in the livers of cephalopods. They include *Dicyema typus* which is parasitic in the octopus. The Orthonectida, less well known and less widespread than the Dicyemida, are smaller than 1 mm (0.04 in) in length and are parasitic in echinoderms (starfish, sea urchins etc), Polychaeta (lugworms etc), nemertines (ribbon worms) and molluscs.

Recently studies have been made of an extremely simple animal, *Trichoplax adhaerans*, formed simply of two layers of cells superimposed one on the other. Some authorities have suggested it should be classified as the only known member of the Placozoa.

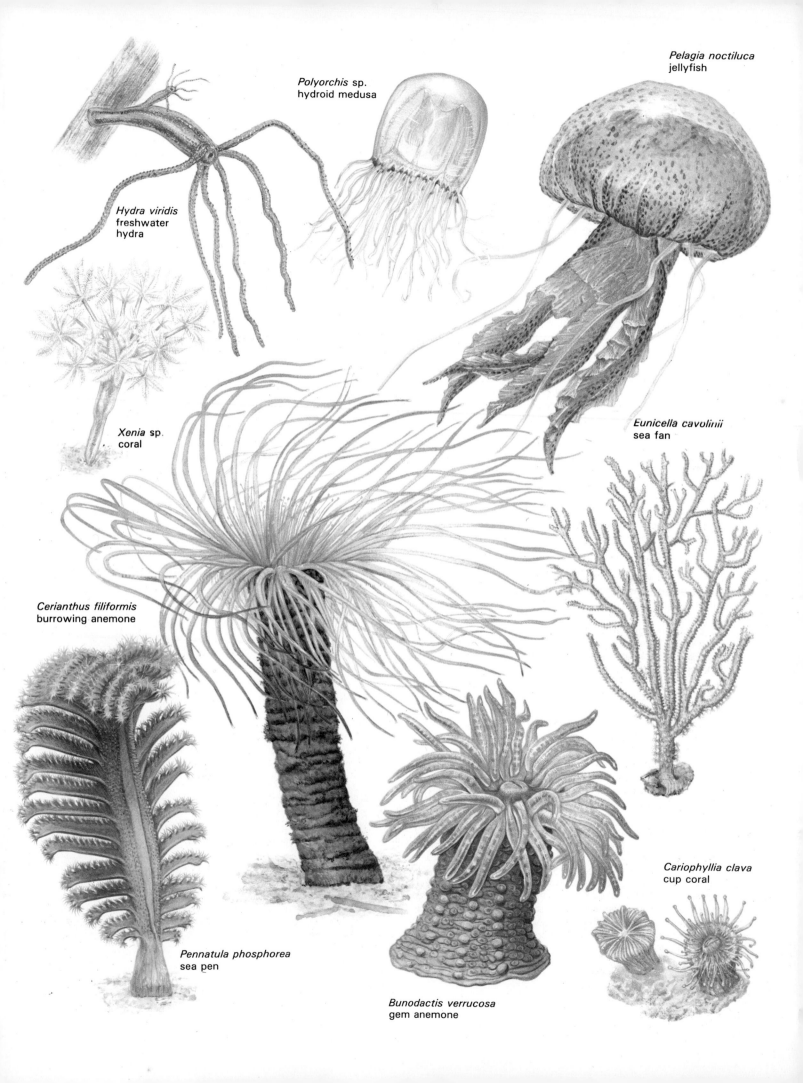

Polyorchis sp.
hydroid medusa

Pelagia noctiluca
jellyfish

Hydra viridis
freshwater
hydra

Xenia sp.
coral

Eunicella cavolinii
sea fan

Cerianthus filiformis
burrowing anemone

Cariophyllia clava
cup coral

Pennatula phosphorea
sea pen

Bunodactis verrucosa
gem anemone

Platyhelminthes

The Platyhelminthes, commonly known as flatworms, are among the first Metozoa to have bilateral symmetry: in their elongated and flattened bodies it is possible to distinguish a right-hand and a left-hand side. They have no coelom or body-cavity – the space between the intestines and the body-wall – and the spaces between the various organs are filled with a connective tissue, the parenchyma. The nervous system consists of a pair of nerve-centres (ganglia) located at the forward extremity from which issue the longitudinal nerve cords.

The sense organs (minute sensitive protuberances called tactile papillae), other sensory fibres and ocelli (simple eye-spots) are present almost exclusively in adult non-parasitic forms. The digestive apparatus, partially present in the Acoelomata but absent in all the Cestoidea or parasitic tapeworms, consists of a mouth situated in the ventral region on the underside of the body, a pharynx and a closed sac-like intestine. The cells of the intestine are provided with cilia and are phagocytic, engulfing and devouring food particles. The Platyhelminthes are usually hermaphrodites. Each individual has both male and female reproductive organs, although it is not capable of fertilizing itself. The advantage of this system is that a male does not have to seek out a female, any partner will do. The animals can exchange sperm to fertilize each other's eggs. This occurs inside the body, so fertilization is internal, whereas in coelenterates, for example, and in many other aquatic invertebrates, male and female sex cells are liberated freely into the surrounding water and fertilization occurs external to the animal. In them appears for the first time internal fecundation, effected by means of a copulatory organ. They are divided into three fairly distinct classes, Turbellaria, Trematoda and Cestoidea.

Turbellaria. The Turbellaria are very common and widely distributed animals, which lead an independent life in the sea, in fresh waters and in moist earth. They are usually carnivorous, though some are commensal, that is, associated with other animals in a less intimate relationship than that called symbiosis, and some are ectoparasitic or external parasites. Their bodies are clad in an epidermis (outer skin) provided with tiny hairs called cilia that wave to and fro to provide locomotion.

The smallest and most primitive of the Turbellaria belong to the Acoela, measuring in general from 1 mm (0.04 in) to 4 mm (0.16 in) in length. They are all marine animals and sometimes green algae live symbiotically in their tissues, as in the case of *Convoluta*, which form a green carpet on the sea bed. The largest members belong to the Triclads, which inhabit cool and temperate seas, fresh water and moist earth. Among the freshwater forms are the Planarians which live under submerged stones and in mud. The terrestrial forms are found principally in the humid soil of tropical forests and can reach remarkable lengths, sometimes attaining up to 60 cm (2 ft).

The Polycladida inhabit the rocky sea beds of the coastal regions of all the seas. This is a group of Turbellaria with more or less discoidal bodies, which in tropical forms display very vivid coloration. They are mostly active hunters and live on small marine animals: one species lives entirely on oysters and is therefore harmful to oyster-breeders.

The Gnathostomulidae, the most primitive animals possessing an apparatus for chewing food, occupy an uncertain position in the animal classification system. They measure 1–2 mm (0.04–0.08 in) in length and live in the sand and mud of the sea bed.

Trematoda. The trematodes are all parasitic, and their physiology and structure are adapted to this way of life. Most of them are provided with suckers with which to attach themselves to their hosts. Although their nervous systems and sense organs are inferior to those of other flatworms, the Trematoda, like the Cestoidea, have a highly developed reproductive apparatus and produce a great number of eggs.

They are either external parasites on fish and other creatures, whose blood they suck, or internal parasites such as *Fasciola hepatica* (liver fluke), living in the bile-ducts of grass-eating animals, and some species of *Schistosoma*, dangerous parasites in man which cause various forms of bilharzia. Different species occur in the Far East, in West Africa and in the tropical zones of America. The adults of these species live in large numbers in the intestines, blood and body cavities of humans; every day the females produce eggs in large numbers which make their way through the intestines and are passed out in the faeces.

Cestoidea. The Cestoidea, or tapeworms, are all internal parasites living in the intestines of vertebrates. They can attain 2–7 m (6–22 ft) in length and are provided at their front end with suckers and hooks with which they attach themselves to the walls of the intestine. Behind the head the body consists of many segments each of which contains a complete male and female reproductive system of its own. When they are sufficiently developed, these segments break off at the hind end of the tapeworm and are passed out with the faeces. Different species of tapeworm specialize in living with different hosts, for instance, fish, dogs, wolves or

A polyclad flatworm on the sea bed. These worms can crawl like slugs or swim with a rippling motion.

jackals. An example is the tapeworm *Diphyllobothrium*, which in its adult form lives in fish-eating birds such as grebes and gulls. Its eggs are dropped into water with the bird's faeces and hatch into larvae, which invade planktonic copepods. When these are eaten by fish, such as stickleback, young pike or salmon, the tapeworm changes again, this time into a pleurocercoid (a flat, white, straplike creature) which occupies much of the body cavity. The fish becomes swollen and is easy prey for a fish-eating bird, in whose gut the tapeworm completes its development to the adult form. This complex cycle cannot be short-circuited, and the tapeworm has to pass through each of the hosts in the correct sequence.

Nemertina

The nemertines, or ribbon worms, are made up of a group of about 600 species of worms with cylindrical bodies, often flattened and elongated, which measure from a few millimetres to some metres in length. They are also known as proboscis worms, because at the head end they have a long muscular tube or proboscis sometimes longer than the worm itself. It is attached by a retractor muscle to the wall of a fluid-filled cavity beside the intestine, and muscular contraction of the cavity wall flings the proboscis forward. The proboscis, which may be provided with a poisonous sting, is used for defence and also for the capture of food, which the proboscis will sometimes wrap itself around and paralyse with its poison.

The principal prey of the proboscis worms is annelid worms, but other invertebrates may be captured, even including fish, which are usually taken during the night hours. These are the first animals to be described that possess a digestive apparatus complete with both mouth and anus. They are mostly marine animals, living on the sea bed, where they hide under rocks or in the sand. There are a few freshwater species, and some terrestrial ones that live only in tropical and sub-tropical regions.

Entoprocta

These are creatures of small dimensions (less than 5 mm/0.2 in long) which resemble Hydroid polyps rather than worms. Their bodies are in fact made up of a stalk (peduncle) and a U-shaped opening, like the calyx of a flower, surrounded by ciliated tentacles; the mouth and anus both open into this cup-like opening. Some Entoprocta live fixed to the bodies of various animals such as sponges and corals, or on seaweeds and rocks. Most are seadwellers, but there are some freshwater varieties.

Aschelminthes

The Aschelminthes, or sac worms, comprise groups of invertebrates which differ from those described above in having a body that is less compact; they are provided with an internal cavity without true walls, in which the organs float freely. Lacking a proper head, they usually have an elongated body covered with a cuticle (tough outer skin). The group includes Gastrotricha, Rotifera, Konorhyncha, Priapulida, Nematoda and Gordiacea.

Gastrotricha. The Gastrotricha are the smallest of the multicellular animals; their cylindrical bodies, covered with cilia – at least in the ventral region – measure 0.06–1.5 mm (0.0025–0.06 in) in length. Most of them live in fresh water, even if it is poor in oxygen, and live on single-celled algae, bacteria and Protozoa; the marine species are less numerous.

Rotifera. The rotifers include forms that are very common in fresh water and of microscopic dimensions, like the Gastrotricha. Their name derives from the fact that their bodies, transparent and saclike in form, have at their forward end a ring of cilia, known as the wheel-organ: when the cilia wave to and fro, the impression is given of a wheel spinning. The rotifers are provided with a chewing organ called a 'mastax' that contains minute jaws studded with teeth. In the species that nourish themselves with particles suspended in the water (such as bacteria and algae), this organ serves to chew or grind down the food, while in the predatory forms it is adapted for grasping the prey, which is then sucked of its nutritional content.

Although a few rotifers exist in sea water (about fifty species out of more than 1500) and some live on mosses, most of the rotifers live in fresh water.

Kinorhyncha. This is a small group of exclusively marine animals, similar in appearance and dimensions to the Gastrotricha. They are distinguished from that group, however, by the absence of cilia. In addition, the cuticle that covers their bodies is divided into thirteen segments and provided with spines and bristles with which they anchor themselves to the substrate. They live in the sand and mud of coastal waters, where they feed on organic particles and unicellular algae.

Priapulida. These are exclusively marine creatures that live in the muddy sea beds of coastal regions down to depths of 100 m (330 ft). The body, which can be up to 10 cm (4 in) long, is soft, squat and cylindrical, and its bulbous front part (prosoma) is separated by a narrower neck from the trunk. The mouth, which opens into the prosoma, is surrounded by spines; the whole can be retracted into the cylindrical trunk. At the rear end the body has two appendages in the form of clusters like bunches of grapes. The Priapulida feed themselves on other sea-bed invertebrates, such as various forms of Polychaete worms. Some varieties live in Arctic and Antarctic waters, others in cool northern waters (such as around the British coasts).

Nematoda. The nematodes, or roundworms, number about 10,000 species, more than any other group of the Aschelminthes. With a slender and elongated body, they possess powerful muscles which enable them to penetrate into very narrow places, not only into cracks in the earth but also into the bodies of animals and plants. They are found everywhere, in fresh water and in the soil, where they live an independent life and are mostly less than 1 mm (0.04 in) long, and in the sea, where some species attain 5 cm (2 in) in length. The free-living species generally live on small invertebrate creatures, although some are plant-eaters and many living in the soil (referred to as eel worms) feed on the juices of plants, causing grave damage to agriculture (the rotting of potatoes and sugar beet, for example).

Many of the nematodes are parasitic on both animals and humans. Among them is the cause of childhood 'worms', *Ascaris lumbricoides*, a parasite of the small intestine. About fifty species of nematodes are parasitic on humans; some of them are fairly harmless but others cause serious disease. Among these are the filaria worms such as *Wuchereria bancrofti*, which causes blockage in the lymph vessels, leading to elephantiasis, which is characterized by immense swellings, particularly of the legs, breast and scrotum. This parasite, which is found throughout tropical and subtropical regions, is transmitted by certain species of mosquito. Another nematode dangerous to man is *Ancyclostoma duodenale*, which is about 1 cm (0.4 in) long and is found throughout Asia and also in the Mediterranean region. Another intestinal parasite, it takes blood from the organism, provoking anaemia and lung haemorrhage, and in children is often the cause of mental retardation. Other harmful nematodes include the trichina worms (*Trichinella spiralis*), which are introduced into the human body from undercooked pork; the hookworms which live in the soil and enter the human body by boring through the skin; and the guinea worms, which are parasitic on minute copepod crustacea living in fresh water and, when introduced into human beings, give rise to ulcerated skin blisters.

Nematodes parasitic on animals include some parasitic in the respiratory tracts of hens, and one, *Placentonema gigantissimum*, which is parasitic in the placenta of whales, can reach a length of 9 m (29 ft).

Gordiacea. The Gordiacea, or Nematomorpha (hairworms), are very long in relation to their diameter. They can reach up to 1 m (39 in) in length, as in *Gordius robustus*, while the diameter is often less than 1 mm (0.04 in). There are some sixty species which live for the most part in fresh water, either in streams or pools or in damp earth. Only a few species live in sea water. The adults live independent lives, but the young are parasitic in arthropods.

Acanthocephala

The Acanthocephala, or spiny-headed worms, comprise over 500 species. They are all internal parasites. They have no mouth and no digestive apparatus and, like the tapeworms, absorb their food through the surface of their body. During their life cycle they live in at least one intermediate host, always an arthropod. After this they may live in another temporary host or move on to the ultimate host, a fish, a bird or a mammal. They live in the intestines of these vertebrates, attaching themselves to the wall of the intestine by means of their proboscis, which is provided with curved spines or hooks. The proboscis can be withdrawn into the forward portion of the trunk.

Annelida

The annelids, or segmented worms, are a group of worms whose bodies are characteristically divided into a number of segments (metameres). The front segment usually forms the head and the last contains the anus. The rest are often alike, each containing a body cavity (coelom) in which all the different organs are to be found. There may however in some species be considerable specialization of function in some segments, this being most marked in the external features. The only function which is not segmental is the digestive apparatus. The body cavity is bounded by a wall called the peritoneum, and is filled with a colourless liquid which strengthens it, so functioning as a kind of liquid skeleton. In the typical annelid this fluid is surrounded by two layers of muscle, one circular and one longitudinal. Co-ordinated contractions of the two layers of muscle send waves along the body, acting on the incompressible fluid within the body cavity and resulting in forward movement of the worm. Depending on the animal's environment, and the ancillary structures such as

setae (bristles), or paddle-like extensions to the body, the muscular contractions permit the worm to swim, thrash from side to side, crawl over a soft substrate such as sand, or burrow rapidly. The entire arrangement is known as a 'hydrostatic skeleton'.

Reproduction is usually sexual; in the Polychaeta and Archiannelids the sexes are as a rule separate, but the earthworms (Oligochaeta) and leeches (Hirudinea) are hermaphrodites in which an individual possesses both male and female sexual organs, although self-fertilization rarely occurs. Many annelids possess the ability to regenerate missing parts, to varying degrees. Some can even reproduce vegetatively by budding heads from certain segments; the heads eventually break away and grow into entire new individuals. The annelid's epidermis is able to fulfil the role of both respiratory exchange surface and protective covering through the secretion of a thin, pliant but porous (to respiratory gases) cuticle. In some of the bigger polychaetes, whose environment is stagnant (oxygen-depleted) water, paired gills may be present. Often the gills have a startling bright-red appearance due to the large amounts of red oxygen-carrying haemoglobin in the blood.

Polychaeta. The polychaetes include the most primitive of the annelids, living mostly in the sea. The Errantia (clamworms, palolo worms, ragworms and leafworms) are capable of movement, attained by means of appendages called parapodia formed by a fold of the body wall extending outwards from the body, and provided with bristles (the setae characteristic of annelids). The setae of *Hermodice carunculata* (illustrated), found in the Mediterranean, have poisonous hooks which when accidentally touched break off; the poison which is discharged provokes burning sensations in the skin. Some of the mobile polychaetes (Errantia), such as *Hermione* (*H. hystrix* is illustrated here), crawl along the sea bed, while others live partly on the sea bed and partly (during the reproductive period) on the surface; among the latter are *Myrianida* (*M. fasciata* is illustrated here) and the edible palolo worm of Polynesia (*Eunice viridis*, also illustrated), which burrows into coral reefs and is noted for its breeding swarms which take place during certain phases of the moon. The posterior sexual parts of the worms become detached and swim to the surface of the sea, where they burst, and the released sexual cells fertilize each other. The heads that have been left behind later re-grow the missing parts.

The heads of some errant polychaetes bear well-developed sensory apparati in the form of eyes and sensitive tentacles; some also have an eversible proboscis equipped with powerful rasp-like teeth. The proboscis and its armoury may be used for scraping algae from the rocks in herbivorous species, and in some carnivorous forms, such as the sizeable king ragworm, the mouth-parts are employed for attacking and tearing at prey. Many fishermen have felt the bite of this worm, which can easily pierce the skin and draw blood.

The other group of Polychaeta, the Sedentaria, live in galleries excavated in the mud or sand, or, like the fan worms *Sabella* (*S. pavonina* is illustrated here), in tubes formed by cementing grains of sand together. The lateral appendages (parapodia) found in the Errantia are either rudimentary or absent, and food is conveyed to the mouth by currents of water set up by movements of the cilia and of the tentacles which surround the mouth. The Sedentaria include parchment worms and feather-duster or fan worms, which live in tubes, and lugworms (*Arenicola* − *A. marina* is illustrated here), which live in burrows in the sand or mud and are much used for bait. They swallow the mud and live on the organic matter it

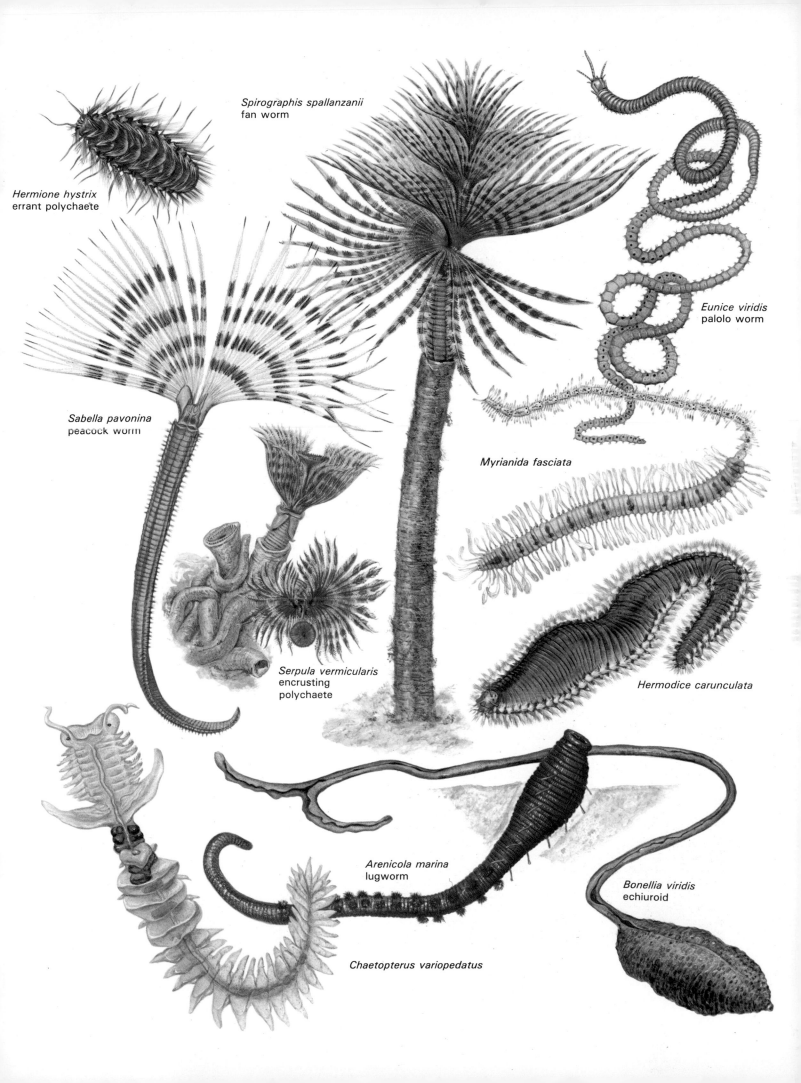

Hermione hystrix
errant polychaete

Spirographis spallanzanii
fan worm

Eunice viridis
palolo worm

Sabella pavonina
peacock worm

Myrianida fasciata

Serpula vermicularis
encrusting
polychaete

Hermodice carunculata

Arenicola marina
lugworm

Bonellia viridis
echiuroid

Chaetopterus variopedatus

contains. The *Spirorbis* and *Serpula* polychaetes (*Serpula vermicularis* is illustrated on p. 19) form the characteristic white, coiled, limestone tubes which are found as encrustations on stones on the seashore. The parchment worm, *Chaetopterus* (*C. variopedatus* is illustrated on p. 19), found in the Atlantic and the Mediterranean coastal waters, is luminescent, the luminescence emanating from a mucus covering its body. Besides the free-living forms there are some parasitic and commensal forms of Polychaeta.

Archiannelida. The archiannelids, a small group of marine worms, some parasitic, were once thought to represent the most primitive annelids, but are now thought to be descendants of oceanic polychaetes which have developed more simplified, instead of more complex, forms. They live mostly in crevices in the sea bed, but one species lives only in underground waters, such as in caverns.

Oligochaeta. The 3000 species of Oligochaeta mostly live in the soil and in the muddy bottoms of freshwater ponds and lakes, and are probably descended from marine polychaetes. All are hermaphrodites. The best known of the oligochaetes is the earthworm (*Lumbricus terrestris*), which is provided with both male and female systems as well as a clitellum; this is a swollen band surrounding the segments in the forward part of the worm and containing glands that secrete mucus. When they mate, the two worms come together head to head; sperms are released by both into grooves and are carried by mucus secreted from the clitellum from one worm to another, where they fertilize the eggs.

The tentacles of a sedentary polychaete fan worm *Spirobranchius giganteus* sweep the water for food.

Earthworms feed under the soil by swallowing the soil ahead of them, extracting any food present in it for their own nourishment, and rejecting it from their hinder ends. By excavating its galleries under the soil the earthworm aerates it and at the same time contributes by its faecal matter to its fertility. Among the terrestrial oligochaetes is the Australian giant worm (*Megascolides australis*), which can attain 3 m (10 ft) in length with diameters of 2.5 cm (1 in) or more.

Aquatic forms of Oligochaeta are much smaller in size than the terrestrial types, some being less than 1 mm (0.04 in) long. They live on the bottom of lakes and ponds with their head buried in the mud and their protruding rear end waving about as an aid to breathing. Among the aquatic forms some are parasitic. One freshwater form, *Tubifex*, is well known for its use as food for aquarium fish. In the wild it is an important food source for fish and diving ducks, being particularly common in polluted water where there is often not much else to eat.

Hirudinea. These are the most evolved of the annelids, living mostly in fresh water. There are a few marine species and some terrestrial ones which inhabit damp soil. There are about 300 species altogether; some are predatory, feeding on invertebrates, but others are external parasites that live on blood. These last attack various invertebrates and also vertebrates such as fish, birds, mammals, some species of Amphibia, snakes and crocodiles. Among them are the terrestrial blood-sucking leeches that are parasitic on birds and mammals including man. *Hirudo medicinalis*, the medicinal leech, was widely used until recent times for blood-letting. The horse-leech (*Limnatis nilotica*), so called because it sucks horses' blood, can reach up to 10 cm (4 in) in length; it is found in Europe and North Africa. The blood-sucking leeches have salivary glands which secrete an anti-coagulant; they inject it into the host in order to prevent the blood from clotting. Many can store up to ten times their own weight of blood and a single feeding may enable them to survive for several months.

Echiuroida

The spoon worms, or echiuroids, are a small group included among the annelids by some scientists but by others regarded as a distinct group of their own. They differ from the annelids in being segmented only in the embryonic stage; the rudimentary segmentation in the larvae disappears in the adult, which resembles a kind of sac with single large body cavity. There are about 150 species, all marine and most of them living along the coastlines. To this group belongs *Bonellia viridis* (illustrated on p. 19), which inhabits rocky sea beds; the sexes are separate and of widely different shapes, the females having round, plumpish bodies provided with a proboscis which may measure up to 1 m (39 in), while the male is minute, with an ovoid body measuring only 2 mm (0.08 in); it lives permanently in the excretory organ of the female.

Sipunculida

The sipunculids are a small group of marine animals which show some resemblance to the echiuroids and like them lack segmentation in the adult stage. They have a worm-like body which can measure from a few millimetres to about 50 cm (20 in) in length. There are about 250 species which live in the sand or in fissures in the rocks. They are sometimes called peanut worms.

MOLLUSCS

After the arthropods the molluscs (Mollusca) are the largest group of invertebrates, numbering more than 100,000 living species and about another 35,000 known as fossils. The first fossil evidence appears in the Cambrian era (over 500 million years ago) but the origin of these animals goes further back, to pre-Cambrian times. The earliest ancestor of the molluscs lived on the rocky beds of the shallow seas of that period. Its body was protected by a dorsal shield or shell which, besides functioning as an external skeleton, gave such an excellent protection to the animal that it has been retained in nearly all the molluscs of the present time. Only in a few groups, as in the Opisthobranchia (sea hares and sea butterflies), some of the Pulmonata and the cephalopods (nautiluses, squids, octopuses etc), is the shell either greatly reduced or absent; these molluscs, however, have adopted other systems of defence such as rapidity of swimming, protective mimicry or the presence of poison glands. In general the molluscs all share features which can be regarded as traces of an original mollusc ancestor. Several parts can be distinguished: the head (often not easily identifiable, however), containing the sense organs, the nerve centres and the mouth; the foot, a broad, ventral muscular structure that provides a slow means of locomotion; and the dome-shaped dorsal hump, the visceral hump, which contains the various digestive and sexual organs. The surface of the dorsal hump has a mantle which secretes calcareous substances to form the shell. The mantle extends as an overhanging rim round the sides of the body, and the space under it is known as the mantle cavity, in which are housed the gills.

The molluscs possess a digestive apparatus; a mouth, often provided with a radula, which is a horny band with curved teeth; a circulatory system, consisting of a heart located in the body cavity (coelom) and surrounded by a pericardial cavity with systems of veins and arteries; and a nervous system with nerve cords to the foot and hump. Reproduction is sexual; many species are hermaphrodites. Primitive molluscs tend to employ external fertilization, simply casting their eggs and sperm into their aquatic surroundings. Some of the more advanced forms (including the common snail) have evolved internal fertilization, which has allowed them to abandon the sea or fresh water and colonize the dry land.

The dimensions of the molluscs vary from a few millimetres to about 20 m (over 60 ft) in some cephalopods. They exist in many forms and in all wet or humid environments, in both fresh water and sea water, in damp ground and even in dry deserts.

Many still follow the way of life of their distant ancestors, living on the hard foundations of the sea bed; some live buried in sand or mud, some have become sedentary and others swim freely. There are species which are adapted to life deep in the oceans, and others which live at altitudes of 5000 m (17,000 ft). Few marine species are distributed over the whole world; generally different species are located in definite areas which differ from each other in their environmental characteristics such as climate, seawater temperatures, existence of warm or cold currents, and salinity.

The molluscs are divided into several different groups: Aplacophora, Monoplacophora, Polyplacophora, Gastropoda, Scaphopoda, Bivalvia and Cephalopoda.

Map showing how groups of mollusc species fall into well-defined geographical regions:
1) Arctic 2) Northern 3) Aleutian 4) Lusitanian 5) Celtic
6) Carolinian 7) Oregonan 8) Californian 9) Japanese
10) Indo-Pacific 11) Panamanian 12) Caribbean
13) Senegalese 14) South African 15) Australian
16) New Zealand 17) Peruvian 18) Argentinian
19) Magellanic 20) Antarctic

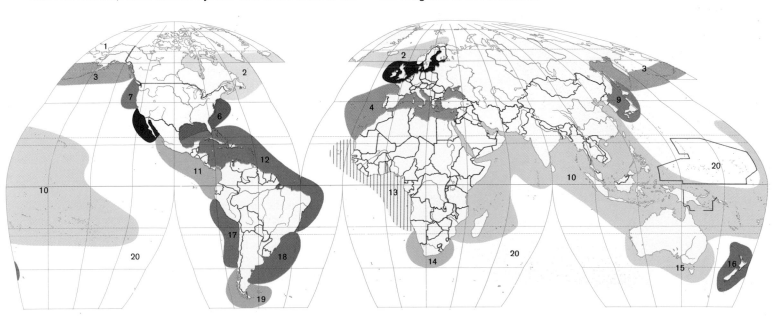

Polyplacophora

The Polyplacophora, or chitons, are a small group of marine molluscs which have preserved some of the characteristics of their remote ancestors. The body, lacking a distinct head, is a flattened ovoid in shape. The shell consists of eight overlapping plates each of which is made up of two calcareous layers. They do not cover the mantle entirely. The mantle cavity is a narrow groove that encircles the animal around its foot. The head, which is not marked off in any way from the body, has no eyes, and tentacles are lacking, but there are cells which function as organs of touch, and sometimes some light-sensitive cells are distributed on the shell-plates.

Like the primitive molluscs, the Polyplacophora live on the rocky sea beds to which they adhere or on which they move by means of the foot. The foot has a very powerful suction-like grip on a firm substrate, and it is almost impossible to dislodge a chiton from a relatively smooth rock. If it is accidentally pulled from its base by a particularly forceful wave, the chiton can roll into a ball, rather like a woodlouse (pillbug), with its vulnerable underparts well protected. The creature can then be rolled about without damage in its aptly named 'coat-of-mail' shell. A few species, however, have the shell enclosed within the mantle and are therefore more easily damaged. The shells of most species are coloured dull green, brown or grey to resemble the rocks and plants on which they live.

The Polyplacophora also resemble the primitive molluscs in their principal food: they mostly live on algae, using their radula to scrape it off rocks and shells. The sexes are separate and no copulation takes place; the sperm emitted by the male travels through the water to reach the mantle cavity of the female, where it fertilizes the eggs. Spawning in some species of chiton is controlled by the phases of the moon. One species from the group is viviparous (bears live, formed young rather than laying eggs); however, in the other species fertilization is external. The fertilized egg produces a planktonic larva called a trochophore which gives rise directly to the adult without passing through the stage of veliger – a larva with a ciliated girdle used for swimming – that

A chiton, *Placiphorella atlantica,* showing the characteristic shell in eight sections.

characterizes all other molluscs. They number about 600 species and range from 1 cm (0.4 in) to about 30 cm (12 in) in length.

Aplacophora

The Aplacophora are probably the most primitive of living molluscs and barely resemble other molluscs at all. They are characterized by the absence of a shell; the body, cylindrical and worm-like in appearance, is nevertheless provided with a mantle containing calcareous spicules. There are about 100 species. Some have no radula, although it is well developed in others, and gills may or may not be present. In one group of Aplacophora the foot is reduced to a kind of longitudinal groove by which movement is achieved with the aid of ventral cilia. Their dimensions range from a few millimetres for one Atlantic species to 30 cm (12 in) for one living in South-East Asia. They may live independently, preying on small marine organisms, or be parasitic; *Nematomenia,* for example, is parasitic on red coral.

Another variety lacks a true foot, but has a shell-plate in the form of a shield, located behind the mouth aperture, which it uses to dig the holes in which it lives. Buried in the sand or mud of the sea bed, it feeds itself on micro-organisms such as algae.

Monoplacophora

Until quite recently the Monoplacophora were believed to have been extinct since the Devonian era, about 300 million years ago. Then in 1952 a specimen of *Neopilina galatheae* was discovered in a deep oceanic trench off the Pacific coast of Costa Rica. It carries a single dorsal shell plate with the apex in front, formed of three layers: an external layer, the periostracum, made of horny material, an intermediate layer and an inner one containing calcareous spicules. The ventral part consists of a large foot encircled by the mantle cavity which contains five or six pairs of gills. The head carries two lateral flaps, two small tentacles and also two pairs of odd-looking tufted tentacles. There is also a radular sac. Members of the Monoplacophora have not been observed alive (which is not surprising, given the depths at which these creatures are found); however, it is postulated that they live on fairly firmly packed abyssal ooze and the head organs function to transfer detritus to the mouth and perhaps carry out some rudimentary sorting of the contents for food.

Since 1952 more species of *Neopilina* have been found in the muddy sea beds off the Pacific coast of America, at depths of between 2500 m ($1\frac{1}{2}$ miles) and 6500 m (4 miles). A specimen of a sub-species (*Neopilina galatheae adenensis*) has more recently been found in the Gulf of Aden. The survival of *Neopilina* is probably due to its ability to live at great depths where there is little competition from more advanced species.

Scaphopoda

The Scaphopoda (tusk shells) are characterized by their conical tubular shells, open at both ends and ranging from 2 mm to 15 cm (0.08 in to 6 in) in length. From the front, which is the larger end, protrude the head and the foot, while the rear aperture houses the hinder part of the body. In appearance they resemble hollow canine teeth or tusks. They live in sandy or muddy sea beds and only the rear part of the shell appears above the substrate.

Scaphopods burrow by lengthening and protruding the pointed, muscular foot through the wider end of the shell and forcing it into the sand. When fully extended, blood is pumped into the tip of the foot to expand it and create an anchorage point; the rest of the shell and the body can then be drawn into the sand by shortening the middle portion of the foot.

Lacking gills, tusk shells breathe through the surface of the mantle; the water is made to enter through the rear aperture into the mantle cavity by the action of cilia on the surface of the mantle, and is expelled after feeding, together with faecal matter. The sexes are separate, unlike many molluscs, and the fertilized eggs give rise to planktonic larvae.

The Scaphopoda live on micro organisms which they capture with the tentacles (captacula) provided with adhesive glands which are carried on the two lobes of the head. The food is conveyed to the mouth where the teeth of the radula grind it down. They live in all seas of the world, some at depths of between 5000 and 7000 m (3 to 4 miles), and number about 350 species.

Gastropoda

The gastropods (limpets, snails, whelks, slugs etc) are the most numerous group of molluscs and are characterized by having a spiral shell and torsion of the body. This is a peculiar feature of gastropods whereby, during embryonic development, the soft parts of the body twist round through 180° so that the gills are brought from the rear to face forwards and the anus opens just behind the head. Although some of the gastropods are partially untwisted and nearly symmetrical; no other group of animal is twisted in this way. They are divided into the Prosobranchia, the Opisthobranchia and the Pulmonata.

Prosobranchia

The Prosobranchia, marine gastropods, are nearly always equipped with a spiral shell provided with an operculum; this is a horny plate on the rear of the foot which serves as a door to close

A species of Aplacophora, the most primitive type of mollusc, showing its worm-like body shape.

the shell aperture when the animal has retreated inside. They owe their name to their having their gills (branchia) placed in front of the heart. They are divided into Archaeogastropoda, Mesogastropoda and Neogastropoda.

Archaeogastropoda. The Archaeogastropoda, which include limpets, abalones and some snails, are the most primitive of the gastropods. For the most part they live on rocky shores, usually on the upper surfaces of rocks but occasionally on the under surfaces of boulders. They feed on algae, scraping them off the rocks with their radula. The algae are mixed with fluids from the salivary glands and passed along the oesophagus to be digested. Limpets

Dentalium vulgare, a species of scaphopod (tusk shell) common in the waters of the Mediterranean.

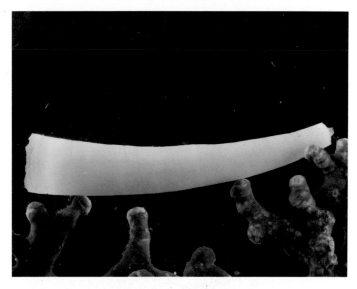

are usually seen attached firmly to rocks but can also be seen creeping over their surfaces. Abalone is the name applied to various species of the genus *Haliotis*, found on the Pacific coast of North America (*H. lamellosa* is illustrated here); they can be up to 25 cm (10 in) long. Their shells have a number of perforations through which water is expelled from the mantle cavity. Smaller abalones, called 'ormers', occur round the Channel Isles. The Archaeogastropoda also include the Pleurotomaria (*Pleurotomaria hirasei* is illustrated here), which inhabit the coastal waters of Japan, and the Fissurellidae, of which the Californian species, *Megatura crenulata*, or keyhole limpet, is illustrated here. This shield-shaped shell, perforated at the apex, measures up to 10 cm (4 in) in diameter.

The limpet family (Patellidae) live generally on rocky coasts. There are about 400 species which are present in all seas of the world. Species of *Patella* are common along European coastlines, and others live on the southern Australian shores and along the Pacific coasts of America. *Nascella mytilina* is found in the Antarctic and *Helcion pectinatus* in South African waters. Members of the Cocculoidinea all live in the deepest areas of the ocean. The Trochidae, noted for their shells shaped like spinning-tops, are almost worldwide in their distribution; the map on p. 26 shows the distribution of various species of the topshell, *Calliostoma* (*C. zizyphinum* is also illustrated here), which are members of the Trochidae.

The Neritacea are a large and successful group of Archaeogastropoda regarded by some zoologists as a separate order. They show a marked advance in the specialization of male and female cells. Not only marine but also freshwater and terrestrial forms are included. The *Nerita* species are amphibious, living largely on tropical coral shores where they have spread widely to occupy any suitable rocky or gravelly sites. *Neritina* live in gently running streams of fresh water, as does *Theodoxus fluviatilis*, illustrated here, while some species of Neritacea in the East Indies have become almost terrestrial.

Mesogastropoda. The process which had already begun in the Archaeogastropoda, where the twisting of the body caused uneven development of organs on the right and left sides, is carried even further in the Mesogastropoda and Neogastropoda, to such an extent that the organs on one side have entirely failed to develop. The animals thus possess only one set of such organs as gills and kidneys. There is also a tendency for the nervous system to be concentrated in definite nerve centres.

Both these groups, living in tidal waters, have developed an operculum, the horny plate on the upper part of the foot. To protect themselves against drying out when the tide falls, they withdraw into their shells and the operculum seals the entrance to the shell, the efficiency of the seal being increased by spreading around the edges of the operculum a mucous fluid secreted by a special gland. Mesogastropods are recognizable by the nacre (mother-of-pearl) lining of their shells. Many have beautiful colours and patterns on the outer surface of the shell.

The Littorinids, members of the Mesogastropoda, include two groups, one marine and the other terrestrial. The marine variety, periwinkles, are distributed widely over the world, particularly along the middle tidal bands of the European and American coastlines. One of these is *Littorina obtusata*, illustrated here. Another species, *Littorina neritoides*, is particularly capable of enduring long periods of exposure to air. *Pomatias elegans* (illustrated) is a terrestrial form living in the Mediterranean area; it is one of a group called the operculates which also includes a number of pond snails.

The Architectonica contain some of the species provided with the most elegant shells, such as *Architectonica perspectiva* (illustrated) of the South-East Asian area and *A. perdix* of the Malaysian coasts. The Cerithiacea are particularly numerous. Among them, the spire shell (*Turritella communis*, illustrated), is common in European waters. Some of the Vermetidae (*Vermetus arenarius*, or worm shell, is illustrated here), found in Europe and in New Zealand, have strangely shaped shells which have lost their spiral form and appear in the shape of a contorted tube.

The Thiaridae are distributed in fresh waters in hot regions; the genus *Thiara*, for example, is present in Africa and Australia. The Ianthinidae are a planktonic family, which feed on floating Hydrozoa. *Ianthina* species (illustrated) are found in warm seas. They secrete a raft of bubbles and drift about with the currents. Most other Gastropods are stuck on the sea bed, but these pelagic (free-floating) types have a thin shell which is light enough to float. The Epithonidae, which include *Epitonium scalare*, or wentletrap, illustrated on p. 27, live on the sea bed and feed on *Actinia*, a genus of sea anemones. In the Strombacea, distributed from the Mediter-

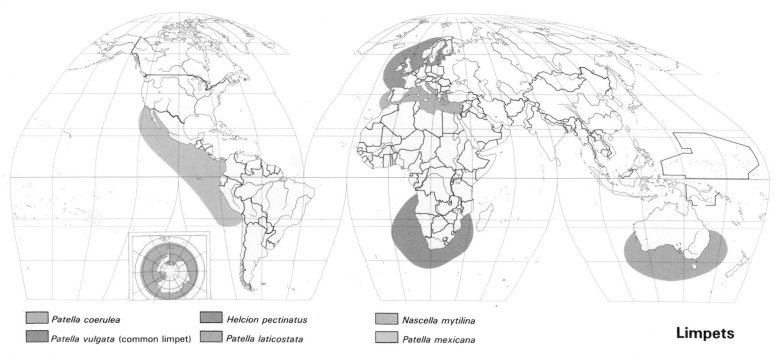

	Patella coerulea		Helcion pectinatus		Nascella mytilina
	Patella vulgata (common limpet)		Patella laticostata		Patella mexicana

Limpets

Pomatias elegans
land winkle

Pleurotomaria hirasei

Ianthina ianthina
violet sea snail

Architectonica perspectiva

Megatura crenulata
keyhole limpet

Calliostoma
topshell
zizyphinum

Haliotis lamellosa
abalone

Littorina obtusata
periwinkle

Thiara amarula

Vermetus arenarius
worm shell

Turritella communis
turret or spire shell

Theodoxus fluviatilis

ranean to the Baltic, the shells sometimes show large wing-like extensions, as in the pelican's foot shell (*Aporrhais pespelecani*, illustrated here). Strombidae, whose shells are much prized by collectors, are particularly widespread in tropical seas such as those of the Caribbean and South-East Asian areas; they include *Strombus gallus* (conch), *Lambis chiragra* (spider shell) and *Tibia fusus*, all illustrated here. The shells of the Calyptraeacea, on the other hand, are not so impressive, some members of the Capulidae, such as *Capulus hungaricus* (illustrated), have shells very similar to one of the half-shells of the bivalves.

The Xenophoridae also have characteristic shells, on which other shells, pebbles, etc. become attached; they live in warm seas, like *Xenophora pallidula* (illustrated), which lives in the seas off Japan. The Heteropoda, like *Ianthina*, are free-floating predators, which feed on plankton and other animals of the open seas. The *Atlanta* species are members of this group, as is *Carinaria* (the sea butterfly, *C. mediterranea*, is illustrated here), an actively swimming form in which the shell is much smaller and lighter, while *Pterotrachea* has lost its shell entirely and become jelly-like. Its foot has been much reduced in size and modified to form a kind of fin to aid in swimming, but it has a residual sucker which is used to grasp its prey of jellyfish and small fishes. Cowries (Cypraeacea) are found principally in tropical seas: the numerous species of Cypraeidae which include *Cypraea cribaria*, illustrated here, are distributed over a vast area of warm seas, while the genus Trivia includes two species found in British waters, *Trivia monacha* and *T. arctica*, which are about 1 cm (0.39 in) long. *Calpurnus verrucosus* and *Volva volva*, illustrated here, belong to another group of cowries, the Ovulidae. Some of the cowries are among the most beautiful and highly prized mesogastropods of coral reefs, with shells showing rich and varied colour patterns. The shell is smooth and glossy so that the mantle can be spread out over it to aid respiration.

Some species of Naticacea also live in British waters, but the group is widely distributed; one, *Naticarius millepunctatus*, is illustrated here. *Natica* is a predator on other molluscs and in particular on bivalves. It lives on sandy shores in Malaysia and elsewhere, and has a greatly enlarged foot with which it ploughs forwards just underneath the surface of the sand; the foot has pores by which sea water can be admitted to an internal network of passages so that the foot can be rapidly expanded and contracted to aid in burrowing. The prey – various species of bivalve living buried in the sand – is seized by the foot of the predator and a hole is drilled in the shell by the teeth of the radula aided by some secret fluid, an acid or an enzyme.

The Tonnoidea are, with the Naticacea, the most highly evolved of the mesogastropods. They are also carnivorous predators living mainly in warm tropical seas and include *Ficus filosa*, *Cypreacassis rufa* (helmet shell), *Tonna galea* and *Cymatium parthenopaeum*, all illustrated on p. 30.

Neogastropoda. The Neogastropods, which include the whelks, are mostly predatory carnivores living in the sea. They are divided into several groups of which one of the most important is that of the Muricacea. These include various species of *Murex* whose shells are often ornamented with spines and ridges, such as *M. troscheli* (spiny murex) of South-East Asia, illustrated on p. 30. Some, such as *Murex brandaris*, have developed a long tubular structure for the intake of water, the siphon, which in burrowing forms can be extended above the soft mud of the ocean bed or may sometimes act as a sense organ. Some Mediterranean *Murex* species were used in classical times as the source of the valuable Tyrian purple dye. For certain species of *Murex* the oyster is the favoured prey; *Murex fulvescens* climbs on the upper flat shell of the oyster and by wedging the outer lip of its own shell against the lower shell drags the two shells apart and devours the oyster by inserting its proboscis through the gap. Another species clasps the oyster with the foot and bores a hole through the shell with the teeth of the radula. *Urosalpinx* eats smaller oysters for preference – their shells are thinner and more easily penetrated – and, owing to the number of young oysters they consume, they are a serious menace to American oyster fisheries. Another neogastropod, *Fasciolaria hunteri*, feeds on *Urosalpinx* as well as on oysters, so that its presence may be advantageous when the *Urosalpinx* are numerous. *Ocenebra* is another predator that attacks its prey by boring, and *Magilus* (such as *M. antiquus* of the Pacific, illustrated on p. 30) are parasitic on coelenterates.

Another family of neogastropods, the Buccinidae, contains some species that are marine scavengers, feeding on dead and decaying flesh which they apparently locate by its smell. The whelk (*Buccineum undatum*) is a large salt-water gastropod of British waters; it is used as a food in some eastern coastal districts, being

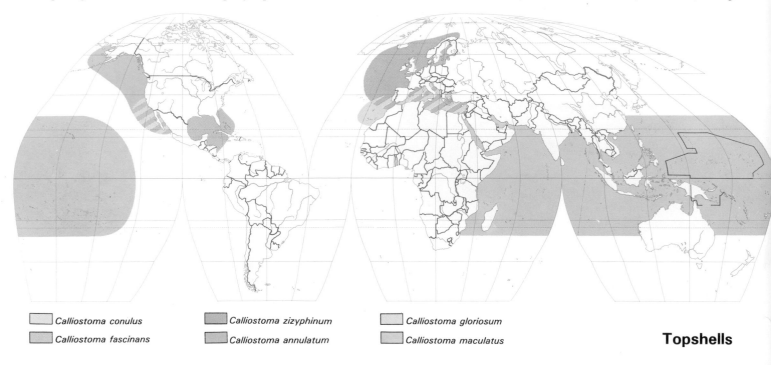

Calliostoma conulus	*Calliostoma zizyphinum*	*Calliostoma gloriosum*
Calliostoma fascinans	*Calliostoma annulatum*	*Calliostoma maculatus*

Topshells

Carinaria mediterranea
sea butterfly

Lambis chiragra
spider shell

Strombus gallus
conch shell

Tibia fusus

Aporrhais pespelecani
pelican's foot shell

Naticarius millepunctatus

Volva volva

Capulus hungaricus

Cypraea cribraria
cowrie

Calpurnus verrucosus

Xenophora pallidula

Epitonium scalare
wendletrap or staircase shell

caught in baited traps. Another close relative attacks oysters in the same manner as that used by Muricaceae; it detects them by the current of exhaled water emitted by bivalves. The Nassaridae include both predatory carnivores and scavengers.

The Volutacea, many of which occur mainly in South-East Asian waters, include species such as *Voluta musica*, which have exceptionally beautiful shells, or whose shells are of exceptionally large size, such as *Melo amphora* (illustrated on p. 30) and *Cymbium cymbium*. The Olividae have smooth shells and wide variations of colouring even within the same species; *Oliva* species are probably the fastest-moving species of gastropods, found in warm and tropical waters such as those of West Africa and South America (*O. porphyria* is illustrated on p. 30). The Olividae live in sandy shores into which they burrow. They feed on small molluscs, but do not drill holes in their shells. They are smooth-shelled and streamlined

in shape, which aids them in burrowing, and have an upright siphon through which they breathe. They are good swimmers, using various extensions of the foot to propel themselves. The Harpidae are similar to the Olividae and include *Harpa amouretta*, illustrated on p. 30. Other volutoids include *Arctomelon*, *Cymbiolacca*, *Cymbiola* and *Guivillea*. The Mitridae are also sand-dwellers and are characterized by the possession of poisonous glands in the radula which aid them in the capture of prey. An example is *Mitra zonata* of the Adriatic, illustrated on p. 30. The *Toxoglossa* species are another group which secrete poison with which they kill their prey before they eat it.

The large family of gastropods known as Conidae are all predatory carnivores and are widely distributed in the Pacific and Indian oceans. Many are noted for the splendid shapes and colours of their shells (the cone shell, *Conus marmoreus*, is illustrated on p. 30). Up

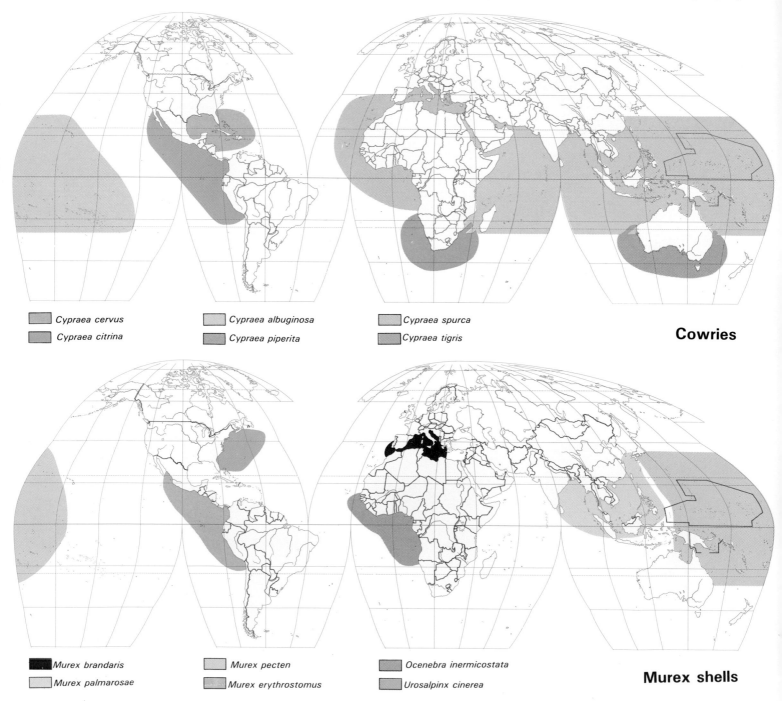

Cypraea cervus	Cypraea albuginosa	Cypraea spurca
Cypraea citrina	Cypraea piperita	Cypraea tigris

Cowries

Murex brandaris	Murex pecten	Ocenebra inermicostata
Murex palmarosae	Murex erythrostomus	Urosalpinx cinerea

Murex shells

to twenty different species of *Conus* may live on the same coral reef, and it is noticeable that in localities where several species are present the feeding habits of each tend to be more specialized. Some species feed exclusively on molluscs, for example, and others on fish.

The Conidae are mostly active by night, concealing themselves under stones or burying themselves in the sand by day. They also store up poison in a duct sometimes several times as long as the animal itself. The poison is discharged into the proboscis from one end of the duct; the other end of the duct is closed and resembles a muscular bulb which, on being contracted, forces the poison along the duct when the *Conus* strikes its prey. Most of the *Conus* species feed on polychaete worms. Some species prey on other gastropods and have lance-shaped teeth lying at the base of the proboscis. When a gastropod is attacked, a single tooth is slid into position

and filled with poison from the duct; it is then propelled at the gastropod like a poison dart, the force being provided by the muscular bulb of the duct. The victim is instantly paralysed, and the *Conus*, placing its mouth against the shell orifice of its prey, sucks out the flesh, leaving an empty shell.

Other species of *Conus* live on fish such as blennies and gobies. They bury themselves in the sand with only the proboscis protruding; then at night, when the fish rest on the bottom, they track down their prey, probably by sensing the chemical substances it discharges into the water, and stab it with the poison-filled radular tooth. The fish, after a brief struggle, subsides and is usually swallowed whole by the *Conus*, which can expand its mouth from a few millimetres to 2 cm (0.75 in) in diameter. Some species of *Conus* can inflict a painful sting on human beings, and that of the Australian *Conus geographus* has sometimes been fatal to unwary

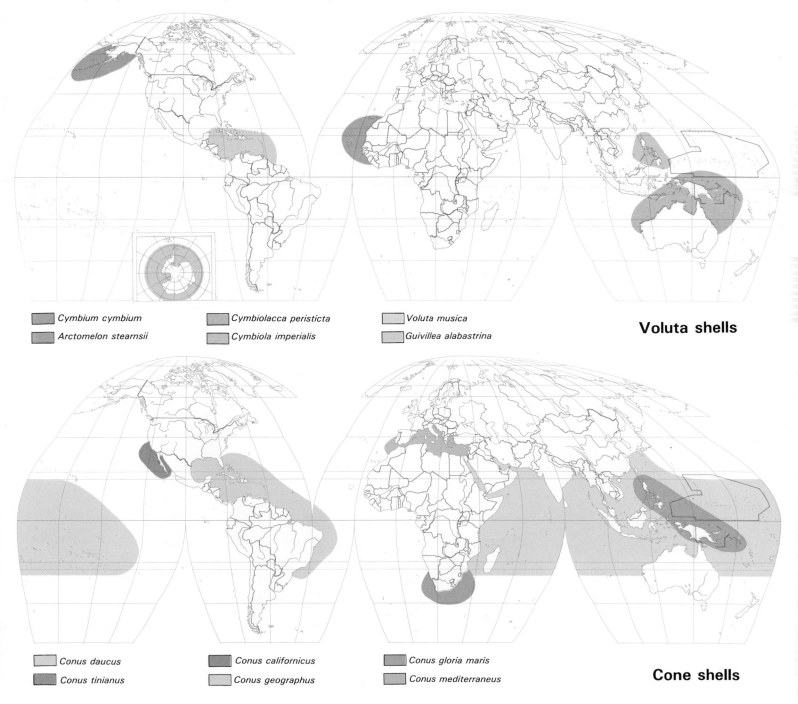

Cymbium cymbium	*Cymbiolacca peristicta*	*Voluta musica*
Arctomelon stearnsii	*Cymbiola imperialis*	*Guivillea alabastrina*

Voluta shells

Conus daucus	*Conus californicus*	*Conus gloria maris*
Conus tinianus	*Conus geographus*	*Conus mediterraneus*

Cone shells

Melo amphora
baler shell

Ficus filosa

Torina galea

Oliva porphyria

Cypreacassis rufa
helmet shell

Conus marmoreus
cone shell

Murex troscheli
spiny murex

Magilus antiquus

Terebra subulata

Mitra zonata

Harpa amouretta

Cymatium parthenopaeum

bathers and careless shell collectors. Another family of predatory carnivores is Terebridae; *Terebra subulata* is illustrated here.

Opisthobranchia

The principal characteristic of the Opisthobranchia is the reduction of the torsion of the body, the torsion being progressively reduced as one passes from the more primitive to the more evolved forms of this group. Reduction and loss of the shell and of the mantle cavity is also characteristic of the Opisthobranchs. In the Nudibranchs, or sea slugs, the shell, mantle cavity and gills have all disappeared by the time the adult stage is reached.

The Opisthobranchia are divided into several different groups. In the Cephalospidea the shell is still present and the head carries an appendage, the cephalic disc, which serves for digging in the sand or mud. There are various sub-groups, the most primitive being the Actaeonidae, which can be found in almost all the oceans. *Actaeon tornatilis* (illustrated on p. 33), which is found in most European waters, feed on micro-organisms in the surface layers of the sand. Other species include *Neactaeonina cingulata*, *Pseudoactaeon albus*, *Rictaxis punctolactaeus* and *Solidula solidula*, whose distribution is shown in the map below.

In the Acochlidiacea and Runcinacea, which contain only a few species of small dimensions, the shell is sometimes lacking.

The Sacoglossa include many different species, which characteristically feed by cutting open the cells of algae and sucking out the contents. The Sacoglossa group resemble the bivalves in having the shell divided into two parts. The family known as Polybranchidae lack both shells and gills, and breathing takes place through the skin; the exchange of chemical substances

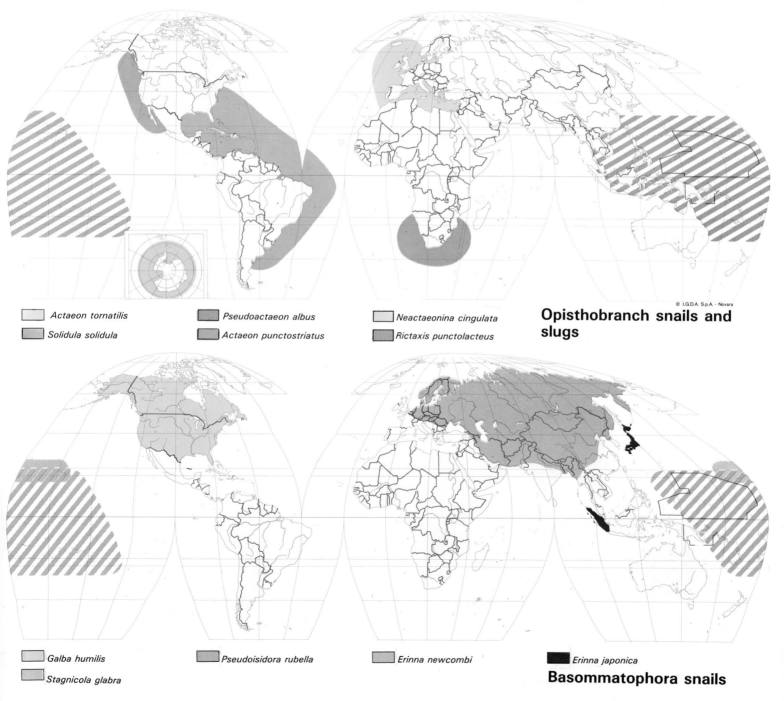

© I.G.D.A. S.p.A - Novara

Actaeon tornatilis	Pseudoactaeon albus	Neactaeonina cingulata
Solidula solidula	Actaeon punctostriatus	Rictaxis punctolacteus

Opisthobranch snails and slugs

Galba humilis	Pseudoisidora rubella	Erinna newcombi
Stagnicola glabra		

Erinna japonica

Basommatophora snails

involved in respiration is aided by the presence of numerous small protuberances (papillae) which give a leaf-like appearance.

The sea hares, Aplysiacea, are characterized by the presence of a thin internal shell and of well-developed parapodia (muscular projections) which make it possible for them to swim. *Aplysia punctata* (illustrated) is a European species. They contain a gland which discharges clouds of purple fluid when the animal is attacked by a predator. They feed on algae by cutting rather than sucking, the algae being grasped by the foot and a strip torn off by the radula and masticated by the muscles of the digestive system.

In the Pleurobranchiacea the shell is so much reduced that it no longer offers any protection. For this reason the members of this group have evolved various other methods of defence. *Tylodina perversa*, for example, a species living along the Atlantic coastline of southern Europe, avoids predators by taking refuge in sponges; *Pleurobranchus membranaceus* defends itself by emitting fluids containing hydrochloric and sulphuric acids. The latter species feeds on sea squirts (ascidians) by cutting a hole in its prey and inserting its proboscis into the interior of the animal. It swims freely by means of extensions of the foot (epipodial lobes), undulating left and right lobes alternately so that it rolls to left and right as it travels along.

The Thecosomata are plant-eaters, feeding on the minute organic particles suspended in sea-water. Among them are the sea butterflies, *Cavolinia tridentata*, *Cymbula peroni* and *Hyloclis striata*, illustrated here. The Gymnosomata on the other hand are predatory carnivores, feeding on Thecosomata and other plant-eaters. The sea butterfly (*Clione limacina*, illustrated), is a planktonic dweller in cold Arctic waters.

The Doridacea have flattened bodies carrying on the posterior part a tuft of secondary gills like a bunch of flowers. They are brightly coloured, often with a yellow nobbly skin, and are called sea lemons. *Glossodoris valenciennesi* and *Chromodoris quadricolor*, illustrated here, belong to this group.

Dendronotacea have a characteristic appearance, often having numerous appendages of varying shapes, such as *Dendronotus frondosus* of the South American coasts, whose body displays a number of branching appendages resembling foliage; a similar form, *Dendronotus arborescens*, is illustrated here.

Some of the hairy-looking sea slugs possess stinging cells similar to those of the coelenterates, and the Aeolidacea also contain species displaying the most striking coloration, such as *Flabellina affinis*, *Coryphella verrucosa* and *Aeolis papillosa* (all illustrated).

Pulmonata

The Pulmonata (snails and slugs) have evolved to colonize fresh waters and terrestrial habitats; their gills are reduced or absent, and the mantle cavity is transformed into a kind of lung. They are divided into Basommatophora (the water snails) and Stylommatophora (land and water snails, edible snails and slugs).

Basommatophora. Basommatophora mostly live in fresh waters or intertidally on the sea shore. They include *Galba*, *Stagnicola*, *Pseudoisidora* and *Erinna*. Some species of Lymnaea, such as the pond snail (*L. stagnalis*, illustrated on p. 35), can breathe either air or water, as can *Physa fontinalis*, while *L. trunculata* is a snail that lives in marshes and breathes only air. Species of *Lymnaea* which live in deeper waters further from the shore-line do not come to the surface to breath air; their mantle cavities are filled with water and they breathe through their gills. Other species breathe air when in shallower waters and water when at great depths. Another of the Basommatophora illustrated on p. 35 is the ram's horn pond snail (*Planorbarius corneus*). The lower map on p. 31 shows the worldwide distribution of various species of Basommatophora.

Stylommatophora. In the Basommatophora the eyes are at the base of tentacles situated on the back part of the head, while in the Stylommatophora the eyes are at the tips of the tentacles. The principal groups of Stylommatophora are the garden snails (*Helix*) and the slugs (*Arion*, *Agriolimax*, *Limax*). The edible snail (*Helix pomatia*), is illustrated on p. 35, as is *H. hortensis*. Both slugs and snails are notoriously voracious eaters of plant material, the more succulent the better. Grey *Limax* slugs feed on bulbs, tubers or roots, while *Arion subfuscus* lives on fungi. The rapid devouring of food is aided by powerful digestive fluids, and rates of growth and of reproduction are correspondingly high. A notorious pulmonate is the giant African snail (*Achatina*), which carries out extensive depredations on human food supplies in many tropical countries, having been accidentally introduced from Africa.

Many snails and slugs will eat flesh, even of their own species, and some are almost entirely carnivorous. *Testacella*, one of the

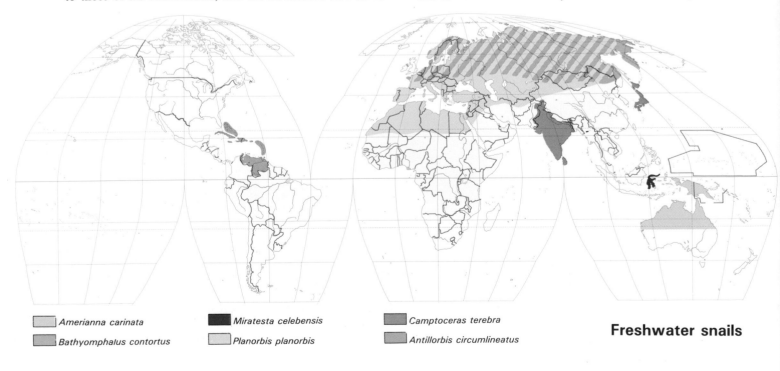

	Amerianna carinata		*Miratesta celebensis*		*Camptoceras terebra*
	Bathyomphalus contortus		*Planorbis planorbis*		*Antillorbis circumlineatus*

Freshwater snails

Actaeon tornatilis

Cymbulia peroni

Hylocylis striata
sea butterfly

Cavolinia tridentata
sea butterfly

*Glossodoris
valenciennesi*
purple sea slug

*Coryphella
verrucosa*
naked sea butterfly

Clione limacina

*Aplysia
punctata*
sea hare

Flabellina affinis

Aeolis papillosa
grey sea slug

Chromodoris quadricolor

Dendronotus arborescens

slugs that has retained a small, flat internal shell, lives mostly below ground and feeds on earthworms and small slugs.

The Succineidae live in fresh waters; *S. putris* for instance lives by the shores of lakes and feeds on green plant tissues. Most of the European slugs belong to the various species of *Arion*, the common garden slug being *A. hortensis*. *A. rufus* is illustrated. The big black slug, common on wet pastures in Britain, is *A. ater*. The map below shows the distribution of various other species including *Hesperarion niger*, *Zacoleus idahoensis* and *Hemphillia glandulosa* of North America and *Oopelta micropunctata* of southern Africa.

Similar to the Arionidae in appearance are the Limacidae, distributed mostly in Europe and western Asia. The giant slug (*Limax maximus*) is illustrated here. The distribution of other groups such as *Trochomorpha*, *Zonitoides*, *Pristiloma* and *Pycnogyra* is shown in the map below.

The Helicacea are a very numerous group, making up 50 per cent of the Pulmonates found in Europe. *Helix pomatia* (illustrated) is the edible snail bred specifically for food on the Continent; it lives wild in chalk and limestone districts of southern England. The garden snail (*Helix aspersa*) is a major horticultural pest. Another common British species is the banded snail (*Cepaea hortensis*), which is very variable in its colouring. *Polymita picta* (illustrated) is a Cuban species.

All snails need a lot of mineral material (mostly calcium carbonate) to form their shell, and those living on calcium-rich soils have thicker and more robust shells than those in other habitats. There are more species on calcareous soils, too, whereas on acid soils (moorlands and mountain grasslands, for example) calcium is at a premium and few snails are able to live. Slugs are then much more abundant since they are not limited in this way.

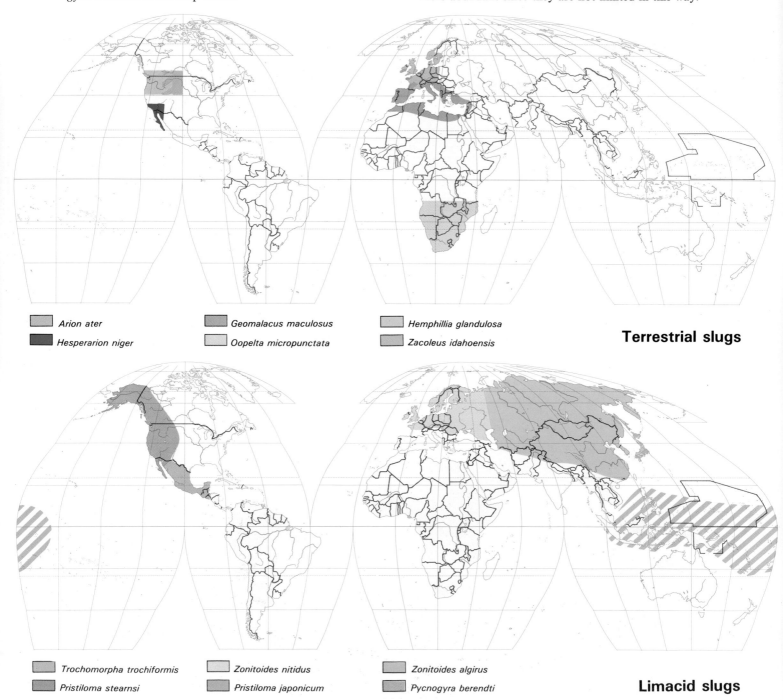

Arion ater	Geomalacus maculosus	Hemphillia glandulosa
Hesperarion niger	Oopelta micropunctata	Zacoleus idahoensis

Terrestrial slugs

Trochomorpha trochiformis	Zonitoides nitidus	Zonitoides algirus
Pristiloma stearnsi	Pristiloma japonicum	Pycnogyra berendti

Limacid slugs

Delima itala

Achatina fulica
giant African snail

Helix hortensis

Succinea putris

Limax maximus
giant slug

Arion rufus
red slug

Polymita picta

Lymnaea stagnalis
common pond snail

Planorbarius corneus
ram's horn pond snail

Liguus dryas

Helix pomatia
Roman or edible snail

Bivalvia

The Bivalvia (bivalves), or Lamellibranchia, include mussels, scallops, oysters, clams and shipworms. They are equipped with a shell consisting of two parts or 'valves', joined at the back by a kind of hinge and closed by means of adductor muscles, situated on the internal faces of the two shells. They have no true head and no radula; the foot is highly developed and the mantle cavity is much larger than in other molluscs. The body is entirely enclosed by two symmetrical mantle flaps. Bivalves are mostly marine: freshwater species are few in number and there are none on land. Nearly all are sedentary. The gills hang in the mantle cavity at either side of the foot. They are equipped with cilia which draw water into the mantle cavity, where food particles are filtered out and carried by other cilia towards the mouth. The stomach is highly developed, but the reproductive, circulatory and excretory systems are much less so, and resemble those in more primitive molluscs. In the virtual absence of a head, the sense organs are located along the fringe of the mantle.

The bivalves are divided into four groups according to the structure of the gills, the musculature and the type of shell hinge.

Protobranchia. The Protobranchia are the most primitive of the bivalves. In *Nucula* (the common nut shell) the gills are used only for breathing. Tentacles which emerge from the shell collect food from the substrate; the food is delivered to a pair of sense organs (labial palps) situated one on each side of the foot.

Nucula live in shallow waters, buried in mud or sand. The foot is quite large and can be used for both movement and burrowing. The respiratory current passes from front to back, whereas in the more advanced *Nuculana* (*N. acinacea* is illustrated here), *Yoldia* and *Malletia* water both enters and leaves the mantle cavity at the rear, which enables them to bury themselves to greater depths.

Filibranchia. This group includes mussels and scallops. It is divided into Taxodonta and Anisomyaria. The first are named in reference to the arrangement of the shell teeth, which are in a long row and of uniform size. Characteristic of the Taxodonta are the Arcacea, known as Noah's ark shells, which produce a byssus, a substance secreted by a gland in the foot which hardens on contact with water. The bundle of filaments so formed acts as a means of anchorage to the rocks or other solid objects. Distribution of Arcacea species is shown on the map below. *Arca zebra* is illustrated here. Arcacea remain, back uppermost, on the surface of the sea bed, and attached to it by the byssus threads springing from the circumference of the foot. *Glycimeris glycimeris* of British waters, on the other hand, burrows to shallow depths in the sea bed, as do the *Limopsis* species (*L. tasimae* is illustrated here).

The Anisomyaria are a large group including the true mussels (Mytilacea), pearl oysters, wing shells and fan mussels (Pteriacea), scallops (Pectinacea), saddle oysters (Anomiacea) and true oysters (Ostreaceae). Some of them cement themselves firmly to the substrate and others remain unattached to it, but the majority attach themselves by means of the byssus.

In the mussels the byssus emerges from the front end and the foot from the rear end. The foot can be used to prise the mussel free from the byssus in order to creep along the surface. The edible mussels of Atlantic and Mediterranean waters are of two different species, *Mytilus edulis* and *M. galloprovincialis* respectively.

Other members of the group, to which the mussels belong, are *Crenella*, *Rhomboidella*, *Brachidontes*, *Modiolus* and *Lithophaga*. Members of the *Modiolus* group still attach themselves in an upright position to the substrate, like mussels (the horse mussel, *Modiolus difficilis*, is illustrated here). *Lithophaga*, the date mussels, are even capable of boring into limestone rocks; they do this by rotating their shells, aided by an acid mucus secreted by glands in the mantle.

The Pterioida, which include the pearl oysters, usually lie on one side, which becomes flattened so that the two halves of the shell are no longer alike. They retain the byssus for attachment. In pearl oysters (*Pinctada margaritifera* of South-East Asia and *Pteria hirundo* of the Mediterranean – illustrated here) the foot has become rudimentary and the half-shells are almost circular but have a long straight hinge. In more advanced members of the group the shells are more elongated. In the hammer oysters (*Malleus malleus*) of the Indian Ocean, illustrated here, the shell has become T-shaped like a hammer. The fan shells, Pinnidae, have long wedge-shaped shells equal in shape, and embed themselves upright in the sand. *Pinna nobilis*, illustrated here, is the largest European bivalve, about 30 cm (12 in) long.

The scallops, or Pectinidae, are present in all the oceans. In *Pecten* the eyes are more highly developed than in any other

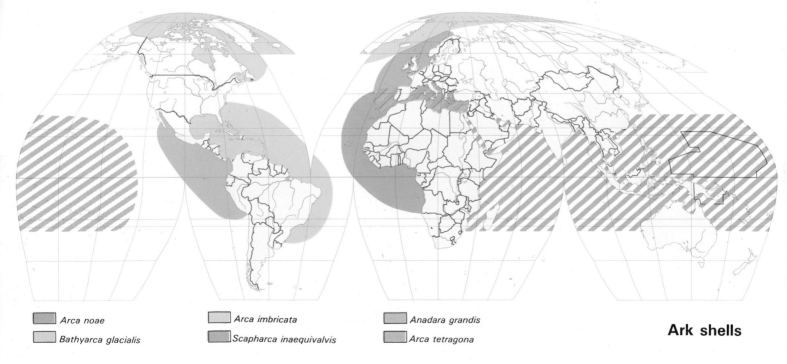

Arca noae

Bathyarca glacialis

Arca imbricata

Scapharca inaequivalvis

Anadara grandis

Arca tetragona

Ark shells

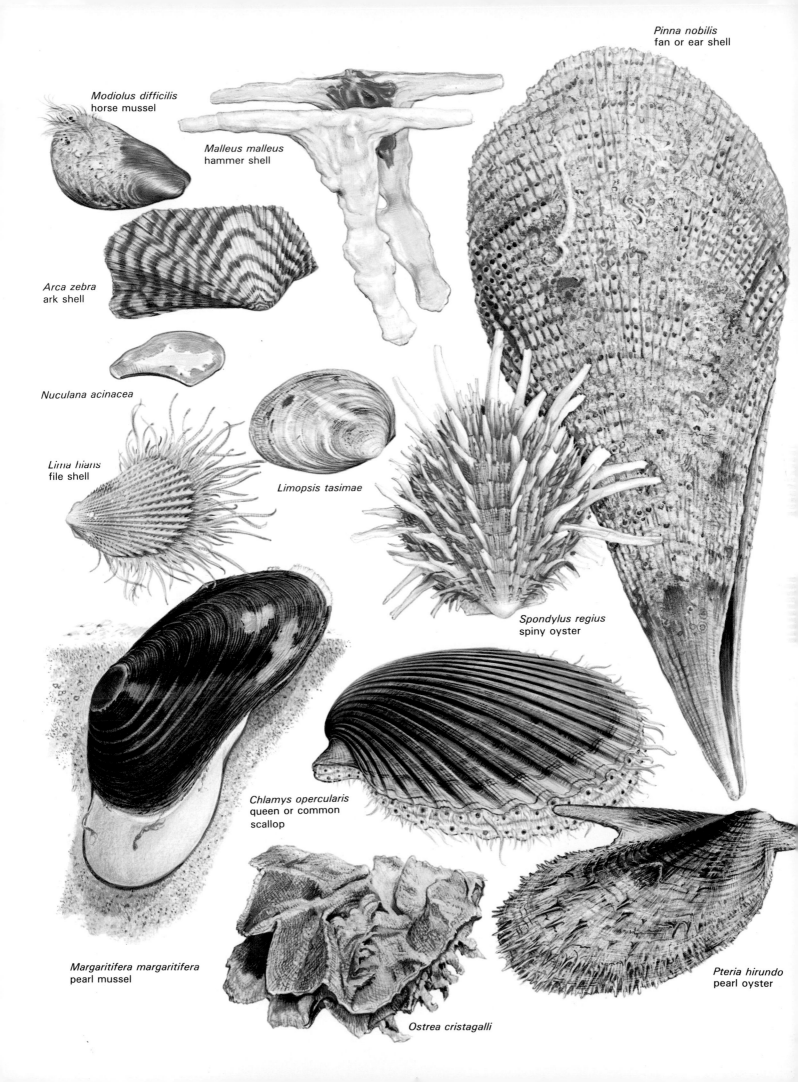

Pinna nobilis
fan or ear shell

Modiolus difficilis
horse mussel

Malleus malleus
hammer shell

Arca zebra
ark shell

Nuculana acinacea

Lima hians
file shell

Limopsis tasimae

Spondylus regius
spiny oyster

Chlamys opercularis
queen or common
scallop

Margaritifera margaritifera
pearl mussel

Ostrea cristagalli

Pteria hirundo
pearl oyster

bivalves. They have a rudimentary brain or nerve centre where impulses are received from eyes in the mantle. They are free-swimming, movement being obtained by clapping the two halves of the shell together to produce a jet of water. *Chlamys opercularis*, illustrated on p. 37, is the common scallop of European waters. The *Spondylus* species, as for instance *Spondylus regius* of South-East Asia, illustrated on p. 37, have shells covered with spines. The Limidae or file shells have numerous tentacles protruding from between the shells. *Lima hians*, illustrated on p. 37, like other Pectinacea has a large number of sense organs along the mantle edge, including complex eyes and tactile tentacles.

The saddle oysters, Anomiacea, include the tropical saddle oyster (*Placuna placenta*) of the South-East Asian area, whose shells were used in place of window-glass. The *Placuna* have no byssus and lie freely on the sea bed.

The oysters, Ostreacea, lose the byssus after their initial floating period when they are known as 'spat'. *Ostrea edulis* is the common edible oyster of European waters; another species is *Ostrea crista-galli*, illustrated on p. 37.

Eulamellibranchia. Some zoologists include oysters in this group, which also contains cockles, clams and shipworms (teredos). The group is divided into Schizodonta, Heterodonta, Adapedonta and Anomalodesmata. Most of these lie freely on the substrate or burrow into the sand or mud. Of the Schizodonta, the Trigoniacea are mostly found as fossils but are represented in Australia by such living specimens as Neotrigonia, which are dwellers in the fresh waters of rivers and lakes. The Unionacea are a very large group of freshwater mussels including the common European species *Unio pictorum* and *Anodonta cygnaea*, and the rarer *Margaritifera margaritifera* (illustrated on p. 37), sought after as a pearl-bearing mussel.

The Heterodonta contain 9500 species; in this group the hinge connecting the two shell halves contains from one to three cardinal teeth and a varying number of lateral teeth. The Heterodonta are divided into numerous subsidiary groups. Astartoidea contain some species inhabiting cold deep waters, such as *Astarte sulcata* of European seas. The cockles (Cardidae) are thick-shelled and globular; in some species the foot, which is long and narrow, can be inserted under the shell and suddenly straightened so that the cockle jumps off the ground. Sphaeriocea, a group inhabiting fresh and brackish waters, also incubate their eggs; they

are small, colourless cockles, usually less than 1 cm (0.4 in) long and worldwide in distribution. *Sphaerium corneum* is common in Eurasia and *Pisidium casertanum* in British and European waters.

The Glossoidea include the heart shell (*Glossus humanus*), of the North Atlantic and Mediterranean, illustrated here. The Arcticoidea include *Arctica islandica*, found only in the Baltic and the North Sea.

The Lucinacea live mostly in burrows in the sandy mud or sea-grass marshes of tropical coasts, though *Loripes lacteus* lives in more temperate seas including the Mediterranean. The foot is used not only for burrowing and movement, but also to construct a breathing shaft.

The cockles sometimes have very marked radial ribs, as in *Cardium costatum* of the West African coasts, and may be furnished with spines, as in the European species *C. aculeatum*, illustrated here. The shell of *Corculum cordissa* of Indo-Pacific waters is of a very unusual shape, flattened from back to front instead of laterally, so that it is roughly heart-shaped. Among other groups are *Acanthocardia*, *Laevicardium* and *Nemocardium*.

The Tridacnidae are giant clams of the coral reefs of the Pacific and Indian Oceans. They are specialized descendants of the Cardiacea (cockles) that have become adapted to living on the surface. To this group belongs *Tridacna gigas*, illustrated here, which may attain 130 cm (4 ft 3 in) in length and 250 kg (550 lb) in weight.

The Veneracea (venus shells) are a large group, of which some 2500 species belong to the sub-group Venericardia. They generally live buried in the sand or mud of the sea bottom. Genera belonging to this group include *Venus*, *Chione*, *Mercenaria*, *Pitar*, *Cyclina* and *Callanaitis* (*Pitar lupanarius* and *Callanaitis disjecta* are illustrated here). The Tellinacea group contains 350 species, which like Cardiacea mostly live on sandy or muddy sea beds.

The Adapedonta have been adapted for deep burrowing and immobility; the mantle is generally fused together to a large extent and the hinge is weak and lacking in teeth. The shells are mostly thin and fragile. The Solenacea, or razor shells, have long, narrow shells shaped like razors; the shape permits them to burrow rapidly through layers of sand. Of this group, *Ensis ensis*, illustrated here, is common in European waters, as is *E. siliqua*. The Mactracea, which include the otter shell (*Lutraria elliptica*, illustrated here), burrow in exposed sandy shores in an area stretching from Norway to Senegal.

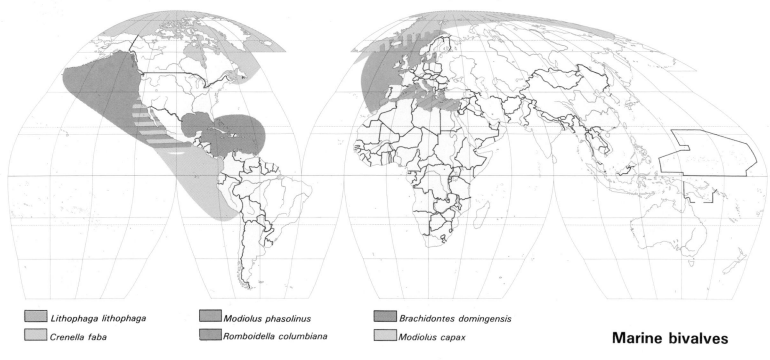

| | Lithophaga lithophaga | | Modiolus phasolinus | | Brachidontes domingensis |
| | Crenella faba | | Romboidella columbiana | | Modiolus capax |

Marine bivalves

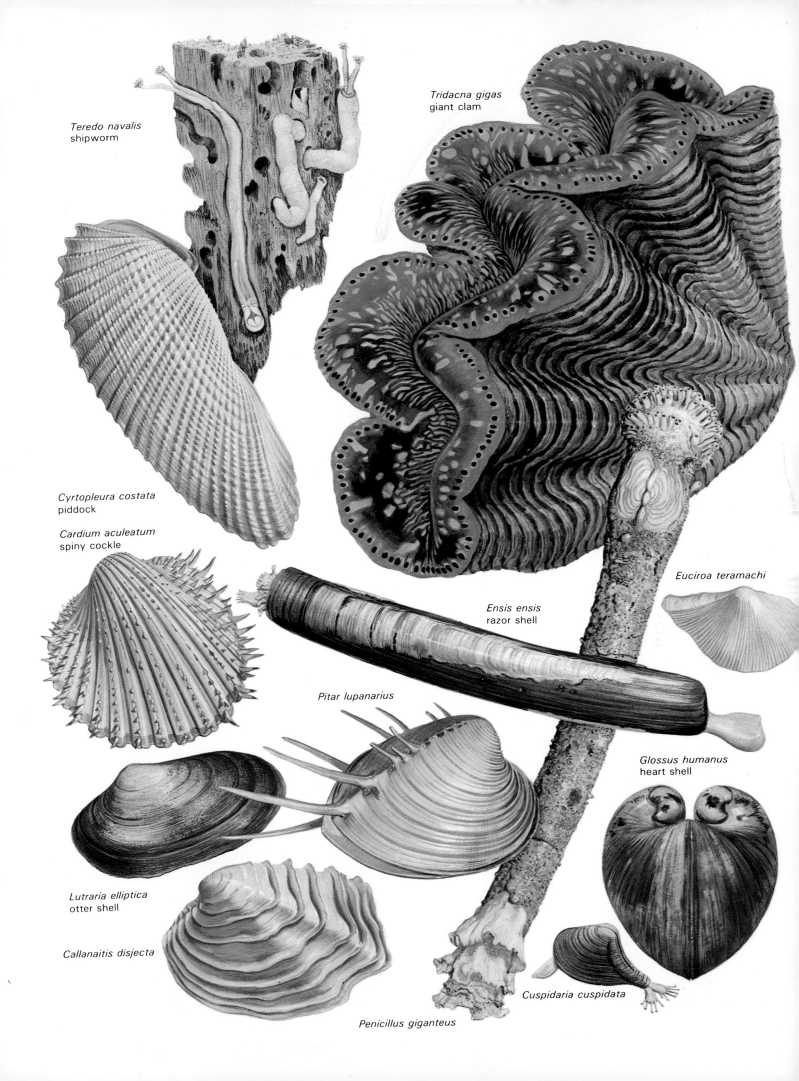

Teredo navalis
shipworm

Tridacna gigas
giant clam

Cyrtopleura costata
piddock

Cardium aculeatum
spiny cockle

Euciroa teramachi

Ensis ensis
razor shell

Pitar lupanarius

Glossus humanus
heart shell

Lutraria elliptica
otter shell

Callanaitis disjecta

Penicillus giganteus

Cuspidaria cuspidata

The Adesmacea include the piddocks, which bore into soft rock or clay, and two groups of wood-borers of which one is the shipworm family, Teredinidae. Although this group (Adesmacea) specializes in boring through hard materials, it possesses neither teeth nor ligaments, and the two halves of the shell are held together only by muscles. The foot is used to attach the animal to the surface and boring is carried out by rocking the valves of the shell to and fro. In *Teredo navalis* (illustrated on p. 39) and *Teredo utriculus*, the siphon is large, the body small, and the shell is used only as an abrasive instrument. Rock and clay borers include *Pholas dactylus* of European waters and the piddock, *Cyrtopleura costata* (illustrated on p. 39), of the Atlantic coasts of Central America.

The group, Anomalodesmata, contains only a few species characterized by the presence of valves of unequal size, as in *Penicillus*

giganteus, illustrated on p. 39, and *Ixartia distorta*, which have shells of irregular shape. *Pandora inaequivalis* has one flat shell while the other is markedly curved; it makes shallow burrows by sliding obliquely into the sand.

Septibranchia. This group consists of forms which lack true gills and do not exceed 2 cm (0.8 in) in length. The gills have been replaced by a muscular partition of septum with pores which is used for pumping water through the mantle cavity. They live at great depths, feeding themselves on small polychaetes and crustacea on the ocean bed. Among sub-groups are *Euciroa* of the Indo-Pacific area and *Cuspidaria* of which some species live in European waters. *Euciroa teramachi* and *Cuspidaria cuspidata* are illustrated on p. 39.

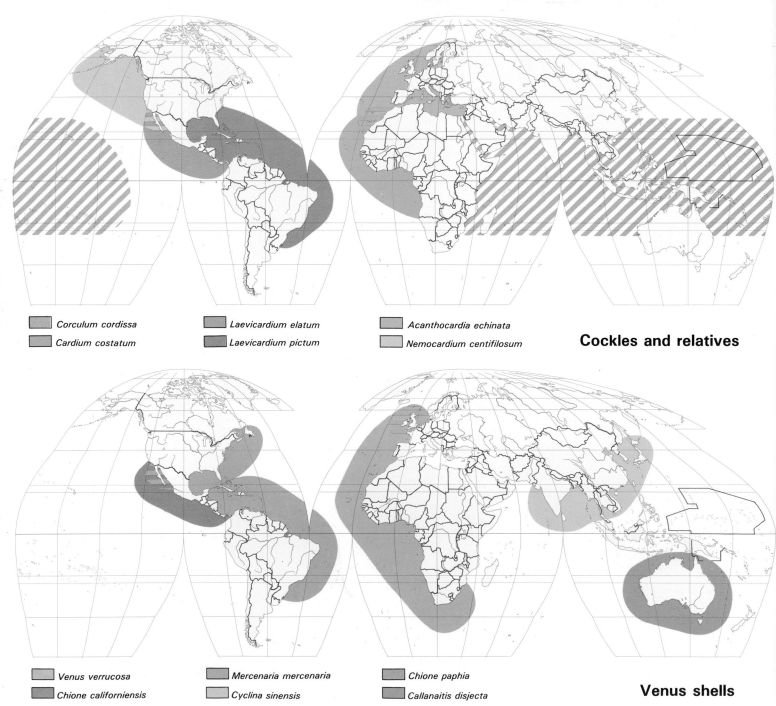

Corculum cordissa	Laevicardium elatum	Acanthocardia echinata
Cardium costatum	Laevicardium pictum	Nemocardium centifilosum

Cockles and relatives

Venus verrucosa	Mercenaria mercenaria	Chione paphia
Chione californiensis	Cyclina sinensis	Callanaitis disjecta

Venus shells

Cephalopoda

The cephalopods – octopuses, squids and cuttlefish – are the most highly evolved group of molluscs, differentiated from all the others by the greater development of the nervous system and the sense organs. In octopuses and cuttlefish the eyes reach a degree of complexity similar to those of the vertebrates.

They live in a marine environment, but not in seas with low salinity, so that they are absent in the Baltic and the Black Sea. Active predators, they are near the end of the food chain and perhaps for this reason represent only a small percentage of all the molluscs. 10,000 fossil species are known, but today they are represented by only about 700 living species, which are divided into the Tetrabranchiata and the Dibranchiata.

Tetrabranchiata

The extinct nautiloids and ammonites belonged to this group, now represented only by the chambered nautilus. As the name implies, the Tetrabranchiata have four gills, in two pairs. Early nautiloids had a long, straight, chambered shell, whereas in the modern forms the shell is coiled. This development occurred at least 200 million years ago and the living forms are little different from ancient fossils. The present genus *Nautilus* contains six species. The shell is a flat spiral, the coil being held above the mantle and mantle cavity. It is divided into several chambers of which the animal occupies the last. The chambers are partly filled with liquid and partly with a mixture of gases similar to air, but containing a greater proportion of nitrogen to oxygen; it is this gas which confers buoyancy.

Like most of the cephalopods, the *Nautilus* moves along by expelling water from the mantle cavity through a funnel formed by a modification of the foot. The mouth and head are surrounded by numerous tentacles which lack suckers but are strongly adhesive; the male has about sixty of these, the female ninety or more. *Nautilus* lives only in the Indo-Pacific region at depths of between 50 and 650 m (150 ft to 2000 ft). The most widely distributed species is the pearly nautilus (*Nautilus pompilius*, illustrated on p. 42). Unlike all other cephalopods, *Nautilus* has no ink sac. It feeds on fish and planktonic crustaceans.

Dibranchiata

The Dibranchiata have one pair of gills and, besides the heart, two branchial hearts which assist the flow of blood through the gills. The shell, always internal, is generally reduced and in the Octopoda has faded away entirely. There are eight arms in both octopods and squids, but in the latter there are also two additional, long, grabbing tentacles. In the region of the mouth, besides the radula, there are two robust, horny jaws, like a bird's beak, capable of grinding down the shells of large crustacea and tearing pieces out of fish prey. The nervous system, strongly centralized, forms a kind of brain enclosed in a cartilaginous capsule. The eyes are highly developed. Lacking the protection of a shell, the Dibranchiata have replaced it by other defensive techniques such as rapidity of swimming and protective mimicry. One of the best known methods of defence is the expulsion of the so-called 'ink', a blackish liquid which, besides concealing the animal, apparently destroys the sense of smell of the predator. In many of the Dibranchiata luminous organs are present, as luminous bacteria live symbiotically with the cephalopod, while other forms are capable of secreting a luminous liquid; it seems that luminescence may serve for recognition between partners and, in species living at great depths, for attracting prey. The group is divided into Decapoda, Vampyroporpha and Octopoda; there are about 120 European species.

Decapoda. The Decapoda – squids and cuttlefish – have ten arms, or to be more exact eight short arms with two much longer tentacles. All are provided with suckers; on the arms these are arranged in two or four rows along the under surface, and on the tentacles in clusters at the tip. The suckers enable them to adhere to anything from solid objects to living prey. The body is elongated and equipped with lateral wing-like extensions, or fins, for swimming and the shell is internal and usually reduced to a single sheet or strip. They are divided into two groups, the Sepioidea and the Teuthoidea. The first is further divided into families including Spirulidae and Sepiidae. Of the first of these the sole representative is *Spirula spirula* (illustrated on p. 42), which has a coiled, chambered shell and lives in the depths of the oceans. The Sepiidae contains about eighty species, many of which live along the Atlantic coasts of Europe. The cuttlefish (*Sepia officinalis*, illustrated on p. 42) is common in the Atlantic and the Mediterranean, and can attain a length of 60 cm (24 in). The shell (commonly known as 'cuttlebone'), though much reduced, clearly shows the original divisions into narrow, flat chambers. The cuttlefish lives on sandy sea beds, where its remarkable ability to vary its colour makes it inconspicuous against its background. It is from *Sepia* that the black ink used to be collected for writing and painting. When it dries, it goes dark brown, hence the painter's term 'sepia'.

The Sepiolidae are similar in appearance to the cuttlefish, the body however is very short and the lateral fins are more developed, since they are used not only as rudders, as in the other cephalopods, but also for swimming. Many Sepiolidae are equipped with luminous organs, including *Sepiola atlantica* of the Atlantic and *S. rondeleti* of the Mediterranean.

The other group of decapods, the Teuthoidea, or squids, are characterized by the presence of a shell reduced to a thin horny plate, or lamella (often called the 'pen'), and of a hook on every sucker, as in *Enoploteuthis diadema*, illustrated on p. 42. They are divided into Loliginacea and Architeuthacea.

The Loliginacea contain many different families, of which the best known is the Loliginidae, to which the common squids belong. Their bodies are distinguished from those of the cuttlefish in being generally more slender and elongated. Highly skilful swimmers (backwards and forwards), they are capable of successfully hunting prey swifter than themselves, several individuals joining together to attack a shoal. Among the species most common along the European coasts are *Loligo vulgaris* (illustrated on p. 42), *L. forbesi*, *Alloteuthis subulata* and *A. media*.

The Architeuthacea also contain numerous families, including the Lycoteuthidae, to which belong various species carrying luminous organs, such as the splendid *Lycoteuthis diadema*, which owes its name to the presence of twenty-two luminous organs mostly situated below the eyes. *Abraliopsis morisii* (illustrated on p. 42), of the Enoploteuthidae, living in the deep waters off California, captures its prey with the powerful hooks on its arms. The Architeutherae include forms of very large dimensions which populate the ocean depths. The most common Atlantic species is *Architeuthis dux*, which reaches an overall length of 2 m (6½ ft). *A. princeps* reaches truly remarkable dimensions. A specimen taken off New Zealand in 1933 measured 22 m (70 ft) in total length; the tentacles of course accounted for a considerable proportion of this. The Histioteuthidae are of much smaller size, less than 30 cm (1 ft) overall, and are liberally studded with luminous organs. They re-

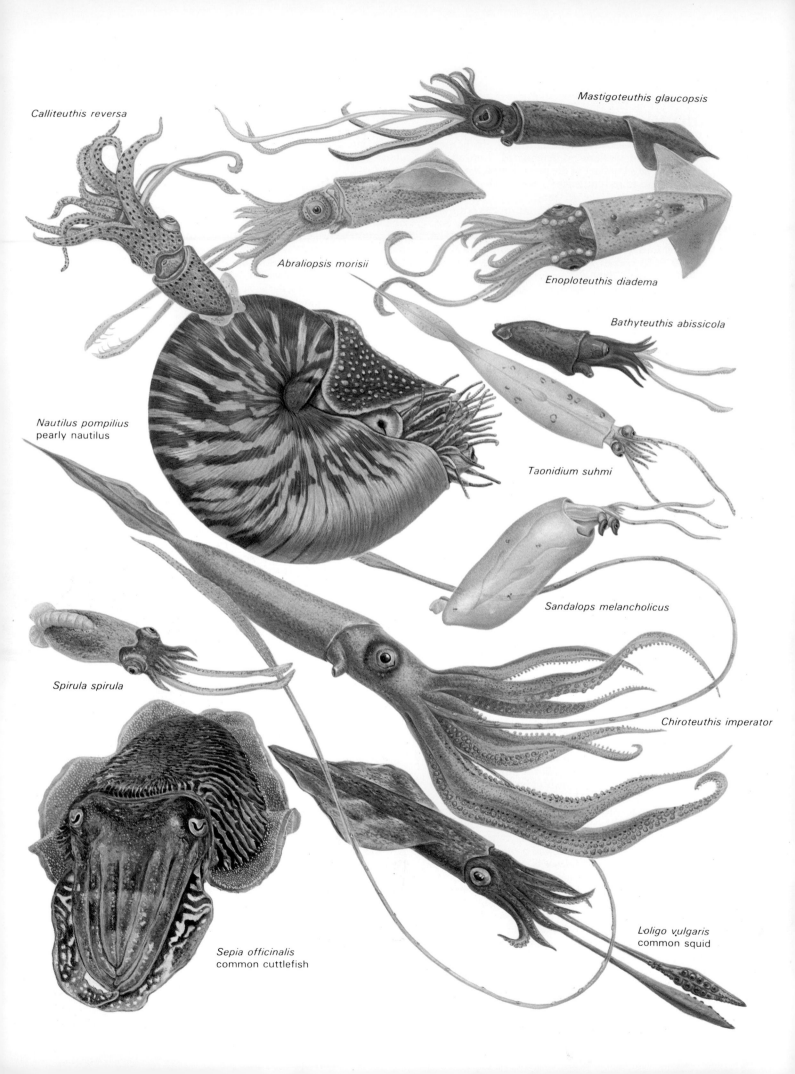

Calliteuthis reversa

Mastigoteuthis glaucopsis

Abraliopsis morisii

Enoploteuthis diadema

Bathyteuthis abissicola

Nautilus pompilius
pearly nautilus

Taonidium suhmi

Sandalops melancholicus

Spirula spirula

Chiroteuthis imperator

Sepia officinalis
common cuttlefish

Loligo vulgaris
common squid

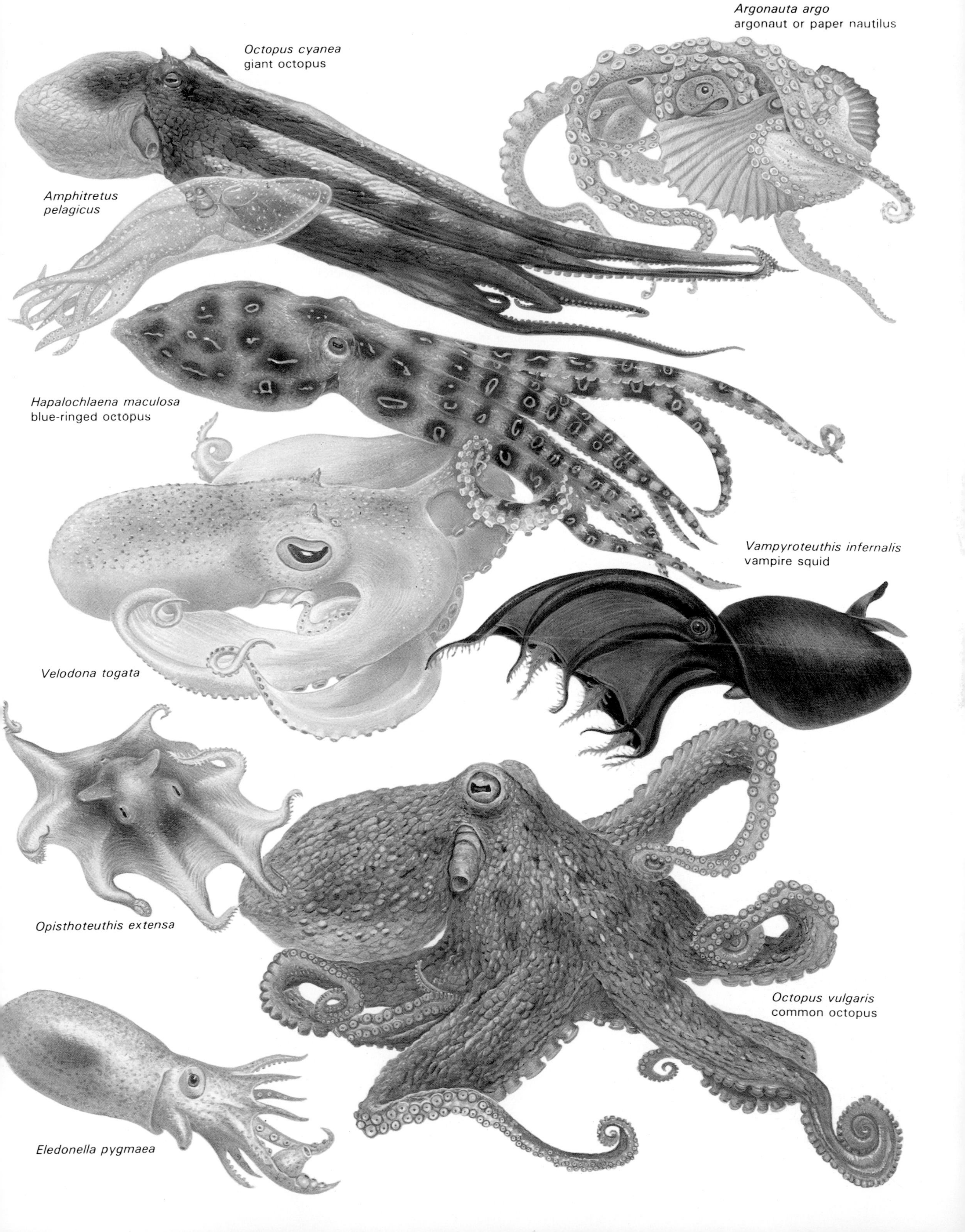

Octopus cyanea
giant octopus

Argonauta argo
argonaut or paper nautilus

Amphitretus
pelagicus

Hapalochlaena maculosa
blue-ringed octopus

Vampyroteuthis infernalis
vampire squid

Velodona togata

Opisthoteuthis extensa

Octopus vulgaris
common octopus

Eledonella pygmaea

semble small vampire squids, with the six dorsal arms joined by a membrane, which enables them to swim in much the same manner as jellyfish. *Calliteuthis*, illustrated on p. 42 by *C. reversa*, is also comparatively small; the eyes are markedly different from each other, the left eye being much larger and the smaller right one being surrounded by a circle of luminous organs.

The Ommastrephidae, like the Loliginidae, also unite in packs to hunt fish. They are powerful swimmers and can take flight into the air when pursued, like flying fish; this is made possible by their stiff fins and leathery arm membranes. Propulsion comes from the powerful expulsion of water jets from the mantle cavity, and can force them high enough out of the water to land on the decks of ships. *Ommastrephes sagittatus* is sometimes found stranded in large numbers along British coasts.

The Chiroteuthidae, small squids living in the ocean depths, have thin cylindrical bodies with long, whip-like tentacles which may measure up to six times the body length, as in *Chiroteuthis imperator* of the Indo-Pacific area, illustrated on p. 42.

In the Cranchiidae the arms are either much reduced or absent. *Cranchia* species, for example, have two long tentacles but the other arms are very short. Most are plankton-eaters, living within 100 m (300 ft) of the surface. Some of the species living at greater depths have entirely lost the ability to swim, and allow themselves to be carried along passively by the current. One of these is *Sandalops melancholicus* (illustrated on p. 42), of the South Atlantic, whose prominent eyes are mounted on stalks bent downwards, giving them the despondent air referred to in their name.

Vampyromorpha. Only one species belongs to this group of vampire squids, *Vampyroteuthis infernalis*, illustrated here, which is considered to be a veritable living fossil. About 30 cm (12 in) long, it lives at depths of between 1500 and 2500 m (1 to 1½ miles) in tropical and sub-tropical seas. There are two large shining eyes and two luminous organs situated at the base of the fins, as well as numerous other light organs on the body.

Octopoda. The Octopoda (octopuses and argonauts), the last group of cephalopods, are characterized by the presence of only eight arms, the tentacles being absent. The octopods of the Cirroteuthacea, living in the greatest ocean depths, have webbed arms, the webs reaching almost to the arm tips. The suckers on the arms are modified to form a double row of curved filaments which are tactile organs used also to collect the fine particles of food. The cirroteuthids, like most deep-sea dwelling octopods, have little bodily strength and the body consists largely of a jelly-like connective tissue. Species equipped with cirri – curled filaments on the arms – include swimming forms such as *Cirrothauma murray* of the North Atlantic, and others such as the various species of *Opisthoteuthis* which have become dwellers in the ocean depths; these last-named have flattened bodies and much-reduced shells (*O. extensa* is illustrated on p. 43).

Other octopods have suckers on their arms but lack cirri. The shell has completely disappeared. Of this group the Bolitenidae contain only a few species, with glassy, transparent, gelatinous bodies. They include *Eledonella pygmaea*, illustrated on p. 43, a species only a few centimetres long which has been found at depths up to 5400 m (3½ miles), and *Amphotretus pelagicus*, also illustrated on p. 43, which inhabits the deepest waters of the Caribbean.

The Octopodidae include the common octopus, (*Octopus vulgaris*, illustrated on p. 43), an active predator which lives principally on crabs but also on bivalves and gastropods. It perforates the shell of its prey with its radula, injects digestive enzymes into the body, and sucks up the partly digested contents. In the two Australian species *Hapalochlaena maculosa*, illustrated on p. 43, and *H. lupolata*, the salivary glands produce an extremely powerful poison which can kill the prey even without contact. The largest octopus is *Octopus dofleini* of the Pacific Ocean, which can weigh up to 60 kg (130 lb). Less well known is *Ozaena moschata*, which owes its name to the odour of musk which it gives off. It lives on the muddy bottoms of the Atlantic and Mediterranean coasts of Europe, and is a scavenger, living on dead animals. The map below shows the distribution of various species of Octopodidae.

The Octopods also include the Argonautacea, found in the open seas from the surface down to 900 m (3000 ft). They include the well-known *Argonauta argo* (illustrated on p. 43), which lives in warm temperate seas including the Mediterranean, as well as the Atlantic and Pacific. In this species two arms of the female are modified to secrete a papery 'pseudo-shell' which since it is not attached to the animal, is held between the two arms and serves as a protection for the mother and her eggs. The males are dwarfs, only one-twentieth the size of the female, and often live inside the shell.

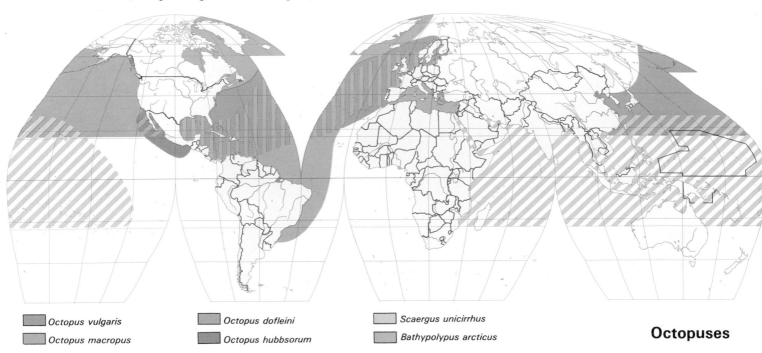

▨ *Octopus vulgaris*	▨ *Octopus dofleini*	▨ *Scaergus unicirrhus*
▨ *Octopus macropus*	▨ *Octopus hubbsorum*	▨ *Bathypolypus arcticus*

Octopuses

ARTHROPODS

The arthropods (Arthropoda) make up the group of invertebrates which has had the greatest evolutionary success. About a million species are known, but it is thought that many more must exist. They have come to occupy the most varied habitats; they live in both salt water and fresh, are the best adapted of the invertebrates to life on the land and the only ones to have conquered the air.

Their fossilized remains go back to the Cambrian era (over 500 million years ago), but their ancestors probably evolved in pre-Cambrian times from the annelids, the segmented worms. Generally the body is divided into three sections, head, thorax and abdomen and each section comprises multiple segments. In many groups, above all in the arachnids and crustaceans, there has been a tendency towards the reduction of metamerism through the fusion of adjacent segments.

The presence of an external cuticular skeleton which encases the whole body and of jointed limbs or other appendages is the principal development which distinguishes the arthropods from the annelids. It seems that the great evolutionary success of the arthropods must stem from the development of the external skeleton, which affords protection to the animal while at the same time a certain mobility is conferred by the many joints or articulations. The rigidity of the external skeleton might form an obstacle to growth, but this is overcome by periodical moultings in which the old outer covering is cast off and replaced by a new one. At such times, however, the animal is unable to support itself properly and is very vulnerable to attack.

Onychophora

The three lines of evolution which show characteristics common to and intermediate between the annelids and the arthropods are represented by the Onychophora, the Tardigrada and the Pentastomida.

The Onychophora, or velvet worms, were discovered only in 1826. They have a long cylindrical body divided into segments each of which, except for the head, is provided with a pair of unjointed legs each terminating in a foot with a pair of claws. The head, which is not marked off from the body by any narrowing, consists of three segments, the front one bearing two antennae and the others two simple eyes and a mouth provided with robust jaws. Onychophorans range from 1.4 cm to 15 cm (0.5 to 6 in) in length, but most are about 2 cm (0.8 in) long. Their excretory apparatus is similar to that of the annelids – each limb bears a pair of excretory tubes – but the circulatory and respiratory systems are similar to those of the arthropods. The legs resemble the parapodia of the annelids, but the robust claws they carry are like those of the insects. They lead a nocturnal life and feed by preying on insects.

Onychophorans live in tropical and semi-tropical countries in damp places such as leaf litter, beneath the bark of dead trees, in crevices in the soil, under stones and in rotting logs. Until examined more closely they resemble slugs, earthworms or other denizens of similar habitats. There are only about seventy species in two families, the Peripatopsidae, found mostly in Australia, and the Peripatidae of the tropical areas of America, Africa and Asia. *Peripatus* is a typical representative of this last group. Superficially it resembles a caterpillar, with about seventeen pairs of legs arranged along the cylindrical body. At the forward end it has two large antennae and two papillae on either side of the mouth which emit the adhesive substance secreted by the glands. This can be shot out over a distance of up to 0.5 m (1.5 ft) and hardens on exposure to the air, forming sticky threads. It crawls along slowly both by using its legs and by extending and contracting its body, the legs of an extending segment being raised off the ground when it is moved forward. *Peripatus* lives in tropical rain forests, hiding under leaves or stones during the day and coming out at night to search for food.

Tardigrada

The tardigrades are a group of very small animals rarely attaining one millimetre (0.04 in) in length. The body is clad with a thick cuticle which presents various types of ornamentation and is often vividly coloured. Their name refers to their characteristically slow and ungainly way of moving. They are sometimes also known as water bears, from their bear-like shape. There are always four pairs of stubby legs, which like those of the onychophorans are simple, cylindrical, movable extensions, each terminating in a group of four to eight sharp-pointed claws. In motion they grasp the substrate with these hooks.

Some tardigrades live among sand particles on the sea bottom, while some live in fresh water or on plants such as mosses and lichens. During dry periods they are able to dehydrate themselves and lower their rate of metabolism; they appear to be dead but are in fact in a state of suspended animation which may last several months. Most species live on the contents of plant cells, the plant being pierced with a sharp 'stylet' in the mouth cavity and the contents sucked out by the action of the muscular pharynx.

Pentastomida

The Pentastomida are a group of less than a hundred species all of which live as parasites, with dimensions ranging between a few millimetres and 14 cm (5.5 in) in length. They have a worm-like appearance with five protuberances at the forward end. The name of the group, which means 'five-mouthed', refers to these extensions, but in fact only one of them is a mouth, the other four terminating in hooks or claws with which they attach themselves to the host. Their life-cycle is often complex and their development may involve living on various hosts in turn. In the adult stage they live in the respiratory tracts of reptiles, birds and mammals. Adult *Linguatula* are parasites in the nasal cavities of dogs and sometimes of other mammals, including man, but in the larval stage they live in various organs of rabbits and hares. When these are eaten by a dog, the adult stage develops in the new host. Other species live all their lives in the lung cavities of snakes.

Crustacea

The crustaceans include the most primitive of the arthropods. The body, which can be divided into head, thorax and abdomen, is made up of numerous segments. The appendages – antennae, mouth-parts and legs – are characteristically bifid (two-pronged) and they have two pairs of antennae instead of the single pair of other arthropods.

The body is covered with a cuticle which forms a carapace – a domed shell – which covers the forward part of the body and sometimes encloses it completely. Some 30,000 species are known at present, divided into various groups.

Cephalocarida

This group contains only a few species, a few millimetres in length, which live in the muddy sediments along the coasts of North America.

Branchiopoda

The branchiopoda include brine shrimps, fairy shrimps and water fleas. Most live in inland waters, but some can tolerate very high concentrations of salt. They are characterized by the possession of flattened appendages, some of which function as gills as well as for locomotion; they also act as filters for feeding. The most primitive group is that of the Anostraca, lacking a carapace, which live in temporary pools of water. One of this group is the fairy shrimp (*Branchipus stagnalis*, illustrated here). It lives in fresh water, but the brine shrimp (*Artemia salina*, also illustrated), lives in salt lakes, like those of Utah and California. These lakes can become filled with enormous numbers of brine shrimps, which provide ample food for bird life such as flamingoes. The Anostraca also include *Polyartemia forcipata*, illustrated here.

The Notostraca comprise a few species characterized by the possession of an ample carapace; they live on the bottom of stagnant pools. One species, *Triops cancriformis*, illustrated here, lives in rice paddies. It can survive long periods of drought in the form of resistant eggs, which hatch immediately it rains and puddles fill up. These big branchiopods thus suddenly appear from nowhere as though by magic. They die when the puddles dry up, but, as long as eggs are produced, the cycle repeats itself when the puddles fill with rain again.

The Conchostraca live in freshwater pools; some species, such as *Limnadia lenticularis*, illustrated here, are widely distributed. The Cladocera live in large numbers in lakes, stagnant pools and rivers, where they make up the principal diet of fish and other aquatic animals such as *Hydra*; some species are inhabitants of the seas. The water flea (*Daphnia pulex*, illustrated here) is one of the commonest creatures of ponds and ditches, and is a major constituent of the food sold for aquarium fish. It is less than ½ mm long, but often occurs in dense swarms where it bobs about in a distinctive manner.

Ostracoda

The Ostracoda comprise some 12,000 species of crustaceans which resemble the bivalves in that the carapace is formed of two parts provided with a hinge, an elastic ligament and an adductor muscle. Most are bottom-dwellers but a few are excellent swimmers. Most are marine but there are some freshwater species. They are all fairly small, about 10 mm (0.4 in) in length, and the largest species, *Gigantocypris agassizi*, illustrated here, attains not more than 30 mm (1.2 in) in length. *Cypris* is a common British freshwater genus, living in the mud at the bottom of ponds.

Copepoda

The Copepoda contain more than 4000 species found in both sea and fresh water. The plankton-eating Copepoda that form enormous shoals in seas and lakes belong to the Calanoida. *Calocalanus pavo*, illustrated here, is a marine form with numerous appendages resembling feathers. *Calanus finmarchicus* is the principal food of the herring and other fish that feed near the surface. *Chondracanthus* species are parasites, living in the gills of saltwater fish, as do the *Caligus* species, which, like some other parasitic forms, are provided with a proboscis. *Penella* are also parasitic, living on fish and whales. *Cyclops* is a group of worldwide distribution; it has one eye, and for this reason is named after the Cyclops, the one-eyed giant of Greek mythology. The *Cyclops* is shaped like a pear with a stalk and lives in both marine and freshwater habitats.

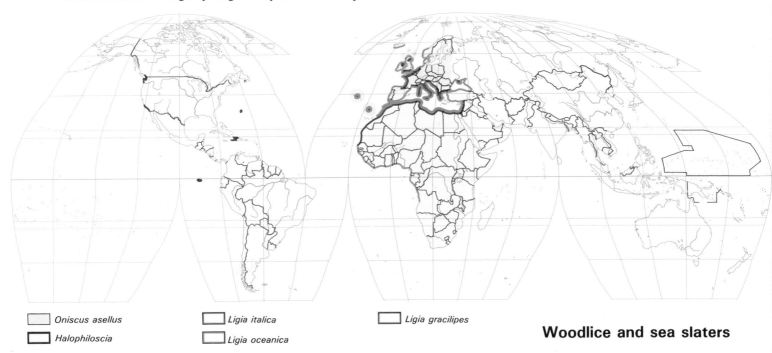

Oniscus asellus

Halophiloscia

Ligia italica

Ligia oceanica

Ligia gracilipes

Woodlice and sea slaters

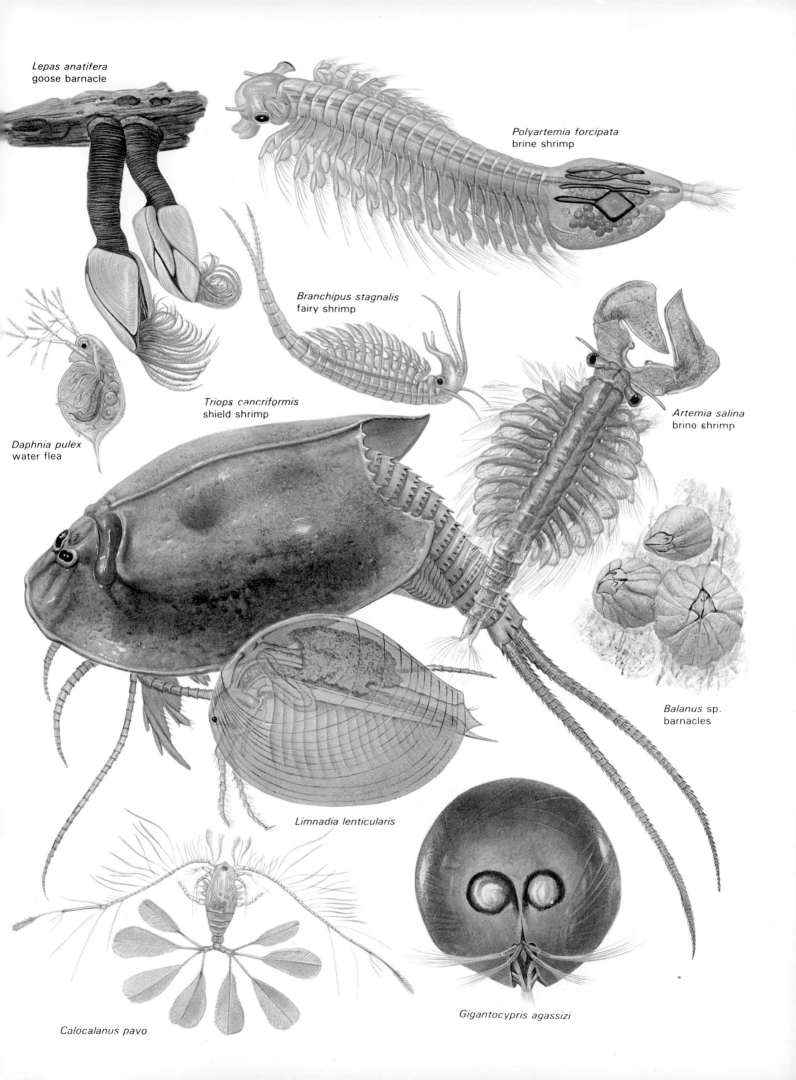

Lepas anatifera
goose barnacle

Polyartemia forcipata
brine shrimp

Branchipus stagnalis
fairy shrimp

Artemia salina
brine shrimp

Daphnia pulex
water flea

Triops cancriformis
shield shrimp

Balanus sp.
barnacles

Limnadia lenticularis

Calocalanus pavo

Gigantocypris agassizi

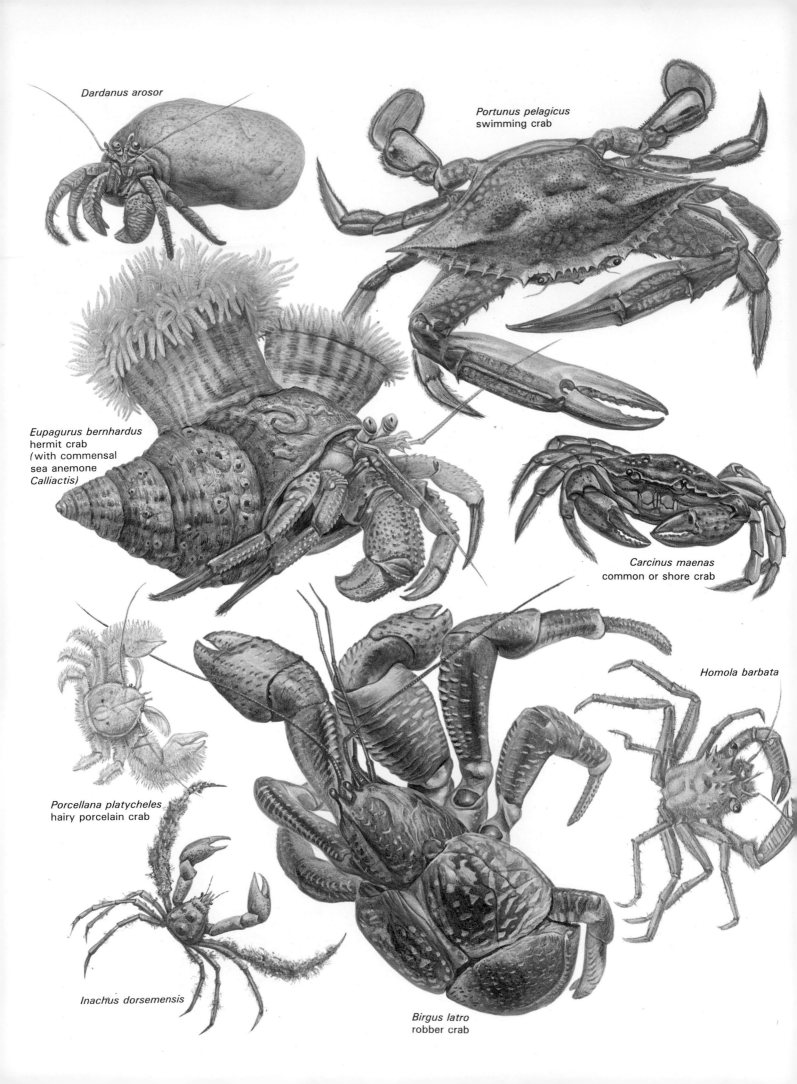

Dardanus arosor

Portunus pelagicus
swimming crab

Eupagurus bernhardus
hermit crab
(with commensal
sea anemone
Calliactis)

Carcinus maenas
common or shore crab

Homola barbata

Porcellana platycheles
hairy porcelain crab

Inachus dorsemensis

Birgus latro
robber crab

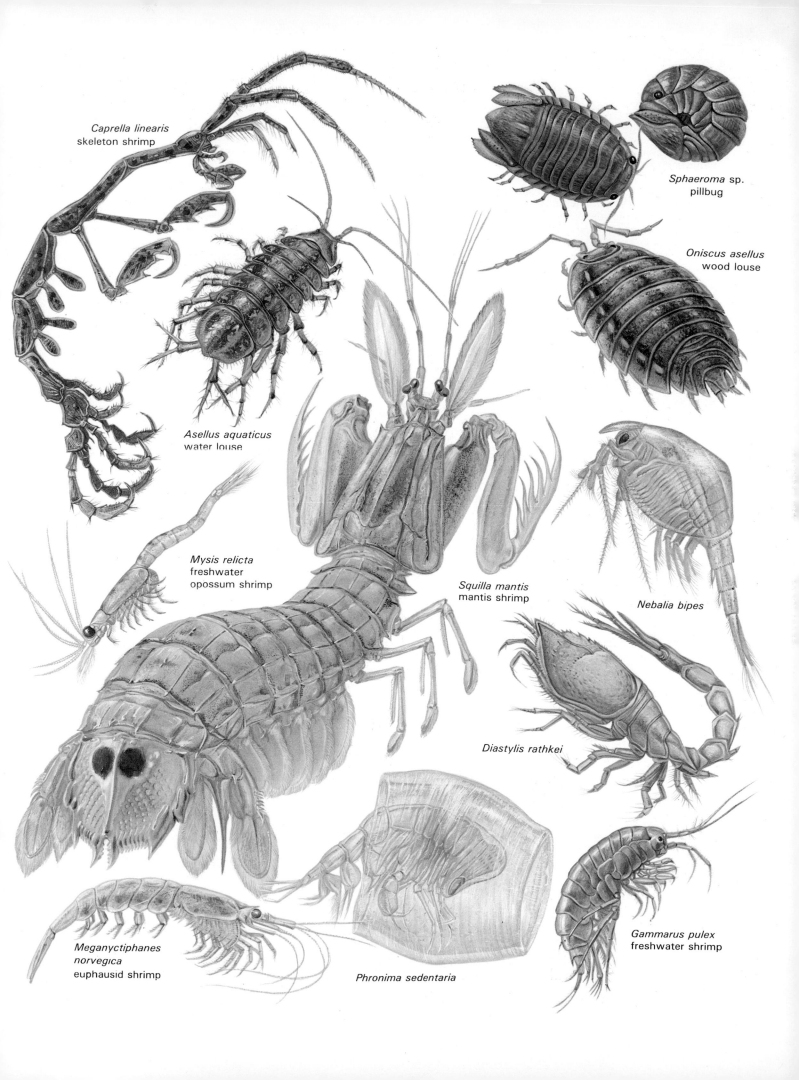

Caprella linearis
skeleton shrimp

Sphaeroma sp.
pillbug

Oniscus asellus
wood louse

Asellus aquaticus
water louse

Mysis relicta
freshwater
opossum shrimp

Squilla mantis
mantis shrimp

Nebalia bipes

Diastylis rathkei

Gammarus pulex
freshwater shrimp

Meganyctiphanes
norvegica
euphausid shrimp

Phronima sedentaria

Branchiura and Cirripedia

The Branchiura group contains only seventy-five species, all external parasites (ectoparasites) living on marine or freshwater fish. They attach themselves to the skin or to the interior of the gills, either by claws or by suckers, and suck the blood of the host.

The Cirripedia, or barnacles, number some 800 species, nearly all marine. They live for the most part attached to a variety of substrates, and many are parasitic. Those that are not are the only non-parasitic crustaceans to have taken to a stationary life as adults, and their structure has been extensively modified to permit this way of life, as is shown by the illustration (on p. 47) of *Balanus*. This group is that of the common barnacles living on rocks along the coast. In them the external skeleton is modified to form a series of overlapping plates. *Balanus* is a member of the larger group Thoracica, which all have a body enclosed in a calcareous shell from which only the cirri emerge. The cirri are the leg-like appendages, furnished with fine bristles, that are periodically thrust out and drawn through the water to collect food particles. The Thoracica have virtually no head or abdomen, the animal consisting almost entirely of a thorax. Another of the Thoracica is *Lepas*, the goose barnacle, which attaches itself to floating objects, notably ships and driftwood, by means of a fleshy stalk. *Lepas anatifera*, illustrated on p. 47, can attain 10 cm (4 in) in length.

The Acrothoracica are small creatures that find refuge in fissures which they excavate in the shells of molluscs. The Rhizocephala are cirripedes which live in the bodies of Decapoda, attaching themselves by a stalk from which roots grow into the host animal. *Sacculina* for example is parasitic on crabs.

Malacostraca

This group comprises at least 18,000 species. The body is typically formed of twenty segments, of which six, fused together, form the head, eight the thorax and six the abdomen. The group includes krill, shrimps, prawns, lobsters, crayfish and crabs. The name is derived from Greek words meaning 'soft shell'.

The most primitive of this group are the Leptostraca, which have a seventh segment at the end of the abdomen. Of this group, *Nebalia*, illustrated on p. 49 by *N. bipes*, is found throughout the world in shallow waters, typically under stones between high and low tidemarks, and particularly in places where there are high concentrations of organic refuse.

The Hoplocarida, which contain only one single sub-group, the Stomatopoda, contain about 350 marine species. They are cunning predators, living concealed in the sand or mud or in fissures in rocks. The mantis shrimp (*Squilla mantis* illustrated on p. 49) is so called because of a supposed resemblance to the praying mantis.

The Peracarida contain about 9000 species, including the animals commonly known as woodlice and sandhoppers. They are divided into several groups. The Thermosbaenacea comprise only a few species that live in the outlets of hot water springs in various parts of the world including the Dead Sea and Texas. Mysidacea number about 500 species, mostly marine and planktonic but found also in fresh and brackish waters. They are free swimmers with a long abdomen and a thin carapace. *Mysis relicta*, are illustrated on p. 49, is very widely distributed in cold and temperate seas and lakes in the northern regions of Europe, Asia and America. It is only about 2 cm (0.8 in) long and is rendered less visible to predators by its semi-transparent body. The Cumacea are marine creatures that live in the sand and mud of coasts and estuaries. They include the genera *Diastylis* (*D. rathkei* is illustrated on p. 49) and *Eudorella*. The Tanaidacea comprise about 250 species, usually living in burrows or tubes in the sand or mud; *Aspendes* and *Tanais* are European and British genera.

The Isopoda are one of the most evolved groups of crustaceans; they include slaters or woodlice. The body, flattened and lacking a carapace, varies in length from a few millimetres to the 35 cm (14 in) of *Bathynomus giganteus*, which lives in the depths of the Gulf of Mexico. Most species live independent lives, but some are commensal or parasitic on fish and crustaceans. There are about 4000 species of Isopoda. These include members of the genus *Ligia*, the sea slater, which lives above the high-water mark on beaches in many parts of the world. Their distribution is shown in the map on p. 46. Other genera are *Tylos* and *Halophiloscia*, the distribution of the last being also shown on the map, as is that of *Oniscus asellus*, the common European woodlouse, which is illustrated on p. 49. *Sphaeroma* (illustrated on p. 49) is another member of this group. The waterlouse (*Ascellus aquaticus*, illustrated on p. 49) is a British freshwater dweller.

The Amphipoda resemble the Isopoda in the lack of a carapace, but differ from them in that the body is flattened from side to side

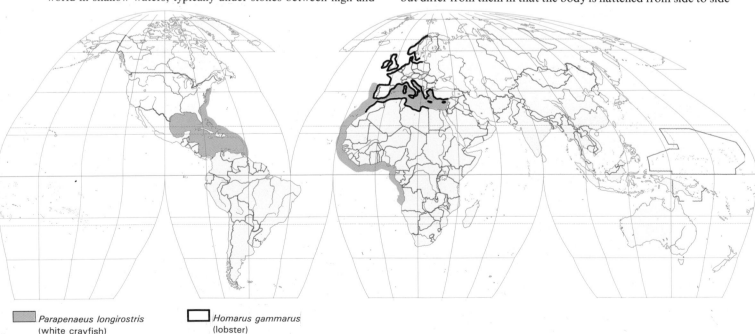

■ *Parapenaeus longirostris*
(white crayfish)

☐ *Homarus gammarus*
(lobster)

instead of from above to below. There are about 4000 species in several groups. Most are marine, but there are some freshwater forms. *Phronima*, illustrated on p. 49 by *P. sedentaria*, is an ocean-dweller, which often lives in jellyfish or tunicates (see squirts); it is noteworthy for its semi-transparency and enormous eyes. *Caprella* species, such as *C. linearis*, illustrated on p. 49, have slender elongated bodies. *Orchestia* and *Talitrus*, the well-known sandhoppers, are common along the coasts, particularly among heaps of damp seaweed on the shore line. *Gammarus* (the freshwater shrimp, *G. pulex*, is illustrated on p. 49) is also adapted for jumping.

The Eucarida – divided into Euphausiacea and Decapods – are also highly evolved crustaceans. Similar in form to shrimps, the Euphausiacea live in large shoals in the open seas. They include the phosphorescent shrimps called krill which form an important part of the food of whales and of many seals and penguins. There are about ninety species of Euphausiacea, of which *Meganyctiphanes norvegica*, illustrated on p. 49, is a denizen of northern waters.

The Decapoda number more than 8500 species. They are sometimes divided into Natantia, or swimmers, and Reptantia, crawlers. The former, which have a fairly light external skeleton, include prawns and shrimps. These may be distinguished from each other by the rostrum, a forward prolongation of the dorsal plate of the head, which is well developed in prawns but much less so in shrimps. Prawns include the common prawn, *Leander*, as well as *Penaeus cheraturus* and *Palaemon serratus*, both illustrated here. The shrimp, with a broader and flatter body and smaller rostrum, is of the genus *Crangon*. The Decapoda are divided into *Macrura*, *Anomura* and *Brachyura*. The first, with a long abdomen, includes, besides prawns and shrimps, lobsters and cray-

fish. *Homarus gammarus*, the true lobster, and *Palinurus vulgaris*, the crawfish or spiny lobster, are illustrated here. The popular food we call 'scampi' is in fact the Norway lobster (*Nephrops norvegicus*). The so-called white crayfish is *Parapenaeus longirostris*, whose distribution along with that of *Homarus gammarus* is shown in the map opposite. A common crayfish of rivers and streams is *Austropotamobius pallipes*, illustrated here.

The Anomura include the squat lobsters and hermit crabs. The latter find refuge in the empty shells of molluscs and sometimes, like *Eupagurus bernhardus*, illustrated on p. 48, live in symbiosis with sea anemones. *Dardanus arosor* (illustrated on p. 48) is a resident of Mediterranean waters. The porcelain crab (*Porcellana platycheles*), which resembles a crab but is one of the Anomura, is also illustrated (on p. 48), as is the robber crab (*Birgus latro*), which has abandoned the sea, having grown too large to inhabit the shells of molluscs, and lives on land in South-East Asia and on many tropical islands, its gills having been modified to permit air breathing.

Finally, the Brachyura, which have short abdomens, comprise about 4000 species, mostly marine. Some, however, live in fresh water, some are amphibious and some have become completely terrestrial. The common crab (*Carcinus maenas*) is illustrated on p. 48. The edible crab of the genus *Cancer* is larger and lacks the ability to swim. Other species include the swimming crab (*Portunus pelagicus*) and *Inachus dorsemensis*, both illustrated on p. 48. The spiny spider crab (*Maia squinado*) lives at depths of up to 200 m (660 ft), *Homola barbat* (illustrated on p. 48) at even greater depths. The Japanese spider crab (*Macrocheira kaempferi*) is the largest living arthropod, measuring 4 m (nearly 13 ft) across with its claws outstretched.

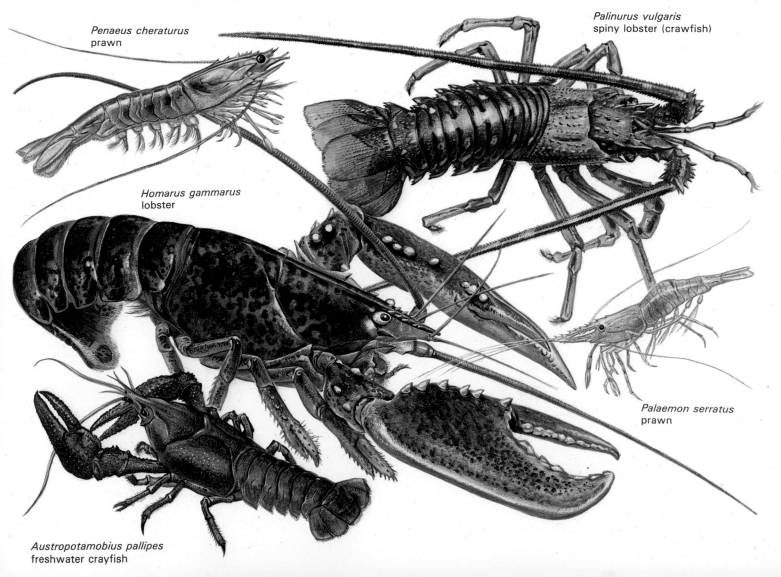

Penaeus cheraturus
prawn

Palinurus vulgaris
spiny lobster (crawfish)

Homarus gammarus
lobster

Palaemon serratus
prawn

Austropotamobius pallipes
freshwater crayfish

CHELICERATA

The group of arthropods known as Chelicerata includes spiders, scorpions and ticks. The Chelicerata were originally marine arthropods which later invaded both fresh waters and the dry land. Their great capacity for adaptation and their wide distribution are evidence of their evolutionary success. The body of the chelicerates is divided into a front portion, the cephalothorax or prosoma, and a rear portion, the abdomen or opisthosoma. The prosoma carries six pairs of appendages of which usually only the last four serve for movement, the first pair having been transformed into chelicerae, kinds of pincers, used for biting or eating. The second pair may be modified to result in organs used for grasping, as in scorpions, or for feeding and as sense organs, as in spiders. The numerous species of Chelicerata may be divided into Merostomata, Arachnida and Pycnogonida (or Pantopoda).

Merostomata

The Merostomata are exclusively marine chelicerates. Most are now extinct and are only known as fossils. There are four living species of which the best known is *Limulus polyphemus*, the king crab or horseshoe crab. It lives on the Atlantic coasts of North America; a veritable living fossil, its body is protected by a substantial carapace of which the forward part is somewhat horseshoe-shaped, giving the creature its American name. It can attain up to 60 cm (24 in) in length and has a long caudal spine resembling a tail. It lives on the sandy or muddy bottoms of the coastal waters and feeds on worms, molluscs and small fish.

Arachnida

The arachnids, which include spiders, ticks, mites and scorpions, are the largest group of chelicerates, with thousands of species, for the most part terrestrial. In spite of the great variety of shapes found in this large group, they present the same basic anatomical plan. The body is divided into the forward part, or prosoma, and the abdomen, or opisthosoma; the prosoma carries the chelicerae, the pedipalps or foot-feelers, and four pairs of limbs used for walking, whereas the opisthosoma has no appendages. Distributed worldwide in all habitats and in particular in the hottest regions, the arachnids are mostly aggressive predators.

Scorpiones

The scorpions are the oldest group of terrestrial arthropods. Their forward part (prosoma) is protected by a dorsal shield and carries, besides the chelicerae, two large pedipalps which terminate in pincers. The abdomen is divided into mesosoma or pre-abdomen and metasoma or post-abdomen. The latter, usually called the 'tail', ends in a poisonous spike, the sting or aculeus. Generally the scorpion's prey is caught and killed by the claws or pedipalps, and the poisonous sting is only used when the prey is too large to be killed in this manner or for defence. They are distributed between latitudes 50° north and south of the equator, and are particularly abundant in hot regions. An example illustrated here is *Hadrurus arizonensis* of Arizona. There are about 600 species.

The largest genus is *Buthus* of the Buthidae family, which contains more than 300 species, extensively distributed. *Microbuthus pusillus*, from the Red Sea coast, is the smallest scorpion, reaching at the most 13 mm (0.5 in) in length. The sting of most scorpions is painful rather than dangerous to man, but that of *Buthus* can be fatal to children, and a few other species are more poisonous still. The sting of *Androctonus australis*, a Saharan species illustrated here, can cause the death of a dog in a few minutes and of a human being in less than eight hours. Scorpions may live in very dry or very humid climates; *Centruroides gracilis*, illustrated here, is a tropical species. The largest scorpion is *Pandinus imperator* (illustrated) of the Scorpionidae family, a species found in West Africa. *Hadogenes bicolor* of the Diplocentridae family, also illustrated here, is an American species. There are some southern European species of which the largest is *Iurus dufourensis* of the Veiovidae family, illustrated here, as are two other European species, *Euscorpius italicus* and *E. flavicaudus*.

Pseudoscorpiones

The pseudoscorpions comprise about 1000 species of small arachnids distributed in all the temperate and warm regions of the world. They vary in length from 1 mm to 8 mm (0.04 in to 0.3 in).

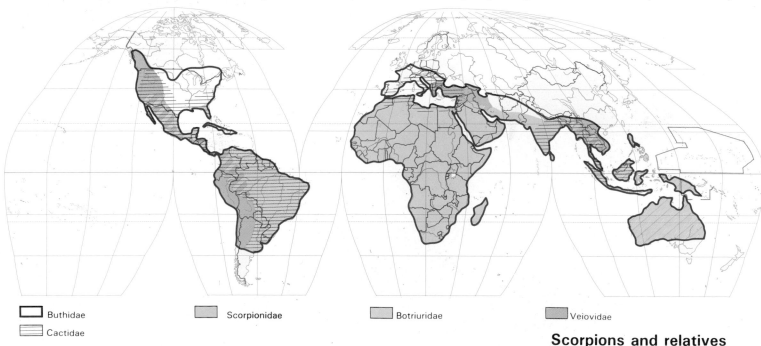

Buthidae Scorpionidae Botriuridae Veiovidae

Cactidae

Scorpions and relatives

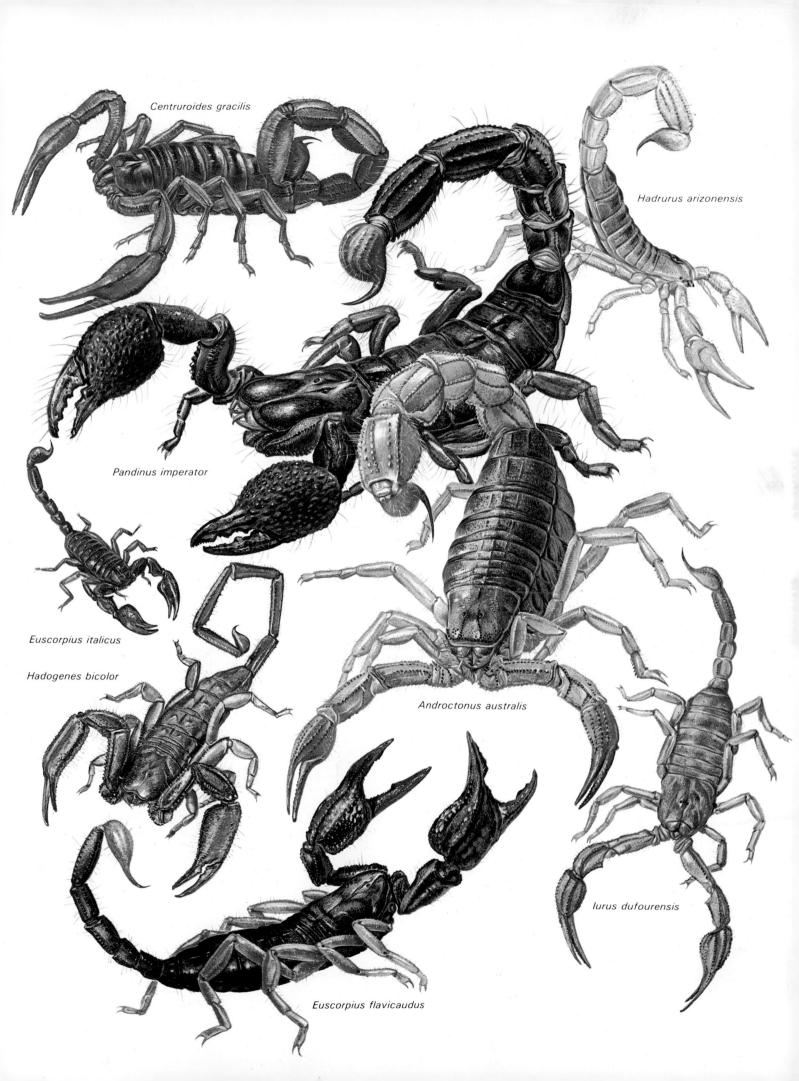

Centruroides gracilis

Hadrurus arizonensis

Pandinus imperator

Euscorpius italicus

Hadogenes bicolor

Androctonus australis

Iurus dufourensis

Euscorpius flavicaudus

They resemble the true scorpions in many respects but differ from them in the absence of a 'tail' and in having a more segmented body. A further characteristic is the possession of two large pedipalps which contain one or two poisonous glands, indispensable for the capture of prey, which includes small spiders, springtails (Collembola) and various insects. The best known species is *Chelifer cancroides*, found throughout the world; the smaller of the two illustrations shows its actual size.

Solifugae and Palpigradi

The solifugids, wind scorpions or sun spiders, are arachnids of large dimensions found mostly in the hot desert regions of Africa and the Americas. Their bodies are covered with a thick down and the prosoma carries the large chelicerae transformed into powerful pincers. Wind scorpions have adhesive organs at the ends of their pedipalps which are used to capture prey which is then torn apart by the chelicerae. The prey consists largely of termites, although small lizards and mammals may also be captured. The third pair of appendages is modified to form tactile organs, or feelers. The solifugids run very fast on the remaining three pairs of legs. There are more than 600 species; *Solfuga* live in South Africa, and *Galeodes* species, of which the sun spider (*G. arabs*) is illustrated here, are European and Asiatic.

The Palpigradi contain only a few species living in temperate and hot regions. They are about 2–3 mm in length (0.08–0.12 in) and have no eyes; the last abdominal segment carries a long whip-like appendage. They live hidden under stones or in caves and lead a nocturnal life.

Uropygi and Amblypygi

The Uropygi live in the humid environments of subtropical and tropical regions. Active only at night, they are predators on various terrestrial molluscs and on insects. More than 100 species are known: the whip scorpion (*Mastigoproctus giganteus*), an American species illustrated here, is the largest living example, measuring 7 cm (2.8 in) in length.

The Amblypygi are distinguished from the other arachnids by their small flattened bodies, by the possession of very long pedipalps furnished with spines, and by the first very long and thin pair of legs, which serve as feelers. Their distribution is limited to warm and tropical zones; they have nocturnal habits, and prefer humid habitats; some are cave-dwellers. There are about 60 species, of which *Prynichus reniformis* is illustrated here.

Araneae

The Araneae, commonly called spiders, are the most numerous group of arachnids. Up to the present time more than 26,000 species have been described, but it is considered that more than 100,000 species must exist. Their body dimensions, excluding the legs, mostly do not exceed about 2 cm (0.8 in), but some tropical varieties are 9 cm (3.5 in) long and with the legs may even exceed 20 cm (8 in). Prosoma and opisthosoma, the forward and posterior parts, are separated by a slight thinning or waist (the pedicel). The prosoma is protected by a carapace which carries eight eyes at the front; the chelicerae are characteristically provided with poisonous glands and the pedipalps of the male have been transformed into copulatory organs. The globular abdomen or opisthosoma, which is not segmented, is provided with appendages modified into spinning organs or spinnerets. These produce the silk which is used for the production of webs in only a small proportion of species; in most spiders the silk is spun into a cocoon to protect the eggs, and also as a lifeline to help in moving from one place to another. When seeking a mate, the male spider is exposed to considerable danger in approaching the female at all, because she is liable to mistake him for prey. He swings on a safety line towards and away from the female and plucks the thread held by her to warn her of his intentions. Spiders are carnivorous and feed principally on insects, which they kill with the poison injected by their chelicerae. They live wherever insects are found, being particularly abundant in tropical regions.

The spiders may be divided into various groups of which the Araneomorphae contain all the ordinary spiders. Of the others the Liphistomorphae, which are distributed in various parts of eastern Asia, are the most primitive, with large bodies provided with two pairs of lungs and articulated chelicerae disposed along the major axis of the body. The Mygalomorphae include the trapdoor and so-called bird-eating spiders, with 1500 species, more than a third of which are found in South America. Trapdoor spiders, such as *Pachylomerus aoudini*, illustrated on p. 57, make silk-lined burrows

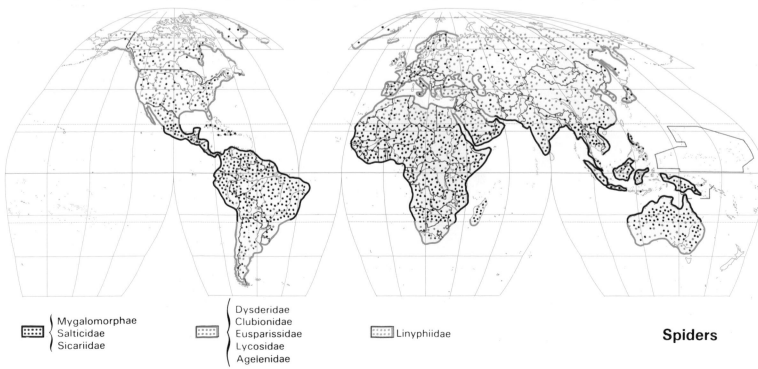

⬚⬚⬚ { Mygalomorphae
Salticidae
Sicariidae

⬚⬚⬚ { Dysderidae
Clubionidae
Eusparissidae
Lycosidae
Agelenidae

⬚⬚⬚ Linyphiidae

Spiders

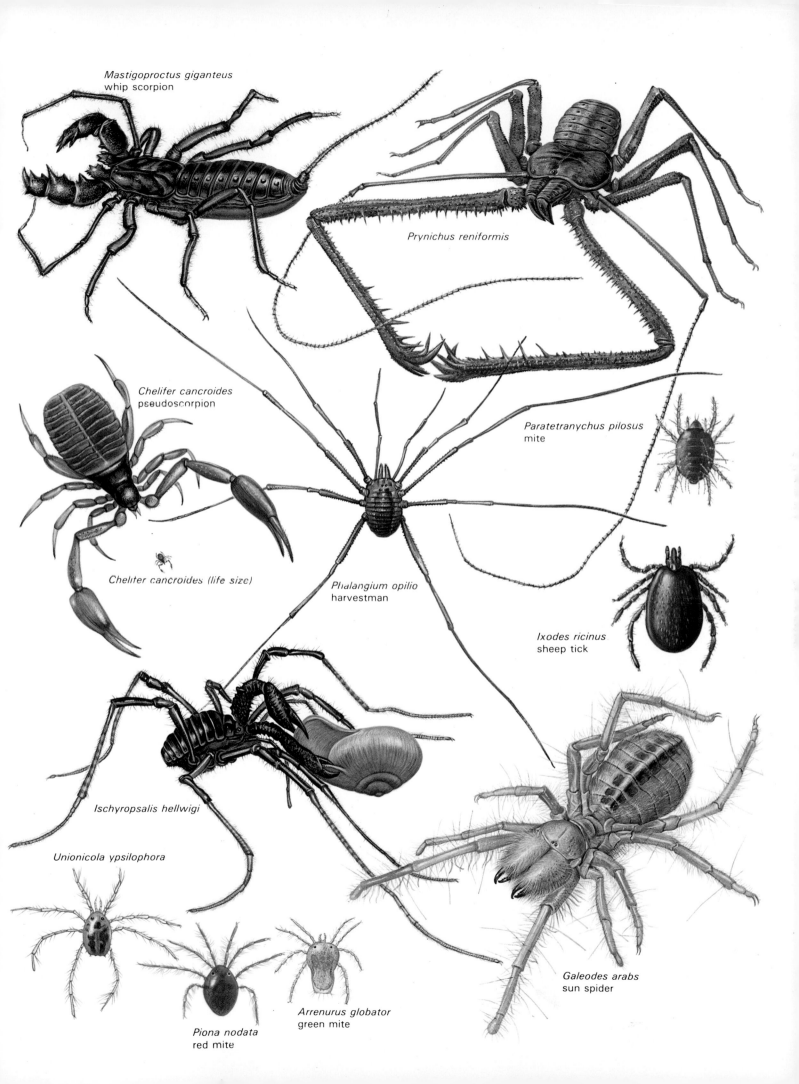

Mastigoproctus giganteus
whip scorpion

Prynichus reniformis

Chelifer cancroides
pseudoscorpion

Paratetranychus pilosus
mite

Chelifer cancroides (life size)

Phalangium opilio
harvestman

Ixodes ricinus
sheep tick

Ischyropsalis hellwigi

Unionicola ypsilophora

Piona nodata
red mite

Arrenurus globator
green mite

Galeodes arabs
sun spider

in the ground with a hinged lid of moss or soil and wait there for passing prey. *Atrax robustus* (illustrated on p. 59), of tropical regions, is feared for its poisonous bite, and the South American bird spiders, such as *Avicularia avicularia* (illustrated here) and *Theraphosa leblondi* (illustrated on p. 59) (sometimes called a tarantula) also have a dangerous bite.

The Araneomorphae contain the greater part of living spiders, being represented by at least 24,500 species. Their chelicerae are articulated along a plane perpendicular to the major axis of the body, and in general they have only one pair of lungs.

The Theridiidae number about 1300 species, widely distributed. In temperate climates they are usually small and often highly coloured, living among the leaves of shrubs and bushes and spinning somewhat untidy and irregular webs. A representative of this group living in hot regions is the notorious black widow spider of the genus *Latrodectes*, whose bite is dangerous to human beings, causing respiratory paralysis. Three different species of this group are illustrated on p. 59.

The Argiopidae are a very extensive family and contain some spiders of very large size. They are also accomplished weavers, constructing intricate webs of surprising strength. In this group are included the tropical genus *Nephila*, of which *N. clavipes*, the largest web-spinning spider, is illustrated here; *Micrathena schreibersi*, illustrated here, which is characterized by the spines on its abdomen; *Argiope*, a genus common in southern Europe, of which *A. bruennincki* is illustrated here; and *Araneus*, of which the most familiar member is *A. diadematus*, the common garden spider, illustrated here.

The Agelenidae are another large family of sedentary spiders which construct webs provided with a kind of funnel in which they take refuge. The cobwebs which appear in our houses are spun by a member of this group, *Tegenaria domestica*, or house spider (illustrated). This is the long-legged spider that appears disconcertingly in baths; it comes up the waste pipe, but is unable to climb up the smooth sides of the bath. Other genera include *Agelena*, which live in social groups.

The Lycosidae include the common wolf spiders which are often to be seen running about in fields and woods in fairly large numbers. They do not build webs, but catch their prey by direct attack. The tarantula of southern Europe (*Lycosa tarentula*) is a member of this family, as is *Lycosa raptoria*, the much more

dangerous South American variety, illustrated on p. 59. Other very poisonous spiders are those of the genus *Ctenus*, of which *C. ferus* and *C. nigriventris* are illustrated on p. 59.

The Thomisidae, known as crab spiders from the characteristic shape of their abdomen, comprise some 16,000 species of 'wandering spiders' distributed throughout the world. *Misumena vatia*, illustrated here, is common in Europe. They have two pairs of strong forelegs stretched out sideways which enable them to run like crabs. They tend to live among flowers with whose colours they blend, or lie flattened against a blade of grass.

The Salticidae, another large group of wanderers, are the jumping spiders. They have excellent eyesight and catch their prey by jumping on it from a distance. They are widely distributed but particularly common in the tropics. There are at least 3000 species, among which are the jumping spider (*Salticus sanguinolentus*) and *Myrmarachne plataleoides* (both illustrated).

The Linyphiidae, living for the most part in cool and Arctic countries, include the small black money spiders, the sight of which is supposed to promise the acquisition of wealth. It hangs upside down in the hedges under a sheet-web.

Loxosceles reclusa, the recluse spider, illustrated on p. 59, is a venomous spider, whose poison breaks up the red corpuscles of the blood and produces serious ulceration.

Ricinulei

The Ricinulei include only fourteen species of little-known arachnids, only 1 cm (0.04 in) long at the most, deprived of eyes and leading nocturnal lives. They are usually found in humid environments in hot climates, mostly in Africa and America.

Opiliones

These are the harvestmen, a group of arachnids with small bodies and exceedingly long thin legs which live in temperate and tropical regions among vegetable detritus and the soil of woodlands, in meadows and in houses. The body, exclusive of the legs, is generally not more than 10 mm (0.4 in) in length; but some forms are less than 1 mm (0.04 in) long, while some tropical species, on the other hand, can measure as much as 20 mm (0.8 in) and have legs up to 16 cm (6.5 in) long. The body has an elliptical shape. The prosoma

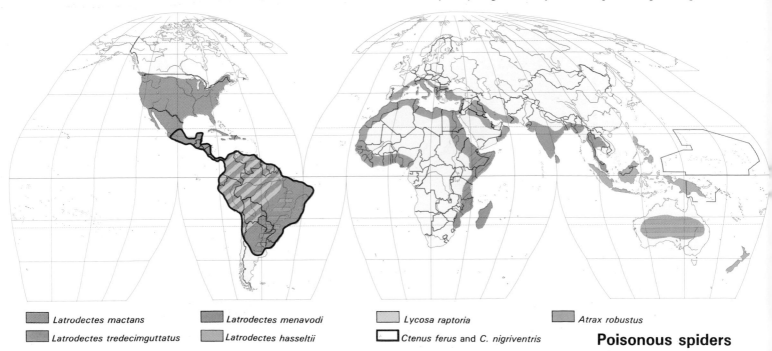

Latrodectes mactans	*Latrodectes menavodi*	*Lycosa raptoria*	*Atrax robustus*
Latrodectes tredecimguttatus	*Latrodectes hasseltii*	*Ctenus ferus* and *C. nigriventris*	**Poisonous spiders**

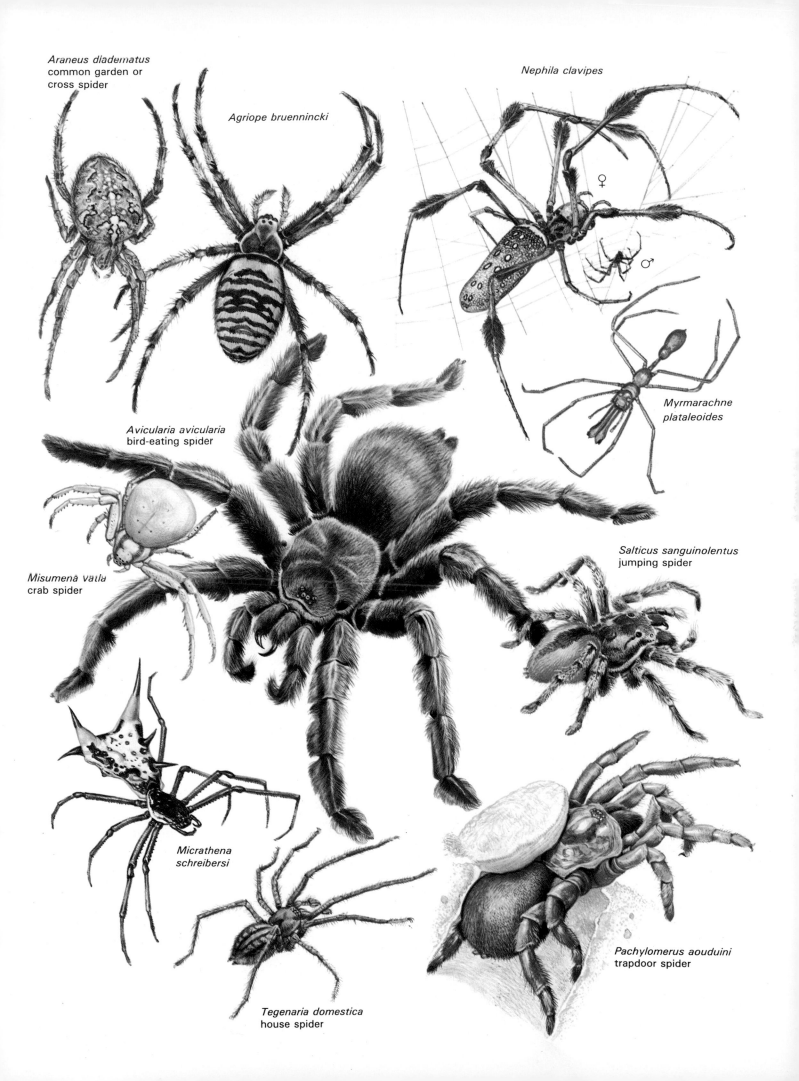

Araneus diadematus
common garden or
cross spider

Agriope bruennincki

Nephila clavipes

♀

♂

*Myrmarachne
plataleoides*

Avicularia avicularia
bird-eating spider

Misumena vatia
crab spider

Salticus sanguinolentus
jumping spider

*Micrathena
schreibersi*

Tegenaria domestica
house spider

Pachylomerus aouduini
trapdoor spider

carries two small eyes at the front and, at the sides, the openings of two scent glands which, in case of danger, emit a secretion with a bitter smell which puts the enemy to flight. There are 2300 species divided into several groups. The Cyphophthalmi are the most primitive, resembling the mites and ticks (Acarina). They do not exceed 2–3 mm (0.08–0.12 in) in length, and live mostly in Europe. The Laniatores live mostly in tropical regions and number about 1500 species. The Palpatores, with about 800 species, are distributed worldwide and include the most common European species, *Phalangium opilio*, the common harvestman, illustrated on p. 55. Another opilionid, *Ischyropsalis hellwigi*, is also illustrated (on p. 55).

Acarina

The Acarina, mites and ticks, are an enormous group of arachnids distributed in all terrestrial habitats and in both fresh and salt water. The terrestrial species are particularly abundant in vegetable detritus, humus, soil and mosses.

The Acarina are divided into various groups some of which are parasitic, such as *Dermanyssus gallinae*, parasitic on poultry, and the sheep tick (*Ixodes ricinus*, illustrated on p. 55), which also infests dogs, hedgehogs, rabbits and man. *Dermatophagoides* is often present in house dust and can cause allergies similar to hay fever. Some are herbivorous, such as the spider mites of the Tetranychidae, whose chelicerae are modified for piercing plant cells, the contents of which are then sucked out. The mange mite (*Sarcoptes scabiei*), causes scabies by burrowing into the human skin, inducing acute itching. The flour mite (*Tyroglyphus siro*) is another harmful species. Others transmit diseases, such as those species of *Trombicula* which spread typhus. Various species of Acarina, *Paratetranychus pilosus*, *Arrenurus globator*, *Piona nodata* and *Unionicola ypsilophora*, are illustrated on p. 55.

Pycnogonida

The Pycnogonida are exclusively marine and are commonly known as sea spiders. They may be between 1 and 10 mm in length (0.04 to 0.4 in), but the deep-sea variety *Colossendeis colossa* has a body 3 cm (1.2 in) long and when the legs are included can measure up to 60 cm (24 in). They are found in all the seas, in all latitudes and at all depths, but for the most part they are dwellers on the sea bottom, living on sponges, corals, sea anemones and Bryozoa, the sea mosses. They comprise about 500 species. They are also found under stones on the shore; *Nymphon gracile* and *Pycnogonum littorale* are British species.

MYRIAPODA

The Myriapoda, millipedes and centipedes, are a large group of arthropods that are either terrestrial or have gone back from the land to an aquatic environment. To this group belong the Diplopoda (millipedes) and Chilopoda (centipedes), together with two minor groups, the Symphyla and the Pauropoda. Common to them all are that they breathe through windpipes, or tracheae, as the insects do; for this reason they are sometimes grouped together with the insects under the name Tracheata. They also all have in common with the insects the possession of a single pair of antennae (whereas crustaceans have two pairs and chelicerates none). Their bodies are divided into numerous segments each of which carries one or two pairs of legs.

Symphyla

The Symphyla, only a few millimetres long, have a slender body with twelve pairs of legs. Lacking eyes, they live hidden under stones, in damp earth and among dead leaves, feeding on vegetable matter or small arthropods. There are about 120 species.

Pauropoda

The Pauropoda, which do not exceed 2 mm (0.08 in) in length, are soft-bodied, grub-like and have in general nine pairs of legs. Like the Symphyla, they live in more humid environments in the soil and among vegetable detritus. They feed on humus, fungi and the corpses of dead animals. There are 370 species.

Diplopoda

The Diplopoda, commonly called millipedes ('thousand feet'), in fact possess at the most 180 legs. They are usually only a few centimetres long, but certain tropical species can reach up to 30 cm (12 in). They prefer humid environments and some species are cave-dwellers; they are scavengers and live on decomposing vegetation and sometimes on the flesh of dead animals. There are 8000 species distributed principally in hot regions. Some of the commonest species belong to the family Iulidae. They include species living in Britain, such as *Iulus*, which lives in damp places, under stones or under the bark of trees, and feeds on decaying organic matter.

Chilopoda

The Chilopoda, commonly called centipedes, comprise about 3000 species distributed virtually everywhere, in cold as well as temperate and hot climates. Characteristically, there is only one pair of legs per segment (two in millipedes) and generally they have fifteen to twenty-three pairs of legs, but in the Geophilomorpha up to 173 pairs are present. Centipedes are carnivorous and the appendages of the first segment of the trunk are modified into two claws provided with a poisonous gland with which the prey is killed. Their food may include arthropods, worms and small vertebrates. The Chilopoda are divided into Epimorpha, characterized by having already fully developed segments and legs at the moment of birth, and Anamorpha, which are born with only a few segments and seven pairs of legs, but grow more later. The best known member of the latter group is *Lithobius*, a common centipede of both temperate and tropical regions, found under stones or under the bark of dead trees. Its body has fifteen segments each carrying a pair of legs. The front pair of appendages is modified to form powerful claws. The centipede is equipped with glands producing poison which is delivered through openings in the tips of the claws. The prey is caught and killed by the claws and cut up by the mandibles before being delivered to the mouth.

Some species of centipedes have bites painful to human beings, and that of *Scolopendra gigantica*, the world's largest species from tropical America which can reach up to 28 cm (11 in) in length, is reported to have been sometimes fatal. *Scutigera coleoptrata* is a fast-moving, long-legged species widespread in tropical and temperate regions, and frequently found in domestic dwellings in Europe.

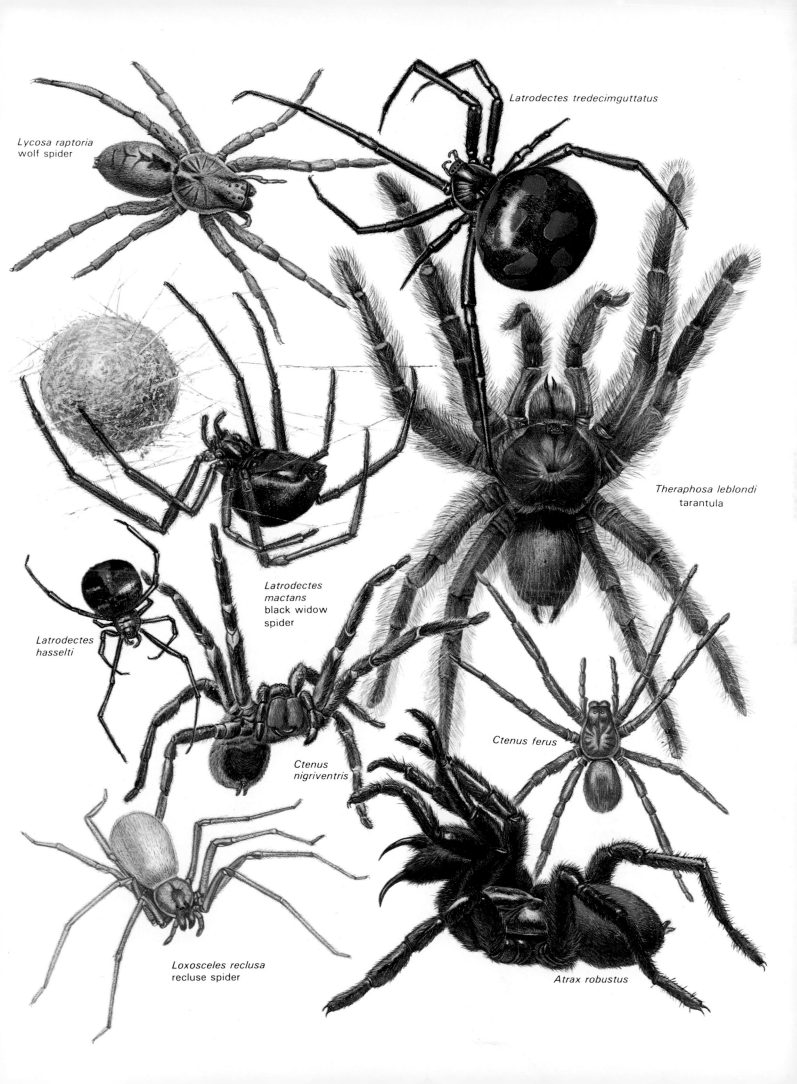

Lycosa raptoria
wolf spider

Latrodectes tredecimguttatus

Theraphosa leblondi
tarantula

Latrodectes mactans
black widow
spider

Latrodectes hasselti

Ctenus nigriventris

Ctenus ferus

Loxosceles reclusa
recluse spider

Atrax robustus

Insecta

More than 750,000 species of insects (Insecta) have been described up to the present time and there must be many more as yet undiscovered. Mostly terrestrial, insects are also found in fresh water. A few live in the sea but none in the deepest waters of the ocean. Existing as far back as the Devonian era (350–400 million years ago), they owe their great evolutionary success to various factors, above all the acquisition of the power of flight. This made possible the conquest of new environments and gave access to new sources of food, besides the possibility of escaping more easily from predators.

Despite the wide variety of forms found among the insects, it is always possible to distinguish three parts of their bodies: head, thorax and abdomen. The head is made up of six segments (metameres) and carries a pair of antennae, two compound eyes, some ocelli (simple eyes) and a mouth-apparatus which consists of a pair of mandibles and two pairs of the feeding appendages called maxillae (a kind of rudimentary jaw), of which the second pair forms the lower lip. The mouth-parts may be modified in various ways according to the type of diet. The thorax is typically formed of three segments, each one furnished with a pair of legs, and the last two normally endowed also with a pair of wings. The abdomen is made up of nine to eleven segments, of which only the last ones generally carry various appendages such as the cerci (tails) and the genitalia. Every bodily segment is armoured with hard cuticle forming a kind of tubular external skeleton which provides protection and supports the body.

Insects have rather complex and diverse life-styles. They are mostly characterized by the process known as metamorphosis, a change from one form to another completely different one as they grow up. Some groups show incomplete metamorphosis (hemimetabolous development), in which the egg becomes what is called a nymph, and the nymph progressively develops into an adult (imago) which resembles it in many respects. Others show complete metamorphosis (holometabolous development), which involves four stages: the egg becomes a larva (often caterpillar-like), the larva turns into a pupa, and the pupa into the adult (imago). The larva is totally unlike the adult in bodily form and way of life, and the transformation from one to the other takes place in the pupa. Complete metamorphosis implies therefore a total change from the larva into an entirely dissimilar adult.

The insects are divided into two major groups, the wingless Apterygota and the more advanced, winged Pterygota (although a few members of this latter group have, during their evolutionary history, lost their wings).

Apterygota

The apterygotes are the most primitive insects, characterized by the absence of wings, the presence of various appendages on the abdomen and, often, a pair of cerci or tail-like appendages. Metamorphosis is either absent or slight, and the young are similar to the adults in all but size. The apterygotes are divided into four groups: Protura, Collembola, Diplura and Thysanura.

Protura

The Protura were described for the first time in 1907, when the species *Acerentomon doderoi* was discovered in a garden in Genoa. They are minute insects, little more than 1 mm (0.04 in) long, distributed throughout the world, and living mostly in humid places such as moist soil, mosses and layers of decaying leaves. They are distinguished from other insects by the lack of antennae. Eyes are also absent and the mouth-parts are transformed into pointed structures capable of pricking or piercing. With the aid of these they live on the internal liquids of the white mass of thread-like fungal cells (mycelium) that coat the roots of plants or other rotting vegetation.

Collembola

The Collembola, or springtails, contain about 4000 species, living mostly in fertile ground, usually on the surface but sometimes at considerable depths. They are very numerous, and with the mites make up over 80 per cent of the arthropods living in the soil. In a square metre of ground there may be anything from a few thousand to 700,000 Collembola, depending on how much organic matter the soil contains. They are of great importance in the initial process of breaking down dead plant remains in the soil. Those species that live on the surface have the largest dimensions, and can attain as much as 5 mm (0.2 in) in length, as in Tetrodontophora; the surface forms are equipped with a kind of forked ventral 'tail' which folds underneath like a spring and enables them to leap into the air. The abdomen is further equipped with a ventral tube which, besides serving for the intake of air and water, secretes a viscous liquid which enables the insect to adhere to the smoothest surfaces. Some Collembola live in water; one of these,

A thysanuran silverfish on moss. These creatures also frequent warm damp rooms such as kitchens.

Podura aquatica, is common in stagnant European waters. Another species is *Isotoma saltans*, known as the glacier flea, which mountain-climbers may have observed on the snow at high altitudes.

Diplura

The Diplura, or two-pronged bristletails, have slender bodies, which are unpigmented and provided with two long antennae. They measure usually about 1 mm (0.04 in) in length, but some tropical species can reach as much as 4 cm (1.5 in). Distributed throughout the world, the Diplura usually live in humid places and are mostly found in temperate and tropical regions. There are about 400 species in two families, Campodeidae and Japygidae. The Campodeidae are characterized by the presence of cerci similar to antennae; the Japygidae on the other hand have cerci transformed into pincers which serve for the capture of prey, either small larvae or other arthropods.

Thysanura

The Thysanura, or bristetails, number about 350 species divided into two groups, Machilidae and Lepismatidae. The first have tapering bodies, large eyes and three ocelli; the second have flattened bodies with eyes either small or absent. Occurring throughout most of the world, like other apterygotes they prefer humid places. They live in the crevices of rocks, on the trunks of

A mayfly (*Ephemera danica*) rests on a stem and shows its characteristic three-bristled 'tail'.

trees, in caves and in the nests of ants and termites. Some species are often present in human habitations. Of these the best known is the common silver-fish (*Lepisma*), which causes damage to books, starchy food and clothing. It is about 1 cm (0.4 in) long and is covered with silver-grey scales. Another thysanuran group that has invaded human habitations in warmer countries is *Thermobia*.

Pterygota

The majority of living insects belong to this group. Characteristics of the Pterygota are the possession of wings (if they have none, this is due to a secondary loss, that is, wings were originally present, but were lost by a past ancestor) and the absence of appendages on the abdomen, except for the external genitalia, situated on the eighth and ninth segments, and the cerci. In certain groups, such as grasshoppers, cockroaches, stoneflies and bugs, metamorphosis is gradual or incomplete (hemimetabolous development) and all the stages from birth to adulthood are called nymphs. Other groups of insects, such as beetles, flies, butterflies and bees, undergo a complete metamorphosis (holometabolous development). From the egg hatches a larva capable of feeding itself. This is subsequently transformed into a pupa and ceases to feed. After undergoing a series of changes within the pupa, during which the definitive structures of the species develop, the adult form (the imago) emerges.

Ephemeroptera

The Ephemeroptera, or mayflies, which are distributed throughout almost all the world, are insects of small or medium dimensions whose life-cycle unfolds for the most part in an aquatic environment. The larvae are fairly long-lived, inhabiting fresh water for periods varying from a few months to three years. They then come to the surface and are transformed into a sub-imago capable of flight, which in a short time – a few minutes to twenty-four hours, according to the species – turns into the adult or imago. The larvae feed on vegetation, but the adults, which may be seen above streams, ponds and lakes in summer, do not eat at all, and their life lasts only a brief time, from a few hours to a few days. They are ephemeral creatures, soon gone, hence their name.

Plecoptera

The Plecoptera, or stoneflies, are a small group of insects varying in length from a few millimetres to some centimetres. They show incomplete metamorphosis, and spend a great part of their lives as immature nymphs living in water. The adult, which lives from a few days to a few weeks, is clumsy in flight but a capable walker, and can be seen making its way rapidly between stones or on trees in the neighbourhood of water. Most of the stoneflies live in hilly or mountainous regions where the vegetation is abundant and the water pure, flowing swiftly in stony beds. *Perla maxima* is a common species in European streams.

Embioptera

This is a small group of insects no more than 2 cm (0.8 in) in length. They often live in tunnels lined with silk that the insects themselves produce, in earth or in the trunks of trees, where they live on rotting vegetation. They prefer warm climates and are mostly found in tropical regions, although a few species are present in warm temperate climates.

Odonata

The Odonata – dragonflies and damselflies – number some 3500 species distributed throughout the world, especially in tropical regions (the map below shows the distribution of various species). Their length varies from 2 cm (0.8 in) to 13 cm (6 in) in some tropical species. They show incomplete metamorphosis. The larvae live in fresh water, in small ponds, in rocky lakes or in streams for a period varying from a few months to three years. They are voracious feeders, living mostly on small arthropods, although the larger species may prey on tadpoles or small fish. The adults have only a brief life, varying according to the species from 2–3 weeks to 3–6 months. The adults are also voracious feeders and prey on small insects such as midges, gnats and mosquitoes. They are assisted in this by their excellent eyesight. The prey is captured in flight by trapping it between the legs, which can be directed forwards; it is generally held in this trap until the dragonfly finds a suitable resting-place at which to devour it.

Anisozygoptera. The Anisozygoptera are represented by only two species of a primitive character, *Epiophlebia superstes* found in Japan and *Epiophlebia laidlawi* in the Himalayas.

Zygoptera. The Zygoptera, or damselflies, have a long slender body, and eyes notably far apart from each other. Their front and rear wings show similar veining; they are slow and irregular in flight and mostly deposit their eggs on the leaves and stems of aquatic plants, although some may deposit them on floating objects. They can be distinguished from dragonflies not only in being usually smaller and more slender, but also by the fact that they hold their wings together upright above the body when at rest, while the dragonflies hold theirs standing out at right angles to the body like the wings of an aircraft. The nymphs of damselflies have a small, slender, cylindrical body with long, slender legs and three, thin, leaf-like appendages at the end of the abdomen – the gills – while the nymphs of dragonflies have a flat or stout abdomen and shorter legs, and the leaf-like appendages are missing. The habit of flying locked together in pairs is also more commonly seen among the damselflies; the male grasps the female by the thorax and accompanies her while she is depositing her eggs, which involves her crawling down the stem of a plant and below

the surface of the water. Damselfly nymphs usually crawl on the bottom of ponds, but are also capable of swimming.

Illustrated here is *Calopteryx splendens*, a species widely distributed from Scandinavia to Algeria and from Spain to Siberia; like all the Odonata this is a territorial insect, and the male defends his own hunting territory. *Agrion puella*, found in Europe, western Asia and northern Africa, and *Pyrrhosoma nymphula*, found in Europe and western Asia, are also illustrated.

Anisoptera. In comparison with damselflies, the Anisoptera, or dragonflies, have a more robust body, eyes that approach each other more closely and front and rear wings which are more noticeably different from each other. The dragonflies are all strong fliers, can remain in the air for several hours and can undertake long migratory journeys. They are the most voracious predators among the Odonata. The male and female are sometimes seen flying joined together, the male in front and the female behind. In some dragonflies this occurs only during mating and the female deposits her eggs alone, flying low across the surface of the water and pausing from time to time to deposit her eggs by dipping the rear end of her abdomen into the water. The eggs are deposited singly or in long gelatinous strings. In other species the male accompanies the female in depositing her eggs, as among the damselflies. The nymphs lurk concealed among water-weeds awaiting the passing of prey, when they dart out to capture it. In transforming into an adult, the nymph climbs up a stalk, reed or other vertical object and clings there until its skin splits down the back and the adult dragonfly emerges.

Illustrated here are *Aeschna cyanea*, or southern hawker, a brilliantly coloured species widely distributed in Europe; the nymph of the species is also shown. As can be seen, the nymph in many respects resembles the adult, a feature of species showing incomplete metamorphosis. *Gomphus vulgatissimus*, or clubtailed dragonfly, is another common European species, which lives in still or slowly moving waters. *Sympetrum pedemontanum*, or red darter, is more often found in hilly and mountainous regions. *Crocothemis erythraea* is a species from India and Ethiopia which sometimes makes its way as far as central Europe. *Orthetrum cancellatum*, or black-tailed skimmer, is another European species; and *Libellula depressa*, or chaser, is a strong flier which both mates and deposits its eggs while in flight.

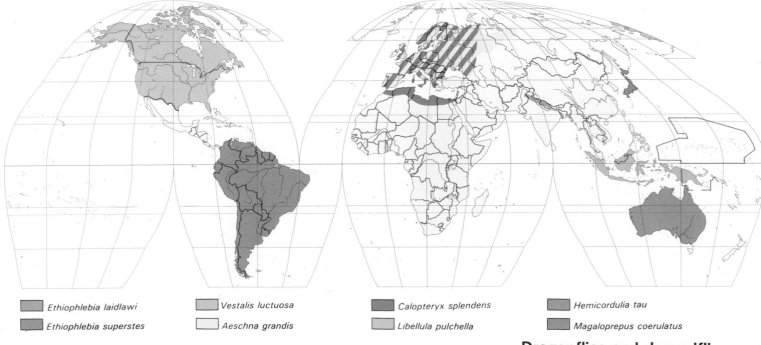

Ethiophlebia laidlawi	Vestalis luctuosa	Calopteryx splendens	Hemicordulia tau
Ethiophlebia superstes	Aeschna grandis	Libellula pulchella	Magaloprepus coerulatus

Dragonflies and damselflies

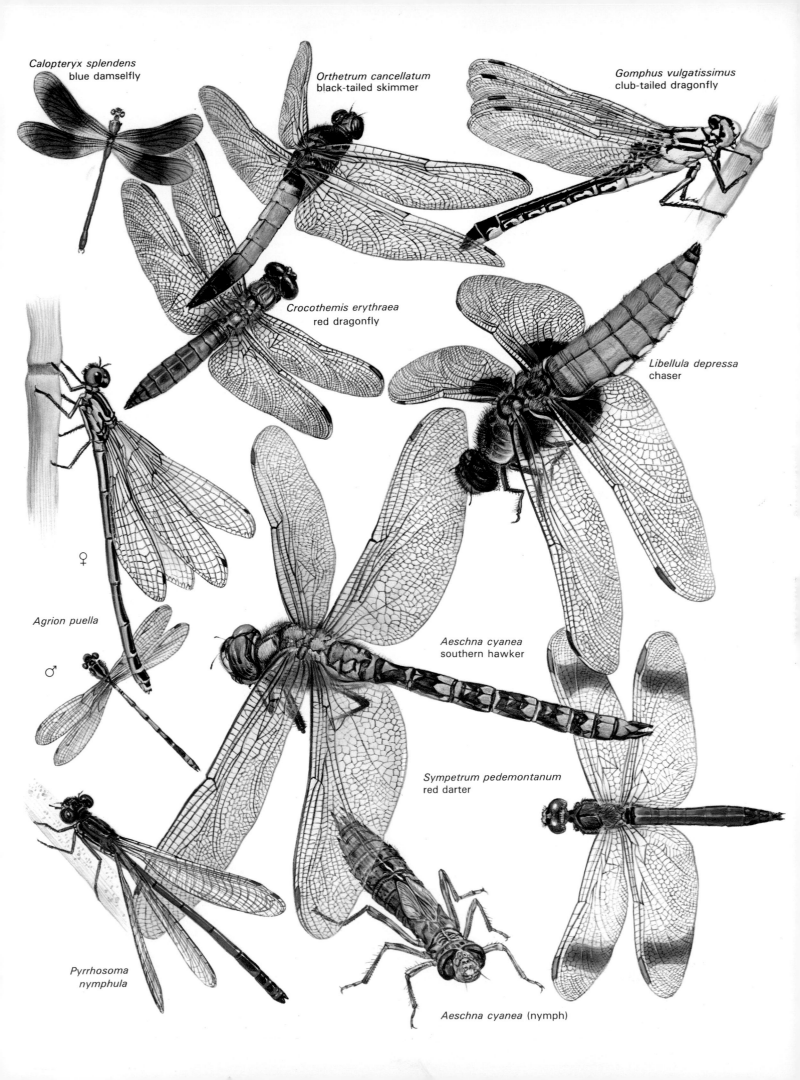

Calopteryx splendens
blue damselfly

Orthetrum cancellatum
black-tailed skimmer

Gomphus vulgatissimus
club-tailed dragonfly

Crocothemis erythraea
red dragonfly

Libellula depressa
chaser

♀

Agrion puella

♂

Aeschna cyanea
southern hawker

Sympetrum pedemontanum
red darter

*Pyrrhosoma
nymphula*

Aeschna cyanea (nymph)

Orthoptera

The Orthoptera – grasshoppers, locusts and crickets – number about 12,000 species distributed nearly everywhere, but particularly abundant in the warmer regions. The great variability of forms is shown in the illustrations of *Acridoxena hewaniana*, from Africa, *Phymateus brunneri*, also from Africa, and *Siliquofera grandis*. Generally not greatly skilled in flight, they move from place to place, for the most part by jumps made possible by their long and highly developed hind legs. Another characteristic of the Orthoptera is their ability to emit sounds which represent an effective method of communication. Most of them have well-developed wings, the first pair being narrow and leathery in texture and the second much broader. Some, however, have very short wings and others have no wings at all. The mouth-parts are well developed with strong jaws; and the female has a prominent egg-laying organ (ovipositor). In many species the abdomen is extendable, so that eggs can be laid below the surface of a softish substrate like loose soil or desert sand.

The Orthoptera are divided into two groups, one of which is characterized by a flattened ovipositor in the form of a sword or sabre; long and slender antennae; hearing organs located in the front tibia; and a ridge on the left forewing (tegmina) which when rubbed against that on the right wing produces a chirping or scraping (stridulant) noise, augmented by a membrane on the right foreleg. The Tettigoniidae are typical grasshoppers of this group, preferring warm climates and widely distributed in tropical

The spread of the migratory locust *(Locusta migratoria)* from central Niger over a seven-year period.

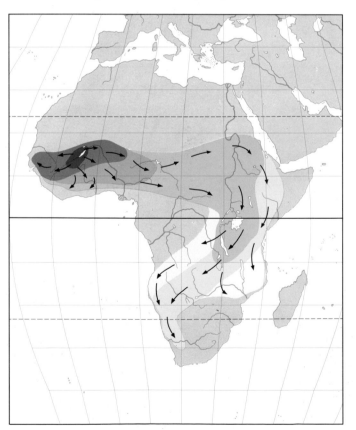

and sub-tropical regions. *Tettigonia viridissima* is the great green grasshopper of Europe, North Africa and Asia, living in the fields and meadows and feeding on buds or young shoots, leaves, grass and also sometimes on insects and larvae. Common in the mountainous regions of Europe is the small grasshopper (*Decticus verrucivorus*), which feeds principally on wheat and sometimes causes extensive damage to crops. Another species is *Saga pedo* which, lacking wings and a voracious predator, attacks and kills its prey with the powerful spikes with which its legs are provided.

The crickets (Gryllidae) also belong to this group. They are most numerous in humid and warm environments, and are able jumpers, having very well developed hind legs. The species most common in Europe, where it is widely distributed, is *Gryllus campestris*, the field cricket, illustrated here. During the day it remains hidden in the tunnels which it excavates in the earth. At twilight it emerges to seek for food, which consists entirely of leaves. In May the males begin their 'singing'; designed to attract the females, which are silent. The female crickets, like those of grasshoppers, deposit their eggs in the ground, in decaying logs or the stumps of dead trees, or in the living tissues of plants. At the end of the summer, when reproduction has been accomplished, the adults die. Another numerous and widely distributed species is *Gryllus domesticus*, the house cricket, which often lives in houses and stables, where its song is heard coming from the darkest and warmest places.

The Gryllotalpidae are a group of large Orthoptera which have a small head and a robust thorax and are protected by a carapace. The principal characteristic of this group is the transformation of the front legs into massive digging organs; hence they are known as mole crickets. Species of this group are distributed throughout Europe and in North Africa, Asia and North America. The largest, *Gryllotalpa gryllotalpa*, digs its burrows in the earth to depths of 5–10 cm (2–4 in) and causes much damage to crops. Other species are cave dwellers.

The other major group of Orthoptera has a short, squat ovipositor, thick, short antennae, stridulating organs situated in the femurs and hearing organs in the abdomen. The most important family in this group are the Acrididae, which include the locusts, notable for their tendency to form large assemblages that move over great distances. There are many species, distributed all over the world. Among those noted for their migrations is *Locusta migratoria* (illustrated), notorious for its devastation of crops in Asia and Africa. Members of this species are often fairly harmless, leading solitary lives (the solitary phase), but when environmental conditions are favourable for a rapid increase in numbers the individuals tend to gather in swarms (the gregarious phase). When they become so numerous that the supply of food becomes scarce, the locusts migrate in search of more favourable conditions, devouring everything edible that lies in their path. What is most remarkable is the difference between the locusts in the solitary phase and those in the gregarious phase; at one time they were even regarded as two distinct species. There are also half-way specimens with a range of characteristics merging at one end into those of the gregarious phase and at the other into those of the less troublesome solitary phase.

Schistocerca gregaria, illustrated here, is the locust that was responsible for the Biblical swarms of locusts that invaded Egypt. Other species belonging to the Acrididae are virtually harmless, like for instance the mottled grasshopper, *Oedipoda germanica*, a European species illustrated here. Another European species which prefers damp meadowlands is the long-headed grasshopper (*Acrida mediterranea*), also illustrated here.

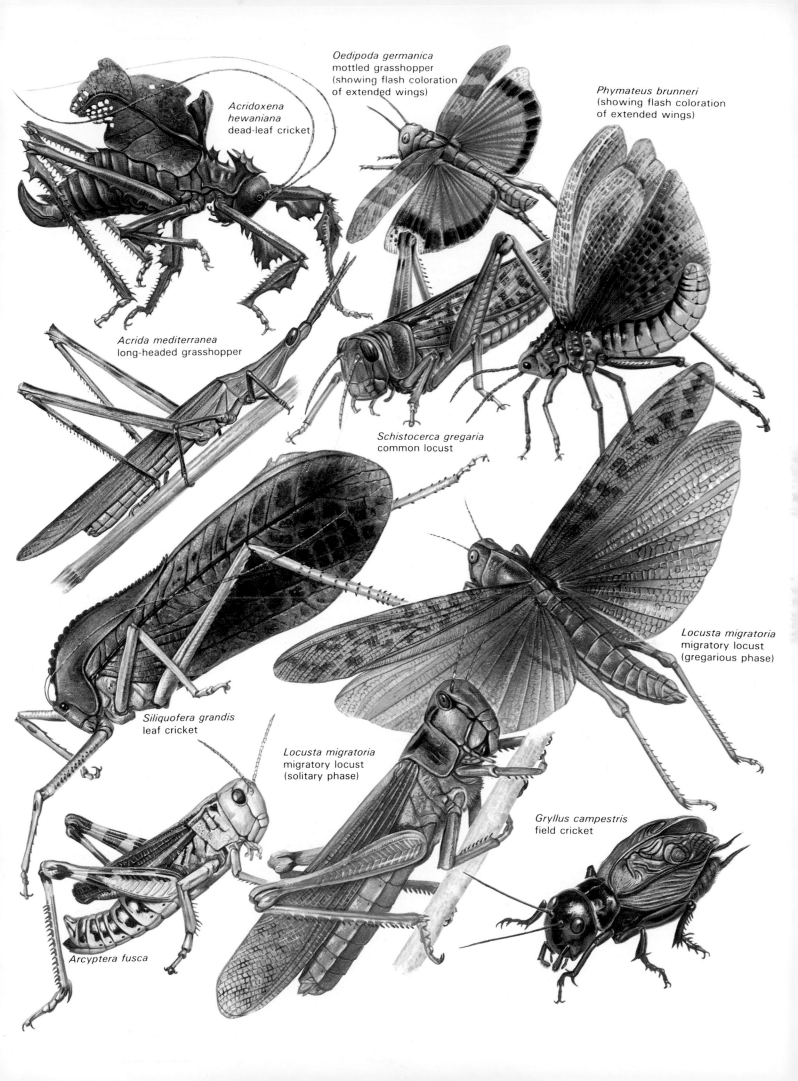

Acridoxena
hewaniana
dead-leaf cricket

Oedipoda germanica
mottled grasshopper
(showing flash coloration
of extended wings)

Phymateus brunneri
(showing flash coloration
of extended wings)

Acrida mediterranea
long-headed grasshopper

Schistocerca gregaria
common locust

Locusta migratoria
migratory locust
(gregarious phase)

Siliquofera grandis
leaf cricket

Locusta migratoria
migratory locust
(solitary phase)

Gryllus campestris
field cricket

Arcyptera fusca

Phasmida

The Phasmida – stick insects and leaf insects – are a group of about 2000 species found in temperate, warm and, above all, tropical regions around the world. Some succeed in maintaining themselves in northerly regions in deep and thickly wooded ravines, as for instance in the Province of Ontario, Canada. They live as a rule among vegetation, perfectly mimicking the twigs and branches on which they rest. They remain immobile during the day and only at twilight do they venture out in search of food, which is made up of buds, shoots and leaves. The females drop their eggs on the ground, and in forests where stick insects are numerous the eggs may be heard pattering on the ground like raindrops. The eggs remain on the ground throughout the winter and in more northerly latitudes only the thick snow covering in deep ravines enables them to survive. In tropical environments the insects assume a remarkable variety of shapes, mimicking to perfection such unappetizing items as dead leaves, twigs and even branches covered with flaking bark.

Leaf insects, which similarly mimic leaves for their protection, are less widely distributed and are found mostly on the islands of the South Pacific and in South-East Asia.

Grylloblattoidea

Grylloblattoidea are very primitive insects which are found at rather high altitudes. Only three species are known; one lives at heights between 450 and 2000 m (1500–6500 ft) in the Rocky Mountains in Canada. The other two are natives of Japan and Russia.

Dermaptera

The Dermaptera, or earwigs, possess a rather thickened external skeleton. The most distinct characteristic of the species is the presence at the rear end of a pair of cerci (tail-like appendages) transformed into pincers, whose purpose is somewhat obscure and the subject of some controversy. The front wings are transformed into sheaths into which the rear wings, large and amply capable of flight, are folded away. There are about 1000 species, distributed more or less everywhere. The common European species is *Forficula auricularia*, which, although it is provided with wings, flies rarely, and only by day. Sometimes it gathers together with others of its kind in large numbers in underground hiding-places. Earwigs live in places where there is a great deal of surface debris, such as leaves and decaying logs; they will squeeze themselves into the narrowest crevices in search of food or to hide themselves from their enemies. They feed mostly on decaying vegetation but some species will eat small insects. No poison glands are associated with the pincers, and the idea that with them earwigs are capable of inflicting stings or bites on human beings is mythical; likewise, the earwig has no motive for entering the human ear.

Diploglossata

The Diploglossata are a small group of insects comprising only eight species; all are parasites. About 1.5 cm (0.6 in) long, they have no wings and are blind. They are furnished with long cerci with no articulations and covered with hairs. They live exclusively in tropical Africa, feeding on the skin of the so-called giant rat (*Cricetomys gambianus*).

Blattaria

The Blattaria number about 3500 species, most of which are found in warm humid regions, notably in equatorial forests. About ten species, known as cockroaches, have been introduced into temperate regions and are common in human habitations, living in such places as kitchens and bakehouses, where they feed on foodstuffs and waste food matter. The bodies of these insects are similar to those of locusts but are flattened from above to below and carry two large eyes and two long whip-like antennae. They do not have the highly developed hind legs of locusts and therefore cannot jump, but depend for escape on their ability to move very fast. The wings, which in some species of Blattaria are very long and in some are completely absent, serve in general only for making brief glides, or as organs of balance. The female carries the eggs for some time between the last two abdominal segments but finally deposits them. The young cockroaches emerge as nymphs resembling the parents but lacking wings; they undergo a series of moults leading finally to the emergence of the adult.

Many species live in small communities of a few individuals of the same age, but the household species form more numerous communities which can number up to some thousands of adults and larvae. Among the household species is the common cockroach (*Blatta orientalis*), which is found almost everywhere. Infestations of cockroaches are dangerous to man since they often carry the agents of infectious diseases. Another type of cockroach is *Periplaneta americana*, found in warmer climates but also now introduced into European coastal cities.

Mantoidea

The Mantoidea, or cockroaches, number about 1800 species, found in regions with a warm climate. The tapered body carries a rather small head, more or less triangular in form, provided with two large compound eyes, a pair of wire-like antennae and a mouth-apparatus well developed for chewing. The first segment of the thorax is particularly long, in some species making up more than half the entire animal. Characteristic of this group is the structure of the forelegs. The first segment (coxa) is very long, and the femur and tibia are furnished with numerous sharp-pointed spines. These two parts of the forelegs can be folded closely together and form an effective instrument for the grabbing and holding of prey.

The best-known species is the praying mantis (*Mantis religiosa*), illustrated here. It can be observed standing perfectly motionless on a grass blade, with the body erect and the forelegs held in front of the body in what looks like an attitude of prayer. Praying mantises are voracious predators, feeding for the most part on various insects, including some of quite large dimensions.

The male mantis is unlucky in love, since the female usually attacks and consumes him after he has performed his function of fertilizing her. After mating she lays an egg capsule containing up to forty eggs; the capsule hardens and looks like a miniature haystack attached to the underside of a rock. The young hatch out after a few weeks.

Other less familiar varieties of mantis illustrated here are *Idolum diabolicum* and *Hymenopus coronatus* of East Africa, which are both highly coloured, but nevertheless mimic their habitual backgrounds; *Choeradodis laticollis* of South America; *Empusa pennata*, found in the Mediterranean region; *Gongylus gongyloides*, of South-East Asia; *Pseudocreobotra wahlbergi*, of Africa, and *Acanthus falcata*, of Brazil.

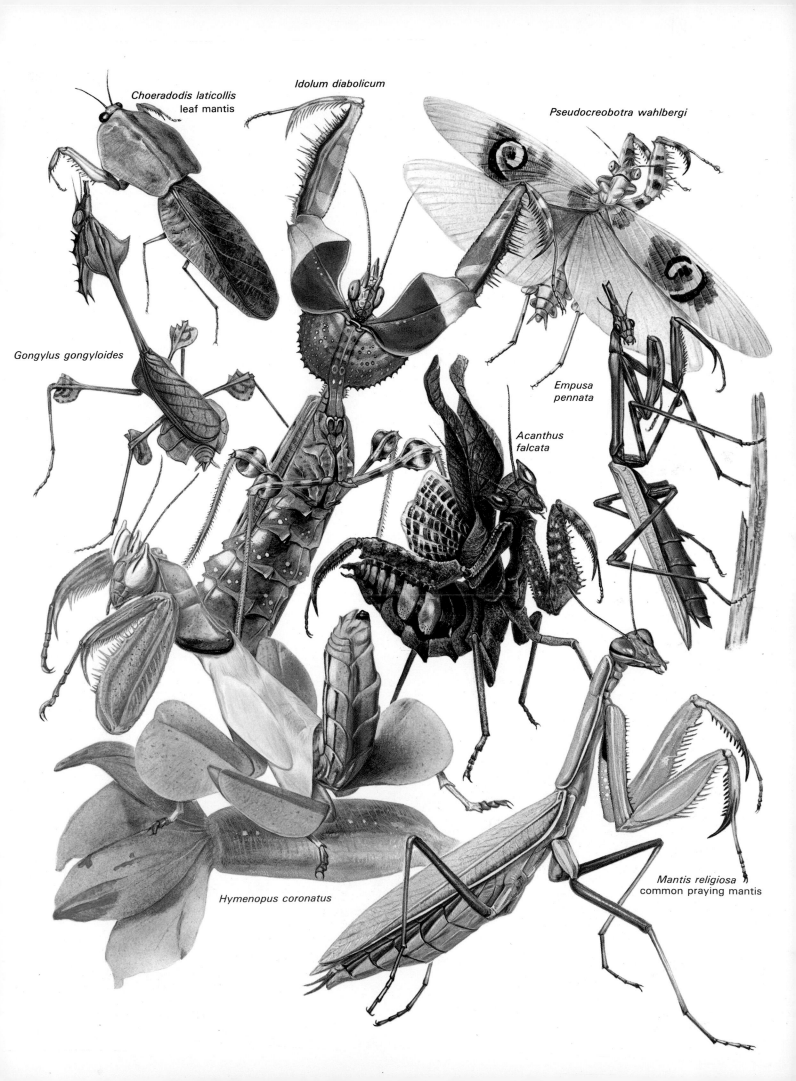

Choeradodis laticollis
leaf mantis

Idolum diabolicum

Pseudocreobotra wahlbergi

Gongylus gongyloides

Empusa pennata

Acanthus falcata

Hymenopus coronatus

Mantis religiosa
common praying mantis

Isoptera

The Isoptera, or termites, number about 1800 species showing incomplete metamorphosis, distributed for the most part in tropical and equatorial regions. They live in colonies formed in some cases of extremely numerous individuals divided into 'castes' differing in both shape and function. Generally these communities are made up of a pair of fertile individuals, the king and queen, and of their progeny, divided into larvae and immature individuals of different ages, some of whom are workers and some soldiers.

At certain times in the life of the colony winged fertile individuals appear whose task it is to found new colonies. The winged forms in several colonies usually swarm at the same time, so that cross-mating between different colonies can take place. Many of the swarming Isoptera are taken by birds or animals. A surviving pair, descending to earth, excavates a small burrow, and both lose their wings. The pair mate and eggs are laid in the nuptial chamber. The first young to hatch, mostly workers, are fed and tended by the parents and then take over the task of bringing up the later young. When fertilized, the female begins to undergo a series of changes. Her abdomen swells up, and after a few days she begins to lay her eggs. She may lay up to 1,000,000 eggs a year. Enormous and helpless (see illustration), she is fed by the workers. The male remains beside her for the whole of her life, which may be more than fifteen years.

Workers and soldiers may be either masculine or feminine, and lack both wings and eyes. Workers are employed on various tasks, such as the care of the offspring, the search for food and the construction, enlarging and repair of the nest. The soldiers, whose task it is to defend the nest, are usually larger than the workers. Their heads are particularly well developed and are provided with a large pair of sharp mandibles. The soldiers of some species are

capable of producing viscous substances used for entrapping the enemy, who are then killed with blows of the mandibles.

Most species of termites feed on vegetable materials, in particular on dead wood, which is initially devoured only by the workers. After it has been partially or completely digested, it is regurgitated to form the food of all the other members of the colony. Some species grow fungus underground for food. The termites' nest is usually partly below and partly above ground and dome-shaped, reaching heights of 4 m (13 ft) above the ground and a diameter of about 3 m (10 ft).

About 70 per cent of the known Isoptera belong to the Termitidae, which include the most evolved species of the group. Many species form enormous colonies, constructing nests of notable size, somewhat variable in form. The compass termite (*Amitermes meridionalis*) of Australia builds wedge-shaped nests (as shown in the illustration), which always have the major axis of the base triangle oriented in the north–south direction. *Cubitermes* and *Eutermes*, of Africa, build nests resembling fungi; these are illustrated here, as are the nests of the African *Macrotermes natalensis*, which are like gigantic towers up to 6 m (20 ft) high, and those of *Nasutitermes arborum*, built in trees.

Termites are sometimes referred to as 'white ants'. Although they are whitish in colour and live in colonies somewhat resembling those of ants, they are louse-like in appearance and are more closely related to stoneflies and cockroaches than to the true ants. The nests are made of earth cemented together with saliva produced by the termites, and in excavating the necessary soil and constructing tunnels and burrows below the earth they perform a useful function in aerating and enriching the soil as earthworms do in temperate countries, but they often remove much of the organic matter from the soil and may also cause extensive damage to various food crops and to the structural timbers of houses.

The different castes in termites' nests

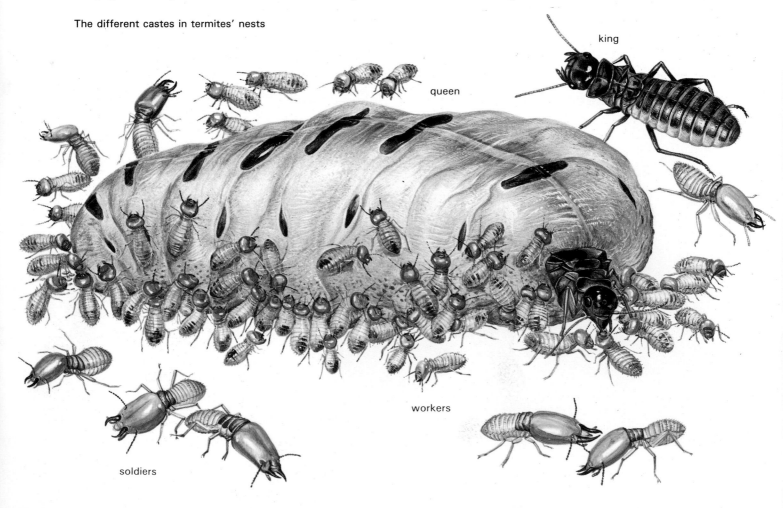

king

queen

workers

soldiers

mound of
Amitermes meridionalis
Australian compass termite

nest of
Nasutitermes arborum
tree termite

mound of
Macrotermes natalensis
African savannah termite
(cut away to show internal
passages and fungus 'gardens')

mound of *Eutermes triodiae*

mound of
*Cubitermes
subcrenulatus*

Mallophaga

The Mallophaga, or biting lice (as opposed to the Anoplura, or suckling lice), comprise a group of small insects 1–14 mm (0.04–0.6 in) long. Their bodies are flattened and are covered with a hard integument (toughened skin). They lack wings, and the head carries short antennae, small eyes and mouth-parts of the chewing (masticatory) type. There are about 3000 species, all external parasites, mostly on birds (for example the feather louse, or *Goniodes colchicus*, illustrated here), but a small proportion live on mammals. Many of the species parasitic on birds are capable of moving very fast along the surface of the body of the host, thanks to the presence of large cushions or suckers on the hind legs. Some species on the other hand clamber over their host on short legs with sharp claws. In the species parasitic on mammals the 'heel' (tarsus) is provided with a claw and a pad on a prolongation of the tibia which permits the animal to cling to the fur of the host; in the species parasitic on birds there are two hooks on the tarsus.

Bird lice feed on fragments of feathers, or on the scales of the skin. They do not feed on blood or puncture the skin of the host, but birds that are infested with these insects lose sleep and appetite and so, through loss of weight and energy, easily become ill.

Other species are parasitic on elephants, both African and Indian, on cats and on dogs; the species parasitic on dogs can be dangerous as carriers of tapeworms.

Anoplura (or Siphunculata)

The Anoplura, or sucking lice, number about 300 species of blood-eating insects, all parasitic, mostly on mammals. Measuring 0.35–6 mm (0.01–0.25 in) in length, they are wingless and have short legs folded inwards and terminating in a hook, which enables them to fasten themselves securely to the fur of the host. They are extremely well adapted to a parasitic life, being provided with mouth-parts suitable for piercing and sucking. The blood which forms the single food supply of the Anoplura is nevertheless lacking in important vitamins, and these substances, which are essential to their lives, are produced by bacteria living symbioti-

One of the Psocoptera, the booklouse (*Liposcelis divinatorius*) which feeds among other things on paper and cloth book bindings.

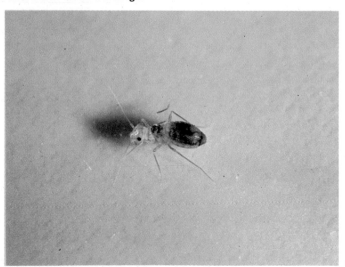

cally within the parasites, either in between their intestinal cells or inside certain organs.

Species of Anoplura are parasitic on various animals including pigs (*Haematopinus suis*, illustrated here), horses, sheep, goats, calves and dogs, besides human beings. The species parasitic on human beings is the louse (*Pediculus humanus*). This is a pale-coloured insect with dark markings along the sides. Its abdomen is flattened, with nine segments having extensible areas along the sides that permit the body to swell to a considerable size when feeding. The louse lays about two eggs a day, and these eggs – commonly called 'nits' – are attached to the skin, hair or clothing of the host by an adhesive substance secreted by the louse. The young hatch in six to nine days and pass through three states of increasing maturity between successive moults (instars) before attaining full maturity in about eighteen days, these times varying according to the temperature. There is no metamorphosis. The entire life cycle of the louse is completed in three or four weeks. The irritation and loss of blood caused by an infestation of these parasites is injurious, but the greatest danger lies in their acting as carriers of various diseases such as typhus and 'relapsing fever'. Trench fever, which was a major menace in all combat areas during the First World War and to a lesser extent in the Second, was also found to be a disease transmitted by a microbe passed into the bloodstream by the bite of this insect.

Most mammals are liable to infestation by only one species of Anoplura. In human beings there is a perceptible difference between those infesting the head and other parts of the body – head lice and body lice – and some authorities regard them as different sub-species, the head louse being named *Pediculus humanus capitis* (illustrated) and the body louse *P. h. corporis*. Others regard lice infesting these and other parts of the body (for example, the pubic louse, *Phthirius pubis*, illustrated here) as members of different species. Body lice are considered to have a greater egg-laying rate and to be more dangerous in the transmission of diseases. They cause intense irritation and itching, and occasionally pus-filled pimples form in the skin.

Thysanoptera

The Thysanoptera, or thrips, are a group of small insects, 0.5–13 mm (0.02–0.5 in) in length and distributed widely all over the world, from sub-polar to desert regions, and present even at high altitudes. Their slender body, either cylindrical or flattened, is covered with a robust external skeleton, often coloured black, yellow or chestnut. The wings, when they are present, are long and narrow and provided, along their edges, with a characteristic fringe of long bristles. The compound eyes are in some species small and situated at the sides of the head, in other species they are larger and situated in the middle of the head. The mouth-apparatus is of the piercing and sucking type. They feed for the most part on plants, sucking the juices, while a few are carnivorous, feeding on the internal liquids of aphids, Acarina, larvae, etc. Most live, in great numbers, in the fields, on blades of grass and on plants, particularly on flowers, on leaves and on buds. Others live on dead tree-trunks and in the bark of trees, in hay, in decaying layers of leaves in the undergrowth and in the tunnels excavated by other insects. If they are present in large numbers they may cause substantial damage to vegetation, and some carry viruses which cause plant diseases. They are therefore regarded as serious pests, since they can cause malformations of plants and inhibit the formation of fruit. On the other hand, many species of thrips feed on uncultivated plants, weeds and fungi and are therefore completely harmless; others, by feeding on the aphids that cause damage to plants, are even beneficial.

Liothrips oleae, illustrated here, lives on olives; the females of this species have no ovipositor and the eggs are simply deposited in cracks or fixed on leaves or other supports with an adhesive secretion. Other species live on tobacco plants, gladioli and various grasses, and there is a South African species that lives in the nests of termites. Many thrips reproduce themselves by the growth of unfertilized eggs (parthenogenesis).

Psocoptera

Psocoptera include the insects called booklice and dustlice. They are small insects that live mostly on the leaves or under the bark of trees, often in orchards and vineyards, in birds' nests, in the lairs of mammals and the nests of wasps and ants. Many species live in human habitations, and they are numerous in warehouses, where they live on cereal products, vegetable and animal debris, dead insects, paste, glue and moulds of all kinds. The majority, however, live outdoors. From 1 to 10 mm (0.04–0.4 in) long, they have a well-developed head provided with slender antennae and a modified chewing apparatus with pointed maxillae and a lower lip in which are found the openings of two silk-producing glands. Some – including booklice – have no wings; others have membranous wings with few if any veins. There are more than 1000 species, of which about 100 are found in Europe. Among these are *Liposcelis divinatorius*, illustrated here, and *Trogium pulsatorium*; both are very common in houses. They live hidden in the more humid places, where the mould they consume is most prevalent, and are often found under carpets, in cupboards, under tiles, in old books and newspapers and sometimes also in corners of the pantry or kitchen where there is food refuse affected by mould. Some species live in beehives, where they feed on honey.

Zoraptera

The Zoraptera contain only one group of eighteen species, mostly living in the tropical regions of the world. They are very small insects measuring at the most 2 mm (0.08 in) in length and provided with a mouth-apparatus of the chewing type. They live in small colonies in vegetable detritus.

Hemiptera

The Hemiptera group contain the true bugs, although many different kinds of insects are referred to as 'bugs'. They have maxillae and mandibles modified to produce two long, pointed parts, or stylets, which are capable of both piercing and sucking and are held when not in use in a sheath, the rostrum. This has a sensitive tip and is used both to select the food source and to guide the stylets into position. Because of the great variety of shapes and ways of life of the Hemiptera they are divided into two groups, Heteroptera and Homoptera.

Heteroptera. The Heteroptera are characterized by the possession of wings differing from each other in shape. The first pair is greatly

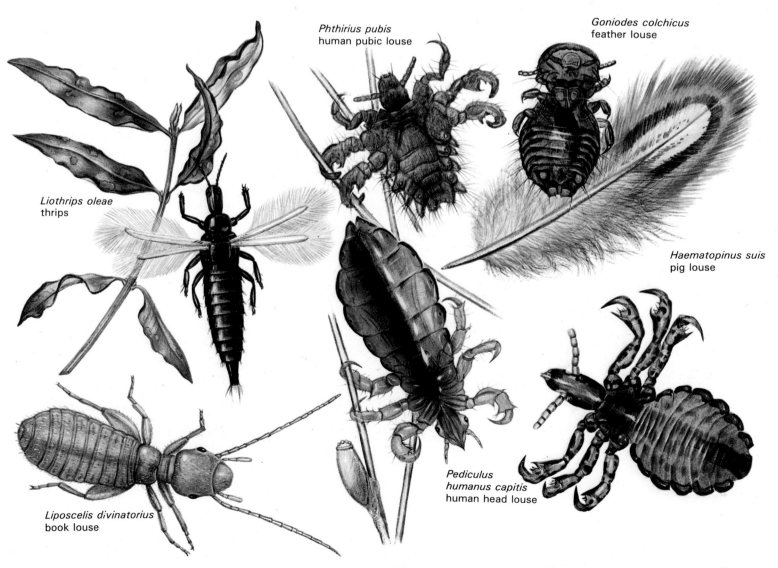

Phthirius pubis
human pubic louse

Goniodes colchicus
feather louse

Liothrips oleae
thrips

Haematopinus suis
pig louse

Liposcelis divinatorius
book louse

Pediculus humanus capitis
human head louse

thickened at the base, while the outer part is membranous and transparent, as are the second pair. When at rest the wings are held flat over the back, with the wings of one side overlapping the other. There are some 25,000 species, both aquatic and terrestrial. The terrestrial forms, the stink bugs, are noted for their evil smell, which is due to a malodorous substance produced by glands in the thorax and is used as a chemical weapon of defence. Some are parasitic, such as the Cimicidae, which live on the blood of reptiles, birds and mammals. *Cimex columbianus*, for example, is parasitic on poultry and doves, while *C. pipistrelli* lives on the blood of parrots. The best known of the Cimicidae, however, is the bed bug (*Cimex lectularius*), parasitic on man. This bloodsucking insect lives in beds and other furniture by day, and emerges to bite and suck the blood of its host at night.

Plant bugs, members of the Heteroptera known as Miridae, number 6000 species of which 300 are common in Europe. Some of them may cause great damage to crops, as *Plesiocoris rugicollis*, originally from the USA and the cause of the dreaded apple-blight that affects orchards. The Lygaeidae (ground bugs) comprise 2000 species which feed on plant sap, causing much damage to crops such as corn and wheat. The Tingitidae or lace bugs generally live in groups on the underside of leaves and when very numerous may give them a frosted appearance. They are white, and when seen under a magnifying lens reveal exquisite lace-like patterns. One of the lace bugs, *Stephanitis pyri*, which damages pear trees, is illustrated here. Another large group of plant bugs are the shield bugs (Pentatomoidae), so called from the large shield-shaped structure extending over the back. They feed on the juices of plants and may impart a nauseating flavour to soft fruit such as raspberries. *Graphosoma italicum*, one of the European species, *Plisthenes ventralis* and *Mozena lunata* are illustrated here. Another family is the squash bugs, Coreidae, so called because some species live on the North American vegetable known as squash. In many species the hind legs are enlarged to form leaf-like extensions, as in *Diactor bilineatus*, a South American species which is illustrated here.

The Gerridae (pond-skaters) are a group of Heteroptera capable of moving on the surface film of water without sinking through it, thanks to the presence of water-repellent hairs on the ends of the second and third pairs of legs. They are found on ponds and still waters almost all over the world; some species live on salt water. They can detect the position of floundering prey by sensing the time differences between surface ripples reaching each of their legs. Many other Heteroptera live on the surface of water, among them the Veliidae and the water striders, Hydrometridae, which move on water with the aid of all six feet.

Fully aquatic Heteroptera capable of immersing themselves and swimming are the Belostomidae, containing about 100 species found in North America and Asia, with a few European species, and the Nepidae (water scorpions) with 150 species. They are not well adapted for swimming and mostly crawl along the bottoms of ponds. Other aquatic groups include the Notonectidae (water boatmen), which swim on their back using their long and bristly third pair of legs as oars. They feed on various insects and larvae, as well as on the young of fish (fry) and tadpoles. The Corixidae (lesser water boatmen) are small aquatic bugs which swim up to the surface of the water to obtain a supply of air, which they trap in a hollow in the abdomen under the wings; they remain on the surface of the pond for a few seconds before swimming back to the bottom, taking their bubble with them. Make corixids 'sing' when courting, by rubbing their hairy front legs against their beak, a process called stridulation.

Homoptera. The Homoptera include a great variety of insects including lantern-bugs, scale insects, plant lice (aphids) and cicadas. They are terrestrial and vegetarian and all four of their wings are always membranous and transparent.

One of the largest groups is that of the lanternflies or lantern bugs (Fulgoridae), which includes 6500 species, mostly tropical. They generally live on the leaves of trees and feed on sap. One of the genus *Lanternaria* is illustrated here. *Lanternaria candelaria* is found in tropical regions; *Fulgora europea* is a European species. Lanternflies have a large head which was once believed to be luminous.

Better known are the cicadas, Cicadidae, represented by about 1500 species and common in warm climates. On the warmer days of summer the males, hidden among the leaves of trees, display their talents by producing a persistent whining or buzzing sound, that continues until the evening. The life cycle of Cicadidae usually takes some years to accomplish, and in one American species full development takes some seventeen years. The only British species is *Cicadetta montana*, which is fairly rare and confined to the New Forest.

The frog-hoppers (Cercopidae) produce the small masses of white froth seen on grasses, bushes and the lower branches of small trees in the summer, commonly known as 'cuckoo-spit'. This is produced by the young nymphs, which surround themselves with a mass of small bubbles resulting from blowing air through a clear fluid secretion. This protects them from their enemies and prevents them drying out. A fairly common European species is *Philaenus spumarius*.

Treehoppers (Cicadellidae and Membracidae), of which there are some 2500 species, mostly tropical, are characterized by the extensive development of the upper surface of the thorax, the pronotum, which results in a broad hood-like covering. The European species *Centronotus cornutus*, the Central and South American *Umbonia spinosa* and *Centrotypus amplicornis* of Sumatra are illustrated here.

The jumping plant lice (Psyllidae) and whiteflies (Aleyrodidae), which are seen jumping or flying about plants when disturbed, resemble the aphids and may cause some damage to plants. The true plant lice or aphids (Aphididae) are however much more destructive. There are more than 3000 species. Characteristic of this group is the ability to produce 'honey-dew', a sugary substance of which ants are particularly fond. Some aphids live at the roots of plants, and ants will sometimes transfer some of them from an infested root to one previously free of aphids, to increase their supply of the honey-dew product. Among the many aphids notorious for the damage they cause to plants are the Phylloxeridae family, one of which, imported from the United States, nearly ruined the European wine industry in the last century by its depredations in the vineyards. *Phylloxera vastatrix* is illustrated here, as is the common greenfly that plagues the gardener's roses, *Macrosiphum rosae*.

The scale insects and mealy bugs (Coccidae) are small Homoptera generally not more than 3 mm (0.12 in) long. They possess glands which produce waxy or silky secretions. Among them are the lac insect (*Laccifer lacca*), which produces shellac and was reared in Asia to produce lacquer, and the cochineal insect, which lives on cactus plants in the West Indies and Mexico and from whose dried bodies is obtained a scarlet dye used in confectionery. The Biblical manna was perhaps a honey-like secretion produced by a swarm of scale insects. Mealy bugs are one of the commonest pests of potted plants, producing a sticky powder resembling corn-meal.

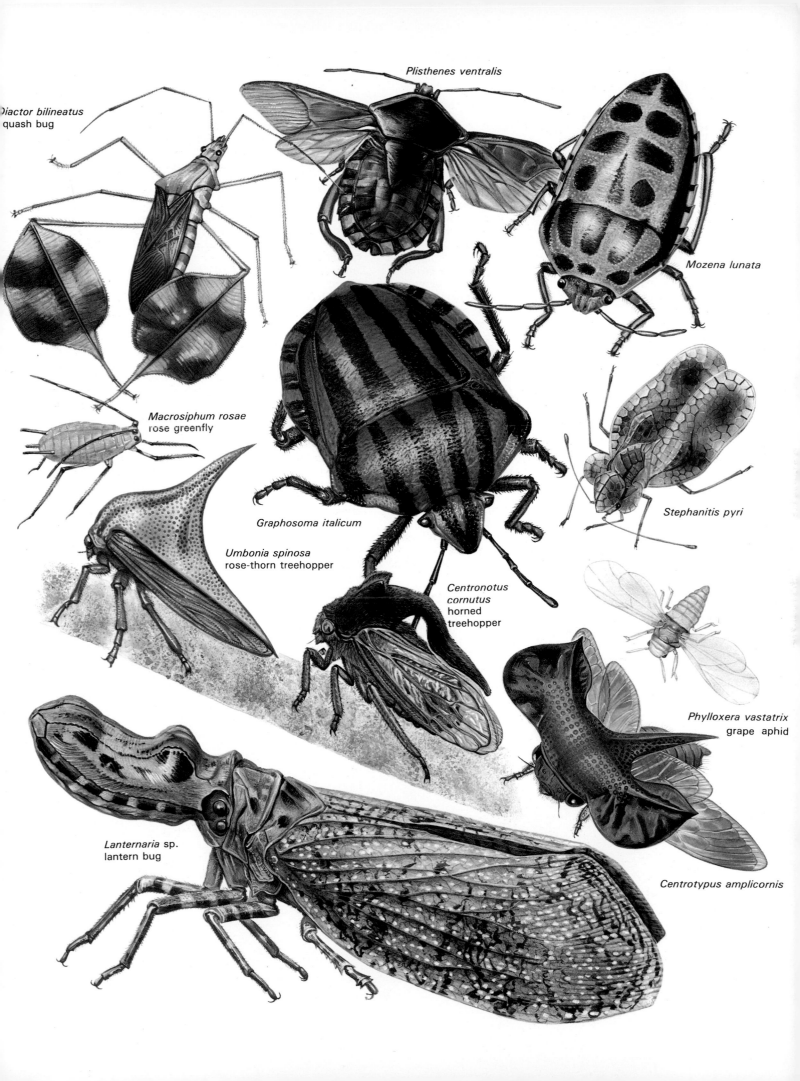

Diactor bilineatus
quash bug

Plisthenes ventralis

Mozena lunata

Macrosiphum rosae
rose greenfly

Stephanitis pyri

Umbonia spinosa
rose-thorn treehopper

Graphosoma italicum

Centronotus cornutus
horned treehopper

Phylloxera vastatrix
grape aphid

Lanternaria sp.
lantern bug

Centrotypus amplicornis

Coleoptera

The Coleoptera, or beetles, are the largest group of insects, containing at least 350,000 known species, a number which some authorities consider will be at least doubled, as more are discovered. About 40 per cent of insects are beetles. Descended from marine ancestors, they are now present in all environments except the sea. Some species have adapted themselves to an underground life, are completely lacking in pigmentation and have lost the use of their eyes. Others, adapted to aquatic life, are able to live without any difficulty in either stagnant or rapidly moving water. Their preferred food similarly varies widely. There are predatory species and others that eat plants, faeces or corpses; there even exist a few which are parasitic. Many species are useful to man because they prey on creatures harmful to growing plants, while others themselves are harmful, such as the Colorado beetle (*Leptinotarsa decemlineata*), which, originating in America, devastates potato crops. There are species, such as *Scolytus scolytus* (illustrated on p. 79), which live beneath the bark of trees, excavating long tunnels with many branches which end by weakening the whole structure, and others which live on the roots of trees. Major enemies of zoological collections in museums are some Coleoptera, such as the larder beetle (*Dermestes lardarius*, illustrated on p. 77), that attack fur, feathers and skin; others will attack either salted or dried meat.

On the whole the bodily structure is the same in all groups; the eyes are generally well developed and the antennae are long, assuming many different forms. The mouth-apparatus is of the chewing type. The thorax carries three pairs of legs adapted to the chosen method of locomotion. Of its three segments the first is free and the other two are provided with wings of which the first pair, those of the second segment, are transformed into a kind of hard 'shell' (the elytra) below which the membranous second pair of wings is folded in a somewhat complicated manner.

There are two major groups of Coleoptera, the Adephaga and the Polyphaga.

Adephaga. The Adephaga include beetles which still show rather primitive characteristics. Among the most important families are the tiger-beetles (Cicindelidae). These are the brilliant green beetles that are seen running swiftly along the ground and take to a

brief flight when approached. There are about 1500 species found in warm temperate and tropical regions. They are voracious predators highly specialized in the chase for prey. The common British species is the green tiger-beetle *Cicindela campestris* which lives on dry heaths and dunes and is active on warm days in spring and summer. It has enormous and powerful mandibles and is a fearsome hunter.

The ground beetles (Carabidae) form the group best known to collectors and the most numerous of the Coleoptera, 30,000 species having been described. They are all terrestrial beetles varying from less than 1 cm (0.4 in) to 10 cm (4 in) in length. They are widespread in equatorial regions and in the northern hemisphere. Most are nocturnal in habits and can be found during the day under logs and stones, particularly in woods and moist places near marshes, lakes and streams. The body is rather long, the legs also long and capable of fast movement; the large head has powerful mandibles which indicate a predatory way of life. A major group of Carabidae is the genus *Carabus*, with many species, found throughout the northern hemisphere, especially in Europe. The coloration is extremely variable and there may be ridges and relief markings adding to the striking appearance of the insect (as in *Carabus variolosus*, illustrated here). As in other Coleoptera, such as *Chlaenius vestitus* (illustrated), the colours are often iridescent. The violet ground beetle *Carabus violaceus* is a large flightless beetle which has iridescent violet or purple edging to its black body and wing cases. This common predator hides under stones or in holes by day but emerges at night to devour worms and many other small soil creatures; it is found in most British gardens. Some species (such as the bombardier beetle) exude an evil-smelling secretion which repels attacks by birds and insectivorous animals.

The diving beetles (Dytiscidae) are fairly uniform in appearance. Their length varies from 1 mm to 5 cm (0.04 to 2 in). They are able swimmers thanks to the hydrodynamic form of the body and to the transformation of the hind legs into a kind of oars. In times of need they are excellent fliers and use this ability when they go in search of new sites to occupy. Incapable of using the oxygen dissolved in the water, they have to visit the surface to breathe. The larvae, sometimes called water tigers, are long and slender and swim through the water with crawling movements of the legs. They are fierce predators of small fish, tadpoles and

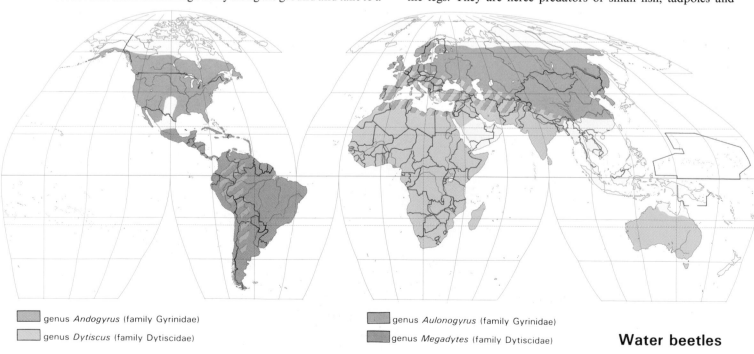

genus *Andogyrus* (family Gyrinidae)
genus *Dytiscus* (family Dytiscidae)
genus *Aulonogyrus* (family Gyrinidae)
genus *Megadytes* (family Dytiscidae)

Water beetles

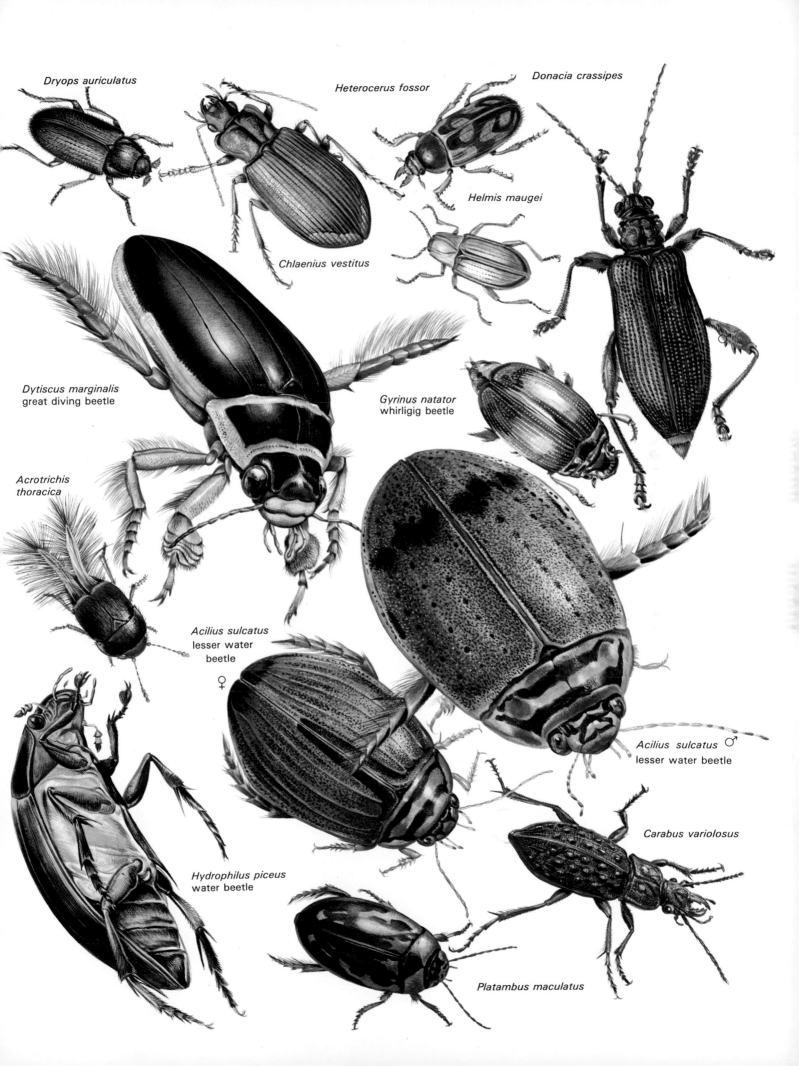

Dryops auriculatus

Heterocerus fossor

Donacia crassipes

Helmis maugei

Chlaenius vestitus

Dytiscus marginalis
great diving beetle

Gyrinus natator
whirligig beetle

Acrotrichis
thoracica

Acilius sulcatus
lesser water
beetle

♀

Acilius sulcatus ♂
lesser water beetle

Carabus variolosus

Hydrophilus piceus
water beetle

Platambus maculatus

various aquatic insects. Some common species, illustrated on p. 75, are *Dytiscus marginalis* (the great diving beetle), *Acilius sulcatus* and *Platambus maculatus*. The great diving beetle particularly is a powerful predator and may give a painful bite when handled; its larva is even bigger and more voracious than the adult and is the top predator in many small ponds.

The whirligigs (Gyrinidae) are usually seen in large colonies swimming together across the surface of a lake or pond. They are perfectly adapted to life in water and excellent swimmers. Swimming is facilitated by the transformation of the second and third pairs of legs into flattened paddles which, moving simultaneously, impart a powerful forward thrust. Their appearance is similar to that of the Dytiscidae, as can be seen in *Gyrinus natator*, illustrated here. The distribution of two groups of Gyrinidae, *Andogyrus* and *Aulonogyrus*, is shown in the map on p. 74.

Polyphaga. About a hundred families belong to the Polyphaga, the Coleoptera that have had the greatest evolutionary success. They include the burying beetles, Silphidae, who devote themselves to the task of demolishing the corpses of dead animals. Many have striking colours, with different parts in contrasting colours of orange or yellow with dark brown or black. A common species is *Oeceoptoma thoracica*, illustrated here, recognizable by the ribs and relief markings on the elytra. Other species illustrated here are *Necrophorus vespillo* and *N. germanicus*, which for their necrophagous diet prefer the corpses of small mammals and birds and very rarely of amphibians and reptiles; and *Thanatophilus sinuatus*, of North America, Europe and the Near East. The genus *Silpha* contains numerous species found almost exclusively in temperate regions. When attacked they spit out drops of a smelly and caustic liquid which defends them from the attacks of enemies.

The appearance of the rove beetles (Staphylinidae) is somewhat different from that of most Coleoptera. The body is very long and the abdomen can be raised up when the insect is alarmed. The elytra are particularly reduced in size, often covering little more than half the body, and the legs are long. Rove beetles are to be found in the bodies of dead animals or in fungi, in decaying logs and beneath the bark of trees. Some are quite large, up to 12 mm (0.5 in) in length, but most measure less than 3 mm (0.125 in). Those illustrated here are the European species *Staphylinus caesa-*

reus, *Emus hirtus*, *Aleochara curtula* and *Ontholestes tessellatus*, and *Creophilus maxillosus* of North America. Members of the genus *Zyras* prey on termites, which they persuade to leave the nest by injecting into it a strongly scented substance which probably acts on the victims like a drug.

The fireflies (Lampyridae) number over a thousand species, although only two of these are found in Britain. The commonest is *Lampyris noctiluca*; the female is a woodlouse-like creature living in sunny, well-drained areas. Both male and female and the larval forms feed on snails. They inject a poisonous liquid into the snail that dissolves its tissues, which the firefly then sucks dry. Their single means of attraction is the luminescent organ which is found in the hindmost segment of the abdomen. It is a very efficient organ, nearly 100 per cent of the energy used is emitted as light, whereas the most efficient human lighting system produces mostly heat, less than 10 per cent being light. Their elytra are very soft and their pronota very large. The female of some species is wingless and worm-like, and this has given them the popular name of glowworm.

Ladybirds belong to the Coccinellidae. They are particularly useful to man for the war they carry on against species of insects that are harmful to agriculture. One species (*Rodolia cardinalis*) is used to combat the depredations of Coccidae on citrus trees. There are several species, identified by the different numbers of spots on a red or yellow wing case. Ladybirds are particularly effective hunters of aphids (greenfly and blackfly) and are rightly regarded as the gardener's friends. Ladybird larvae are also voracious predators of aphids.

Blister beetles (Meloidae) are mostly tropical species and have the ability to discharge from various joints of the body an oily secretion with a nauseating odour that causes the skin to blister.

The darkling beetles (Tenebrionidae) lead a nocturnal life, as the name implies; their coloration is usually black or brownish-blue. Many have the habit of raising the abdomen vertically when alarmed, and most have a disagreeable smell. Mealworms, sold as food for animal pets of various kinds, belong to this group, as do flour beetles, which infest food products in storage. These last are dangerous to man, as they can carry various disease-bearing parasites.

Dung beetles (Scarabaeidae) feed on the droppings of animals. Many present singular ornaments on the head, such as horns,

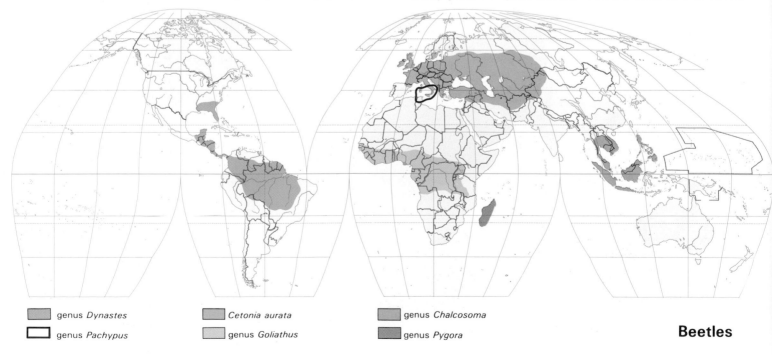

| | genus *Dynastes* | | *Cetonia aurata* | | genus *Chalcosoma* |
| | genus *Pachypus* | | genus *Goliathus* | | genus *Pygora* |

Beetles

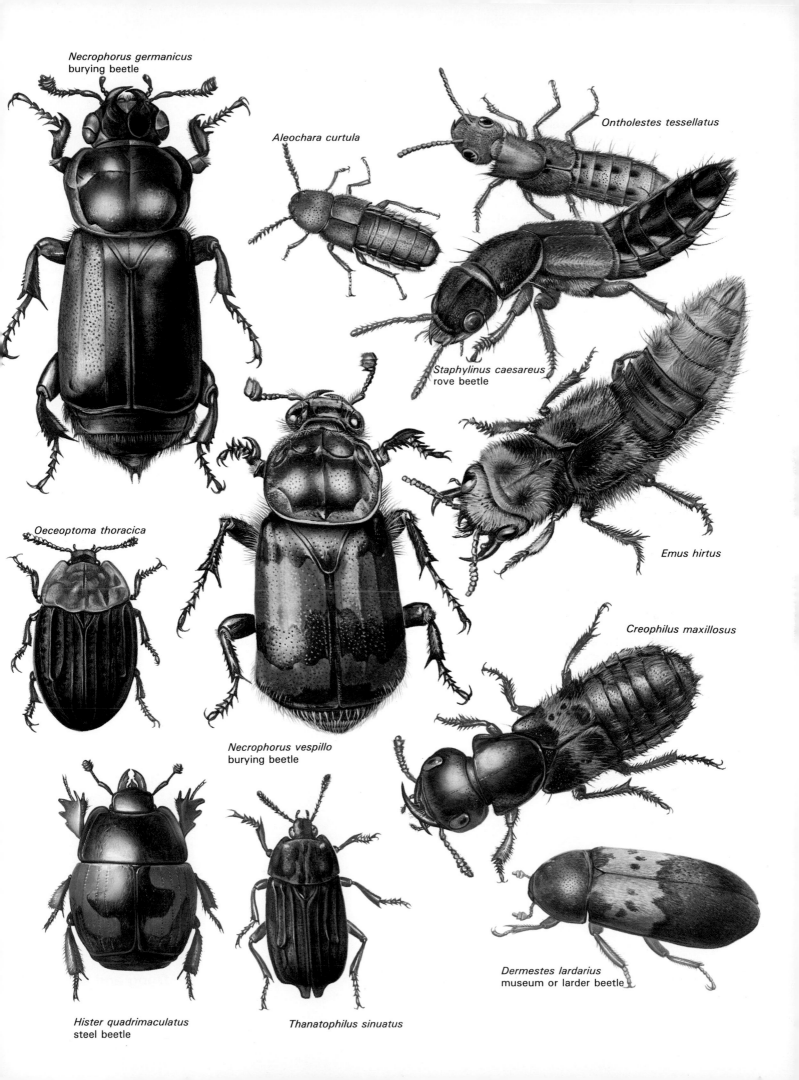

Necrophorus germanicus
burying beetle

Aleochara curtula

Ontholestes tessellatus

Staphylinus caesareus
rove beetle

Emus hirtus

Oeceoptoma thoracica

Necrophorus vespillo
burying beetle

Creophilus maxillosus

Hister quadrimaculatus
steel beetle

Thanatophilus sinuatus

Dermestes lardarius
museum or larder beetle

spikes or swellings, often accompanied by spots or stripes of different colours, sometimes with a metallic sheen. Their diet is notably varied, some being strictly flower-eaters, while others specialize in dung-eating, like the genus *Copris* which spends its life in the collection of dung. This it rolls into balls which it then transports to a suitable place where it will serve the larvae as a reserve of food. The Scarabeidae include *Scarabeinus termitophilus*, which lives in termites' nests, and the genus *Pachypus*, which can be both dung-eating and flower-eating. One species, which feeds solely on plants, is *Phyllopertha orticola*, illustrated here. This is the garden chafer, or June bug as it is sometimes called. This beetle is not as common in Britain as it once was; it tends to be plentiful only every few years, and lives mainly in areas of wood and bracken. Chafers are much used by fishermen as bait and have many colourful local names.

The Dynastidae are represented in Europe by the rhinoceros scarab (*Oryctes nasicornis*), the male possessing a large horn which makes it look particularly monstrous and dangerous; it is in fact harmless. Tropical scarabs are similar in appearance but of enormous size, as *Dynastes hercules* which can be up to 20 cm (8 in) in length. Species of the genus *Chalcosoma*, gaudily coloured and with elongated and branching horns, are found in the rain-forests of South-East Asia. Such protuberances on the head are present also in the stag beetles, Lucanidae, and horned beetles, Passalidae. In the stag beetles pronounced sexual dimorphism is observed, the male having enormously developed mandibles while those of the female are short and inconspicuous.

The North American goldsmith beetle, which feeds on willow and poplar trees, is a member of the Cetoniidae. It is a brilliant golden-green in colour with a splendid metallic sheen. Another species, *Trichius fasciatus*, is clad in yellow and black stripes, probably to imitate wasps and so dissuade attacks by predators.

Cockchafers, May bugs or June bugs belong to the Melolonthidae. The larvae (known as white grubs) feed on the roots of plants and the adults on their leaves. Large numbers of May bugs are attracted to lights at night in early summer.

The leaf beetles (Chrysomelidae) form a very numerous group containing about 30,000 species of a widely varying form, characterized in most species by showy coloration with a metallic sheen. They are plant-eaters and, in years particularly favourable to their reproduction, they migrate in great numbers and cause grave damage to agriculture. The Colorado beetle, previously mentioned, belongs to this family. Another member is the genus *Donacia* whose larvae inhabit sheets of water where they feed on submerged vegetation. Among particularly harmful species are those which attack asparagus, garlic and onions; illustrated here are *Dlochrysa fastuora*, found in Europe and in Japan, and *Lilioceris lilii*.

Perhaps the most beautiful and elegant beetles are the longhorns, belonging to the family Cerambycidae. The typical characteristic of this group is the extraordinary development of the antennae, which can reach a length much greater than that of the body. Nearly all skilful in flight, they live in wooded habitats, where they feed on plants and wood. *Oberea oculata* of this group, found from Europe to Siberia, is illustrated here. Some species can be harmful to agriculture; but the main group of Coleoptera which is so harmful as to be a constant preoccupation of agriculturists is that of the weevils (Curculionidae), recognizable by a long rigid proboscis to which are attached the angled antennae. *Lixus iridis*, illustrated here, belongs to this family. The larvae of weevils feed on either the roots or the internal tissues of plants and thus are harmful to living plants; while others feed on stored grain. There are about 500 species of weevil in Britain; one of the most likely to be seen is the speckled leaf weevil *Polydrosus cervinus*. It is a small, greeny-brown mottled beetle that comes out in the June sunshine, frequenting young trees.

Carpet beetles, belonging to the Dermestidae, attack carpets, rugs, clothing and furniture; *Dermestes lardarius* is illustrated on p. 77, as is *Hister quadrimaculatus*, one of the steel beetles (Histeridae) that live in the droppings of animals, under bark or in ants nests. Also illustrated here are *Triplax aenea*, one of the Erotilidae from northern Asia; *Elater sanguineus*, a click beetle (one of the Elateridae), which, when placed on their backs, will press the front part of the thorax against the underside of the body, producing a clicking sound and at the same time causing themselves to spring into the air; and *Ancyclocheira octoguttata*, a metallic woodborer, one of the Buprestidae, a mostly tropical group that excavate long flat tunnels in the trunks, branches and roots of trees. Some other species that are illustrated – *Dryops auriculatus*, *Heterocerus fossor*, *Hydrophilus piceus* (the great silver water beetle) (all illustrated on p. 75) and *Corymbites cupreus* illustrated here – can be found in Europe. A few species are found in Britain.

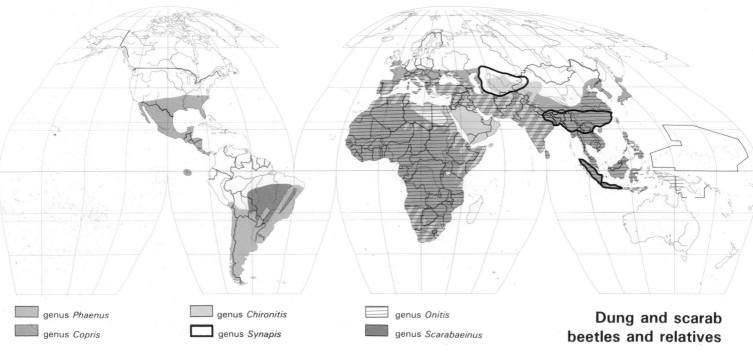

genus *Phaenus*

genus *Copris*

genus *Chironitis*

genus *Synapis*

genus *Onitis*

genus *Scarabaeinus*

**Dung and scarab
beetles and relatives**

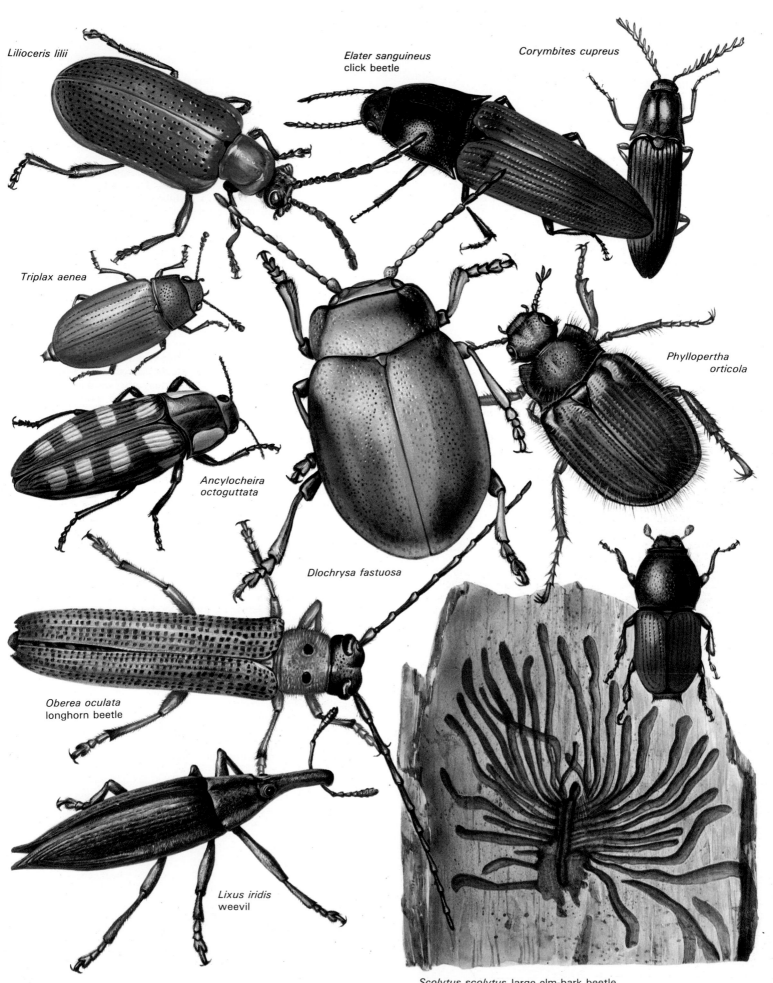

Lilioceris lilii

Elater sanguineus
click beetle

Corymbites cupreus

Triplax aenea

Ancylocheira octoguttata

Phyllopertha orticola

Dlochrysa fastuosa

Oberea oculata
longhorn beetle

Lixus iridis
weevil

Scolytus scolytus large elm-bark beetle
(showing burrows in wood under bark)

Hymenoptera

The Hymenoptera – ants, bees and wasps – are a large group of insects which comprises more than 200,000 species distributed in every part of the world. Generally of medium dimensions, they have a distinct head and carry two antennae, usually wire-like, two large composite eyes, in some species three ocelli and a mouth-apparatus, adapted either for chewing and sipping (lapping) or chewing and sucking. Skilful fliers, they have two pairs of transparent membranous wings, the forward pair being larger than the rear pair. Typically the female is provided with a long ovipositor which in many species has been transformed into a poisonous sting. Many of the Hymenoptera have a highly developed social life and live in communities where the individuals, divided into castes, have different functions aimed at fulfilling the particular needs of the group. All terrestrial creatures, they feed generally on pollen and nectar, but some species hunt small animals. The group is divided into the Symphyta and the Apocrita.

Symphyta. The symphyta – wood wasps and sawflies – are distinguished from the Apocrita by the lack of the narrow waist between the thorax and the abdomen (the peduncle). The wood wasps or horntails (Siricidae) belong to this group; the giant wood wasp (*Uroceros gigas*) is illustrated here. During the summer the female goes in search of suitable dead trees in whose trunks she may lay up to 1000 eggs. The ovipositor is inserted into the trunk of the tree and the eggs are deposited either in the bark or in the wood. Sometimes the female finds it difficult to withdraw the ovipositor and female wood wasps may be found trapped in this way, the male – who usually accompanies her – lurking close by. Wood wasps may occasionally attack healthy trees but usually the trees chosen are either sickly or recently felled.

The sawflies (Tenthredinidae) are the largest group of Symphyta, numbering some 4000 species of which about 1000 are present in Europe. They are 2.5–14 mm (0.1–0.6 in) long and are often vividly coloured. Many of the Tenthredinidae are harmful to agriculture, and some species devastate fruit trees. The female deposits her eggs in the leaves and fruit, and from them emerge caterpillars which at once begin to devour the vegetable matter close to hand. Various species prefer different fruit trees such as pears, apples and plums. The larvae of the gooseberry sawfly (*Nematus ventricosus*, illustrated here) live on soft fruit, such as gooseberries and red and black currants. The numerous members of the Diprionidae, of which there are about seventy species, include the pine sawfly (*Diprion piri*, illustrated here). Sawflies live in conifer woods and infestations of them may sometimes defoliate hundreds of acres of trees in Europe and North America.

Apocrita. All the Apocrita – ants, bees and wasps – are pedunculate (have a narrow waist) and are extremely mobile. The first section of the abdomen is fused to the thorax, while the second, very slender, segment constitutes the peduncle or waist.

Some of the Apocrita possess an ovipositor in the form of a piercing or boring instrument (terebra) which, besides serving for the deposition of eggs, can be used for paralysing the prey. Most of these terebrant Apocrita have a very brief life and are parasitic on various insects, so that they can be helpful to man in preventing the excessive multiplication of species of insects harmful to agriculture and forestry. Among the numerous species are the Pelecinidae, found only in the Americas. The female of *Pelecinus polyturator*, illustrated here, has an immensely long abdomen which can reach an overall length of 50–60 mm (2–2.4 in).

The chalcid wasps (Chalcididae) include many species that are parasitic on plant-eating insects. In the larval stage they live on the eggs and larvae of various insects. The adults have a metallic sheen and their diet is purely vegetarian. *Phlebopenes longicaudatus*, a Brazilian species illustrated here, is characteristic of this group.

The family Leucospididae contains some large species which may reach 16 mm (6 in) in length and in their black-and-yellow coloration somewhat resemble wasps. *Leucospis gigas* is a parasitic species that lives in the nests of bees of the genus *Chalcidoma*.

The Chinipidae include species which live on other insects and also plant-eating species. The plant-eaters are responsible for the formation on plants of the characteristic 'galls' at the centre of which the larvae can be found. *Biorrhiza aptera* produces ovoid galls on the roots and buds of oak trees; the galls produced by *Rhodites rosae* (illustrated) are thread-like in form. *Evania* species are distinguished by a short, laterally compressed abdomen. A member of this group, *Evania appendigaster*, illustrated here, is parasitic on cockroaches.

The ichneumon flies (Ichneumonidae) include species of medium and large dimensions, all parasitic on various insects, especially moth caterpillars, many of which are harmful defoliators of forest trees. The ovipositor varies in length from one species to another; in some it may greatly exceed the length of the entire body, in others it is short and may also serve as a sting. Among European forms of large dimensions is the persuasive burglar fly (*Rhyssa persuasoria*, illustrated here) which can reach 40 mm (1.5 in) in length; it is common in pinewoods in summer. *Protichneumon pisorius*, illustrated here, is parasitic on the larvae of moths, in particular those of hawk moths, the Sphingidae.

Other groups of Apocrita possess a poisonous sting, derived from a transformation of the ovipositor, which has the function of paralysing the prey, besides serving as a weapon of defence. Among these Apocrita are the bees, wasps and ants – Apoidea, Vespoidea and Formicoidea – which have social habits of living.

The velvet ants (Mutillidae) contain several thousand species, mostly distributed in tropical regions. The females deposit their eggs in the nests of other Apocrita, where the larvae live as parasites on the larvae of the hosts. *Mutilla europea*, illustrated on p. 83, is parasitic on the larvae of silkworms.

The ruby-tailed or cuckoo wasps (Chrysididae) are parasitic on bees and wasps, the larvae feeding on food material stored up in the hosts' nests. They are all characterized by a splendid metallic sheen, green, blue-green or copper-coloured. *Euchroreus purpuratus* and *Stilbum cyanurum*, illustrated on p. 83, are in this group.

The scoliid wasps (Scoliidae) which, together with the Pompilidae, Sphecidae and Vespidae, are the insects commonly referred to as wasps, comprise species distributed predominantly in tropical climates, while in Europe hardly more than ten species are present. The scoliid wasps are parasitic on the large, white larvae of May bugs which are actually beetles. They burrow into the ground in search of their prey, which they first paralyse, and then deposit their eggs on them. *Scolia procer*, illustrated on p. 83, is a member of this group.

The Sphecidae, or mud daubers, distributed throughout the world, are solitary wasps, usually predatory, which hunt not only a large variety of insects but also several other arthropods. The digger wasp (*Ammophila sabulosa*, illustrated on p. 83) is a common European species. The long thin waist is a distinguishing feature of this group. Mud daubers build nests made of mud which are found stuck to rafters and ceilings in attics, woodsheds or similar places. One species, *Philanthus triangulum*, is feared by beekeepers since it feeds on the larvae of domestic bees.

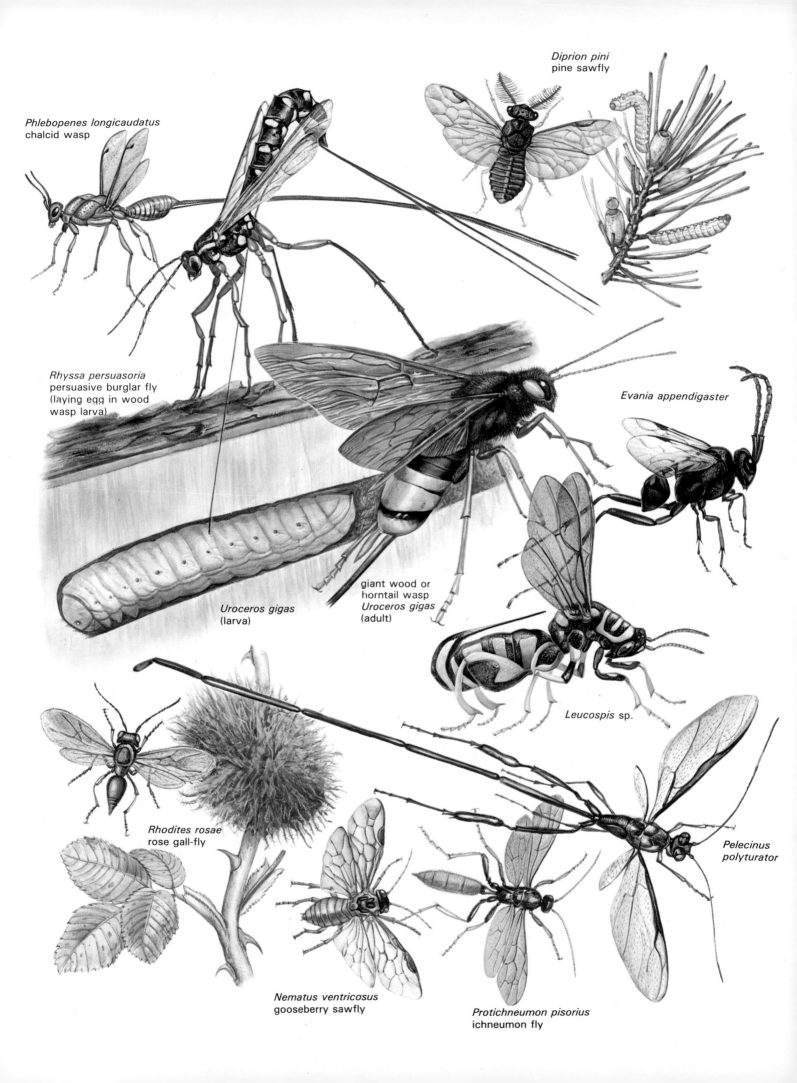

Phlebopenes longicaudatus
chalcid wasp

Diprion pini
pine sawfly

Rhyssa persuasoria
persuasive burglar fly
(laying egg in wood
wasp larva)

Evania appendigaster

Uroceros gigas
(larva)

giant wood or
horntail wasp
Uroceros gigas
(adult)

Leucospis sp.

Rhodites rosae
rose gall-fly

*Pelecinus
polyturator*

Nematus ventricosus
gooseberry sawfly

Protichneumon pisorius
ichneumon fly

The Pompilidae are another large group found all over the world but concentrated in tropical and sub-tropical regions. They are all predators, living exclusively on spiders, and include some forms of notable dimensions, as for example species of the tarantula hawk moth (*Pepsis*, illustrated here) of northern Central America, which with its wingspan of 10 cm (4 in) is the largest known Hymenopteran.

The Vespoidea, wasps, with their characteristic yellow and black colouring, are divided into numerous families. The Eumenidae, potter wasps, differ from the others in leading solitary lives. Some species build nests resembling small jugs or vases attached to twigs or planks; these contain caterpillars or grubs which have first been paralysed by the female wasp, which then lays her eggs on the body. All members of this group build their nests of mud. Illustrated here is *Eumenes coarctata* which lives on flower nectar.

The Polistinidae are all social insects. Various species are known in Europe, such as the common *Polistes gallicus* whose nests can be found in the shelter of walls or stones, or in trees. Their communities last for only a year; their members come together in the spring and scatter in the late autumn.

A similar way of life is led by the 'paper wasps', the Vespidae. The best-known member of this group is the common wasp (*Vespa vulgaris*), which generally constructs its nest underground out of a paper-like material. Another well-known member is the hornet (*Vespa crabro*), whose sting can be dangerous even to man. The nests of hornets, which are usually found in holes in trees but also under the beams of houses, are made of a material resembling cardboard. As with the Polistinidae, the communities of Vespidae comprise a breeding female, the queen, who is the original founder of the colony; numerous sterile females, who fulfil the role of workers, and usually, towards the end of summer, some males and other females capable of reproduction. The workers and males die when the winter sets in, but the fertilized females disperse and seek a suitable sheltered place in which to spend the winter, to emerge again and found new colonies in the spring.

The honey bees (Apoidea) are among the most evolved groups of Hymenoptera, and comprise numerous species found all over the world but in the greatest numbers in warm climates. Good fliers and provided for the most part with a poisonous sting, the Apoidea feed on pollen and nectar which they take from flowers. The pollen is gathered by brush-like structures present on the legs and sometimes on the abdomen; in certain species it is accumulated in a kind of basket. There are several sub-groups of Apoidea; the most advanced forms belong to the family Apidae which include solitary as well as social species. The bumble-bees (Bombidae) are all social and live in small communities which last only a year. They build nests in a wide variety of places according to the species. For example, *Bombus terrestris* (illustrated) prefers the earth, *B. lapidarius* often nests under stones, *B. pratorium* in brushwood or mosses. In the Meliponidae, bees which are without stings, the communities last for several years and may consist of an enormous number of individuals, sometimes more than 100,000. Some species are bred for their honey, as for instance *Melipona beechii* of South America.

The Apidae also contain the highly evolved and social honey bees. The population of honey bee communities is made up of three principal castes, which differ both in shape and in function, namely a fertile female (queen), sterile females (workers), and in certain periods of the year fertile males (drones), which have the sole duty of reproduction.

Another large group of Hymenoptera which show highly evolved social behaviour are the ants (Formicoidea). Ant communities are also organized in three basic castes, queen, workers and fertile males. While the queen is dedicated to the laying of eggs and the males to the fertilization of future queens, the workers have to undertake the most diverse tasks: care of the young, the provision of food, the maintenance and defence of the nest, etc. Many species are carnivorous, others essentially vegetarian, but most are omnivorous, preferring the sugary substances contained in flowers and fruits and the honey-dew produced by aphids and scale insects (Coccidae) which some species rear for this product.

The Formicoidea are divided into several families of which the most primitive is that of the Poneridae. The Dorilidae are mostly tropical and include hunting species famous for their migrations during which they capture the most varied prey with their sharp mandibles. The Myrmicidae, which with 3000 species is the largest ant family, sometimes form complex communities. The best known of this group is the harvester ant (*Messor barbarus*) which collects the seeds of various grasses for its nourishment, and the leafcutter ant (*Atta sexdens*) which lives on fungi that it specially cultivates on heaps of freshly cut leaves. The Dolichoderidae are mostly small species. They are omnivorous, as is for instance the silvery ant (*Iridomyrmex humilis*) which often infests houses. This species, originally from South America, has spread throughout North America and has reached as far as Europe.

The most evolved forms of Formicoidea are those of the family Formicidae, distributed throughout the world and numbering some 2500 species. Common all over Europe is the red ant (*Formica rufa*) which lives in pinewoods, where it builds its nests as giant mounds incorporating pine-needles, twigs and dry brushwood. The garden or black ant is also common in England, building its nest in soil or under stones. Other species build nests of cardboard, or they use the secretions of their larvae to bind leaves together to form a nest. Others are slave-makers, one species capturing pupae from colonies of another species which on emergence act as slaves in the colony which has captured them.

Neuroptera

The Neuroptera are a primitive group of insects that were already present on earth in the Permian era 250 million years ago. They include three suborders: the Megaloptera, the Raphidiodea and the Planipennia.

Megaloptera. The Megaloptera, fishflies and alderflies, comprise about 120 species, almost all tropical. In Europe the group is represented by the alderflies (Sialidae) common in stagnant waters and marshes. Their brief lives are dedicated principally to reproduction. The females deposit about 2000 eggs on vegetation growing out of water. At birth the larvae allow themselves to fall into the water and sink to the bottom, where they complete their development. Some exotic species attain a wingspan of 16 cm (6.5 in). The British species is the alderfly (*Sialis lutaria*).

Raphidiodea. The common name of the Raphidiodea – snake flies – arises from their long necks, which in fact are a remarkable elongation of the thorax. About 80 species are known, of lengths between 1 and 2 cm (0.4–0.8 in) which all inhabit the northern hemisphere except for one South American species. They are carnivorous, preying on aphids and other small insects, and spiders. A typical representative of the group is *Raphidia notata*, illustrated overleaf, in which the characteristic elongation of the neck can be seen. Before coupling the females are particularly aggressive and may attack the males with little hesitation. When

Scolia procer

Mutilla europea
velvet ant

Bombus terrestris
bumble bee

Euchroreus purpuratus.
cuckoo wasp ♂

*Euchroreus
purpuratus.*
♀

Vespa crabro
common hornet

Stilbum cyanurum
velvet cuckoo wasp

Pepsis sp.
tarantula hawk wasp

Ammophila sabulosa
digger wasp

*Eumenes
coarctata*
potter wasp
(on its mud nest)

Dinoponera gigantea

the reproductive period arrives the encounters between the sexes are more cordial allowing mating to occur.

Planipennia. The Planipennia, the lacewings and ant-lions, contain many diverse species which resemble the butterflies (Lepidoptera), mantids (Mantoidea) and dragonflies (Odonata). The larvae are similar in all members of the group and share the peculiarity of possessing no anus; the excrement accumulates in the body and is only expelled on metamorphosis to the adult stage. The smaller Planipennia include the Coniopterigidae, whose species are no more than 2–4 mm (0.08–0.16 in) in length. There are about a hundred species found in all parts of the world. The only species whose larvae lead an aquatic life are those of the Sisyridae, which are parasitic on freshwater sponges (*Spongilla*). The insects with fine transparent yellowish-green wings and golden eyes that are seen at night outside lighted window-panes belong to the genus *Chrysopa*, of which the common or green lacewing (*Chrysopa vulgaris*) is illustrated here.

Species belonging to the Mantispidae much resemble mantids, not only in appearance but also in their habit of lying in wait for their prey. About 400 tropical species belong to this group, including *Mantispa styriaca*, illustrated here.

The curious creatures called ant-lions belong to the Myrmeleonidae, of which *Myrmeleon formicarius* is illustrated here. The larvae live at the bottom of small conical pits which they dig for themselves. Ants fall into these and are instantly seized in the huge jaws of the insect larva, hence the name 'ant-lion'. If the ant looks like escaping, the larva hurls sand grains at it till it is buried or falls back into the waiting jaws. The group contains at least 2000 species distributed in warm temperate zones. The adults closely resemble dragonflies or damselflies but the antennae are large and club-shaped and the wings are longer and broader. They are not as skilled in flying as damselflies and are most often seen resting on grasses or small shrubs. The species *Palpares libelluloides*, illustrated here, shows the same resemblance to dragonflies or damselflies. A resemblance to butterflies can be noticed in the family Ascalaphidae, of which *Ascalaphus macaronius* is illustrated here.

In the Nemopteridae, of which *Nemoptera sinuata* is illustrated here, the rear wings are greatly elongated and are ribbon-like or wire-like. Finally, the Osmilidae contain about 100 species, including *Osmius fulvicephalus*, illustrated here. A characteristic of this group is that the males possess a pair of odoriferous glands in the abdomen which serve to attract the female.

Mecoptera

The Mecoptera, scorpionflies, are found in almost all parts of the world. The most important family is the Panorpidae, to which the genus *Panorpa* belongs. These insects are very common among bushes on the edges of woods. They are most often seen resting on the broad leaves of bracken or other woodland plants and have two pairs of membranous wings with conspicuous brown spots. The front of the head is elongated, giving it a beak-like appearance. In the males the abdomen terminates in a kind of claw or hook resembling a scorpion's tail, though it does not function as a sting.

Strepsiptera

The small order of Strepsiptera includes hardly 250 species which live a parasitic life. They measure no more than 1–5 mm (0.04–0.2 in) in length. The males possess large rear wings while the forward wings are reduced to small stumps used for balancing while in flight. The females, on the other hand, are practically no more than larvae that have attained sexual maturity. They live as parasites in other insects, adhering to the abdomen.

Trichoptera

The Trichoptera, caddisflies, like the Neuroptera, also present archaic characteristics. The two pairs of wings are equally developed and are thickly covered with hairs with a silken sheen. The composite eyes are large and the antennae, wire-like and longer than the body itself, are held in a forward position when the insect is at rest. The mouth apparatus is of the lapping type, adapted to sucking the sugary liquids that ooze from plants. The larvae, which live in fresh water, have much longer lives than the adults (about 10 months) and are notable for their habit of encasing themselves in small houses of sticks or stones which they cement together by means of a fine silk thread. The sticks may be placed lengthwise, parallel to the body, or crosswise, different species adopting different patterns of construction. The species that build their houses of small stones usually live in rocky pools. Others use small shells to coat the cocoon in which they live. Some species do not build at all, but live below rocks, spinning small webs to catch the aquatic invertebrates on which they feed. Other species are plant-eaters. The larvae breathe by means of thread-like gills. The adults are weak fliers and usually only fly when the females are depositing their eggs on the surface of the water. At other times they mostly rest on twigs or leaves by the side of pools or streams, and fly only for short distances when disturbed. Most are dull brown or black in colour, though a few species have white or brown wings with brown or yellow spots.

They live in all parts of the world and about 4450 species are known, with 189 British species and nearly 1000 North American species. Among the principal groups are *Limnophilus* and *Phryganea*. The larvae of *Macronema trasversum*, of the eastern United States, procures its food by erecting remarkably complicated and efficacious snares on the beds of streams.

Lepidoptera

There are some 100,000 species of Lepidoptera – moths and butterflies – of which about 4000 are present in Europe. Moths and butterflies are not usually regarded as distinct groups, scientifically speaking, but there are general distinctions apart from the nocturnal habits of many moths as against the diurnal habits of butterflies. The butterflies have a slight thickening at the end of the antennae, giving them a club-like form; the antennae of moths lack the club at the apex, and are usually either feathery or thread-like. The course of development also differs in the two groups; both have four stages of life, egg, larva – usually known as a caterpillar in both cases – pupa and adult, but in the moths the shiny pupa is usually surrounded by a silk cocoon, whereas the pupa of butterflies is not covered and is called a chrysalis. The larvae of nearly all Lepidoptera are destructive plant-eaters.

Zoologists divide the Lepidoptera into Homoneura, in which the front and rear wings have almost identical vein-patterns, and Heteroneura, in which the veins of the rear wings have become greatly reduced. The great majority of moths and butterflies come within this latter group.

Lepidoptera are found in all parts of the world, but favour tropical regions, where the greater number of species and the

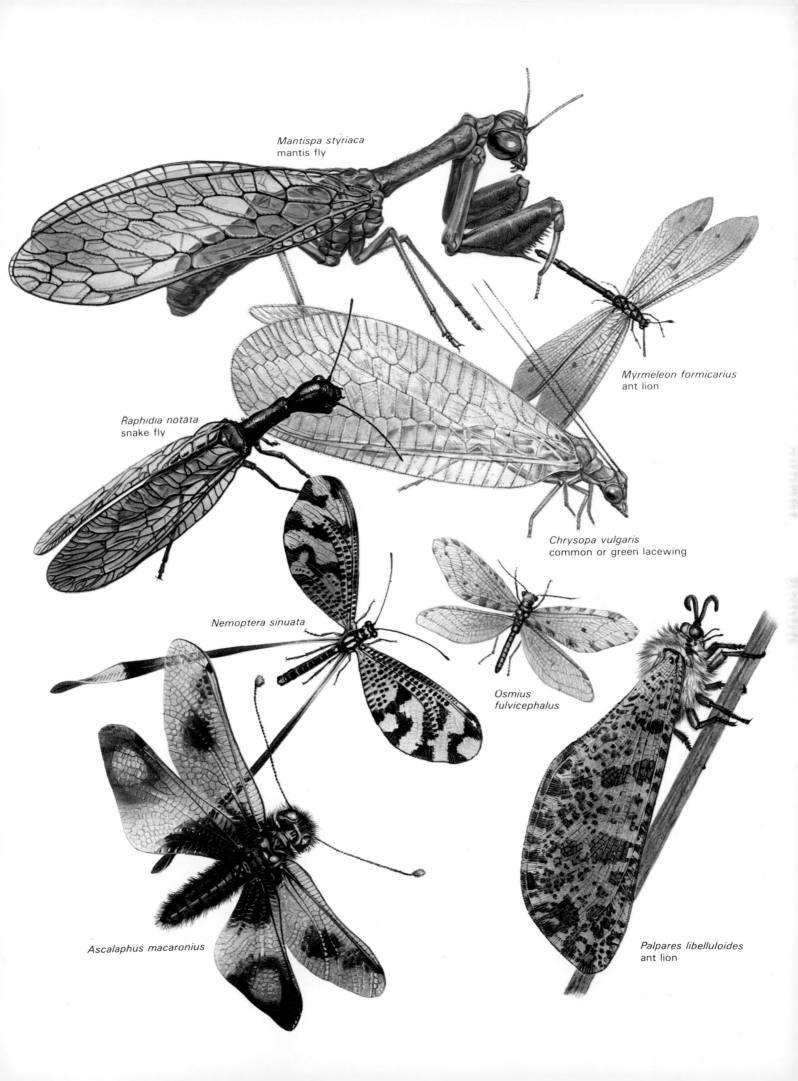

Mantispa styriaca
mantis fly

Myrmeleon formicarius
ant lion

Raphidia notata
snake fly

Chrysopa vulgaris
common or green lacewing

Nemoptera sinuata

*Osmius
fulvicephalus*

Ascalaphus macaronius

Palpares libelluloides
ant lion

largest and most richly ornamental species are to be found. Southern Central America is particularly rich in Lepidoptera. Species present in temperate regions are generally smaller and less imposing. A few penetrate to colder regions and in the Himalayas some species live at levels up to 6000 m (18,000 ft) above sea-level. Lengths vary from 1 mm to 10 cm (0.04–4 in), while in the largest specimens the wingspan can reach 30 cm (12 in). The elongated body is covered with a fine velvety fur, and the wings are provided with a multitude of small scales from which the Lepidoptera ('scaly-wings') derive their name. These scales easily become detached when a butterfly or moth is touched or handled, and fall as 'dust'. In species which have very brief adult lives, the mouth-parts are much reduced or even absent, but in most species, which live on the nectar of flowers, a highly specialized proboscis has been developed from the greatly elongated maxillae. When at rest the proboscis is tightly curled below the head and when feeding it is extended in order to suck nectar from within a flower.

The power of flight of some species is noteworthy, and some 2000 species are capable of performing long migratory journeys. The map on the left-hand side below shows the migrations undertaken by the painted lady butterfly (*Vanessa cardui*) of the family Nymphalidae. The right-hand map shows the migrations undertaken by the silver 'Y' moth (*Autographa gamma*), the convolvulus hawk moth (*Herse convolvuli*) and clouded yellow butterflies (*Colias* spp.) in order to reach the areas where they breed. The return journey is undertaken by their offspring. Other species, however, such as the hummingbird hawk moth (*Macroglossum stellatarum*) perform both the outward journey and the return journey from the breeding area. The monarch butterfly (*Danaus plexippus*) breeds in the northern parts of North America and at the end of the breeding season sets out (as the map on p. 88 shows) on a journey to Mexico, Cuba and the Bahamas, covering distances of the order of 3000 km (2000 miles) or more, some of them crossing wide stretches of the ocean on their way. At the end of the winter, during which a large proportion of them die, the survivors set off on the return journey to the breeding zone.

The eggs of Lepidoptera hatch into larvae which are often vividly coloured. In some species the larvae have ocelli which resemble large eyes. Often the caterpillars are covered with hairs or bristles which connect with poison glands that secrete an irritant substance that makes them repellent to predators.

The vivid coloration of the wings of many Lepidoptera (such as *Chrysiridia madagascariensis*, illustrated on p. 89) may be produced by the particular pigmentation present on the scales or be due to interference colours caused by the microscopic structure of the surface. The colours and patterns are sometimes used for sexual attraction but more often form a defensive system. The red underwing moth (*Catocala nupta*, illustrated here) and *C. fraxini* perfectly mimic their backgrounds when the wings are closed, but when the wings are opened for flight they reveal vivid colours which confuse a possible predator. 'Eye' designs such as are present on the silk moth (*Automeris io*) and the owl butterfly (*Caligo eurilochus*) both illustrated here, make the insect seem larger and more terrifying than it really is. The particularly showy coloration of the burnet moth (*Zigaena filipendula*, illustrated on p. 89) seems intended to warn predators that the butterfly is far from appetizing. Among caterpillars that show defensive patterns are the puss moths (genus *Cerura*), of which the adult is illustrated here. The caterpillar's head is vividly coloured. One of the Lepidoptera whose camouflage is so good that it easily confused with its background is the leaf butterfly of South-East Asia (*Kallima inachus*, illustrated here). With its wings folded it resembles a dry leaf, while on opening its wings it discloses a striking pattern of colour. A classic example of cryptic coloration is provided by the northern European peppered moth (*Biston betularia*) which has two sub-species, *insularia* and *carbonaria*, living together in the same type of habitat. *Insularia* is white speckled with black, *carbonaria* completely sooty black. The *insularia* variety imitates perfectly the predominantly white bark of the birch trees on which it lives and used to be more numerous than *carbonaria*, which was more often taken by predators because its dark form was easily visible on pale clean tree trunks. With industrial development and the consequent pollution of the air the trunks of the trees in certain areas darkened in colour. The *insularia* sub-species became more visible and was more likely to be taken by predators, while the *carbonaria* was now more difficult for predators to see. As a result *carbonaria* is now much more common than *insularia* in urban and industrial areas. Other forms notable for their cryptic coloration are *Thecla linus*, *Thysania agrippina*, *Anophylla magnifica* (illustrated here) and *Phalera bucephala*.

Most Lepidoptera obtain their nourishment from liquid foods, and water is of great importance for their survival. The proboscis

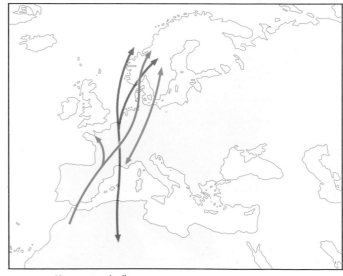

Migratory routes of the painted lady butterfly *Vanessa cardui* (above) and other lepidoptera (above right) in Europe and western Asia.

———— *Herse convolvuli* (convolvulus hawk moth)

———— genus *Colias* (clouded yellow butterflies)

———— *Autographa gamma* (silver 'Y' moth)

Automeris io
silk moth

Thecla linus

Caligo eurilochus
owl butterfly

Catocala nupta
red underwing moth

Kallima inachus
leaf butterfly

Thysania agrippina

Kallima inachus
(wings folded)

Cerura vinula
puss moth

Anophylla magnifica

Acherontia atropos
death's-head hawk moth

serves to collect the nectar from flowers, but some species suck their nourishment from mature fruits, from dung, from decomposing corpses and from animal perspiration. Others insert the proboscis between the closed eyelids of sleeping animals and drink in the tear-liquid. A few species will actively defend an occupied territory. For example, some of the fritillaries (Nymphalidae) that live in tropical America attack invaders on the wing; while swallowtails (Papilionidae) control their territory by continually patrolling its borders. *Mesosemia croesus* and *Agrias claudia*, illustrated on p. 91, are two of the territorial species.

Homoneura. The Homoneura are a small group of Lepidoptera showing some primitive characteristics. The moths of the Micropterygidae have a mouth-apparatus of the chewing type and feed on pollen during the daylight hours. The ghost moths or swifts (Hepialidae) are nocturnal and have less developed mouth-parts; some are vividly coloured. In *Hepialus humuli* the female goes in search of the male, who attracts her by emitting pheromones, minute secretions ('scent') which travel through the air and are detected by the female at remarkable distances. A similar mechanism of sexual attraction is used by many moth species.

Heteroneura. The group contains all but the most primitive of the Lepidoptera. The Tineoidea include the common clothes moth, of which there are two different kinds. The larvae of the case-making clothes moth (*Tinea pellionella*) construct a cylindrical case which encloses its body; that of the webbing clothes moth (*Tinea bisselliella*) spins a loose web over the material on which it feeds. The female adults usually remain close to the material on which they fed as larvae, and rarely fly, but the male is more active and is

the clothes moth usually seen in flight. Under natural conditions, these moths live in old bird nests and among owl pellets. It is the larvae that do damage to cloth by eating it.

This group also includes the leaf miners, moths of very small dimensions whose larvae excavate tunnels in the interior of leaves. The moths lay their eggs on the surface of the leaves and the larvae burrow into them, making tunnels that may be straight or twisted, according to the species. If they restrict themselves to a small area of the leaf if acquires a typical blotched appearance. Other species cause withering or yellowing of the foliage. The Hyponomeutoidea include the apple moth, which deposits its eggs on the leaves of various fruit-trees; the larvae of various species of Torticoidea feed on the leaves of vines and oak trees.

The clearwings (Aegeniidae) have wings which lack scales and are for this reason transparent. Their bodies are often ringed with red, black and yellow, making them look not unlike wasps, which grants them a certain amount of freedom from the attacks of predators. The female lays her eggs on the bark of trees and the larvae burrow into the wood, so that the presence of clearwings in considerable numbers can be harmful to trees and bushes.

The Gelechiidae are dark-coloured moths whose larvae are mostly plant-eaters, but there are some species that are parasitic on arthropods. Other species are among the insects that produce galls on various plants, as are some species of Tortricidae. The Gelechiidae galls take the form of swellings on the ends of branches of the oak tree.

The larvae of the Tortricidae are commonly known as leaf-rollers from their habit of rolling the leaves of the plant on which they live into a cylindrical form. Some species of Tortricidae produce galls on ragwort, poplars and willows. The Mexican jumping bean is inhabited by the larvae of one of the Tortricidae, which eats out a cavity inside the seed and, by its twitching and writhing, causes the seed to move about. Another species feeds on the needles and buds of the balsam fir, and has demolished thousands of acres of forest in Canada. Leaf-rollers have also caused extensive damage to fruit-trees in North America, New Zealand and Australia.

The plume moths (Pteroforidae) have peculiarly feathered wings. The larvae are furry and encase themselves in tubes or spin webs about themselves.

The Pyralidae include the wax moth (*Galleria mellonella*) a species much feared by bee-keepers for the immense damage it causes in beehives. The larvae feed on wax, destroying the cells in a short time and forcing the bees to abandon the hive. Another of the Pyralidae attacks maize, destroying the entire substance of the plants; other species are damaging to crops such as rape and radishes. But it is only the caterpillars that cause the damage, the adults like most caterpillars and moths are liquid feeders.

The geometers (Geometridae) are a large group containing up to 12,000 species. The adults are mostly not highly coloured but rich in ornamentation. The caterpillars lack the legs that caterpillars of other species possess in the middle sections of the body, between the three pairs at the front end and the large grasping pair at the rear. They are therefore unable to crawl like other caterpillars but have to progress by drawing the rear end of the body up to the front end, then raising the forepart up and reaching forwards to grasp the leaf or twig with the front legs. The arching of the body resulting from this method of locomotion has given them the name of 'loopers'. The magpie moth (*Abraxes grossulariata*, illustrated here), attacks gooseberries, red and black currants, plums and hawthorn trees. Other loopers are common inhabitants of the forest canopy and cause considerable damage among the foliage.

Migratory routes of *Danaus plexippus*, the Monarch butterfly

Areas of development

Summer locations

Hibernating locations

Zygaena filipendula
six-spot burnet moth

Ephestia kuehniella
wax moth

Celerio lineata
hawk moth

Alucita sp.
plumed moth

Argema mittrei
giant moon moth

Abraxas grossulariata
magpie moth

Plusia gamma autographa
silver 'Y' moth

Tortrix viridiana
oak tortrix

Lasiocampa quercus
oak moth

Arctia caja
garden tiger moth

Chrysiridia madagascariensis
swallowtail

Phalera bucephala

The tussock moths (Lymantriidae) are so called from the tufts of hair or bristle that in many species stick up on the backs of the caterpillars. The larvae cause immense damage to plants, often completely defoliating them. The adults are of medium size with squat bodies covered with white or ivory-coloured down; the wings of the males are usually deep brown or grey with markings of lighter shades. In some species the females are almost wingless and are incapable of flight. The proboscis is almost or entirely absent, a sign that the adults do not feed. Many species show a marked fluctuation in numbers from one year to another, depending on the climatic conditions and the prevalence or otherwise of parasites and predators. A typical species is the gypsy moth (*Lymantria dispar*) whose larvae are much feared by foresters. It is sometimes possible when passing through a wood infested by these creatures to hear the sound produced by the millions of larvae chewing the leaves and by their droppings falling to the forest floor.

The tiger moths (Arctiidae) are primarily nocturnal but often also fly by day and are distinguished by unusually brilliant colours, as in the garden tiger moth (*Arctia caja*, illustrated previously) which has white forewings with brown spots, the rear wings being reddish with black spots.

The noctuid moths (Noctuidae) are night-fliers, the numerous species including the brightly coloured red underwing moth (*Catocala nupta*) and the silver 'Y' moth (*Plusia gamma autographa*, also illustrated on p. 89).

The hawk moths (Sphingidae) can reach noteworthy dimensions, especially tropical species which sometimes attain a wingspan of 20 cm (8 in). They are also sometimes known as hummingbird moths from their habit of hovering in front of flowers. Some seventeen species live in Britain, of which the biggest is the death's head hawk both (*Acherontia atropos*, illustrated on p. 87), so called from the skull-like markings on the back. It is now rather rare in Britain. The caterpillar is about 12 cm (4.5 in) long and feeds mostly on the leaves of potatoes and woody nightshade. The poplar hawk moth (*Laothoe popului*) also has a fairly large caterpillar, about 7 cm (3.0 in) long, which is brilliant green in colour and lives on poplars, sallows and willows. *Celerio lineata*, illustrated on p. 89, is another species of Sphingidae.

The Thaumetopeidae are moths of modest dimensions whose larvae are extremely destructive. Large numbers of the larvae of certain species such as the processionary moths (*Thaumetopoea pityocampa*) and (*T. processionea*) may sometimes be seen on the continent of Europe processing in a single file across the ground or on trees, the head of one in contact with the tail of the one in front.

The giant silkworm moths (Saturniidae) sometimes, as in the case of members of the genus *Attacus*, attain a wingspan of 25 cm (10 in). The body is short and squat and the proboscis is either much reduced or absent. The wings are often brightly coloured and ornamented with large 'eyes' whose alarming appearance tends to repel predators. Most of the family live in Asia, and there are several species in North America, including the Cecropia moth (*Hyalophora cecropia*), the largest moth on the North American continent. The emperor moth (*Saturnia pavonia*) is the only member of the group living in Britain. The adults do not feed, living on body-fat long enough to breed before dying. The larvae live on the leaves of various fruit-trees. The cocoons of Saturniid moths are not used for making silk thread or cloth since the threads are of uneven diameters and are not continuous. The Chinese silkworm moth which produces usable silk is *Bombyx mori* and belongs to a different group, the Bombycidae.

The tent caterpillars (Lasiocampidae) are so called from the large tent-like webs that the larvae of many species weave in trees. The adults are heavy-bodied and of insignificant coloration, some species being notably camouflaged, for example the oak moth (*Lasiocampa quercus*, illustrated on p. 89), which is difficult to detect in the oak trees in which it lives, and the pine tree lappet moth (*Dendrolimus pini*), whose larvae feed on the leaves of pine trees. The lackey moth (*Malacoma neustria*), a member of this group, is a common pest of fruit-trees and also attacks forest trees and ornamental shrubs. The caterpillar has a dark blue back with a whitish line along the middle and the sides carry a black stripe outlined in reddish orange.

The goat moths (Cossidae) have heavy bodies and wings well marked with veins; *Cossus cossus* is the common European species. The eggs are laid on the trunks or branches of trees and the larvae burrow inwards, making large tunnels in the wood.

The best-known of the puss moths (Notodontidae) is *Cerura vinula*, illustrated on p. 87, whose larvae have already been mentioned. The adult is greyish in colour and furry, of an appearance that can be imagined to be cat-like.

The blue and copper butterflies (Lycaenidae) are small in size but brilliant in colour. The 'hairstreak' butterflies, so called from the hair-like projections from the rear of the rear wings, are also members of this group. The larvae produce a substance which forms the food of some species of ants, who cultivate them in order to procure supplies. An African species, *Jolans prometheus*, is illustrated here.

The swallowtails (Papilionidae) mostly have tail-like projections at the rear edge of the rear wings, from which their name is derived. The group contains some butterflies of notably large dimensions, such as the giant swallowtail (*Papilio cresphontes*) of the southern USA with a wingspan of 13 cm (5 in). In some species there is a marked difference in the appearance of the two sexes. Some of the larvae possess scent organs at the front of the head which are extended when the creature is alarmed and give off an odour similar to that of the plant on which the larva is feeding. *Papilio machaon*, a European species, is the only member of the group found in Great Britain, but it is now very rare in the fen country of East Anglia, where it used to be found, due to loss of suitable habitat. *Bhutanitis lidderdalei*, a Himalayan species, is illustrated here, as are three other species of Papilionidae, *Papilio ulisses*, *P. childrenae*, and *P. androcles*.

The most notorious member of the white and sulphur butterflies (Pieridae) is the cabbage white (*Pieris brassicae*). These butterflies can produce three broods during the summer. Leguminous plants are attacked by caterpillars of the clouded yellow butterflies (genus *Colias*). Brimstone butterflies also belong to the Pieridae.

The fritillaries (Nymphalidae) are large butterflies possessing somewhat atrophied forelegs. Many species are brown in colour with attractive patterns of lighter shades. Emperor, peacock and tortoiseshell butterflies are among the more brilliantly coloured European species. The Camberwell beauty (*Nymphalis antiopa*) rare in Britain but common in North America, also belongs to this family. *Morpho didius*, illustrated here, is a species from the forests of the Amazon; other species illustrated here are the small tortoiseshell butterfly (*Aglais urticae*), whose larvae feed on nettles, *Erihoea dehani* and the purple emperor butterfly (*Apatura iris*) a territorial European woodland species, whose adults feed on dung.

Other well-known butterflies are the skippers (Hesperiidae), monarchs (Danaidae) already mentioned for their migratory habits, and meadow browns (Satyridae).

Morpho didius
morpho

Apatura iris
purple emperor

Jolans prometheus
hairstreak

Aglais urticae
small tortoiseshell

Rhutanitis lidderdalei
Indian swallowtail

Papilio androcles
swallowtail

Mesosemia croeus

Agrias claudia

Papilio childrenae
swallowtail

Erihoea dehani

Papilio ulisses
swallowtail

Diptera

The flies (Diptera) number some 85,000 species distributed in all parts of the world. They are distinguished from all other insects by possessing only one pair of wings, the forewings; the hind wings have in fact been transformed into what are called 'halteres', after the dumb-bells held by athletes when jumping in classical Greece; they take the form of knobbed stumps and are used to preserve the equilibrium while in flight. Diptera are equipped with two large compound eyes and a mouth-apparatus which may be of the lapping and sucking type or of the piercing and biting type.

Nematocera. Nematocera, which include crane-flies, mosquitoes and midges, have a slender body and are provided with long legs and thin antennae. A typical member of the group is *Tanyptera atrata*, illustrated here.

A crane fly. The larva of this insect is called a leather-jacket and lives in the soil.

The crane-flies (Tipulidae) commonly called daddy-long-legs in Britain, vary greatly in size. The smaller ones resemble mosquitoes, but the adults are in fact harmless. The larvae on the other hand do great damage to the roots of plants. They are brownish in colour with tough leathery skins, which has given them the common name of leather-jackets. *Ctenophora festiva*, illustrated here, is a typical member of the group.

The Bibionidae are another family whose larvae cause damage to crops, attacking the roots of numerous horticultural plants. A member of the family is *Bibio hortulanus*, illustrated here. The adults are small, black and hairy and are often called 'March' flies, being common at that time of year. The Psychodidae include some species harmful to man, such as the moth flies or owl midges, minute creatures which can be seen around the drain-openings of kitchen sinks and the larvae are enormously abundant in sewage filter beds. Some species of this group carry diseases; among them various forms of leishmaniasis. Related to the Psychodidae, but with aspects more resembling the Tipulidae, are the Ptychopteridae, represented in Europe by *Ptychoptera contaminata*, illustrated here.

The mosquitoes (Culicidae) are one of the most important groups of Diptera in that they include many species that are harmful to man, carrying numerous diseases. The female mosquito may lay her eggs in early summer on the surface of small pools of water; the adults of these species hibernate during the winter. Other species lay their eggs on ground that will be the site of a temporary pool in spring or early summer; these mosquitoes mature earlier, in midsummer. The larvae often have a long slender tube, the siphon, protruding from the rear of the abdomen; this is extended through the surface of the water and the larva hangs from it, as it were, while taking in a supply of air. After breathing the larva sinks to the bottom of the pond to feed. They turn into pupae from which the adult mosquitoes finally emerge. The mosquito that bites is the female.

The anopheles mosquito (*Anopheles maculipennis*, illustrated here) is responsible for the transmission of malaria, while *Aedes aegypti*, also illustrated, carries the virus of yellow fever, besides several other diseases. The common mosquito of Europe (*Culex pipiens*) familiar in summer, is annoying but not dangerous.

The phantom midges (Chaoboridae) have long worm-like larvae which live in water and feed on small invertebrates, including planktonic crustaceans and other mosquitoes. The midges (Chironomidae) also have aquatic larvae and include 400 British species. They are the non-biting midges; many do not feed at all as adults. *Endochironomus tendens* is illustrated here with its larva.

The black flies (Simuliidae) live on the blood of mammals, including man. In Europe and North America, the bites of black flies, while painful, rarely cause more than secondary infections leading to swellings, but among domestic animals and poultry the results are more serious, and many fatalities are caused. In Africa, black flies transmit river blindness, a serious and debilitating disease. Illustrated here is *Simulium equinum* which favours horses as victims. Other mosquito-like Diptera are the Mycetophilidae, which are fungus-eaters. Among them is the fungus gnat (*Mycetophila fungorum*, illustrated here).

Brachycera. Brachycera, which include horseflies, robber flies and bee flies, are distinguished by their short, squat body and shorter antennae. Some have antennae with more than three segments; these include the horseflies, robber flies and bee flies. Horseflies (Tabanidae) live on the blood of various animals; *Tabanus bovinus*, illustrated on p. 95, attacks cattle and horses. Deer are also

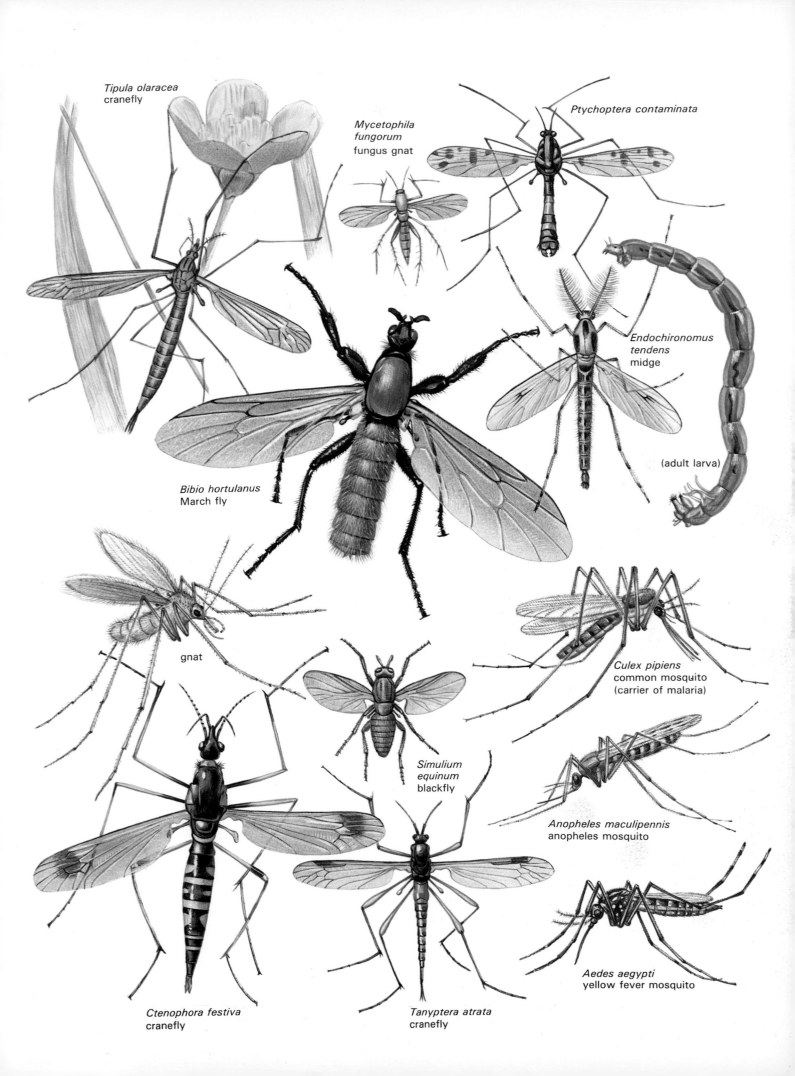

Tipula olaracea
cranefly

Mycetophila fungorum
fungus gnat

Ptychoptera contaminata

Endochironomus tendens
midge

(adult larva)

Bibio hortulanus
March fly

gnat

Culex pipiens
common mosquito
(carrier of malaria)

Simulium equinum
blackfly

Anopheles maculipennis
anopheles mosquito

Ctenophora festiva
cranefly

Tanyptera atrata
cranefly

Aedes aegypti
yellow fever mosquito

subject to their attacks. Horseflies of the genus *Chrysops* are small and fairly light in colour; *Tabanus* species are larger and deeper brown. The eyes are very large and often green in colour with a metallic sheen. Another common name for the group is gadflies.

Others of this group are the robber flies or assassin flies (Asilidae), predators which live on the internal liquids of their prey, having first killed them with injections of poisonous secretions. The prey largely consists of other insects. The larvae live under the bark of dead trees and in decaying wood along the banks of streams and in forests. Like the adults, they live on other insects and their larvae. The females often devour the males after or even during copulation, as happens with the largest species *Asilus crabroniformis* of the Palaearctic region, illustrated here. Others of this group are the Acroceridae, represented in Europe by *Cyrtus gibbus*, illustrated here, whose larvae are parasitic on spiders, and the bee flies (Bombyliidae).

Schizophora. Schizophora, which include fruit flies, blow flies, house flies etc., are squat-bodied flies whose antennae have only three segments.

Fruit flies (Trypetidae) are small Diptera whose larvae, such as the apple maggot, bore long winding tunnels in fruit. A characteristic fruit fly, *Ceratiris capitata*, is illustrated here.

The bee lice (Braulidae) number only three European species among which is *Braula coeca*, illustrated here, and one rare species in North America. The adults are external parasites on bees, while the larvae feed on the pollen contained in the wax of the honeycombs.

The vinegar and fruit flies (Drosophilidae) live on decomposing materials and deposit their eggs in rotting fruit or other fermenting substances. Among the best-known species is the common fruit fly (*Drosophila melanogaster*) which is found wherever fruit is stored. It is also famous as the fruit fly which has been much used by biologists in experiments in breeding.

The Muscidae are one of the largest families of Diptera and include many of the commonest flies. One of the best-known species is the ordinary house-fly (*Musca domestica*) which is present wherever food is available. Provided with a mouth-apparatus of the sucking type, it feeds exclusively on liquid substances, preferably sugary liquids. It can sometimes act as a carrier of various pathogenic germs, such as those of dysentry and tuberculosis. Much more dangerous, however, is the tsetse fly (*Glossina palpalis*) which transmits sleeping-sickness in Africa.

The blow flies (Calliphoridae), characterized by the metallic blues and greens of thorax and abdomen, include the bluebottle (*Calliphora erythrocephala*) one of the most common species in Europe, whose females deposit their eggs in decomposing substances and also in festering wounds. The larvae of the warble fly (*Hypoderma bovis*, illustrated here) grow from eggs laid below the skin of various cattle. Another meat-eater is the flesh fly (*Lucilia caesar*, also illustrated here) one of the Sarcophagidae; these resemble very large house flies.

The Larvevoridae have well-developed wings and a squat, hairy body. European representatives include *Ocyptera brassicaria*, illustrated here. Another species is the North American velvety shore bug (*Ochtera mantis*) whose forelegs resemble those of the mantids. Other families include the hover flies and drone flies (Syrphidae), soldier flies (Stratomyiidae), stable flies (Stomoxyidae), bot flies (Gasterophilidae), and dung flies (Scatophagidae).

Siphonaptera

The Siphonaptera, fleas, include over a thousand species of small terrestrial insects, undergoing complete metamorphosis, which live as parasites, sucking the bood of numerous birds and mammals. They are active insects rarely exceeding 3–5 mm (0.12–0.20 in) in length and equipped with long hind legs well adapted for jumping up to 100 times their own length. The mouth-apparatus is of the piercing and sucking type and has three sharp members protruding from it, two mandibles and the labrum-epipharynx; with these they puncture the skin of the victim and the blood is drawn up through the channel formed by the three mouth-parts. Saliva is injected on making the first puncture so that the blood does not coagulate.

One of the most important families is that of the Pulicidae, to which belongs the infamous human flea (*Pulex irritans*) which also attacks pigs, dogs, rats and poultry. Other common fleas are of the genus *Ctenocephalides*, including the dog flea (*C. canis*) and cat flea (*C. felis*). These cannot flourish on human beings and do not remain on them long. The most dangerous of the fleas is the Oriental rat flea (*Xenopsylla cheopis*) which transmits bubonic plague from rats to human beings.

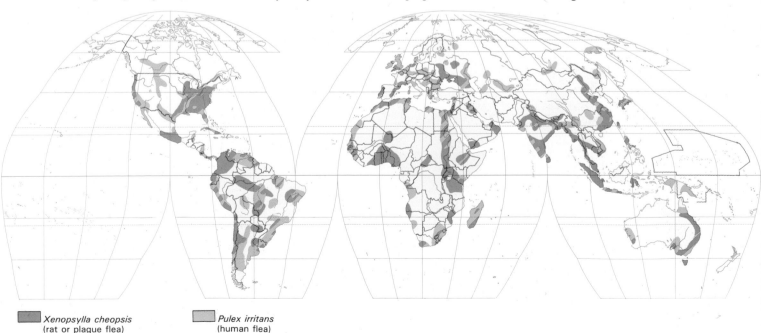

■ *Xenopsylla cheopsis* (rat or plague flea)

■ *Pulex irritans* (human flea)

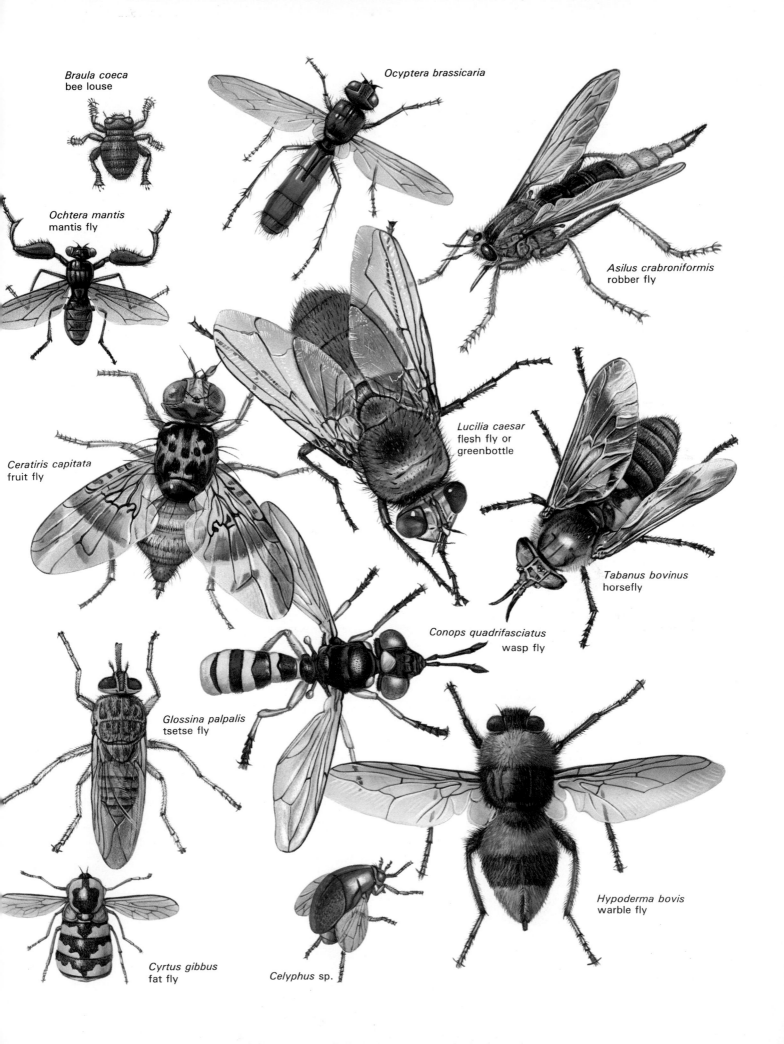

Braula coeca
bee louse

Ocyptera brassicaria

Asilus crabroniformis
robber fly

Ochtera mantis
mantis fly

Ceratiris capitata
fruit fly

Lucilia caesar
flesh fly or
greenbottle

Tabanus bovinus
horsefly

Conops quadrifasciatus
wasp fly

Glossina palpalis
tsetse fly

Hypoderma bovis
warble fly

Cyrtus gibbus
fat fly

Celyphus sp.

PROTOSTOMIA AND DEUTEROSTOMIA

All animals consisting of more than a single cell are grouped in the Metazoa. Apart from the sponges, coelenterates and ctenophores, the Metazoa can be divided into Protostomia and Deuterostomia mainly because of differences in development. The Protostomia are bilaterally symmetrical animals whose mouth is derived directly from the blastopore, that is, the orifice formed by the inward curving of the wall of the newly developing egg. They include most invertebrates as well as the tentaculates, which are dealt with below. In the Deuterostomia the mouth orifice is of secondary origin and is not derived from the blastopore. The Deuterostomia include the other animals – the Chaetognatha, Pogonophora, Pterobranchia and Enteropneusta, as well as the Echinoderms and Chordates, dealt with in the following chapters.

Tentaculata

The last representatives of the Protostomia to be considered here are the tentaculates (Tentaculata), which comprise a rather mixed collection of animals whose aquatic larvae are trochophores, that is, long-lived, free-swimming and shaped something like a Catherine-wheel or spinning-top. At a certain point in its development the larva divides into three segments (metameres), a division that remains in the adult form. The three segments are a small first segment that overhangs the mouth, a segment with a mouth surrounded by tentacles (called a lophophore) and a third segment

A bryozoan of the species *Bugula turbinata.* These colonial animals are sometimes called sea mosses.

which is the main portion of the body, containing the viscera. The tentaculates, also called Lophophora, are divided into three phyla, Bryozoa (sea mosses), Phoronida (horseshoe worms) and Brachiopoda (lampshells).

Bryozoa

The Bryozoa, sea mosses, which are animals but strongly resemble plants, are extremely common in marine and fresh waters. The many species include hornwrack or sea-mat (genus *Flustra*), which resembles bleached seaweed and is often found washed up on the tideline. Other species of sea moss such as those of the genus *Bugula*, illustrated here, grow on underwater structures including the hulls of ships. The individual Bryozoa are microscopic in size, and an entire assemblage or colony is rarely more than 10 mm (0.4 in) thick. Each individual is surrounded by an external skeleton formed by calcareous or horny secretions. The colonies are formed by the asexual budding of one individual and may be erect and branching, like a plant, or lie as an encrustation on the sea bed. They have no circulatory or excretory systems. Marine species feed on plankton captured by means of the lophophore, the system of tentacles forming a circle round the mouth. The tentacles are equipped with cilia which create a current which drives water and food-particles down towards the mouth.

Phoronida

The Phoronida, or horseshoe worms, include only a few species, all marine and sedentary. As in the Bryozoa, the mouth aperture is close to the anus and between the two are found the principal nerve centres. In contrast to the Bryozoa, however, they have red blood due to the presence of haemoglobin flowing in a closed circulatory system. The first larval period is free swimming, after which the larva fixes itself to the substrate. The Phoronida resemble worms and have no external appendages except a horseshoe-shaped ring of tentacles surrounding the mouth, the lophophore. They live in shallow waters, in tubes that they excavate and line with a horny secretion. Some make their burrows in sand, others in calcareous rocks or in mollusc shells.

Brachiopoda

The Brachiopoda, lampshells, include the largest tentaculates. They closely resemble bivalve molluscs, since the body is enclosed by two calcareous valves or shells. However, the valves of the Brachiopoda are dorsal and ventral – enclosing the animal above and below – rather than lateral, as in the molluscs. There are two classes; one (Articulata) in which the shells are connected by a hinge as well as muscles, the other (Inarticulata) in which they are connected only by muscles. In the position of the hinge there is a hole through which issues a foot (peduncle) that adheres to the substrate. The mouth-tentacles of other tentaculates are modified in most of the Brachiopoda into two long arms (the name Brachiopoda means arm-feet). The sexes are separate; the larvae,

after a free-swimming period which may be quite short, begin their metamorphosis after they have fixed themselves to the substrate and so begun their sedentary life. At the present time about 260 species are known, but these are only the remnant of a much more numerous group, with 30,000 fossil species. Some of the present species are found in the sea at depths of 5000 m (16,000 ft).

Chaetognatha

The Chaetognatha, arrow worms, are transparent, shaped like long, slender torpedoes, and have a pair of lateral fins and a tail fin. The mouth has a set of grasping spines giving them their scientific name which is derived from the Greek meaning 'bristle jaws'. They live in the sea and move by rapid jerks, due to contractions of powerful muscles running longitudinally along their upper and lower surfaces. They are carnivorous, feeding on planktonic animals such as copepods, and are themselves eaten by other plankton feeders, such as young fish. There are only about fifty species, but some of them, particularly those of the genus *Sagitta*, are so numerous that they form one of the principal animal components of plankton.

Pogonophora

The Pogonophora, beard worms, have only recently been discovered; the first was found in the mid-1930s in material dredged up from the deep-sea bed. They are thread-like animals, with lengths up to 1.5 m (5 ft) but diameters of no more than 1 mm (0.04 in). A tuft of tentacles at the front end gives them their name; but they have no mouth or digestive tract. It seems that they may collect food by arranging the tentacles into a tube and drawing water through it by the action of cilia, the food particles being digested outside the body and the products of digestion absorbed

Phoronid or horseshoe worms (*Phoronis hippocrepia*) at different stages of tentacle extension.

through the body wall. Beard worms live in long tubes of material held together by secretions; the tubes are believed to stand vertically in the sea bed ooze.

Pterobranchia

The Pterobranchia, together with the following group, the Enteropneusta, are classed as Hemichordates. The Pterobranchia are minute marine animals, a few millimetres in length, whose bodies are divided into three sections, a proboscis, a collar and a trunk, each section containing a part of the body cavity (the coelom). There are few genera and only two are well known. In one, *Rhabdopleura*, multiplication is attained by budding. All new buds remain in contact with the parent forming a colony. In the other, *Cephalodiscus*, buds formed in the same way become free of the parent body and lead solitary lives. Both genera live in tubes formed in sand bound together with secretions produced by the animal, and collect food by means of cilia-bearing arms protruding from the collar. The body is vase-shaped and the gut U-shaped so that the anus opens upwards.

Enteropneusta

The Enteropneusta, acorn worms, are larger than the pterobranchs and as their name suggests, are worm-like in form. As with pterobranchs there is the same division into proboscis, collar and trunk, with the mouth at the base of the proboscis. The proboscis is used to excavate the U-shaped burrows in which the animals live. The excavated sand forms characteristic spiral piles on the surface. The lengths vary from a few centimetres to 2 m (6½ ft).

ECHINODERMS

Most of the known 20,000 species of echinoderms are fossils with only 5000 living species. Echinoderms are divided into two main groups. The first, the Pelmatozoa, lead a sedentary life and are commonly called sea-lilies (Crinoidea). The second, the Eleutherozoa, can move about freely and are divided into four classes, sea-cucumbers (Holothuridea), sea urchins (Echinoidea), brittle stars (Ophiuridea) and starfish (Asteroidea).

All are marine animals, and are the only coelomates – animals with a body-cavity – to show radial symmetry. The body, which takes various forms, is usually made up of five parts radiating from a central axis. The body wall usually has an internal skeleton of calcareous plates lying within the wall, and in many species the skeleton possesses numerous spines or small lumps which project above the outer surface, giving it a spiny or knobbly appearance. The surface containing the mouth is known as the oral side and the opposite surface, the aboral side. Echinoderms have a water-vascular system, a ring round the mouth connected by a number of tubes filled with seawater. The exterior parts of this system are formed into numerous hollow tube-feet (podia) arranged in rows. Echinoderms lack a definite head region and centralized brain; instead, body activity is coordinated by a branching network of nerves. Most echinoderms live on the sea bed either fixed to the substrate or slow moving. A few species are free-swimming.

Crinoidea

The Crinoidea, sea-lilies, number about eighty living species. They are usually fastened to the sea bed by a stalk or peduncle, with the mouth and tube-feet directed upwards. The body, often spectacular in shape and highly coloured, is shaped like a calyx, or goblet, from which extend numerous fragile arms, made up of jointed segments. The calyx is usually held up by a stalk (peduncle) and the pedunculate species live at great depths, between 500 and 10,000 m (0.3 to 6 miles), where they form vast 'meadows' containing thousands of individuals. The species present in coastal waters, the feather stars, are usually free-swimming and lead a sedentary life only in the larval stage.

The feather stars are generally regarded as mobile relatives of the sea-lilies. They cling to the substrate with a circle of tiny tentacles and pull themselves along with their arms. Feather stars have been described as 'starfish turned upside down', with ten feathered arms able to catch floating edible particles and also propel the animal in short bursts by waving up and down.

Sea-lilies illustrated here are *Rhizocrinus lofotensis*, *Cenocrinus asteria* and *Antedon mediterranea*.

Holothuroidea

There are about 500 living species of Holothuroidea which include sea cucumbers or cotton spinners. They have an elongated sausage-like body, 1–5 cm (0.4–2 in) long, provided with calcareous platelets of various forms, and tube-feet either scattered about the body surface or formed into rows, usually three on the lower surface and two on the upper. Most species have separate sexes, with some hermaphroditism, so that besides sexual reproduction there may also be asexual reproduction by splitting of cells, as in *Cucumaria planci*, illustrated here. Some species, such as *Pelagothuria ludwigi*, illustrated here, have the tentacles joined by a membrane which enables them to swim like jellyfish. Other species live in close contact with the substrate; *Rhopalodina lageniformis*, illustrated here, buries itself completely, leaving nothing above the surface but the end of its long proboscis.

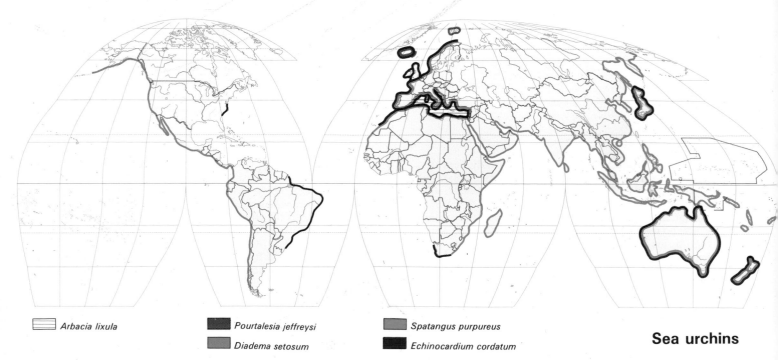

▭ *Arbacia lixula*	▬ *Pourtalesia jeffreysi*	▬ *Spatangus purpureus*
▬ *Diadema setosum*	▬ *Echinocardium cordatum*	

Sea urchins

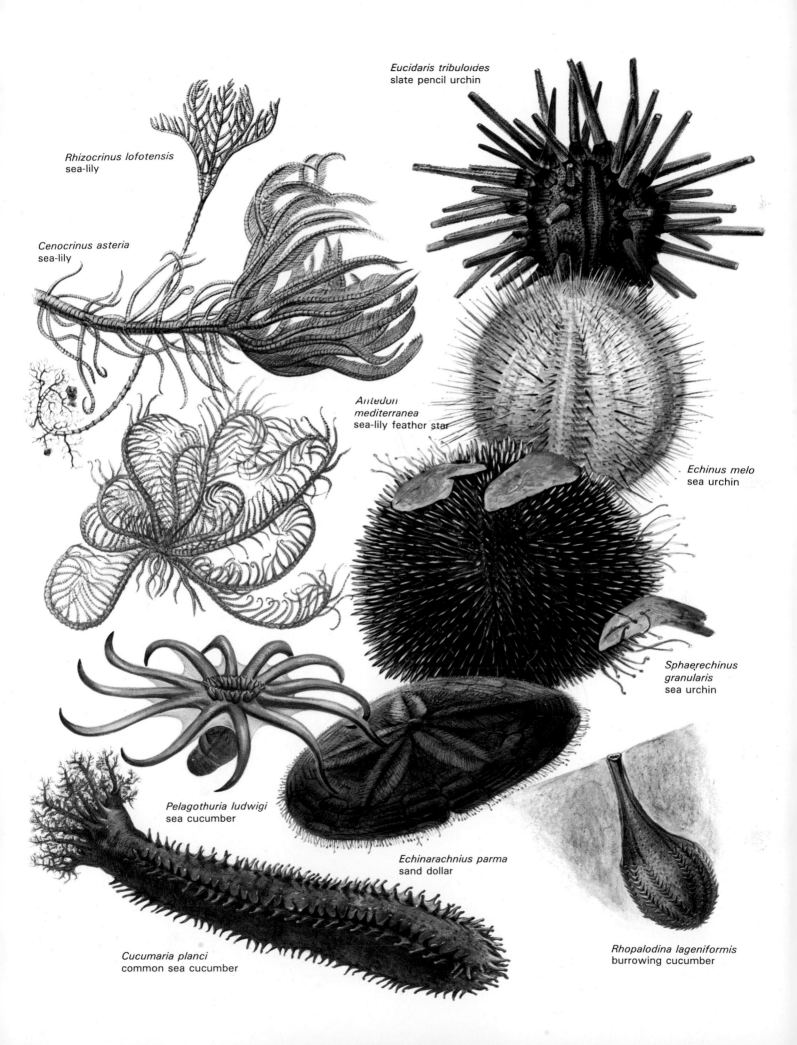

Rhizocrinus lofotensis
sea-lily

Cenocrinus asteria
sea-lily

Eucidaris tribuloides
slate pencil urchin

*Antedon
mediterranea*
sea-lily feather star

Echinus melo
sea urchin

*Sphaerechinus
granularis*
sea urchin

Pelagothuria ludwigi
sea cucumber

Echinarachnius parma
sand dollar

Rhopalodina lageniformis
burrowing cucumber

Cucumaria planci
common sea cucumber

Echinoidea

The Echinoidea – sea urchins, sand dollars and heart urchins – are globular, cushion-shaped or disc-shaped, without arms but with numerous long spines and tube-feet ending in suckers. In the centre of the circle is the mouth, where the sea urchins have a complex chewing organ, known as 'Aristotle's lantern', consisting of a ring of small bars (ossicles) and sharp-pointed teeth pointing inwards. It uses this organ to scrape edible material off the rocks. The body is entirely protected by a skeleton within the skin, consisting of calcareous plates jointed to form a shell or 'test'. In some species, long, sharp spines project from small rounded knobs and terminate in poisonous sacs. Some species have much shorter and softer spines, and these generally live buried in the sand. Some groups, the heart urchins (*Spatangus*) and sea potatoes (*Echinocardium*), have species which carry their own eggs to incubate them, up to the development of the larvae. Most sea urchins are found at depths not greater than 200 m (650 ft), but some species, such as those of the genus *Pourtalesia*, have been gathered from depths of 7000 m (22,000 ft). The diet varies with the habitat. Some are omnivorous, others are herbivorous or predatory, devouring animals which are captured by the tube-feet. Others filter the sand in search of minute diatoms and foraminifera.

The form of the body can vary considerably, as can be seen from the illustrations on p. 99 of *Echinus melo*, which is almost spherical; *Sphaerechinus granularis*, a typical sea urchin almost circular in section with rather shorter spines; *Eucidarius tribuloides*, which has very large, fairly stiff spines; and *Echinarachnius parma*, whose spines have been transformed into a kind of fur. An Australian species, *Phyllacanthus parvispinus*, also has large stiff spines, and when these are detached from the dead animal and washed up on the beach they resemble the old-fashioned slate crayons – hence the local name of the slate pencil urchin.

Ophiuroidea

The ophiurids, or brittle stars, are the most successful of the echinoderms, with just under 2000 living species. Somewhat similar in appearance to starfish, they have long and very slender, mobile arms. These radiate from a distinctly separate central disc.

Some species are hermaphroditic; in others the sexes are separate, sometimes with a marked sexual dimorphism, as for instance in *Amphilycus androphorus*, illustrated here, in which the female is relatively large while the much smaller male stays attached to her throughout life.

The ophiurids generally grow very slowly, and species of the genus *Ophiura* (of which *O. albida* is illustrated here) may take as much as five or six years to attain maturity. The coloration of the ophiuroids is often varied and brilliant, as is shown here in *Ophioderma longicaudata* and *Ophiothrix fragilis*.

As the name brittle star implies, the arms of these creatures are prone to snapping and detachment (the shallow-water species *Opiothrix fragilis* seems to fall to pieces almost as soon as it is touched). However a large proportion of the broken-off arms, as well as the original central discs, regenerate into new individuals.

Asteroidea

The Asteroidea or starfish contain approximately 1700 living species. The coloration of the body is often very vivid: bright red, yellow, orange, blue for example. They have thick muscular arms and lack a distinct central disc. Dimensions vary considerably and the diameter may measure from a few centimetres to nearly 1 m (39 in). They have five pairs of sex organs, one on each arm. Some mate by copulation but most species multiply by spawning: eggs and sperm are released into the water where fertilization takes place. Starfish are active predators who prey particularly on bivalve molluscs and are thus a nuisance in commercial oyster beds. They seize the mollusc, prise it open and insert their stomach. This releases digestive juices which dissolve the prey and allow it to be absorbed by the stomach wall. Some species attack other echinoderms such as sea cucumbers, while the crown-of-thorns starfish (*Acanthaster planci*, shown here) feeds also on decaying vegetable matter. *Cossaster papposus*, also illustrated, swallows the prey whole and later rejects unwanted matter. Vividly coloured species illustrated here are *Astropecten aurantiacus*, *Luidia ciliaris* and *Fromia ghardaqana*. The heaviest starfish known is *Oreaster reticulatus* found off the coast of Florida and the Bahamas. It is like a massive five-rayed cushion 50 cm (20 in) across.

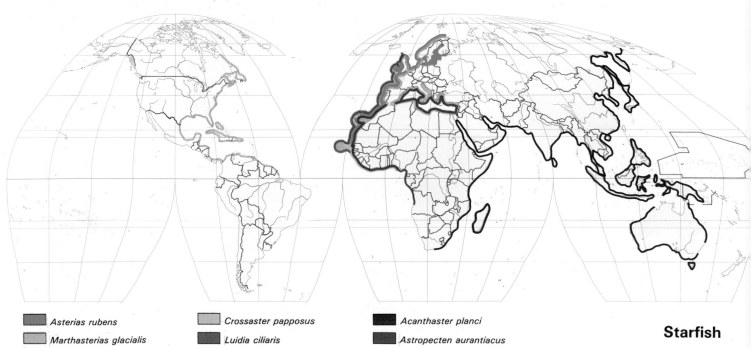

Asterias rubens

Marthasterias glacialis

Crossaster papposus

Luidia ciliaris

Acanthaster planci

Astropecten aurantiacus

Starfish

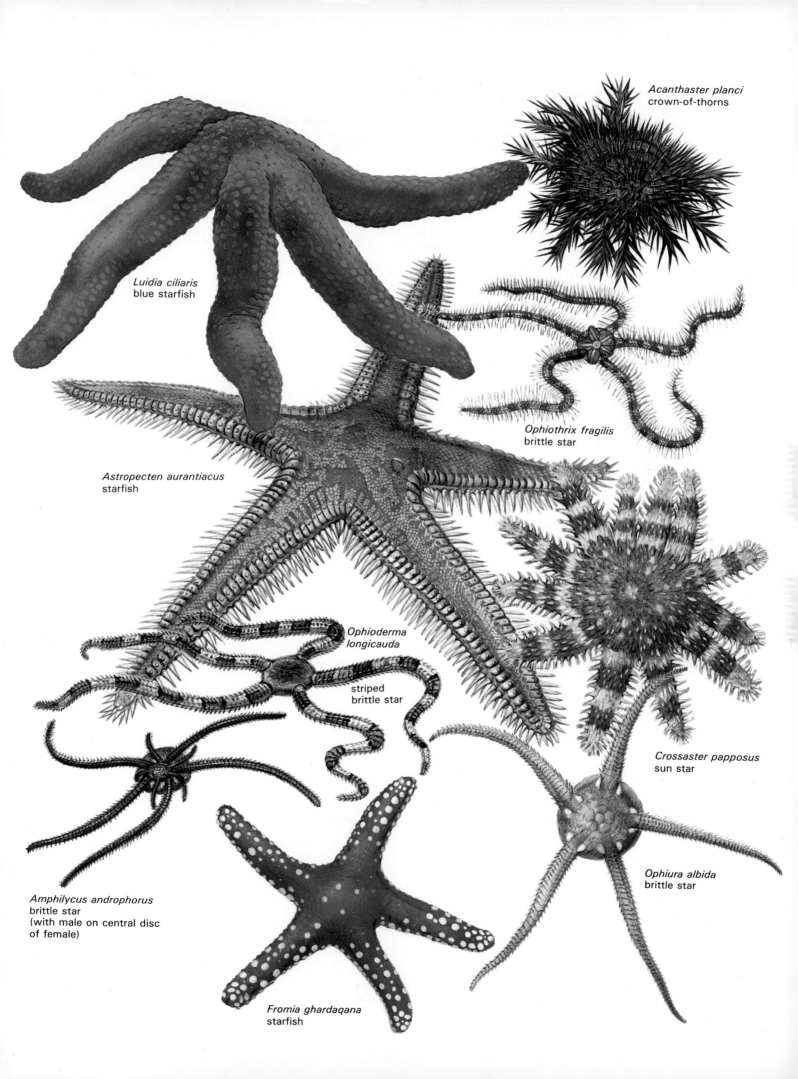

Acanthaster planci
crown-of-thorns

Luidia ciliaris
blue starfish

Ophiothrix fragilis
brittle star

Astropecten aurantiacus
starfish

*Ophioderma
longicauda*

striped
brittle star

Crossaster papposus
sun star

Amphilycus androphorus
brittle star
(with male on central disc
of female)

Ophiura albida
brittle star

Fromia ghardaqana
starfish

CHORDATES

The chordates are a very large group, comprising a small number of animals which lack vertebrae, as well as all the vertebrates, including man. Chordates are relative newcomers to the evolutionary stage – for example, the earliest vertebrates first appear as fossils only 500 million years ago as against 1600 million years for invertebrate fossils. Chordates have in many ways assumed a dominant position in the animal kingdom, even though arthropods are still more numerous both as species and as individuals. One of the distinguishing features of the chordates is the possession at some time in their lives of a notochord – a strong but flexible central support able to strengthen the body and serve as a point of attachment for the musculature.

Urochordata

The urochordates or tunicates, also known as sea squirts, were thought for a long time to be most closely related to the molluscs because of their appearance and way of life. They are mostly sedentary creatures of the sea bed, though some are planktonic, of sizes varying from a few millimetres up to about 10 cm (4 in). In general they are shapeless, sack-like creatures, and the body is covered with an elastic skin known as a tunic. In the larval stage, however, they show all the features of a chordate, having a notochord, gill slits and a nervous system which features a hollow dorsal nerve cord (the forerunner of a spinal cord and brain). There are three groups of urochordates, the Ascidiacea, Thaliacea and Appendicularia (Larvacea).

Ascidiacea. Some 2000 species of ascidiaceans, or sea squirts, are known. They live in coastal waters where they attach themselves to rocks, piers and the sea bed for the whole of their adult lives. In this adult stage there is no trace of any fish-like form, but the larvae are free swimmers resembling transparent tadpoles, and possess a rudimentary backbone (notochord) in the tail and other chordate features. When the planktonic larva is fully grown the tail is lost and the ascidian fixes itself firmly to the substrate by its head end. It then assumes the sedentary adult way of life.

Larvacea. Larvacea are very small, transparent, free-floating animals that retain a tadpole-like form throughout their lives, and never lose the tail and the notochord contained within it. None of the seventy species attains a length of more than a few millimetres.

Thaliacea. The thaliaceans, or salps, are small planktonic creatures resembling small barrels of transparent jelly, with the mouth siphon at one end and the anal siphon at the other. By closing the anal cavity and expanding the body wall, water is drawn in through the mouth cavity; on contracting the body wall, the water is driven out through the anal cavity. Food particles are trapped in a cone of mucus, oxygen is absorbed from the water and the jet of water expelled from the rear propels the animal forwards. Some thaliacea form colonies, sometimes of considerable length. There are only about thirty species, most tropical.

Cephalochordata

The cephalochordates, which include the lancelets, are small segmented animals living on the sea bed, where they bury themselves in the mud leaving only the head visible. They are the closest to fish of the non-vertebrates; the body is laterally compressed, and the notochord runs through the entire length of the body with the central nervous system located below it. The mouth, which opens below the forward end, lacks jaws but is provided with a bundle of filaments (cirri). There are only about twenty species; the commonest is the lancelet, *Branchiostoma lanceolatum*, also called amphioxus, which measures about 5–6 cm (2–2.4 in) in length. Lancelets are pale whitish animals with an iridescent sheen. They live buried in the sea bed, filtering planktonic food particles through an extensive system of delicate gill bars in the pharynx. They can swim, and also burrow, by contracing the powerful muscles of the body wall, alternately on either side, giving them a wriggling motion rather like that of an eel. There are two separate sexes and reproduction is sexual.

Vertebrata

The Vertebrata, the most advanced group of chordates, is characterized by a segmented backbone made up of separate vertebrae. In the embryonic stage there is a notochord but in most species this is replaced by the vertebral column in adults. The skeleton is bony except in two groups (Agnatha and Chondrichtheys) in which it is cartilaginous. The front end of the nerve cord is expanded to form a brain, and a bony structure – the cranium (skull) – is developed to protect it. Typically the skeleton of the trunk is made up of the spinal column and the ribs; two pairs of limbs are attached to the spinal column which are used for locomotion, though in some early forms these are absent and in others are much reduced.

The skin of vertebrates is formed of two layers, a dermis (skin) and epidermis (outer skin); generally the epidermis is thin and the dermis much thicker. In aquatic animals the epidermis consists mostly of living cells, but in terrestrial animals the outer layers are usually dead cells. In many terrestrial vertebrates the epidermis forms a waterproof protective layer over the dermis. The dermis also produces scales (reptiles), feathers (birds), or fur (mammals) which offer further protection and insulation. The dermis also contains glands which may secrete scent, sweat, milk (in mammals) and other chemical substances.

The nervous system is made up of the spinal cord, the brain and the peripheral nervous system, with various sense organs. The circulatory system is a closed one, consisting of a pumping organ (the heart), blood vessels, and in the higher vertebrates, in particular the mammals, a lymphatic system. Birds and mammals that generate heat internally and maintain a warm body are referred to as endothermic, whereas reptiles, amphibians and fish derive most of their heat from their environment and are referred to as ectothermic. If the environment cools, ectotherms cool too and become less active.

FISH

Fish (Pisces) breathe by means of gills, and have bodies generally elongated and spindle-shaped, usually covered with scales and provided with fins for locomotion. They were the first vertebrates to populate the earth, from the Lower Silurian period, 400 million years ago. There are three major groups, Agnatha (jawless fishes), Chondrichthyes (cartilaginous fishes) and Osteichthyes (bony fishes – comprising the Chondrostei, Holostei and Teleostei).

AGNATHA

The Agnatha, or jawless fishes, are the most primitive of living vertebrates and are represented today by only two groups, lampreys and hagfish. They are collectively known as cyclostomes (round-mouths), and are descended from a much larger group, the ostracoderms, known only as fossils from the Paleozoic period. These ancestors were covered with an armour of bony plates which their descendants have lost, being now covered with bare skin. Thus they lack scales as well as a skull, jaws, limbs and vertebrae. Both lampreys and hagfish resemble eels in appearance. The former are parasites on other fish, the latter are scavengers. The mouth, lacking jaws, is circular in form and in the lampreys lies at the bottom of a large conical fleshy sucker, while in the hagfish it opens directly to the exterior. The tongue of hagfish and the entire mouth apparatus of lampreys are furnished with a set of small, sharp, replaceable horny teeth. Lampreys pierce the skin of living fish with their teeth and suck their blood, which remains fluid thanks to an anticoagulant substance contained in the saliva. Some remain attached to the fish, and cause considerable damage to economically important species, particularly in the Great Lakes of North America which they reached by invasion from the sea when the Niagara Falls bypass-canal was built. The fisheries owners went to great lengths to kill off the lampreys that had invaded the Great Lakes, and they also built more weirs and dams to prevent further migration. In the extermination programme many lampreys were electrocuted but the breakthrough came when a poison was developed that killed lamprey larvae only, leaving most other fish unharmed. Hagfish live mostly on dead or dying fish, burrowing into their bodies, often through the mouth, and eat out the entire contents of the body. More than a hundred hagfish have been found in a single fish. They also eat worms and crustaceans. Unlike lampreys, hagfish have no eyes, though sensitive reveptors in the skin make them aware of changes of light intensity.

The distribution of lampreys (Petromyzontidae) is shown in the map below. They are widely distributed in the northern hemisphere, while in the southern hemisphere they are present only in small areas of Australia, New Zealand and South America. The adults, about 30 cm (12 in) long, live in the sea, probably for about two and a half years, and then travel to fresh waters to breed. The eggs hatch into larvae which live buried in the mud, feeding on micro-organisms. They then travel downstream to the sea where they metamorphose into adults. The commonest species in Europe is *Lampetra fluviatilis*. Lampreys used to be caught in large numbers in the rivers for food but are now much rarer. It is often said that King John of England died from lamprey poisoning because he ate so many of these fish; in fact it was Henry I who met his death in this way. King John did have the reputation of fining his subjects because they paid insufficient taxes in the form of live lampreys for food. Hagfish (Myxinoidea) are also present in both hemispheres. Unlike lampreys they do not have a distinct larval stage and pass their entire lives in the sea. An individual hagfish has both male and female sexual organs and is therefore a hermaphrodite. However, it is thought that only one set of organs is functional and so a 'male' hagfish must mate with a 'female' one in order to fertilize the eggs.

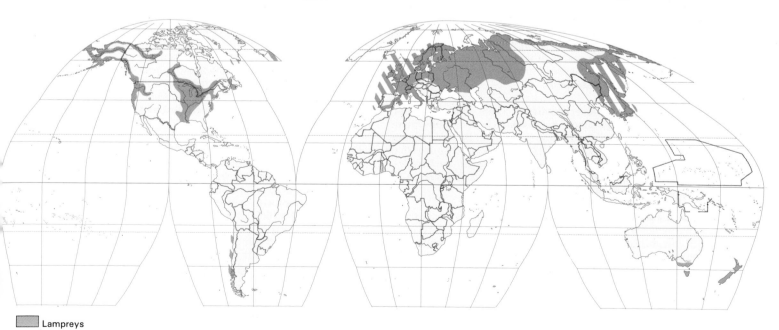

Lampreys

CHONDRICHTHYES

Up to about 400 million years ago all fish (then the only vertebrates) were jawless (agnathous). There later evolved fish with jaws (Gnathostomata) and fins in pairs, which gave them a much greater capacity for accuracy of direction and manoeuvring in swimming. An early group to appear was that of the cartilaginous fishes (Chondrichthyes) belonging to the elasmobranchs (Elasmobranchii or plate-gilled fishes) of which there were two kinds: sharks and dogfish (Pleurotremata), and skates and rays (Hypotremata), all characterized by a cartilaginous skeleton.

Pleurotremata

The body of the pleurotremata, which include sharks and dogfish, is hydrodynamically well designed, perfectly adapted for swift and continuous swimming. Continuous swimming is essential since in the absence of buoyant swim bladders they have to swim without interruption to avoid sinking though most have a huge oily liver which helps them float. The 250 species are marine, and tend to be found in the open seas. They are particularly numerous in tropical waters where there is an abundance of prey – other fish, molluscs and crustaceans. Their preference for a carnivorous diet is shown by their powerful array of teeth. Some are notorious for their attacks on swimmers.

Of the 250 species of sharks and dogfish, only a handful have been reliably documented as being responsible for attacks on humans. Among the most dangerous are the great white shark, variously called the white shark and white pointer (*Carcharodon carcharias*, illustrated here), the tiger shark (*Galeocerda cuvieri*) of the Carchariidae, found in tropical waters, and some of the whaler sharks such as the bronze whaler and the black-tipped whaler. One particularly fast and dangerous shark of southern waters is the mako. There are several other species that have the reputation for attacking swimmers and divers but attacks by them have rarely, if ever, been reliably documented. Such species include the grey nurse and the various hammerheads (*Sphyrna* spp.).

Heterodontidae and Hexanchidae. The Heterodontidae include the Port Jackson sharks and the Hexanchidae, the six or seven gill sharks. The Port Jackson shark or horn shark (*Heterodontus*) is probably the most primitive of all, found mainly in the Indian Ocean. The Hexanchidae include the sixgill sharks (*Hexanchus*), and the comb-toothed sharks (*Heptranchias*); both are long-bodied and slow-moving sharks of warm European waters. The frilled shark (*Chlamydoselachus*, illustrated here) is a deep-sea shark that preys on cephalopods.

Cetorhinidae and Rhinocodontidae. The basking shark (*Cetorhinus*) and whale shark (*Rhincodon*) – both are illustrated – are the sole representatives of these two genera. Both are gigantic in size, 15 m (50 ft) and 18 m (63 ft) long respectively – the whale shark being the largest known fish. Both these fish are harmless, feeding solely on plankton. The basking shark is found in the North Atlantic, the whale shark is worldwide.

Carcharinidae. The group most feared by man is that of the family Carcharinidae which populate tropical waters in all parts of the world. Besides big marine species, such as the great white shark which can grow to more than 10 m (36 ft) and weigh up to 3000 kg (3 tons) and the tiger shark already mentioned, some species also live in fresh water. For example, *Carcharinus nicaraguensis* lives in lakes and rivers of tropical America, *C. zambesensis* in Africa, and *C. gangeticus* in India. A typical and dangerous inhabitant of warm seas is the lemon shark (*Megaprion brevirostris*). In southern European waters the green shark (*Prionace glauca*), sometimes called the blue shark, is easily recognizable by its habit of swimming just below the surface of the water with its dorsal fin and tail fin exposed. It is sometimes seen off western Britain but does not come inshore. Members of this family are the most abundant of the sharks, and are hunted by men for food, oil and leather. They live on various fishes and also attack men.

Squalidae and Triakidae. The Squalidae include sharks of cold, deep waters, such as the spiny dogfish (*Squalus acanthias*) which has a spine in front of each dorsal fin. It travels around in large shoals and is an important food species. A less well-known member is the pig-fish (*Oxynotus centrina*, illustrated on p. 107). Some species have luminous organs and large scales armed with spines. The Triakidae includes the smooth hound (*Mustelus*), common off the Atlantic coast of N. America but not caught for food.

Orectolobidae and Scyliorhinidae. The Orectolobidae, nurse sharks (*Ginglymostoma*), are distinguishable by the deep furrows joining the nostrils to the mouth and by the fleshy feelers along the mouth, which are most visible in the marbled shark (*Orectolobus maculatus*). They are inhabitants of the warm zones of the Atlantic, Pacific and Indian Oceans.

The Scyliorhinidae or cat sharks have two dorsal fins which lie behind the ventral ones. A common example is the lesser spotted dogfish (*Scyliorhinus canicular*, illustrated here) of the Atlantic and Mediterranean, also known in fishmongers' shops as rock salmon. It can attain about 76 cm (30 in) in length. Its eggs are almost rectangular, with a horny shell carrying long tendrils at each corner which anchor it to the vegetation of the seabed. The young dogfish spends six months developing inside the egg case, and when it hatches it is a miniature of its parents but only three inches long. The empty capsules are commonly washed up on the shore and are known as mermaids' purses.

Alopidae and Sphyrnidae. The Alopidae include the thresher sharks and the Sphyrnidae, the hammerheads. The typical heterocercal tail of the sharks (one which produces lift as well as forward motion) reaches its maximum development in the threshers, such as *Alopias vulpinus*, illustrated here. It stuns its prey by delivering powerful blows of the tail. Several threshers may work together to herd fish into a shoal. A modification of the basic shark-structure can be seen in the hammerheads, such as *Sphyrna zygaena*, illustrated on p. 107. Lateral extensions of the head enable the nostrils to be set far apart, perhaps aiding the location of food by smell. Some hammerheads grow to 5 m (16 ft) in length, though most are about 3 m (10 ft) long.

Pristiphoridae and Squatinidae. The Pristiphoridae include the saw sharks and the Squatinidae, the angel sharks. The saw sharks or saw-toothed sharks (*Pristiophorus*) also show extensive modifications of the head region which is elongated into a long flattened 'beak' (rostrum) with toothed edges, like a saw-blade. They are found in the Pacific and in South African coastal waters where they are regarded as a delicacy.

In sharks the gill slits are situated on the side, behind the head, and in rays they are below the head. This feature leads to the classification of the angelfish among the sharks rather than among

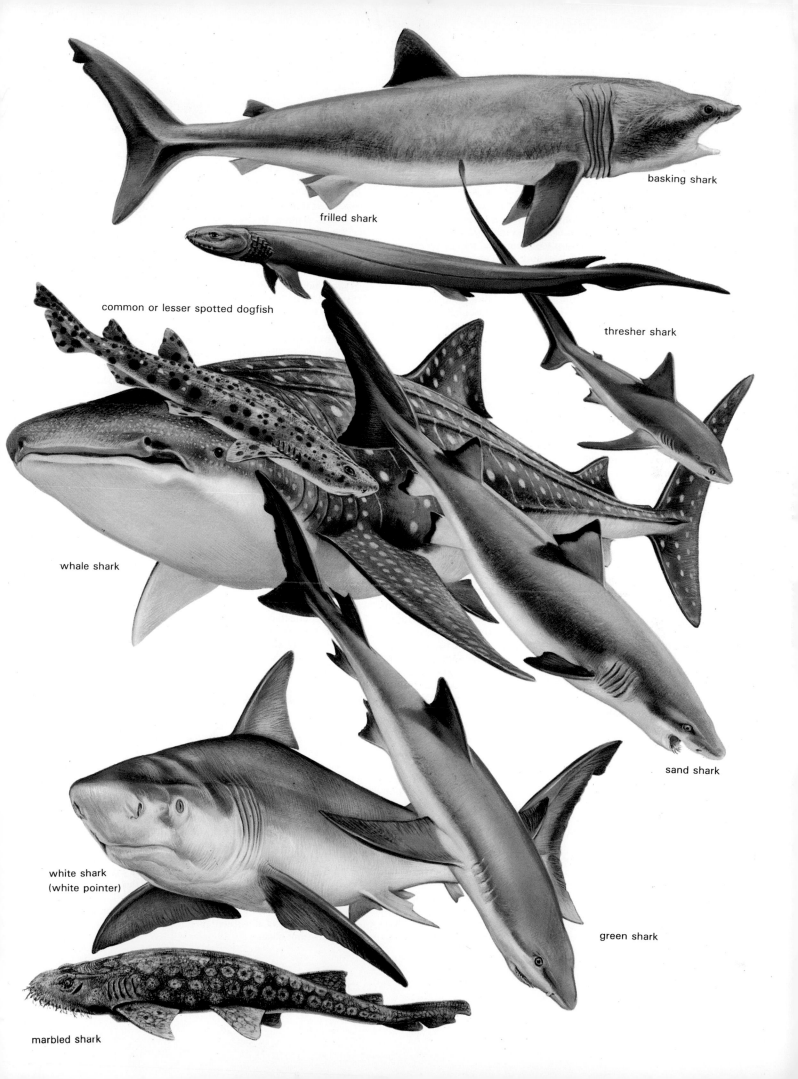

basking shark

frilled shark

common or lesser spotted dogfish

thresher shark

whale shark

sand shark

white shark
(white pointer)

green shark

marbled shark

the rays, which they superficially resemble. Angelfish or monkfish (*Squatina*, illustrated here) are bottom-feeders, found in temperate and tropical waters.

Hypotremata

Unlike the sharks, the Hypotremata, which include the rays and skates, are relatively sluggish fish found mainly on the sea bed of coastal waters. They have blunt teeth and feed mostly on invertebrates such as shelled molluscs and crustaceans. The body is extremely flattened, and the much reduced tail is incapable of producing any propulsion for swimming. The front fins (pectorals) are enormously developed and are attached along the sides of the head. Movement is effected by waves of muscular contraction passing backwards along the pectoral fins which act almost like wings in some species, enabling the rays to 'fly' gracefully through the water.

Pristidae and Rhinobatidae. The Pristidae include the sawfish and the Rhinobatidae, the banjo-rays. The transition from sharks to rays is probably best represented by the sawfish (*Pristis*, illustrated here) which somewhat resembles the saw shark (*Pristiophorus*). In sawfish the body still resembles that of a shark but the lateral fins are much enlarged and the mouth and gill slits are ventral, i.e., situated on the under side. The dorsal fins and tail are still well developed. This group of rays can reach lengths of 9 m (30 ft) and their beak or saw, armoured with teeth, may be 3 m (10 ft) long.

A further transformation has taken place in the banjo-rays, in which the pectoral fins are larger and are attached to the hinder part of the body. The violin-fish (*Rhinobatus rhinobatus*, illustrated here) is also in this group.

Torpedinoidae. The Torpedinoidae, electric rays, attain a completely flattened aspect typical of the rays. Electric rays usually inhabit warm seas, and of the ten or so known genera the most typical is the genus *Torpedo*, of which some members are found in warmer European waters, including *Torpedo torpedo*, illustrated here. The most remarkable characteristic of the electric rays is the possession of an electric organ situated between the head and the pectoral fins. Through nervous impulses, at the animal's will, it can effect a discharge of up to 50 V, capable of stunning fish larger than itself, which it then eats. This is enough to give a human a nasty shock, but the fish is safe to pick up by the tail where there are no large electric organs.

The electric ray has featured prominently in medical history. Physicians in ancient Rome used the fish to treat patients with gout, headaches and many other illnesses. The ray was captured and kept in an aquarium, and the patient either stood on it or had the live fish pressed to his temples. Needless to say he received a shock, though how effective this was in curing the illness we do not know. It was not until the mid-1700s, following the invention of the Leyden jar and the discovery of the nature of electricity by Galvani, that the power of the *Torpedo* was understood.

Rajoidae. In the Rajoidae, true rays, the flattened 'disc' of the body and the pectoral fins joined to it is quite distinct from the reduced, slender tail. European species include *Raja clavata*, with its large dorsal spines, *R. miraletus* illustrated here, and the larger *R. batis* which can reach 2 m (6½ ft) in length. The egg cases of this group are similar to those of dogfish, but the corner extensions that attach the eggs to the substratum are rigid instead of tendril-like.

Dasyatidae. The Dasyatidae, sting rays such as *Dasyatis*, and *Trygon*, illustrated here, have flattened and very extended bodies in which the tail is reduced to a defensive whip, and the dorsal fin has become a highly poisonous spike. Some species ascend rivers, and in South America the genus *Potamotrygon* lives exclusively in fresh water. In the butterfly rays (*Gymnura*) the lateral fins are so expanded that they resemble wings. The species of sting ray that is found around British coasts is *Dasyatis pastinaca*. Like its relatives it is a bottom-living fish, frequenting sandy or muddy areas and feeding on molluscs and crustaceans. It has a venomous spine at the base of its long whip-like tail.

Myliobatidae and Mobulidae. The Myliobatidae include the eagle rays and Mobulidae, the devil rays. The eagle rays include species such as *Myliobatis aquila*, illustrated here, whose 'wings' have a pointed shape like those of birds. Other modifications have occurred in some such as the displacement of the eyes, which are situated at each side of the head on fleshy protuberances.

The manta rays and sea devils have expanded fins at the front of the head which are used to steer plankton towards the mouth, as is seen in *Manta birostris*, illustrated here. Some manta rays are equipped with long poison stings that can be dangerous and sometimes fatal to man. In these two groups the largest dimensions of rays are reached, with spans of up to 5 m (16 ft).

Chimaeriformes

The Chimaeriformes, rat fish, rabbit fish and elephant fish, are close to the sharks and skates in their evolutionary history and body structure. They still have the five gill slits but here they are covered by a flap of skin. They are bottom-feeders, living on molluscs and other invertebrates. The tail is long and thin. There is no stomach and the gut is a straight tube leading from pharynx to anus. The mouth is a small aperture surrounded by lips, giving them a parrot-like appearance. A spine in front of the dorsal fin is sometimes poisonous. The skin is soft and lacks spines and propulsion is effected by a rowing action of the pectoral fins. They include the rat fish (*Chimaera*), rabbit fish (*Hydrolagus*) and elephant fish (*Callorhynchus*). There are about 35 species, of which the best-known is *Chimaera monstrosa*, illustrated here.

CHONDROSTEI

The Chondrostei, sturgeons and paddle fish, contain both cartilage and bone. They are classified as Osteichthyes (bony fish) and are the most primitive members of that group.

One group of Chondrostei – the Acipenseroidei – is represented by the sturgeon (*Acipenser*, illustrated on p. 109) found in Europe, Asia and North America. The best-known species is *Acipenser sturio*, whose undeveloped eggs provide the much-prized caviare. Another source of caviare is the beluga (*Huso huso*) which can attain 9 m (30 ft) in length and weigh up to 1000 kg (1 ton). It is one of the largest of all freshwater fish. All the sturgeons are big fish with no scales but five rows of bony plates; the snout is elongated and has a bunch of sensitive barbels below it which are used to search for the fish on which the sturgeon preys. The tail is of the heterocercal kind, giving lift as well as forward motion, the upper lobe being much larger than the lower, as in the shovelnose sturgeon (*Scaphirhynchus platorhynchus*, illustrated on p. 109) which lives in the rivers of the Mississippi basin.

spiny dogfish

rat or rabbit fish

hammerhead

eagle ray

angelfish
(monkfish)

cuckoo
ray

sawfish

pig-fish

manta ray

banjo-ray
(violin-fish)

electric ray

sting ray

In the paddle fish (*Polyodon spathula*, illustrated here) of the eastern USA, an exceptional prolongation of the snout is observed. This is a fresh water, filter feeding species.

Another group of the Chondrostei is represented by the West African bichir (*Polypterus senegalensis* and *Calamoichthys calabaricus*, both illustrated). A notable characteristic of these fishes is the presence of a kind of lung situated ventrally and communicating with the gut, which enables them to cope with a dearth of dissolved oxygen in the water – often a problem in warmer parts of the world because oxygen dissolves less readily in warm water.

HOLOSTEI

The Holostei, garpikes and bowfins, are bony fishes, which, like the Chondrostei, are survivors of a primitive group known mostly by fossils. Both the garpike (*Lepisosteus*) and the bowfin (*Amia*) are illustrated here. In the garpikes the snout is so much elongated as to resemble that of a crocodile, hence they are often called 'alligatorgars' in North America where they live. These fish are able to breathe air, thanks to a modification of the swim bladder. The garpike (*Lepisosteus osseus*) can attain a length of 60 cm (2 ft). The bowfin (*Amia calva*) which has a long dorsal fin and rounded tail fin, reaches only 25 cm (10 in) in length.

Sarcopterygii

Most members of the Sarcopterygii, lobe fins and lung fishes, are extinct. The first were known only as fossils until 1938 when a fish of a previously unknown type was caught off the mouth of the River Chalumna in South Africa. Weighing 50 kg (100 lb) and 1.5 m (5 ft) long, it was the first lobe fin or coelacanth to be seen living in modern times; the second, a more complete specimen, was not caught until 1952. It is illustrated here. The name *Latimeria chalumnae* recalls the name of a Miss Latimer of the East London Museum who first examined it, and the river near the mouth of which it was caught. Since then several dozen have been obtained and many of the world's museums now possess a specimen. Coelacanths produce eggs the size of tennis balls – the largest

eggs that have been produced by any species of bony fish.

Fossil coelacanths lived from about 450 to 70 million years ago, and scientists always viewed them as a possible link between fish and the earliest land creatures, the amphibians. This was due mainly to the fossil coelacanth's possession of lobed fins, which look like the precursors of legs, and a swim bladder which seemed (in the fossil species) that it might be the beginnings of lungs. When the live coelacanths were examined, however, the swim bladder was found to be very small and filled with fat, so that it could not function as an air-breathing organ, as it does in the lung fish mentioned below. Some excitable scientists declared that the newly-discovered coelacanth was a 'missing link' of great importance and that it shed much light on man's ancestry. However, modern evidence shows that the living coelacanth is the sole known surviving member of an offshoot from the main line of evolution and that it is not on the evolutionary path from fishes to land creatures.

Only three groups of lung fishes are known. Representatives of each group, the Australian lung fish *Neoceratodus forsteri*, *Protopterus aethiopicus* of Africa and *Lepidosiren paradoxa* of South America, are illustrated here. All have elongated bodies, and possess both gills and lungs, the swim bladders having been transformed into a kind of lungs rich in blood vessels. All live in lakes or rivers that tend to dry out in some seasons. *Neoceratodus* species breathe mainly through their gills if the water contains sufficient oxygen, but if this becomes too scarce they use their lungs. *Protopterus* and *Lepidosirena* breathe only with their lungs, and when the river or lake in which they live dries out they bury themselves in the mud and breathe air through a small breathing-tube that connects the mud hole with the outer air. They can survive in this way for over four years, with most of their body systems inactive, until the rains come.

The Australian species, often called the Queensland lungfish, was originally found in only two rivers, the Mary and the Burnett, but has been introduced into other river systems. At one time it was under threat of extinction; partly because of diversion and disturbance of the slow, sluggish streams in which it lives, and partly because it was collected as a zoological curiosity and caught as a source of food. This fish is now protected by law and its future seems assured.

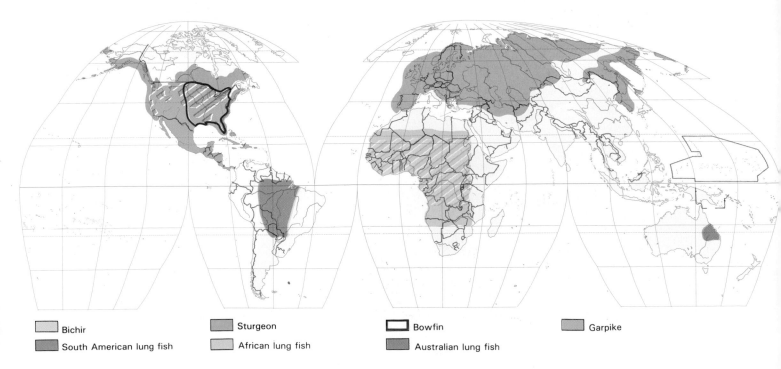

Bichir	Sturgeon	Bowfin	Garpike
South American lung fish	African lung fish	Australian lung fish	

Australian lung fish

garpike

bowfin

paddle fish

African lung fish

South American lung fish

sturgeon

shovelnose sturgeon

bichir

bichir (reed fish)

coelacanth

TELEOSTEI

The Teleostei, the bony fish, have achieved the greatest evolutionary success and include most of the fish familiar in everyday life. Unlike the Chondrostei, the Teleostei present an enormous variety of forms and colours, corresponding to their many different habitats and ways of life. There are about thirty major groups containing over 20,000 species – this accounts for over 40 per cent of all living vertebrate species.

Clupeiformes

The order Clupeiformes is assumed to be the oldest living group in the Teleostei. It contains the herring, trout and many other more or less related fishes.

Clupeoidea

The Clupeoidea, herring group, includes many of the fish that are important as human food. Among these are the herring itself (*Clupea harengus*), the sprat (*Sprattus sprattus*), the sardine or its larger version the pilchard (*Sardina pilchardus*), the gilthead or gilt sardine (*Sardinella aurita*), the alewives or greybacks that have become lake-dwellers (*Alosa ficta*), gizzard shad or hickory shad (*Dorosoma cepedianum*, illustrated here) and anchovies (*Engraulis encrasicholus*). There are over 100 species of anchovy, with a maximum size of about 20 cm (8 in). They are possibly the most numerous of all marine fish.

The tarpons (*Megalops*) resemble gigantic herrings, reaching lengths of 2 m (6½ ft) and weights of 100 kg (220 lb). The Atlantic tarpon (*Megalops atlanticus*) is illustrated on p. 113.

Closely related to these are the bonefish, banana fish or ladyfish (*Albula vulpes*) marine gamefish from whose eggs are born larvae similar to those of eels. Another related group is the slickheads, Alepocephalidae, some of which have luminescent organs.

Salmonoidea

The Salmonoidea include several groups, the most important of which is the Salmonidae, comprising both freshwater and sea fish.

Among them are the Atlantic salmon (*Salmo salar*) and the Pacific salmon (*Oncorhyncus nerka*), both illustrated. Both live in the sea and reproduce in rivers. When adult they migrate from far out in the ocean back to the coast and upriver to the exact place where they were hatched several years before. It is not known exactly how this migration is guided, though smell is probably the main sense responsible. Pacific salmon make the journey once then spawn and die. Atlantic salmon can breed in several successive years. The rainbow trout (*Salmo gairdneri*) is a North American species, now introduced to Europe and fish farms. Another notable member of the group is the brown trout (*Salmo trutta*) common in European waters. The whitefish (*Coregonus*, illustrated here) inhabit cold inland waters. The grayling (*Thymallus thymallus*) is another freshwater fish, found in cool, clear rivers.

Salmon is considered a great delicacy and has been called 'the king of fish', not only for its taste but also for the spectacular leaps it makes on its journey upriver, to spawn. Jumps of 3 m (10 ft) have been recorded.

The Osmiridae are another group of Salmonoidea which include some purely marine and some purely freshwater forms, but also some that can pass freely from one environment to the other. The great silver smelts, found off the north and west coasts of Scotland and Ireland (Argentinidae), however, live only in a marine habitat. *Bathylagus* species prefer fairly deep waters.

Chirocentroidea, Channoidea and Esocoidea

The Chirocentroidea group contains only the single member, the wolf herring (*Chirocentrus dorab*, illustrated here on p. 113). It grows up to 3 m (10 ft long) and inhabits the coastal waters of the Indian Ocean. The Channoidea include three families, among them the Channidae, found in Africa and Asia, long-bodied fishes with a cylindrical cross-section, 10-90 cm (4-36 in) in length, which can breathe air with the aid of vascular cavities situated under the gills. They are carnivorous and can survive for long periods out of water.

The principal member of the Esocoidea is the pike (*Esox lucius*, illustrated here), the great predator of the fresh waters of North America and Europe. In hunting it plays a waiting game; when the prey is within range it swims very slowly towards it and only when it finds itself a short distance away does it give a powerful flick of

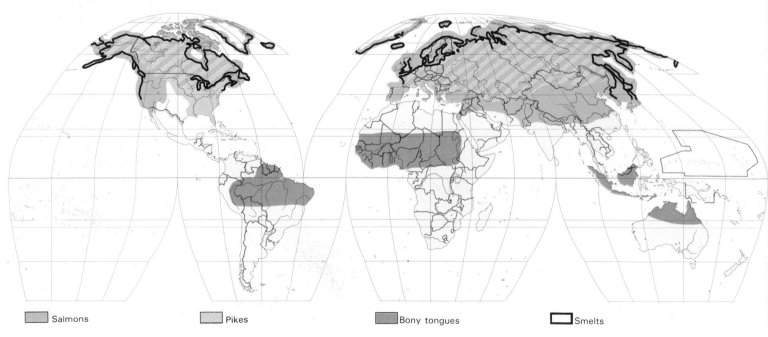

Salmons   Pikes   Bony tongues   Smelts

shad

mooneye or toothed herring

Pacific salmon

grayling

whitefish

pike

Alaska blackfish

Atlantic salmon

gizzard or hickory shad

the tail which enables it to dart forwards and capture its victim. The Alaska blackfish (*Dallia pectoralis*, illustrated on p. 111) inhabits the northern regions of America and Siberia, where it lives in the stagnant waters of the tundra. Another group of the Esocoidea is that of the mudminnows (Umbridae). These small fish, which live in North America and North-East Asia, as well as in the basins of the Danube and Dniester in Europe, can bury themselves in the mud either to avoid a predator or to survive rainless periods when the ponds in which they live dry up.

Stomiatoidea

The stomiatoid fishes include light fishes, angler fish, and hatchet fishes, sea-fishes that inhabit the levels between 150 and 1200 m (500 and 4000 ft) in depth. Many of them have rows of light organs along their sides. In many the mouth can open very widely to permit the ingestion of enormous prey. Nearly all have a larval period in which the young are very different from the adults. The Stomiatidae and Chauliodontidae have bodies almost snake-like in form and a mouth armed with very long pointed teeth, as can be seen in the illustration of the luminous viper fish (*Chauliodis sloanei*). The Stomiatidae also possess a long filament dangling from the mandibles and terminating in a luminous organ, as can be seen in the illustration of *Stomias boa*.

The light fishes, Gonostomatidae, are also elongated in form, though to a lesser degree. *Cyclothone signata* and *Maurolicus*

muelleri of this group, illustrated here, are creatures of the deep oceans. Another group found in the same regions is that of the Sternoptychiidae; a curious member of this group is the large-mouthed silvery hatchet fish, illustrated here. This has rows of large luminous organs which produce a reddish-tinted light.

Some families such as the Idiacanthidae are characterized by the absence of scales on the body. A member of this group illustrated here is the ribbon sawtail fish (*Idiacanthus fasciola*) whose larvae possess large feet (peduncles) at the extremities of which are found the eyes. An example from another family is the scaleless dragon-fish of the Melanostomiatidae.

Opisthoproctoidea and Notopteridea

The Opisthoproctoidea group contains the barrel eye fish of the middle depths, characterized by eyes on stalks, which give them excellent vision, and luminous organs placed on the lower (ventral) surface. The Notopteridea consists of two families, moon-eyes (Iodontidae) and knife fishes or featherbacks (Notopteridae). The first are freshwater fishes of North America, also called toothed herring. They have sharp teeth, large eyes and deeply forked tail fins. The Notopteridae consist of two genera. The first is *Notopterus*, air-breathing freshwater fishes of Africa and South-East Asia, known as knife fishes or featherbacks. The latter may attain 80 cm (32 in) in length. Undulations passing along the anal fins allow them to swim either forwards or backwards. The second

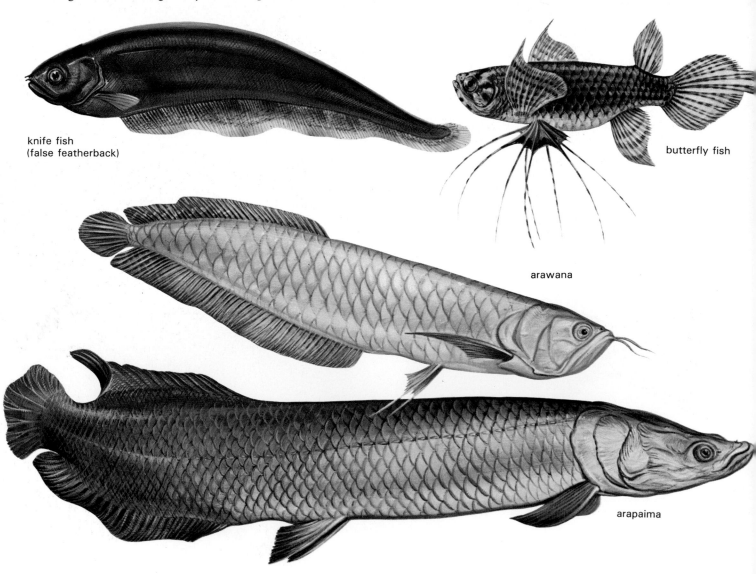

knife fish
(false featherback)

butterfly fish

arawana

arapaima

herring

Atlantic tarpon

anchovy

wolf herring

ribbon sawtail fish

viper fish

boa fish

light fish
Maurolicus muelleri

light fish
Cyclothone signata

large-mouthed
silvery hatchetfish

genus is *Xenomystus*. In this species the dorsal fin is absent and the caudal fin has become joined to the much elongated ventral-anal fin to form a continuous fin passing round the tail.

Osteoglossoidea

The Osteoglossoidea, bony tongues, contain some of the largest freshwater species. They have elongated bodies, thin from side to side, a large head and a broad mouth, and a tongue armed with powerful teeth. The giant of the family Osteoglossidae is the arapaima (*Arapaima gigas*, illustrated on p. 112) of the Amazon and Orinoco rivers and their tributaries. It can attain an overall length of 5 m (16 ft) and weigh 200 kg (450 lb). Arapaimas are great predators and consumme immense quantities of fish. In the mating season the partners prepare a nest in which up to 1100 eggs may be deposited; the young when hatched are defended by the parents. In another South American species, the arawana (*Osteoglossum bicirrhosum*, illustrated on p. 112), the eggs are incubated in the mouth of one of the parents. Parental care is met with also in *Heterotis niloticus*, an African fish of the Heterotidae; it is the male who occupies himself with the young, and it is also his task to construct a circular nest with walls some 50 cm (20 in) high sometimes visible at the water surface.

Pantodontoidea

The Pantodontoidea, of which the butterfly fish (*Pantodon buchholzi*, illustrated on p. 112) is the sole species, is found in the rivers of Central Africa. It is small, less than 10 cm (4 in) and is characterized by the enormous development of the pectoral and ventral fins. With the aid of the pectoral fins the butterfly fish is capable of undertaking fairly long 'flights' (in fact, prolonged glides) above the water.

Bathyclupeiformes and Galaxiiformes

The Bathyclupeiformes consist of the single genus *Bathyclupea* found in waters 250–750 m (775–2325 ft) deep in the Pacific and Indian Oceans and in the Gulf of Mexico. The body is compressed and of small dimensions, while the head occupies a third of the overall body length. They are predators and the mouth, which has a prominent lower jaw, is armed with long, slender teeth.

The Galaxiiformes also comprise one single family, the Galaxiidae, scale-less and trout-like fishes that live exclusively in the Southern Hemisphere. The genus *Galaxias*, to which belongs *Galaxias attenuatus* illustrated here, lives in fresh waters in New Zealand, Australia, South America and South Africa. The unusual distribution of the group is due to the ability of these fish to migrate at will through salt waters to brackish and fresh water.

Ateleopiformes and Giganturiformes

The Ateleopiformes are represented by the family Ateleopidae to which the genera *Ateleopus*, *Parateleopus* and *Ijimaia* belong. They live in deep waters off Japan and the Philippines, in the Indian Ocean and the Caribbean, and off the Moroccan coast. So little is known of them that many ichthyologists believe that the genus *Ijimaia* consists in fact of the females of *Ateleopus*.

The Giganturiformes are also represented by a single family, the Giganturidae, which in their turn consist of a single genus, *Gigantura*. Denizens of very deep waters, they prey on deep-sea fish with the aid of long teeth inclined in different directions. The body is elongated and the large pectoral fin is placed well forward; the telescopic eyes are large and protuberant.

Mormyriformes

The Mormyriformes, elephant-nosed fish etc, are slimy freshwater fish found in muddy African rivers, such as in the Nile and in the Congo and Senegal river basins. Their eyes are often degenerate and when searching for food they utilize the elongated snout to rummage about in the mud.

Some species of Mormyridae, such as *Mormyrus kannume* and *Gnathonemus petersi*, illustrated here, have highly developed snouts; *Campylomormyrus curvirostris*, also illustrated, has an even more pronounced elongated proboscis. The genera *Petrocephalus* and *Marcusenius* show a reduction in the size of the snout which finally disappears in the genus *Mormyrops*. The Mormyridae sense the proximity of obstacles or of prey thanks to the presence of an electrical organ in the tail which sets up an electric field entirely surrounding the fish. By means of their electric organ, they can feed and navigate in total darkness or in very muddy water as though they possessed radar – a distinct advantage over many other fish.

A similar organ is present in the Nile knife fish (*Gymnarchus niloticus*, illustrated here), a fish attaining up to 2 m (6½ ft) in length which has also the power to store up air in its swim bladder and can swim both forwards and backwards at will.

Myctophiformes

The Myctophiformes, lantern fish and lancet fish, possess luminous organs. The Myctophidae are the most important and also the most 'luminous' family. Their species are gregarious, forming enormous shoals which live in the ocean depths by day but at night come nearer to the surface to feed, and are sometimes attracted by light. They are rather elongate with large mouths and eyes and numerous light organs situated in the head, underside and base of the tail. One example illustrated here, is *Electrona rissoi*, in which only the male possesses luminous organs. *Myctophum punctatum* is another species of Myctophidae illustrated here.

Another group of the Myctophiformes is the Alepisauridae, the lancet fish. They are elongated and slender, with a long, tall dorsal fin and a large mouth with fang-like teeth. They are carnivorous, feeding on various fish and invertebrates, and can attain lengths of 1.8 m (6 ft) although the extremely slender body means they weigh only 0.5 kg (about 1 lb). The stomach of one specimen caught on a long line contained: several octopuses, a number of prawns or similar crustaceans, several salps, a horse mackerel, twelve young boarfish – and one young lancet fish. It seems that such a swift and predatory fish as this may have few enemies and cannibalism is one way the species keeps a check on its numbers. The long-nosed lancet fish (*Alepisaurus ferox*) is found in the Atlantic; other species of *Alepisaurus* in the Pacific:

electric fish

Nile knife fish

elephant-nosed fish

mormyrus

Gnathonemus petersi

lantern fish
Electrona rissoi

lantern fish
Myctophum punctatum

Galaxias attenuatus

Anguilliformes

The Anguilliformes comprise some 350 species of eels – marine fish with elongated bodies, snake-like in form, in which the scales are much reduced or even entirely absent. The back fin is continuous with the tail fin, which in its turn is united with the anal fin; the ventral fins are reduced and often missing, while in the moray eels the pectoral fins are also absent. The body is rendered virtually impossible to seize by the abundant mucus which covers it, whose function is to assist respiration through the skin. Two genera are exceptions to the rule that eels are exclusively creatures of the sea: one of these is *Anguilla* (*A. anguilla* is the European species). Species of these two genera ascend freshwater streams and rivers in search of the food necessary for their development, and remain there until they have attained sexual maturity, before returning to the sea and readapting to saline water.

Most eels live in tropical and equatorial waters; only a few eels penetrate cooler seas, where they prefer deep waters where the thermal variations during the course of the year are minimal. The genus *Anguilla* is again an exception to this rule, as is the genus *Conger*, which chooses to live along rocky coasts. The adult Anguilliformes feed on plankton, on bottom-dwelling animals and on a great variety and quantity of fish.

Nemichthyidae

The Nemichthyidae, snipe-eels, are sea-fishes with very elongated bodies which live at depths greater than 1000 m (3200 ft).

Anguillidae

The Anguillidae comprise sixteen species of eels all belonging to the genus *Anguilla*. The eels of British and European waters belong to the species *Anguilla anguilla*, which breed only in the Sargasso Sea, in mid-Atlantic. The eggs are laid in water 400–700 m (1300–2300 ft) deep. The larvae, 5–6 mm (0.2–0.24 in) long at hatching, gradually rise through the water, drifting eastwards on the prevailing currents. By the time they are near the surface they are about 10 mm (0.4 in) long and are flat, thin, transparent and leaf-like in appearance. The larvae are called leptocephalus (narrow-headed). They feed on the smaller plankton. After about two and a half years they reach European North American coastal waters, partly by swimming and partly borne on the currents. By now they are about 7.5 cm (3 in) long and have begun to metamorphose into young eels (elvers), changing from their leaf-like form to a cylindrical one closer to that of an eel. They ascend rivers and, growing in size, become yellowish in colour. They encounter and overcome many barriers, both natural and artificial, in this journey upstream. During their period of change the larvae cease to feed, but now the young eels feed on crustaceans, molluscs, insect larvae, small fish and fish eggs. These yellow eels live in lakes or rivers, buried in the sand or concealed among stones during the day, but feeding at dusk. The ability to move about in damp places – eels cannot in fact travel to any great extent on dry land – is due to their ability to breathe through the skin, to an extent which provides them with up to 50 per cent of all the oxygen they need. After ten to fifteen years they migrate downstream to estuaries where sexual maturity is attained and the eels, ceasing for a time to feed, undergo another change, becoming dark on the back and silvery on the sides. They begin to return to the sea to breed. They travel to the depths of the Sargasso Sea to breed and there, presumably, die, though the details of the return journey and its end are still unknown.

Muraenidae and Congridae

The moray eel (*Muraena helena*) and conger eel (*Conger conger*) are two other widely known species of the Anguilliformes, with similar ways of life. Powerful predators, they remain inactive during the day but are active at night, hunting fish, molluscs and crustaceans. Moray eels are rare in north European waters, living normally in warmer temperate and tropical waters. The eel-like appearance is rendered more attractive by the coloration of the skin, which is richly ornamented with stripes, spots and eye-like patterns. The head is rather large and the mouth is armed with long, curved and pointed teeth, capable of dealing with the most difficult prey. Divers who molest these creatures have received serious wounds. Adults can attain a length of 1.5 m (5 ft).

Migration of eel larvae from the Sargasso Sea to Europe

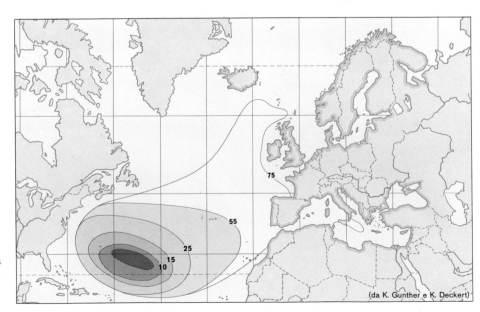

■ Breeding area of adult eels.

15 Numbers indicate the length in millimetres of the larvae at various stages of their journey, prior to changing into elvers.
  Stretches of coastline where the elvers swim into rivers.

(da K. Gunther e K. Deckert)

The conger eels occur all round the British Isles and off the Atlantic coast of North America, living along rocky parts of the coast. It remains hidden among rocks during the day and emerges at night to hunt for fish such as pollack, wrasse, hake and sole. Spawning takes place at great depths in a wide area of the Atlantic, and the larvae (in the leptocephalus stage) migrate to rocky coastal regions. After metamorphosis they feed until mature. After sexual maturity is attained some degeneration of tissues takes place. The female has very large ovaries; the eggs all develop at the same time, and may form half the total weight of the fish. The number of eggs laid may be from three to eight million.

Simenchelyidae to Derichthyidae

Other groups of the Anguilliformes are less well known, largely because most of them live in the deepest waters of the oceans. These lesser-known families include, besides the Simenchelyidae, the Ophichthyidae, a group which includes some parasitic forms; the Muraenosocidae, which resemble conger eels; the Nettasto-midae, characterized by a long narrow snout and powerful teeth; and the Derichthyidae.

Saccopharyngiformes

The Saccopharyngiformes, gulpers, comprise species that live in the Atlantic, Pacific and Indian Oceans at depths of between 2000 and 5000 m (1.2 to 3 miles). The eyes are much reduced, there is no swim bladder and the body is covered with bare skin, lacking scales. In some species the mouth is of normal proportions, but in others it opens to an enormous size, denoting a predatory way of life. They are soft-bodied, of a tapering shape, with long tails and greatly expandable stomachs to contain a large volume of prey. They measure up to 1.8 m (6 ft) in length, most of this being the tail. Some species are included by fish biologists among the Anguilliformes.

Above A freshwater eel rests on the bottom.
Below A moray eel of the species *Echidna nebulosa* emerges from its coral lair. Morays are generally shy but will retaliate if molested, hence their reputation.

Cypriniformes

The Cypriniformes include about 5000 living species which are divided into four major groups, Cyprinoidea, Characoidea, Gymnotoidea and Siluroidea.

Cyprinoidea

The most important group of the Cypriniformes is that of the Cyprinoidea, characterized by having a protractile mouth – one that can be thrust forward, and lacking teeth, which however are present in the pharynx. The skin is bare or covered with circular scales. The family Cyprinidae includes many species common in American and European fresh waters, such as the carp, tench, barbel, gudgeon, chub and roach. Some popular aquarium fish are included, such as the Sumatran barb or tiger barb (*Puntius tetrazona*) from South-East Asia, and the zebra fish (*Brachydanio rerio*) with its blue and yellow stripes. Both are illustrated on p. 121.

Many species, such as carp and tench, are interesting for the ease with which they can be reared for human food. Others are much favoured by sporting fishermen and at the same time are important links in the food chain in fresh waters, where they form the most important part of the fish biomass.

Among representatives of the group is the goldfish (*Carassius auratus*) which so many people have at one time or another kept in the house in a bowl of water.

The original 'goldfish' is an ordinary-looking fish of dull green or brown coloration. However red or reddy-gold individuals are sometimes seen in nature, as a result of a mutation occurring in the genes of the fish. The ancient Chinese collected these coloured fish and bred them, and in the sixteenth century they were introduced to Japan to bring more beauty to the ornamental gardens. The first goldfish probably reached Britain by the beginning of the eighteenth century and they were introduced to the United States around 1859.

Selective breeding has produced innumerable varieties of goldfish with names such as telescope, lionhead, tumbler, water bubble eye and fantail. Some pet fish have lived for twenty-five years in captivity. When released to the wild (either accidentally or on purpose), as has happened in parts of France and Portugal and in the United States, they breed but in a few generations the descendants have returned to the drab coloration of the original wild fish; the bright reds and golds are far too easy for a predator to spot.

Another common species is the minnow (*Phoxinus phoxinus*) found throughout most of Europe and the British Isles except for the northernmost highlands of Scotland. It lives in streams, lakes, ponds and rivers in shoals of about 100 fish, moving near the surface and feeding on insects and their larvae and on algae. Most reach sexual maturity at about two years of age, when they are about 4 cm (1.5 in) long. The male puts on brilliant colouring in the breeding season, in mid-March onwards. Orfe (another popular aquarium species), ide and chub, members of the genus *Leuciscus*, live in lakes and slow-moving rivers; they feed on crustacea, insect larvae, water snails, worms and other invertebrates, and also on aquatic vegetation.

A mainly vegetarian species is the rudd (*Scardinius erythro-phthalmus*) which lives in slow-moving waters. It is a voracious browser, feeding mostly on plants, but also on small planktonic invertebrates. The bleak (*Alburnus alburnus*) found in Wales and in England south of the Tees, is a fast-moving fish of the upper layers of the water, which can reach up to 20 cm (7.5 in) in length. Some species of *Barbus* can attain a great size, as for instance the mahseer of India which may reach up to 2 m (6½ ft) in length.

The suckers, Catastomidae, are a group of Cyprinoidea containing 80 to 100 species found exclusively in North America except for a few in Asia. They are distinguishable from the Cyprinidae by the absence of teeth in the pharynx (their teeth form a single row in the throat) and by the large fleshy lips surrounding the mouth, which opens ventrally. They live on the bottoms of slow-moving lakes and streams and suck up invertebrates and detritus.

The Cobitidae include about 200 species all known by the common name of loach. Most live in Asia, but a few species are present in Europe and in North Africa. They are bottom-dwellers of small size, with an elongated body compressed from side to side and a ventral mouth, with three to six pairs of whisker-like barbels. Some do not only feed on the bottom but also bury themselves in it, leaving only a part of the back showing. *Cobitis taenia* of Europe and Asia has a short movable spine over each eye. Aquarium fish of this group are useful for keeping the bottom of the tank free of detritus and include the clown loach (*Botis mac-*

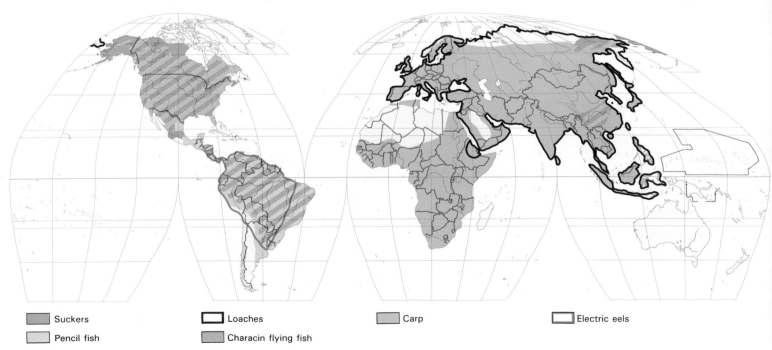

| Suckers | Loaches | Carp | Electric eels |
| Pencil fish | Characin flying fish | | |

racanthus), coolie loach (*Acanthophthalmus kuhlii*, illustrated on p. 121) and stone loach (*Noemacheilus barbatus*).

Characoidea

The Characoidea include many families, among them the Characidae of South America and Central Africa, the Anostomidae and Gasteropeledicae (Characin flying fish) of America and the Citarinidae which live only in Africa.

Numerous African species of Characoidea are predatory in habit and, besides having powerful teeth, are of notable size, reaching 1 m (3¼ ft) in length. Other African species on the other hand are plant-eaters. American waters also harbour some notorious predators of this group. Among them is the piranha (*Serrasalmus piraya*) best known carnivorous fish of fresh waters. Not more than 30 cm (12 in) long, it has strong jaws armed with triangular and very sharp teeth. It is made more dangerous by its habit of swimming around in large shoals, numbering from 100 to as many as 1000 individuals. They usually attack only other fishes or animals in difficulties, but they are capable occasionally of attacking large mammals, including man, and those of Brazilian waters are reported to have stripped a cow of all flesh in less than five minutes.

Some families of the Characoidea contain numerous species which, by reason of their small size and vivid coloration, are much sought after for aquaria. Among the Characidae, commonly called pencil fish, are small slender South American species such as the neon tetra (*Hyphessobrycon innesi*), much admired for its coloration of red and a dazzling blue; *H. rubrostigma*, illustrated on p. 121, with its long dorsal fin; *Thayeria obliqua*, black and silver, which tends to swim at an angle instead of horizontally; those of the genus *Metynnis*, which have a laterally compressed body and shiny silver coloration, they resemble piranhas but are plant eaters; and *Cheirodon axelrodi* (illustrated on p. 121) which is tri-coloured in red, blue and green. Another aquarium species illustrated here is *Poecilobrycon eques*, of the Hemiodontidae.

Among the different reproductive habits may be mentioned those of *Copeina arnoldi* in which species the male chooses the locality for breeding. Shortly afterwards the female arrives, and the two fishes leap out of the water until they succeed in reaching a leaf on which the female deposits her eggs, which the male immediately fertilizes before falling back into the water. The eggs are then kept moist by the male with sprays of water produced by energetic blows of his tail, hence their common name of splashing tetra. Other fish which make a habit of leaving the water are those of the genus *Carnegiella*, among them *C. striata*, illustrated on p. 121, which carries out short skimming flights across the water, beating its highly developed pectoral fins like wings with such vigour as to produce a humming sound.

Gymnotoidea

The Gymnotoidea are known as knife fish, being knife-shaped, with a very elongated body, ending in a sharp tail, and an anal fin that extends along most of the underside. They have no pectoral fins and the dorsal and caudal fins are much reduced. Swimming is achieved by rippling movements of the long anal fin, propelling the animal without movements of the body. The Gymnotoidea are to be found only in the New World, in Central and South America.

The family Gymnotidae include large species such as *Gymnotus carapo* of the River Plate, that attains 60 cm (24 in) in length. This group have nocturnal habits and live on small fish and invertebrates of the depths; they are characterized by the possession of electric organs.

Highly developed electric organs are present in the electric eel (*Electrophorus electricus*, illustrated on p. 121) which is not in fact an eel of the family Electrophoridae. It can grow up to 2 m (6½ ft) long. In specimens only a quarter of this length discharges of between 40 and 300 volts have been measured, and it may be supposed that larger individuals would be able to emit more powerful discharges. The South Americans call the fish 'tremblador'. The discharges serve to stun the prey on which the electric eels feed. This and the knife fish also use small electric pulses to help find their way about.

The Ramphichthyidae of South America are smaller and either lack teeth or have them only slightly developed.

Siluroidea

The Siluroidea are commonly called catfish from the presence of long barbels around the mouth which are reminiscent of cats'

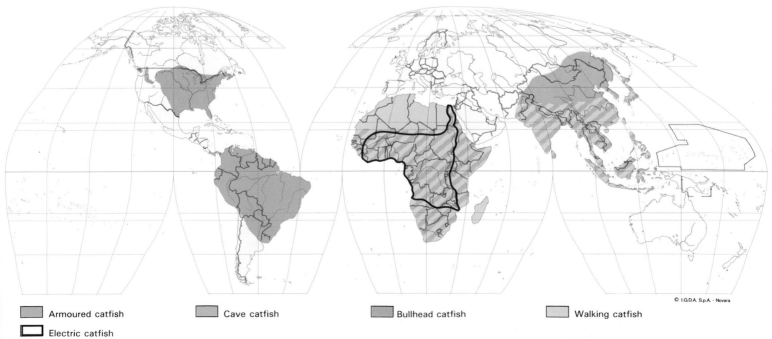

□ Armoured catfish   □ Cave catfish   □ Bullhead catfish   □ Walking catfish
□ Electric catfish

© I.G.D.A. S.p.A. - Novara

A species of loach, *Gyrnocheilus aymoniere*, from Thailand. These fish are well suited to life in an aquarium, where they rasp algae from the glass sides and keep them clean.

whiskers. The skin is smooth and scaleless but there are often sharp bony spines present which support the fins and provide an excellent system of defence. Catfish are mostly freshwater fish found in almost all parts of the world, and in view of the widely diversified habitats they occupy this indicates a wide adaptability to different conditions. Some species, for example, inhabit turbulent and torrential rivers and streams at high altitudes, and in order to avoid being swept away, attach themselves to the stream bed by means of a ventral sucker or with the mouth. These two different types of adaptation have led to different ways of breathing; in the first the water enters through the mouth and issues from the gills, whereas in the second the water is restricted to passing through the gills obliquely.

Other species prefer calm and muddy waters which are often low in oxygen content. This has made necessary a modification which enables them to breathe atmospheric oxygen. In *Heteropneustes fossilis*, a member of the Saccobranchidae, air-breathing has been made possible by a major development of the gill cavity which has ended up by occupying a great part of the body of the fish. In the Clariidae, a family of labyrinthine or walking catfish, of which the species *Clarias batrachus* is illustrated here, the gill chamber is small but is enriched by numerous branches profusely furnished with blood vessels which enables them to breathe air. Other catfish come to the surface frequently to swallow air; the air is taken into the intestine and oxygen is absorbed from it through the wall of the gut.

Some siluroids have taken to life in caverns. Typical examples are the Bagridae, of Africa and Asia, and the Trichomyctidae, small scaleless freshwater catfish of South America, less than 10 cm (4 in) in length. Naturally cave-dwelling catfish show characteristic modifications caused by the total darkness, such as reduction of the eyes and complete depigmentation of the skin, so they appear a ghostly pinkish white. Others, such as the glass catfish (*Kryptopterus bicirrhis*, illustrated here) of the family Schilbeidae, have developed a body that appears to be totally transparent.

The catfish have a reproductive output rather lower than that of other fish, and as a result they undertake a considerable degree of parental care in order to limit mortality in the first phase of growth. So in the Ariidae, which with the Plotoxidae are the only marine Cypriniformes, incubation of a few eggs the size of marbles takes place in the mouth. Other examples of parental care are found in the Siluridae, to which group the common European catfish or wels (*Siluris glanis*) belongs. The female deposits up to 100,000 eggs which adhere to the underwater vegetation and are tended by the male. Another European species, *Parasilurus aristotilis*, excavates a nest in which the female lays her eggs. The bullhead, family Ictaluridae, which live in still or stagnant waters in Central and North America, excavate a nest somewhat larger than their own bodies. In this the female deposits her eggs, which are immediately fertilized by the male. The nest is then oxygenated by the male, by vibrations of his pectoral and ventral fins. From time to time he takes the eggs into his mouth and spits them out again to change their position, or more frequently turns them over with the barbels on his chin. After hatching, the newborn young remain for a few days in the neighbourhood of the nest and then begin to move off in large groups under the careful supervision of one or both of the parents.

Parental care can also be observed in some American groups in which the female carries first the eggs and then the newborn young in the shelter of folds of skin in the ventral part of the body. On the whole, parental care is unusual among bony fish, so these examples are of some interest.

Many siluroids are predators, but other types of diet may be observed, as in the bottom-browsers of the Bagridae and the armoured catfish Loricariidae, one of the latter group, *Loricaria parva*, being illustrated here. Others are the Doradidae and the Callichthyidae, the latter being a group of small South American catfish found in slow-moving rivers. They possess two overlapping rows of smooth armour plates on each side, and two pairs of short barbels, with spines in front of the dorsal, adipose and pectoral fins. Some of the genus *Corydoras* are kept in aquaria, as for instance *C. arcuatus*, illustrated here, known to aquarists as useful scavengers, which clean organic refuse from the bottoms of the tanks.

The catfish include some parasitic species, such as those of the Trichomyctidae already mentioned, which live on blood sucked from the gills of other fish. The Mocochidae, denizens of African streams, are characterized by the possession of branched barbels and are able to produce sounds by rubbing their pectoral spines against a sound-box in the body. This group includes the 'upside down catfish' (*Synodontis angelicus*, illustrated here) which when young swims in the normal fashion with the ventral region downwards, but when adult reverses itself and swims with the ventral region uppermost. Finally the electric catfish, a whole family (Melapteruridae) represented by a single African species *Malapterurus electricus*. this has the ability to emit intense electric discharges reaching 350 volts, generated by an electric organ which forms a gelatinous jacket round the body under the skin.

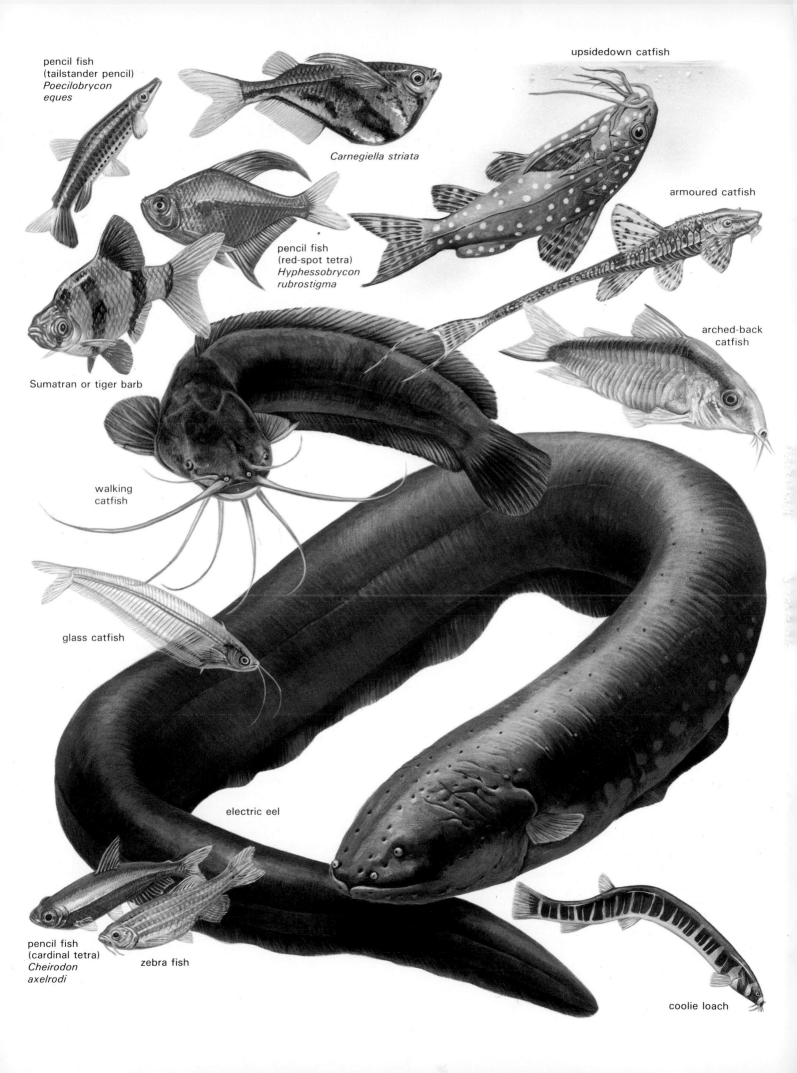

pencil fish
(tailstander pencil)
*Poecilobrycon
eques*

Carnegiella striata

upsidedown catfish

armoured catfish

pencil fish
(red-spot tetra)
*Hyphessobrycon
rubrostigma*

arched-back
catfish

Sumatran or tiger barb

walking
catfish

glass catfish

electric eel

pencil fish
(cardinal tetra)
*Cheirodon
axelrodi*

zebra fish

coolie loach

Beloniformes

The Beloniformes comprise groups characterized by beak-like prolongations of the mouth, of various lengths and forms. The common garfish or needle fish (*Belone belone*, illustrated here), which has a very elongated body terminating at the front end in a slender beak armed with sharp teeth, belongs to the family Belonidae. Its distribution includes the coastal waters of the Atlantic, the Mediterranean and the Black Sea.

The beak-like form of the mouth is present also in the Scomberesoxidae, which include the skipper or saury pike (*Scomberesox saurus*). Somewhat smaller than the garfish, the skipper differs from it also in the decreased length of the beak and the presence of some smaller fins behind the anal and dorsal fins. It is a fish of the Atlantic and Mediterranean that migrates in shoals to shallower waters in summer, appearing occasionally in British waters. It lives near the surface and has the habit of skimming over the surface of the sea, the tips of its pectoral fins brushing the water, and propelling itself by violent oscillations of the lower lobe of the tail which just enters the water.

In the halfbeak family, the Hemiramphidae, the beak is still further reduced and only the lower jaw is much prolonged, while the upper is normal or only slightly elongated. This group lives in the coastal waters of the western Pacific and eastern Indian Ocean. Some species prefer a freshwater environment and are unusual in being ovoviviparous. This is a feature of some cartilaginous fish (e.g. certain sharks) and a very few bony fish in which eggs are produced and are hatched within the body of the mother so that the young are born fully formed.

The last family to be mentioned of the Beloniformes is that of the Exocoetidae, or flying fish, characterized by an expansion of the pectoral fins so great that they resemble wings and are capable of sustaining the fish in gliding flight. They are found in tropical zones of the Atlantic and Pacific but occasionally appear as far north as the south-western coastal waters of the British Isles. Flying fish fly by approaching the surface at high speed with the pectoral and pelvic fins folded into the body, using vigorous thrusts of the tail. After most of the body has left the water a stroke of the tail confers a final acceleration that propels the fish into the air, up to a metre ($3\frac{1}{4}$ ft) above the surface. It then opens the pectoral fins and glides without further movement of the fins. The larger flying fish can cover in this way more than 30 m (100 ft) above the water. The species illustrated here, *Cypselurus heterurus*, can reach some 30 cm (12 in) in length.

Percopsiformes

The Percopsiformes group comprises freshwater fishes living in North America which attain at the most a length of about 15 cm (6 in). They are divided into two groups each containing only a few species. The Percopsidae comprise only the single genus *Percopsis* of which the most important is *P. omiscomaycus*, illustrated here, which has an upper jaw longer than the lower, a translucent body and small scales armed with spines. Its diet consists of small invertebrates and fish. It is nocturnal and lives in deep lakes.

The other family is that of the Aphredoderidae, with the single species the pirate fish (*Aphredoderus sayanus*) in which the adipose fin seen in the preceding group is not present and the anus opens far forward in the throat region. The male and female build a nest in which the eggs are laid, which the pair then defend. They live in muddy creeks in the south and east of North America.

Notacanthiformes

The Notacanthiformes, or spiny eels, are deep-sea fish with an elongated body that becomes slenderer from head to tail, the tail being pointed and sometimes carrying a terminal spine. They have a protruding snout and can be up to 50 cm (20 in) in length.

Gadiformes

The Gadiformes are one of the groups of greatest economic importance as a source of human food. It includes the cod (*Gadus morhua*, illustrated here), bib, burbot, haddock, whiting, hake, ling and pollack. Except for the burbot (*Lota lota*), now very rare in British rivers, all are marine. The most important species are divided into two groups distinguished by the presence or absence of a caudal fin, the Gadoidea and Macruroidea.

Gadoidea

The Gadoidea comprise three families. The Muraenolepidae contain the single genus *Muraenolepis*, with three species, all of the Southern Hemisphere, characterized by the fusion of the dorsal fin with the caudal and anal fins.

The Moridae, deep water codfish, are to be found in nearly all the oceans. Their swim bladder is prolonged forwards in two lobes which end up in contact with the auditory capsule. *Mora mora*, 50 cm (20 in) long, is found in the Atlantic and Mediterranean.

The most important family of the Gadoidea is the Gadidae, which can be distinguished from each other by the number of fins and by the presence or absence of barbels on the chin. All have soft-rayed fins; the pelvic and pectoral fins are close together, and the tail fin is reduced or absent in some members.

The cod (*Gadus morhua*, illustrated here) is widely distributed in cold waters of the Northern Hemisphere and is especially numerous in the North Atlantic. It is one of the most commercially important fish. Cod form large shoals in areas where the sea bottom is of sand or mud and the food supply abundant. The young mostly eat small crustaceans but adults eat a greater proportion of fish, up to 70 per cent of their intake. Cod can live as long as 20 years and attain a length of up to 90 cm (3 ft) and a weight of up to 20 kg (44 lb).

The pollack (*Pollachinus pollachinus*) is also widely distributed in the colder waters of the Northern Hemisphere. It lives on cephalopods and small fish and can attain a length of about 42 cm (18 in) and a weight of up to 10 kg (22 lb).

Haddock (*Melanogrammus aeglefinus*) are found in the North Atlantic and all around the British Isles, but most commercial fishing is done in the North Sea and off the coast of Newfoundland. They feed mostly on creatures living on or near the sea bed, such as echinoderms, worms, crustacea, molluscs and fish. They can live up to ten years or more and attain up to 1.1 m (44 in) in length and weigh up to 16 kg (35 lb), but are usually much smaller.

Pouting or bib (*Trisopterus luscus*) are present in British waters. So are the Norway pout (*Trisopterus esmarkii*) and the blue whiting (*Micromesistus poutassou*). These are not commercially fished to any great extent though they are taken by rod-fishermen and a commercial fishery for blue whiting is being developed.

Whiting (*Merlangius merlangus*) are present all around the British Isles and are fished commercially. They usually attain a length of 50 cm (20 in) and weigh up to 1 kg (2.2 lb) but can be bigger. They may live up to eight years, and are not bottom feeders

rat-tail (grenadier)

common garfish (needle fish)

ribbon fish

snipe fish

John Dory

flying fish

sea horse

South American eel-fish
Synbranchus marmoratus

trout-perch
Percopsis omiscomaycus

opah (moonfish)

fifteen-spined
stickleback

broad-nosed pipefish

cod

like haddock but live mainly on fish such as sand eels, smaller whiting and pollack.

The 'poor cod' (*Trisopterus minutus*) common off the Labrador coast and in British waters, is the smallest of the cod family.

Hake (*Merluccius merluccius*) are found all around the British Isles and in the Mediterranean. The adults feed mainly on blue whiting, smaller hake and other fish, and can attain ages of over twelve years, lengths of 100 cm (40 in) and weights up to 10 kg (22 lb).

Ling (*Molva molva*) are deep-water fish found mostly off the west and north coasts of the British Isles. Commercially valuable fish, they are bottom-feeders, preferring rocky ground, and live mainly on fish such as mackerel and dabs. They can attain lengths of 180 cm (72 in) and weights up to 32 kg (70 lbs).

Coalfish or coley (*Pollachius virens*) are found in waters around the British Isles but less frequently off southern coasts. They are bottom-feeders, living off young fish, sand eels and cephalopods, and can reach an age of ten years, lengths of 120 cm (48 in) and weights up to 16 kg (35 lb). They are also caught off the United States where they are known as pollack.

The greater forkbeard or forked hake (*Phycis blennoides*) is a deep-water Atlantic fish that migrates to British coastal waters in winter. The five-bearded rockling (*Ciliata mustela*) is found in British coastal waters, where it can be found beneath stones in intertidal rock pools. The four-bearded rockling (*Rhinonemus cimbrius*) is found off the Atlantic coasts of the British Isles. The darker three-bearded rockling (*Gaidropsarus mediterraneus*) lives in rocky offshire waters along the south-western coasts of the British Isles and can be found in rock pools at low water.

The burbot (*Lota lota*) is, as has been said, an exceptional member of the cod family since it lives in fresh water. In England it is found in eastward-flowing rivers from Durham to the Great Ouse but is rare or even possibly extinct. It prefers deep, clear waters and is quiescent during the summer, feeding mainly in winter. In Europe it also lives in lakes, preferring cold, deep waters, and occurs in similar habitats in Canada and Alaska and in the United States as far south as Kansas.

Macruroidea

The Macruroidea comprise only one family, the Macruridae or rat-tails. These have a body that tapers from head to tail, the tail being long and slender. They are luminescent owing to the presence of symbiotic luminous bacteria. In many species the snout is particularly well developed, as in *Coelorhynchus coelorhynchus*, illustrated on p. 123.

Gasterosteiformes

The Gasterosteiformes – sticklebacks, pipefishes and sea-horses – are small fish usually having an elongated body encased in bony armour. Other fish in the group are comet fish, shrimp fish, snipe fish and trumpet fish.

Gasterosteoidea

The stickleback (*Gasterosteus aculeatus*) is found in fresh water and in sea water of weak salinity – coastal and brackish waters – throughout the British Isles. It also occurs, with other similar species, in the USA. It is a small fish growing slowly to a maximum length of about 7 cm (2.8 in) in its third year. Its name is derived from the three characteristic spines in front of the dorsal fin, which is displaced to a rearwards position. In spring time sticklebacks move upstream to shallow waters and the males leave the shoal. Each male marks out his territory which he defends against all intruders. He builds a nest by digging a shallow hole in the stream bed with his mouth and roofing it with algae. At the same time he changes colour, the back becoming bluish grey, the eyes a brilliant blue-green and the ventral region bright red. The female is silvery in colour and at this season swollen with eggs. The male entices her with elaborate courtship dances into the nest, where she lays her eggs and the male fertilizes them. He then chases her away and another pregnant female takes her place. As many as five females may be induced to deposit their eggs in one nest. The male looks after them, defending the nest and aerating the eggs by creating a current of water with vibrations of his pectoral fin. When the young are hatched, if some stray too far from the nest he pursues them and brings them back in his mouth. Sticklebacks are predators, feeding mainly on small crustacea, insect larvae and oligochaetes.

Other Gasterosteoidea of Europe are the fifteen-spined stickleback (*Spinachia spinachia*) which lives in seawater, in rock pools,

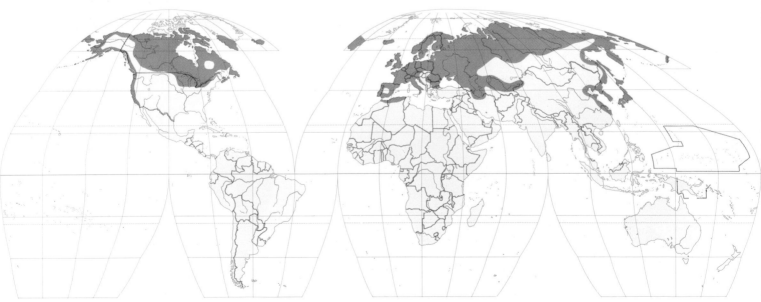

Sticklebacks

and the ten-spined stickleback (*Pungitius pungitius*), a freshwater fish of a retiring and non-aggressive disposition unlike its three-spined cousin.

The tubenoses, Aulorhynchidae, are Gasterosteoidea that live along north Pacific coasts, the genera *Aulorhynchus* and *Aulichthys* have characteristic tubular snouts and armoured rows of bony plates below the skin. They are tiny fish only a few inches long that sometimes occur in vast shoals.

Syngnathoidea

The Syngnathoidea, pipefishes, are a group characterized by the elongation of the snout and by their tubular pipe-like body. The Macrorhamphosidae are all sea-dwellers, with an oval elongated body terminating in a long tubular snout which has given them the name of trumpet fish. The Aulostomidae also possess an elongated body and snout, as do the Fistularidae, in which the snout is very long and the dorsal and anal fins much reduced. The Centriscidae, shrimpfish, on the other hand have compressed and less elongated bodies; they swim in the vertical position, the ventral region foremost, propelled by tiny fin movements. They occur in the Southern Pacific and Indian Oceans.

The family Syngnathidae, pipefishes and sea-horses, have a small mouth at the end of a long tubular snout. The body is enclosed by bony jointed rings. The males possess a sort of pouch in which they incubate the eggs and carry the young. They feed mostly on small crustaceans that are sucked into the mouth, and live among underwater vegetation in which, resting immobile in an upright position, they are most effectively concealed. They can endure considerable variations in salinity. The greater pipefish (*Syngnathus acus*) is found in seas all around the British Isles at depths of 30–100 m (100–325 ft), as is the snake or ocean pipefish (*Entelurus acquoreus*). The broad-nosed pipefish (*Syngnathus rostellatus*) lives among seaweed where the seabottom is sandy, in the southern and western coasts of England and Ireland. A similar species is common off the New England coast The straight-noted pipefish (*Nerophis phidion*) is widely distributed from Norway to North Africa, and the worm pipefish (*Nerophis lumbriciformis*) from Norway to the English Channel.

Sea-horses, of the genus *Hippocampus* (*H. guttulatus* is illustrated on p. 123), are distinguished by the position of the head, which is at right angles to the body; there is a 'neck' between body and head, and the rolled tail is used as a prehensile organ for holding on to seaweed and coral. The dorsal and pectoral fins oscillate, allowing the fish to manoeuvre slowly with no discernible movement of the body.

Lampridiformes

Some species of Lampridiformes, ribbon fish and moon fish, may have been the origin of the legend of the sea-serpent. The ribbon fish (*Trachipterus trachipterus*, illustrated on p. 123) is laterally flattened and tapers gradually from head to tail. It resembles a long silvery ribbon, its dorsal fin forming a prolonged crest along its back. The oarfish (*Regalecus glesne*), a member of the Regalecidae is similar in shape and can reach a length of 10 m (32 ft); the fins are red and the dorsal fin, which again runs the whole length of the body, rises up near the head in the form of a crest.

The opah or moon fish (*Lampris regius*, illustrated on p. 123) lives in the warmer waters of the Atlantic at depths of 100 to 200 m (350 to 700 ft). It is a large, flattened, brilliantly coloured fish that can attain lengths of over 1 m (39 in). It feeds largely on oceanic squid, besides crustaceans and other fish.

Zeiformes

The Zeiformes comprise species with laterally compressed bodies, in which the mouth can be pushed forwards something like a bellows. The best-known member of the group is the John Dory (*Zeus faber*, illustrated on p. 123), a remarkably ugly fish which is much prized for its flavour. It lives in waters up to 300 m (950 ft) deep, in the middle or bottom layers of the water, but comes closer inshore in summer. Its usual length is about 30-40 cm (12-16 in) and its weight 4-6 kg (9-13 lb). It swims slowly when approaching its prey – small fish including pilchards and herrings – and then shoots its mouth forward with great rapidity to seize the prey.

Synbranchiformes

The Synbranchiformes resemble the eels, with their elongated bodies almost circular in cross-section. They are freshwater fishes that live in South America, West Africa, South-East Asia and Australia. They live in pools liable to dry out, and so are well adapted for breathing atmospheric air. Like other species, *Synbranchus marmoratus*, illustrated on p. 123, endures the lack of oxygen by breathing through its skin, and passes the dry periods immersed in mud.

Beryciformes

The Beryciformes are a group of sea fishes that inhabit warm coastal waters, except for a few genera that live in the deep waters of the oceans. These – *Beryx*, *Hoplopteryx* and *Diretmus* – do not possess light organs, whereas strangely enough some of the coastal fishes do. These include the Anomalopsidae, commonly known as lantern-eyed fishes, spiny-rayed fishes that have luminous organs below the eye, and the Holocentridae, squirrel fish or soldier fish, large-eyed and brightly coloured fish of the tropical reefs, with spiny fins and rough prickly scales, some having a large spine on each cheek. Most are red with white, yellow or black markings. The largest is *Holocentrus spinifer*, a Pacific squirrel fish which reaches lengths up to 60 cm (24 in). Carnivorous and nocturnal, they hide themselves among the reefs by day.

Stephanoberyciformes

Among the fish of the lower depths are the Stephanoberyciformes, characteristically reddish-black or black in colour. The appearance varies from species to species; the prickle fish (Stephanoberycidae) have a scaly snout and a body covered with spines and ridges, while the whale fishes (Rondeletiidae) have an enormous head, taking up a quarter of the whole body length, and have neither spiny excrescences nor scales.

There are about thirty species of whale fish, living in mainly tropical waters. The eyes are tiny or even absent in some species. They move and feed by detecting vibrations in the water using the lateral line, a channel containing touch-sensitive organs that runs down each side of the fish's body.

Cyprinodontiformes

The Cyprinodontiformes possess fins without spiny fin rays. The ventral fins are either abdominal or absent, and the tail fins are homocercal – having the upper and lower lobes alike – and not forked. The young are frequently born alive, hence the name 'livebearers'. Fertilization is often internal and some rays of the forward part of the anal fin of the male are modified to form a copulatory organ, the gonopod.

The most characteristic group is that of the Cyprinodontidae, of which the genus *Aphanius* is found in western Asia and in parts of Africa and Europe. The southern European species is the tooth carp (*A. fasciatus*), a small fish about 8 cm (3 in) long which can tolerate waters with a wide range of salinity around the Mediterranean coast and moves from salt water to brackish and fresh water without difficulty. In South-East Asia and the Indo-Australian archipelago the genera *Aplocheilus* and *Oryzias* (the medaka) are present in all kinds of pools, ponds and lakes, feeding at the surface on prey consisting largely of the larvae of Diptera. The female attaches the fertilized eggs, gathered together in small bunches, to the stalks of floating aquatic vegetation, where they stay until they hatch.

An African genus is *Aphyosemion*, one of whose species, the lyretail (*A. sjostedti*), is illustrated here. The species is much sought after by aquarists for the beautiful colouring of the males, made more attractive by the tail fin in the form of a lyre. Because of the type of environment – pools of water which habitually dry out – the eggs can endure for long periods in an inactive state buried in mud until the rains come when they then complete their development.

Durable eggs subject to similar environmental changes are also encountered in the genera *Cynolebias* and *Pterolebias* of America. *Cynolebias bellotti* lays its eggs one by one in holes dug in the mud at the bottom of ponds which dry out in the summer. The American flagfish (*Jordanella floridae*, illustrated here) shows a different pattern of behaviour; the male sometimes collects the eggs together in a hole in the mud and aerates them. He also defends them against intruders, including the female, whose intention is to eat them. *Fundulus* species are well known for their complex courting behaviour; their eggs undergo a complete embryonic development immediately after being laid.

Among the species favoured by aquarists are the members of the genera *Lebistes* and *Mollienisia*, such as the guppy (*L. reticulatus*) and the sailfin molly (*M. velifera*), both illustrated here. Both belong to the family Poeciliidae, the viviparous topminnow family; confined to the Americas and containing many species. Other denizens of aquaria are those of the genus *Xiphophorus*, of which the male and female swordtail (*X. helleri*), are illustrated here; the male has an extraordinary development of the lower lobe of the tail fin. The Poeciliidae also include the genus *Gambusia*, whose species are useful in all parts of the world as active destroyers of mosquito larvae; and the genus *Belonesox*, of which the pike topminnow (*B. belizanus*) is illustrated here.

Among other families mention must be made of the *Anableptidae*, of which the four-eyed fish (*Anableps anableps*) is illustrated here. These are fish of the tropics of Central America whose eyes are adapted for seeing both above and below the surface of the water. The eyes are on top of the head and the fish swims just below the surface with the eyes half above and half below it, the upper half of the eyes being adapted for seeing in air and the lower half for seeing in water. The cave fish, Amblyopsidae, on the other hand, are blind; they live in subterranean waters in the limestone caves of North America. They have small eyes which however are non-functional, and orient themselves by means of tactile organs distributed over the body.

Phallostethiformes

The Phallostethiformes, comprising the two groups Phallostethidae and Neostethidae, of South-East Asia and the Philippines, are characterized by the possession of a copulatory organ, the 'priapus'; this structure, rendered rigid by the presence of a skeletal support, is situated in the region of the throat. Fertilization is naturally internal and the eggs when deposited adhere to the substrate, anchored to it by means of filaments.

Perciformes

The most evolved level reached by the fishes is seen in the Perciformes, a very large group of spiny-finned fish containing

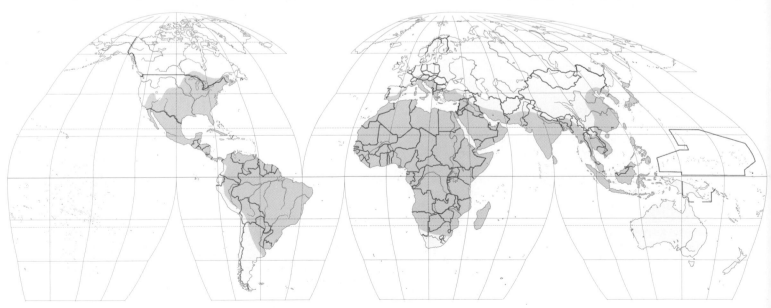

Tooth carp

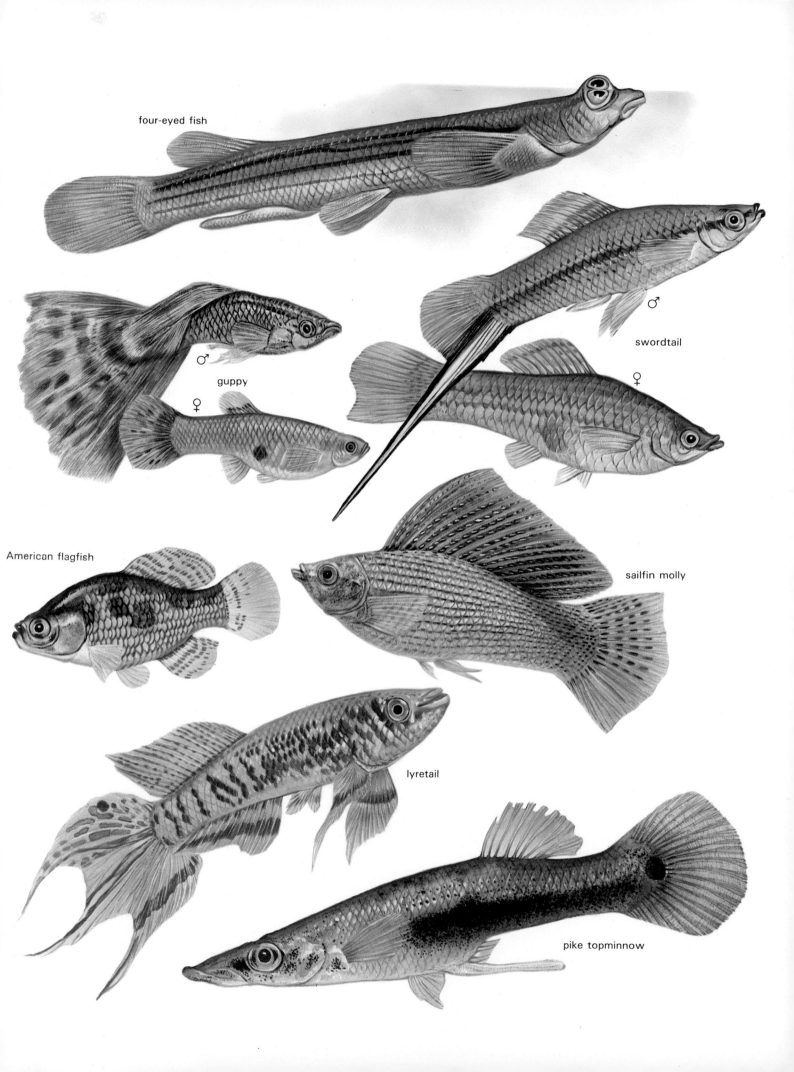

four-eyed fish

guppy ♂ ♀

swordtail ♂ ♀

American flagfish

sailfin molly

lyretail

pike topminnow

over 6000 species including tuna, mackerel, blenny, perch, sea bass and many other marine and freshwater species.

Percoidea

The most important group is that of the Percoidea, which contains many typical perciform fish, both marine and freshwater species, living in both tropical and temperate zones. Many fish of the coral reefs belong to the group, such as those of the Pomacentridae, Chaetodontidae including the long nosed butterfly fish (*Chelmon rostratus*, illustrated here) and the finger fish (Monodactylidae). Others, such as the jacks and pompanos (Carangidae) and croakers (Scienidae), are fish of the open seas. The swallowers (Chiasmodontidae) are present in deep waters and can swallow huge meals, while the weaver fish (Trachinidae) and stargazers (Uranoscopidae) are bottom feeders. The stargazers have huge eye muscles than can produce a big electric shock, an effective defence against predators. The croakers can emit loud sounds by vibrations of their swim bladders.

The Percoidei also have a wide range of feeding habits. Some are predators, including the perch (*Perca fluviatilis*), common in British rivers, which gives its name to the whole group, and the bass (*Dicentrarchus labrax*), both of which pursue their prey. The archer fish (*Toxotes jaculator*), of the rivers and lagoons of India and South-East Asia, catch insects settled on vegetation above the water level by spitting out a jet of water which makes them fall into the stream, where they are easily seized. Others such as the leaf fish, Nandidae, catch their prey by mimicking the vegetation among which they lurk. Reproduction is also carried out in diverse ways. Some species deposit an enormous number of eggs which are then abandoned to their fate without any defence, while others take care of their progeny; the latter include many of the Cichlidae, mentioned later, and the Apogonidae, such as the cardinal fish (*Apogon imberbis*, illustrated here). These take the eggs into their mouth both for safe-keeping and to aerate them. Finally, the surf perch, Embiotocidae, of the northern Pacific bear live young.

The most important family of the Percoidei is that of the Percidae which, apart from the perch already mentioned, includes the pike-perch or zander (*Stizostedion lucioperca*), introduced to Britain from eastern Europe, and the ruffe or pope (*Gymnocephalus cernua*).

The Serranidae family includes the bass, as well as the groupers such as the dusky perch (*Epinephelus guaza*, illustrated here) and the gigantic stone bass or wreckfish (*Polyprion americanus*) which descends to depths of 1000 m (3000 ft) and can reach lengths of 2 m (6½ ft) and weigh 45 kg (100 lb). In some of the Serranidae hermaphroditism can be observed; members of various species are both male and female at the same time. In spite of this they achieve cross-fertilization, since an individual does not fertilize the eggs it has itself deposited. In certain families, for instance in species of the Sparidae (sea bream), there is a different type of hermaphroditism in which the same individual passes one period of its life as a male and the next as a female, or vice versa. Another member of the Sparidae, the dorado or gilt-head (*Sparus aurata*, illustrated here) is protandrous; that is, it is male in the juvenile period and, having ripened and shed its male organs, is then transformed into a female which can lay eggs.

The Centrarchidae, freshwater sun fish of North America, have plump, oval bodies, more or less elongated. They inhabit shallow waters where there is plenty of vegetation, and their diet consists of small animals of the river-bed. There are some predatory species, among them the largemouth bass (*Micropterus salmoides*, illustrated on p. 133) which has been introduced into the streams of southern England and is an important angler's fish in North America.

Numerous members of the Labridae family, commonly called wrasse, are found in the coastal waters of warm and temperate seas. The rainbow wrasse (*Coris julis*, illustrated here) is a member of this group common in the Atlantic waters off France and Spain, and in the Mediterranean. The ballan wrasse and cuckoo wrasse of the genus *Labrus* are common in northern European and British coastal waters.

A similar environment is favoured by the Scaridae, a family which includes the parrot fish, so called from the characteristic beak-like shape of the mouth, resulting from the fusing of the teeth of the jaw, as in *Scarus vetula*, illustrated here. Their diet is made up of algae and corals which they succeed in scraping from the rocks thanks to their robust beak; the food is ground up by the plate-like teeth in their throats.

The Pomacentridae, the brightly coloured tropical fish known as damsel fish, mostly live among the rocky reefs in warm waters, but some of the anemone fish and clown fish (such as *Amphiprion percula*, illustrated here) live among sea-anemones. They deposit

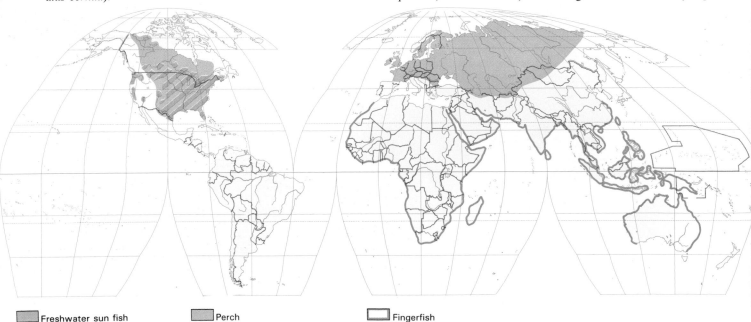

Freshwater sun fish   Perch   Fingerfish

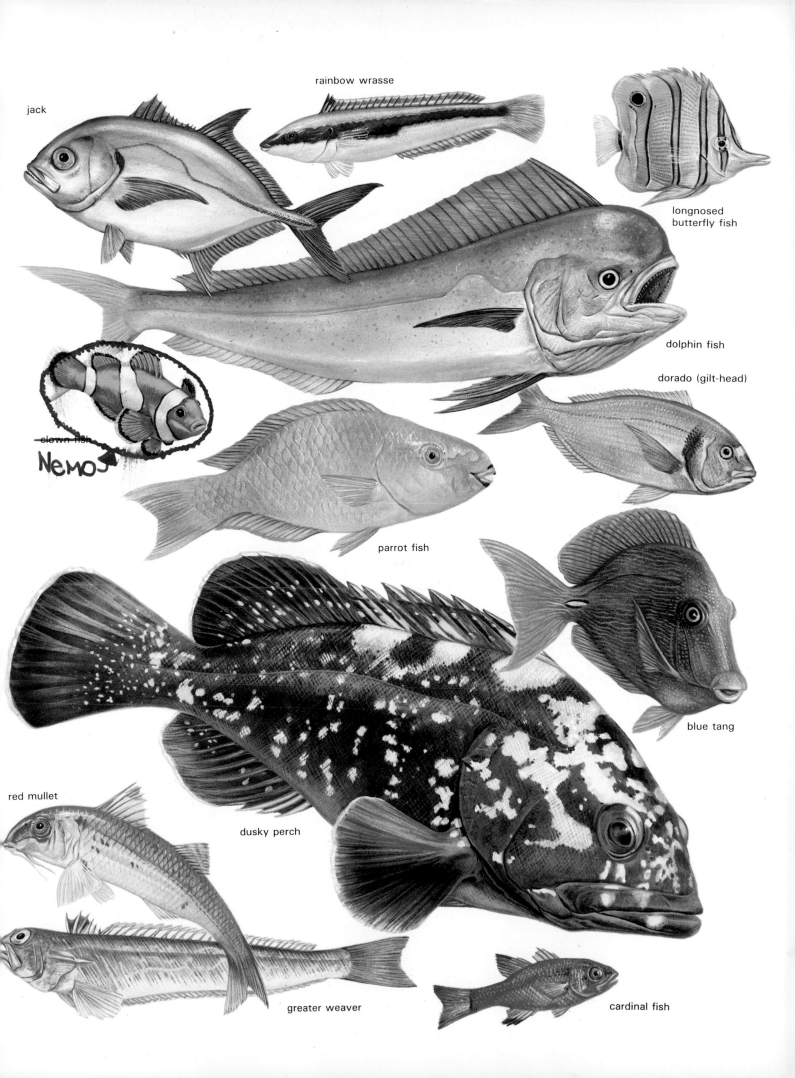

jack

rainbow wrasse

longnosed
butterfly fish

dolphin fish

dorado (gilt-head)

clown fish
NEMO

parrot fish

blue tang

red mullet

dusky perch

greater weaver

cardinal fish

their eggs in the basal disc of the anemone and can swim around among the tentacles unharmed by the poison that these contain, though it can be fatal to other fish. The dangerous tentacles provide a protection for the eggs from predators.

The Mullidae group includes the red mullet (*Mullus surmuletus*, illustrated on p. 129), a regular visitor to British waters, which can measure up to 40 cm (16 in) in length. It rakes the sea-bottom with its barbels in search of food hidden in the sand, such as shrimps, small crustaceans and bivalves, gastropods and cephalopods. A similar species occurs off the American coast and is referred to as the goatfish. Another species is the grey mullet (*M. barbatus*).

The Trachinidae, which include the greater weaver (*Trachinus draco*, illustrated on p. 129) and the lesser weaver (*T. vipera*) inhabit shallow coastal waters where they often half bury themselves in the sand, where they are excellently concealed by their camouflage colours. They have elongated bodies, and the dorsal and pectoral fins are held up by rays transformed into spines, at the base of which there are glands which secrete a poisonous substance. These are capable of inflicting painful wounds on, for instance, the bare feet of human beings.

The dolphin-fish, Coryphaenidae, are found in all tropical and sub-tropical waters. *Coryphaena hippurus* (illustrated on p. 129) and *C. equisitis* are voracious predators, the former hunting flying fish which often succeed only temporarily in escaping from them by leaping out of the water. Dolphin-fish also eat cephalopods and crustacea. The Carangidae, which include pilot-fish, scad or horse mackerel and amberjack, travel around in fairly large shoals. The pilot fish (*Naucrates ductor*) is noted for its habit of accompanying sharks, turtles and sometimes ships. The scad or horse mackerel (*Trachurus trachurus*), which resembles the mackerel but has a larger head and a deeper body, is common around the British Isles. The amberjack (*Seriola dumerili*) is usually found in the warmer waters of the Atlantic. The jack (*Caranx hipos*, illustrated on p. 129) is a Mediterranean species.

The Cichlidae are exclusively freshwater fish with about 600 species in Asia, America and Africa. Many are kept in aquaria, including angel fish (*Pterophyllum*) and discus (*Cichlasoma*), both illustrated on p. 133, *Haplochromis* and *Aequidens*. The greatest concentration of different species is found in the great lowland lakes of Africa. Here they have been much studied, particularly as examples of mouthbrooders such as the genus *Tilapia*, in which the female carries the eggs in her mouth until they are hatched – a specialized form of parental care. Other studies have concentrated on their complex nuptial dances, their nests, and their methods of communication, which in some species, such as the red cichlid (*Hemichromis bimaculatus*, illustrated on p. 133) is assisted by chemical substances discharged into the water.

Acanthuroidea and Siganoidea

The Acanthuroidea comprise fish of the coral reefs, the best-known members being of the family Acanthuridae, called surgeon fish because of the presence of sharp flat spines located on either side of the tail base, that can inflict sharp cuts on human beings and are reminiscent of surgeon's scalpel blades. In the genus *Acanthurus*, of which the blue tang (*A. coeruleus*) is illustrated on p. 129, the spines are erectile. The diet is largely vegetarian, and the fish move about in shoals to browse on the algae. They are often very brightly coloured.

The rabbit-fish, Siganidae, are found among rocks in warm shallow waters from the Red Sea to the South Pacific. Some have in recent years penetrated the Suez Canal to the Mediterranean.

Trichiuroidea and Stromateoidea

The Trichiuroidea, called cutlass fish from their long, thin shape and silvery colour, comprise about 20 species, some found in European waters.

The Stromateoidea, butterfish, live in warm and temperate seas. Some species, such as the dollarfish, commonly move among the tentacles of jellyfish, to whose poison they seem to be completely immune.

Ophidioidea and Ammodytoidea

The Ophidioidea, so-called cusk eels, have long eel-like bodies and are found all over the world in warm and temperate seas. Most are deep-water fish attaining lengths no greater than 60 cm (2 ft). The dorsal, anal and tail fins are united into one long continuous fin. The pelvic fins are long and thin and hang from the throat, acting as feelers in the search for food on the sea-bottom. The pearl fish and fieraspers (Carapidae) belong to the same group. They mostly

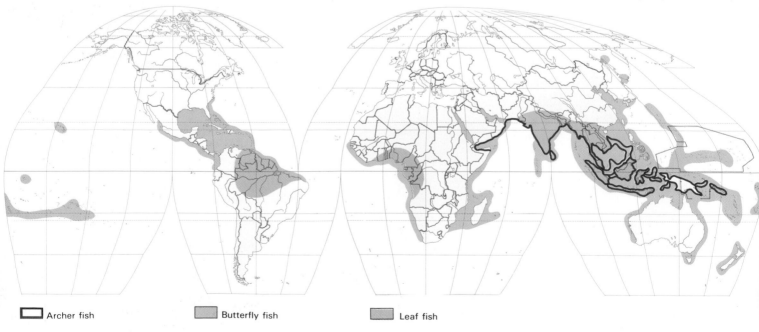

Archer fish   Butterfly fish   Leaf fish

barracuda

sand eel (sand lance)

sand smelt

bluefin tuna

swordfish

lumpsucker

common mullet

wolf fish

lion fish

flying gurnard

gurnard

inhabit shallow tropical waters and spend some part of their lives in the bodies of invertebrates such as sea cucumbers, pearl oysters and starfish, feeding on the internal organs of the hosts.

The Ammodytoidea are represented by only one group, the sand eels (Ammodytidae, illustrated on p. 131) which are small slim, silvery elongated fish, mostly of northern waters. They live in large shoals, often burrowing under the sand of the sea-bed for concealment from their enemies. They are often used as bait for cod by long-line fishermen, and form an important part of the food supply of some other fishes and many sea-birds.

Dactylopteroidea and Scombroidea

The few species of Dactylopteroidea, flying gurnards, live in warm tropical seas and possess highly developed pectoral fins, sometimes brightly coloured, which enable them to glide for short distances above the surface of the water. However, they mostly feed on the sea bottom. The flying gurnard (*Dactylopterus volitans*, illustrated on p. 131) is found in European waters.

The fish best adapted for rapid swimming belong to the Scombroidea. The swordfish (*Xiphias gladius*, illustrated on p. 131) of the Xiphiidae family, is a large, fast-swimming member of the group. The sword extending from its snout is used to slash at its prey; the swordfish otherwise has no teeth. They can be up to 4.5 m (15 ft) long. Others of the family Istiophoridae include the marlin, sailfish and spearfish. Marlin have a short rounded spear extending from the snout, as against the flat and much longer sword of the swordfish. Sailfish are slimmer and have large dorsal fins resembling sails; they are found in warm and temperate waters all round the globe. Spearfish are mostly smaller and have shorter snouts.

The most familiar of the swift-moving fishes is however the mackerel (*Scomber scombrus*) of the Scombroidea group. They average about 30 cm (12 in) in length and travel sometimes in enormous shoals. They are predators, feeding on other fish and on marine animals. Tuna fishes and bonito also belong to this group and are important both as food fish and for sport. The commonest tuna is the bluefin tuna (*Thunnus thynnus*, illustrated on p. 131) which can grow to about 4.5 m (15 ft) in length and attain a weight of 800 kg (1800 lb). Other tunas include the albacore (*T. alalunga*) and skipjack tuna (*Katsuwonus pelamis*). Bonito are fast-moving predators attaining lengths of about 75 cm (30 in).

The above fish are all fast and powerful swimmers due to the arrangement of strong muscles which may account for up to 70 per cent of the body weight of the fish. They are also very smooth skinned and perfectly streamlined. The highly streamlined sailfish is credited with being the fastest fish in the world with bursts of speed of over 100 km per hour (60 mph).

Sphyraenoidea and Mugiloidea

Another group of successful swimmers is that of the barracudas (Sphyraenidae). There are some twenty species found mostly in warm and tropical waters. All are slender and have many big sharp teeth, and are swift and powerful swimmers. They have been known to attack bathers, though they are not of great size; the largest, *Sphyraena barracuda*, illustrated on p. 131, does not as a rule exceed 2 m (6½ ft) in length. Their main diet is fish.

The Mugiloidea or mullet – not related to the red mullet – are a group of fish which search for their food in the mud of the sea bottom and can endure considerable variations in salinity, so that they can pass easily from the sea to brackish waters. The common mullet (*Mugil cephalus*, illustrated on p. 131) is bred as food.

The Atherinidae, silversides, of which the sand smelt (*Atherina hepsetus*) is illustrated on p. 131, are also called whitebait. Some are found in fresh water, e.g. the brook silverside (*Labidesthes*) of the eastern United States.

Cottoidea

The Cottoidea are a group of fish with tapering bodies and large, heavy heads. They are known by various popular names including bullhead, sculpin and miller's thumb. The last-named are freshwater fish common in European streams and rivers. They can act as indicators of water pollution, since they are very sensitive to it. They are noted also for their aggressive attitude towards fish of any kind that approach their nests.

The same group includes the scorpion fish or rockfish (Scorpaenidae). These are saltwater fishes characterized by a massive body and a large head armoured with spines. The fins are supported by spines connected to poisonous glands secreting a substance which is sometimes lethal. The lion fish (*Pterois volitans*, illustrated on p. 131) is often kept in aquaria for its splendid appearance, despite its venomous fin spines. The fish spread and display their fins if disturbed and may go on to attack the source of the disturbance. They grow to about 30 cm (12 in) long, and live in the coral reefs of the Indian Ocean and Red Sea.

The gurnards or sea robins (Triglidae) have an unmistakable appearance thanks to their large polygonal head armoured with bony plates. The fan-shaped pectoral fins have the front fin rays separated as 'feelers', used for walking on the sea-bottom and for sensing the presence of prey such as molluscs and crustaceans. Many species emit audible sounds by vibrating their swim bladder. Some are highly coloured, like the European tub gurnard (*Trigla lucerna*), with its reddish colour and blue and green spotted pectoral fins.

The lumpsuckers and snail fish (Cyclopteridae) live in the Atlantic and Pacific. The males acquire an orange-red colour during the reproductive period. The lumpsucker (*Cyclopterus lumpus*, illustrated on p. 131) is also known as the sea hen from the practice of the male guarding the eggs for several weeks without eating, until they hatch. The pelvic fins are modified to form a sucker by which it attaches itself to a rock. This enables it to resist being swept away by wave action while it guards the eggs. Snail fish, living in cold Arctic and Antarctic waters, have, like the lumpsuckers, a ventral sucker with which they can attach themselves to the sea bed.

Gobioidea

The Gobioidea, mudskippers and gobies, are a large group containing about 600 species. They are sedentary fish that live mostly in contact with the sea bed. The Pteriophthalmidae include the mudskippers such as *Pteriophthalmus koelreuteri*, illustrated here. This and other similar species can leave the water and climb up over stones and vegetation, thanks to the muscles that support their pectoral fins. They live in the mangrove swamps that fringe tropical shores, and spend much of their time out of water basking and displaying on exposed mudbanks.

The Eleotridae are commonly called sleepers, because their usual way of life is to lie quietly on the sea-bottom. They mostly live in the tropical or subtropical regions of America, South-East Asia and Australia.

The gobies belong to the family Gobiidae. Most gobies inhabit the reefs and rockpools of tropical and temperate seas. They are

mudskipper

climbing perch

largemouth bass

archer fish

perch

red cichlid

angelfish

discus

pearl gourami

flag cichlid

Siamese fighting fish

egg-layers and stand guard over their eggs, each of which is attached to the substratum. Many are mud-dwellers, some of them sharing mud-burrows with other animals.

Blennioidea

The Blennioidea, blennies, are also bottom-dwellers. In this group the dorsal fin is much developed in length, and the anal fin even more so. The ventral fins are situated under the throat and are supported by five rays. Some larger species belong to the family Anarhichidae, wolf fish, of northern Atlantic and Pacific waters, which grow to lengths of about 2.5 m (8 ft). *Anarhichus lupus* is illustrated on p. 131. They have formidable teeth and live on crabs, starfish, sea urchins and similar creatures of the sea bed.

The Blennidae are often localised in their distribution, as for example *Ophioblennis atlanticus* of the Caribbean. Many species have local names, such as the hairy blenny (*Labrisomus nuchipinnis*) of the equatorial Atlantic and the shanny (*Blennius pholis*), a European species. The eelpout (*Zoarces viviparous*), of Arctic waters, gives birth to up to 400 live young at a time.

Anabantoidea

The Anabantoidea, labyrinth fish, have a complex, deeply folded accessory structure connected with the gill cavity that functions as a lung and permits the breathing of atmospheric oxygen. This structure gives them their common name. The climbing perch or walking fish, of the genus *Anabas*, lives in ponds and ditches in Asia and sometimes emerges from the water for short periods, moving on the ground with a jerky motion, with the aid of its tail and the spines on the lower edges of its gill covers. *A. testudineus* of this group is illustrated on p. 133. The members of the genus *Betta* are well known as aquarium fish, including the Siamese fighting fish (*B. splendens*, illustrated on p. 133) which is famous for the remarkable territoriality that leads the male to launch himself into ferocious duels with competitors. Other species often kept in aquaria include the gouramis of the genera *Trichogaster* and *Colisa*, in which the pectoral fins are transformed into long filaments, as is seen in the pearl gourami (*Trichogaster leeri*, illustrated on p. 133). Mention should also be made of the paradise fish (*Macropodus*) which were the first exotic fish after the goldfish to be imported into Europe.

Kurtoidea, Ophicephaloidea and Luciocephaloidea

Finally a few small groups of the Perciformes must be mentioned, such as the Kurtoidea of New Guinea. The male of one species, the nurseryfish (*Kurtus gulliveri*) carries the eggs on his head, secured by a cartilaginous hook. The Ophicephaloidea, of central Africa and southern Asia, take particular care of their offspring. The snakehead (*Ophicephalus punctatus*) of India, constructs a bowl-shaped nest by interlacing the stalks of aquatic plants and watches over the young, which number up to fifty at a time. The Luciocephaloidea contain only one species, *Luciocephalus pulcher* of Indonesia; it possesses a tube-shaped mouth which it extends to catch insects on the surface.

Pleuronectiformes

The Pleuronectiformes, the flatfish group, has undergone the greatest adaptation of any of the fishes. Life in contact with the sea bed has led to an extraordinary flattening of the body, with a consequent displacement of some organs that has rendered these fish asymmetrical. The Pleuronectiformes are descendants of perciform ancestors that had the habit of resting on one side on the sea bed; resulting in the fish we know today – soles, dabs, flounders, halibut, turbot and plaice.

The eggs of the Pleuronectiformes hatch into symmetrical, transparent larvae that swim freely in surface waters of the sea. After a while the larvae begin to develop some pigmentation and descend to deeper waters; at the same time a metamorphosis begins in which one eye migrates to the upper part of the head. The mouth undergoes a twisting, the swim bladder disappears and the body enlarges and flattens. The upper part of the body (the zenithal side) becomes pigmented; the lower part (the nadiral) remains white. The typical habitat is a sandy sea bed in which the fish can almost bury themselves, making them virtually invisible.

The members of the group vary greatly in size, from the few centimetres of the scald fish (*Arnoglossus*) to the 2.8 m (9 ft) in the halibut (*Hippoglossus hippoglossus*, illustrated on p. 137).

Some species undergo an identical metamorphosis so that the zenithal side may be either the left or the right. For example, the

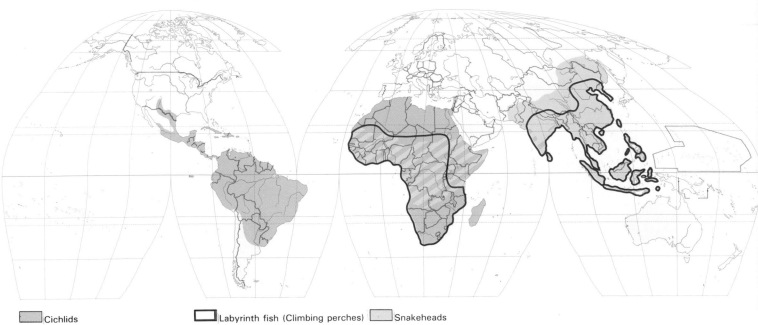

Cichlids Labyrinth fish (Climbing perches) Snakeheads

common plaice lies on its left side, with its right side uppermost, and brill and turbot lie on their right side. Plaice thus have both their eyes on their right side and are called 'right-eyed' or dextral flatfish. Others can present different zenithal sides within the same species or even within the same local population. The Pleuronectiformes are active predators. As a defence they bury themselves rapidly in the sand and sometimes change colour to blend with different backgrounds.

The Soleidae, soles, and Cynoglossidae, tongue soles, are more restricted to warm waters, while the Pleuronectidae, plaice, and Bothidae, flounders, halibut and sand dabs, have a much wider distribution.

The most common species of sole of European waters is the Dover sole (*Solea solea*, illustrated on p. 137) which grows to about 50 cm (20 in) in length. It is brown with darker blotches and a black spot on each pectoral fin. It lives on sandy bottoms at depths up to some hundreds of metres. The variegated or thickback sole (*Monochirus variegatus*) is found from the Mediterranean to the south-west of the British Isles, as is the sand or French sole (*Pegusa lascaris*). The hogchoker (*Trinectes maculatus*), is common along the American coast from New England to Panama.

The tongue soles are sinistral, having the eyes on the left side of the head. They live in tropical seas, mostly in Asia, and grow only to about 30 cm (12 in).

The Scophthalmidae include the turbot (*Scophthalmus maximus*, illustrated on p. 137) and brill (*S. rhombus*). Turbot, which are sinistral, inhabit sand and gravel shores and most are caught in shallow waters less than 100 m (325 ft) deep, but in winter they tend to migrate to much deeper waters. Brill are found in still shallower waters, mostly at about 40 m (130 ft). The megrim (*Lepidorhombus whiffiagonis*) is an inhabitant of deeper and more northern waters.

The Bothidae are right-eyed (dextral) some, like the flounder (*Platichthys flesus*), are common in all British waters, living in creeks and estuaries where the bottom is rich in mud and sand. They travel up and down with the tides and can tolerate fresh water, being found as far up the River Thames as central London. They live on crabs, shrimps, molluscs, lugworms and smaller fish, feeding by day. The halibut, already mentioned above, is an Arctic and sub-Arctic fish, living on rough ground with rock ledges and sandbanks. It is the largest member of the Pleuronectiformes; a massive specimen caught off the Massachusetts coast weighed 280 kg (600 lb). They eat mostly haddock and whiting. Sand dab (*Citharichthys*) are members of the Bothidae of the American Pacific coast; the common topknot (*Zeugopterus punctatus*) and scald fish (*Arnoglossus laterna*) are other, smaller members.

The Pleuronectidae include plaice, witch, lemon sole and dabs. Plaice live in all the shallower coastal waters of northern Europe, most abundantly in the North Sea. They feed on crustaceans, echinoderms and fish. Witch (*Glyptocephalus cynoglossus*) is a bottom feeder found off the American and western British coasts. The lemon sole (*Microstomus kitt*) occurs in shallow waters all round the British Isles and is important commercially. It feeds largely on polychaete worms and crustacea. When feeding it lifts up its head and the front part of its body from the bottom, and scours an area for prey with its back arched ready to pounce. The dab (*Limanda limanda*) is found from Iceland to the Bay of Biscay, sometimes living close inshore. As with other flatfish, much of its life is spent on the muddy bottom, but it can swim rapidly over short distances. Like the lemon sole it is an abundant and valuable source of food. A similar species, the yellow-tailed flounder, occurs off the rocky shores of Labrador and New England.

Echeneiformes

The Echeneiformes contain only the remoras, family Echeneidae. They are slender and active elongated fish with the dorsal fin lying far back opposite the anal fin. The pectoral and ventral fins are well developed and the large mouth has a prominent mandible and is armed with small, sharp teeth.

The remoras have a flat oval sucking disc on top of the head, derived from a modification of the spiny portion of the dorsal fin. With it they attach themselves to larger marine animals, with a preference for squid or whales, but also other large fish, turtles or even ships. Some species prefer to fasten themselves to a particular host, as for instance *Remiligia australis* and *Rhombochirus osteochir*, which seem to prefer whales and marlins respectively.

Remoras gain distinct advantages from attaching themselves to larger hosts. Firstly, they are offered protection and also a free means of transport which saves them the effort of searching for food. They also pick up the leftovers of the host's meal or eat external parasites, such as copepods, from the host's body; which may even involve them entering the host's mouth and gill chambers. There are about ten species, all are thin, elongated, rather dark-coloured fish measuring, according to the species, from about 30 cm to 1 m (1 ft to $3\frac{1}{4}$ ft).

Tetraodontiformes

The Tetraodontiformes are a group of strange looking fishes with anatomical peculiarities. They include porcupine fish, puffer fish, box fish, ocean sunfish, trigger fish and file fish. There are about 300 species in several families. The Tetraodontiformes have a characteristic stomachal sac, made up either of the stomach itself or of an attached organ which can be filled with air or with water. When the fish is threatened it swells up until it appears monstrous in size. In this way the fish appears much larger than in fact it is to potential predators. It also becomes too big and fat for most predators to tackle. Also, many have toxins in their flesh which cause illness and even death if they are eaten.

Diodontidae. The Diodontidae, porcupine fish, have bodies covered with spines; the ventral fin is missing and the teeth are fused together into a robus beak visible even when the mouth is closed. They are short and broad-bodied with large eyes and can inflate their bodies when disturbed. *Diodon hystrix* is the most widely distributed species, a brown fish with dark spots measuring about 90 cm (3 ft) in length. The closely related *Diodon holacanthus* is illustrated on p. 137.

Tetraodontidae. In the Tetraodontidae, puffer fish, the skin is bare or covered with minute spines. The stomachal sac is separate from the true stomach but is dependent on it. The puffer fish can inflate itself suddenly with water until it is like a prickly football, making it virtually impossible for a predator to seize it. *Tetraodon palembangensis*, illustrated on p. 137, is from South-East Asia.

Ostraciontidae. The Ostraciontidae, box fish, also known as trunk fish or cowfish, live on the bottom of warm and tropical seas throughout the world. They are characterized by a mosaic of bony plates that covers the body like a carapace. In section they are pentagonal; in many species (as in *Ostracion cornutus*, illustrated on p. 137), there are spines resembling horns above the eyes and also behind the anal fin. Many species live among coral reefs, feeding on small animals such as corals and molluscs, which are finely ground up by the strong beak. The shape and stiffness of the body makes swimming difficult and for movement the fish rely solely on tiny movements of the fins.

Molidae. The Molidae, ocean sunfish, also called molas or head-fish, are fish of a very strange appearance and sometimes of enormous size. *Mola mola*, for example (illustrated here), has a roundish, short body, laterally compressed, with a tough skin, small mouth and teeth fused together into a beak; its length can be up to 3 m (10 ft) and its weight 2000 kg (4400 lb). The dorsal and anal fins are long and narrow, pointed at the ends, and the tail fin is so tiny that it is almost invisible, since what would normally be the rear part of the body seems to be missing, the body terminating immediately after the dorsal and anal fins.

These gigantic and indolent creatures like to rest on one side on the surface of the sea and allow themselves to be carried along by the currents. They prefer the open sea, but prior to reproduction they come inshore to deposit their eggs, which may number (as in the case of *Mola mola*) up to 300 million.

Balistidae. The Balistidae, trigger fish, have bodies oval in section, much compressed from side to side, and covered with rather thick scales or plates. They swim by rippling their dorsal and anal fins, not by side to side movement of the tail. There are two dorsal fins, the first armoured with three spines, the second with soft rays. Trigger fish take refuge in fissures or holes in the rocks, in which they inflate themselves. When erected the first spine of the front dorsal fin is locked into place by the second, and presses against the walls of the cavity making it impossible to pull the fish out. Only when the trigger mechanism of the second spine is released can the fish withdraw itself or be withdrawn from its shelter. Two species of trigger fish are illustrated here, *Oxymonacanthus longirostris* and *Odonus niger*.

The Monacanthidae, filefish, are sometimes classed together with trigger fish in the Balistidae. Like the trigger fish, they can lock the first dorsal spine, which is long and erectile, in an upright position with the second spine. They are found in warm waters in all parts of the world.

Lophiiformes

The Lophiiformes – angler fish, batfish, goosefish, and frogfish – have evolved the art of ambush to perfection. They lie resting on the sea bed, perfectly disguised thanks to their brown or greyish colouring, and wait unmoving for passing prey. But, to hasten matters, they wave a lure about in the water, a filament derived from the first ray of the dorsal fin, at the end of which is a shred of fleshy material which may also be luminous and attracts the attention of the small fish. The victim approaches and is at once caught and swallowed. The batfish *Ogcocephalus vespertilio*, illustrated here) is a form of angler fish in which the 'fishing rod' can be withdrawn into a tube when not in use.

Lophiidae. The Lophiidae, goosefish, are angler fish found in warm and temperate seas. In some regions they are much prized for their delicate flavour. *Lophius piscatorius* is illustrated here. They are soft and flabby with large, flat heads and tapering bodies.

Ceratidae. The Ceratidae, deep-sea anglers, are usually luminescent. In a few species the female is more than 1 m (3 ft 3 in) long and the male less than 10 cm (4 in); the male attaches himself to the female by biting her, when his mouth becomes fused to her skin and the bloodstreams of the two become interdependent, so that the male remains permanently attached as an ectoparasite, his sole function being to fertilize the eggs. He is nourished via a placenta-like arrangement with the female's blood system.

Antennaridae. The Antennaridae, frogfish, are another group of angler fish, very strange in appearance, with a ragged or lumpy outline. They are strongly patterned to blend with their surroundings and some species change colour to improve camouflage.

Gobiesociformes

The Gobiesociformes, clingfish, live in warm and temperate seas. Their most typical feature is a suction disc, derived from the ventral fin and located on the under surface, which enables them to attach themselves to the substrate. There is only one family, the Gobiesocidae, most of which deposit their eggs under stones or in mollusc shells. Some tropical American species of the genus *Gobiesox* live in fast-flowing freshwater streams.

Batrachoidiformes

The Batrachoidiformes, toadfish, live among the seaweeds of rocky coasts, of warm seas. The sole family is the Batrachoididae. They have heavy bodies, broad heads, large mouths and strong teeth, and are carnivorous. Most species can produce croaking or grunting sounds. Some Central and South American species have poisonous spines on the dorsal fins and gill covers; many may bite when touched. The true toadfish (*Opsanus tau*) lives along the eastern coasts of North America and has the curious habit of depositing its eggs in material abandoned by man, such as boxes, cans and broken bottles. The midshipman (*Porichthys*) has light organs in rows along its body like buttons on a uniform.

Pegasiformes

The Pegasiformes, dragon fish, also known as sea moths, comprise only one family, the Pegasidae, and one genus, *Pegasus*. There are about five species living in the warm coastal waters of the Indian and Pacific Oceans. They have a very distinctive appearance, being completely covered with bony plates or rings except for the tail, which is flexible. The head is pointed and ends in a kind of beak under which the small mouth opens. The pectoral fins are large and are held spread out horizontally, resembling wings. They do not grow to more than about 16 cm (6.5 in) long.

Mastacembeliformes

The Mastacembeliformes, spiny eels, are fish of fresh and brackish waters of Africa and south and South-East Asia. There is only one family, the Mastacembelidae. The body is eel-like, compressed laterally. They are carnivorous and nocturnal, and usually burrow into the bed of a stream or lake during the day. They are not closely related to the deep-sea spiny eels, Notacanthiformes. One of the largest species is *Mastacembelus armatus*, illustrated here, which can reach a length of 75 cm (28 in).

spiny eel

trigger fish
Odonus niger

porcupine fish

trigger fish
*Oxymonachanthus
longirostris*

puffer fish

ocean sunfish

box fish

halibut

bat fish

turbot

Dover sole

goosefish

AMPHIBIANS

The amphibians represent an important stage in the evolution of terrestrial vertebrates but should not be viewed as unsuccessful because of their dependence on water or moist environments for their development.

There are three major groups of amphibians: Apoda, those that have a tail but lack legs; Urodela, the newts and salamanders which have a tail and legs; and the Anura, the frogs and toads, which have legs but no tail. The Anura contain approximately 90 per cent of the known 2000 species. Though of diverse forms, the amphibians comprise a very homogeneous group. Their life consists of two phases: following the hatching of the egg is an aquatic larval period during which breathing is by means of gills; after metamorphosis the adult breathes by lungs and can leave the water for long periods. To increase oxygen uptake in water and heat exchange in air, the skin is naked, unlike that of other vertebrates. For example, the skin of fishes and reptiles is covered with scales, birds have feathers and mammals have hair. This makes most frogs and toads susceptible to drying out in hot weather and so most species frequent damp, shady habitats.

Apoda

The Apoda or Gynophiona are tropical amphibians specialized for living underground in mud and sand, and characterized by an elongated cylindrical body, a short, thick head and a short tail. The absence of limbs makes them resemble worms, but unlike these they have jaws and two eyes. They vary in length from a few centimetres to 1.5 m (5 ft). They are found mostly in forests and marshes of equatorial regions of America, Africa and Asia.

The form of the body and the presence of rings which divide the length into segments indicates an evolution convergent with two groups very remote from them: the earthworms (annelids) and the snake-like lizards called Amphisbaenia.

Fertilization is internal and the eggs are laid in soft earth; the larvae which emerge complete their metamorphosis in water. In ovoviviparous species (those in which the eggs are hatched in the body of the parent) the larvae do not leave the mother's body but remain in the oviduct, where they live on 'uterine milk'. The young are born when almost fully developed and change their skins immediately after birth. The Apoda are carnivorous and eat insects and other arthropods, as well as earthworms and small vertebrates such as frogs, toads and small snakes. There are three families, the Ichthyophidae, Typhlonectidae and Caecilidae, containing altogether 164 species. In common terminology all apodans are referred to as caecilians.

Ichthyophis glutinosus, of the Ichthyophidae, is well known for its parental care. At the moment of deposition the female rolls itself round the eggs and protects them until they hatch. This 'brooding' takes place in a small enlargement of the burrow; at birth the young immediately make for the water, where they undergo development.

The Typhlonectidae are more aquatic; the illustration shows *Typhlonectes compressicaudata* of Guyana and Venezuela, which is completely aquatic. The Caecilidae, such as *Caecilia tentaculata* of Surinam and *Geotripetes seraphini* of central and west Africa, are more terrestrial. Caecilidae are worm-like, legless and lack a pelvis, and their colour ranges from black to a pinkish tan. They feed on earthworms and termites.

Opposite above   The tropical South American apodan (*Typhlonectes compressicaudata*) is entirely aquatic.
Opposite below   One of the caecilians, tropical worm-like burrowing amphibians (this one is from West Africa).

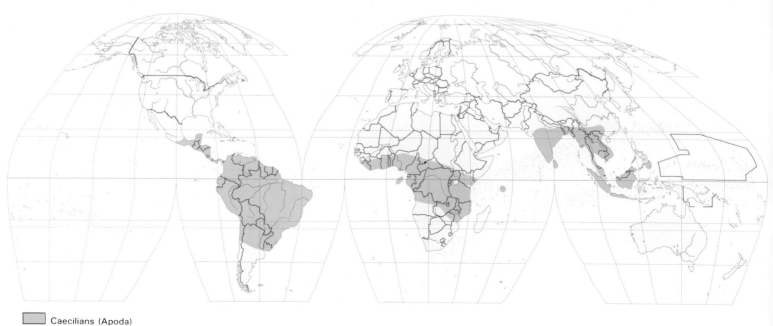

Caecilians (Apoda)

Urodela

The Urodela or Caudata are lizard-shaped and have a tail, both as larvae and as adults. Fertilization is external in some species, internal in others; the larvae possess feathery gills, which are reabsorbed during metamorphosis. There are also cases of neoteny – prolonged retention of larval or immature characteristics – in which the adults retain external gills, lack lungs, and live exclusively in water. The Urodela are sub-divided into the Cryptobranchoidea, Ambystomoidea, Salamandroidea and Sirenoidea, with eight families in all. They are almost all inhabitants of northern regions; only the Pletodontidae are found south of the equator.

Cryptobranchoidea

The Cryptobranchoidea are the most primitive of the Urodela. They comprise two families called the Hynobiidae and the Cryptobranchidae.

Hynobiidae. The Hynobiidae resemble the salamanders and their area of distribution is in Europe and Asia. *Hynobius keyserlingii*, illustrated here, is adapted to cold climates; it is the only member of the Urodela to live beyond the Arctic Circle. Before it hibernates it reduces the water content of its body, which increases the density of the body tissues and helps prevent it freezing at very low temperatures. It emerges early from hibernation and is already active when the temperature reaches 3°C. Breeding behaviour consists of the female depositing a firm-walled egg-case (octheca) on a branch or stone immediately above the surface of the water. The male then fertilizes the eggs and, after a few days, the newly born 'tadpoles' fall into the water. Other species belonging to this family are *Onychodactylus japonicus*, of Japan, and *O. fischeri*, of eastern Siberia and Korea – the only members of the Urodela provided with claws.

Cryptobranchidae. The Cryptobranchidae are the giants of the group, and can exceed 150 cm (5 ft) in length. Aquatic animals, of a heavy and clumsy appearance, they do not possess eyelids and retain some larval features. The largest species is the giant salamander of Japan (*Megalobatrachus japonicus*), which can weigh more than 25 kg (55 lb). Of only slightly smaller dimensions is Father David's salamander (*M. davidianus*) of central western China. This species lives in deep, fast flowing streams. The hellbender (*Cryptobranchus alleganiensis*, illustrated here) of the eastern USA, also lives in torrential streams and can reach a length of over 45 cm (18 in). The adults possess some gill slits in the folds of the skin of the neck.

In summer female cryptobranchids deposit a gelatinous string of some hundred eggs that are fertilized by the male who guards over them until they hatch.

Ambystomoidea

Adult ambystomids are terrestrial and bear an extraordinary resemblance to the European black and yellow salamander both in coloration and in behaviour. They are widely distributed throughout North America, but are difficult to observe, as they leave their refuges only at night or on rainy days. They travel to ponds or lakes to reproduce; fertilization is internal and takes place by means of spermatophores, packets of sperm transferred from the male to the female.

The great Pacific salamander (*Dicamptodon ensatus*, illustrated here) is the largest species, 30 cm (12 in) long. Despite its heavy and clumsy appearance, it is very agile and can climb nimbly up trees. Besides invertebrates, its diet includes amphibians and small mammals. The genus *Rhyacotriton* includes the Olympus salamander (*R. olympicus*), characterized by its large eyes. The genus *Rhyacasiredon* contains four species of very limited distribution.

The most numerous genus is *Ambystoma*, found throughout North America. The best known member is the tiger salamander (*A. tigrinum*, illustrated here) in both the larval and the adult stages. The larval stage of this amphibian was named axolotl by the Aztecs of Mexico, where it lives today, in lakes in the neighbourhood of Mexico City. When some specimens were taken to Europe for study, after a few years some specimens metamorphosed into adult tiger salamanders, thus revealing their true identity. The spotted salamander (*A. maculatum*) migrates in large numbers in the breeding season to freshwater ponds and pools, where the two sexes meet each other. A similar behaviour is shown by *A. jeffersonianum*. *A. californiense* is adapted to dry climates and arid habitats; *A. gracilis* prefers meadows and humid forests, while *A. talpoideum* lives in burrows dug by other animals.

Salamandroidea

The Salamandroidea are the dominant group of the Urodela, and are distributed throughout America, Eurasia and Africa. They comprise the families Salamandridae, Amphiumidae, Proteidae and Plethodontidae.

Salamandridae. The typical salamander appearance is common to all the representatives of the Salamandridae. *Tylototriton* is probably the most primitive genus, with its Asiatic species of rather squat and spiritless forms. Primitive characteristics are present in the genus *Pleurodeles*, found in Spain, Portugal and Morocco. The yellow and black salamander (*Salamandra salamandra*, illustrated on p. 143) is the best known European species; it visits water solely to give birth to its young, who are already partly developed when born. *Salamandra atra*, found in Alpine regions, is particularly well adapted to arid environments, in that the young are born already metamorphosed and thus do not need to complete a larval period in water. The spectacled salamander (*Salamandrina terdigitata*, illustrated on p. 143) is another European species, easily recognized by its slender body and very long tail. The genus *Chioglossa* is represented in Spain and Portugal only by *C. lusitanica*, characterized by its long tail, which it sheds as a reflex action when alarmed, later growing a new one to replace it.

The newts live a more aquatic life than the salamanders. At breeding time male newts become brightly coloured, their tails broaden out and their crests tend to enlarge and become exaggerated. For example, the most common British species, the male smooth newt (*Triturus vulgaris*, illustrated on p. 143) puts on a nuptial finery of black spots which show up particularly well against the yellow back, and orange and white edge to the tail fin. The crested newt (*T. cristatus*, illustrated on p. 143) is decorated with such a well-developed crest as to resemble some prehistoric reptile. The alpine newt (*T. alpestris*, illustrated on p. 143) sports a fiery red stomach and turquoise flanks, with smooth spotted crest. The marbled newt (*T. marmotus*, illustrated on p. 143) is patterned a mossy green. The females of all species are duller and do not have a broad tail. The Italian newt (*T. italicus*) is the smallest species, not exceeding 8 cm (3 in).

The genus *Euproctus* has some primitive characteristics. There are only three species, of which *E. montanus*, illustrated on p. 143,

great Pacific salamander

hellbender

red salamander

red eft

Texas blind newt

worm salamander

tiger salamander (adult)

greater siren

mud puppy

tiger salamander
(larva or axolotl)

Hynobius keyserlingii

inhabits the mountainous regions of Corsica in remote and fast-flowing streams.

The red eft (*Diemictylus, viridescens*, illustrated on p. 141) is a species of eastern North America which lives on land for two or three years before taking permanently to the water. On doing so it turns from bright red to dull green, with a row of red spots on the sides. The giant Californian newt (*Taricha torosa*) of western North America, grows to 15 cm (6 in) in length. The Japanese newt (*Cynops pyrrhogaster*) is somtimes kept as a pet, as are several of the other urodeles.

Amphiumidae. The family Amphiumidae comprises a single genus *Amphiuma*, with three species, distributed in the south-eastern part of the USA. They have a somewhat strange appearance, with a cylindrical eel-like body, reaching up to 90 cm (36 in) in length, with small claws on much reduced legs. They are neotenic, preserving some juvenile characteristics, for example, they have lost the external gills but still have a gill slit and four gill covers. They live in still waters such as swamps, and are nocturnal in habit. The two-toed amphiuma (*A. means*) is not exclusively aquatic and abandons the water for limited periods.

Proteidae. The family Proteidae contains only two genera, *Proteus* and *Necturus*, the first European and the second North American. They have a long slender body and a long tail; they are neotenic and the adults possess external gills. The sole European species is the olm or proteus (*Proteus anguinus*, illustrated here) which lives in the caves of the Carpathians and the limestone areas of Yugoslavia. It is totally unpigmented with very small limbs, red gill plumes, a narrow head and a blunt snout. Its eyes are vestigial and covered with skin, but are still sensitive to light.

The olm is Europe's only cave-dwelling amphibian and lives mainly in limestone caves in Yugoslavia and Italy. When it was first discovered scientists realized its resemblance to the axolotl; and when experiments on axolotls revealed that under certain circumstances they could be encouraged to develop into salamanders, the same kinds of experiments were carried out on olms. They failed, however. It seems that the olm is not the larval form of some other amphibian which has halted its physical development but continued its sexual development, so that it can breed while still a 'larva' (that is, neoteny in the same way as the axolotl).

Olms are now considered to be very primitive members of the Urodela – they are the original aquatic model from which the terrestial salamanders have evolved. In this sense the olm is therefore an evolutionary 'missing link'.

The mud puppy (*Necturus maculosus*, illustrated on p. 141) of eastern North America, lives in surface waters – lakes, rivers and swamps – and leads a nocturnal life.

Plethodontidae. The Plethodontidae, lungless salamanders, are the most numerous family of Salamandroidea, with twenty-three genera, all American except one, which is European. All lack lungs, or else the lungs are much reduced, so that respiration is exclusively through the skin. In Europe there are two species, living in caverns but not in water, of the genus *Hydromantes*; the Italian cave salamander (*H. italicus*, illustrated on p. 141) is found in the Apennines, *H. genei* in Sardinia. The American red salamander (*Pseudotriton ruber*, illustrated on p. 141) is reddish-orange in colour, with small black spots, while *Aneides aeneus* is brown spotted with green; the latter is well known for its ability to climb about on plants. The blind newt of Texas (*Typhlomolge rathbuni*, illustrated on p. 141) is neotenic and lives permanently in underground waters. There is a similar blind cave-dwelling species of the genus *Haideotriton* which was described from one individual animal found in Georgia, in a well 60 m (200 ft) deep. The grotto salamander (*Typlotriton spelaeus*) is another blind cave species from the Ozark area of the United States. The worm salamander (*Batrachoseps attenuatus*, illustrated on p. 141) gets its name from its very slender and elongated body. The genus *Batiglossa* should also be mentioned; it is the only one of the Urodela to be found in the Southern Hemisphere, in the Amazon basin.

Sirenoidea

Sirenidae. The last family of the Urodela is that of the Sirenidae, of the Sirenoidea group whose species resemble a mixture of larval and adult forms. The eyes lack eyelids, and there are lungs but external gills also persist. The body is long and the tail short; the hind legs are absent and the forelegs much reduced. Three species are known, among them the greater siren (*Siren lacertina*, illustrated on p. 141), 50-90 cm (20-35 in) long, found in the eastern and southern states of the USA but particularly in Florida.

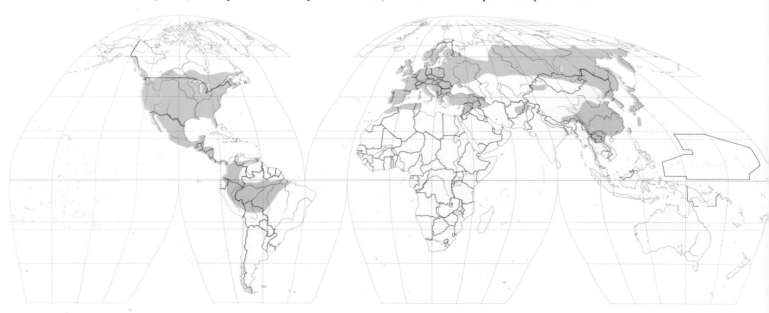

☐ Newts and salamanders

crested or warty newt

smooth or common newt

olm (proteus)

alpine newt

marbled newt

Corsican brook salamander *Euproctus montanus*

Italian cave salamander

spectacled salamander

yellow and black salamander

Anura

The Anura – frogs and toads – have an unmistakable appearance; globular body, hind legs more developed than the forelegs, absence of a tail in the adult stage, head hardly if at all distinct from the body, protruding eyes. Most lay their eggs in water and the development of the embryo may take quite a long time, depending on the temperature of the water in which the eggs are deposited. The embryo emerges from the egg as a tadpole and undergoes a slow metamorphosis involving the loss of the tail, the development of the limbs, the modification of the blood circulation, the regression of the gills and the development of the lungs, and the change from a vegetarian diet to a carnivorous one.

Leiopelmatidae

The Leiopelmatidae, Hochstetter's frog and others of the genus *Leiopelma*, are found only in New Zealand, and represent the only amphibians of that region except for species of the genus *Hyla* that have been introduced by man. They are small frogs that deposit their eggs at some distance from the water. The tadpole stage of development is lacking and the young are born already metamorphosed into adults. The adults are unusual in that they have no eardrum or vocal sacs.

Ascaphidae

The Ascaphidae include the tailed frog (*Ascaphius truei*, illustrated here) of North America. The 'tail' of the male is in fact an external prolongation of the cloaca, the cavity in which the intestinal and urinary ducts terminate, and is used as a copulatory organ, making possible internal fertilization.

Pipidae

The Pipidae, tongueless frogs, comprise some fifteen South American and African species that never leave their watery environment. The best known species is the Surinam toad (*Pipa pipa*, illustrated here) of tropical South America. It has a large flattened body and the hind feet are amply webbed. The eggs fall on to the stomach of the male, who fertilizes them and presses them on to the back of the female. Pouches of skin grow around them in which they remain until metamorphosis is complete. After hatching the young remain near the mother, who defends them from predators. Another interesting species is the South African clawed toad (*Xenopus laevis*, illustrated here) which is characterized by a very smooth skin and the presence of small black claws on the inner three toes of the hind feet. The mouth can be opened very wide, permitting large prey to be swallowed. This species was used in the first successful test for pregnancy; it was found that when the urine of a pregnant woman was injected into an unmated female clawed toad it would immediately produce eggs. *X. laevis* is also valuable for mosquito control since it eats their eggs and larvae.

Discoglossidae

The Discoglossidae, midwife toads and fire-bellied toads, are present in Eurasia, North Africa and the Philippines. The midwife toad (*Alytes obstetricans*, illustrated on p. 147) found in Western Europe, is notable for its mating habits; the female lays the eggs in two strands which the male, having fertilized them wraps round his hind legs. He then returns to his burrow, emerging at night to feed and to dampen the eggs. He takes to the water for the hatching of the young, which he then leaves there to develop. The 'midwife' is therefore the male and, if disturbed when walking with his eggs, he will not hesitate to jettison them in order to make good his escape.

The fire-bellied toads (*Bombina*) live in Europe and Asia. There are two European species, the yellow-bellied toad (*B. variegata*, illustrated on p. 147) and the red-bellied toad (*B. bombina*). The painted frogs (*Discoglossus*) of Europe closely resemble the common frogs but do not have a horizontal pupil in the eye. The fourth genus of Discoglossidae is *Barbourula* of the Philippines.

Rhinophrynidae

The Rhinophrynidae, burrowing toads, comprise the single species *Rhinophrynus dorsalis* of Mexico and Guatemala. It possesses near the first toe of the hind legs a horny excrescence called a 'spade' with which it digs out the earth or the nests of termites, to find food, or when it burrows for shelter in order to avoid intense heat.

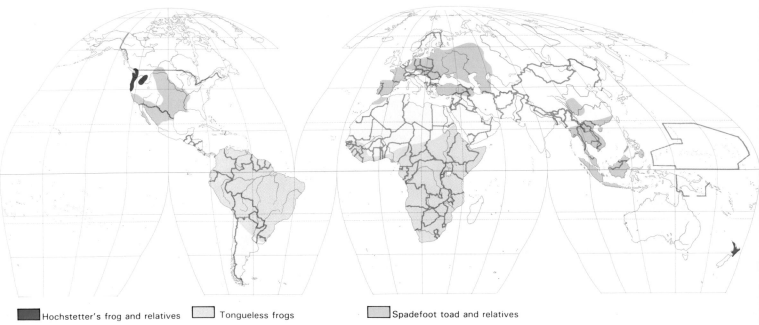

■ Hochstetter's frog and relatives   □ Tongueless frogs   □ Spadefoot toad and relatives

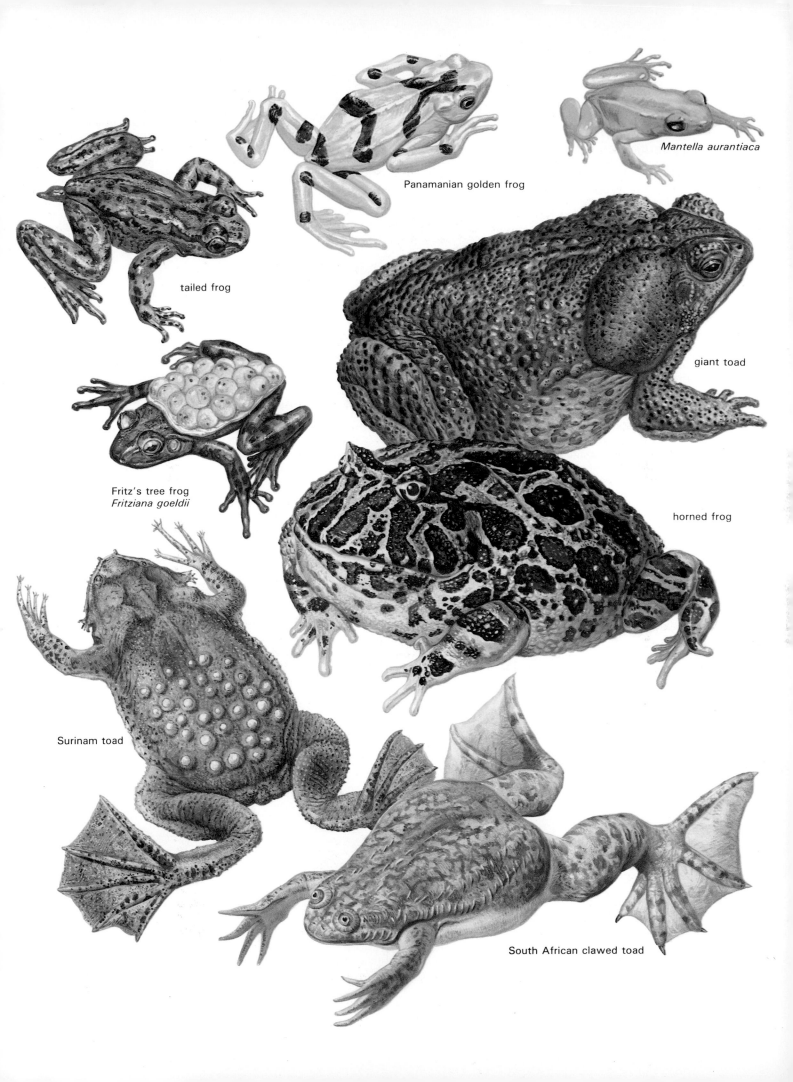

tailed frog

Panamanian golden frog

Mantella aurantiaca

giant toad

Fritz's tree frog
Fritziana goeldii

horned frog

Surinam toad

South African clawed toad

Pelobatidae

Like the Pelodytidae, the Pelobatidae are characterized by the absence of ribs, and by not possessing true teeth on the upper jaw. The best known species is the spadefoot toad (*Pelobates fuscus*, illustrated here) which is found throughout much of lowland Europe and western Asia. It is well adapted to fairly arid conditions with sandy soil. It is nocturnal and at dawn burrows out a den with the aid of a horny 'spade' projecting from the inner edge of each hind foot. The corresponding American genus is *Scaphiopus*, of which there are six species. A third similar group is *Megophrys* of central and southern Asia.

Pelodytidae

The Pelodytidae comprise two species of the genus *Pelodytes*, one of central southern Europe and the other of the Caucasus. Both lack the specialized digging organ of the Pelobatidae.

Ranidae

This is the family of true frogs, distinguished from toads by being smooth-skinned, long-legged, and progressing by leaps, whereas the toads have warty skins and move by crawling or hopping. They are found all over the world except in Greenland and New Zealand. The green frogs are represented in Europe by the marsh frog (*Rana ridibunda*, illustrated here) and the edible frog (*Rana esculenta*). The bullfrog (*R. catesbeiana*) is of American origin but has been imported into various other regions, largely for food. Another important group is that of the 'red frogs', whose way of life is rather less aquatic.

The common frog (*R. temporaria*, illustrated here) is the most familiar British species. In continental Europe, where it is also common, it is known as the brown frog or grass frog. Other European species are *R. dalmatina* and *R. latastei*. The giant among frogs is the goliath frog (*Gigantorana goliath*) of the humid forests of West Africa, with a body over 15 cm (6 in) long.

Other species of Ranidae include *Mantella aurantiaca* of Madagascar, illustrated on p. 145, with its brilliant orange coloration, and the furry frog (*Trienobatrachus robustus*) of West Africa, whose males during the reproductive period acquire a dense 'fur' on the legs and sides. The genus *Sooglossus* of the Seychelles, comprises three species whose tadpoles climb up on to the male's body and remain there until their development is complete. This behaviour is similar to that of the arrow-poison frogs *Dendrobates* of South and Central America, whose skins secrete a toxic substance used by the Indians to coat their arrow tips. The toxin acts as a nerve poison and paralyses the muscles, including the diaphragm and other breathing muscles; death is by suffocation. Another wide ranging member of the family is *Hemisus marmoratus* of South Africa, which digs its burrows in the sandy soil with its snout.

Rhacophoridae

The Rhacophoridae are tree and gliding frogs; the finger ends are supported by cartilage which assists the grip of the adhesive discs present on the tip of each finger. The typical genus is *Rhacophorus* of southern and eastern Asia. Some species such as *R. nigropalmatus* and *R. pardalis* have webbed feet and are also equipped with a membrane that joins the front and hind legs, which permits a gliding flight over distances up to 7 m (22 ft).

Microhylidae

About forty genera make up the tropical family of Microhylidae, the narrow-mouthed toads. They are found in the Americas, Africa, Madagascar, Asia, New Guinea and parts of Asia. Many species make use of the lairs of various animals; some dig their own burrows with their snouts, and some, such as *Kaloula pulchra* of South-East Asia and *Hypopacheus ceneus* of Mexico, with the aid of a horny excrescence on the hind legs.

Phrynomeridae

The Phrynomeridae are another family of narrow-mouthed toads containing only six species of the genus *Phrynomerus* of central and southern Africa. They are unusual in having a mobile neck.

Pseudidae

The Pseudidae comprise two South American genera which have one extra joint in the fingers. The larvae are much larger than the

True frogs Rhacophorid tree and gliding frogs

marsh frog

European green tree frog

green toad

common toad

yellow-bellied toad

spadefoot toad

midwife toad

common frog

adults: in *Pseudis paradoxus* the adult is 6 cm (2.5 in) long and the tadpole 25 cm (10 in) long. This species is found in a few high-altitude lakes in South America.

Bufonidae

The Bufonidae – toads – are found all over the world, even in Australia. The body is squat, clumsy and of a rough texture, and the legs short, so that they walk or hop rather than jump. The common toad (*Bufo bufo*, illustrated on p. 147), the most representative of the group, is distributed in Europe, Asia and North Africa. Another European species is the green toad (*B. viridis*, illustrated on p. 147). Rapacious devourers of insects, the toads are useful to man, and some such as the giant toad (*B. marinus*, illustrated on p. 145) have been employed to combat insect pests. Toads have glands on the back and above the eyes that secrete poison, and that of the giant toad can be lethal to animals as large as dogs.

The only toad in Australia is called the cane toad, but it is in fact *Bufo marinus*, the giant toad mentioned above. It acquired its new name and home through being introduced from South America to eradicate the cane beetle which was seriously affecting the sugar cane crop in north-western Australia. In 1935 a batch of cane toads were released in Queensland in the hope they would act as a 'biological controlling agent' and rid the plantations of the beetle pest.

Unfortunately the toad failed in its appointed task: it ignored the cane beetles and instead devoured the predators of the insect pest, so that the beetles became even more numerous. The toads quickly spread and bred successfully, and they now take a heavy annual toll of pet dogs and cats and also deprive the rare native Australian wildlife of food. The original high hopes for biological control were not realized, therefore, and there are now two pests – toad and beetle – instead of one.

An interesting group is the genus *Nectophrynoides*, which, unusually among the Anura, reproduce in a similar way to mammals; the development of the egg and the larva take place inside the body of the mother, who is provided with modified oviducts (egg ducts) that resemble the uterus (womb) of a mammal and nourish the young as they develop within. There is no free-living tadpole stage, therefore, and the young are born fully-formed as miniatures of their parents.

Atelopodidae

The Panamanian frog (*Atelopus zeteki*, illustrated on p. 145) is also known as the golden frog from its characteristic colour. It is one of the few representatives of the Atelopodidae.

Hylidae

The Hylidae, tree frogs, are known by their croaking as well as for their arboreal habits. They are found in America, Europe, New Guinea and Australia. The typical genus is *Hyla*, with about 200 widespread species, the European green tree frog (*Hyla arborea*, illustrated on p. 147). The marsupial frog (*Gastrotheca marsupiata*) of South America, is a tree frog of which the females carry the fertilized eggs in a pouch on the back, the young being released from the pouch at the tadpole stage, but in another species, *G. ovifera*, the young remain in the pouch until they are fully metamorphosed. Another tree frog that acts in a similar way is *Fritziana goeldii*, illustrated on p. 145.

To assist their clambering through the trees, tree frogs have fingers and toes that are expanded into adhesive discs at the tips. They are commonly seen clinging to the outsides of window panes at night, feeding on insects drawn by the lights of the room within. As might be expected, most tree frogs are greenish or mottled green-brown for effective camouflage.

Leptodactylidae

The Leptodactylidae are common in South and Central America and in Australia. One genus, *Heleophryne*, lives in Africa. Some of the best-known species are *Leptodactylus pentadactylus*, which acquires vivid colours during the breeding season, and *L. fallax*, prized for the excellence of its flesh. Some species lay their eggs in a frothy mass; the young live in the foam until rain washes them down to the nearest pool of water. The young of the genus *Eleutherodactylus* are among those of the Anura that are born as babies instead of hatching from eggs laid previously. The horned frogs of the genus *Ceratophrys* of South America are aggressive and prey on other frogs. They may bite when disturbed. Their common name is derived from the projecting flaps of skin above each eye, as can be seen in the illustration on p. 145 of *C. ornata*.

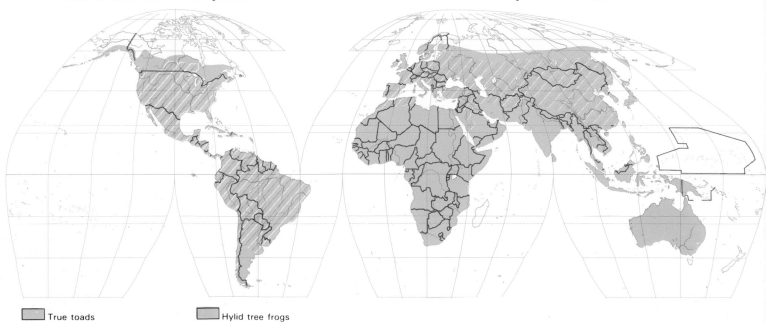

☐ True toads   ☐ Hylid tree frogs

REPTILES

The Reptilia, reptiles, are of enormous importance in the history of evolution, since they were the first group of vertebrates to become fully terrestrial. This step was made possible by the development of the amniotic egg, one in which a membrane, the amnion, envelops the embryo and maintains it in a liquid environment so that the embryo can develop floating in an aquatic medium without the egg having to be laid in water.

Reptiles are ectothermic creatures, ones which derive most of their body heat from the environment by basking. When the ambient temperature falls, so does their own body temperature. This is in contrast to birds and mammals which, by physiological processes, can generate heat to keep their body at a high and constant temperature even when the air around them is quite cool. Reptiles strive to keep warm by judicious basking in the sun, but are at a disadvantage in places where cloudy or cool weather reduce the prospects for successful basking. They are therefore most abundant in the warmer parts of the world; comparatively few species penetrate the higher latitudes of the temperate zones.

Chelonia

The Chelonia – turtles and tortoises – appeared some 300 million years ago and since then have undergone little change, so that those now living are very similar to their remote ancestors. The body, short and squat, is covered by a protective shell made up of two parts, the upper section being called the carapace and the lower section the plastron. The two are joined at the sides by bridges of bone or, in some cases, by elastic ligaments. This shell is formed of bony plates clad by a horny substance. The mandibles, which lack teeth, are transformed into a beak similar to that of the birds. There are some differences in the form of the legs, due to the type of habitat. The Chelonia are divided into two groups, Pleuro-

dira and Cryptodira. The name tortoise is commonly applied to land-dwelling members of the group while those living in water are called turtles or terrapins.

Pleurodira

In the Pleurodira the neck is bent sideways when the head is withdrawn into the shell, whereas in the Cryptodira the head when being withdrawn is held vertically and the neck is bent into an S shape. There are thirteen genera with about fifty species grouped into the Pelomedusidae (side-necked turtles) and Chelyidae (snake-necked turtles). They are aquatic tropical turtles that live in South America, Africa, Madagascar and Australia. In Australia they are the sole representatives of the Chelonia.

Pelomedusidae. The Pelomedusidae, side-necked turtles, do not usually reach large dimensions and are all aquatic reptiles. *Pelomedusa* and *Pelusios* are African genera; the genus *Podocnemis* includes one freshwater species of Madagascar and about seven river turtles of South America. *Pelusios* turtles, living in lakes and rivers, are characterized by a hinged section of the front part of the lower shell which they can close tightly, to shut themselves in. Their carapaces range from 12 to 45 cm (5 to 18 in) in length. *P. niger* (illustrated on p. 150) lives in ponds and slow-moving rivers in West Africa.

Chelyidae. The seat turtles of the family Chelyidae are notable for the length of their neck. Typical representatives are the snake-necked turtle (*Chelodina longicollis*, illustrated on p. 150) of Australia, and *Hydromedusa tectifera* (illustrated on p. 150) of Argentina. The matamata of Guyana and Brazil (*Chelys fimbriata*) captures its prey by creating a sudden whirlpool by opening its mouth and sucking in its prey. *Phrynops* is another South American genus.

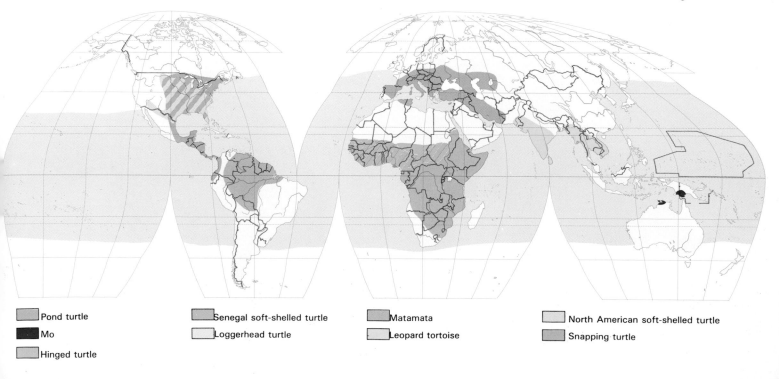

Pond turtle	Senegal soft-shelled turtle	Matamata	North American soft-shelled turtle
Mo	Loggerhead turtle	Leopard tortoise	Snapping turtle
Hinged turtle			

gopher tortoise

snake-necked turtle
Chelodina longicollis

snake-necked turtle
Hydromedusa tectifera

side-necked turtle

leatherback turtle

box turtle

leopard tortoise
Geochelone pardalis

Platysternum megacephalum

North American
soft-shelled turtle

Cryptodira

Dermatemydidae. The Cryptodira comprise nine families among which the Dermatemydidae contains only one species, *Dermatemys mawii*, from the rivers of Mexico, Honduras and Guatemala.

Kinosternidae. The four genera of Kinosternidae live in the ponds and freshwater streams of North and South America. The mud turtles (*Kinosternon* sp.) have a hinged portion at either end of the lower shell which they can raise up to protect themselves like closing a door at the front and back of their shell. Like the musk turtles (*Sternotherus* sp.) they can exude a strong musky odour.

Chelydridae. The Chelydridae include the snapping turtles (*Macrochelys temminckii* and *Chelydra serpentina*) from North America. Both have a rather reduced shell, rough in texture, and both are large, aggressive reptiles. The former is the largest freshwater turtle in the USA, reaching 70 cm (28 in) in length; the latter is usually quiescent in water but on land may snap at intruders.

Platysternidae. There is only one representative of the Platysternidae, *Platysternum megacephalum* of eastern and southern Asia, which is characterized by its inability to withdraw its rather large head into its shell.

Testudinidae. The Testudinidae, with the Emydidae, comprise 33 genera and include the land-dwelling tortoises. The Emydidae are mostly aquatic reptiles and include the diamondback terrapin and red-eared turtles of North America. An exception is the terrestrial box turtle (*Terrapene carolina*, illustrated here) which can shut itself into its shell with hinged portions of the plastron. The pond turtle (*Emys orbicularis*) is a European species.

The Testudinidae are hard-shelled tortoises, well adapted to a terrestrial environment. The leopard tortoise (*Geochelone elegans*) and *G. pardalis* (illustrated here), of Asia and Africa respectively, have highly ornamented carapaces. Another member of the same genus is *G. elephantopus*, the giant tortoise of the Galapagos. The gopher tortoise (*Gopherus polyphemus*, illustrated here) has flattened front limbs adapted for burrowing and lives in deep lairs that it excavates in the sand. The hinged turtle (*Kinixys belliana*) is able to fold down the hinder part of its carapace. The common tortoises of southern Europe, imported into Britain as pets, belong to the genus *Testudo*. *T. graeca* is one species often taken; it is about 18–25 cm (7–10 in) long, and is now rare in its Mediterranean home owing to excessive collecting to supply the pet trade.

Cheloniidae. Most of the marine turtles belong to the Cheloniidae. They are characterized by a flattened shell and forelimbs transformed into paddles. Among them are the well-known green turtle (*Chelonia mydas*), which makes long migrations by sea and is the basis of turtle soup, and the loggerhead (*Caretta caretta*).

Dermochelydae. The leatherback turtle (*Dermochelys coriacea*, illustrated here) is the largest of living turtles, attaining up to 2 m (6½ ft) in length. It has no visible shell but a leathery skin in which the bones of the shell are buried.

Carettochelydae. The Carettochelydae comprise only one species, *Carettochelys insculpta*, which lives in Papua–New Guinea, where it is known as 'mo'. The snout is provided with a proboscis, the carapace is leather and the forelegs are paddles or flippers.

Trionychidae. The Trionychidae, soft-shelled turtles, comprise about twenty-five genera found in the rivers of America, Africa and Asia. Distinctive in appearance, they have flat, leathery shells, the snout is much elongated and the lips are fleshy. A typical species is the North American soft-shelled turtle (*Trionyx spiniferus*, illustrated here). Another species is the Senegal soft-shelled turtle (*Cyclanorbis senegalensis*).

LEPIDOSAURIA

The Lepidosauria include the Squamata, lizards and snakes, and also the Rhynchocephalia with only one surviving representative, the tuatara.

Rhynchocephalia

The Rhynchocephalia are a group that appeared in the Triassic era and were believed to be extinct until the end of the last century, when the tuatara (*Sphenodon punctatus*, illustrated here) was discovered on a few small islands off New Zealand. It is a reptile some 60 cm in length (24 in), with a squat body and rather clumsy movements. The head is robust, and the back is ornamented with a toothed crest. It feeds on vegetation and insects, not disdaining sometimes the eggs of the shearwater (*Puffinus carneipes*), a bird with which it sometimes shares its burrow. Its metabolism is very slow; it can endure cold and can live as long as a hundred years. It is an example of a true living fossil, since it is a representative of a group all other members of which became extinct millions of years ago.

The tuatara (*Sphenodon punctatus*) of New Zealand is almost a living fossil — a primitive lizard which owes its survival to its occupation of rocky offshore islands.

Squamata

The Squamata, lizards and snakes, are characterized by having skin-bearing horny scales, a flexible skull and a male copulatory apparatus made up of two hemipenes (paired sexual organs). Squamates are found all over the world, except for Antarctica, and are ecologically very diverse. There are two sub-groups, Sauria, lizards, and Ophidia or Serpentes, snakes.

Sauria

The Sauria usually have an elongated body provided with well-developed legs and a long tail. Together with the snakes they make up 95 per cent of living reptiles. Many forms are adapted to life in the soil and in some cases a reduction in the limbs has been followed by the disappearance of the eyes. Many species of gecko and lizard are able to shed the tail voluntarily as a means of escape from predators. The tail usually regrows after several weeks but may not be as long as the original one.

Gekkonidae. The Gekkonidae, geckos, have some archaic characteristics. In the most primitive forms the eyes possess mobile eyelids while in the more evolved forms the eyes are protected by a transparent covering derived from the eyelids, which are thereby able to remain permanently open. Unlike most reptiles they can emit audible sounds, varying from chirps to barks. They usually have toe pads furnished with minute hooks that enable them to cling to very small irregularities in a surface, so that they can run up walls and across ceilings. They live mostly in the warmer areas of the world, in habitats ranging from deserts to jungles and houses. The geckos lay small numbers of brittle-shelled eggs. The tokay gecko (*Gekko gecko*, illustrated here), of South-East Asia, is the largest species; it can attain 35 cm (14 in) in length. *Gonatodes albogularis* of Central America, illustrated here, has a yellow head and a blackish body. *Tarentola mauritanica*, whose distribution is shown in the map below, is a south European and north African

Pygopodidae. The Pygopodidae are lizards in which there only remain small vestiges of the rear legs. They live underground in soil and under rocks. The group is found only in Australia. In the legless lizards, genus *Pygopus*, the limbs have almost completely

disappeared, as in *P. lepidopodus*, illustrated here. *P. nigriceps* resembles a snake and for defence often imitates their behaviour.

Xanthusidae. The xanthusidae, night lizards, are nocturnal reptiles, mostly living on insects. Among them is *Cricosaura typica*, which is one of the rarest animals in the world, living only in a small area of south-west Cuba, and *Klauberina riversiana* of California, illustrated here, which lives on flowers and fruit.

Anelytropsidae. The only known member of this group is *Anelytropsis papillosus* of central and eastern Mexico. It is very rare and only a few specimens have been found. It is worm-like in appearance and blind.

Dibamidae. The Dibamidae are a group of blind, earless and limbless lizards, snake-like, with short tails, the head being indistinguishable from the neck. Three species are known, belonging to the genus *Dibames*: *D. novaeguineae* of South-East Asia, illustrated on p. 155, lives in the damp earth of forests.

Iguanidae. The Iguanidae, iguanas, live in America and Madagascar, the Agamidae in Africa, Asia and Australia. There are many cases among the iguanas of similar adaptation to similar habitats and consequently of similar behaviour, causing them to resemble members of the Agamidae found in Africa, Asia and Australia.

The Iguanidae include the Sceloporinae of Northern and Central America, which are ground-dwellers and insect-eaters living at altitudes up to 4000 m (13,000 ft). Typical representatives are the fence lizards, members of the genus *Sceloporus*, with 300 species. The horned toads (*Phrynosoma*) have dagger-like horns, and mostly eat ants. Living in sandy desert country in western North America and Central America, they conceal themselves by wriggling sideways until the whole body except the head is covered with sand. When grasped by a predator, they jerk their head violently, jabbing their sharp spines into their attacker. *Tropidurus* species occupy the same niche in South America as *Sceleropus* in North America; they are very agile, so much so as to be able to capture the prey in flight.

The true iguanas are distributed throughout the warmer regions of the Americas. Among them is the green iguana (*Iguana iguana*, illustrated here) which can reach 2 m (6½ ft) in length. They are

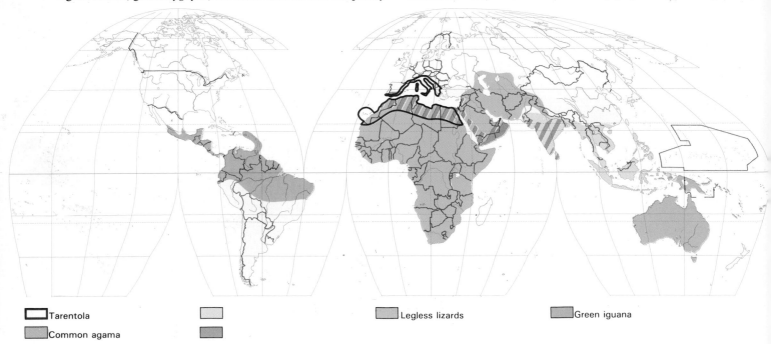

Tarentola
Common agama
Legless lizards
Green iguana

green iguana

Meller's chameleon

Fischer's chameleon

water dragon

legless lizard
Pygopus sp.

tokay gecko

night lizard
Klauberina riversiana

Gonatodes albogularis

common agama

thick-tongued tree-dwellers. The two genera *Conolophus* and *Amblyrhynchus* live on the Galápagos Islands, the former being terrestrial, the latter marine and feeds on seaweed. The most curious member of the Iguanidae is perhaps the basilisk (*Basiliscus basiliscus*) living in trees near rivers and streams in the tropical regions of the Americas. The body is laterally compressed, the tail whip-like, and the rear of the head extended into a lobe like a cock's comb. Basilisks can run across the surface of the water on their hind legs, the body being held almost upright.

The Anolinae are an important group containing twenty-two genera. They live in the warm regions of the Americas, in particular in the West Indies. As in the geckos, the fingers and toes have enlarged pads covered with minute hooks, and they are able to climb smooth surfaces with great agility. They can change colour from brown to green and yellow, and are sometimes mistaken for chameleons. Many have elaborate colour patterns used for aggressive and sexual displays.

Agamidae. More than 300 species belong to the Agamidae. Some are adapted to an arboreal life. The flying lizard (*Draco volans*) of southern India and South-East Asia, is an outstanding example of this, possessing a scaly membrane along its flanks that permits it to glide from tree to tree. A watery habitat is preferred by other species such as those of the water dragons (*Hydrosaurus*) of the Philippines, Celebes and New Guinea, including *H. amboiensis*, illustrated on p. 153. The genus *Agama* is present in Africa and Asia, the common agama (*A. agama*) being numerous in Africa. *Agama stellione* lives in the Mediterranean region.

Chamaeleontidae. The eighty-five species of Chamaeleontidae, chameleons, are well known for their ability to change the colour of their bodies, either to blend with the background or to display their state of mind. Very well adapted to an arboreal life, they have feet like pincers, a prehensile tail, and eyes that function independently, each one capable of performing a complete rotation. About half the species are found only in Madagascar, most of the others in Africa south of the Sahara. One is found in southern India, and another in western Asia, north Africa and southern Europe. This last is the common chameleon (*Chamaeleo chamaeleo*). In the males the head is often helmet-shaped. Meller's chameleon and Fischer's chameleon are illustrated on p. 153.

Scincidae. The Scincidae, skinks, are mostly found in tropical regions but some occur in temperate regions of North America. The greatest number are in South-East Asia. There is a marked tendency in some groups towards the reduction of the limbs and the assumption of a snake-like appearance. Most are very smooth and often shiny. They are generally under 20 cm (8 in) long, though a few may attain 66 cm (26 in). Some are aquatic or live in trees but the majority live close to the ground, sometimes in burrows. They mostly live on insects and other invertebrates, though some larger species are herbivorous. They may lay eggs or give birth to live young.

The Australian stump-tailed lizard (*Tiliqua rugosa*, illustrated here) has a squat body covered with thick shiny scales. Its tail is of similar mass to its head, potentially confusing to a predator unsure which end is which. *Scincus scincus*, also illustrated here, is one of the sand-skinks of the genus *Scincus*, adapted to an arid environment. The keeled skinks (*Tropidophorus*), mabuyas (*Mabuya*), prehensile-tailed skinks (*Corucia zebrata*), slender skinks (*Lygosoma*) and snake-eyed skinks (*Ablepharus*) are other widespread species.

Feylinidae. The Feylinidae comprise only one genus with four species all lacking feet, the most important being *Feylinia currori*, illustrated here, of tropical Africa.

Cordylidae. The Cordylidae, girdle-tailed lizards, are found in southern Africa and Madagascar. They include the armadillo lizard (*Cordylus cataphractus*) which, when threatened, rolls into a ball by taking its tail into its mouth. It has hard, bony scales and spines on the head. Strong, pointed scales are characteristic of this group, as is shown in the illustration of the spiny lizard (*Cordyles gigantus* of South Africa.

Lacertidae. The Lacertidae group contains about 170 species of typical lizards including most of the European species. The genus *Lacerta* have well-developed limbs and a deeply notched tongue; they include the sand lizard (*Lacerta agilis*, illustrated here), the green lizard (*L. viridis*) and the common lizard (*L. vivipara*) whose distribution extends north to the Arctic Circle; the world's most northerly reptile. Species of the genus *Podarcis* include the European wall lizard (*P. muralis*); *P. sicula* is illustrated here.

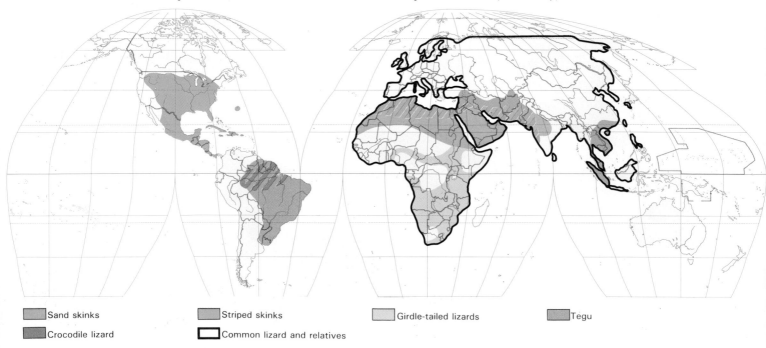

Sand skinks   Striped skinks   Girdle-tailed lizards   Tegu

Crocodile lizard   Common lizard and relatives

Chilean cave lizard

Australian stump-tailed lizard

sand lizard

legless skink
Feylinia currori

tegu lizard

Podarcis sicula

Dibamus novaeguineae

sand skink

spiny lizard

Teiidae. The Teiidae lizards, found in the Americas from the USA to Argentina, are very similar in appearance to the Lacertidae. The genus *Tupinambis* includes four species living in forests including the tegu or teguexin of South America (*T. teguixin*, illustrated on p. 155), which is considered a delicacy, and *T. nigropunctatus*. The crocodile lizard (*Crocodilurus lacertinus*) lives in water. A lizard that lives underground is the Chilean cave lizard (*Callopistes maculatus*, illustrated on p. 155).

Anguidae. The Anguinomorphae groups together species which only on close examination can be shown to be related. There are six families, Anguidae, Anniellidae, Xenosauridae, Varanidae, Helodermatidae and Lanthanotidae.

The family Anguidae include eight genera with sixty species divided into Anguinae and Gerrhotinae. Among the former is the slowworm (*Anguis fragilis*, illustrated here), also called the blindworm, living in grasslands and woodlands throughout Europe. It usually does not exceed 30 cm (1 ft) in length. Though often mistaken for a brown snake, its ability to shed its tail when attacked confirms that it is in fact a legless lizard. Closer inspection reveals that it also has eyelids: snakes do not. The genus *Diploglossus* contains about twenty species living in the Antilles, among them *D. tenuifasciatus*. In the Gerrhotinae there are notable differences between one genus and another; *Abronia* species are arboreal with well-developed claws and prehensile tails; the grass snakes (*Ophisaurus* species) are legless lizards. The Gerrhosus lizard (*Gerrhosus coeruleus*) is ovoviviparous, producing eggs hatched out in the parent's body.

Anniellidae. These are burrowing lizards all of the genus *Anniella*: *A. pulchra*, illustrated here, and *A. geronimensis* of California. The eyes and limbs are much reduced, and the body snake-like.

Xenosauridae. The Xenosauridae comprise *Xenosaurus grandis* of Mexico and Guatemala, and another Chinese species.

Varanidae. The Varanidae, monitor lizards, comprise only one genus, *Varanus*, characterized by a small head and great mobility of the neck. About twenty species are known, living in Africa, Asia and Australia. The Nile monitor (*Varanus niloticus*) and the perenty (*V. giganteus*) which grows to 2 m (6½ ft), are African species. The former is a voracious carnivore and regularly eats crocodile babies and eggs. The bright green *V. prasinus*, illustrated here, is from New Guinea and Sonda. The Komodo dragon (*Varanus komodoensis*, also illustrated) of Indonesia is the largest of all lizards, attaining lengths of more than 3 m (10 ft).

Helodermatidae. The Helodermatidae comprise the only two species of venomous lizards. One, the Gila monster (*Heloderma suspectus*), lives in the south-western USA and northern Mexico. It grows to about 50 cm (20 in) long. The Mexican beaded lizard (*H. horridum*, illustrated here) grows to about 80 cm (30 in). Like the Gila monster, it is sluggish but has a strong bite; both live on small mammals and birds and their eggs. Their poison is rarely fatal to human beings.

Lanthanotidae. The sole representative of the Lanthanotidae is the earless lizard of Borneo (*Lanthanotus bornensis*, illustrated here) which is rare and was discovered in 1878. It grows to 40 cm (16 in).

Amphisbaenidae. The Amphisbaenidae are a family of burrowing reptiles, snake-like, with a small head and very small eyes and a body covered with tiny, smooth scales. Apart from the Mexican genus *Bipes*, all are limbless. Two species live in Europe. *Amphisbaena alba*, the giant of the group, 60 cm (24 in) long, lives on the eastern slopes of the Andes. Illustrated here are *Trogonophis wiegmanni* of north-west Africa and *Agamodon anguliceps* of Ethiopia and Somalia.

Ophidia or Serpentes

The Ophidia or Serpentes, snakes, are found almost all over the world. The body is cylindrical, elongated, lacks limbs apart from a few very rare exceptions, and is covered with scales. Like the lizards, the surface coating of the scales is periodically moulted (sloughed). Most live on the ground, a few burrow in soil; many are arboreal and a few strictly aquatic.

The use of poison is of primary importance in the capture of food in some species, and its use in defence is only secondary.

Typhlopidae. The Typhlopidae and Leptotyphlopidae, blind snakes, are burrowing reptiles; their eyes are atrophied and the

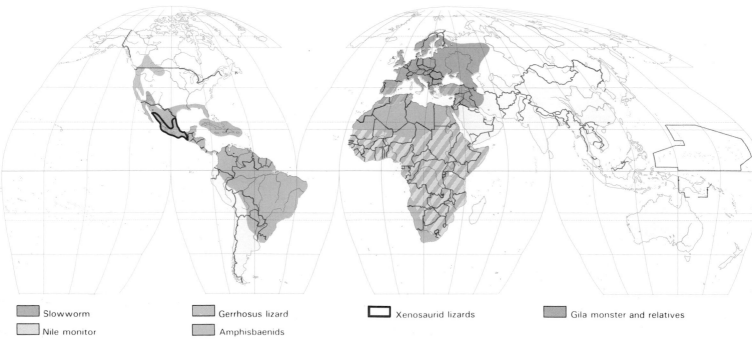

Slowworm	Gerrhosus lizard	Xenosaurid lizards	Gila monster and relatives
Nile monitor	Amphisbaenids		

green monitor

Mexican
bearded
lizard

*Diploglossus
tenuifasciatus*

komodo dragon

Borneo earless lizard

Xenosaurus grandis

slowworm (blindworm)

amphisbaenid
Agamodon anguliceps

burrowing lizard

amphisbaenid
Trogonophis wiegmanni

head is almost indistinguishable from the tail. They live in most tropical regions and feed on small invertebrates, mainly ants and termites. *Typhlops vermicularis* of Greece, sometimes called the worm snake, illustrated here, is the only European species; it can be found in soft earth with plenty of vegetation. As its name implies, it is worm-like in appearance.

The Leptotyphlopidae, thread snakes, or slender blind snakes, are superficially similar in appearance to the Typhlopidae, but are of different descent. They are 10–50 cm (4–20 in) long and live in Africa and America. *Leptotyphlops humilis* of America, illustrated here, is a typical representative of the group. A West African species is *Rhinoleptus koniagui*. Thread snakes feed on insect larvae, and some lay their eggs in termite nests, ensuring a food supply and a protective environment for the young.

Aniliidae. This and the next four families are grouped together as a superfamily, the Booidea. They often show vestiges of a pelvic girdle and residues of associated limb bones such as femurs, which may even be visible on the exterior as small appendages.

The Aniliidae are primitive forms with reduced eyes, a cylindrical body and a short head almost indistinguishable from the tail. They are burrowing snakes, and, like all the snakes, are predators. They possess poison glands but since the teeth are not grooved the poison cannot be injected.

Three genera are known, *Cilindrophis*, the pipe snake, with seven species, which live in the rice paddies of South-East Asia; *Anomalochilus*, with a single species *A. weberi* of Sumatra and Malaysia; and *Anilius*, the false coral snakes of South America. Some species are ringed with red, black and yellow or with red and black, as in *A. scytale*, illustrated here.

Uropeltidae. The Uropeltidae, shield-tail snakes, are also burrowing snakes, found in India and Sri Lanka. The group is characterized by a modification of the tail; in more primitive forms it ended as a cone, but then became flattened and finally was ornamented with spines and crests. In *Uropeltis ocellatus* the end part is flattened and covered with scales that form a spiny shield used to stop up the entrance to the den.

Xenopeltidae. The sunbeam snake (*Xenopeltis unicolor*, illustrated here) of southern India and South-East Asia is the only known species of the Xenopeltidae. It is 1 m (3¼ ft) long and lives on small mammals, amphibia and other reptiles.

Acrochordidae. The Acrochordidae, wart snakes, comprise two Asian genera, *Acrochordus* and *Chersydrus*, both aquatic. They do not leave the water even in order to lay their eggs, having become ovoviviparous, hatching out the eggs internally. *Acrochordus javanicus* of Java (illustrated here) like the other wart snakes hunts fish and for this reason has modified its teeth into long fangs.

Boidae. The Boidae – pythons, boas and wood snakes – have small eyes, the pupils elliptical and vertical, and small nostrils. Under the nostrils are two sensitive grooves which function by 'reading' the temperature of the surroundings making it possible for the snake to detect and intercept warm-blooded prey.

The subfamily Loxoceminae has only one species, the dwarf python (*Loxocemus bicolor*) of southern Mexico and northern Central America.

The Pythoninae, pythons, live in the Old World from Africa to the Philippines, and in Australia. The genus *Python*, which is the most representative and rich in species, is found in Africa and Asia. The females curl round their eggs to protect them. Unlike most reptiles, they also generate heat within their body to help speed the incubation of the eggs. The reticulated python (*P. reticulatus*) of South-East Asia can attain lengths of 8 m (26 ft). Good swimmers, at times they take to the sea; reticulated pythons were among the animals who plunged into the sea to escape when the island of Krakatoa was destroyed by the eruption of its volcano. The Indian python (*P. molurus*, illustrated here) is smaller; African species include the rock python (*P. sebae*) which reaches a length of 7 m (23 ft), and the royal or ball python (*P. regius*) which curls itself into a tight ball with its head inside and can be rolled along the ground in this position. Pythons wrap around their prey and crush it; tackling animals as big as pig and antelope. Such a meal may take several months to digest, during which time the snake rests and sleeps. Other genera are *Morelia* and *Liasis* of Australia, New Guinea and Indonesia.

The Boinae (boas) live in the Americas and in Madagascar. They have a stout body and rather a short tail. Many have a green, brown or yellow body with patterns of diamonds or blotches. The young are mostly born alive rather than as eggs. These snakes kill

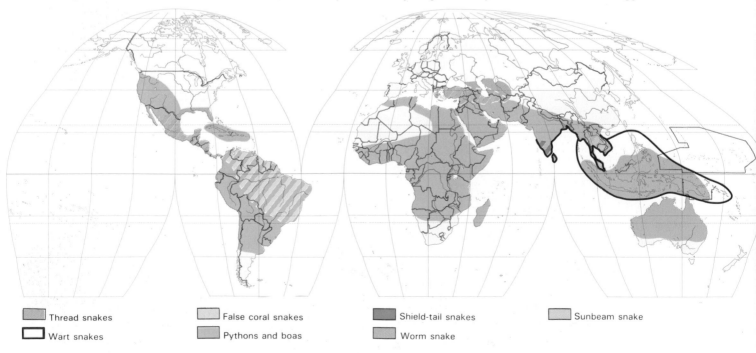

Thread snakes   False coral snakes   Shield-tail snakes   Sunbeam snake

Wart snakes   Pythons and boas   Worm snake

South American
green tree boa

slender blind snake
(thread snake)

boa constrictor

blind worm snake

wart snake

Indian python

false coral snake

anaconda

sunbeam snake

their prey by squeezing; they have no poison fangs though the prey is often bitten first. Despite their reputation, they are not dangerous to man. They differ from the pythons in having the thermally sensitive receptors situated between the labial scales rather than in one of them. Snakes of the genus *Boa* are tree-dwellers and have long teeth for catching birds.

The South American green tree boa (*Boa canina*, illustrated on p. 159) has a body colouring that perfectly matches its background. The boa constrictor (*Constrictor constrictor*, illustrated on p. 159) lives from Mexico to Argentina, and can attain 5 m (16 ft) in length. The anaconda (*Eunectes murinus*, illustrated on p. 159) can be up to 6 m (20 ft) long. It is typically dark green with black markings, and lives in the river basins of the Orinoco and Amazon, where it lies by night in the water waiting for prey such as pigs to come down to drink. Occasionally it hunts birds in the trees.

Colubridae. The superfamily Colubroidea, containing the majority of the snakes, includes three families that are very different in some ways but have in common the development of progressively more efficient poison fangs and glands. The poisonous forms belonging to the family Colubridae have grooved teeth set at the rear of the jaws and are often called back fanged snakes (opisthoglyphs). The Elapidae (cobras, kraits, mambas and coral snakes) have a channelled fang in the front part of the jaw; the Viperidae (vipers, rattlesnakes and moccasins) have the channel for poison running inside each fang of the upper jaw.

The Colubridae are found all over the world except in polar regions and in Australia. There are about 250 genera and 2500 species. The burrowing species have a thickset body, a short tail and reduced eyes; arboreal species are slender and agile, with a long tail and good eyesight; aquatic species show in certain cases a movement of the nostrils from the front to the upper part of the head. Some Colubrids have an extremely specialized diet: for example, the Pareinae eat only snails, and so have developed mandibles adapted to dealing with the shell. The Pareinae are Asian species; the Dipsadinae, similarly specialized in snail-eating, are American. The Calamarinae, reed snakes, of South-East Asia, have a cylindrical body, small eyes, and head indistinguishable from the body, giving a worm-like appearance. They eat insects and worms. Among them is *Calamaria smithii* of Borneo, 10 cm (4 in) long, and one of the smallest living snakes.

Snakes of the genus *Dasypeltis* are egg-eating and primarily arboreal. Their teeth are much reduced and peg-like. The mouth can be enormously distended so that the egg – sometimes as large as a chicken's egg and much wider than the snake's head – can be taken in. It is swallowed or rather engulfed with some difficulty and then broken by spines extending from the vertebrae into the oesophagus. The fragments of shell are first taken into the stomach with the rest and later regurgitated. An egg-eating snake is illustrated here. Of the two genera one, *Dasypeltis*, lives in Africa, the other, *Elachistodon*, in north-eastern India.

The Homalopsines are very specialized back-fanged snakes. They do not have storage glands for the poison, which means that the amount they have for use is always small. The poison is neurotoxic, affecting the heart and lungs of the victim, and can sometimes be dangerous even to man. Some forms are aquatic, others arboreal. *Homalopsis buccata*, which looks like a boa, is nocturnal and catches fish and amphibians along the banks of ponds and rice-paddies in South-East Asia, the East Indies and Australia. The tentacled snake (*Herpeton tentaculatum*, illustrated here) is strictly aquatic and prefers the brackish waters, rich in vegetation, of Asia. In these last two species the nostrils are situated on the hinder part of the snout. The mangrove snake (*Boiga dendrophila*, illustrated here) lives in Malaysia and neighbouring islands, where it hunts birds, mammals and reptiles. It can exceed 2 m (6½ ft) in length and produces a great quantity of poison. *Thelotornis kirtlandii*, *Dryopsis nasuta* and *Chrysopela ornata* are among those species of the Homalopsinae that are adapted to arboreal life. The boomslang (*Dispholidus typus*, illustrated here) is found in tropical Africa; adapted to life in the trees, it is slender and very agile. A back-fanged snake, it has three fangs on each side and its poison must be considered more dangerous to man, than that of any of the other Colubridae. It waits, perfectly immobile and very well camouflaged, in trees for chameleons and birds. The cat snakes, genus *Telescopus*, of Africa and South-West Asia, are nocturnal and their eyes have vertical pupils, like a cat's; they mostly hunt lizards. One species, *T. fallax*, illustrated here, is found in southern Europe. The Montpellier snake or lizard snake (*Malpolon monspessulana*) is also found in southern Europe as well as in Asia Minor; it is back-fanged and lives on lizards, snakes and small mammals.

The water snakes, of the genus *Natrix*, include the common grass snake (*N. natrix*) of Britain and western Europe, north Africa and western Asia, usually less than 1 m (39 in) long, a non-poisonous snake. It lives largely on frogs, newts, toads and small mammals, but it will also enter streams in search of tadpoles and fish. Females often seek out heaps of manure and rotting vegetation in which to lay their eggs. The heat of decomposition helps to speed their development. The *Thamnophis* genus, the garter snakes, are the commonest snakes of North America; the ribbon snake, *T. sauritus*, of this genus, is illustrated here. The Colubrinae, an important group, include the king snakes of North America (*Lampropeltis getulus*, illustrated here), which imitate the ornamentation of the coral snakes (Elapidae) in order to discourage predators. They themselves eat other snakes, including poisonous ones, to whose venom they are mostly immune, killing them by constriction. They are terrestrial and rather slow-moving. The genus *Coluber* includes the horseshoe snake (*C. hippocrepis*, illustrated here). Rather similar in appearance to *Coluber* species are the rat snakes or chicken snakes of the genus *Elaphe*, which often live around farm buildings, eating rats, mice and sometimes birds, which they kill by constriction. The corn snake (*E. guttata*, illustrated here) is one of the commonest snakes in the central and southern states of North America. It is largely nocturnal and frequently found beside roads.

Elapidae. The Elapidae – cobras, mambas, kraits and coral snakes – are found all over the world except in Europe. There are two sub-families, Elapinae and Hydrophiinae. The Elapinae are abundant in Asia, Africa and Central and South America. They are usually of small or medium size but some species are veritable giants. The only species living an aquatic life is the African *Boulengerina annulata*. The king cobra (*Ophisphagus hannah*) is the world's largest poisonous snake often over 4 m (13 ft) long; at least two specimens over 5.5 m (18 ft) have been recorded, but in general the true cobras do not exceed 1.5 m (5 ft).

Characteristic of the cobras is the expansion of the neck ribs to form a hood. The Indian cobra (*Naja naja*, illustrated on p. 163) has designs on its hood resembling a pair of spectacles. The common or Egyptian cobra (*Naja haje*) is found in much of Africa and also in Arabia. It is probably the snake once known as the asp. Cobras have a short, hollow poison fang in the front part of the upper jaw. In some species the opening of the fang faces forwards so that the cobra can actually spit poison at anything that disturbs it. The fine

boomslang

tentacled snake

corn snake

mangrove snake

ribbon snake

egg-eating snake
Dasypeltis sp.

horseshoe snake

king snake

cat snake

spray of poison can blind an attacker at a range of up to 2 m (6 ft) and it may be many days before sight is regained, if at all. This is the case with the black-necked cobra (*Naja nigricollis*) and the ringhals or spitting cobra (*Hemachatus hemachatus*) both of northern and central Africa.

The mambas, of the genus *Dendroaspis*, are very agile arboreal snakes of Africa, noted for their highly dangerous bite. The black mamba (*D. polylepis*) can be up to 4 m (13 ft) long; its bite is nearly always fatal unless snakebite serum is immediately available. The green mamba (*D. angusticeps*) is smaller and less aggressive. The coral snakes are the only representatives of the Elapinae in the New World. The eastern coral snake or harlequin snake (*Micrurus fulvius*, illustrated here) banded in red, yellow and black, is a nocturnal burrowing snake of the south-eastern USA. Similar snakes, the false coral snakes, occur in Africa and other parts of the Old World; a South-East Asian species, the krait (*Bungarus flaviceps*) is illustrated here. Kraits are unaggressive but highly poisonous, so that the rare victims of their bite have only a 50 per cent chance of survival even if serum is available. In Australia the Elapidae include primitive forms such as the death adder (*Acanthophis antarcticus*, illustrated here) which is extremely poisonous.

The Hydrophiinae, are sea snakes mostly found off the coasts of South-East Asia. They are highly specialized fish-eaters. Many species are known; some are ovoviviparous and never leave the sea, others are oviparous and come to land to lay their eggs. The common sea snake (*Laticauda laticaudata*, illustrated here) is among the least well adapted to aquatic life and always stays near land. The yellow-bellied sea snake (*Pelamis platurus*), on the other hand, is at home in the open sea and is found widely distributed in the Pacific and Indian Oceans.

Viperidae. The Viperidae – vipers, rattlesnakes and moccasins – are the most highly evolved of the snakes; in them the poisonous apparatus is brought to its highest efficiency. There are two groups, the Viperinae of the Palearctic and African regions, and Crotalinae, which are almost exclusively of the New World. Vipers possess two long, hollow fangs for the injection of venom. They are attached to the upper jaw, and can be folded back in the mouth when not in use. Some of the Viperinae are tree-dwellers, like the African tree vipers of the genus *Atheris*, which are slender and have a prehensile tail. Most, however, are ground dwellers,

fairly stout, and slow in their movements. Characteristically there is a narrow neck and the head is thus quite distinct from the body. The tail is short and thick. The genus *Bitis*, also of Africa, includes the puff adder (*B. arietans*) which announces its presence by inflating its body and hissing loudly, the Gaboon viper (*B. gabonicus*, illustrated here), which can be up to 1.5 m (5 ft) in length, and the rhinoceros viper (*B. nasicornis*). They are all heavy snakes which lie in wait to ambush unwary animals that pass by. They are well camouflaged and easily escape notice despite their considerable size. Some vipers have chosen a desert habitat, like the members of the genus *Cerastes*, which include the common or Sahara sand viper (*C. cerastes*) and the horned viper (*C. cornutus*), which has a spine-like scale above each eye. Another desert-dweller is the highly venomous saw-scaled viper (*Echis carinatus*). The genus *Vipera* includes the common adder (*V. berus*) widespread in Britain, Europe and Asia, and found even north of the Arctic Circle, in Norway.

The Crotalinae are distinguished from the Viperinae by the presence of thermally sensitive pits between each nostril and eye, that enable them to detect warm-blooded prey, similar to those of the Boidae; they are often referred to as pit vipers for this reason. They are almost exclusively American, though a few are found in Asia. Several of the Crotalinae possess rattles on the tail, derived from modified scales. The most important genus of Crotalinae, numerically, is *Bothrops*, with forty-eight species, the best known being the fer-de-lance or lancehead of tropical America (*B. atrox*, illustrated here), 1.8 m (6 ft) long, whose bite can be fatal to human beings. The bushmaster (*Lachesis muta*) is the longest of the hollow-toothed snakes (solenoglyphs), sometimes attaining lengths of 3.5 m (12 ft) with fangs 4 cm (1.5 in) long. Among the Crotalinae furnished with rattles the most important genus is *Crotalus* with some 25 species, among them the very poisonous Mexican west coast rattlesnake (*C. basiliscus*, illustrated here). The timber or banded rattlesnake (*C. horridus*) of the eastern and southern USA and the prairie rattlesnake (*C. viridis*) of the western state are well known. The only South American representative is the cascavel (*C. durissus*), probably the most poisonous of the group. The sidewinder or horned rattlesnake (*C. cerastes*, illustrated here) strongly resembles the African sand viper (*Cerastes cerastes*). The moccasins are American aquatic snakes of the genus *Agkistrodon*.

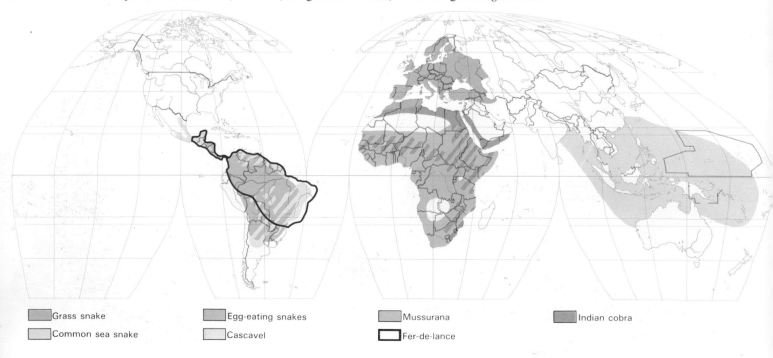

Grass snake   Egg-eating snakes   Mussurana   Indian cobra

Common sea snake   Cascavel   Fer-de-lance

Gaboon viper

Mexican west coast rattlesnake

common sea snake

krait

sidewinder

death adder

fer-de-lance

Indian or spectacled cobra

eastern coral snake

Crocodilia

The group known as Archosauria – crocodiles, alligators, dinosaurs and pterodactyls – underwent their major developments during the 'age of reptiles', when the reptiles dominated the Earth and the birds and mammals were only just beginning to evolve. Most are known only as fossils now, but the crocodiles and alligators survive, and form the Crocodilia. They appear at first glance to resemble somewhat clumsy and indolent lizards of considerable dimensions, that range from little more than 1 m (39 in) in the smooth-fronted caiman (*Paleosuchus trigonatus*), of South America, to the 10 m (32 ft) of the estuarine crocodiles.

The body, somewhat flattened, is covered with horny plates reinforced with flat bones. Along the tail, which is compressed from side to side, there may be ridges and knobs or lumps. The legs are short and massive. The lungs are highly developed and are capable of storing up an enormous stock of air, necessary for long periods without breathing. The heart is unique among the reptiles in being divided into four chambers, so that the venous and arterial blood are kept separate.

Extremely able swimmers, they seem awkward and uncomfortable on land. Their habitat is water, and for this reason the hindfeet, and often the forefeet also, are webbed, serving to maintain control of direction when swimming; the propulsion is effected by the tail, richly endowed with powerful muscles. The sense organs are placed high up on the head, so that the reptile can make full use of them while remaining almost completely submerged; eardrums, eyes and nostrils remain above the surface of the water. The eardrum is protected by a fold of skin; the olfactory organ can be isolated by suitable valves; the eyes possess a nictitating (winking) membrane, moving at right angles to the eyelids, which covers them during immersion.

The adults are highly skilful predators and they will eat every kind of animal, even large ones, that approach the water. The young feed first on insects, later on fish and gradually progress to larger and larger prey. Crocodiles are present in America, Africa, Asia and Australia and are divided into two families, Gavialidae and Crocodilidae.

Gavialidae. The Gavialidae comprise a single species, the gavial or gharial of the Ganges (*Gavialis gangeticus*, illustrated here), which lives in the rivers of northern India including the Ganges, Brahmaputra and Indus. It has a long, very slender snout, jaws with numerous sharp teeth, weak legs and a crested tail, and can reach lengths of 6 m (19 ft). It is the crocodile best adapted to an aquatic life. It catches fish and amphibians by sideways blows of its jaw, afterwards forcing them down its throat. The female leaves the water to deposit eggs numbering about forty in a nest in the sand. The gavial does not normally attack human beings but has been known to do so, possibly after feeding on corpses floating down the Ganges after funeral ceremonies.

Crocodilidae. The Crocodilidae have shorter snouts than the Gavialidae, the legs are more massive and the body much heavier. There are two subfamilies, Crocodilinae and Alligatorinae, distinguishable by their teeth; in the crocodiles some large teeth in the forward part of the mouth are always visible with the mouth closed. Usually the fourth tooth in each lower jaw can be seen projecting in a crocodile; in the alligator these teeth fit into sockets in the upper jaw when the mouth is closed, and so cannot be seen. There are other general differences in body shape and appearance but these are not consistent enough for reliably distinguishing the two groups.

The Crocodilinae live in Asia, Africa, Australia and America. They comprise the three genera *Crocodilus*, *Osteolaemus* and *Tomistoma*. *Crocodilus acutus*, the American crocodile of North, Central and northern South America, is nocturnal in habit and can reach 7 m (23 ft) in length. The male defends its territory, warning approaching intruders by bellowing and beating the surface of the water. Courtship is usually initiated by the female, who approaches the male maintaining a submissive posture in order to avoid attack. After mating, which occurs in the water, the female prepares a nest on the land where she deposits twenty to sixty eggs which are incubated for three months. The nest is watched over by the mother, who makes it her business to keep away all possible predators, which include monitor lizards. When the female senses that the birth of the young is imminent she digs out the nest and collects the young, carrying them carefully to the river in her mouth. In their early stages the young are vulnerable and fall prey to many animals, so that the mother has to be constantly on her guard to protect them and she frequently collects and shelters them in her mouth.

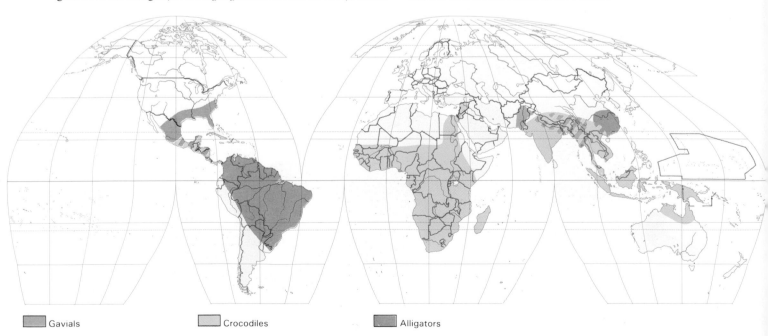

Gavials   Crocodiles   Alligators

Ganges gavial

false gavial

Nile crocodile

dwarf crocodile

Crocodilus cataphractus has a long snout and in some ways resembles the gavial. It lives in African rivers where it hunts fish, catching them often in the hollows of the river banks with the aid of its slender snout. The biggest existing crocodile is the estuarine crocodile (*C. porosus*, illustrated here) – the average size of a male is 4.5 m (14 ft), but there have been reports of individuals measuring twice this size – making them the largest of all reptiles. It lives in the mouths of rivers, whose course it ascends from time to time to hunt, and along the coasts, from which it often travels outwards so that it is quite often seen in the open sea. It is found along the Australian coast, in the Solomon Islands and Fiji, and along the coasts of China, India and Sri Lanka. It preys on animals that come down to the water to drink, and has been known to attack people. The Nile crocodile (*C. niloticus*, illustrated on p. 165) is now extremely localized through the ruthless way in which it has been hunted by man, though at one time it was common from Madagascar to the whole of equatorial Africa. Like the estuarine crocodile, it has a bad reputation for its attacks on people. The Orinoco crocodile (*C. intermedius*) lives in the Orinoco and Amazon river basins. *C. johnsoni* is a species of northern Australia; *C. moreletii* lives in Mexico, Honduras and Guatemala. The mugger, or marsh crocodile (*C. palustris*), lives in India and Sri Lanka; it is a freshwater species and is broad-snouted. It is regarded as sacred in some localities – these crocodiles are kept in tanks and attended by priests. Other species of *Crocodilus* inhabit waterways of Cuba and New Guinea.

The dwarf crocodile (*Osteolaemus tetraspis*, illustrated on p. 165) of West Africa attains a length of only 1.5 m (5 ft). It is not much at home in the water, preferring the African forests, and has a broad, short snout. It is the only representative of its genus. The false gavial (*Tomistoma schlegelii*, illustrated on p. 165) of South-East Asia is reminiscent of the gavial because of its long and slender snout. It lives on fish and attains 4.5 m (14 ft) in length.

The Alligatorinae group contains four genera with six New World and one Asian species. They have broader snouts than the Crocodilinae. The genus *Alligator* includes the Mississippi alligator (*A. mississippiensis*, illustrated here) which can attain over 5 m (16 ft) in length. It was formerly very common but was ruthlessly hunted for its hide and its young sold as pets. It became very scarce in many of its haunts and is now locally protected in certain small areas. As a result of continued protection, alligators have once again become common in parts of Florida and the southern states where they are something of a nuisance and a potential source of danger. Studies have shown that these reptiles have complex social behaviour patterns with established hierarchies within the groups.

Others of the Alligatorinae are the spectacled caiman (*Caiman sclerops*, illustrated here), which has a bony ridge between the eyes resembling the nosepiece of a pair of glasses; and the broad-snouted caiman (*C. latirostris*) both of Central America and the tropical regions of South America. The South American black caiman (*Melanosuchus niger*, illustrated here), the largest and most dangerous of the caimans, can attain a length of about 4.5 m (15 ft). It is notable for its ability to make rapid changes in its own body colour.

The genus *Paleosuchus*, the smooth-fronted caimans, comprises two species, *P. trigonatus*, already mentioned, and *P. palpebrosus*, illustrated here, which can reach 1.4 m (5 ft) in length. These species lack the bony ridge of the spectacled caiman, and live in the swift, rocky streams of the Amazon region, living on fish, birds, insects and other animals.

The estuarine crocodile, the giant of the group, is found along Asian coasts from India to China. It does not hesitate to attack humans, looking on them as fair game, the same as any other prey.

black caiman

Mississippi alligator

smooth-fronted caiman

spectacled caiman

BIRDS

The birds (Aves) are a group of warm-blooded (homeothermic) animals whose origins can be traced to the reptiles, more precisely to the dinosaurs. According to some zoologists they are, in fact, the dinosaurs of the present day, though much modified of course, particularly in respect of their outward appearance. Their principal characteristic is the presence of plumes or feathers forming a covering for the body. The feathers are in reality scales of the reptilian type that have been expanded and lightened in order to conserve body heat. The most important adaptation achieved by the group is still, however, the transformation of the forelimbs into wings covered with long feathers which can sustain the animal in flight. The pectoral muscles that lower the wings during flight, providing lift, are exceedingly well developed and are attached to a flange-like extension of the breastbone (sternum) called the keel. The rear limbs are generally covered with scales (betraying the group's reptilian ancestry) and bear claws that are used for gripping, hunting, feeding and perching.

The birds have occupied every region of the planet, succeeding in adapting themselves to the most disparate climates, from the frozen wastes of the Antarctic to the scorching heat of the desert, and even, in some cases, the great oceans.

Some groups have lost the ability to fly and have become swift runners. Others again are principally swimmers. A great number however have perfected the art of flight so far as to achieve an extraordinary power of manoeuvre and great speeds.

The group sometimes called the Ratites comprises the running birds that have lost the power of flight and have a flat, keel-less breastbone. Four kinds survive today, Struthioniformes (ostriches), Rheiformes (rheas), Casuariiformes (cassowaries and emus) and Apterygiformes (kiwis). With these may be grouped the Tinamiformes (tinamous), which, though they have keeled breastbones, are otherwise very similar to the Rheiformes. Ratites do not have flight feathers of course and those that cover the wings and body are soft and shaggy. They are quite unlike the flat feathers of normal birds in which the feather barbs are interlocked to form a fairly stiff structure.

Struthioniformes

The Struthioniformes consist now of only one family, the Struthionidae, with one species, the ostrich (*Struthio camelus*, illustrated here). This is the giant of the whole group of flightless birds, since the extinction three centuries ago by human hunters of the moa (*Dinornis maximus*) of New Zealand, which reached 3 m (9½ ft) in height and weighed up to 250 kg (550 lb). The male ostrich attains 2.5 m (8 ft) in height and may weigh 130 kg (285 lb), while the female is about a third smaller. The male's plumage is black with white wings and tail, and his legs and neck are bare. The female's plumage is greyish brown, the neck being thinly covered with down.

The four extant sub-species of ostrich live in Africa. All live in similar habitats: arid regions, sandy deserts, savannah, and woodlands that are dry even if thickly wooded. The diet is very varied, with a preference for vegetation and small animals. Stones are also swallowed to aid in the grinding up of the food in the gizzard. Among the enemies of the ostrich are hyenas and lions, which attack the young, although these fierce predators are wary of an encounter with the parent birds. The eggs, weighing 1.5 kg (3.3 lb), are the largest laid by any living bird and are also preyed on by various animals, including the Egyptian vulture (*Neophron percnopterus*) which breaks them open with stones, letting the stones drop on them from a height.

Mating is preceded by courtship with the male displaying his fine black and white plumage. Finally he collects together several females who usually deposit all their eggs in the same nest, consisting of a simple hole in the earth. The male ostrich broods the eggs and cares for the chicks, and only the preferred female is allowed to give him occasional help. The young are looked after for a year except in particularly favourable years, when they leave and form a group of their own, followed by females who have not found mates or have passed the reproductive age. Abandoned chicks are frequently adopted by these solitary females.

Ostriches are farmed commercially in South Africa for their plumes and hide, the latter being used to make high quality leather goods.

The ostrich is the largest flightless bird, and one of the biggest birds in the world. When fleeing from danger it can reach speeds as high as 90 km/hr (55 mph) in short bursts.

Rheiformes

The Rheiformes contain a single family, the Rheidae, rheas, with two species, both South American. The rheas strongly resemble small ostriches. The common rhea or 'American ostrich' (*Rhea americana*) which is the largest American bird, lives in South America from Brazil to Argentina. It attains 1.7 m (51 in) in height and weights of 25 kg (55 lb). The smaller Darwin's rhea (*Pterocnemia pennata*) lives between Patagonia and the uplands of Peru. Accomplished runners, and skilful swimmers when the need arises, they live on vegetation and small animals. They live most of the year round in large flocks. When the breeding season begins the flocks break up, the males compete and the strongest succeed in winning over large harems. The females all deposit their eggs in the same nest, where they are incubated for about six weeks by the male, who then tends the young and defends the nest.

Casuariiformes

The Casuariiformes are divided into two living families, the Casuariidae (cassowaries) and Dromaiidae (emus).

Casuariidae

The cassowaries live in the dense forests of New Guinea and the neighbouring islands, and in the eastern coastal districts of Australia. The legs are shorter than those of the ostrich but equally powerful; the feet are armed with the sharp nails on the three toes of each foot. The small head is surmounted by a bony casque or helmet. The male occupies himself with the incubation of the eggs and the bringing up of the young, which are active from the moment of hatching. Their dense and impenetrable habitat makes it difficult to study their behaviour, and it is much easier to hear their resonant call than to actually see them. Unlike ostriches and rheas, cassowaries are monogamous, the females being larger than the males. There are three species, *Casuarius casuarius*, the Australian species, with two brightly coloured wattles, *C. unappendiculatus* with one wattle and *C. bennettii*, Bennett's cassowary, with none, the last two being from New Guinea.

Dromaiidae

The Dromaiidae comprises only one species, the emu (*Dromaius novaehollandiae*) of Australia, which, being 1.8 m (5 ft 2 in) in height and weighing 50 kg (110 lb), is the second largest bird after the ostrich. Eggs are laid communally by the harem of females and tended by the males. These are birds of open brush and grassland, and live in small groups.

Apterygiformes

The Apterygiformes, kiwis, are included among the Ratites although in many respects they form a group of their own, probably related to the extinct moas. There is one family, Apterygidae, whose three species, all from New Zealand, measure from 35 cm to 60 cm (14 in to 24 in) in length, are squat in shape, have tiny vestigial wings buried among the feathers and no tail, and possess robust legs. The head is small with a long curved bill with nostrils at the tip. They are rare among birds in having a good sense of smell, and are nocturnal forest-dwellers by habit. The brown or common kiwi (*Apteryx australis*) lives on North, South and Stewart Islands, the great spotted kiwi (*A. haasti*) and little spotted kiwi (*A. oweni*) on South Island only.

Tinamiformes

The Tinamiformes contain a single family the Tinamidae, tinamous, whose species resemble in appearance game birds such as grouse or partridges, rather than the ostriches. The breastbone is keeled, and in fact these birds can fly but not very strongly. They spend most of their time running about on the ground. In some species couples are formed, in others the harem still persists. All live in South America. *Crypturellus variegatus* lives in Guyana and Brazil, *Nothoprocta ornata* in the uplands and high grasslands of the Andes. The crested tinamou or martineta (*Eudromia elegans*) lives on the Argintine pampas and Bonaparte's tinamou (*Nothocercus bonapartei*) in the mountain forests of Colombia and Venezuela.

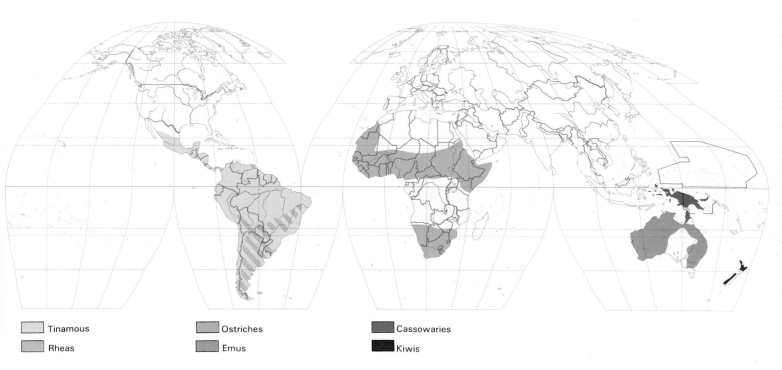

	Tinamous		Ostriches		Cassowaries
	Rheas		Emus		Kiwis

Sphenisciformes

The sole family of the Sphenisciformes is that of the Spheniscidae, penguins, flightless marine birds of the Southern Hemisphere. The seventeen species are all of a similar appearance; the body is entirely covered with feathers that are almost thread-like in form, and the wings are transformed into stiff flippers that can no longer be folded or twisted as in a normal bird, but are movable principally at the shoulder. The curious posture of the penguins is because the hind legs are so far to the rear that the bird has to stand upright. It cannot bring its legs below the body any other way. The toes are joined by a web, and the feet are generally used as rudders while the flippers provide propulsion in the water. The beak is elongated and very strong. The tail, short and stiff, is used as a support in standing. Clumsy on land, walking with a typical waddling gait or sliding on their bellies, they are highly skilled swimmers. The typical coloration is black and white, with varied ornamentation, sometimes of a striking yellow-orange; the dimensions vary from 30 to 120 cm (12 to 48 in) in height.

Penguins nest in colonies that may contain millions of individuals. Often the areas occupied by the colonies are at some distance from the sea, though it is only from the sea that the penguins derive their food. Feeding trips thus necessitate a long overland hike to the water and back. The nests may be lined with vegetable material or simply with stones, but more often they are merely sheltered places or even completely exposed; some species however nest in burrows or rock crevices. The family is subdivided into six genera which inhabit the Antarctic and the southernmost coasts of Africa, Australia and South America; one single species, the Galápagos penguin, is found further north on the Equator. The distribution of the various species is shown in the map below. The two largest species belong to the genus *Aptenodytes*. These are the emperor penguin (*A. forsteri*, illustrated here), attaining 120 cm (4 ft) in height, which lives exclusively on the Antarctic continent where it breeds during the winter; and the king penguin (*A. patagonia*) whose colonies are found in the Falkland Islands at the southern tip of South America as well as in Antarctica and the sub-antarctic islands.

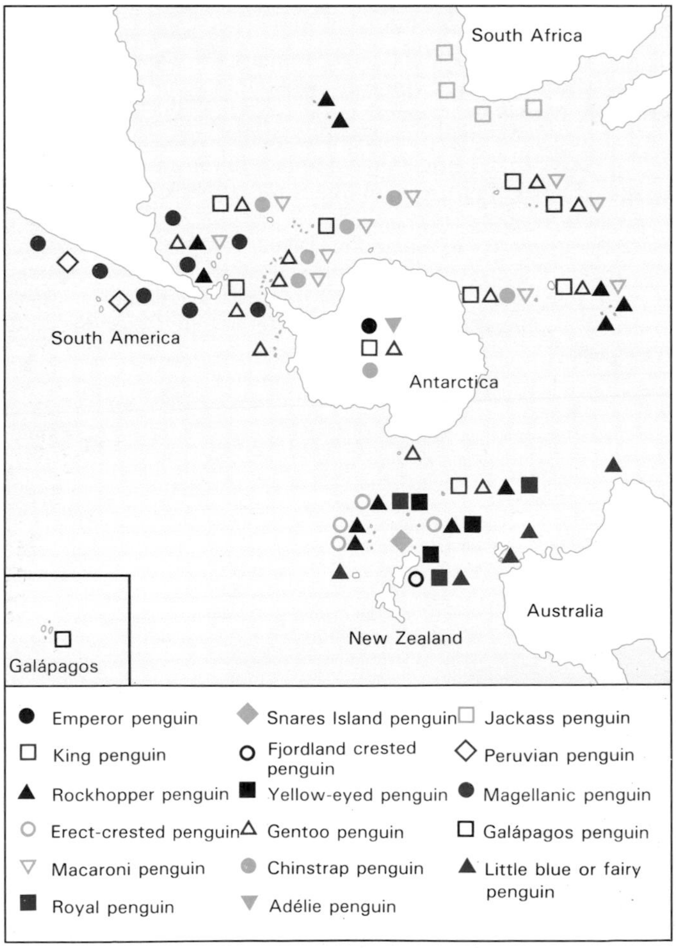

The Adélie penguin (*Pygoscelis adeliae*, illustrated here), 70 cm (28 in) high, breeds in vast rookeries on stony beaches. The chinstrap penguin (*P. antarctica*) is similar, but found only on the Antarctic continent. The gentoo (*P. papua*, illustrated here) is larger than the other two, breeds further north and has a circumpolar distribution. All three species usually lay two eggs and they feed on krill and small squids.

The crested penguins belonging to the genus *Eudyptes* are characterized by ornamentations of thread-like feathers on the head. The thick-billed penguin (*E. pachyrhynchus*) has a particularly strong beak and lives only in New Zealand, while the rockhopper penguin (*E. cristatus*, illustrated here) is found as far north as Tristan da Cunha and the Falklands. Other species are the macaroni penguin (*E. chrysolophus*) and the Royal penguin (*E. schlegeli*). These crested penguins are comparatively small and have muscular feet and strong claws which enable them to scramble over boulder beaches and even climb cliffs. Another New Zealand species is the yellow-crested penguin (*Megadyptes antipodes*, illustrated here). The little blue penguin (*Eudyptula minor*, illustrated here), with its slender beak and bluish coloration of the back, nests in sandy burrows on the southern coasts of Australia, Tasmania and New Zealand and is the smallest penguin species. Its height is only 30 cm (12 in).

The genus *Spheniscus*, which has given its name to the whole family of penguins, comprises two South American species, one of South Africa and one of the Galápagos. The jackass penguin (*S. demersus*, illustrated here) inhabits the islands off the southern coasts of Africa. Others of the same genus are the Galápagos penguin (*S. mendiculus*, illustrated here) which in singular contrast to the rest of the family lives on the Equator (though the water around the Galápagos is very cold), the Magellan penguin (*S. magellicanus*) and the Peruvian penguin (*S. humboldti*).

The inhospitable climate of Antarctica constrains the emperor penguin to nest during the winter of the Southern Hemisphere, in order that the chicks can take advantage of the abundance of food in the slightly more clement season from November to April. The emperor penguin lays only one egg, which the male incubates for two months (amongst the longest time of any bird); standing motionless in the world's coldest air. The bird presses the egg on to his feet and wraps it round in a fold of skin that acts as a kind of pouch to protect it and keep it warm, perhaps 50°C warmer than the ice on which the bird stands. In the depths of the Antarctic winter, July and August, the young hatches and the father feeds it with a secretion from his crop, until the return of the females, who have been out at sea, feeding. They take the males' place for three weeks, during which time the males, by now reduced almost to a skeleton, go off to the sea to restore themselves. At the age of about a month the growth of the young is accelerated since both parents are actively caring for the young. In another two months

South Africa

South America

Antarctica

New Zealand

Australia

Galápagos

● Emperor penguin	◆ Snares Island penguin	▫ Jackass penguin
▫ King penguin	○ Fjordland crested penguin	◇ Peruvian penguin
▲ Rockhopper penguin	■ Yellow-eyed penguin	● Magellanic penguin
○ Erect-crested penguin	△ Gentoo penguin	▫ Galápagos penguin
▽ Macaroni penguin	● Chinstrap penguin	▲ Little blue or fairy penguin
■ Royal penguin	▼ Adélie penguin	

little blue penguin

yellow-crested penguin

Adélie penguin

jackass penguin

rockhopper penguin

emperor penguin

gentoo penguin

Galápagos penguin

the young penguins lose their juvenile plumage. In species living in more temperate climes reproduction takes a somewhat different course owing to the greater availability of food and the absence of the stringent conditions imposed by the icy hostility of the Antarctic.

Gaviiformes

The Gaviiformes comprise the single family of Gaviidae containing the divers or loons. They live only in the Northern Hemisphere with only a single extant genus, *Gavia*. The four species are strictly aquatic and resemble each other in appearance: a streamlined body, a tapered head ending in a sharply pointed beak, and webbed feet. Their length varies from 60 to 80 cm (24 to 30 in); their wings are not large, and they are hampered in flying by their heavy bones, which are not extensively honeycombed like most birds'. The robust legs are housed too far within the body – as far down as the ankle joint – to make walking easy, but they are used in swimming (in contrast to the penguins, which use the forelimbs or flippers), for which they are extremely well adapted. The breeding plumage, which is similar in the two sexes, consists of strong bold contrasts of black and white and also subtle degrees of shading. At the time of moulting, when they shed their longest feathers, they are incapable of flight. They are well known for their wild and eerie calls.

The breeding season is spent in cold inland waters – lakes, ponds – especially in northern North America, Iceland, Scotland and Scandinavia – and they winter in the sea, along the coasts. The nest is usually simple and at the water's edge; on emerging from the two eggs after about thirty days the chicks enter the water as soon as the down dries. Divers are generally solitary in winter and only form pairs in spring, but sometimes larger groups are formed.

The great northern diver, or common loon (*Gavia immer*), the largest bird of the genus, nests in large lakes in Iceland, Greenland and the northern parts of North America. In winter it moves south to ice-free waters in Lower California, Florida, the North Sea and the British coasts. The white-billed loon (*G. adamsii*), also of large size, lives all round the polar region, but is commonest in Northern Europe. The black-throated diver or Arctic loon (*G. arctica*, illustrated here) is about 62 cm (25 in) long, also lives in all the southern parts of the Arctic regions, and moves southwards in autumn to winter in offshore waters. The red-throated diver or loon (*G. stellata*), circumpolar in distribution, nests also in Scotland, Iceland and Greenland.

The nest is looked after by both parents. The young, in the first stages of life, are often carried on the backs of the parents, even when diving. Divers cam swim long distances under water and can dive to depths of 60 m (200 ft). Mating is preceded by nuptial displays, sometimes remarkably complex, which take place in flight and in the water.

Podicipediformes

The Podicipediformes are closely related to the Gaviiformes and comprise the single family of Podicipedidae, grebes. Unlike the divers, the grebes have a worldwide distribution except in Antarctica. During cold periods they migrate to more welcoming regions. Besides their normal habitat, areas of fresh water, they also frequent brackish and coastal waters. Their appearance also recalls that of the divers: a streamlined body with short wings, the beak more or less elongated according to the diet, and legs housed partly within the body, but the toes are not fully webbed, each having an enlarged fringing lobe.

Courtship includes nuptial parades during which the two sexes perform spectacular ritual dances on the water, showing off their plumage, which is particularly bright during this period. In winter the species look very similar, grey-brown above and white below. The nest, constructed of reeds and other plants, is in fact a floating raft of plant material anchored to growing aquatic plants. By its nature the nest tends to sink, and for this reason the grebes continue to add further material to it, so increasing its thickness. When the eggs are left unguarded, even for a brief period, the parents carefully cover them up with fragments of vegetation. As with the divers, the young grebes are often carried on the back of the parents.

A particular habit of these birds is to eat feathers pulled from their own bodies. Even the young are fed with feathers by the parents. The reason for this behaviour is rather obscure, but the feathers may act as a digestive aid, or serve to gather together fishbones or the arthropod shells that have been swallowed.

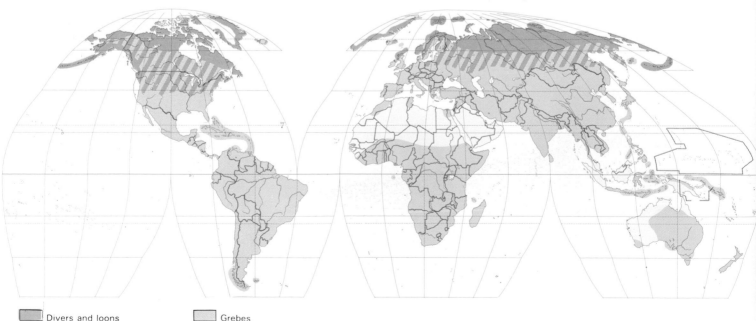

Divers and loons   Grebes

The division of the family into genera is still debated. According to some authorities there are four or five genera with seventeen to twenty-one species. The western grebe (*Aechmophorus occidentalis*) lives in the north-western regions of North America, moving to the south and along the coast in winter in large flocks. It has a long pointed beak suitable for spearing the fish on which it feeds. The genus *Podylimbus* has two species, the pied-billed grebe (*P. podiceps*) breeding from Canada to Argentina and wintering on both the Pacific and Atlantic coasts of North and South America; and the less numerous great pied-billed grebe (*P. gigas*), confined to a small area of Guatemala. The flightless short-winged grebe (*Centropelma micropterum*) lives on Lake Titicaca on the borders of Bolivia and Peru, 3800 m (12,500 ft) above sea level.

The genus with the most species is *Podiceps*, which includes the little grebes or dabchicks. The dabchick (*P. ruficollis*) is widely distributed in Europe, Asia and Africa, with associated species in Australia, New Zealand, South-East Asia and Madagascar. Other species of *Podiceps* are present in South America, Eurasia and North America. *P. andinus* is a grebe of the mountain lakes of Colombia. The Slavonian or horned grebe (*P. auritus*) lives in the circumpolar regions and migrates northwards to Europe, Asia and North America in the autumn, mostly wintering offshore. It is a buoyant swimmer and dives frequently in pursuit of small aquatic animals; it is a good flier but needs a long take-off. The black-necked grebe (*P. nigricollis*) breeds in Europe and is an occasional visitor to Britain, as is the Slavonian grebe (*P. auritus*). The red-necked grebe (*P. griseigena*) is another European species. The great crested grebe (*P. cristatus*, illustrated here) is widespread in the Old World, including British waters. It measures 48 cm (19 in) in length. It practises spectacular courtship displays

Above A black-throated diver or Arctic loon (*Gavia arctica*) in summer breeding plumage.
Below A great crested grebe sitting on its nest in the reeds. Divers and grebes are well adapted to an aquatic habitat; the diver prefers large inland lakes while the grebe frequents reed-fringed lakes and rivers.

including head-waggling with calls resembling barking or groaning. The grebes are looked on as ecological indicators, since their presence on a sheet of water is a sign of a thriving fish population and hence little pollution.

Procellariiformes

The Procellariiformes display many particular adaptations to their marine habitat. The name of the group means tube-nosed, referring to the nostrils, which are carried in external tubes along the top or sides of the upper mandible, which suggests a well-developed sense of smell. There are four families: the Diomedeidae (albatrosses), Procellariidae (shearwaters, fulmars and larger petrels), Hydrobatidae (stormy petrels) and Pelicanoididae (diving petrels). All the representatives of the group spend their lives on the sea, from which they derive their food, and they come to land solely for nesting. Living in colonies, they pair for life; the same partners have been observed for several consecutive years occupying the same nest, though what they do outside the breeding period is a mystery. The distribution of the group is worldwide; diving petrels are found exclusively in the Southern Hemisphere, so are the albatrosses except for a few species which penetrate the North Atlantic and North Pacific. Shearwaters, fulmars and the other petrels are found in all the oceans.

Diomedeidae

The Diomedeidae, albatrosses, are the largest marine birds, reaching in the wandering albatross (*Diomedea exulans*, illustrated here) lengths of 1.4 m (4 ft 7 in) and wing spans greater than 3 m (10 ft). The body is heavy and massive, the head large, armed with a powerful beak, the legs short with webbed feet, the tail short and the wings very long, which permits an exceptional capacity for gliding flight (one specimen was captured 10,000 km (6250 miles) from where it was ringed). Without beating their wings, albatrosses can travel great distances simply by gliding, making use of the winds. They seldom alight on the water, but dive to feed; though in calm weather they find it difficult to support their heavy bodies in the air and may descend to rest on the water. They mostly live on cuttlefish, though they are attracted by ships' garbage and are sometimes caught by seamen using hooks baited with meat. They drink seawater, as do other seabirds, excreting the excess salt using special glands on the head.

Breeding takes place on oceanic islands where the colonies may consist of a large number of pairs. The nest varies little among the various species and may consist of a hillock of earth or a simple natural hollow in the ground. A single egg is laid, from which, after two to three months, a chick emerges, already covered with feathers. The rearing of the young is slow, and it may take up to five months for the young of the smaller species to acquire fully developed flight plumage, and as much as nine months for the larger ones. They are cared for by both parents alternately. The offspring then spend five or ten years at sea, learning the arts of flying and navigation, before returning to land to breed. Courtship entails wing-stretching and bill-fencing displays.

The first to reach the nesting area is the male, who usually lands near the nest used on previous occasions. The female arrives later and after inspecting the nest takes up her place by the side of her mate. They greet each other by stretching out their wings. The female then flies out to sea to feed, while the male puts the old nest in order. On her return the female gives the finishing touches to the nest, using materials which the male brings her. After the single egg is laid the female incubates, and from then on the two partners take it in turns approximately one week at a time. The chick, when it is large enough to be left on its own for fairly long periods, defends itself against attackers by spitting an oily substance at them which is secreted by the stomach. This substance is normally used by the Procellariiformes to render the feathers waterproof.

Apart from the wandering albatross there are eleven other species of the genus *Diomedea*, among which are the laysan albatross (*D. immutabilis*) and the black-footed albatross (*D. nigripes*, illustrated here) of the Northern Hemisphere, while the royal albatross (*D. epomophora*) is of the Southern Hemisphere. Albatrosses are wide-ranging outside the breeding season. Even the black-browed albatross (*D. melanophris*, illustrated on p. 177) has been seen in northern waters, though it normally lives between the 30° and 60° south parallels. Typical of the cold southern seas are the two species of the genus *Phoebetria*, the sooty albatross (*P. fusca*) and the light-mantled sooty albatross (*P. palpebrata*).

Procellariidae

The Procellariidae – shearwaters, fulmars, and large petrels – are the largest family of the Procellariiformes. The six species of fulmars have a short, heavy body with a large head and short tail. The beak shows a sheath-like reinforcement formed of several extremely hard, horny plates arranged in various ways in the different species. Similar plates are present in other groups of Procellariiformes. The largest forms belong to the genus *Macronectes*: the giant petrel (*M. giganteus*), which lives in the Antarctic Ocean, reaches wing spans of 2.5 m (8 ft); the northern giant fulmar (or petrel) (*M. halli*), as its name implies, penetrates further north but even so it rarely reaches the tropic of Capricorn.

The genus *Fulmarus* is represented by the fulmar (*F. glacialis*, illustrated here). It nests in the Arctic regions and along the coasts of Britain, Scandinavia, Greenland, Iceland and other northern islands of the Atlantic and Pacific Oceans. It is notable for its enormous increase in population during this century. The silvery or southern fulmar (*F. glacialoides*) lives exclusively in the Antarctic. The coloration of the fulmars ranges normally from grey to brown, but it is not uncommon to find brighter-coloured forms sometimes of a dazzling white spotted with black. The basic diet is plankton, crustaceans, small fish and squid, but they will eat almost anything and follow ships to feed on the garbage thrown overboard. They nest ashore, from May to September, on ledges, shelves, buildings or even level ground if in large numbers.

The snow petrel (*Pagodroma nivea*) is easily recognizable by its pure white colour. It lives only in the Antarctic region, nesting in Antarctica and in a few of the surrounding islands, such as the South Shetlands, South Sandwich Islands and South Orkneys. The pintado petrel or Cape pigeon (*Daption capensis*, illustrated here) is a sub-Antarctic species with bold black and white markings that nests in Antarctica and various southern islands, pressing as far north as New Zealand.

The prions or whalebirds are a group of small, elegant Antarctic seabirds, all blue-grey above and whitish below, living on plankton scooped up by their bills from the water while in flight, and characterized by the typical plates alongside the beak. The several species belonging to the genus *Pachyptila* – the Antarctic prion (*P. desolata*), broad-billed prion (*P. rittata*) and narrow-billed prion (*P. belcheri*) – are practically indistinguishable from one another by simple observation in flight. All inhabit Antarctic waters and nest on islands and archipelagoes as far north as New Zealand.

pintado petrel
(Cape pigeon)

great shearwater

black-footed albatross

wandering albatross

Wilson's petrel

fulmar

The third group of Procellariidae are of tropical distribution and comprises the genera *Pterodroma* and *Bulweria*. They are called gadfly petrels because of their fluttering flight. The black-capped petrel or diablotin (*Pterodroma hasitata*) which breeds in Hispaniola, was long believed to be extinct but is now known to number several thousand.

The last group comprises about fifteen species including the true shearwaters. The genus *Procellaria* contains birds with relatively long legs, large wings and rounded bodies; *Puffinus* species have shorter legs, tail and wings. Cory's shearwater (*Procellaria diomedea*) and the Manx shearwater (*Puffinus puffinus*) both nest in British and European coastal regions. The great shearwater (*Puffinus gravis*, illustrated on p. 175) visits the eastern North Atlantic from Iceland to Portugal in summer and autumn, but breeds in burrows on Tristan da Cunha in the South Atlantic. The sooty shearwater (*Puffinus griseus*) also breeds in burrows on islands in the Southern

Hemisphere but visits the North Atlantic in summer and autumn, ranging as far north as Iceland and Norway.

Hydrobatidae

The Hydrobatidae, storm petrels, are the smallest birds of the great ocean. The appearance and structure of the webbed feet are similar except in size of those of the shearwaters. The body colouration is usually grey, blackish or brown and white; sometimes the back is white. The legs are slender and rather long, the tail often forked and the beak long and slender, ending in a hook. They are found in both Northern and Southern Hemispheres. The best known southern storm petrel is probably Wilson's petrel (*Oceanites oceanicus*, illustrated on p. 175). It breeds on Antarctica and on neighbouring islands but visits the North Atlantic in summer, venturing as far north as the Bay of Biscay and the waters off

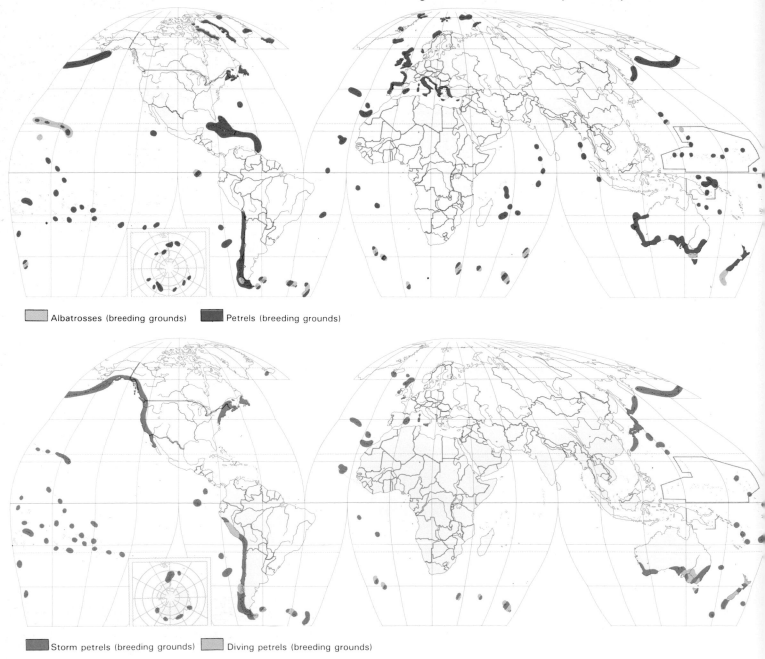

Albatrosses (breeding grounds)   Petrels (breeding grounds)

Storm petrels (breeding grounds)   Diving petrels (breeding grounds)

south-west Ireland, and may sometimes be seen in British waters. Storm petrels are active day and night and rarely rest on the water but skim across the surface on pattering feet, picking their prey from it with their beak. They follow ships, hunting zooplankton disturbed by the ship's passage or feeding on the discharged refuse. Seamen named them Mother Carey's chickens, after the divine guardian of sailors (*Mater cara*). The name petrel (little St Peter) has a similar origin. The storm petrel (*Hydrobates pelagicus*) is the smallest and commonest of the Hydrobatidae, measuring 15 cm (6 in) in length. It lives in the North Atlantic east of Iceland and nests in sea caves, burrows, or in piles of stones or stone walls, on bare islands and headlands. The pairs disperse after breeding. They feed mainly on plankton but also follow ships for scraps. Leach's petrel (*Oceanodroma leucorrhea*) is larger than Wilson's petrel and normally does not follow ships; it excavates nest burrows in peaty ground. It is distinguished by its forked tail. The frigate petrel (*Pelagodroma marina*) breeds on islands in the Southern Oceans and the North Atlantic; it is easily recognized by its entirely white undersurface.

Pelecanoididae

The last family of Procelliformes is that of the Pelecanoididae, diving petrels, present in the Southern Hemisphere with five species of the single genus *Pelecanoides*. They strongly resemble the auks (*Alcidae*), with stout bodies, short wings and rapid, whirring flight. Like the other Procellariiformes, the diving petrels nest in holes in

Breeding seabirds: a mixed nesting colony of black-browed albatrosses ('mollyhawks') and penguins.

soft ground; they live in sub-Antarctic and southern temperate oceans, breeding in the Kerguelen and Crozet Islands, the Falklands, Tristan da Cunha and the islands off New Zealand, as well as along the southern coasts of Australia and South America.

Pelecaniformes

The Pelecaniformes have had a considerable evolutionary success, as is demonstrated by the six living families belonging to this group. They are represented in all parts of the world; the Phaethontidae (tropic-birds and frigate birds) inhabit only the tropics, the Anhingidae (darters) are found between 35°N and 40°S, while the pelicans, gannets, boobies and cormorants are distributed more widely over the two hemispheres. All the Pelecaniformes move more or less awkwardly on land, but in the air they are fine fliers. All have the unique characteristic of webbing between all four toes.

Phaethontidae

The Phaethontidae possess only one genus, *Phaethon*, with three species known as tropic-birds or bosun-birds. The constant climate of the tropics where they live allows them to nest practically all the year round. This reproductive behaviour also makes it easier to search for food, since all the young are not born at the same time, so that the demand for food in a breeding area is not exceptional at one period of the year, as happens with other colonial species. Courtship takes place in the air, and mating in the vicinity of the nest; the nest is dug in the earth by the feet, shortly before the laying of the single egg. Incubation, undertaken by both partners, lasts for about a month and a half, and the young remain in the nest for about three months after being hatched, leaving it only when they are fully capable of flying and finding food of their own.

The largest of the family are the red-tailed tropic-birds, (*Phaethon rubricauda*, illustrated here) whose wing-span is as much as 1 m (3 ft 3 in); they inhabit a few islands in the Pacific and Indian Oceans. The red-billed tropic-bird (*P. aethereus*) has a red beak and a white back ornamented with black bars, and white tail-feathers. It is present in the Antilles, in the Atlantic tropical belt, in the Red Sea and in the Indian Ocean, as well as in the Galápagos. It is the national bird of Bermuda. The last and smallest species is the yellow-billed tropic-bird (*P. lepturus*) with a similar distribution to the preceding species but a somewhat further range to the south-eastern part of the Pacific. There is a variety of this species with bright orange-pink plumage (*P. l. fulvus*) on Christmas Island. All the tropic-birds spend most of their time in the air above the sea, though they are capable swimmers and often dive for fish close to the surface.

Pelecanidae

The Pelecanidae, the family to which familiar pelicans belong, is of very ancient phylogenetic origin. The appearance of the pelican is known to all: large body with very ample wings, short, robust legs with webbed feet, long neck with a small head provided with a long beak, slightly hooked, and with the characteristic distensible sac under the lower mandible. Clumsy on land, they are very capable in the water, as also in flight. The coloration is generally white with the points of the wings black, or at least dark; the bare parts, during the reproductive season, assume fairly vivid red, orange or yellow colours. The Pelecanidae are present in all the continents except Antarctica. Some species prefer salt water, others fresh water. The diet consists of fish and other aquatic animals.

The brown pelican (*Pelecanus occidentalis*) is capable of nose-diving into the sea and immersing itself completely in the pursuit of its prey. The other species often fish in groups and search for food while in flight; once a shoal of fish has been sighted, the pelicans swoop down to the surface of the water and arrange themselves in a semicircle and, raising their wings, encircle the terrified fish. They are very sociable, they nest in large colonies, often in remote localities. The nests are made of large piles of branches, and two to three eggs are laid. The young are fed with predigested food which the parents regurgitate from the sac below the beak, which can contain more than twice as much as the stomach. In eastern and south-eastern Europe, there are colonies of Dalmatian pelicans (*P. crispus*, illustrated on p. 180) and less often of white pelicans (*P. onocrotalus*), this latter species being more common in Asia and Africa. The Australian pelican (*P. conspicillatus*, illustrated here) and the grey or Asian pelican (*P. philippensis*) is of the Philippines. In America, besides the brown pelican already mentioned, there is the white pelican (*P. erythrorhynchus*). The pink-backed pelican (*P. rufescens*) is found in southern Arabia and in Madagascar.

Phalacrocoracidae

The Phalacrocoracidae include the well-known cormorants and shags. Cormorants are used in the East for fishing; the bird is held by a leash, and a ring round the neck is sufficient to prevent the fish once caught from being swallowed. The birds are allowed to satisfy their hunger abundantly when, at the end of their labour, the owner removes the collar. In China and Japan it has been found possible to tame and train the birds to catch fish for human consumption without subjecting them to a collar.

The appearance is similar in all the species; elongated body, legs short and robust with webbed feet, tail almost rigid and wings relatively short, long neck and elongated beak with hooked tip. Excellent swimmers, they stay in the water only for as long as they need to fish, then take to land and spread out their wings to dry the feathers, which are apparently less waterproof than those of other birds. It has been suggested that this characteristic posture, with outstretched wings may aid balance or even digestion.

The most widespread species is the common cormorant (*Phalacrocorax carbo*) which is found from Canada and Greenland to

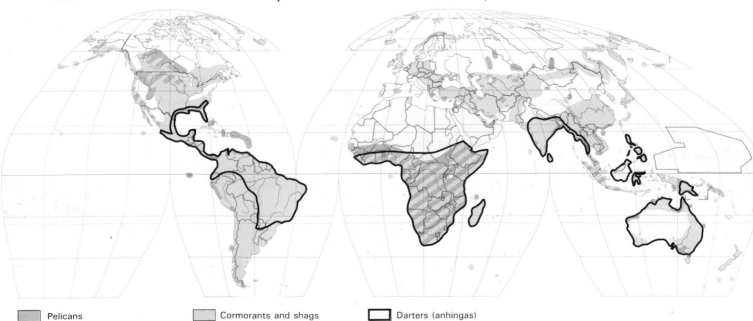

Pelicans   Cormorants and shags   Darters (anhingas)

red-tailed tropic-bird

double-crested cormorant

Australian pelican

lesser frigate bird

brown booby

red-legged cormorant

anhinga (darter)

the Eurasian continent, in Africa and in the Australasian region. It and the slightly smaller Japanese cormorant (*P. capillatus*) are the species trained for fishing. The shage (*P. aristotelis*) is also present in European waters, while the double-crested cormorant (*P. auritus*, illustrated on p. 179) is North American. The red-legged cormorant (*P. gaimardi*, illustrated on p. 179) is from South America. One species, *Nannopterum harrisi* of the Galápagos, has much reduced wings and is incapable of flight. Other shags include the long-tailed shag (*Phalacrocorax africanus*) and the blue-eyed shag (*P. atriceps*). The pied cormorant (*P. varius*) is from Australia and New Zealand.

Anhingidae

The family Anhingidae comprises the single genus *Anhinga*, whose species are commonly called by several alternative names: darters, anhingas (the Amazonian Indian name), snake-birds – from the curious form of their long snake-like necks – or, in North America, water-turkeys. The general appearance resembles that of the cormorants, but the tail is longer and the beak straight and pointed, suitable for spearing fish. They are birds of fresh or brackish water, living mainly on lakes or rivers. They swim very well, remaining semi-submerged over long distances. Like the

Left A nesting colony of common gannets, each individual just out of beak's range of the neighbours.
Below Dalmatian pelicans (*Pelecanus crispus*) rest and sun themselves in their tree-top nesting colony.

cormorants, they have to dry their feathers after each immersion. Their distribution is worldwide except for Europe, Polynesi, New Zealand and Antarctica. The anhinga (*A. anhinga*, illustrated on p. 179) lives in the Americas, *A. rufa* in Africa, Madagascar and the Middle East, *A. melanogaster* in Asia and *A. novaehollandiae* in Australasia.

Sulidae

The Sulidae, gannets and boobies, comprise a single genus, *Sula*, which contains nine marine species of very similar appearance. Three species are found in northern temperate waters: these are the gannets, with white plumage and black wing-tips. The immature birds are grey with pale brown spots. The other six species, which are smaller, are the boobies and live in the tropics and the temperate waters of the Southern Hemisphere. They are predominantly brown but have bright coloured feet. The familiar gannet of British waters is *Sula bassana*, illustrated here; the young birds migrate to warmer climes in winter but the tendency declines in the adults. They have a spindle-shaped body, highly streamlined, with a long, strong beak with slight sacs under the throat. The legs are short and strong and the feet webbed. The tail and wings are long and straight. The gannets are highly accomplished fliers and swimmers, admirably designed to kill fish by plunging down from a considerable height in a nose-dive. Their courtship is rather brutal and their fights over territory violent; nesting takes place in colonies containing large numbers of birds, and the nests are built sometimes on inaccessible rocky ledges, sometimes on level ground if the locality is sufficiently remote. The nesting area stretches in an arc from Newfoundland to Iceland and south-western Norway, and across Britain and Ireland to the Channel Islands and Isles of Scilly. The headquarters of the northern gannet are undoubtedly around Britain and Ireland; the largest colony is found on the sea stacks of St Kilda where gannets have nested for at least 1000 years, with over 55,000 pairs. The Cape gannet (*S. capensis*) in contrast nests on fairly flat, low islands off South Africa. Along with the Cape cormorant and black-footed penguin, the Cape gannet is an important guano producer – a phosphate-rich, fish-based fertilizer, gathered from the accumulated droppings of thousands of seabirds. The Australian gannet (*S. serrator*), less numerous than its relatives, breeds on

islands in the Bass Strait, off Tasmania and also off North Island, New Zealand.

Three of the six species of booby are well represented in the tropics: the masked or blue-faced booby (*S. dactylatra*), the red-footed booby (*S. sula*) and the brown booby (*S. leucogaster*, illustrated on p. 179). Other species have more restricted ranges. The Peruvian booby (*S. variegata*) nests on islands off Peru where it can occur in vast colonies. It is another major producer of guano. The blue-footed booby (*S. nebouxii*), the largest species, nests on islands from Mexico south to Ecuador and Peru.

Fregatidae

The Fregatidae – frigate birds, man-o'-war birds or pirate birds – are the Pelecaniformes best adapted to an aerial life. There is only a single genus, *Fregata*. Though they have webbed feet they spend little time on the sea, but spend more time in the air than any other birds except swifts, tirelessly soaring and alighting only to sleep or tend the nest. They rarely venture into the open sea but stay within sight of the land, living along tropical and sub-tropical coasts. They feed on fish or zooplankton taken from the sea surface, and on the young of other seabirds. They also specialize in snatching the prey from other birds by chasing them and forcing them to drop or disgorge their prey. Refuse from ships floating on the surface of the sea is also eagerly taken, as are newly hatched turtles.

Male frigate birds are brilliant black with a bright red throat pouch which they inflate during the breeding season to attract the female. They can sit for hours on end with the pouch inflated while the larger females fly overhead. As a female approaches, the male spreads his wings, calls, and rattles his bill, a display accentuated by his brilliant throat pouch. Species include the magnificent frigate bird (*Fregata magnifiscens*) of the tropical Atlantic and the eastern Pacific, which has a wingspan of up to 2.5 m (8 ft), the largest wingspan of any bird in relation to its body size. The great frigate bird (*F. minor*), and the lesser frigate bird (*F. ariel*, illustrated on p. 179) are both widespread species of subtropical and tropical islands. At some archipelagoes in the eastern Pacific, islanders have taken advantage of the birds' tameness and have trained them to carry messages from island to island.

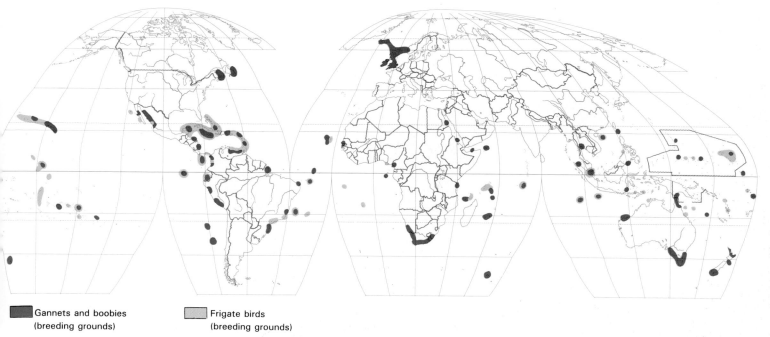

☐ Gannets and boobies
(breeding grounds)

☐ Frigate birds
(breeding grounds)

Ciconiiformes

The Ciconiiformes are a group of birds of medium and large size characterized by having long legs, large non-webbed feet and long beaks. The members of all five families live in aquatic habitats, their diet consisting in large measure of fish, amphibians, crustacea and other small water creatures. The distribution is more or less worldwide, excluding only the polar regions and high altitudes. The families include herons, egrets, bitterns, shoebills, hammerheads, storks, ibises, spoonbills and flamingoes.

Ardeidae

The Ardeidae comprise the herons, egrets and bitterns. This is divided in turn into Ardeinae and Botaurinae. The herons belong to the first group, birds which can be 1.60 m (5 ft) tall and are easily identified by their long legs and big feet with four long toes, long beak and long neck, the last characteristically folded in flight with the head brought back between the shoulders. The wings are large and confer a powerful though slow flight. The general colour of the plumage varies from white to black, blue, purple, fawn or grey. In some species the head is adorned with long feathers which can be erected and which are of great importance during courtship or for exchanging signals between members of the same species. The backs may also be adorned by long silky feathers which were at one time much used for decorating ladies' hats.

The herons live in shallow waters, where their long legs permit them to wade in search of food. According to the species, they hunt in groups or singly. When hunting in groups, several individuals move in a line or semicircle, forcing the prey into shallower water where it can be seized more easily. Solitary herons on the other hand hunt by standing in wait for their prey; remaining immobile waiting for the victim to approach closely enough to be seized with the beak. Some species spread their wings forward to create a shadow in front; in this way they eliminate distracting reflections and create a dark zone which attracts fish since it resembles a hole or cavern. The greatest expert in this method of fishing is certainly the African black heron (*Hydranassa ardesiaca*). The cattle egret (*Egretta garzetta*) feeds mainly on insects, especially grasshoppers disturbed by the hoofs of cattle and game animals. Originally found in Africa and Asia it has now spread widely to southern Europe, Australia, and from the Caribbean to North America.

The giant of the group is the goliath heron (*Ardea goliath*) of East and South Africa which stands nearly 2 m (6.5 ft) tall; of the same genus is the grey heron (*Ardea cinerea*), familiar in Britain and breeding across temperate Eurasia, Africa and Madagascar. The purple heron (*A. purpurea*) also breeds in Europe and is a summer visitor to Britain. The genus *Egretta* includes the majestic great white egret (*E. alba*) and *E. garzetta* already mentioned. A very rare visitor to western Europe is the slate-coloured reef heron (*E. gularis*, illustrated here). The stockier and shorter-legged night heron (*Nycticorax nycticorax*) is another summer visitor. The yellow-crowned night heron (*Nyctanassa violacea*) of the Americas, is illustrated here. Another night heron is the tiger heron (*Tigriorhis leucolophus*, illustrated here) of West Africa. The squacco heron (*Ardeola ralloides*), stocky and thick-legged, is another occasional summer visitor to Britain.

The Botaurinae comprise the bitterns, shy and solitary birds whose plumage is cryptically coloured so that the birds are difficult to see even close to, unless they move. Their presence is more often made known by the booming call, made by the larger species in spring. The bittern (*Botaurus stellaris*) nests in Britain, in reed-beds fens and marshes but is now rare due to loss of habitat. The little bittern (*Ixobrychus minutus*) is a summer visitor though it used to breed in Britain. The American *Botaurus lentiginosus* is another occasional visitor to Britain.

Ciconiidae

The Ciconiidae, storks, are large Ciconiiformes and look similar to herons, from which however they differ in holding their necks straight out in flight. The diet is varied, many living on fish and frogs and small mammals, while some live on carrion, the classic example being the marabou (*Leptoptilos crumeniferus*) of Africa. This is the largest of the family and one of the world's largest flying birds. The white stork (*Ciconia ciconia*) nests in Europe, as does the black stork (*C. nigra*); both these species migrate to Africa in winter. The close cohabitation of the white storks with man allows us to study their behaviour, and in particular their 'language'. Like most of the Ciconiidae they do not make sounds with the throat, and to communicate they clatter their beaks, reinforcing or clarifying their message with displays and ritual movements.

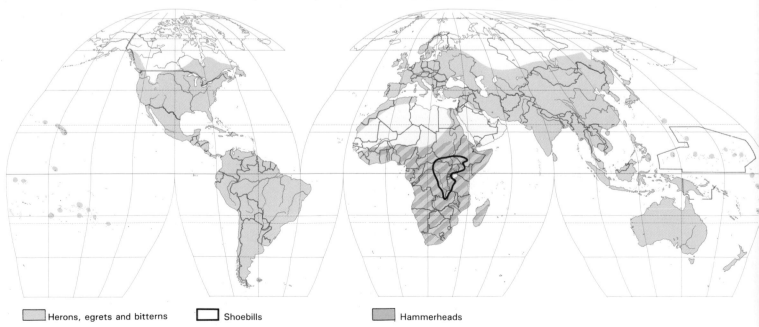

Herons, egrets and bitterns	Shoebills	Hammerheads

reef heron

yellow-crowned
night heron

tiger heron

scarlet ibis

marabou

shoebill

roseate spoonbill

Among other species is the white-necked or woolly-necked stork (*Dissoura episcopus*) of Ethiopia and southern Asia, and the saddlebill (*Ephippiorhynchus senegalensis*) of Africa. The wood stork (*Mycteria americana*) is an American species ranging from Argentina to Florida, dispersing further north after breeding.

Threskiornithidae

The Threskiornithidae comprise ibises and spoonbills. The former have long legs and a long, slender, curving beak. Nesting usually takes place in colonies near water, and the nests are built in trees or bushes, in reedbeds or on rocks. There are about twenty-five species, six of the genera being American, one worldwide – the glossy ibis (*Plegadis falcinellus*) – and the rest distributed in Europe, Asia and Africa. The most famous species, venerated by the ancient Egyptians, is the sacred ibis (*Threskiornis aethiopica*), which is still abundant south of the Sahara and in Madagascar. The waldrapp (*Geronticus eremita*) was at one time common in the Alps, but the nearest population to Europe is now in south-eastern Turkey. The bald ibis (*G. calvus*), very similar to the waldrapp, is a southern African species. Two endangered species are the giant ibis (*Thaumatibis gigantea*) of South-East Asia and the Japanese ibis (*Nipponia nippon*). The scarlet ibis (*Guara rubra*, illustrated on p. 183) or tropical America, is the only ibis to have a vivid red colour, but this rapidly fades to white if the birds are not fed on a natural diet, as often happens in zoos.

The spoonbills comprise six species, the distribution being mostly tropical and sub-tropical. The name refers to the curious shape of the beak, adapted to the birds' peculiar diet. This consists of small creatures dwelling in the mud at the bottom of ponds, in marshes and on riverside beaches, and the beak is swept from side to side through the mud in search of food. Nesting is colonial and the young hatch with a normal beak; only as they mature does the beak take on its typical flattened shape. The commonest of the five Old World species is the Eurasian spoonbill (*Platalea leucorodia*), which nests in the Low Countries, Spain and south-eastern Europe. While ths species has always had a scattered European distribution, its overall range has been reduced by drainage of reed beds and by the pollution of its freshwater feeding grounds. The one American species is the beautiful roseate spoonbill (*Ajaia ajaia*, illustrated on p. 183).

Scopidae

The Scopidae have one representative, the hammerkop or hammerhead (*Scopus umbretta*), which is found in equatorial Africa. It has a long tail and wings but rather short legs, and the beak, short for one of the Ciconiiformes, is slightly hooked and compressed from side to side. The head has a crest that makes the bird look like a hammer. It lives in marshes or by stretches of water, eating frogs and other aquatic animals which it sometimes watches for while resting on the back of a hippopotamus. It is active at twilight and nests in trees, building enormous spherical nests 1.5 m (5 ft) in diameter. The entrance to the nest is by a tunnel, and the interior is plastered with mud and dung. No other bird builds a nest quite like this huge domed structure of twigs, mud and water plants. During incubation the birds collect decorative items such as paper, rags and old tins to add to the nest.

Balaenicipitidae

The last family of the Ciconiiformes is that of the Balaenicipitidae, which again contains one single species, the shoebill (*Balaeniceps rex*, illustrated on p. 183). A bird of curious appearancce, the shoebill reaches a height of 1.3 m (4½ ft), has long legs with large toes, a large head and an enormous beak, broad and thick, whose adaptative significance is uncertain. Its plumage is slaty in colour on the back, paler underneath. It lives in tropical East Africa in the area between Zaire, Uganda and the borders of Sudan, especially in and around the great swamp known as The Sudd, a vast wetland area dominated by giant stands of papyrus. The shoebill feeds on a variety of aquatic animals including frogs and young crocodiles, but its main food is fish, especially lungfish which it digs out of dry mud with its massive beak.

Phoenicopteriformes

The Phoenicopteriformes contain only one family, the flamingoes, Phoenicopteridae. The appearance of the flamingo is unmistakable: very long legs, beak of a strange angled form, with the head placed on a long sinuous neck which is carried outstretched in flight. Its colour is from rosy to deep red, the wings being

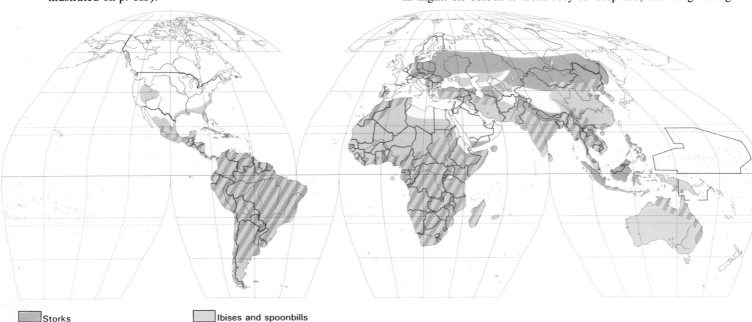

Storks | Ibises and spoonbills

generally darker than the rest of the body. The toes are short and webbed. The beak has platelets along the edges which serve to filter out food particles from the water.

The greater flamingo (*Phoenicopterus ruber*, illustrated here) like all the flamingoes, searches for its food on the bottoms of lakes, mostly of salty water. The beak is held upside-down and food – molluscs, crustacea and small plants – is filtered from the water. The young are hatched with a normal beak, which only later develops the typical shape. Flamingoes nest in colonies sometimes containing several thousand individuals. *P. ruber* is the species with the widest distribution, ranging from Africa and the West Indies to South America, South-West Asia and some parts of southern Europe. The most numerous species, however, which contains 75 per cent of the individuals of the entire family, is the lesser flamingo (*Phoeniconaias minor*) of Africa. There are probably over four million of these birds nesting on and around the soda-lakes of the East African Rift Valley. Lake Magadi and Lake Nakuru both have populations of over one million birds. Other high concentrations exist in South-West Africa and Botswana. Lesser flamingos exist solely on minute blue-green algae,

that are especially plentiful in alkaline lakes. The rarest flamingo (but still with an estimated population of around 50,000) is James' flamingo (*P. jamesi*) which is restricted to a few high-level lakes in the Peruvian Andes. The other South American species, the Andean flamingo (*P. andinus*) and the Chilean flamingo (*P. chilensis*), have more extensive ranges also along the Andes.

All flamingos nest in large colonies. The nest is built in shallow water and consists of a truncated cone made of mud which is collected by the birds and skilfully shaped with their bills. A single egg is usually laid, sometimes two, incubated by both parents. The nestlings are covered with grey down at birth and are completely helpless, but by two or three days they may form large juvenile flocks together with those birds that have failed to nest. Sixty days after birth the young can fly and their bills are sufficiently developed to obtain their own food. The young do not develop the typically pink plumage until a year old and do not breed for several years.

Nesting greater flamingoes, showing the adults, the grey chicks and the white eggs in the low nest mounds.

Anseriformes

The Anseriformes include geese, ducks and swans (Anatidae) and another family (Anhimidae) which at first sight may seem very unlike the former group, since they are more similar in appearance to game birds or domestic poultry. Characteristics common to them all are the laying of eggs of uniform colours, from which hatch fully developed young.

Anhimidae

The Anhimidae, screamers, have relatively long legs, the toes widely spread and on the same plane. They prefer a habitat which is a mixture of marsh and dry land. They are vegetarian, often perch in trees above their wet habitats, and are very noisy. A characteristic is the presence of two pointed spurs about 5 cm (2 in) long on the forward edge of each wing. They are found in South America and there are three known species, the northern or black-necked screamer (*Chauna chavaria*) of north-western Venezuela and north Colombia, the collared screamer (*C. torquata*) and the horned screamer (*Anhima cornuta*, illustrated here), distributed from Guyana to Argentina.

Anatidae

The Anatidae, geese, ducks and swans, include altogether about 150 species whose appearance has many similar aspects in the three sub-groups: heavy body, short legs with webbed feet, a longish neck and a flattened bill.

The magpie goose (*Anseranas semipalmata*, illustrated here) is unusual in having separate, not webbed toes. It lives in Australia.

The whistling or tree ducks live in the tropics and are represented by eight species belonging to the genus *Dendrocygna*, among which are the whistling tree duck (*D. arcuata*, illustrated here) and the fulvous tree duck (*D. bicolor*) with a wide distribution in America, Africa and Asia. Together with the tree ducks, the swans and geese form the sub-group Anserinae. The swans are mostly white and noted for their graceful movements in the water. Species familiar in Europe include the mute swan (*Cygnus olor*), Bewick's swan (*C. bewickii*), a winter visitor from Siberia, and whooper swan (*C. cygnus*). The black swan (*C. stratus*) is Australian in

origin; the black-necked swan (*C. melanocoryphus*, illustrated here) and coscoroba swan (*Coscoroba coscoroba*) are both South American; but all three are kept in Europe.

The geese have shorter necks and a more modest deportment. In Europe the greylag goose (*Anser anser*) is common and from it is derived the domestic grey goose. The white-fronted goose (*A. albifrons*, illustrated here) has a wide distribution; nesting in the Arctic but wintering further south, in Britain for example. The bean goose (*A. fabilis*), pink-footed goose (*A. brachyrhynchus*) also nest in the north but winter in Britain. The snow goose (*A. caerulescens*) is another migratory species familiar in North America, but rarely seen in Europe. The brent goose (*Branta bernicla*), barnacle goose (*B. leucopsis*) and Canada goose (*B. canadensis*) are all known in Britain, though the latter is an introduced species and the only one to breed here. The néné or Hawaiian goose (*B. sandvicensis*, illustrated here) is found only in the Hawaiian islands and has only been saved from extinction by urgent conservation measures.

The Anatinae, dabbling ducks, feed mainly on water plants which they gather by tipping up in shallow waters, but they also feed on land. They occur all over the world but are commonest in temperate regions of the Northern Hemisphere. They include the shelduck (*Tadorna tadorna*) and ruddy shelduck (*T. ferruginea*). The greater number however belong to the genus *Anas*, including the mallard (*A. platyrhynchos*), pintail (*A. acuta*), teal (*A. crecca*, illustrated here), garganey (*A. querquedula*), shoveler (*A. clypeata*), wigeon (*A. penelope*) and gadwall (*A strepera*).

Diving ducks include pochard (*Aythya ferina*), tufted duck (*A. fuligula*). scaup (*A. marila*) and red-crested pochard (*Netta rufina*). These birds live in deeper water and dive to feed off the bottom. Among the Anatinae kept in gardens is the decorative mandarin duck (*Aix galericulata*), originally from China. The eider duck (*Somateria mollissima*) is famous for its plumage which is collected and used for making eiderdowns. It is a maritime bird, though found inland locally, and breeds along rocky coasts. The smew (*Mergus albellus*), red-breasted merganser (*M. serrator*) and goosander (*M. merganser*) are fish eaters. The goldeneye (*Bucephala clangula*), scoter (*Melanitta nigra*) and velvet scoter (*M. fusca*) are often seen at sea round the British coast. The hooded merganser (*M. cucullatus*, illustrated here) is a North American species.

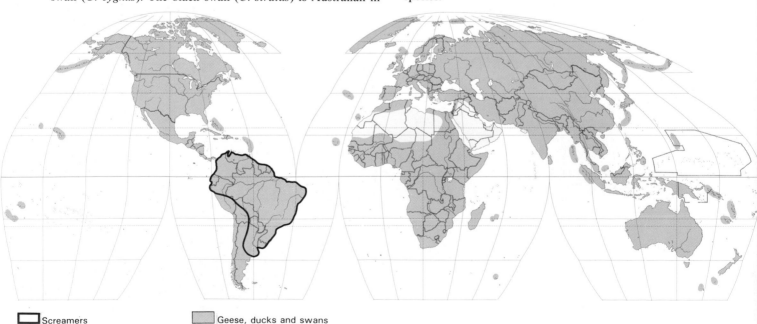

☐ Screamers   ▨ Geese, ducks and swans

néné (Hawaiian goose)

horned screamer

magpie goose

white-fronted goose

teal

whistling tree duck

black-necked swan

hooded merganser

Falconiformes

The Falconiformes are predatory or scavenging birds with hooked beaks, highly developed eyesight and extreme skill in flight. The four families are: Cathartidae, Accipitridae, Falconidae and Sagittaridae.

Cathartidae

The family contains the vultures of the New World, all of which feed on carrion. The most striking is the South American king vulture (*Sarcoramphus papa*, illustrated here); among the five other species the best known are the Andean condor (*Vultur gryphus*) and the turkey vulture (*Cathartes aura*).

Accipitridae

The Accipitridae is the largest family of the Falconiformes. It comprises the vultures of the Old World, and the eagles, buzzards, hawks, kites, harriers and ospreys, though this species is often put in its own family, the Pandionidae. Their wings are broader than those of the falcons and the upper mandible is not notched the way it is in falcons. Most build substantial nests. The females are much larger than the males. Typical hawks nesting in Europe include the sparrowhawk (*Accipiter nisus*), goshawk (*A. gentilis*), and buzzard (*Buteo buteo*). Eagles mate for life and use the same nest each year. The golden eagle (*Aquila chrysaëtos*) nests in Scotland and many countries of Europe. Eagles are found all over the world: the wedge-tailed eagle (*A. audax*, illustrated here) is Australian, while the harpy eagle (*Harpia harpya*) is South American. European eagles include Bonelli's eagle (*Hieraëtus fasciatus*) and the sea eagle (*Haliaëtus albicilla*). The sub-group Circaetinae comprises birds of prey that live mostly on reptiles, such as the crested snake-eagle (*Spilornis cheela*, illustrated here) of Asia, and the bateleur (*Terathopius caudatus*, illustrated here) of Africa. The harriers include Montagu's harrier (*C. pygargus*) and marsh harrier (*C. aeruginosus*) both of which nest in Europe as does the hen harrier (*Circus cyaneus*). This species also occurs in North America where it is often called the marsh hawk. The kites, of worldwide distribution, are lightly built, graceful fliers. They include the black kite (*Milvus migrans*) and red kite (*M. milvus*) both of which used to

occur in Britain, though only the latter does now, confined to a few breeding pairs in Wales. Another well-known kite is the Everglade kite (*Rostrhamus sociabilis*, illustrated here) of Florida.

The sea eagles, largely carrion-eaters which also take fish, include the bald eagle (*Haliaëtus leucocephalus*), the national bird of the USA, and the white-fronted sea eagle (*H. leucogaster*, illustrated here) of Asia and Australia.

The honey buzzard (*Pernis apivorus*), a summer visitor to Britain, eats bee and wasp larvae, and small birds and their eggs. The bat hawk (*Macheiramphus alcinus*, illustrated here) is found in Africa and Asia. Another well-known species of southern Europe and Asia is the lammergeier (*Gypaëtus barbatus*); this often drops bones from a great height onto rocks so that they smash and expose the marrow, which is eaten. The cinereous vulture (*Aegypius monachus*) of southern Europe, Africa and Asia, is one of the largest and heaviest flying birds. The Egyptian vulture (*Neophron percnopterus*) follows cattle, waiting for the death of the weaker members. The osprey (*Pandion haliaetus*) is a fish-eater.

Falconidae

The falcons have long, pointed wings and are swift and powerful in flight. They include the laughing falcon (*Herpetotheres cachinnans*) a noisy snake-eating bird of Mexican and Brazilian forests. The smallest members of the family are the falconets and pygmy falcons, of which *Microhierax caerulescens* of South-East Asia is illustrated here. The gyrfalcon (*Falco rusticolus*, illustrated here) of Arctic regions, is the largest of the falcons, reaching 60 cm (24 in) in length. It hunts hares, rodents and birds of the tundra and seacoasts. Other falcons nesting in Britain and Europe are the hobby (*F. subbuteo*), merlin (*F. columbarius*), kestrel (*F. tinnunculus*), and the peregrine (*F. peregrinus*) called the duck hawk where it occurs in North America.

Sagittaridae

This family comprises the sole species, the secretary bird (*Sagittarius serpentarius*). Its popular name is derived from the few large black plumes which project from the back of the head, like a quill pen. It lives on the open savannah country south of the Sahara and eats ground-living animals especially snakes.

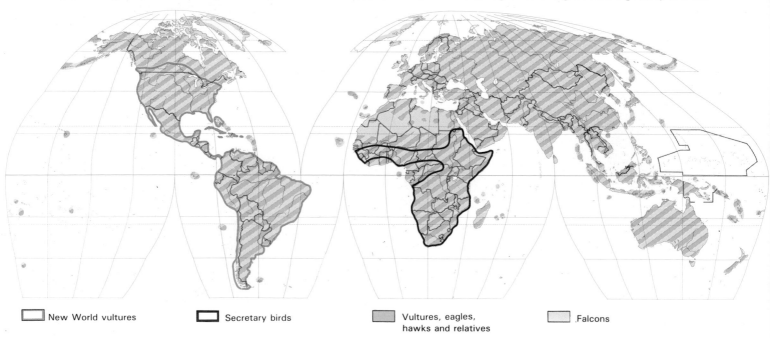

New World vultures   Secretary birds   Vultures, eagles, hawks and relatives   Falcons

bat hawk

everglade kite

bateleur eagle

white-fronted
sea eagle

wedge-tailed eagle

South American
king vulture

crested snake
eagle

pygmy falcon

gyrfalcon

Galliformes

The Galliformes group is of worldwide distribution and comprises a large number of chicken-like species of very similar structure: squat body, short wings, short legs, and strong toenails adapted for digging. The head has a lightly curved beak and often sprouts crests, or wattles. They usually have abundant feathers and the plumage is often brightly coloured, especially the males.

There are seven families, of which the first is the Megapodidae: megapodes or mound-builders, known by various common names such as brush turkeys and jungle fowl, and include the Mallee fowl (*Leipoa ocellata*, illustrated here). They live in Australia and the islands to the north-east. They are unique among birds in not incubating the eggs or keeping the young warm by body heat. Instead, they build incubators consisting of holes in the earth in which the eggs are deposited, often colonially, then covered with sand or various plants. In this way the eggs are incubated by the heat of the sun or rotting vegetation. All the parents have to do is to see that the temperature is suitable at all times of the day, by covering or exposing the eggs as necessary. It is also their task to help the newly hatched chicks out of the earth. The maleo (*Megacephalon maleo*) of Sulawesi uses holes dug obliquely 1 m (3¼ ft) into warm sand, and does not visit the eggs again once they are buried within the mound.

The Cracidae – curassows, guans and chachalacas – are tropical American birds, often having the head ornamented with tufts of curly feathers. Frequently the beak bears protuberances of one kind or another. The great curassow (*Crax rubra*, illustrated here), for example, has a crest of feathers bent forwards and a large protuberance on the beak in contact with the forehead. It lives from Mexico to Ecuador. The guans are smaller, and the chachalacas, mostly of the genus *Ortalus*, are smaller still.

The Tetraonidae, grouse and ptarmigan, are fat-bodied birds sometimes reaching weights of 7 kg (15 lb). There are eleven genera but only twelve species, all living in temperate and Arctic regions of the Northern Hemisphere. They are distinguished by feathered nostrils and in some species by legs feathered down to the toes. In North America the spruce grouse (*Canachites canadensis*, illustrated here) and sage grouse (*Centrocercus urophasianus*) are common. In Great Britain the red grouse (*Lagopus lagopus*) and black grouse or black-cock (*Lyrurus tetrix*) both nest in northern and western areas, but ptarmigan (*Lagopus mutus*) and capercaillie (*Tetrao urogallus*) occur only in Scotland; all are found in Europe, the red grouse under the name of willow grouse (and willow ptarmigan in North America). The ptarmigan occurs only in the mountainous parts of Scandinavia, the Alps and the Pyrenees, and in North America where it is known as the rock ptarmigan.

The family Phasianidae includes pheasants, partridge, peacocks, quail and francolins, with a worldwide distribution. They are good runners and the sexes are often markedly unlike each other, the males being very showy, the females cryptically coloured. The common pheasant (*Phasianus colchicus*) originates from Asia but has been widely introduced into Europe and America as a game bird. The common or grey partridge (*Perdix perdix*) is widespread across Europe from Scandinavia, Ireland and Spain and eastwards to Central Asia. The peacocks are noted for their decorative plumage which is displayed during courtship. The familiar peacock of ornamental gardens is *Pavo cristatus*; the African Congo peafowl of Zaire (*Afroparvo congensis*, illustrated here) also has beautiful colouring. Among the smallest of the Phasianidae are the quails, including the common quail (*Coturnix coturnix*) and tufted quail (*Oreotrix pictus*, illustrated here). Species of the genus *Tragopan* are found in Eastern and Central Asia. The attractive satyr tragopan (*T. satyra*) is illustrated here.

The Numididae, guinea-fowl, are distributed in Africa, Madagascar and parts of Arabia. The tufted guinea-fowl (*Numida meleagris*) of Africa is the ancestor of the domestic guinea-fowl.

The Meleagridae are represented only by the wild turkey (*Meleagris gallopavo*) of North America. The ocellated turkey (*Agriocharis ocellata*, illustrated here) is found in Central America. From the former, originally of USA and Mexico all domesticated turkeys are derived. The body is massive and the length can attain 110 cm (44 in); the head is bare, vividly coloured and ornamented with wattles. The tail can be opened into a wheel-like form and the large males open it out in courtship or to demonstrate their superiority to intruders.

The family Opisthocomidae is represented only by the hoatzin (*Opisthocomus hoatzin*, illustrated here) of the Amazon. Its nestlings have a small claw on each wing which is used for scrambling about in trees; vestiges of these claws persist in the adult bird.

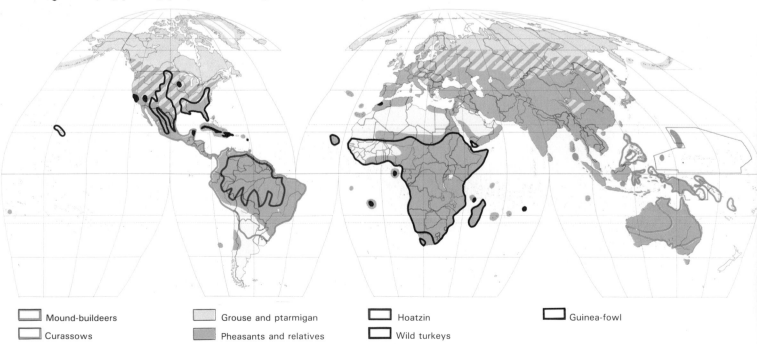

☐ Mound-buildeers	☐ Grouse and ptarmigan	☐ Hoatzin	☐ Guinea-fowl
☐ Curassows	☐ Pheasants and relatives	☐ Wild turkeys	

hoatzin

Congo peafowl

ocellated turkey

tufted quail

mallee fowl

satyr tragopan

great curassow

spruce grouse

Gruiformes

The Gruiformes comprise twelve families, including cranes and bustards, which resemble each other only in a few particulars of the skeleton and the general anatomy. Common characteristics are the long neck, beak and legs; feet which are never webbed but sometimes lobed; the sexes are similar and most species characteristically spend a lot of their time on the ground, walking rather than flying.

Gruidae

The family Gruidae, cranes, contains five genera. They are elegant birds up to 1.5 m (5 ft) tall, with long legs, neck and beak. The plumage is often striking, and the head often partly bare. One of the principal characteristics of the family is the remarkable courtship displays, one of the most extraordinary among the birds. It is a highly ritualized dance which includes loud and penetrating calls on the part of the male, with simulated embraces, flights and returns, bowing, pirouetting, short running steps, and offerings of grass stems and twigs; the rituals may be repeated many times.

The common crane (*Grus grus*) nests from Eastern Europe across northern Asia to Siberia and China. Some species, such as the sandhill crane (*G. canadensis*) of Canada and eastern Siberia, the whooping crane (*G. americana*) of North America, the Japanese or Manchurian crane (*G. japonensis*), and the Siberian white crane (*G. leucogeranus*) are endangered mostly due to loss of habitat. The smallest species is the demoiselle crane (*Anthropoides virgo*) that breeds in North Africa, south-eastern Europe and Central Asia. The crowned crane (*Balearica pavonina*) is found in most of sub-Saharan Africa, and the wattled crane (*Bugeranus carunculatus*) in eastern and southern Africa. The other genus is *Tetrapterix* of Africa. The remarkable cries uttered by the cranes are made possible by the elongated trachea or windpipe, which is of normal length in the chick but grows until in the adult it can reach a length of 1.5 m (5 ft); it is coiled up in the hollow keel of the breastbone and provides resonance to the call like the coiled tubes of a French horn. Several species of crane are on the endangered list due to shooting, nesting disturbance and loss of habitat.

Otididae

The Otididae, bustards, look rather like small, dumpy ostriches. They are however capable of sustained flight, despite their bulk, which is sometimes notable, as in the case of the Kori bustard (*Ardeotis kori*), which at 15 kg (33 lb) is the heaviest of the flying birds. They have strong legs and broad feet with only three toes. The neck is rather long and thick. The great bustard (*Otis tarda*) lives on the steppes and cultivated fields of southern Europe and central and western Asia and formerly occurred in England. The little bustard (*O. tetrax*) occupies much the same area. Various species live in Africa including the Houbara (*Chlamydotis undulata*) and the white-bellied bustard (*Eupodotis senegalensis*, illustrated here). Two very elegant species, *E. bengalensis* and *Sypheotides indica*, live in India.

Rallidae

The Rallidae – rails, crakes, coots and gallinules – are the largest and most diverse Gruiformes family, found all over the world except in polar regions. The most numerous genus is *Rallus*, to which belongs the water rail (*R. aquaticus*), common in Britain and western Europe, though it is difficult to observe and more often heard than seen. The spotted crake (*Porzana porzana*) is smaller and even more difficult to observe though it nests in south-eastern England. The little crake (*P. parva*) and Baillon's crake (*P. pusilla*) are summer visitors or vagrants to Britain. The corncrake (*Crex crex*) used to be common in cornfields and haymeadows but now breeds only in north and north-western Britain and Ireland. The most familiar members of the family are the moorhen (*Gallinula chloropus*), called Florida gallinule in the USA, and coot (*Fulica atra*); with similar species *F. americana* in North America. The purple gallinule (*Porphyrio porphyrio*) is a bird of southern and eastern Europe that is occasionally seen in northern France. Others of the same genus are present in Asia. A very similar species lives in New Zealand, the takahé (*Notornis mantelli*, illustrated here). Pigs, dogs and weasels introduced to New Zealand soon devastated populations of defenceless ground birds including the takahé. By 1900 it was thought to be extinct but in 1948 it was rediscovered in a remote valley, now part of an extensive nature reserve appropriately called Takahé Valley.

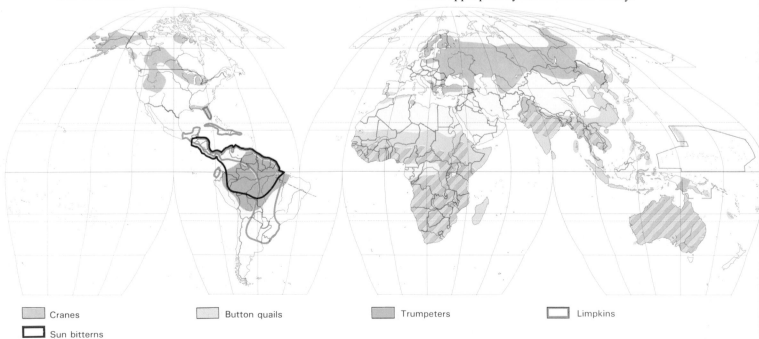

Cranes Button quails Trumpeters Limpkins

Sun bitterns

crested seriema

sun bittern

kagu

white-bellied bustard

trumpeter

finfoot

button quail

limpkin

takahé

Turnicidae

The Turnicidae, button quails, occupy much of the Old World, strongly resembling the true quails in appearance and habits. They are small and short-tailed with rounded wings. They are distributed from south-eastern Europe and through Africa and Asia to the Far East and Australia. In contrast to other groups, in the button quails it is the female, larger than the males, who are more highly coloured and take the initiative in courtship. The male incubates the eggs and busies himself with the chicks. The best-known genus is *Turnix*, comprising thirteen species, among them the painted button quail (*T. varia*) of Australia, *T. suscitator* of Asia, illustrated on p. 193, and the Andalusian hemipode (*T. sylvatica*) of Spain.

Heliornithidae

The Heliornithidae, finfoots or sun grebes, live in some limited tropical and sub-tropical areas. They are aquatic birds with lobed toes and a long thin neck. They are reluctant fliers, awkward on land but excellent swimmers. The nest is built in dense vegetation some metres above the ground. As with the grebes, the young are carried on the backs of the parents and often stay there even during dives. Three genera are known, each with only one species: the African finfoot (*Podica senegalensis*, illustrated on p. 193) has a low booming call, heard especially during the breeding season.

Mesitornithidae

The Mesitornithidae, mesites or monias, live only in Madagascar. Weak fliers, they move about on the ground and build their nests in low bushes. Of the three known species one lives in the bushy savannah in the west of the island, two in the eastern forests.

Aramidae

The Aramidae comprises only one species, the limpkin (*Aramus guarauna*, illustrated on p. 193), which lives from the USA to Argentina. It resembles a heron, with its long legs, neck and beak. It lives in marshy regions where it finds its preferred food, water snails, which it extracts skilfully from the shell without cracking it.

Psophiidae

The Psophiidae – trumpeters – contain only one genus with three species, which live in South America. In size half way between cranes and rails, they measure 43 to 53 cm (18 to 22 in) in length and are rather dark in colour, ranging from black with a purple sheen to black with a greenish or bronze sheen. The curved beak is short and robust. They have an upright posture and the three species rarely fly, preferring to run on the earth when escaping from predators. One of them, *Psophia leucoptera*, is illustrated on p. 193.

Eurypygidae

The Eurypygidae again comprise only one geuns but with only one species, the sun bittern (*Eurypyga helias*, illustrated on p. 193), which lives between southern Mexico and central Brazil, in the humid forest zones near to rivers, up to 1000 m (3200 ft) above sea level. They most resemble herons, live alone or in couples, and are easy to observe while they catch fish and small invertebrates along the banks of the rivers.

Cariamidae

The Cariamidae, seriemas, comprise two species whose appearance recalls the cranes, the bustards and, very distantly, the secretary birds. The legs and tail are very long, while the neck and head are like those of a bustard. The wings are rounded and short, and on the forehead there is an erectile tuft of feathers. The crested seriema (*Cariama cristata*, illustrated on p. 193) is the most widely distributed species, found in Brazil, Argentina and Uruguay. The other species is Burmeister's seriema (*Chunga burmeisteri*) found in north-western Argentina and Paraguay.

Pedionomidae

The family Pedionomidae also has only one species, the plains wanderer or collared hemipode (*Pedionomus torquatus*) found in the grasslands and plains of south-eastern Australia. It is the male who incubates the eggs while the female defends the nest and procures food.

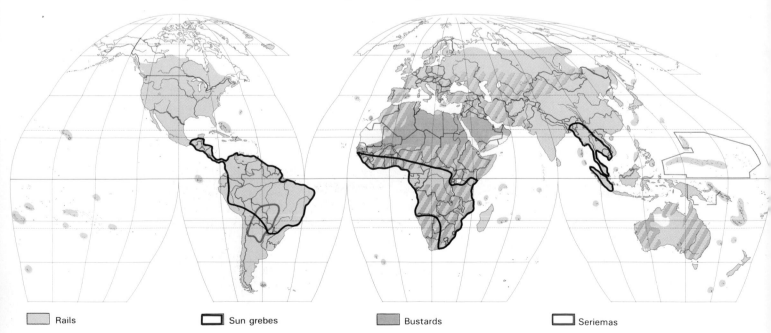

Rails   Sun grebes   Bustards   Seriemas

Rhynochetidae

The Rhynochetidae again comprise only one species, the kagu (*Rhynochetos jubatus*, illustrated on p. 193), found only in the mountains of New Caledonia. Little is known of its biology, except that it runs rapidly and indulges in complicated displays which involves it seizing the fathers of its wings and tail with its beak.

Charadriiformes

The Charadriiformes groups together birds variable in appearance but linked with the Gruiformes. There are many species, grouped into sixteen families. The Charadriiformes have a worldwide distribution and their habitat is in general coastal, but many species inhabit freshwater habitats and even deserts and moorlands.

Jacanidae and Rostrulidae

The Jacanidae, jacanas or lily-trotters, much resemble the rails. Thanks to their long legs and long toes, the jacanas can walk on floating vegetation, in particular on water-lilies. The wings are fairly long and have on the wrist a protuberance which in some species is a real spur. The family is found in Africa, Madagascar, Asia, tropical America and Australia. The African jacana (*Actophilornis africana*) is a well-known species.

The Rostratulidae, painted snipe, are represented by *Rostratula bengalensis*, illustrated on p. 196, found in Australia, Africa and southern Asia, and the South African *Nycticryphes semicollaris*. They are effectively camouflaged against the marsh vegetation in which they live. The male incubates the eggs and cares for the young, while his mate defends the territory.

Haematopididae

The single genus of the Haematopodidae is *Haemotopus*, the oystercatchers, with about four species. They are distributed widely along the coasts and sometimes in the interiors both of the Old and the New World. They are largely wading birds with brightly coloured legs, beak and eyes. The powerful beak is well adapted for striking or prising open molluscs. The European species (*Haematopus ostralegus*) is black and white, with pink legs and red beak. Other species include the black oystercatchers (*H. niger*, illustrated on p. 196) of South America and *H. moquini* of Africa.

Charadriidae

The family Charadriidae comprises three distinct groups of birds: plovers, lapwings and dotterels, Capable fliers, on the ground they flock and are rapid in their movements. They search for worms, molluscs and other small animals in the sand, or mud or in the fields. The plovers belong to the genus *Vanellus* among which is the European and Asian lapwing (*V. vanellus*). The spurwing plover (*Hoplopterus* (or *Vanellus*) *spinosus*, illustrated on p. 196) lives in Africa. The grey plover (*Pluvialis squatarola*) is a winter visitor from the north to Britain, while the golden plover (*P. apricaria*) is a resident of northern Britain and northern Ireland. Also included among British species are the ringed plover (*Charadrius hiaticula*) and the little ringed plover (*C. dubius*). The dotterel (*Eudromias morinellus*) is a mountain bird which breeds in north-eastern Scotland and Norway.

Scolopacidae

The seventy species, in twenty-four genera, that make up the family of the Scolopacidae – long-billed waders, sandpipers, woodcock, and snipe – nearly all breed in the temperate or Arctic regions of the Northern Hemisphere. They both live and breed on open ground and shorelines in wet localities. Most form winter flocks, sometimes in enormous numbers and often on estuaries.

There are four sub-families. The Tringinae include the largest waders – curlews, sandpipers and red- and greenshanks. There are two genera. *Numenius* includes the common curlew (*N. arquata*), the whimbrel (*N. phaeopus*) and the Tahitian curlew (*N. tahitiensis*, illustrated on p. 196). *Tringa* includes greenshanks (*T. nebularia*), redshank (*T. totanus*) and common sandpiper (*T. hypoleucos*), all of which breed in Britain.

The Scolopacinae include the woodcock (*Scolopex rusticola*), which breed over a wide area from western Europe to Japan, and snipe (*Gallinago gallinago*). The Calidritinae include the black-tailed and bar-tailed godwits (*Limosa limosa* and *L. lapponica*), the little stint and Temminck's stint (*Calidris minuta* and *C. temminckii*), other *Calidris* species such as pectoral and curlew, sandpipers, knot, and dunlin sanderling, ruff (*Philomachus pugnax*, illustrated on p. 196) and dowitchers (*Limnodromus* sp.). The Arenariinae which include the turnstone (*Arenaria interpres*).

Recurvirostridae, Phalaropodidae and Dromadidae

The Recurvirostridae comprise birds with long, slender beaks and legs. They include stilts and avocets. The black-winged stilt (*Himantopus himantopus*) has a straight beak, while in the avocets – (*Recurvirostra avosetta*), breeding on European coasts, including that of south-eastern England, and the American avocet (*R. americana*, illustrated on p. 196) – it is turned upwards.

The Phalaropodidae comprise three species of the genus *Phalaropus*. They are aquatic birds and excellent swimmers. The European species are the grey phalarope (*P. fulicarius*) and red necked phalarope (*P. lobatus*), while Wilson's phalarope (*P. tricolor*, illustrated on p. 196) nests in America.

The Dromadidae comprise only the crab plove (*Dromas ardeola*, illustrated on p. 196) which lives on the East African coasts.

Burhinidae

The nine species of Burhinidae, thick-knees or stone curlew, have broad heads with enormous yellow eyes, revealing their nocturnal habits, and short beaks. The stone curlew (*Burhinus oedeicnemus*, illustrated on p. 199) breeds from south-eastern England across Europe to North Africa, Arabia, Sri Lanka and Burma. It is a shy bird and lives in open habitats – shingle heaths, riverbeds and dry salt marshes.

Glareolidae

Coursers and pratincoles form two sub-familes (Cursoriinae and Glareolinae) belonging to the Glareolidae. They are small and mottled brown or sandy-golden. The Cursoriinae are gregarious, nesting in colonies and defending their territory. The pratincole (*Glareola pratincola*) is found in southern Europe. The cream-coloured courser (*Cursorius cursor*) is a desert species, seen sometimes on sandy beaches in Europe as far north as Scandinavia. *Cursorius coromandelicus*, illustrated on p. 199, is an Asian species.

spurwing plover

crab plover

Wilson's phalarope

black oystercatcher

American avocet

painted snipe

Tahitian
or bristle-thighed
curlew

African jacana
(lilytrotter)

ruff
(male in breeding
plumage)

Thinocoridae and Chionididae

The Thinocoridae, seedsnipe, are South American. They eat seed and grain. The piping seedsnipe, *T. rumicivorus*, is illustrated on p. 199.

The Chiomididae, looking like a cross between a seagull and a white dove, are called Antarctic pigeons or sheathbills. There are only two species, the yellow-billed sheathbill (*Chionis alba*, illustrated on p. 199) and *C. minor* with a black bill. They are found on the southernmost coasts of South America and a few Antarctic islands, and on the Antarctic continent. They are the only seabirds without webbed feet.

Stercorariidae

The Stercorariidae comprise the skuas, or jaegers, birds of cold seas and polar regions. They have strongly hooked bills and are accomplished fliers. Of the four species found in the northern hemisphere, the largest is the great skua (*Sterocarius skua*) 58 cm (23 in) long. It is a heavily built bird identified by its size and by white wing patches which are visible in flight. Though it will harry other seabirds to force them to disgorge their catch, it also scavenges after ships and takes eggs and young of other birds; the southern race often nests near penguin colonies on which it preys. Of the other species, the pomarine skua is the largest, being some 53 cm (20 in) in length, and is distinguished by its very large bill and curiously twisted tail feathers. The smallest species is the long-tailed skua (*S. longicaudatus*, illustrated on p. 199) with a length of 50 cm (20 in) excluding the 20 cm (8 in) tail feathers. Its range extends further north than any of the species, and is unusual in that its food consists primarily of small mammals – lemmings that are especially abundant on the Arctic tundra. The Arctic skua (*S. parasiticus*) is probably the

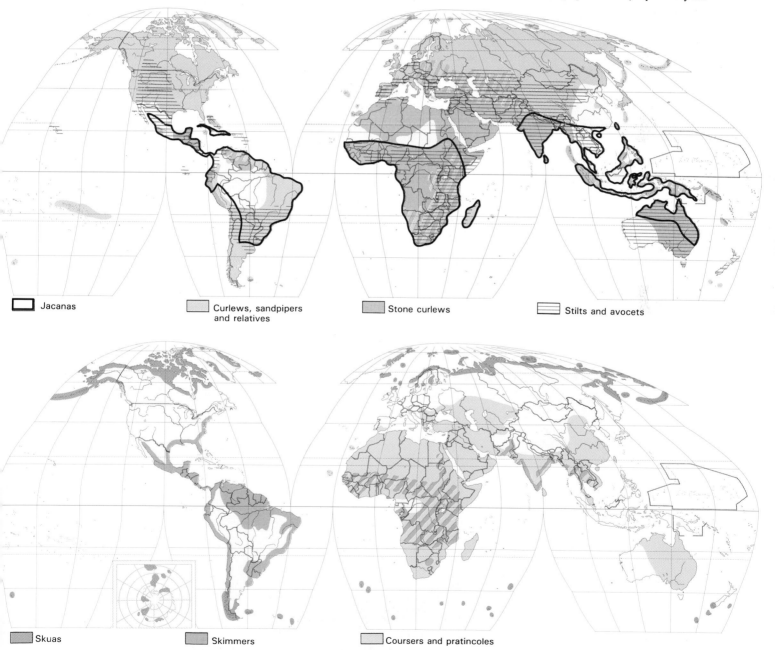

☐ Jacanas

▨ Curlews, sandpipers and relatives

▨ Stone curlews

▥ Stilts and avocets

☐ Skuas

☐ Skimmers

☐ Coursers and pratincoles

commonest species. As its names suggests it relies heavily on other birds for food. After a brief chase, a gull or tern will readily disgorge its food and continue unmolested while the skua swoops down to feed. Skuas are great wanderers and, outside the breeding season, tran-equatorial migrations are commonest.

Laridae

The Laridae include seventy-eight species in four genera of which *Larus* contains most of the seagulls and *Sterna* the terns. They have long wings, webbed feet and slightly hooked beaks. Dimensions vary from the 20 cm (8 in) of the white-winged black tern (*Chlidonias leucopterus*) to the more than 70 cm (28 in) of the great black-backed gull (*Larus marinus*). All the Laridae live near water, either fresh or salt, and some are essentially ocean-going. Nesting takes place, as a rule, in very large colonies and mating is preceded by nuptial parades and displays. The swallow-tailed gull *Creagrus furcatus* is illustrated here.

The gulls comprise the sub-family Larinae. The black-headed gull (*Larus ridibundus*) nests in the more northerly parts of Europe and is commonly seen inland; the herring-gull (*L. argentatus*) is the commonest coastal gull of Europe.

The terns belong to the sub-family Sterninae. They are small, delicate birds with long pointed wings, an elongated beak and a tail which is often forked. The common tern (*Sterna hirundo*), little tern (*S. albifrons*), roseate tern (*S. dougalli*), and Arctic tern (*S. paradisaea*) are often seen in British waters. The Arctic tern breeds in Britain and in Arctic latitudes, then migrates far into the Southern Hemisphere to spend the winter. The round trip exceeds 32,000 km (20,000 miles); among the longest migrations of any species. Other genera are *Chlidonias*, to which the white-winged black tern already mentioned belongs, *Gygis* with the fairy or white tern (*G. alba*) of the Southern Hemisphere, and *Thalasseus* with the royal tern (*T. maximus*, illustrated here), of the western coasts of North America.

Rynchopidae

The Rhynchiopidae, skimmers, are a small interesting family consisting of three species of the genus *Rynchops*. The black skimmer (*R. nigra*, illustrated here) nests along the south-eastern seaboard of North America south to Argentina. The African skimmer (*R. flavirostris*) is found on the coast and on inland waters of Africa, and the Indian skimmer (*R. albicollis*) lives by rivers and large lakes of India and Burma.

The skimmers' most distinguishing feature is the large bill, with the lower mandible developed into a scoop. When feeding, this part of the bill ploughs through the water, and when a fish is caught it is tossed into the air and swallowed on the wing.

Alcidae

The Alcidae – auks, guillemots and puffins – differ markedly in appearance from other members of the Charadriiformes. Chubby, medium to small-sized birds, they live in the colder waters of the northern hemisphere. Most species are found in the Pacific and Bering Sea. The largest species was the great auk (*Pinguinis impennis*) at 76 cm (30 in), thought to have become extinct in 1844 off Iceland when two adults were killed and a single egg was destroyed. One of the smallest members at 20 cm (8 in) is the little auk. It is also one of the most numerous seabirds of the North Atlantic, sometimes nesting in enormous colonies.

Nest sites vary considerably, for example the common guillemot (*Uria aalge*) uses narrow ledges, the razorbill (*Alca torda*) prefers crevices and the hollows under boulders, while puffins such as the tufted puffin (*Luna cirrhota*, illustrated here), is a burrow nester.

The black guillemot (*Cepphus grylle*), pigeon guillemot (*C. columba*), and the spectacled guillemot (*C. carbo*) differ from other auks in not having a particularly upright stance and when at rest look almost duck-like. They also have weak calls and tend to be more solitary in their nesting habits.

The six species of auklets as their name suggests are rather like auks in miniature. Some species such as the rhinoceros auklet (*Cerorhinca monocerata*) have streamers of feathers growing from the base of the beak. The whiskered auklet (*Aethia pusilla*) is probably the rarest and least known of the tribe. It nests on the Aleutian Islands.

Murrelets are small, rather drab-looking birds of the North Pacific. Because of their remote islet breeding grounds, little is known of their behaviour – indeed the nest site of the marbled murrelet (*Brachyramphus marmoratus*) has never been discovered.

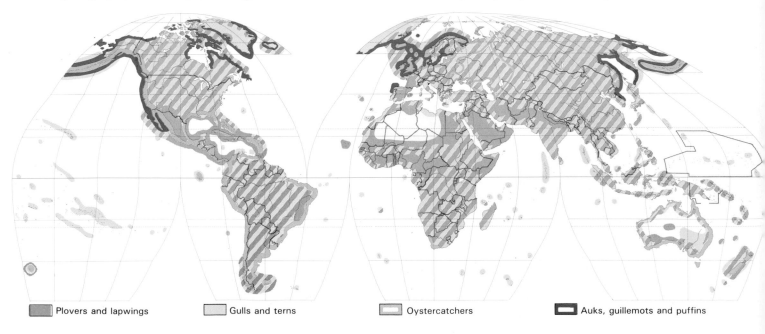

| Plovers and lapwings | Gulls and terns | Oystercatchers | Auks, guillemots and puffins |

black skimmer

piping seedsnipe

royal tern

Indian courser

stone curlew

swallow-tailed
gull

tufted puffin

yellow-billed
sheathbill

long-tailed skua

Columbiformes

The Columbiformes have a squat body supported on short legs, a small head with a short neck and long, pointed wings which permit fast and dextrous flight; though some are flightless or nearly so and spend most of their time on the ground. Bred for food by man since ancient times, the rock dove and the domestic pigeons evolved from it have, thanks to their talent for orientation, been also used through the ages for the carrying of messages. A characteristic of the group is the ability to breathe in water when drinking, so that they do not need to raise the head to swallow. There are three families, Raphidae, Pteroclidae and Columbidae.

Raphidae

The Raphidae are birds that became extinct in historic times through the actions of man. Nothing remains of them but bones, a few skin fragments and some contemporary illustrations. Unable to fly, they retained only rudiments of wings, but had very strong beaks. The known species are the dodo (*Raphus cucullatus*) of Mauritius, the solitaire of Réunion (*R. solitarius*) and the solitaire of Rodrigues (*Penzophaps solitaria*).

Pteroclidae

The sixteen species of sandgrouse, the Pteroclidae, are terrestrial birds, with very short feathered legs, generally three-toed; they are unable to run but walk rapidly, and fly well once they are on the wing. The plumage is coloured to match the open, often desert country in which they live in southern Europe, Asia and Africa. They are gregarious, and the flocks may contain up to 400 individuals. The young are able to leave the nest and feed themselves almost as soon as they hatch, but depend on the parents for drinking. In view of the aridity of the nesting areas, the parents have to make long journeys to find water; at the same time they take a bath in order to soak their feathers with water which they then offer the young to drink on their return to the nest. The Tibetan sandgrouse (*Syrrhaptus tibetanus*) is a Central Asian species; Pallas's sandgrouse (*S. paradoxus*) lives in southern Russia and occasionally populations irrupt north temporarily into other countries, including Britain. The Lichtenstein's sand-grouse (*Pterocles lichtensteini*, illustrated here) lives in the savannah country south of the Sahara, and the pin-tailed sandgrouse (*P. alchata*, illustrated here) frequents areas of Spain, North Africa and Asia Minor.

Columbidae

The plumage of the Columbidae, pigeons and doves, is sometimes highly coloured, and the feathers detach themselves easily, probably as an adaptive device against predators. Many attacks by birds of prey end up in fact with a mouthful of feathers for the raptor and the 'victim' escapes. The young, born featherless and with eyes still closed, are fed by the parents with 'pigeon's milk', a substance secreted in the crop. There are three sub-families, Treroninae, Gourinae and Columbinae.

The Treroninae are fruit-eating pigeons, living in the tropics of the Old World and feeding exclusively on fruit and berries. Members of the genus *Treron* live in groups guided by an adult individual and move continually in the search for food. Among the various species is the green pigeon (*T. capella*, illustrated here). The Gourinae, crowned pigeons, all come from New Guinea and are essentially terrestrial; *Goura victoria* is illustrated here.

Of the Columbinae, three species of the genus *Columba* are well known in Britain, the rock dove (*C. livia*), woodpigeon (*C. palumbus*), and stock dove (*C. oenas*). The rock dove is the ancestor of the domesticated types of pigeons and the feral 'wild' pigeons of towns and cities. These birds have regular habits: they fly in flocks to feed and drink in the morning, then return to a midday perching area during the hottest part of the day, then feed again in the late afternoon before retiring to a communal roost. Such a routine, plus the fact that they fight little even during the breeding season, has well fitted them for captivity. The genus *Streptopelia* includes turtledoves and ringdoves such as the turtledove (*S. turtur*) and palm dove (*S. canadensis*, illustrated here). Also illustrated here are the pheasant dove (*Otodiphas nobilis*) and tufted ground dove (*Lophophas plumifera*). The bleeding heart pigeon (*Gallicolumba luzonica*) of the Philippines has white underparts except for a red marking on the upper part of the chest. The formerly abundant passenger pigeon (*Columbigallina passerina*, illustrated here) of North America became extinct owing to human activities as recently as 1914 when the last zoo specimen died.

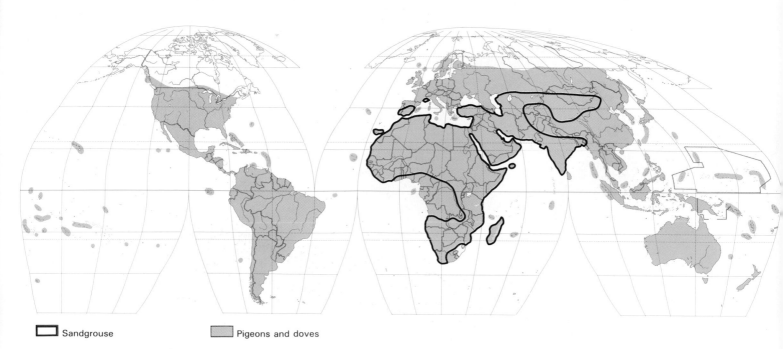

☐ Sandgrouse   ▨ Pigeons and doves

pin-tailed sandgrouse

pheasant dove

palm dove

tufted ground dove

green pigeon

crowned pigeon

Lichtenstein's
sandgrouse

passenger pigeon

Psittaciformes

The Psittaciformes comprise the single family of Psittacidae, the parrots, made up of over 300 species whose appearance is very similar even though their lengths can vary from 10 cm (5 in) to more than 1 m (3 ft 3 in). Perfectly adapted for arboreal life, the parrots have short legs with two forward toes and two backward, giving them a powerful grip and a capacity for manipulation superior to that of other birds. The beak is hooked and the upper jaw is much more developed than the lower. With strong, rounded wings, they are not exceptional fliers; some species are completely adapted to a non-aerial life, as is the ground parrot (*Pezoporus wallicus*) of Australia and Tasmania. The plumage is often vividly coloured with white, red, green, blue, black and many intermediate shades. Many of the parrots live in large colonies and nest in holes in rocks or in trees Their distribution is tropical and subtropical in Africa, South America, Asia and Australia. The family contains more than 300 species in eighty-two genera which can be subdivided into seven sub-families.

The Nestorinae have only one genus with two species, both living in New Zealand: the kea (*Nestor notabilis*, illustrated here), which sometimes attacks sheep, and the kaka (*N. meridionalis*), a gentler bird that lives on fruit and insect larvae. Many tales have grown up concerning the kea. Farmers and livestock managers say that it attacks and kills sheep and lambs, and is especially fond of tearing out and eating the fatty flesh around the kidneys. Conservationists counter that the kea will only feed on dying or already dead prey, and that it is innocent of its notorious reputation. Whichever version is true the kea is certainly a large and powerful bird, named for its raucous cry that echoes among the mountains. The Psittrichasinae contain only one species, the vulture parrot (*Psittrichas fulgidus*) of New Guinea. Little is known of its biology; it is greyish-black with red wings and underparts. The Strigopinae are also monotypic, being represented only by the kakapo of New Zealand (*Strigops habroptilus*, illustrated here); a terrestrial bird, it usually spends the day sheltering between the roots of trees, while at night it goes in search of food. Incapable of flight, it sometimes launches itself in a downward glide from trees. It is now one of the world's rarest birds with probably fewer than 100 alive today in the wild. The Cacatuinae, cockatoos, all of Australia and New Zealand, have as their most important genus

Cacatua, among whose species is the magnificent sulphur-crested cockatoo (*C. galerita*), an inmate of many zoological gardens. It lives on hard-shelled nuts that it cracks with its powerful beak. Most of the genus are white. The black palm cockatoo (*Probosciger aterrimus*, illustrated here) is the largest of the cockatoos; its beak is as large as the rest of its head. The males of the raven cockatoos of the genus *Calyptorhynchus* are also all black, but the females are marked with yellow bars; an example is the black cockatoo (*C. funereus*).

The smallest parrots belong to the subfamily of the Micropsittinae, pygmy parrots; they average about 10 cm (4 in) in length with weights of about 13 gm ($\frac{1}{2}$ oz). The single genus is *Micropsitta* of New Guinea, which exhibits a pronounced sexual dimorphism, the female being much more brightly coloured than the male. The diet consists of fruit, the sap of plants, and probably also fungi and insects. The ornamentation of the plumage is often very beautiful.

The Trichoglossinae include the lories (with a short tail) and lorikeets (with a longer, pointed tail), found in Australia, New Zealand and Polynesia. They live on nectar which they extract from flowers with a brush-tipped tongue. The rainbow parakeet (*Trichoglossus haematodus*, illustrated here), common in Oceania, frequents an area only when certain species of plants are in bloom and there is an abundance of nectar. When the nectar source is exploited, it moves on in large flocks in search of new supplies.

Finally, the Psittacinae are by far the largest subfamily, containing all the typical parrots. Among them is the blue and yellow macaw (*Ara ararauna*) of the South American forests, and the sun conure or golden parrot (*Aratinga guarouba*, illustrated here). The familiar green parrots of the genus *Amazona* are among the best imitators of the human voice; they include the Hispaniola parrot and the blue-cheeked or blue-headed parrot (*A. brasiliensis*). The best imitator of the human voice is however the African grey parrot (*Psittacus erithacus*). The parakeets include the budgerigar (*Melopsittacus undulatus*) commonly kept as a cage-bird.

The rosellas, such as the crimson rosella (*Platycercus elegans*, illustrated here) of Australia, are highly skilled fliers. The hanging parakeets, among which is *Loriculus galgulus* of South-East Asia, illustrated here, are more terrestrial. Finally among the Psittacinae are the true lovebirds of the genus *Agapornis*, found in Madagascar and Africa, which include the black-masked lovebird (*A. personata*, illustrated here).

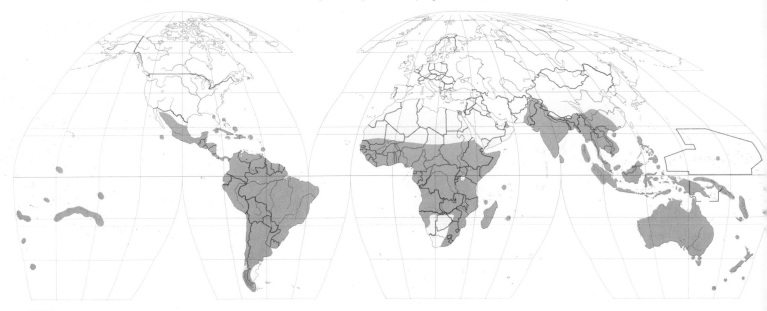

Parrots

kakapo

black palm cockatoo

crimson rosella

kea

rainbow parakeet

sun conure
(golden parrot)

hanging parakeet

black-masked lovebirds

Cuculiformes

The Cuculiformes, touracos and cuckoos, comprise two families, Musophagidae and Cuculidae, very different from each other but having certain characteristics in common, for example they both have a discontinuous moult (when a feather falls out, the two adjacent ones remain intact), a unique feature among the birds.

Musophagidae

The Musophagidae, touracos, are arboreal birds of Africa south of the Sahara. Five genera are known with eighteen species whose dimensions vary from those of a woodpigeon to the 70 cm (28 in) of the great blue touraco (*Corythaeola cristata*). The members of the *Touraco* and *Musophaga* genera have brilliant colouring with different tones of blue, green and violet. Ross's touraco (*Musophaga violacea*, illustrated here) lives in Africa from Gambia to Nigeria. The *Touraco* genus comprises about ten species among which is Prince Ruspoli's touraco (*T. ruspolii*) of Ethiopia and the Guinea touraco (*T. persa*), with various subspecies including Livingstone's touraco (*T. p. livingstonii*, illustrated here).

Cuculidae

The Cuculidae – cuckoos, couas, coucals and roadrunners – are present in nearly all tropical and temperate parts of the world. Most of the species live almost exclusively in trees. About 40 per cent of the species are parasitic, laying their eggs in the nests of other birds; this evolutionary adaptation is highly perfected and the egg is often very similar in colour and dimensions to that of the host. The choice of host is also very accurate. The great spotted cuckoo (*Clamator glandarius*) of Europe lays its eggs in the nests of magpies, there being a notable similarity between the eggs of the two species. In Africa other members of the crow family are its victims. Research has shown that in some cuckoo species there are several sub-groups of birds; individuals from one sub-group lay their eggs in the nests of only one host species. The idea that a female cuckoo can lay one of several different kinds of eggs at will, to match her host's eggs, is therefore a myth.

The acceptance of other birds' eggs as their own is made possible by the exceptionally strong urge to incubate that the host birds show during the reproductive period. Furthermore, the inside of the beak of the young cuckoo is an intense red which, when displayed, functions as a super-visual stimulus inducing an immediate feeding response on the part of the adoptive parent, in preference to its own nestlings. In some species, also, the baby cuckoo, soon after hatching pushes the eggs of the adoptive parents out of the nest.

Six sub-families are known. The first, the Cuculinae of the Old World, contains only parasitic cuckoos. The common cuckoo (*Cuculus canorus*) of Europe and Asia lays its eggs in nests of several dissimilar species such as reed warblers, dunnocks and pipits. The tufted cuckoo (*C. coromandus*, illustrated here) of India is of the same subfamily. The didric or emerald cuckoo (*Chrysococcyx cupreus*, illustrated here) lives in Africa; in China, India and New Guinea is found the koel (*Eudynamis scolopacea*, illustrated here) which lays its eggs in the nests of crows. Three other species of parasitic cuckoos, all of South and Central America, belong to the sub-family Neomorphinae. *Carpococcyx radiceus*, one of the ground cuckoos, which build nests of leaves and sticks on the ground, is illustrated here. Living in South-East Asia, it has a large bill and a kind of hood on the head.

The Crotophaginae include the anis, large-billed, glossy black birds of tropical America. The common or smooth-billed ani (*Crotophaga ani*) is illustrated here. They lead a gregarious life and build communal nests of twigs in which several females may lay their eggs and share in incubating the eggs and raising the young.

The non-parasitic Phaenicophaeinae comprise nine genera including *Coccyzus*, to which genus the yellow-billed cuckoo (*C. americanus*) and black-billed cuckoo (*C. erythrophthalmus*) of North America belong.

The couas of the genus *Coua* are found in Madagascar. They are long-tailed, weak-flying birds living on insects and fruit. Coucals belong to the genus *Centropus* and are found from Africa across southern Asia to Australia. They also are weak fliers and escape from predators by running along the ground. The black-faced coucal (*Centropus melanops*) of the Philippines is illustrated here. The great or common coucal (*C. sinensis*) called crow pheasant in India, lives from India to South China and Malaysia. The road-runner (*Geococcyx californianus*) of the south-western USA and Mexico is often seen running along the roads in Arizona and other desert states. It feeds on insects, lizards and snakes.

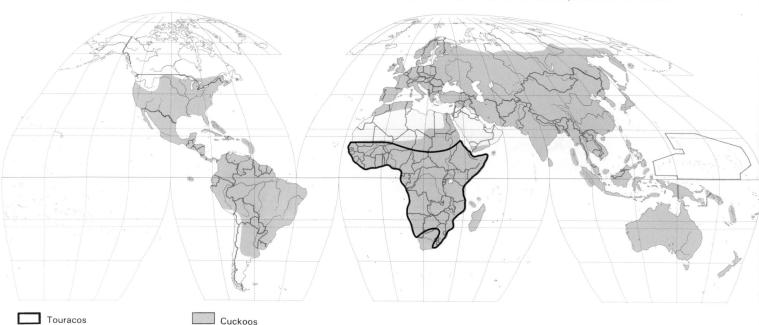

Touracos   Cuckoos

black-faced coucal

common or smooth-billed ani

ground cuckoo

Ross's touraco

Livingstone's touraco

tufted cuckoo

♂

didric cuckoo

koel

♀

Strigiformes

The Strigiformes, owls, are nocturnal birds of prey characterized by having the eyes on the front of the head and circled by a sort of disc of soft and silky feathers, with a hooked beak and sharp claws. Nocturnal life has brought about a series of adaptations, in the first place a sharpness of hearing which has become extremely refined, capable of distinguishing the source and origin of the smallest sounds. The eyesight, already extremely good in the birds and particularly well developed in the birds of prey in general, is finally perfected to enable the owls to see in almost absolute darkness. Furthermore, flight is silent, since the wing feathers, like all the others, are extremely soft and have frayed edges so as not to produce any sound either in beating the wings or in gliding, so that prey animals are taken entirely by surprise.

These birds have significant effects on populations of small mammals particularly. Many are taken, so that the number of those that remain is kept in check. Conversely the abundance of their prey significantly affects the breeding success of owls. In some areas the hunting of owls by man has created havoc in the form of plagues of rodents which are difficult to control having escaped their natural check.

The Strigiformes are subdivided into two families, Tytonidae and Strigidae.

Tytonidae

The Tytonidae include as their typical member the barn owl (*Tyto alba*, illustrated here), recognizable at first glance by its characteristic heart-shaped facial disc. It may hunt all night by moonlight, or, especially in winter, limit its activity to twilight and the early hours of the morning. It has a worldwide distribution except for Antarctica and Micronesia. The bay owls of the genus *Phodilus* include *P. badius*, and live in dense forests from India to South-East Asia. They live on insects, lizards, frogs, birds and small mammals.

Strigidae

The Strigidae include all the other species of owl. In them, orientation is aided by tactile bristles situated on either side of the beak,

as well as by eyesight and hearing. The eagle owl (*Bubo bubo*) is among the largest species, 70 cm (28 in) in length; it lives from Scandinavia and Spain across Europe and Asia to the Pacific, and in Africa north of the Sahara. It inhabits open areas bordering on forests, nesting in cliffs and rock walls, and also in ruins. Its plumage is golden brown with dark patches and streaks; long-lived, it can attain an age of up to sixty years. It has prominent ear-tufts and large orange eyes. Among the other species of this genus is the Verreaux's eagle owl (*B. lacteus*, illustrated here), living in nearly the whole of Africa, and the great horned owl (*B. virginianus*) of the Americas from the Arctic ice limit to the Magellan Straits, but absent from the West Indies.

The fishing owls, whose dimensions are similar to those of the eagle owls, belong to the genera *Ketupa* in Asia and *Scotopelia* in Africa. Their diet consists mainly of fish but they do not disdain other small vertebrates. Another large owl is the snowy owl (*Nyctea scandiaca*) of the Arctic regions, living mostly north of 60°N and even north of 80°N in Greenland. It lives on rodents and snow hares and other birds up to ptarmigan size, but above all on lemmings, to the extent that where lemmings are absent the snowy owl is rarely to be found. The female is white with dark brown or grey markings, the male an immaculate white for perfect camouflage.

The little owl (*Athene noctua*) is found across Europe and Asia from south-eastern Britain and Spain to Manchuria, Arabia and the nearby parts of Africa; it was introduced into Britain in the nineteenth century from southern Europe. The pygmy owl (*Glaucidium passerinum*, illustrated here) also lives in northern regions from Scandinavia to Manchuria. The scops owl (*Otus scops*) is seen as a vagrant in Britain, as is Tengmalm's owl (*Aegolius funereus*, illustrated here), but the tawny owl (*Strix aluco*) is a resident. Among other owls resident in Britain are the long-eared owl (*Asio otus*), which breeds from Ireland to Japan, and the short-eared owl (*Asio flammeus*), which lives mostly in northern Europe and Asia but has isolated colonies in the West Indies and the Southern Hemisphere. Two American species are the spectacled owl (*Pulsatrix perspicillatae*) and burrowing owl (*Speotyto cunicularia*), both illustrated here. On the North American prairie burrowing owls are often found in association with prairie dogs, using their abandoned burrows. On the South American pampas they may cohabit with viscachas or armadillos.

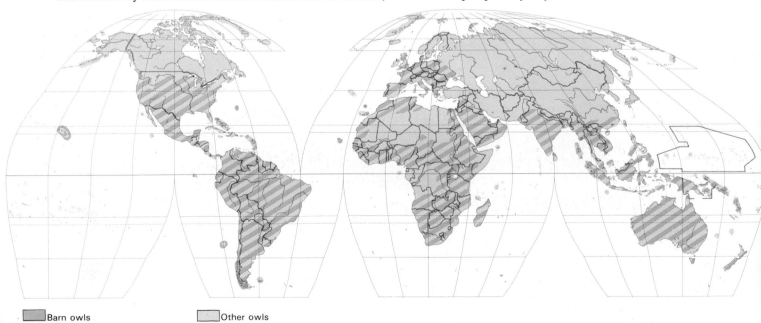

Barn owls

Other owls

spectacled owl

Verraux's eagle owl

Tengmalm's owl

pygmy owl

barn owl

burrowing owl

Caprimulgiformes

The Caprimulgiformes are present throughout the world except the polar regions. They have a large head with a very broad beak and large eyes, evidence of the nocturnal habits of most of the species. The coloration of the plumage is decidedly cryptic, matching dead leaves and of the utmost importance for creatures that nest on the earth. Some species are capable of hibernating during the winter months, reducing their own body temperature by about 20°C (38°F). There are five families.

Steatornithidae

The oilbird, guacharo or diablotin (*Steatornis caripensis*, illustrated here), of Trinidad and northern South America, is the sole representative of this family. Its habitat is forests with caves and grottoes suitable for nesting colonies. It is nocturnal, and like the bat uses an echo-location system. The sounds, audible to the human ear, are reflected from obstacles and returned to the ear. In this way the bird manoeuvres when flying in darkness.

Podargidae

The Podargidae, frogmouths, are birds of medium size with a large hooked beak, living in South-East Asia and Australia. Among the larger species is the Papuan frogmouth (*Podargus papuensis*), 54 cm (22 in) long, found in New Guinea and northern Queensland. The tawny frogmouth (*P. strigoides*, illustrated here) is of Australia and Tasmania. The frogmouths sleep upright on stumps or branches by day, and at night hunt insects, lizards and mice. They have the ability to lower their own temperatures and so endure the heat of the equatorial day more easily. The genus *Batrachostomus* of Malaya, Sumatra and Borneo is richer in species; the large frogmouth (*B. auritus*) about 40 cm (16 in) long, is equipped with long bristles around its beak that give it a bearded look.

Nyctibiidae

The Nyctibiidae live in Central and South America and are represented by the single genus *Nyctibius* (potoos). The mouth aperture is enormous and is provided with a small and slightly hooked beak. Their camouflage is remarkably effective: by freezing in an upright position, they resemble (due to coloration and posture) the extension of a branch, broken tree trunk or post. They have a range of calls which have been described as mournful and strangely beautiful. The largest species is the great potoo (*Nyctibius grandis*), with an 80 cm (32 in) wingspan. The common potoo (*Nyctibius griseus*, illustrated here) has the peculiar habit of laying just one egg in a cavity just large enough to contain that one egg and nothing more. It also perches bolt upright on tree stumps; most nightjars perch along branches or logs.

Aegothelidae

The Aegothelidae, owlet frogmouths, also have a disproportionately large mouth aperture, with a small beak almost hidden by stiff bristles. They live mostly in New Guinea, are nocturnal, and hunt insects, spending the day in holes in trees. The owlet frogmouth or moth-owl (*Aegotheles cristatus*, illustrated here) lives in Australia; it looks like a small long-tailed owl.

Caprimulgidae

The Caprimulgidae, nightjars and nighthawks, represent 70 per cent of the entire group of Caprimulgiformes, with almost worldwide distribution, absent only from Australia. They are compact and elongated, with a very short neck, and do not build nests, the eggs being laid directly on the ground. With large eyes, a wide mouth and long wings, they make agile and efficient hunters, preying on flying insects by night. The common nighthawk (*Chordeiles minor*) lives from Central America north to Canada and, despite its name, is often active by day.

The nightjar (*Caprimulgus europaeus*, illustrated here) lives in Europe, Asia and Africa. Its nocturnal habits and cryptic coloration make it difficult to observe. The pennant-winged nightjar (*Macrodipteryx longipennis*, illustrated here) is an African species; during the breeding season the male's ninth primary wing feathers become elongated and wire-like, terminating in a feather resembling a banner. The length of these feathers can reach 45 cm (18 in). When the period of courtship is over the two elongated feathers fall, probably pulled out by the male himself.

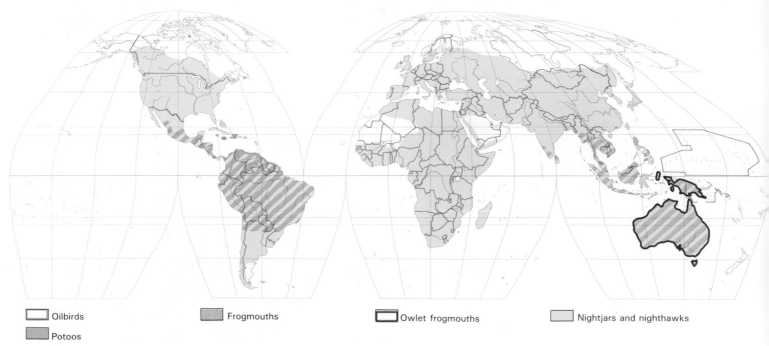

Oilbirds   Frogmouths   Owlet frogmouths   Nightjars and nighthawks
Potoos

owlet frogmouth

pennant-winged nightjar

nightjar

common potoo

tawny frogmouth

oilbird

Apodiformes

The Apodiformes are a heterogeneous group of birds characterized by long wings and a capacity for exceptional flight. The three families, Apodidae, Hemiprocnidae and Trochilidae are in fact extremely well adapted to an aerial life. The first family are best at sheer speed, the second at rapidity of hunting through dense vegetation, and the third are capable of moving their wings with such rapidity as to hover in the air and even fly sideways or backwards.

Apodidae

The Apodidae are best known by the name of swifts. Their structure is the most refined that nature has evolved for flight. Their shape is streamlined, the head small, the wings very long and the humerus (near the end of the wing) short in relation to the length of the 'hand'. Swifts are insectivorous and prey is captured in flight; the structure of the eye permits acute stereoscopic vision which facilitates hunting for small insects in the air. When hunting swifts may fly at speeds of over 100 km/hour (65 mph). Even drinking is performed in flight, the bird flying over a sheet of water, collecting the liquid with its lowered mandible.

The family has a worldwide distribution, and among the seventy or so species the common swift (*Apus apus*) is certainly the best known. It nests in fissures in rocks or under the eaves of roofs. In Britain it is a summer visitor, arriving in spring to breed and leaving in August, to migrate to its winter quarters in West and southern Africa. The Alpine swift (*A. melba*, illustrated here) breeds in southern Europe, eastwards to Turkestan, wintering in Africa, Arabia and India. Larger than the common swift and with broader wings, it is sometimes seen as a vagrant in Britain. Other European species are the pallid swift (*A. pallidus*) and white-rumped swift (*A. cafer*). The Indian swift (*A. affinis*) nests in colonies containing numerous nests in contact with each other. The cave swiftlet (*Collocalia fuciphaga*) of South-East Asia builds a nest in dark caverns where it has to use an echo-location system to enable it to fly about, without crashing into the cave walls. Its nests are collected and made into bird's nest soup, a Chinese delicacy. Swifts' nests are made of twigs or feathers glued together with saliva, and it is only the latter which is extracted and turned into soup. Some are attached to walls or trees, or even to palm fronds; the Asian palm swift (*Cypsiurus parvus*) glues its eggs to the nest, which in turn is glued to the surface of a palm leaf.

Hemiprocnidae

The Hemiprocnidae, crested swifts, are represented by three species of the genus *Hemiprocne*, including the Indian crested swift (*H. longipennis*, illustrated here), which lives in the area between the Malaysian peninsula and the Philippines. They are less exclusively aerial than the common swifts and perch on branches waiting for their prey: when an insect passes they pursue and catch it after a brief but rapid flight. They also join together in small flocks for hunting flights. The nests, each holding a single egg, are attached to the side of a branch.

Trochilidae

The Trochilidae, hummingbirds, are like tiny jewels as they dart in and out of the tropical foliage with their iridescent plumage. They are mostly very small, with a rounded head, well-developed eyes and a beak, whether straight or curved, sometimes as long as the entire body. The tongue, which is long and flexible and tubular at the tip, serves to collect nectar, pollen, and small insects from inside the corollas of flowers. Flight has been perfected to the point at which the hummingbirds can move in any direction, including backwards, or remain hovering in the air. The brilliance of their iridescent coloration results from the diffraction of light through black or reddish feathers rather than from actual pigmentation.

All are residents of the New World. The sword-billed hummingbird (*Ensifera ensifera*, illustrated here) of the mountains of Venezuela and Colombia is among the largest species; 20 cm (8 in) in length. The sylphide (*Loddigesia mirabilis*, illustrated here) is an inhabitant of the Peruvian forests. The sicklebill (*Eutoxeres aquila*) is found from Costa Rica to Ecuador and the black-headed streamertail (*Trochilus polytmus*) in Jamaica. Among the smallest hummingbirds are the red-headed Anna's hummingbird (*Calypte anna*) of California and the Andean hillstar hummingbird (*Oreotrochilus estella*). All these last four species are illustrated here. The hillstar lives at high altitudes and can go torpid, with a reduced body temperature, at night.

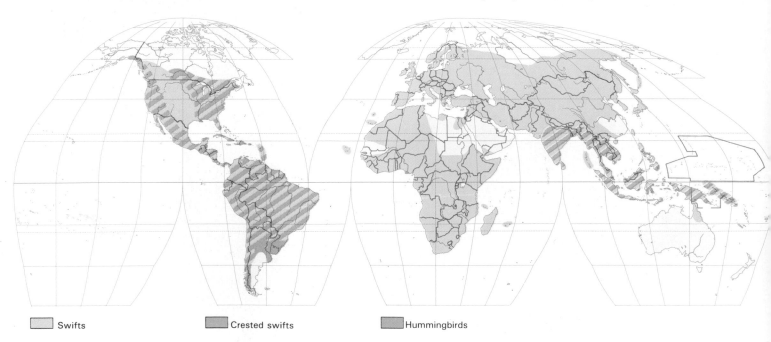

Swifts   Crested swifts   Hummingbirds

blackheaded streamertail

Anna's hummingbird

Andean hillstar hummingbird

sylphide

Indian crested swift

sword-billed hummingbird

alpine swift

sicklebill

Trogoniformes

The Trogoniformes are found in the equatorial and tropical areas of South America, Africa and South-East Asia. The single family of the group is that of the Trogonidae, trogons, with about forty species which range in size from a blackbird to a pigeon. The usual habitat is dense and very humid forest, the diet consisting of insects and fruit, though at times some small vertebrates may be taken.

The unique characteristic of the Trogoniformes is their foot structure. The toes are arranged in two pairs; the first and second point backwards, while the third and fourth toes point forwards. This arrangement is markedly different from other birds, and is known as heterodactyly. Trogons are generally quiet and shy birds and are rarely seen – even in areas where they are quite common – due to the denseness of their forest habitat.

One of the most beautiful birds in the world, the quetzal (*Pharomachrus mocino*, illustrated here) of the Central American forests, belongs to this family. It is the national bird of Guatemala. It reaches 40 cm (16 in) in length, excluding the tail. The male's head is covered with a sort of soft crest of erectile feathers and the tail coverts can measure 80 cm (32 in) in length. Each male defends his territory against all intruders, and the limits of the area he occupies are marked by flying tours of the border in which he displays the metallic colour of his plumage, which can be seen from a considerable distance. The quetzal's flight is often quoted as the most beautiful sight in the bird world.

The trogons belonging to the genus *Trogon* in some ways resemble the shrikes – with their stout, slightly hooked bill and sturdy body. The violet trogon (*T. violaceus*) uses a beehive as its nest site, chasing away the original occupants; besides offering the birds an excellent defensive site, the beehive provides an abundance of food in the form of the bee larvae. The white-tailed trogon (*T. viridis*, illustrated here) of the Amazonian basin builds its nests in the hollows of dead trees, the entrance consisting of a long oblique tunnel. Two species live in the Antilles, the Cuban trogon (*Priotelus temnurus*, illustrated here) and *Temnotrogon roseigaster*.

The African trogons number only three species belonging to the genus *Apaloderma*. The narina trogon (*A. narina*, illustrated here) occupies an area between Ethiopia and South Africa. The equatorial narina bare-cheeked trogon (*A. aequitoriale*) lives in Tanzania and Kenya and penetrates the forests of the plains as far as the coasts of the Indian Ocean. The last species is the bar-tailed trogon (*Heterotrogon vittatus*) which lives in the forests of the Congo basin.

In Asia there are six species of trogons, all of which belong to the genus *Harpactes*. Among them is the red-naped trogon (*H. kasumba*, illustrated here) found in the Malaysian forests. In this group there is marked sexual dimorphism, the males being brilliantly coloured while the females are brownish with lighter markings.

Coliiformes

The Coliiformes are represented by a single family, the Coliidae, colies or mousebirds, with characteristics that clearly separate them from all the other groups. The single genus, *Colius*, has six species all the size of sparrows and is found in Africa south of the Sahara. The head is ornamented with a crest of erect feathers like a helmet, while the tapering tail is sometimes two or three times as long as the body. Exceptionally among the birds, the colies have four toes that can change their position; either two forward and two back, three forward and one back, or all four in one direction. This particular adaptation is an aid to living in their habitat of densely interlaced leafy branches demanding particular movements and grips to climb about and penetrate them.

Gregarious in habit, the colies live in groups containing large numbers of birds. The pairs are stable for several years; mating is preceded by a simple parade of the male, and the nest is built of twigs and grass-blades in the dense bushes. The beak is short, resembling that of a finch, and the soft plumage grows evenly on the body instead of in tracts. This, together with the creeping movements between the branches, is reminiscent of mice and gives them the name mousebirds. A typical example of the whole family is the blue-naped coly or mousebird (*Colius macrourus*, illustrated here), whose head, surmounted by a thick tuft, recalls that of a waxwing.

All the colies are regarded as agricultural pests, since they often descend on cultivated fields in search of food, causing considerable damage, particularly to orchards.

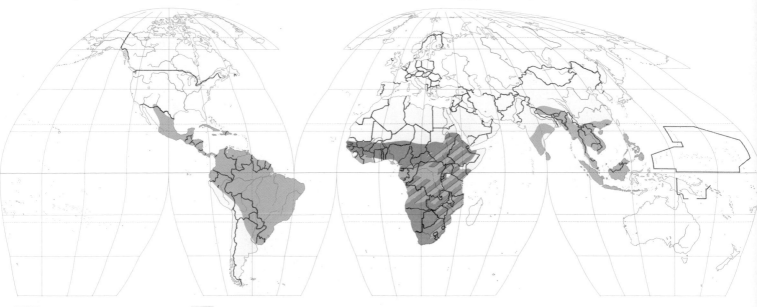

Trogons   Mousebirds (colies)

blue-naped coly

quetzal

narina trogon

white-tailed trogon

Cuban trogon

red-naped trogon

Coraciiformes

A very mixed group, the Coraciiformes comprise about 200 species belonging to seven families with fifty-three genera. The distribution of the group is mainly African and Asian, and only to a lesser extent in Europe, America and Australia.

The groups included in this order are the kingfishers, bee-eaters, rollers, todies and hornbills. They are mostly brightly-coloured birds that tend to nest in holes; consequently they usually have white or pale eggs, since there is no need to camouflage them if they are hidden away. A characteristic common to all representatives of the group is the possession of short legs with three toes pointing forwards and one backwards, not at all well adapted for walking; and a beak specialized for the capture of living prey. Some are fish-eaters, others insect-eaters; the fish are taken by diving, the insects may be taken in flight or on the ground.

Alcedinidae

The Alcedinidae, kingfishers, subdivided into Alcedininae and Daceloninae, are found everywhere except in the Antarctic. They are characterized by a long straight beak which is laterally compressed in the fish-eating species and flattened top-to-bottom in the species that hunt insects or small vertebrates. The wings are short and adapted to rapid flight in a straight line; the head is large, and the legs too small for walking, so that hunting is done on the wing. Only in the case of the shovel-billed kingfisher (*Clytoceix rex*) of New Guinea does the pursuit of prey, consisting of insects, take place on the ground. The Alcedininae are mostly fish-eaters; they are found all over the world, and near rivers, lakes, rapid streams and sea coasts.

The European kingfisher (*Alcedo atthis*) is a small but very fast bird 13 cm (5 in) long, of a metallic blue and orange colour easily visible at a distance. Common along clear rivers and streams rich in fish, it is often seen perched a couple of metres above the surface watching out for its prey. It plunges headlong into the water after its prey of small fish, plus the occasional water insect and crustacean. It then returns to its perch to feed, and always swallows the meal head-first. The kingfisher excavates its nest (a tunnel ending in a chamber) in the steeper stretches of river banks, where it lays clusters of pearly white, almost spherical eggs. The male keeps the female supplied with food during incubation, and sometimes sits on the nest himself. Both parents feed the young until they fledge at about four weeks.

The Daceloninae, found all over the world, are hunters of insects and small vertebrates. They are found in a variety of habitats, from coastal plains to montane forests. The white-breasted kingfisher (*Halcyon smyrnensis*, illustrated here) lives from Asia Minor to the Far East. The Daceloninae are often gifted with a melodious song, or at least with a very varied repertoire; the kookaburra or laughing jackass (*Dacelo gigas*) of Australia, which measures up to 45 cm (18 in) in length, sometimes indulges in its loud, raucous laugh throughout the day from dawn to sunset. Its diet includes insects, crabs, and small reptiles including poisonous snakes. It is the largest of the kingfishers.

Coraciidae

The Coraciidae, rollers and ground rollers, comprise three sub-families with a strong, hooked beak and a forked tail. The Leptosomatinae are represented solely by the cuckoo roller or courol (*Leptosomus discolor*) which lives in Madagascar and the Comoro Islands. The Brachypteraciinae, ground rollers, all of Madagascar, live in the dense forests and nest in holes in the earth or in hollow trees; the best known is *Atelornis crossleyi*, a beautiful green colour on the back with a red neck, head and chest.

The Coraciinae live in Africa, Asia and Australia and the eleven species belong to two genera, *Coracias* and *Eurystomus*. The first is represented in Europe and Asia by the European roller (*C. garrulus*) which occasionally strays north-west as far as Britain. It is a heavy-looking bird, the beak is large and elongated, the plumage blue with a chestnut back, and the wings blue with black edges; the tail is blue-green with brown central tail feathers. Its diet consists of insects, particularly grasshoppers, locusts and termites. It breeds from Central Europe to the Caspian, and winters in southern Africa, where the lilac-breasted roller (*C. caudata*, illustrated here) can also be seen. The genus *Eurystomus* comprises birds whose appearance is somewhat different from that of the other rollers. It includes the broad-billed roller or dollar bird (*E. orientalis*, illustrated here) living between north India and Japan, and a summer visitor to Australia. It eats mainly cicadas, moths and beetles.

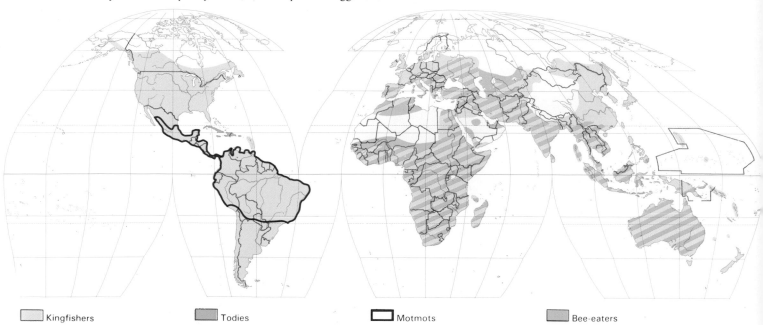

Kingfishers   Todies   Motmots   Bee-eaters

white-breasted kingfisher

carmine bee-eater

green wood hoopoe

broad-billed roller

lilac-breasted roller

great pied hornbill

blue-crowned motmot

broad-billed tody

A hoopoe (*Upupa epops*) uses its long sword-like bill to seek out insects on the ground.

Meropidae

The plumage of the Meropidae, bee-eaters, is the most colourful and beautiful of this order. Their preferred habitat is open woodland in warm climates; in tropical and sub-tropical Eurasia, Africa and Australasia. Unlike the other Coraciiformes, bee-eaters are colonial in habit, excavating their nest-holes in walls of earth. They feed largely on bees, wasps, and occasionally other insects. The European bee-eater (*Merops apiaster*), vividly coloured yellow, green and blue, breeds in Europe and North Africa and eastward to Kashmir, but has also occasionally bred in Britain. The carmine bee-eater (*M. nubicus*, illustrated on p. 215) is similar but has a longer tail; it is found from Senegal to Somalia. Others of the Meropidae are the little green bee-eater (*M. orientalis*) of Asia and Africa, and the rainbow bird (*M. ornatus*) of Australasia.

The flight of bee-eaters is distinctive, consisting of long glides followed by a quick acceleration to capture prey. The bee-eater returns to its perch and batters its prey to death before swallowing it.

Todidae

The Todidae, todies, live only in the Greater Antilles and the five known species belong to the one genus. *Todus*. They are small birds with a flattened beak which, when at rest, they hold turned upwards. The broad-billed tody (*T. subulatus*, illustrated on p. 215) is found only in Hispaniola.

Motmotidae

The Motmotidae, motmots, are found in Central America, Bolivia and Argentina. These birds never clean their nest, so that after a short time it becomes so dirty and messy that it has to be abandoned. Another feature is that the vanes of the two longest tail feathers break off, leaving spoon-shaped tips, as shown by the blue-crowned motmot (*Momotus momota*) illustrated on p. 215.

Upupidae

The Upupidae, hoopoes, are divided into Upupinae and Phoeniculinae. The Phoeniculinae, wood hoopoes, are African and include the genera *Phoeniculus* and *Rhinopomastes*, characterized by long claws which enable them to clamber up and down tree trunks like woodpeckers. The green wood hoopoe (*Phoeniculus purpureus*, illustrated on p. 215) lives in groups and has a harsh chattering call. The hoopoe (*Upupa epops*, illustrated here) breeds in most of Europe but only rarely in Britain and Scandinavia.

Bucerotidae

The Bucerotidae, hornbills, found in Africa south of the Sahara, India and South-East Asia, have enormous curved beaks surmounted by a sort of casque or helmet. Their broad wings permit a slow but powerful flight; many species have loud calls resembling the howls of monkeys; and they will eat almost anything. Among the various species is the red-billed hornbill (*Tockus erythrorhynchus*) of Africa, in which the female is walled up inside the nest – a hole in a tree – during the period of incubation and part of the nesting period, and is fed by her mate through a small aperture. Another species is the great pied hornbill (*Buceros bicornis*, illustrated here) of India and Malaysia.

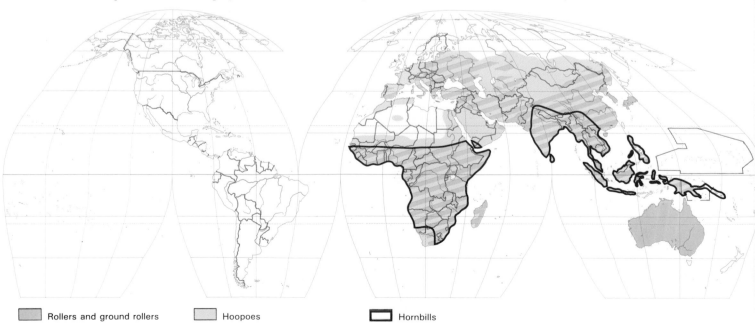

░ Rollers and ground rollers   ░ Hoopoes   □ Hornbills

Piciformes

This is another rather heterogeneous group. It comprises birds related to each other by certain anatomical peculiarities not immediately identifiable. One common characteristic is the arrangement of toes termed zygodactyly: the second and third digits point forwards while the first and fourth are directed backwards. Members of the Piciformes tend to nest in holes and eat insects, though some species are exclusively vegetarian. There are two sub-groups, Galbuloidea and Picoidea, the first containing five families and the second only one.

Galbulidae

The Galbulidae, jacamars, a tropical American family of fifteen species, have long pointed beaks and an iridescent plumage reminiscent of the hummingbirds. Typical representatives are the rufous-tailed jacamar (*Galbula ruficauda*) and the paradise jacamar (*G. dea*, illustrated on p. 218). They live on insects captured in flight, which they catch with a loud snap of the beak and then return to the bough they have been perching on, to pound the insect before eating it. In the mating season the males display the brilliant colours of their wings and opened tail. The song, which is always melodious, is territorial and also attracts the female.

Bucconidae

The appearance of the thirty-two species of Bucconidae, puffbirds, another tropical American family, differs from that of the jacamars in that they are more squat and thickset and more modestly coloured. They are named for their habit of puffing out the neck and head feathers while perching. The white-necked or large-billed puffbird (*Notharcus macrorhynchus*), one of the most widely distributed species, lives from Mexico to the Amazonian forests.

There are six other genera including *Bucco*, to which the collared puffbird (*B. capensis*, illustrated on p. 218), with its large orange beak, belongs. In contrast to the jacamars, the puffbirds emit only low, weak sounds. The nests are excavated in termites' nests or in the earth itself. Some species have other names besides that of puffbirds. The nunbirds of Venzuela (*Monasa* sp.), dull-coloured, quiet puffbirds, conceal the entry to their subterranean nests with a great pile of vegetation. Other species are the nunlets (*Nonnula* sp.) and the swallow-wing (*Chelidoptera tenebrosa*). The smallest species is the lanceolated monklet (*Micromonacha lanceolata*), 14 cm (5.5 in) long.

Capitonidae

The Capitonidae are called barbets from the tuft of feathers around the base of the beak. They live in the tropical forests, and also frequent cultivated fields, in Africa, South-East Asia and northern South America. Their diet is mostly vegetarian, consisting of fruit, berries and seeds, but they will also eat some insects. Their song consists only of a few notes, rarely musical; the coppersmiths (*Megalaima haemacephala*) of Asia and tinkerbirds (*Pogoniulus* sp.) of Africa are so called because of their ringing calls reminiscent of a hammer beating on metal. Others with maddeningly repetitious notes are called brain-fever birds.

Indicatoridae

The Indicatoridae, honeyguides, are so called because the presence of two African species in a locality indicates that there are beehives in the neighbourhood, and the birds in their own interest guide men and other animals such as honey badgers (ratels) to locate the hive. After the hive is broken into the birds feed mainly on the wax, but also on the adult bees or wasps and their larvae. There are twelve species in four genera, the most important genus, *Indicator*, includes two Asiatic species, of the Himalayas and Malaysia. Honeyguides are small birds with a short, slightly down-pointed beak, short legs, pointed wings and the tail usually has the outer feathers shorter than the others, except in the case of the lyre-tailed honeyguide (*Melichneutes robustus*). Another feature is the thick skin, probably related to the diet which exposes them to being stung by venomous insects. The best-known species is the greater or black-throated honeyguide (*Indicator indicator*, illustrated here), widely distributed in Africa except for the West African rain-forests and the Kalahari.

Six species of honeyguide are parasitic, laying their eggs in other birds' nests. The first young to hatch kill the other young in the nest with a hook on the beak which disappears after use.

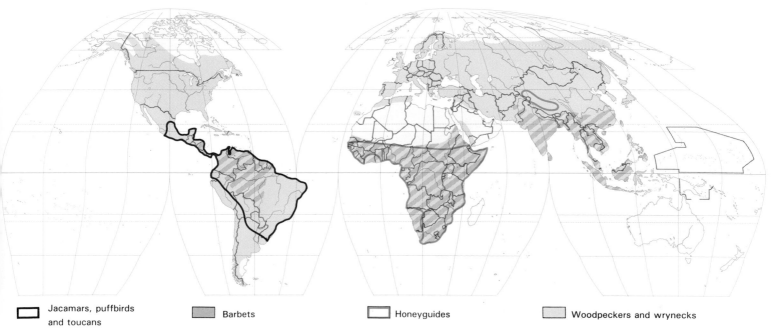

Jacamars, puffbirds and toucans

Barbets

Honeyguides

Woodpeckers and wrynecks

plate-billed
mountain toucan

toco toucan

double-collared araçari

collard puffbird

paradise jacamar

wryneck

black-throated honeyguide

ivory-billed woodpecker

great-spotted
woodpecker

red-headed
woodpecker

yellow-shafted flicker

arrowhead piculet

red-winged woodpecker

black woodpecker

Ramphastidae

The Ramphastidae, toucans, have disproportionately large beaks, the upper part being usually saw-toothed along the edges. The tongue is long, notched at the sides and bristly at the tip. The diet consists mainly of fruit and berries, plus some insects and small vertebrates. The fruit is gathered with one foot and minced up by the beak. The largest species belong to the genus *Ramphastos*, among them the toco toucan (*R. toco*, illustrated on p. 218), which can reach 60 cm (24 in) in length.

The araçaris are generally brightly coloured, as for example the double-collared araçari (*Pteroglossus bitorquatus*, illustrated on p. 218), found in rain-forests from Mexico to Venezuela. All the toucans also tend to have highly coloured beaks shown here by plate-billed mountain toucan (*Andigena laminorostris*, illustrated on p. 218).

Picidae

The last family of the Piciformes is that of the Picidae, woodpeckers and wrynecks, with more than 200 species, nearly all vividly coloured and many of them crested. The tail with its coverts is wedge-shaped and stiff in the true woodpeckers, which use it as a support when clinging upright against the trunk of a tree. The tongue is very long; the tip is stiff and can secrete a sticky mucus to which insects adhere. The beak is usually long, straight

A pair of African red and yellow barbets (*Tracyphonus erythrocephalus*) on a termite mound.

and very strong, but in the wrynecks and the piculets it is shorter and weaker. The legs are short and strong, armed with sharp claws. Normally they are non-migratory birds, except for a few, including the wryneck (*Jynx torquilla*, illustrated on p. 218).

There are three sub-families, the first of which is the Jynginae, to which the wrynecks belong. The Picumninae comprise the piculets, including the Asian arrowhead piculet (*Picumnus minutissimus*, illustrated on p. 219) while the true woodpeckers belong to the Picinae. Some species, such as the red-winged woodpecker (*Picus puniceus*) and yellow-shafted flicker (*Colaptes auratus*) have a vivid coloration which shows up particularly well in flight. Both these species are illustrated on p. 219. The common woodpecker of Britain is the green woodpecker (*Picus viridis*) while the greyheaded woodpecker (*Picus canis*) occasionally seen in Britain, ranges from Central Europe to Japan and southwards to Sumatra. The much rare black woodpecker (*Dryocopus martius*, illustrated on p. 219) nests ion the temperate regions of Europe and Asia, while other species well known in Britain include the great spotted woodpecker (*Dendrocopus major*, illustrated on p. 219) and lesser spotted woodpecker (*Dendrocopus minor*). American species include the largest of all, the ivory-billed woodpecker (*Campephilus principalis*) and red-headed woodpecker (*Melanerpes erythrocephalus*), both illustrated on p. 219.

Passeriformes

More than half of all existing birds belong to the Passeriformes, perching birds, whose great evolutionary success has been due in part to the great diversity of flowering plants and the multitude of insects that are associated with them. The Passeriformes are generally small, with a slender body, a small head, a beak of varied form according to the diet, and four-toed feet, adapted for perching, with three toes pointing forward and one well-developed hind toe, all provided with strong claws; and soft and abundant plumage of various colours. The reproductive habits are extremely varied; the nest, of widely differing form, may be placed on the ground, in holes in trees, among the branches or on cliffs. The young emerge from the egg naked and with closed eyes, and are therefore dependent on the parents for some time. There are more than 5600 species in the order Passeriformes, divided into four sub-orders, Eurylaimi, Tyranni, Menurae and Oscinae, containing in all fifty-six families.

Eurylaimidae

The Eurylaimidae, broadbills, are represented by a few species of non-migratory forest birds. They have a stout body with short rounded wings, large eyes, and rather short, pointed beak. The banded broadbill (*Eurylaimus javanicus*) is illustrated on p. 223. A characteristic of the family is the pear-shaped nest which hangs from a branch of a tree and can measure 2 m (6ft 6 in) in length.

Dendrocolaptidae and Furnariidae

The first family of the tyrannids is that of the Dendrocolaptidae, woodcreepers, which contains about fifty species whose appearance recals that of the woodpeckers and treecreepers. The beak is strong and may be short and straight or long and curved, as in the scythebills that form part of the family. The legs are short and the toes provided with sharp claws suitble for climbing. They are forest-dwellers climbing up the trunks in a spiral fashion, as the treecreepers do in Europe. The red-billed scythebill (*Campyloramphus trochilirostris*, illustrated on p. 223) lives in Central and South America.

The ovenbirds are among the least known Passerines of of South America, but are a large family of fifty-eight genera and 228 species, all of which are rather small birds. Some birds. Some species nest in holes in the ground, others build hollow globular, domed nests out of mud and vegetable detritus with an entrance tunnel leading to the incubation chamber. Most members of the family are forest dwellers living between Mexico and southern Argentina. One species of wiretail (*Sylviorthorhynchus desmursii*) has a tail twice as long as its body; another, the sharp-tailed streamcreeper (*Lochmias nematura*, illustrated on p. 223), always holds its tail erect, while members of the *Cinclodes* genus behave like European dippers, walking through and under water in search of food.

Formicariidae, Conopophagidae and Rhinocryptidae

The Formicariidae, ant birds, owe their name to the habit of some species of following the migrations of ants. They live in the tropical forests of Central and South America and have a hooked and notched tip to the upper mandible. The use of sound to communicate in the dense forest habitat is highly developed, as in the barred antshrike (*Thamnophilus doliatus*, illustrated on p. 223), which has a varied and melodious song. In contrast to the ovenbirds there is a marked sexual dimorphism, the males being more highly coloured and decorated with stripes and bars, while the females are mostly various shades of brown.

The Conopophagidae, gnat-eaters, are closely related to the antbirds but have a flatter beak, broader at the base. Eleven species are known, grouped in two genera, *Conopophaga* and *Corythopis*, ground-dwellers living on insects. The two *Corythopis* species walk rather than hop as the *Conopophaga* do. Sexual dimorphism is again present in the *Conopophaga* species.

The Rhinocryptidae, tapaculos, are another New World family of small brown birds, but live in the more temperate regions of Central and South America. They live on the ground, scratching for insects and their larvae among the leaf litter; even when escaping from a predator they prefer to run through the vegetation and hide rather than taking to the wing. Their song is resonant and has the peculiar characteristic that it is impossible on hearing the song to locate the bird emitting it. The Latin name arises from the operculum, or moving cover, which hides the nostrils probably as a protection against dust. The ocellated tapaculo

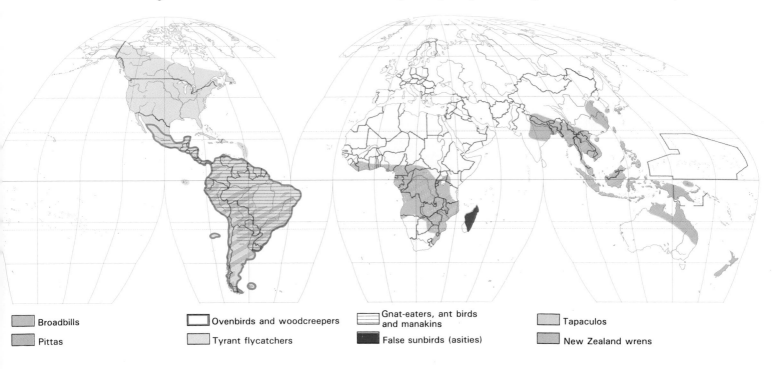

Broadbills

Pittas

Ovenbirds and woodcreepers

Tyrant flycatchers

Gnat-eaters, ant birds and manakins

False sunbirds (asities)

Tapaculos

New Zealand wrens

(*Acropternis orthonyx*) of the Andes and grey gallito (*Rhinocrypta lanceolata*) of Argentina and Paraguay are typical representatives.

Pittidae, Philepittidae and Acanthisittidae

The Pitidae, pittas, contained twenty-six species, all of the genus *Pitta*, of the Old World tropical forests. They resemble thrushes, from whom they can be distinguished by the particular structure of the legs and the muscles of the vocal organ (syrinx). The plumage is highly coloured and there are erectile feathers on the head. The best-known species are the blue pitta (*P. caerulea*, illustrated here) and the garnet pitta (*P. granatina*), which has fiery red underparts.

The Philepittidae, false sunbirds or asities, resemble the pittas and number only four species in two genera. The velvet asity (*Philepitta castanea*) lives in the eastern forests of Madagascar, where it flutters from bush to bush in search of berries and fruit. The false sunbird (*Neodrepanis coruscans*, illustrated here) of the western forests of Madagascar is much smaller – only 10 cm (4 in) long – and feeds on nectar which it collects with its long curved beak.

Only three species belong to the Acanthisittidae, the tiny New Zealand wrens. The rifleman (*Acanthisitta chloris*) and bush wren (*Xenicus longipes*) are found on both islands but the rock wren (*X. gilviventris*) only on South Island. They are agile, insectivorous forest birds.

Tyrannidae

The Tyrannidae, tyrant flycatchers, are the dominant family of the tyrannids, containing 345 species in 116 genera. Found all over the Americas, they resemble the flycatchers of the Old World. The nests are of very varied forms, spherical, domed or pear-shaped, in holes or fissures, or even the disused nest of another bird. Among the best-known species is the great kiskadee or Derby flycatcher (*Pitangus sulphuratus*, illustrated here), 23 cm (9 in) long, found from South Texas to Argentina, which sometimes catches tadpoles or fish by diving into shallow waters. Among the most striking in appearance of the tyrannids are the members of the genus *Muscivora*, in particular the swallow-tailed flycatcher (*M. tyrannus*, illustrated here).

Pipridae, Cotingidae and Phytotomidae

The Pipridae, manakins, forest dwellers of the New World, show a clear sexual dimorphism, the females being greenish in colour while the males are usually black with various parts in red, white, orange and blue. The males have also evolved some modifications to the flight feathers which make metallic clicking sounds. In many species these sounds accompany the elaborate nuptial displays, which are among the most choreographic birds. In *Manacus* species such as the golden-collared manakin (*Manacus vitellinus*) the bird clears a space on the forest floor, leaving a small tree as a display perch, and there performs its dance and sings until it has drawn the attention of the female (behaviour reminscent of some of the birds of Paradise). The white-bearded manakin (*M. manacus*, illustrated on p. 225) performs similar displays, flying between saplings on his cleared ground with his 'beard' puffed out and making clicking and whirring noises with his wings. The female joins him in the dance and mating finally takes place on the principal perch on one of the saplings. The male swallow-tailed manakin (*Chiroxiphia caudata*, illustrated on p. 225) joins with another male in dancing up and down on a low bough, the two skilfully changing places; the female may also join in. Generally, it is the female that builds the nest, often slung from the low fork of a tree, and it is she alone that takes care of the young.

The Cotingidae, cotingas, becards, tityras and bellbirds, are also forest dwellers, nearly all of the tropical forests of the New World, but two species of thickbills or becard (*Pachyrhamphus*) are found in the southern USA and the West Indies. There is again marked sexual dimorphism, the males, more brilliantly coloured, being ornamented with plumes, crests and ruffs. The best-known species are the cock of the rock (*Rupicola rupicola*) of Guyana, the ornate umbrella-bird (*Cephalopterus ornatus*) with its erectile crest and ruff, the bearded bellbird (*Procnias averano*), the lovely cotinga (*Cotinga amabilis*) with its splendid blue colour, and the Pompadour cotinga (*Xipholena punicea*). All these last five species are illustrated on p. 225.

Dimorphism is also evident in the three species of the phytotomidae, plant-cutters, of more temperate regions of South America, which possess a fine-toothed beak for stripping a plant of its buds and shoots. A typical representative is the white-tipped plant-cutter (*Phytotoma rutila*, illustrated on p. 225).

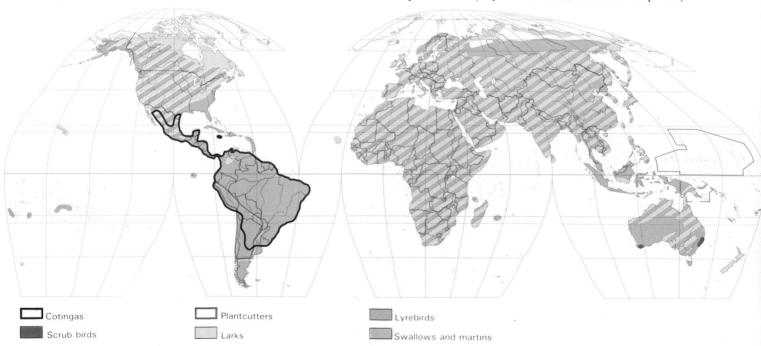

☐ Cotingas   ☐ Plantcutters   ▨ Lyrebirds
■ Scrub birds   ☐ Larks   ▨ Swallows and martins

banded broadbill

red-billed scythebill

false sunbird

blue pitta

barred antshrike

swallow-tailed
flycatcher

sharp-tailed streamcreeper

great kiskadee

Menuridae

The third sub-order of Passeriformes, the Menurae, consists of only two families. One is the Menuridae, lyrebirds, with only two species, both found in south-eastern Australia. These are the superb lyrebird (*Menura novaehollandiae*, illustrated on p. 227), the Australian national bird, and a rarer and less obtrusive species, Albert's lyrebird (*M. albertti*). The lyrebird looks like a pheasant but the male's lyre-shaped tail is longer than his body. The females lack this ornament. They live in sub-tropical forests and feed on insects, worms, and crustacea. In the mating season the males exhibit strong territorial behaviour and will not tolerate the presence of other males. They clear a patch of ground in a forest glade to serve as a stage on which they display their remarkable tails, dance and sing to attract the females. The song is an extensive medley of original and imitative sounds, the birds being highly skilled mimics.

Atrichornithidae

The other family of the Menurae is the Atrichornithidae, scrub birds, also of Australia. There are two species, the rufous scrub bird (*Atrichornis rufescens*) and the noisy scrub bird (*A. clamosus*). The latter was thought to be extinct but was rediscovered in south-western Australia in 1960. They are about the size of blackbirds with long tails and legs, and are hardly able to fly.

Alaudidae

The fourth sub-order of the Passeriformes is that of the Oscines or song-birds, whose members possess a semilunar membrane of the syrinx (vocal organ) moved by five to eight pairs of muscles. About half of the living species of birds belong to the Oscines, but their exact classification is controversial.

There are forty-one families of oscinine birds. The first is the Alaudidae, larks, characterized by the scales that cover the back of the tarsus and a very long hind claw. The most familiar species in Europe is the skylark (*Alauda arvensis*, illustrated on p. 227), which nests all across Europe and Asia from the British Isles to Kamchatka and southward to India and North Africa. Other common species include the wood lark (*Lullula arborea*), favouring wood-

land, and the crested lark (*Galerida cristata*) of open country. The most striking-looking member is the shore lark (*Eremophila alpestris*), with yellow and black markings on the face and chest, a bird of the tundra, stubble fields and seacoasts of the Northern Hemisphere. This is the only species of true lark native to North America, where it is known as the horned lark.

Hirundinidae

The Hirundinidae, swallows and martins, are particularly well adapted to aerial life and specialize in catching insects on the wing. The best-known species is the swallow (*Hirundo rustica*), which breeds throughout the north temperate zone; the American species, *H. erythrogaster*, is known as the barn swallow. North American birds winter in South America, European birds in Africa. The house martin (*Delichon urbica*) makes a nest of mud, commonly attached to houses, but formerly cliffs were used (as they still are in some places today). The red-rumped swallow (*Hirundo daurica*) and the crag martin (*Hirundo rupestris*) breed in southern Europe, and are occasional visitors to Britain. Much more common is the sand martin (*Riparia riparia*) which nests in tunnels dug in the river banks. American species include the cliff swallow (*Petrochelidon pyrrhonota*), the tree swallow (*Iridoprocne bicolor*), and the purple martin (*Progne subis*). The latter bird is the largest species of North American martin.

Motacillidae

The Motacillidae, pipits and wagtails, are slender, elegant birds with long tails. They are insect-eaters which search for their prey mainly on the ground, where they also nest in the shelter of a stone or a bush. Of the two groups, pipits and wagtails, the first belong to the genus *Anthus* and are characterized by brown camouflage colours. Common European species are the meadow pipit (*A. pratensis*) and tree pipit (*A trivialis*), very similar in appearance; the rock pipit and water pipit (both *A. spinoletta*, of different sub-species) and tawny pipit (*A. campestris*). The African long-claws of the genus *Macronyx* show strong resemblance to the American meadowlarks (Icteridae). The wagtails, apart from the Asian forest wagtail (*Dendromanthus indicus*), all belong to the genus *Motacilla*. In Europe they are represented by the white wagtail

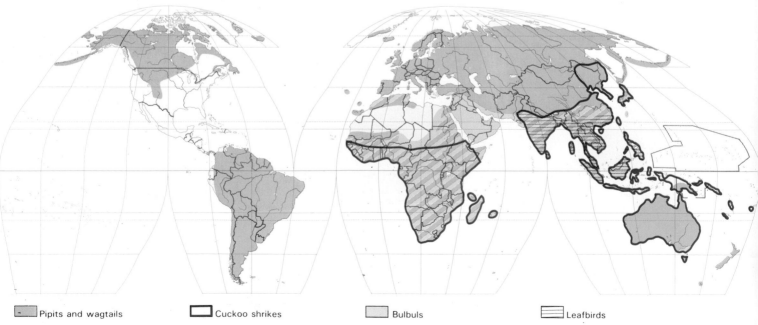

Pipits and wagtails   Cuckoo shrikes   Bulbuls   Leafbirds

white-tipped
plantcutter

ornate umbrella-bird

bearded bellbird

lovely cotinga

cock of the rock

pompadour cotinga

white-bearded manakin

swallow-tailed manakin

(*M. alba*, illustrated here), the pied wagtail (a subspecies of *M. alba*), the yellow wagtail (*M. flava*) and grey wagtail (*M. cinerea*).

Campephagidae and Pycnonotidae

The Campephagidae, cuckoo shrikes, bear a slight resemblance to cuckoos and also have the hooked beak of shrikes. The Australian ground cuckoo shrike (*Pteropodocys maxima*) nests in high trees and travels in family groups. The minivets of the genus *Pericrocotus*, also in this family, are neat, slender birds of the tree-tops, living from Afghanistan to the Philippines. All the Campephagidae tend to live in trees and are insect-eaters.

The Pycnonotidae, bulbuls, of southern Asia and Africa are perhaps better known and are sometimes kept as cage birds. They live in large flocks and have a very melodious song. During the breeding season the males become very aggressive towards one another and because of this they have been used as fighting birds in the same manner as fighting cocks. They are forest birds by origin but have spread their range and adapted well to gardens, orchards and parks. Among the best-known representatives are the red-whiskered bulbul (*Pycnonotus jocosus*), living from India to South China, the African white-vented or black-eyed bulbul (*P. barbatus*) and the yellow-streaked greenbul (*Phyllastrephus flavostriatus*); this latter bird eats beetles, in contrast to most bulbuls, which are fruit-eaters.

Irenidae

The Irenidae, leaf birds, are fourteen species of arboreal birds of India to South-East Asia, living in forests, woods and gardens and having a series of varied and brilliant calls. The ioras, such as the common iora (*Aegithina tiphia*) and the fairy bluebird (*Irena puella*, illustrated here), engage in striking aerial displays at breeding times.

Laniidae and Vangidae

The Laniidae, shrikes, are active predators, many of the seventy species have the habit of impaling the prey – insects, reptiles, small mammals and birds – on thorns or broken branches to be used as a food reserve. They are principally birds of open woodlands and scrub in the Old World, with two North American species. The red-backed shrike (*Lanius collurio*) nests in south-eastern England in summer (though it is now extremely rare), migrating to Africa in the autumn; other occasional visitors are the woodchat shrike (*L. senator*) and lesser greyshrike (*L. minor*). African species include the helmet shrikes (*Prionops*), which are sometimes classed as a separate family, bush shrikes (*Malaconotinae*) and puff backs (*Dryoscopus*). The Borneo brittlehead (*Pityriasis gymnocephala*) is noted for its mournful call. The American species are the northern grey shrike (*Lanius excubitor*) and loggerhead shrike (*L. ludovicianus*).

The Vangidae, vanga shrikes, are a Madagascan family that resemble the true shrikes. Some of the thirteen species, such as the blue vanga shrike (*Leptopterus madagascarinus*, illustrated here) and the green vanga shrike (*L. viridis*) hang their victims on spikes like the true shrikes; others catch insects on the wing.

Bombycillidae, Dulidae and Cinclidae

The Bombycillidae – waxwings, silky flycatchers, and hypocolius – number only eight species, among which are the waxwing (*Bombycilla garrulus*). This bird lives in the birch and conifer forests of northern Europe and northern North America. A second species, the cedar waxwing (*B. cedorum*) also occurs in North America. Waxwings migrate in close-knit flocks and are noted for the irregularity of their appearances; sometimes in hard winters they appear in large numbers far south of their normal wintering range. The silky flycatchers, all Central American, include the genera *Ptilogonys* and *Phainopepla*. The grey hypocolius (*Hypocolius ampelinus*) is a rare species that lives in the deserts between Arabia and Afghanistan.

The Dulidae are represented solely by the palm chat (*Dulus dominicus*) of Hispaniola, a fruit-eater living in large flocks. Up to thirty pairs of these birds may build a communal structure that resembles a large basket of twigs, often located at the top of a palm tree trunk; each pair has its own entrance and nesting chamber.

The Cinclidae, dippers, contains four species in one genus, *Cinclus*. The sole European representative is the dipper (*C. cinclus*) of mountain streams from North Africa and Western Asia to Britain. They have a water-repellent plumage, eyes capable of seeing both in air and under water, ears protected by a membrane

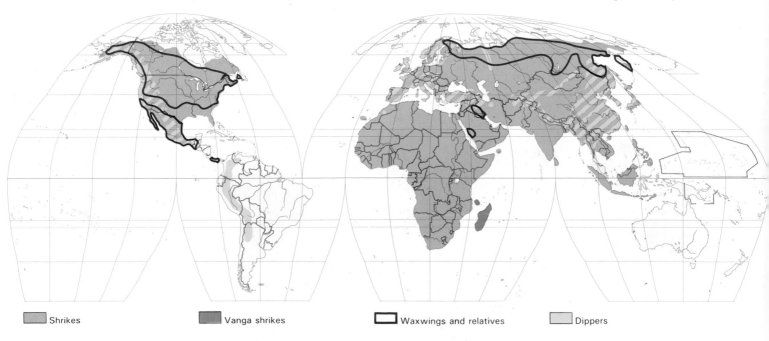

Shrikes   Vanga shrikes   Waxwings and relatives   Dippers

cactus wren

brown thrasher

blue vanga
shrike

fairy
bluebird

superb lyrebird

skylark

white wagtail

and nostrils provided with an operculum. They swim, dive and move about under water with ease to find their diet of aquatic insects and other small invertebrates. The three other species live in northern Asia and Japan, the brown dipper (*C. pallasii*), western North America, the American dipper (*C. mexicanus*), and the Andes, the white-headed dipper (*C. leucocephalus*).

Troglodytidae, Mimidae and Prunellidae

The Troglodytidae comprise the wrens, small birds with a short body and short rounded wings (typicals of birds of woods and thickets). Their tail is usually short and points upwards. Most wrens are American, the family being represented in Europe solely by the wren (*Troglodytes troglodytes*) about 9 cm (3¾ in) long, found over most of Eurasia and in North Africa as well as in North America. The cactus wren (*Campylorhynchus brunneicapillus*, illustrated on p. 227), lives only in the arid regions of the western USA and Mexico, the zapata wren (*Ferminia cerverai*) is found only in one marsh in Cuba, and the house wren (*Troglodytes aëdon*) occurs everywhere from Canada to Tierra del Fuego.

The Mimidae, mockingbirds, or mimic thrushes, are named from their ability to imitate the songs of other birds. They comprise thirteen genera with thirty species of woodland birds, all of the New World. The best-known species is the mockingbird (*Mimus polyglottus*) which chases off intruders from its territory and delights in attacking domestic cats and dogs. The brown thrasher (*Toxostoma rufum*, illustrated on p. 227) occurs from Maine to Florida; the blue mockingbird (*Melanotis caerulescens*) lives in Mexico.

The Prunellidae, accentors, contain only one genus, *Prunella*, with twelve species of medium dimensions with a squat body and strong legs. They are ground-dwellers, living on insects in summer and fruits and seeds in winter. The birds that occupy more northerly areas migrate southwards when the cold season arrives, while the more southerly populations are sedentary. Two species are present in Europe, the dunnock or hedge accentor (also called, misleadingly, hedge sparrow) (*Prunella modularis*), familiar in Britain, and the Alpine accentor (*P. collaris*) of high mountain slopes, known in Britain only as a chance vagrant. The black-throated accentor (*P. atrogularis*) and the Siberian accentor (*P. montanella*) inhabit the north of the Soviet Union.

Muscicapidae

This family is the largest of all birds, with 1,500 species in nine sub-families. The sub-family Turdinae include the song-thrushes (*Turdus philomelos*) with the mistle thrushes (*T. viscivorus*), redwings (*T. ilacus*) and fieldfares (*T. pilaris*, illustrated here), the blackbird (*T. merula*) and ring ouzel (*T. torquatus*). Other genera and species in this same sub-family are the robin (*Erithacus rubecula*), nightingale (*Luscinia megalorhynchus*) and the rock thrushes of southern Europe (*Monticola* spp.). The redstart (*Phoenicurus phoenicurus*) of woodlands, parks and gardens, black redstart (*P. ochrurus*) of stonier localities, and wheatear (*Oenanthe oenanthe*) of open country are others of the group; as are the stonechat and whinchat (*Saxicola torquata* and *S. rubetra*). In North America the American robin (*Turdus migratorius*) is the size of a blackbird rather than a robin; it was called a robin by early settlers on account of its orange breast. The eastern bluebird (*Sialia sialis*, illustrated here) is a resident of woodlands and gardens in the eastern USA.

The Timaliinae, babblers and wren tits, are birds of the Old World tropics, including Australia, such as the white-crested laughing thrush (*Garrulax leucolophus*) of the Himalayas to South-East Asia, with one New World species, the North American wren tit (*Chamaea fasciata*). The Cinclosomatinae are a small group from Australia and New Guinea with nine genera including rail babblers, scrub robins, quail thrushes and logrunners. The Panurinae comprise two genera, of which *Panurus* includes the bearded tit or reedling (*P. biarmicus*) nesting in south-east England. The Polioptilinae, gnatcatchers, are insect-eating birds that live in the New World.

The sub-family Sylviinae, Old World warblers, number over 300 species in about thirty genera, nearly all of Eurasia and Africa. Many live near water, such as the reed warbler (*Acrocephalus scirpaceus*) and marsh warbler (*A. palustris*, illustrated here). Others live in bushy habitats, such as the blackcap (*Sylvia atricapilla*, illustrated here), garden warbler (*S. borin*), whitethroat (*S. communis*) and lesser whitethroat (*S. curruca*), chiffchaff (*Phylloscopus collybita*) and willow warbler (*P. trochilus*). Also in this sub-family are the tailor birds (*Orthotomus* sp.) of southern Asia, which 'sew' leaves together to make their nests, and the goldcrests, firecrests and kinglets (*Regulus* sp.).

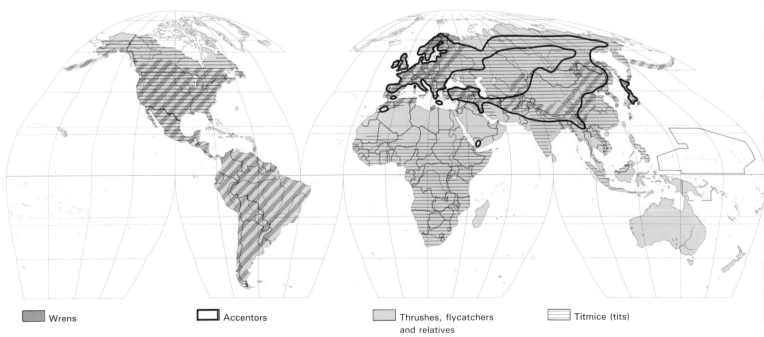

Wrens   Accentors   Thrushes, flycatchers and relatives   Titmice (tits)

white-crested
laughing thrush

golden whistler

pied flycatcher

eastern bluebird

marsh warbler

fieldfare

variegated wren

blackcap

The Malurinae, Australian wren warblers, live exclusively in Australia, New Zealand and New Guinea. There are twenty-five genera and eighty-three species. The most highly coloured forms are of the genus *Malurus*, including the blue wren and variegated wren (*M. cyaneus* and *M. lamberti*, illustrated on p. 229). The fly-catchers, sub-family Muscicapinae, include the spotted flycatcher (*Muscicapa striata*) pied flycatcher (*Ficedula hypoleuca*, illustrated on p. 229) and collared flycatcher (*F. albicollis*). The last sub-family is that of the Pachycephalinae, thickheads or whistlers, typical of the islands between Asia and Australia; illustrated on p. 229 is the golden whistler (*Pachycephala pectoralis*).

Paridae

The Paridae, titmice, are small birds, with short conical beaks; many species are common in Britain, including the great tit (*Parus major*, illustrated here), blue tit (*P. caeruleus*), coal tit (*P. ater*), marsh tit (*P. palustris*) and willow tit (*P. montanus*). The crested tit (*P. cristatus*) lives in conifer forests in Europe, but in Britain is quite rare, found only in some Scottish pinewoods. The long-tailed tit (*Aegithalos caudatus*) and – rare vagrant to Britain – the penduline tit (*Remiz pendulinus*), which hangs its nest like a small sack from branches, are sometimes classed in separate families as they are rather different in appearance and nesting habits from other tits of the family Paridae. Among exotic tits is the southern black tit (*Parus niger*, illustrated here) of East Africa. American species include the bush tits (*Psaltriparus* species), the verdin (*Auriparus flaviceps*), inhabiting semi-desert country, and several *Parus* species, called chickadees, found in temperate areas.

Sittidae

The Sittidae, nuthatches, resemble small woodpeckers. They nest in holes in trees, often using the old nests of woodpeckers and reducing the size of the entrance with a mud surround. They climb about the tree trunks in any position, including head downwards, not using the tail for support like woodpeckers but relying solely on the claws. They include the nuthatch of Europe (*Sitta europaea*), the velvet-fronted nuthatch (*S. frontalis*, illustrated here) of South-East Asia, and the wall creeper (*Tichodroma muraria*) of the mountains of Europe and Central Asia.

Certhiidae and Climacteridae

The Certhiidae include the treecreeper (*Certhia familiaris*) of the forests of North America and Europe, and the short-toed treecreeper (*C. brachydactyla*, illustrated here). The six species of treecreeper all look very similar. They are small, slender brown birds with a thin, curved bill, that hunt insects by spiralling round a tree-trunk supporting themselves, like woodpeckers, with their stiff tail.

The Climacteridae are the six species of Australian treecreepers, more brightly coloured than the European and American species, with longer legs, but a soft tail which they do not use for support. A typical representative is the Australian brown treecreeper (*Climacteris picumnus*).

Dicaeidae and Nectariniidae

The Dicaeidae are arboreal Asian and Australian birds known as flowerpeckers from their diet of nectar. An example is the mistletoe bird (*Dicaeum hirundinaceum*) of Australia and some Indonesian islands.

A similar diet is typical of the sunbirds family Nectariniidae. Typically of hot tropical climates, they sometimes occupy mountain habitats, and in Africa, on Kilimanjaro, they extend above the 4000 m (13,000 ft) level. The best-known representatives belong to the genus *Nectarinia*, among which are the tropical Asian van Hesselt's sunbird (*N. sperata*) and the green-headed sunbird (*N. orientalis*) both illustrated here. Unlike hummingbirds, sunbirds do not hover in front of flowers to obtain nectar and pollen, but perch on them and reach inside with their curved beak.

Zosteropidae

The Zosteropidae, white-eyes, are residents of the tropical areas of the Old World and Australasia. They are small birds, 10 to 13 cm (4 to 5.5 in) long, with a ring of white feathers round the eye. They live on insects, fruit and nectar; the beak is correspondingly thin, pointed and slightly decurved, and used most effectively to break open the skin of fruits. Except in the breeding season white-eyes are gregarious. The biggest genus is *Zosterops* with fifty-seven of the seventy-nine species.

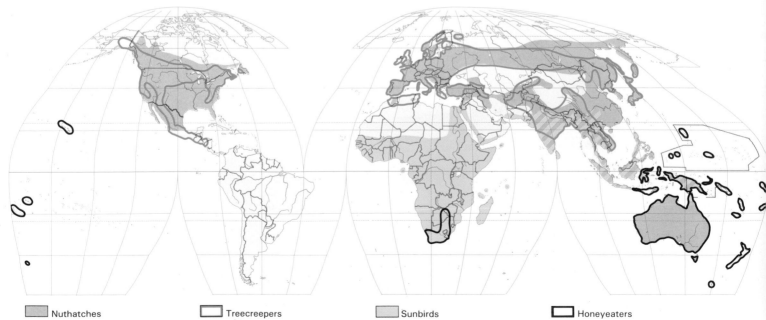

Nuthatches   Treecreepers   Sunbirds   Honeyeaters

southern black tit

great tit

van Hesselt's sunbird

green-headed sunbird

short-toed treecreeper

noisy friarbird

tui

velvet-fronted nuthatch

Meliphagidae

The Meliphagidae, honey-eaters, are characterized by having a tongue which is cleft at the tip and bristle-tipped like a paintbrush, ideal for extracting flower nectar and pulp from fruits. Some species, such as those of the genus *Philemon*, on the other hand, are carnivorous and live on insects, small animals and birds. The family numbers thirty-eight genera with 167 species, some of which have colonial habits even during the breeding season. Some species of *Meliphaga* and *Melithreptes* upholster their nests with animal fur plucked directly from the owner such as a cow or marsupial. The colouring is often rich and varied as in the tui (*Prosthemadera novaeseelandiae*, illustrated on p. 231) of New Zealand. Many have melodious voices, others disagreeable ones, as in the noisy friarbird or leatherhead (*Philemon corniculatus*, illustrated on p. 231) of eastern Australia. The sole South African genus is *Promerops* (containing the two species of Cape sugarbirds).

Emberizidae

The Emberizidae contain 280 species divided into seven sub-families. The first of these, the Emberizinae, are the buntings (known as sparrows in the USA), found in the Americas, Africa, Europe and parts of Asia. They prefer open or thinly wooded country. European species include the yellowhammer (*Emberiza citrinella*), corn bunting (*E. calandra*), cirl bunting (*E. cirlus*), ortolan bunting (*E. hortulana*), rock bunting (*E. cia*), reed bunting (*E. schoeniclus*) and the black-headed bunting (*E. melanocephala*, illustrated here), known only as an occasional vagrant in Britain.

Other well-known species include the Lapland bunting (*Calcarius lapponicus*) known as the Lapland longspur in Arctic regions of North America and snow bunting (*Plectrophenax nivalis*) of the north.

The Geospizinae are the Darwin's finches, six genera found only on the Galápagos and the Cocos Islands; one is *Geospiza*. Darwin's finches have evolved specializations of the beak as adaptations to different diets. The heavy seed crushing beak of the medium ground finch (*G. fortis*, illustrated here) is typical. Two species of *Camarhynchus*, the woodpecker finch (*C. pallidus*) and mangrove finch (*C. heliobates*) use cactus spines to prise insects

from the folds in bark. The Cardinalinae are characterized by a tuft of feathers on the head, as in the pyrrhuloxia (*Cardinalis sinuatus*) of North America and the red-crested cardinal (*Paroaria coronata*) of South America, both illustrated here.

The Thraupinae, tanagers, live only in South America. Among them is the seven-coloured tanager (*Tanagra chilensis*) and the crimson-collared tanager (*Rhamphocelus sanguinolenta*, illustrated here). The South American swallow-tanager (*Tersina viridis*, illustrated here) is the sole member of the sub-family Tersinae. Another sub-family with only one member is the Catamblyrhynchinae with the South American plush-capped finch (*Catamblyrhynchus diadema*).

Parulidae and Drepanididae

The Parulidae, American or wood warblers, are a varied group. One common characteristic is the insectivorous diet, though hunting methods and the sites chosen for nesting vary. Among the 120 species are the magnolia warbler (*Dendroica magnoliae*, illustrated here) of the USA, that winters from Mexico to Panama, the ovenbird (*Seiurus aurocapillus*), also of the Americas, which makes a large domed mud nest on a tree stump or fence post.

The Drepanididae, Hawaiian honeycreepers, are a nectar-eating family that lives only in Hawaii and seems to be dying out. Many species are already extinct, while others are rare, such as the Hawaiian honeycreeper or iiwi (*Vestinaria coccinea*, illustrated here), the apapane (*Himatione sanguinea*) and amakihi (*Viridonia virens*). Their native names derive from renderings of their calls.

Vireonidae

The Vireonidae – vireos, shrike vireos and peppershrikes – comprise thirty-nine species of small New World birds of modest colouring. There are three sub-families. The Vireoninae of North America live in foliage, continuously searching for insects. They include the white-eyed vireo (*Vireo griseus*). The Vireolaninae include the chestnut-sided shrike vireo (*Vireolanius melitophrys*) of southern Mexico to Guatemala; it holds large insects with one foot while it tears them to pieces with the beak. The two *Cyclarhis* species include the rufous-browed peppershrike (*C. gujanensis*), living from Mexico to Argentina.

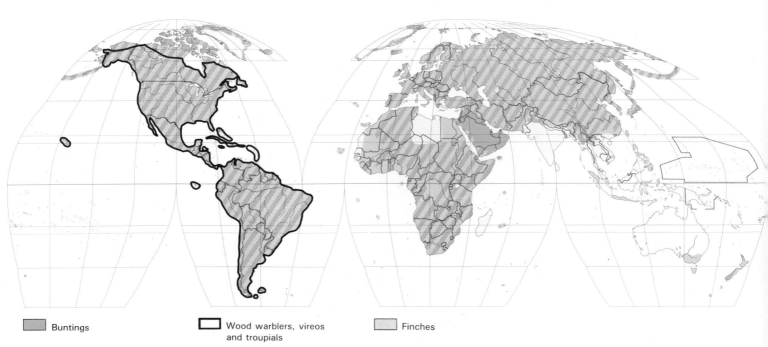

Buntings   Wood warblers, vireos   Finches
                  and troupials

Hawaiian honeycreeper

Darwin's medium
ground finch

spot-breasted
oriole

black-headed bunting

swallow-tanager

pyrrhuloxia

red-crested cardinal

magnolia warbler

crimson-collared tanager

Icteridae

Many species of the Icteridae, troupials, are omnivorous, such as the grackles (*Quiscalus* sp.) and *Euphagus* species such as the rusty blackbird (*Euphagus carolinus*), which nests in Alaska and northern Canada and winters in the southern USA. Others live on nectar, such as the caciques (*Cacicus* sp.) of Central America to Brazil. Others again, such as the chestnut-headed oropendola (*Psarocolius wagleri*) and Montezuma oropendola (*Psarocolius montezuma*), the troupial (*Icterus icterus*) and the spot-breasted oriole (*I. pectoralis*, illustrated on p. 233), are fruit-eaters. Another northern species, the bobolink (*Dolichonyx oryzivorus*), lives on insects in spring and summer and seeds in autumn, wintering in Argentina. Others like the brown-headed cowbird (*Molothrus ater*) of Canada to Mexico are parasitic and lay their eggs in other birds' nests like cuckoos, whereas related species limit themselves to laying their eggs in other birds' nests but incubating the eggs themselves. Among them is the bay-winged cowbird (*M. badius*) which takes care of the eggs and chicks of the nest's owner. The meadowlarks (*Sturnella* sp.), solitary birds, are well liked in North America for their sweet voices.

Fringillidae

The Fringillidae, finches, comprise arboreal grain-eating birds with short, strong, slightly hooked beaks. The first sub-family, Fringillinae, contains only the genus *Fringilla*, which in its turn consists of the chaffinch (*F. coelebs*) whose song is familiar in hedges, woods and gardens; the brambling (*F. montifringilla*); and the Canary Islands chaffinch (*F. teydea*). The Carduelinae contain 122 species in several genera, among them *Carduelis* with the goldfinch (*C. carduelis*), greenfinch (*C. chloris*) and siskin (*C. spinus*). *Acanthis* species include the linnet (*A. cannabina*), redpoll (*A. flammea*) and twite (*A. flavirostris*). Other well-known species are the bullfinch (*Pyrrhula pyrrhula*) and serin (*Serinus serinus*). The hawfinch (*Coccothraustes coccothraustes*) has the heaviest and strongest beak of all the finches, and the beak of the crossbill (*Loxia recurvirostra*) enables it to extract seeds from spruce cones. Other species are adapted to extract the seeds from other conifer trees, for example the two-barred crossbill (*L. leucoptera*) feeds on larch and the parrot crossbill (*L. pytopsittacus*) on pine.

Estrildidae

The Estrildidae, grass finches and waxbills, are small seed-eating birds with often varied and vivid colouring. Some species inhabit humid forests, some semi-arid savannahs and others the most torrid deserts. The Erythrurinae of Australasia include the long-tailed grass finch (*Poephila acuticauda*, illustrated here) and Gouldian finch (*P. gouldiae*). The waxbills include the common African waxbill (*Estrilda astrild*) and Sydney waxbill (*E. temporalis*). The waxbill group also contains the avadavats of southern Asia, including the red avadavat (*E. amandava*, illustrated here) and the blue-faced parrot finch (*Erythrura trichroa*). Another genus of the family is *Lonchura*, the mannikins of South-East Asia, Australia and Africa.

Ploceidae

The Ploceidae, weavers and sparrows, the last of the families of Old World seed-eaters, is divided into five sub-families. The house sparrow (*Passer domesticus*, illustrated here), is found in many parts of the world, and its plumage is typical of the genus *Passer*, light on the underparts and reddish-brown on the back. Another dull-coloured common species is the tree sparrow (*P. montanus*). An exception to this is the golden sparrow (*Passer luteus*, illustrated here) of Africa south of the Sahara. In the mountainous parts of Europe and Asia lives the snow finch (*Montifringilla nivalis*), whose white wings stand out from the brown body. The rock sparrow (*Petronia petronia*) is resident from the Canary Islands, across the mountains and deserts of Asia to Tibet and China. The house sparrow has been introduced into many countries; notably to the USA at the turn of the century, and it is now widespread there across the whole continent. The tree sparrow has also been introduced to the USA, but is neither common nor widespread. Some members of the Ploceidae are notable pests: the African quelea (*Quelea quelea*) descends in millions on seed crops.

The sub-family Ploceinae comprise the weaver birds of the genera *Ploceus*, *Bubalornis* and *Textor*, of Africa and Asia. Some build nests by skilfully interweaving grass blades and straw, though others make untidy twig nests. The Euplectinae of Africa are also clever weavers of complex nests which are often built in reeds and rushes in swampy areas, rather than in trees. The best-

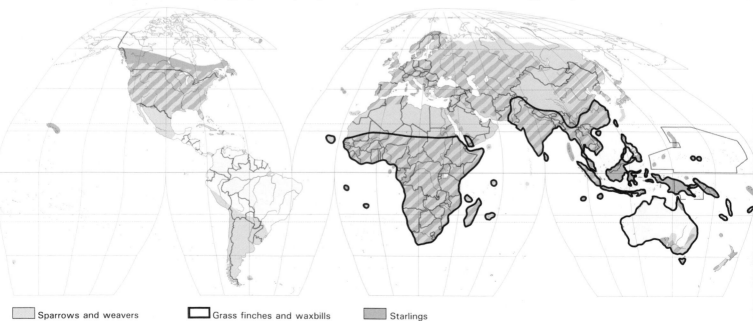

Sparrows and weavers   Grass finches and waxbills   Starlings

paradise whydah

♂

♀

long-tailed grass finch

red
avadavat

golden sparrow

red bishop

house sparrow

giant racket-tailed drongo

known representatives are the red bishop (*Euplectes orix*, illustrated on p. 235) and black-winged red bishop (*E. hordaceus*). Others are the long-tailed and yellow-backed widow birds (*E. progne*) and (*E. macrourus*). The Ploceopasserinae, such as the sociable weaver (*Philetarus socius*) build very large communal nests. The Viduinae, all African, are parasitic; the male of the paradise whydah (*Vidua paradisea*, illustrated on p. 235) is polygamous; during the breeding season he grows four long tail feathers and mates with several females who, like cuckoos, lay their eggs in other birds' nests.

Sturnidae

The Sturnidae, 106 species of starlings, mynahs and oxpeckers, move about in large flocks in search of food, sometimes causing appreciable damage to crops. There are two sub-families, Buphaginae and Sturninae; to the first belongs only the genus *Buphagus*, with two species of African oxpeckers, which search for ticks and mites on large mammals, wild or domestic, even mating on the backs of the hosts. The Sturninae contain more than 100 species among which is the common starling (*Sturnus vulgaris*), widespread throughout the world. Others are Asian mynahs or grackles (*Gracula* sp.) and various African genera, many of which have glossy iridescent plumage.

Oriolidae

The orioles number some thirty species of sizes between starlings and jays. They are mainly tropical tree-dwellers, living on insects and fruit, and are often brilliant yellow or golden in colour with dark wings. They show marked sexual dimorphism. Some species are sedentary, others migratory. The latter include the golden oriole (*Oriolus oriolus*) common in continental Europe and occasionally seen in south-east Britain, with a characteristic fluting song; it lives in woods and is rarely seen in the open.

Dicruridae

The Dicruridae, drongos, combine about twenty species in two genera, of sizes ranging from those of a starling to those of a jackdaw. Some species, such as the giant racket-tailed drongo (*Dicrurus paradiseus*, illustrated on p. 235) of Asia, have two long tail-feathers ending in banner-like feathers. They are highly terrestrial birds that defend their own areas furiously even against large birds of prey. Their aggression pervades their entire lifestyle; they hunt insects on the wing, in the manner of flycatchers, but with a definite ferocity. Such is their success in battle, even against eagles, that the tree where a drongo nests is likely to be inhabited by several other, less forceful birds that gain protection if they are left in peace by the drongo. Among other members of this family is the only species of the *Chaetorhynchus* genus, the mountain drongo (*C. papuensis*) of New Guinea.

Callaeidae and Grallinidae

The Callaeidae, wattlebirds, all of New Zealand, contain only three genera, each with only one species. They are omnivorous birds whose appearance recalls that of crows. The most widely distributed species is the kokako (*Callaeus cinerea*), while only a small population of the saddleback (*Creadion carunculatus*) survives, and the huia (*Heteralocha acutirostris*) is probably extinct.

The Grallinidae, magpie larks, mudlarks or mudnest builders, are also a small Australian family of only four species. Their appearance resembles that of the crows, but the legs are more slender and the tail longer. They are gregarious in habit and the flocks may contain very large numbers. The black and white magpie lark or mudlark (*Grallina cyanoleuca*) lives in areas near watercourses and searches for arthropods and molluscs along their banks. The habitat of the apostle bird (*Struthidea cinerea*) is by contrast the arid semi-deserts of Australia; it derives its name from its habit of moving about in small flocks of about twelve birds, among which a strict hierarchical order is observed. The white-winged chough (*Corcorax melanorhamphos*) also exhibits an unusual gregarious habit: several individuals join together to build an enormous nest and take turns at sitting on the eggs. The fourth species is the torrent lark (*Grallina bruijni*) of New Guinea.

Artamidae

The Artamidae, wood swallows or swallow-shrikes, mostly of Australia, contain only one genus (*Artamus*) with about ten species. The streamlined appearance underlines the great flying skill of these birds. Their habitat is the humid tropical forests from

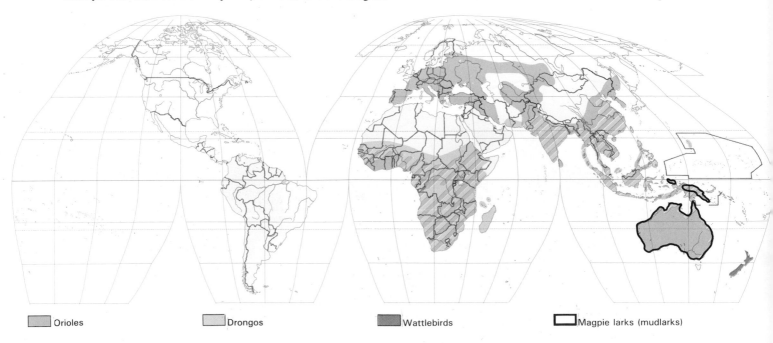

Orioles   Drongos   Wattlebirds   Magpie larks (mudlarks)

magnificent riflebird

king bird of paradise

orange-crested gardener

greater bird of paradise

superb bird of paradise

emperor bird of paradise

six-wired bird of paradise

Australia to China and India. They live in large flocks and tend to be insectivorous. They include the white-breasted wood swallow (*A. leucorhynchus*), living from the Andamans to Australia, and the white-browed wood swallow (*A. superciliosus*) of Australia.

Cracticidae

The Cracticidae, currawongs and Australian butcherbirds are another small Australian family containing some species that can easily be confused with crows, from whom they are distinguished only by the greater length of the beak and greater development of the tail. They have a melodious song and are skilful imitators of the songs of other birds. Among the best songsters is the Australian black-backed bell magpie (*Gymnorhina tibicen*).

Ptilonorhynchidae

The Ptilonorhynchidae, bower birds, are noted for the behaviour of the males, who devote much time preparing an arena in which they later perform their courtship displays. Some species build platforms, while others prepare avenues or bowers, sometimes even painting their walls, to make a 'theatre' in which to attract and hold the attention of the female. These edifices are made with interwoven twigs, sticks or grasses. They are decorated with coloured flower petals, shells, beetle wings and even pieces of brightly coloured plastic and bottle tops. The arena and bower are sometimes enclosed by walls of plant material, as in the case of the orange-crested gardener (*Amblyornis subalaris*, illustrated on p. 237) of south-east New Guinea, which also adds fresh flowers every day. The highest level of bower building is achieved by the golden bowerbird (*Sericulus aureas*) of northern Australia and New Guinea, and the satin bowerbird (*Ptilonorhynchus violaceus*) of eastern Australia, which paint them with coloured liquids.

Paradisaeidae

The Paradisaeidae – the forty species of birds of paradise – are perhaps the most spectacular bird family of all. They live in the depths of forests; the nest is usually made of a pile of branches in the fork of a tree; the diet can be considered omnivorous, since it consists of fruit, insects and small vertebrates. A characteristic of the birds of paradise is the strong sexual dimorphism (except in some genera such as *Loboparadisea*, *Loria* and *Phonygammus*) and the unequalled spectacle of the courting displays.

The smallest known bird of paradise is the king bird of paradise (*Cicinnurus regius*, which, with the following six species, is illustrated on p. 237), of the coastal regions of New Guinea. The six-wired bird of paradise (*Parotia sexpennis*) is also found in New Guinea, as are the greater bird of paradise (*Paradisaea apoda*), and the emperor bird of paradise (*P. quilielmi*), which puts on the most spectacular displays. The superb bird of paradise (*Lophorina superba*) comes from the same region, while the magnificent riflebird (*Ptiloris magnificus*) has colonized northern Australia.

Corvidae

The Corvidae – crows, magpies and jays – are considered to be the most highly evolved birds; they lack a true song, and are gifted only with raucous voices, quite disagreeable in some species. The dimensions are often medium to large, but some species are much smaller, as is *Pseudopoces humilis* of the high plateaux of Central Asia, which is only as big as a sparrow. The beak is always large and fairly long, and is sometimes exceptionally powerful; the habitats occupied are very varied and the diet is often omnivorous. This non-specialization is largely responsible for the success of the family, with over 100 species. The plumage is normally dark in the crows, but can be spectacular in the jays, such as the turquoise jay (*Cyanolyca turquosa*, illustrated here) of the Andes.

In the Palaearctic region – the Old World part of the north temperate and Arctic zones – the commonest species (the first four are illustrated here) are the jay (*Garrulus glandarius*), the common magpie (*Pica pica* – also occurs in west USA as the black-bellied magpie), the jackdaw (*Corvus monedula*), the raven (*C. corax*), the carrion crow (*C. corone corone*; *C. brachyrhynchus* in North America), and the hooded crow (*C. corone cornix*). A magpie similar to that of Europe but more brilliantly coloured lives in Sri Lanka, the Ceylon blue magpie (*Cissa ornata*, illustrated here). Pander's ground jay (*Podoces panderi*, illustrated here) lives in the deserts of Central Asia, while a resident of northern European pinewoods is the nutcracker (*Nucifraga caryocatactes*). Clark's nutcracker (*N. columbiana*, illustrated here) lives in coniferous forests from Alaska to Lower California.

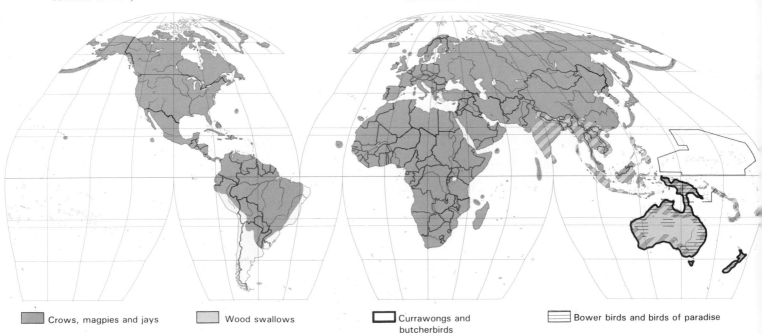

Crows, magpies and jays   Wood swallows   Currawongs and butcherbirds   Bower birds and birds of paradise

Clark's nutcracker

turquoise jay

Ceylon blue magpie

common magpie

jackdaw

Pander's ground jay

raven

jay

MAMMALS

The mammals are descended directly from the reptiles, and the relationship of the two groups is so close that some fossil forms are difficult to place in either category. The most obvious mammalian characteristic is the presence of hair or fur covering the skin, but there exist 'naked' mammals and others covered with scales. Except for a few very primitive forms, they do not lay eggs but bring forth their young alive, and the newly born are suckled, nourished by the mother with milk secreted by special glands usually located on the thorax or abdomen. After birth the young are usually looked after for a period varying from group to group, during which time they are protected and taught. Capable of adapting to the most diverse environments, mammals may live under the ground or on its surface, and may run, jump or fly. This is the animal group that has undergone the greatest evolution and it is at present in a dominant position over the whole animal kingdom. At the present time more than 4500 species are known, distributed over all the continents and at all latitudes. Three sub-classes can be distinguished, of which only two survive, Prototheria (the monotremes) and Theria (the marsupials and the placental mammals). The last-named include at least twenty-six orders, of which sixteen are surviving, a number which in itself testifies to the success of the group.

Monotremata

Fossils of the monotreme order (Monotremata) have been found exclusively on the Australian continent, signifying that they appeared at some time after the continents of Australia and South America drifted apart. It is possible nevertheless that their origin can be attributed to an independent branch developing during the triassic period (200 million years ago) from the synapsid (extinct and mammal-like) reptiles. They are the only egg-laying mammals. The monotremes comprise the families Ornithorhynchidae (platypuses) and Tachyglossidae (echidnas or spiny anteaters).

Ornithorhynchidae

The Ornithorhynchidae are represented solely by the duckbilled platypus (*Ornithorhynchus anatinus*, illustrated here), characterized by a spatulate bill and webbed feet. It lives in fresh water in Australia and Tasmania, and when it is under water the eyes and ears are protected by a fold of skin. The young have temporary milk teeth, which disappear in the adult state, to be replaced by strong horny plates. The platypus also makes burrows in the river bank, consisting of a long gallery leading to a grass-lined den. Here the female lays her eggs and incubates them for fourteen days. The young are protected and fed by the mother, sucking the milk from the hairs surrounding her mammary glands. The males have on the hind legs a horny spur which is the terminal portion of a poison-gland whose exact function is not known.

Tachyglossidae

Two genera belong to the Tachyglossidae, echidnas: *Tachyglossus*, of which there are two species, of Australia, Tasmania and New Guinea, and *Zaglossus*, illustrated here, with three species, all of New Guinea. *Tachyglossus aculeatus* resembles a porcupine, its body being covered with spines as much as 6 cm (2.5 in) long. It has a long, slender snout with which it probes the earth in search of ants and termites, which it locates by its sense of smell and picks up with its sticky tongue. The female deposits an egg which is kept in a pocket analogous to the pouch of the marsupials, but which exists only for a brief period during each breeding season. This 'incubator' contains the glands which secrete the milk whose production is simulated by the newborn. *Tachyglossus setosus* lives in Tasmania. The species of the genus *Zaglossus* (*Z. bruijni*, *Z. bubensis* and *Z. bartoni*) are differentiated from those of *Tachyglossus* by their longer, curved snout, more robust body and longer limbs. They are also furry with scattered spines among the dense fur. All echidnas are well adapted for digging.

The only two mammals that lay eggs:
Left A duckbilled platypus from Australia.
Right A long-snouted echidna (spiny anteater) with its spines partly buried in its dense fur.

Marsupialia

The marsupial order is limited to the Americas and Australia (feral individuals – escaped from captivity – exist in Britain and New Zealand). Its species possess a primitive placenta: the young are born at an early stage of development, and find refuge in a pouch, where they attach themselves to the nipples until they are completely developed. However, some marsupials (the American species) have a poorly developed pouch or none at all. The order comprises nine families.

Didelphidae

The didelphids, opossums, are the most primitive of these families. They are found in the Americas and comprise arboreal animals with teeth of the carnivorous type, a fairly long snout and a long tail which is prehensile and sparsely haired. The woolly opossum (*Caluromys lanatus*) possesses particularly soft and woolly fur. Another species is the Virginia opossum (*Didelphis virginianus*, illustrated here), which has yellowish-grey fur; the tail, covered with scales, gives the animal assistance in climbing. The young, after suckling, remain clinging to the mother's fur. If attacked *Didelphys* responds by going limp and pretending to be dead – 'playing possum' – till left alone. This is a poor defence against motor traffic and many are killed on American roads. There are several species of the genus *Marmosa*, the mouse opossums, all of South and Central America. The thick-tailed opossum or little water opossum (*Lutreolina crassicaudata*) lives along watercourses in South America east of the Andes. The water opossum or yapok (*Chironectes minimus*), found from Mexico to Argentina, has a pouch which it can close up to keep the young dry.

Dasyuridae

The Dasyuridae, dasyures and marsupial mice, are exclusively Australian and, like the opossums, present some primitive characteristics. All are carnivorous, generally nocturnal, and very lively and aggressive, their behaviour resembles in some respects that of shrews, cats, dogs and badgers. Some of the planigales (*Planigale* sp.) have a flattened skull which enables them to creep into crevices in the rocks in which they live. The yellow-footed marsupial mouse (*Antechinus flavipes*, illustrated here) is a skilful tree- and rock-climber; the eastern jerboa marsupial (*Antechinomys laniger*) is a true acrobat, specially adapted for life in savannahs, steppes and deserts. The crest-tailed marsupial rat (*Dasyuroides byrnei*) also lives in dry grassland and deserts. The black-tailed phascogale or tuan (*Phascogale tapoatafa*) is a tree-dweller; the spotted dasyure or native cat (*Dasyurus maculatus*, illustrated here) of south-eastern Australia and Tasmania preys on the smaller marsupials and birds; the Tasmanian devil (*Sarcophilus harrisi*, illustrated here) lives only in the most inaccessible regions of that country. The marsupial wolf or thylacine (*Thylacinus cynocephalus*, illustrated here) is probably extinct but may still survive, also in Tasmania; its resemblance to a dog is striking.

Notoryctidae

The Notoryctidae, marsupial moles, are of a single genus with two species, *Notoryctes typhlops* (illustrated here) and *N. caurinus*. Similar in size and behaviour to the European moles, they live in sandy regions. Unlike American and European moles they have a horn pad on the snout used for pushing earth aside. Their fur is prized for its softness.

Myrmecobiidae

The marsupial anteater or numbat (*Myrmecobius fasciatus*, illustrated here) is the only species of this family. It lives among the eucalyptus trees in forest regions and feeds on ants and termites, which it catches with its long, slender, sticky tongue. Lacking a pouch, it carries its young hidden in its fur.

Peramelidae

The Peramelidae, bandicoots, contain eight genera with about twenty species distributed in Australia, Tasmania, New Guinea, and New Zealand. The bandicoot resembles a long-snouted guinea pig. The genus *Perameles*, with the long-nosed bandicoot (*P. nasuta*, illustrated here) as a typical example, has the peculiarity, unique among the marsupials, of possessing a more developed placenta; the young are born more fully developed and hence pass a briefer period of time in the pouch.

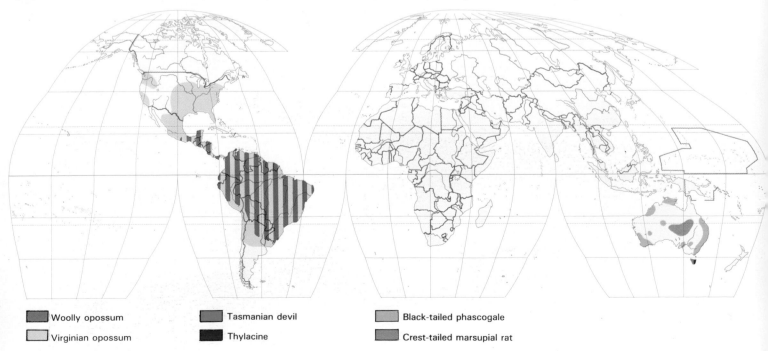

Woolly opossum

Virginian opossum

Tasmanian devil

Thylacine

Black-tailed phascogale

Crest-tailed marsupial rat

long-nosed bandicoot

spotted dasyure cat

Virginia opossum

thylacine

Tasmanian devil

yellow-footed marsupial mouse

numbat

marsupial mole

Caenolestidae

The Caenolestidae, rat opossums, look very similar to shrews. *Caenolestes* species live in the high forests and valleys of Ecuador and Bolivia, *Lestoros* in Peru, *Rhyncholestes* in Chile. Strangely, the marsupial pouch is present only in the young, who are carried clinging to their mother's fur.

Phalangeridae

The Phalangeridae, phalangers (called possums in Australia), are a much larger family with fifteen genera and about forty species. They are tree-dwellers and possess well-developed toes (phalanges), the big toes on the hind feet and sometimes the first and second toes on the forefeet being opposed to the others, so that they have a strong grip on branches. Some species have membranes between fore and hind legs that permit gliding flight.

The brush-tailed phalanger or possum (*Trichosurus vulpecula*), found in Australia and Tasmania and introduced into New Zealand, is the commonest species. The spotted cuscus (*Phalanger maculatus*, illustrated here) of Australia and New Guinea resembles a monkey and lives in the forest canopy; it has a prehensile tail, dense fur (spotted in the male) and large eyes which betray a nocturnal habit. The pygmy flying phalanger (*Acrobates pygmaeus*) of northern Australia lives on the eucalyptus trees, between which it glides, while the short-headed flying phalanger (*Petaurus breviceps*, illustrated here) can glide up to 50 m (160 ft). The largest species is the greater glider (*Schoinobates volans*) which may be 50 cm (20 in) long excluding the equally long tail. The honey phalanger (*Tarsipes spenserae*) of south-western Australia, feeds by sucking nectar from flowers. There are many species of *Pseudocheirus*, the ring-tails, found in New Guinea, Tasmania and Australia. The koala (*Phascolarctos cinereus*, illustrated here) is nocturnal and feeds on eucalyptus leaves.

Phascolomyidae or Vombatidae

There are two species resembling marmots: the common wombat (*Phascolomis* or *Vombatus ursinus*, illustrated here) which lives in south-eastern Australia and Tasmania, and the hairy-nosed wombat (*Lasiorhinus latifrons*) of southern Australia and Queensland. Both dig large burrows and are thus a nuisance to farmers.

Macropodidae

The family Macropodidae is the last marsupial order and comprises mainly the kangaroos and wallabies, found in Australia, New Guinea, New Zealand, the Bismarck Archipelago east of New Guinea, and nearby islands.

The hind legs, very long and strong, permit rapid bounding movement with the stout tail used as a balance. Herbivorous and generally nocturnal, the Macropodidae are grouped in three subfamilies. The musky rat kangaroo (*Hypsiprymnodon moschatus*) of Queensland belongs to the Hypsiprymnodontinae. The rest of the rat kangaroos, of which there are four genera with eight species, belong to the Potoroinae. The brush-tailed rat kangaroo (*Bettongia penicillata*) is little larger than a rabbit; once a serious pest, it is now rare since the introduction of the European fox. The potoroos that give their name to the sub-family are longer-nosed and shorter-tailed. The largest species is the rufous rat kangaroo (*Aepyprymnus rufescens*). All rat kangaroos live in undergrowth and forage at night for grass, tubers and fungi; some also eat grubs and worms.

The true kangaroos and the tree kangaroos belong to the Macropodinae. The tree kangaroos of the genus *Dendrolagus* are the only arboreal members of the family; they live mostly in New Guinea and Queensland. About 95 to 175 cm (37.5 in to 70 in) long, they spend the day in trees and may come down at night to forage for food. Bennett's tree kangaroo (*Dendrolagus bennettianus*) is illustrated here.

The wallabies are medium-sized members of the kangaroo family, found mostly in Australia. The rock wallabies of the genera *Petrogale* and *Peradorcas*, including the ring-tailed rock wallaby (*Petrogale xanthopus*, illustrated here), live among rocks, usually near water; they thump their feet when alarmed. The mountain wallabies (*Dorcopsulus* and *Dorcopsis* sp.) live in New Guinea; the pademelons of the genus *Thylogale* also in Australia and Tasmania. Most members are of the genus *Wallabia*, the brush wallabies, living in bushlands and open woods.

The largest members of the group are the grey kangaroo or forester (*Macropus major*, illustrated here), found mostly in open woodlands, and standing sometimes more than 2 m (6 ft 6 in) tall; and the red kangaroo (*M. rufus*) which lives in the grasslands of the interior. Somewhat smaller, the wallaroo or euro (*M. robustus*) lives in rocky areas throughout Australia, except Victoria.

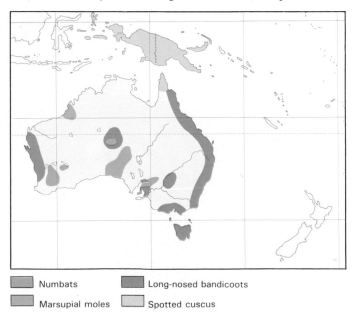

Wombats · Wallabies · Grey kangaroo

Rat kangaroos · Red kangaroo

Numbats · Long-nosed bandicoots

Marsupial moles · Spotted cuscus

spotted cuscus

common wombat

Bennett's
tree kangaroo

ring-tailed
rock wallaby

short-headed
flying phalanger

grey kangaroo

koala

Insectivora

Insectivores, being placental mammals, have the characteristic of allowing the embryo to develop completely inside the body of the mother, nourished through the placenta, which acts as a means of metabolic exchange for oxygen, food and waste products between the developing individual and the parent. Placentals comprise all the living mammals except the monotremes and the marsupials.

The insectivores are the probable ancient ancestors of all the other placentals. There are about 370 species in the order Insectivora, in eight extant families. The snout is generally elongated, and the teeth small and sharp. Many burrow, and all are carnivorous. Insectivores are adapted to diverse habits, but prefer the humid environment of woodland undergrowth. In nearly all species eyesight is poor but sense of smell excellent, and the fingers and toes have claws although the grasp is weak. Some have an aquatic habitat: the Potamogalidae (otter shrews) have webbed feet, flattened tails and valves to close their nostrils.

Solenodontidae

Solenodons are the most primitive of the Insectivora. Only two species survive, both are ratlike mammals about 28 cm (11 in) long, with a tail almost as long as the body. They live on invertebrates dug up with their claws. *Solenodon paradoxus* lives in Hispaniola; *S. cubanus* lives in Cuba. Both have toxic saliva.

Tenrecidae and Potamogalidae

The Tenrecidae, tenrecs, are exclusively of Madagascar and the Comoro Islands. They are round-bodied, big-headed mammals with a pointed snout, which they use to root up worms and grubs, foraging at night. The common or tailless tenrec (*Tenrec ecaudatus*, illustrated here) is up to 40 cm (16 in) long; the female bears usually twelve to sixteen young at a time but sometimes as many as twenty-one. The hedgehog tenrec (*Setifer setosus*) has stiff, prickly spines; it lives in dense forest undergrowth.

The otter-shrews, Potamogalidae, are long-bodied, carnivorous, semi-aquatic animals living in equatorial West Africa. There are three species, the largest (up to 64 cm (25 in) long) is the giant otter shrew (*Potamogale velox*, illustrated here).

Chrysochloridae

The Chrysochloridae, golden moles, live in Africa from Cameroon to the Cape. They are blind, burrowing mammals showing a curious evolutionary convergence with the common mole of Eurasia. Most species eat worms.

Erinaceidae, Soricidae and Talpidae

The common spiny hedgehog of Europe and Asia is *Erinaceus europaeus*. It eats mainly insects, worms, snails, slugs and is a valuable killer of pests. The gymnures of Asia, hairy hedgehogs, have coarse hairs rather than spines. African spiny hedgehogs include the Ethiopian hedgehog (*Paraechinus aethopicus*, illustrated here).

The family which has had the most success is that of the shrews, Soricidae. There are 290 species found throughout the northern hemisphere and in some mountainous regions of South America. Most are terrestrial; some are burrowers, a few semi-aquatic or arboreal; and they mostly live on invertebrates. The smallest, which may be the smallest of all mammals, is Savi's pygmy shrew (*Suncus etruscus*) of southern Europe, Asia and Africa, measuring as little as 35 mm (1.4 in) overall. The common shrew of Europe and Asia is *Sorex araneus*, illustrated here. The European water shrew (*Neomys fodiens*) is an excellent swimmer, not more than 4 cm (1.6 in) long. A North American species is the short-tailed shrew (*Blarina brevicauda*), illustrated here.

The common mole of Europe and Asia (*Talpa europaea*, illustrated here) is a typical member of the family Talpidae. Other well-known species are the Pyrenean desman (*Galemys pyrenaicus*) and the Russian desman (*Desmana moschata*), found in south-eastern Europe and parts of Asia. The star-nosed mole (*Condylura cristata*, illustrated here) of North America has twenty-two pink, tentacle-like sense organs round its nose.

Macroscelididae

The Macroscelididae, elephant shrews, are found all over Africa. A typical representative is the North African elephant shrew (*Elephantulus rozeti*, illustrated here), found from Morocco to South Africa.

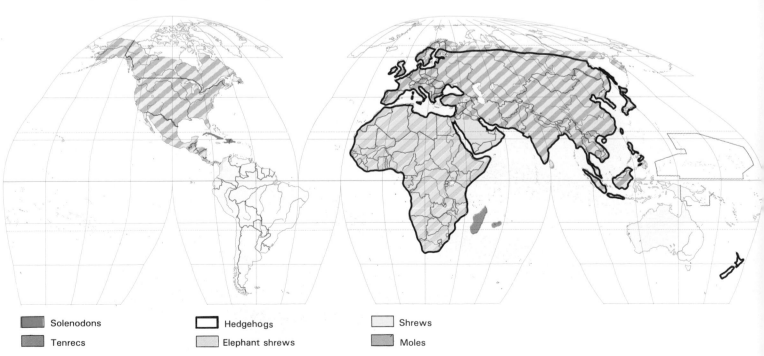

	Solenodons		Hedgehogs		Shrews
	Tenrecs		Elephant shrews		Moles

common or tailless tenrec

Ethiopian hedgehog

common shrew

North African
elephant shrew

short-tailed shrew

star-nosed mole

giant otter shrew

common mole

Dermoptera

The Dermoptera, flying lemurs, are a small order with only one family, Cynocephalidae, containing two species *Cynocephalus variegatus* and *C. philippinensis*, the former found from South-East Asia to Borneo and the latter in the Philippines. They are cat-sized herbivorous tree-dwellers with pointed snouts and large eyes and ears. A membrane extends along the sides from the cheeks to the tail, permitting glides of up to 60 m (190 ft).

Chiroptera: Megachiroptera

The Chiroptera comprise the only truly flying mammals, the bats. The wings are elastic membranes attached to the sides of the body and extended by the forelimbs and the elongated finger bones. Bats use echo-location to 'see' in the dark and locate their prey by the emission and reception of high-frequency sounds. They are divided into two sub-orders: the first, Megachiroptera, contains the many species of fruit bats and flying foxes of the family Pteropidae. They are comparatively large, dog-faced, mostly depending not on echolocation but more on their excellent eyesight to avoid obstacles. They live in the tropical Old World, Australia and Polynesia. A typical species is the Indian flying fox (*Pteropus giganteus*, illustrated here).

Chiroptera: Microchiroptera

The first family of the Microchiroptera is that of the Rhinopomatidae with the sole genus *Rhinopoma*, among whose species is the mouse-tailed bat (*R. microphyllum*, illustrated here). Like most others of the sub-order it is insectivorous. The Emballinuridae, sac-winged bats, comprise forty species among which is the tomb bat (*Taphozous perforatus*), found (as the map shows) in Arabia and north-east Africa. The bulldog bats (Noctilionidae) of Central and South America include the fishing bat (*Noctilio leporinus*, illustrated here) which skims across the surface of the water locating its prey by the echo of ripples below. The Nycteridae (slit-faced bats) contain the sole genus *Nycteris* in which there are twenty species.

The false vampires, Megadermatidae, are large, tail-less, broad-winged bats of the tropical Old World, living in dark caves or buildings. *Megaderma spasma*, illustrated here, is found in south and South-East Asia. Unlike the true vampires, the false vampires eat insects rather than blood. The horseshoe bats, Rhinolophidae, are found in Europe, Africa, Asia and Australasia; they include the greater horseshoe bat (*Rhinolophus ferrumequinum*, illustrated here). Closely related are the leaf-nosed bats, Hipposideridae, found in tropical and subtropical zones of the Old World. Some of the Phyllostomatidae are also known as false vampires, such as Linnaeus's false vampire (*Vampyrum spectrum*), the largest American bat. The true vampires however belong to the Desmodontidae, of Central and South America. They feed at night on mammals and sometimes birds, making an incision with their teeth and lapping the blood as it flows out of the wound. Their bites are not in themselves harmful but may transmit diseases (notably rabies). The vampire bat (*Desmodus rotundus*) is illustrated here. Also from South America are the smoky bats, Furipteridae, the funnel-eared bats, Natalidae, and the disc-winged bats, Thyropteridae, which have suckers on their wrists and feet.

The familiar bats of Britain and Europe belong to the worldwide family Vespertilionidae. The largest is the mouse-eared bat (*Myotis myotis*) of the worldwide genus *Myotis* containing some seventy-one species. Like most bats they are nocturnal and colonial. Species living in temperate regions either migrate to warmer regions in winter or hibernate. Most species produce a single offspring each year; hibernating species mate in autumn but do not produce young until next spring. Other European genera are the pipistrelles (*Pipistrellus*), noctules (*Nyctalus*), called in America serotines, big brown bats (*Eptisicus*), long-eared bats (*Plecotus*), barbastelles (*Barbastella*) and, somewhat rarer, parti-coloured bats (*Vespertilio*). American species include the American fish-eating bat (*Pizonyx vivesi*) and the silver-haired bat (*Lasionycteris noctivagans*).

The New Zealand short-tailed bat (*Mystacina tuberculata*) has two pockets along its sides in which it can fold its wings and is sometimes accorded its own family Mystacinidae. The free-tailed bats of the family Molossidae, are mostly of tropical regions of America, Africa and Asia, but include the genus *Tadarida* which is worldwide except in Polar regions; a species illustrated here is the Mexican free-tailed bat (*T. brasiliensis*).

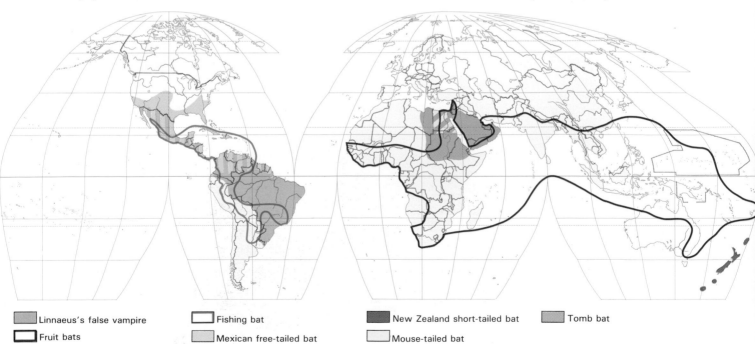

| Linnaeus's false vampire | Fishing bat | New Zealand short-tailed bat | Tomb bat |
| Fruit bats | Mexican free-tailed bat | Mouse-tailed bat | |

mouse-tailed bat

Indian flying fox

fishing bat

vampire bat

false vampire bat

Mexican free-tailed bat

greater horseshoe bat

Chinese pangolin

tree pangolin

giant pangolin

Edentata

The edentates, anteaters, sloths and armadillos, though related, are strikingly different in appearance and habits. The name means 'without teeth', but in fact only the anteaters are entirely toothless. All live in tropical Central and South America except the nine-banded armadillo, which extends into the southern USA.

The Myrmecophagidae are the anteaters of the tropical forests from Mexico to Paraguay. They feed on ants and termites, breaking open the nests with their powerful claws and inserting their long, sticky tongue into the nest. There are four species including the giant anteater (*Myrmecophaga tridactyla*), the tamandua (*Tamandua tetracdactyla*) and the dwarf anteater (*Cyclopes didactylus*), all of which are illustrated here.

The Bradypodidae, sloths, live in the trees, clinging erect to the trunks or hanging upside down from the branches. They rarely descend to the ground, since they cannot walk but can only pull themselves along by their claws. The three-toed sloths include *Bradypus tridactylus*, the two-toed sloths, *Choloepus didactylus*, both of which species are illustrated here. All are leaf-eaters.

The Dasypodidae, armadillos, are armoured with bony plates arranged in transverse bands. Mostly nocturnal, they live in burrows and feed on termites, other insects, and occasional small vertebrates. They include the nine-banded armadillo (*Dasypus novemcinctus*), the giant armadillo (*Priodontes giganteus*) and the fairy armadillo (*Chlamyphorus truncatus*), all of which are illustrated here; and the three-banded armadillos of the genus *Tolypeutes*, which are able to roll up into a ball.

Pholidota

The only living members of the order Pholidota are the pangolins or scaly anteaters of the family Manidae, with the sole genus *Manis*. They are from 30 to 90 cm (12 to 36 in) long exclusive of the tail. The body is covered with scales made of hairs cemented together; when the animals are threatened they roll themselves into a ball. They can run swiftly and climb well, aiding themselves with the tail. The species illustrated here are the Chinese pangolin (*Manis pentadactyla*), the tree pangolin (*M. tricuspis*) of Africa and the giant pangolin (*M. gigantea*) of West Africa.

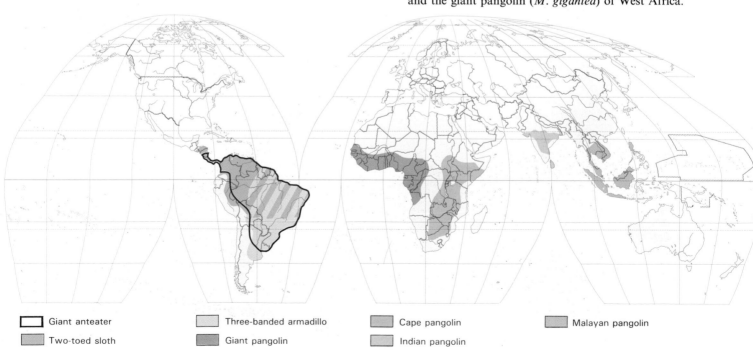

Giant anteater

Two-toed sloth

Three-banded armadillo

Giant pangolin

Cape pangolin

Indian pangolin

Malayan pangolin

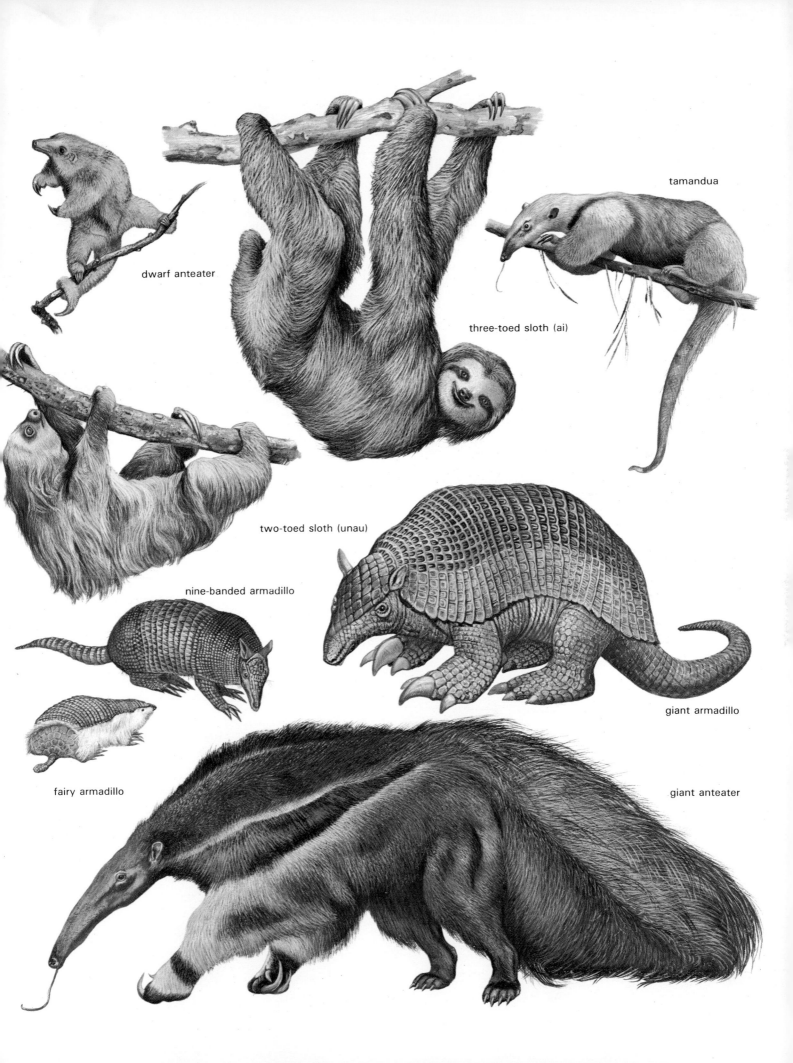

dwarf anteater

tamandua

three-toed sloth (ai)

two-toed sloth (unau)

nine-banded armadillo

giant armadillo

fairy armadillo

giant anteater

Lagomorpha

The lagomorphs – pikas, hares and rabbits – are distributed worldwide with the exception of Antarctica and Australia / New Zealand; though their introduction by man to the latter region has proved lamentably successful. They are of small to medium dimensions with weights varying from 100 gm to 1 kg (0.2 to 2¼ lb). The diet is herbivorous and the teeth have undergone important modifications such as the loss of the canine teeth and the development of the incisors, which are in a state of continuous growth, as are the premolars and molars, which have no roots. Unlike rodents, lagomorphs have two pairs of upper incisor teeth, a small pair behind the larger front teeth. There are two families, Ochotonidae and Leporidae.

Ochotonidae

The Ochotonidae, pikas, also sometimes called rock rabbits or conies, are in some ways more primitive than the Leporidae. At the present time only the genus *Ochotona* is known, with fourteen species. Two species are American, the rest live in Asia from the Urals to Kamchatka and Korea. Most live in rocky, mountainous areas, but some of the Asian species live in burrows in forests, and others in desert areas. They are not good at running. They tend therefore to remain in the vicinity of their dens where they can take refuge in case of need. They are usually active during the day, and live either alone or in small groups. In the summer months they gather vegetation and dry it in the sun, hiding it under rocks if it rains, so that it does not rot. Once it is dry, the pikas store their harvest also under rocks or other shelter, where it provides a source of food for the winter.

One of the American species, the American pika (*Ochotona princeps*), about the size of a guinea-pig, builds a nest-like shelter by lining a rocky cavity with grass, though if the terrain permits it will excavate a long burrow. The Altai pika (*O. alpina*, illustrated here), which lives in the mountains of Central and north-eastern Asia, emits high-pitched calls to which other members of the species respond, forming an easily heard chorus, especially in the evenings. The calls communicate alarm or danger. This habit of pikas in general has led to their being given the names whistling hare, or squeak rabbit.

Leporidae

The Leporidae, an expanding family at the present time, contain the two forms generally known as hares and rabbits. The principal difference is that hares deliver their young in the open; they have eyes already open and are fully haired, and can hop about within a few minutes after being born. The young of rabbits are naked, blind and helpless at birth, and are born in the den or burrow. In the hares the ears are longer and the hind legs much more developed. There are more than sixty species of Leporidae occupying very diverse habitats. The cottontail rabbits of America, so called from the white on the underside of their tails, are mainly a woodland species, though some are adapted to marshy and others to arid environments. Among the well-known species are the eastern cottontail (*Sylvilagus floridanus*, illustrated here) and forest rabbit (*S. brasiliensis*), both of North and South America. Among the species most skilled in fast running are the black-tailed jackrabbit (*Lepus californicus*, illustrated here), the antelope jackrabbit (*L. alleni*) and the white-tailed jackrabbit (*L. townsendi*), which can attain speeds of 70 km/hr (45 mph) without difficulty. The black-tailed jackrabbit is a desert species whose huge ears act as radiators to dissipate excess body heat. The common hare of Europe (*L. europaeus*, illustrated here) has enlarged its area of distribution due to man having introduced it into many areas for the purpose of hunting. However, in Britain its numbers are decreasing as a result of changed farming methods. The Cape hare (*L. capensis*), closely related, is found from Africa to China. The varying hare (*Lepus timidus*) is sometimes regarded as being the same species as the European hare. It is illustrated here in its summer and winter coats, which, like most hares of northern latitudes, is grey-brown in summer and white in winter, a change favouring its concealment. The common European rabbit is *Oryctolagus cuniculus*, illustrated here. Originally of southern Europe, it has spread across Europe and North Africa and has been introduced by man to Australia, New Zealand and the Americas. A social animal, it lives in warrens made up of the burrows of many individuals. The reproductive potential of the rabbit is legendary. A female bears five to ten young at a time and may have four litters each year; the young doe is ready to breed after about six months. Enemies include foxes, badgers, birds of prey, muskelids, cats, dogs – and man.

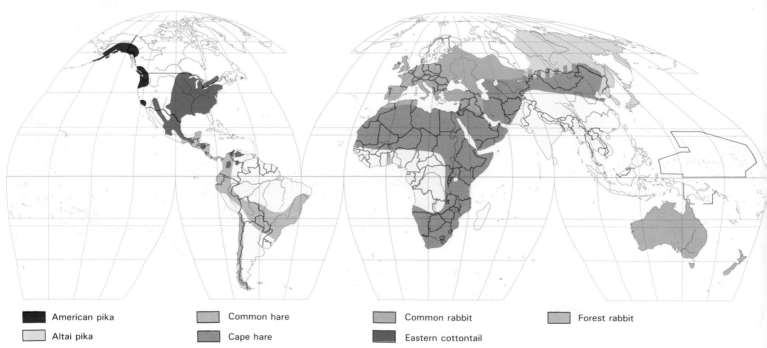

■ American pika	Common hare	Common rabbit	Forest rabbit
Altai pika	Cape hare	Eastern cottontail	

varying hare

(summer coat)

(winter coat)

eastern cottontail

black-tailed jackrabbit

altai pika

common rabbit

common hare

Rodents: Sciuromorphs

The largest order of mammals is Rodentia (the rodents) with thirty-two families, 354 genera and about 2000 living species. The rodents are gnawing animals (from the Latin *rodere*, to gnaw). Their unique feature is the teeth: the front incisors, which grow continually, have strong enamel on the front surface, the rest being of softer dentine, so that as the tooth wears down the front edge lasts longer than the back, giving them a sharp chisel-like shape. Canine teeth and pre-molars are absent and there is a gap (diastema) between the front teeth and the cheek teeth. The lower jaw can be moved forward, bringing the two pairs of incisors opposite each other for gnawing, and the back part of the mouth can be cut off by drawing in the cheeks in the region of the gap. This means that the rodent can gnaw for a long time without wearing out its cheek teeth or swallowing lumps of earth or wood.

There are three sub-orders, the squirrel-like rodents (Sciuromorpha), rat-like (Myomorpha) and porcupine-like (Hystricomorpha). The sciuromorphs comprise seven families.

Aplodontidae, Sciuridae and Geomyidae

The mountain beavers (*Aplodontia rufa*, illustrated here) are the only living species of the Aplodontidae. They live in the humid forests in the extreme north-west of America, from British Columbia to central California. The Sciuridae, on the other hand, are a numerous family with fifty-one genera and 260 species. Among the best-known genera are: *Marmota*, with the common marmot (*M. marmota*, illustrated here) and the bobak (*M. bobak*) and woodchuck (*M. monax*). The genus *Cynomys* comprises the prairie dogs of North America, now much reduced by poisoning. There are also the ground squirrels of several different genera living in Africa, America, Asia and Europe, including the suslik of the plains of eastern Europe (*Citellus souslicus*, illustrated here), which excavates complex systems of galleries; and the chipmunks of the genera *Tamias* and *Eutamias*, living in the northern regions of America and Asia. Chipmunks are distinguished by their striped backs and capacious cheek pouches in which seeds are carried. The members of the genus *Sciurus*, the tree squirrels, of which the best-known members are the grey squirrel (*S. carolinensis*) and red squirrel (*S. vulgaris*, both illustrated here),

are perfectly adapted for an arboreal life. There are several genera of flying squirrels, which possess a membrane on each side between the forelegs and hind leg that enables them to make long gliding flights from tree to tree; a typical species is the North American flying squirrel (*Glaucomys volans*, illustrated here). The giant squirrels found from South-East Asia to Borneo include *Ratufa bicolor*, illustrated here. The gophers of North and Central America belong to the Geomyidae; they have large, fur-lined cheek pouches. The main North American genera are the eastern and western pocket gophers, *Geomys* and *Thomomys*.

Heteromyidae and Castoridae

The Heteromyidae comprise the kangaroo rats and kangaroo mice (of the genera *Dipodomys* and *Microdipodops*), typically inhabiting desert or arid regions, and the spiny pocket mice (*Heteromys*) of tropical forests. They are all American and they bound along upright, making long jumps, such as the kangaroo rat (*Dipodomys deserti*, illustrated here).

The only genus of the family Castoridae is *Castor*, the beavers, with two (or possibly one) species, the North American (*C. canadensis*) and European (*C. fiber*). Beavers build large houses (lodges) from twigs and branches in the water of lakes or streams. The entrances are below water, and to keep the water level up they build dams above and below the site, of branches and mud reinforced with stones. They are among the largest rodents, reaching 30 kg in weight (66 lb) and 130 cm (52 in) in length, including the tail. The latter is large and flat, hairless, and is used to give an alarm signal by slapping the surface of the water before diving.

Anomaluridae and Pedetidae

The Anomaluridae are the scaly-tailed squirrels of Africa, all of which are gliders except for *Zenkerella insignis*. The gliding membranes differ from those of other gliding species in being attached at the elbow instead of the wrist. They do not glide very far and always land on vertical surfaces such as the trunks of trees.

The family Pedetidae comprises two species of springhares or springhaas, both of sub-Saharan Africa, living in open sandy country in burrows and emerging at night to feed on roots and other vegetation.

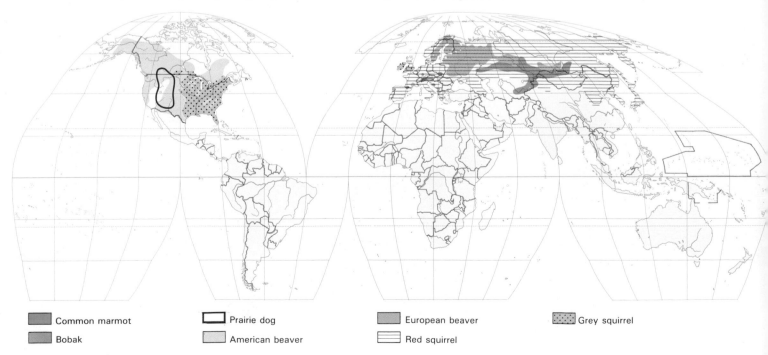

Common marmot   Prairie dog   European beaver   Grey squirrel
Bobak   American beaver   Red squirrel

gopher

giant squirrel

North American
flying squirrel

kangaroo rat

mountain beaver

common marmot

red squirrel

grey squirrel

suslik

Rodents: Myomorpha

The myomorphs comprise nine families including rats, mice, and similar creatures.

Cricetidae, Spalacidae, Rhizomyidae and Muridae

The Cricetidae – rats, mice, hamsters, lemmings, voles etc – are widely distributed in the Old and New Worlds with ninety-seven genera and over 560 species grouped together in five sub-families. The Cricetinae, one of which is the well-known hamster (*Cricetus cricetus*), are animals of small dimensions. The largest of the family is the giant pouched rat (*Cricetomys gambianus*) which can reach 90 cm (36 in) in length. The only native rodents of Madagascar are those of the sub-family Nesomyinae, the Malagasy rats. The Lophiomyinae comprises only the one species, the maned rat (*Lophiomys imhausi*) which lives in the forests of East Africa. The Microtinae sub-family includes the lemmings, such as the common lemming (*Lemmus lemmus*, illustrated here) famous for its mass migrations, and the muskrats of North America, including *Ondatra zibethicus*. The common field voles of Europe, Asia, North America and North Africa belong to this sub-family; the common British species is the field vole (*Microtus arvalis*). Another familiar vole is the water vole (*Arvicola terrestris*) and the bank vole (*Clethrionomus glareolus*). The gerbils, including the tamarisk gerbil or jird (*Meriones unguiculatus*), often kept as a pet, are properly of the African and Asian deserts; the largest genus, *Gerbillurus*, has thirty-seven species.

The Spalacidae are represented by the genus *Spalax*, containing three species of mole rat, of south-eastern Europe and Asia Minor. Burrowing animals, they have reduced eyes covered by skin, and no external ears. *Spalax leucodon* is illustrated here, and, typical of mole rats, uses its huge incisor teeth for digging.

The Muridae are second only to the Cricetidae in the number of species they contain, and are divided into six sub-families. The Murinae contain forms which have colonized any environment that man has. Among them are the black rat (*Rattus rattus*); the brown or Norway rat, also known as sewer or wharf rat (*R. norvegicus*), which is larger than the black rat and an excellent swimmer; and the house mouse (*Mus musculus*). Other familiar members of the Murinae are the common wood mouse (*Apodemus sylvaticus*) and the harvest mouse (*Micromys minutus*, illustrated here). The striped mice (*Lemniscomys*) are found in nearly the whole of Africa; *L. striatus* is illustrated here. The African tree mice, Dendromurinae, live in the humid forests of sub-Saharan Africa and include the African climbing mice of the genus *Dendromus* and others. The Otomyinae include the vlei rats of sub-Saharan Africa. The Phloeomyinae include the bushy-tailed rats of the Philippines (*Phloeomys* and *Crateromys*), the pencil-tailed tree mice (*Chiropodomys*) and prehensile-tailed rats (*Pogonomys*) of South-East Asia, New Guinea and Borneo. The Philippines shrew rat (*Rhynchomys soricoides*) is the sole representative of the Rhynchominae; and the Hydromyinae comprise the water rats of Australia, New Guinea and the Philippines.

Gliridae, Platacanthomyidae and Seleviniidae

The Gliridae, dormice, have one African genus, *Graphiurus*; the rest are European or Asian. The fat (or edible) dormouse (*Glis glis*) is the largest, and was prized as food by the Romans. The common dormouse (*Muscardinus avellanarius*, illustrated here) is rarely half that size. Both live in trees, walls or nests of plant material and hibernate for much of the winter. Other European species are the garden dormouse (*Eliomys quercinus*) and forest dormouse (*Dryomys nitedula*). Dormice are normally arboreal and strictly nocturnal. The spiny dormice, Platacanthomyidae, include the Malabar spiny dormouse of India (*Platacanthomys lasiurus*) and the Chinese pygmy dormouse (*Typhlomys cinereus*). The Seleviniidae are represented by the Asian desert dormouse or Betpakdala dormouse (*Selevinia betpakdalaensis*, illustrated here).

Zapodidae and Dipodidae

The jumping mice, Zapodidae, have long hind legs and long tails. American jumping mice are of the genus *Zapus*, including the meadow jumping mouse (*Z. hudsonianus*) and *Napaeozapus*. The European genus is *Sicista*; the birch mouse (*S. betulina*, illustrated here) lives in the Scandinavian forests and hibernates for eight months of the year. The last family of the Myomorpha is that of the Dipodidae, jerboas. The desert jerboa (*Jaculus jaculus*) is illustrated here.

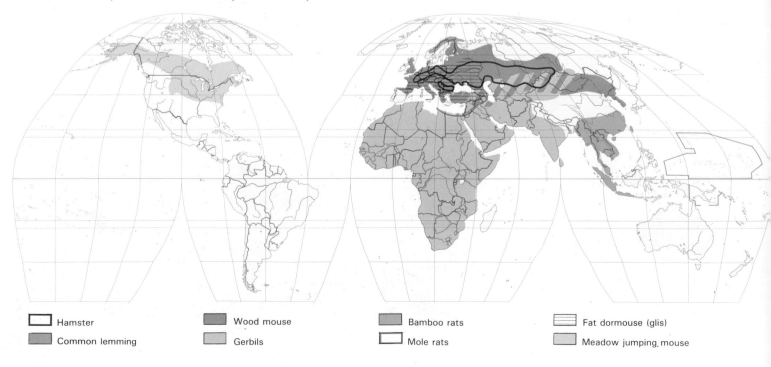

Hamster
Common lemming
Wood mouse
Gerbils
Bamboo rats
Mole rats
Fat dormouse (glis)
Meadow jumping mouse

desert jerboa

lemming

birch mouse

mole rat

desert or betpakdala
dormouse

harvest
mouse

common dormouse

striped mouse

Rodents:Hystricomorpha

The third sub-order of the rodents, that of the Hystricomorpha, comprises sixteen varied families.

Hystricidae to Dasyproctidae

The Hystricidae, Old World porcupines, are characterized by having skin covered with erectile spines as well as flexible bristles and fur. There are two sub-families, the brush-tailed porcupines (Atherurinae) of Africa and South-East Asia, and crested porcupines (Hystricinae) of Africa, southern Europe and south and South-East Asia. The African crested porcupine (*Hystrix cristata*), illustrated here, is the largest terrestrial rodent of Africa and Europe, attaining lengths of 80 cm (32 in).

The American porcupines, Erethizontidae, have shorter barbed spines (quills). They include the North American porcupine (*Erethizon dorsatum*), the tree porcupines (*Coendou* sp.) of Central and South America, and the upper Amazon porcupine and thin-spined porcupine of South America.

The Caviidae are a South American family that includes the well-known cavies, including the domestic guinea pig (*Cavia porcellus*) and its wild relative *Cavia aperea*; both are illustrated here. Another of the Caviidae is the marà of South America (*Dolichotis patagonum*, illustrated here), a large hare-like rodent of open pampas. The capybaras of the Hydrochoeridae family are the largest living rodents, attaining lengths of 120 cm (4 ft) and weights of up to 50 kg (110 lb). *H. hydrochaeris*, illustrated here, is common in waterside habitats in South America. The Dinomyidae family contains the single species, the pacarana (*Dinomys branickii*) of the Brazilian and Peruvian forests.

The Dasyproctidae are long-legged rodents found from Mexico to the Amazonian forests and in the Antilles. They are divided into the Cuniculinae (including the paca, *Cuniculus paca*, and the mountain paca) and the Dasyproctinae (agoutis and acouchis).

Chinchillidae to Abrocomidae

The Chinchillidae, resembling long-tailed rabbits, have long, soft fur, the most prized being that of the chinchilla (*Chinchilla laniger*, illustrated here), which lives high in the Andes. Another well-known species is the viscacha (*Lagostomus maxiumus*) of the plains. The nutrias, coypus, and now-rare hutias of the New World belong to the family Capromyidae. The nutria (*Myocastor coypus*), of some value in the fur trade, originated in South America but has been introduced as an escapee in some other regions including East Anglia, in England, where it has become a serious pest, eating crops and burrowing into river banks causing erosion and collapse.

The Octodontidae are small, stout, ratlike South American rodents, living in burrows and eating plants, sometimes causing damage to crops. The best known is the degu (*Octodon degus*); other species are known as cururos, rock rats or viscacha rats. The Ctenomyidae are represented by only one genus, *Ctenomys*, found from Brazil to Tierra del Fuego. They are known as tucotucos, from the cry which can be heard from their underground burrows. The Peruvian species *C. peruanus* is illustrated here.

The chinchilla rat or rat chinchilla (*Abrocoma*) is of the Abrocomidae family; it is found in rocky areas of the Andes.

Echimyidae to Ctenodactylidae

The large South American family of the Echimyidae contains some fourteen genera with forty-three species, including the spiny rats (*Proechimys*) and crested spiny rats (*Echimys*). The Thryonomyidae have only one genus, *Thryonomys*, the African cane rats. The great cane rat or 'cutting grass' (*T. swinderianus*, illustrated here) has large incisors that can deal with the toughest vegetation. Its heavy and clumsy appearance belies its remarkable turn of speed when alarmed, though it will take to the water if possible. It lives in marshy regions and along the banks of rivers.

The Bathyergidae are the African mole rats, living almost entirely underground. Like moles, they throw up mounds of earth at regular intervals. They have no external ears and very small eyes, short legs and a short tail. They differ from the moles most markedly in their teeth and their diet, having large and formidable incisors and living on underground vegetables such as potatoes, sweet potatoes, roots and bulbs, which they store up in underground chambers in their burrows. The most widely spread genus is *Cryptomys*, which expels the excavated earth in the form of large compact pellets. The Ctenodactylidae are the gundis, resembling guinea pigs, that live in dry, rocky regions in North Africa.

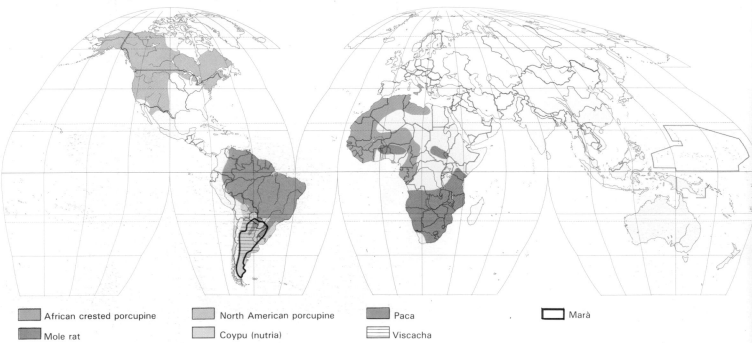

| African crested porcupine | North American porcupine | Paca | Marà |
| Mole rat | Coypu (nutria) | Viscacha | |

marà

African crested porcupine

Peruvian tucotuco

chinchilla

capybara

domestic guinea pig

wild guinea pig (cavy)

great cane rat

Carnivora: Fissipedia

The Carnivora include numerous species of varied dimensions – from as small as a weasel to as big as a bear – with a complete array of variously shaped teeth specialized to fulfil different functions. There are canine teeth to tear the food with, six small incisors on each jaw, and some of the cheek teeth are modified to become what are called carnassials, sharper shearing teeth that can chop and slice the meat and even the cartilage and bone instead of grinding it down slowly. The Carnivora are above all predators and have refined techniques for attacking animals on which they feed; some however are omnivorous and others feed on vegetable matter. They are divided into the sub-orders Fissipedia and Pinnipedia.

The Fissipedia are so called because its members have divided toes. They comprise the terrestrial carnivores, though some, such as the otters, are semi-aquatic; nearly all are carnivorous in diet, or omnivorous; some, however, such as the pandas, are plant-eaters. The digits of the feet are independent; in most the nails take the form of claws, in some species these are retractile. The method of locomotion may be plantigrade – walking on the soles of the feet, with the heels touching the ground – as in bears and badgers; semiplantigrade, as in mongooses; or digitigrade, walking on the toes, as in dogs and cats. All have characteristic-scent producing glands, especially the anal glands, which are particularly developed in the viverrids (genets, mongooses) and mustelids (weasels, skunks and badgers). Of the senses, that of smell is pre-eminent, but all senses are generally well developed and reflect the versatile hunting way of life. Most species hunt alone or in pairs; an example of hunting in packs is shown by the wolves and lions. The populations of carnivores sometimes undergo strong fluctuations which relate to similar fluctuations in the numbers of their prey. One spectacular example of these population cycles is the Arctic fox, which depends on small rodents such as lemmings that also show regular changes in numbers. The sub-order is divided into nine families.

Canidae

The Canidae, dog family, is particularly homogeneous and the fifteen genera that belong to it are similar in form: head with an elongated and pointed snout or muzzle, large ears held upright,

long legs and tail; they are digitigrades. The long legs and strong musculature of the body permit high running speeds which facilitate the pursuit of prey or flight from enemies. Their area of distribution is very wide, in Europe, Asia, Africa and America. In Australia is found the dingo, a dog returned to the wild, descended from the domestic dogs imported probably in prehistoric times. Some species show no preference for any particular habitat, such as the jackals, who are found in the most diverse environments; others are specialized for particular niches from which they never remove themselves, such as the fennec foxes of the desert.

The genus *Canis*, with six species, is present in Europe, Asia, Africa and North America. The species which reaches the largest dimensions is the wolf (*C. lupus*, illustrated here), which, because of its wide distribution in North America, Europe and Asia, has many sub-species differing among themselves in dimensions and the colour of the coat. The wolves live in packs in which males and females are divided in various hierarchical orders; dominant males and females have the possibility of reproducing at their pleasure and of suppressing breeding in individuals of inferior rank. The females deliver the cubs in a den dug in the earth. Some weeks after the birth the cubs come out into the open and are protected by other adults besides their parents. At the age of six to seven months the cubs already are the same size as the adults and take part in the hunt, at first only in the pursuit of the prey and later also in its capture. Hunting is a cooperative affair with some individuals driving prey towards others waiting in ambush. In North America, the coyote (*C. latrans*, illustrated here) is also present; its behaviour is similar to that of the wolves though it is less social.

The jackals are light, active canids. The golden jackal (*C. aureus*, illustrated here) lives from North Africa to the whole of southern Asia and is found in every environment from humid forests to arid deserts, and from sea-level to 3500 m (11,500 ft). The side-striped jackal (*C. adustus*) and the black-backed jackal (*C. mesomelas*) are both African, living in savannah country; they catch various kinds of prey and feed also on carrion. Their diet often includes vegetable matter. The domestic dog (*C. familiaris*) is of this genus. The last species to be mentioned is the Simien jackal (*C. simensis*), which inhabits a restricted area of the Ethiopian mountains.

The genus *Alopex* contains one species, the Arctic fox (*Alopex lagopus*, illustrated here), which lives in the Arctic polar regions

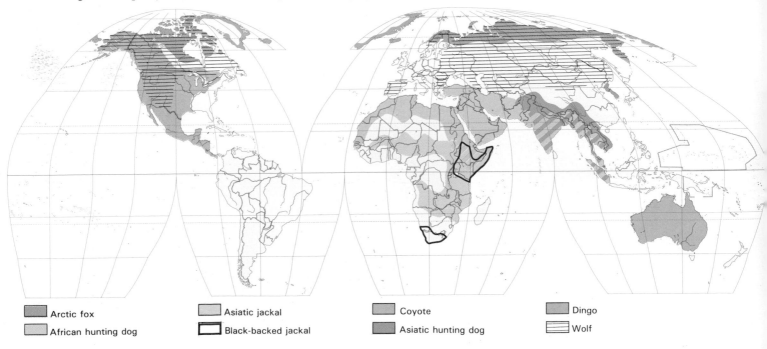

Arctic fox	Asiatic jackal	Coyote	Dingo
African hunting dog	Black-backed jackal	Asiatic hunting dog	Wolf

steppe fox (corsac)

Arctic fox

coyote

kit fox

red or common fox

pale fox

golden jackal

wolf

where two colour forms occur depending upon season. In winter the fur is long and pure white, in summer it is brown ranging to blue-grey. The fur is much sought after, for fashionable coats and trimmings and this has been the cause of a decrease in population, which in places is somewhat limited. They mainly hunt lemmings and other rodents, but also insects, fish that venture inshore, birds and hares, and on occasion scavenge the remains of the prey of bears. The steppe fox or corsac (*V. corsac*, illustrated on p. 261) lives on the steppes of Mongolia and Manchuria. They are more social than Arctic foxes and hunt in small groups, the prey consisting of hares, marmots and birds.

The genus *Vulpes* contains ten species with many sub-species. The red fox (*V. vulpes*, illustrated here and on p. 261) lives in North America, Eurasia and North Africa. The colour of the coat varies considerably from region to region, but usually it is brownish-red with whitish yellow underparts. The red fox is usually a solitary animal and only joins together in couples during the breeding season. Very beneficial to agriculture because of its high intake of small mammals that cause damage to crops, it has come to be regarded as a harmful animal by the great majority of people and hence has been heavily persecuted.

Among the commoner foxes, besides the red fox, are Blanford's fox (*V. cana*), found in Pakistan and Afghanistan; the Tibetan sand fox (*V. ferrilata*) of Nepal and Tibet, and the Bengal fox (*V. bengalensis*) of India and the Himalayas. North American species include the plains kit fox (*V. velox*) of the north-western plains and deserts, and the kit fox (*V. macrotis*, illustrated on p. 261). These animals also, although very useful to agriculture owing to their diet which comprises many rodents, have been persecuted and thoughtlessly reduced in numbers. In Africa and parts of Asia Minor are

A red fox carefully stalks its prey, pausing motionless to listen for sounds and watch for movement.

found Rüppel's fox (*V. ruppelli*), the pale fox (*V. pallida*, illustrated on p. 261) and the Cape fox (*V. chama*).

The fox with the strangest appearance is the fennec (*Vulpes zerda*, illustrated here), which is also the smallest canid, hardly reaching 40 cm (16 in) in head and body length. It is highly specialized for its life in the deserts of North Africa and Arabia. Its most remarkable feature is its enormous ears, as large as the head itself. Unable to hunt during the heat of the day, it ventures out at night, when keen hearing is essential. Another major adaptation is its ability to endure the scarcity of water, by making use of the liquids present in the body of the prey – desert mice, reptiles and birds – or in the few available plants. South of the Sahara lives a large canine whose appearance and behaviour distance it somewhat from other representatives of the family. This is the African hunting dog (*Lycaon pictus*, illustrated here). The head is robust and equipped with large ears, the body lean, the legs very long, the tail terminates in a tuft of hair, and the coat is short-haired with blotches of black, orange and white. Hunting dogs live in open country, in savannahs and in mountains. They live and hunt in packs of up to sixty individuals in a highly organized manner, the pack running alongside the prey while first one animal and then another increases its speed to leap at its flanks. The weakened animal finally drops behind the herd and is surrounded by the pack. In this way hunting dogs can overcome prey much larger than themselves. On their return from the hunt the adults regurgitate some of the food for the cubs and those adults who have stayed behind to guard them.

The Asiatic wild dog (*Cuon alpinus*, illustrated here) lives in the eastern parts of Asia, from Siberia to India and as far as Indonesia. It inhabits tropical and sub-tropical forests up to 4000 m (13,000 ft) above sea-level, both living and hunting in packs. The prey having been located, the wild dogs follow it, keeping it in sight and scattering to close avenues of escape, keeping in touch with each other by a series of calls.

The only species that shows a kind of hibernation is the raccoon dog (*Nyctereutes procyonoides*, illustrated here), originally of Siberia, China and Japan but imported into Europe for its fur, and now acclimatized in Scandinavia, Russia, Germany, Poland and Romania. The grey foxes of the genus *Urocyon*, resembling red foxes in all but colour, are found in the Americas: the grey fox (*U. cinereoargenteus*, illustrated here) of Canada and Venezuela and the island grey fox (*U. littoralis*), living on the islands off the southern coasts of California. The South American foxes of the genus *Dusicyon*, including the colpeo fox (*D. culpaeus*) and Azara's fox (*D. gymnocercus*, illustrated here) are, on the other hand, widespread. The small-toothed dog (*Dusicyon vetulus*) of the Brazilian savannah is fairly common but its biology is little known. The crab-eating fox (*Dusicyon thous*) and small-eared fox (*Dusicyon microtis*) are found in the forests of South America. Perhaps the rarest of the Canidae is the bush dog (*Speothos venaticus*, illustrated here) of Colombia, Bolivia and Paraguay. The maned wolf (*Chrysocyon brachyurus*, illustrated here) is of a strange appearance, with a pointed muzzle, very large, erect ears, a coat of long, reddish-brown hair and a white-tipped tail and, above all, very long, black legs, so that it looks like a fox on stilts. It is a secretive, retiring animal, living in patches of forest in Brazil, Argentina and Uruguay. One of the Pampas foxes used to be found on the Falkland Islands, where it was first discovered by Charles Darwin and later called the Falkland's fox or wolf. It was tame and easily exterminated to protect sheep, and is now extinct. The bat-eared fox (*Otocyon megalotis*, illustrated here) lives in the dry uplands of Africa from Somalia to South Africa.

bush dog

Azara's fox

fennec fox

African
hunting dog

grey fox

raccoon dog

maned wolf

bat-eared fox

Asiatic wild dog

Ursidae

The largest of the terrestrial carnivores belong to the family Ursidae, which comprises the bears, whose area of distribution is limited to the northern hemisphere except for one species in S. America. The various members of the group show a notable similarity of structure: massive head with small ears, large body of a clumsy appearance supported by solid legs. They are plantigrade animals, and their toes are provided with strong claws. The diet is omnivorous but is made up in great part of vegetation with a preference for fruit. Occasionally a bear will attack an animal even of medium size. The most developed sense is that of smell and the eyesight is particularly weak.

The winters, in regions which have little to offer in the way of food supplies, are passed in dens in a state of lethargy. Normally a bear lives alone in a territory which it delimits with its own scent, but where food is abundant several individuals may live peacefully in the same area. A classic case is that of grizzly bears fishing for salmon intent on swimming upstream to their spawning-place. At this time the bears may live together in great numbers in a quite restricted area. During the winter the females deliver two young, and it is often the task of the female to rear and protect them for a couple of years. The family is divided into two groups, the Tremarctinae and Ursinae.

Tremarctinae. The Tremarctinae comprise one species only, the spectacled bear (*Tremarctos ornatus*, illustrated here), which is also the only one of the Ursidae living in South America. Its distribution is from Venezuela to Chile, along the chain of the Andes. It lives alone or in groups in the forests, is an excellent climber and builds its nest on the branches of a tree. It lives largely on leaves, fruit and nuts, though on occasion it may attack and eat lamas or cattle.

Ursinae. The genus *Ursus* is the most important of the sub-family and is found in Europe, Asia and North America. The brown bear (*Ursus arctos*, illustrated here) is the best known, with various sub-species. Formerly brown bears ranged over most of western Europe but only a few now survive in such remote localities as northern Scandinavia and the Pyrenees. Two sub-species living in America are the kodiak bear (*U. arctos beringianus*), the largest of all living

land carnivores, and the grizzly (*U. arctos horribilis*), now limited to a few areas of North America. Though they are carnivores of enormous dimensions, they rarely prey on large animals, and their food consists largely of berries, fruit, tubers, fish and insects. They also dig up mice and ground squirrels. The most widely distributed American bear is however the American black bear (*U. americanus*, illustrated here), found from Alaska to Mexico. Smaller than the brown bears, they are mostly vegetarian, though they will eat small mammals and also sometimes carrion; but their usual diet is berries, acorns, grasses, bulbs, roots, briars, and also honey and grubs from wasps' and bees' nests. They have learned to hang about rubbish tips for food scraps.

The Asiatic black bear (*Selenarctos thibetanus*, illustrated here), lives in the forests from the Himalayas to Japan. Its diet is again omnivorous, but its need for meat is greater than that of the preceding species and for this reason it will sometimes attack domestic animals. One of the giants of the family is the polar bear (*Thalarctos martimus*, illustrated here), with lengths exceeding 2.5 m (8 ft) and weights which may reach 700 kg (1500 lb). Adaptation to a semi-aquatic life has made the coat impermeable; the soles of the feet are provided with fur to prevent slipping on the ice, and between the toes is a membrane which acts as an aid in swimming. It lives on the shores of the Arctic Ocean, spending much of its time on the pack-ice. Its diet is therefore of necessity mostly carnivorous, and its preferred prey is the ringed seal, but it will also consume fish and seabirds, and sometimes a little lichen or moss. The females spend much of the winter sleeping in a den which they dig out under the snow, but the males travel during the winter, moving southward.

The sloth bear (*Melursus ursinus*, illustrated here) lives in the forests of southern India and Sri Lanka. Its lower lip is prolonged, giving it a strange appearance. It feeds largely on termites and bees, ripping open the nest with its claws, inserting its nose through the hole and sucking up the insects with its lips aided by its long tongue. The sun bear (*Helarctos malayanus*, illustrated here) lives in the tropical forests of southern Asia, in Assam, Burma, Malays, Sumatra and Borneo. It is the most lightly built of all the bears and an excellent climber, spending much of its time in the trees. It feeds on lizards and birds, fruit and, above all, on honey which it extracts from wild bees' nests in the same way as the sloth bear.

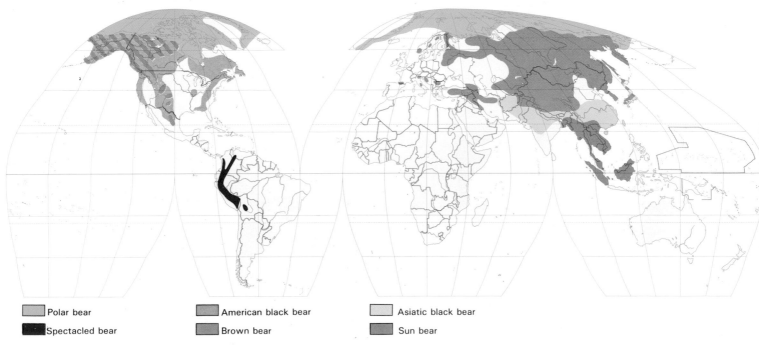

| Polar bear | American black bear | Asiatic black bear |
| Spectacled bear | Brown bear | Sun bear |

sloth bear

Asiatic black bear

spectacled bear

sun bear

brown bear

polar bear

American black
bear

Procyonidae

The Procyonidae, raccoons, inhabit the American continent, and comprise several genera with some sixteen species and at least eighty-five sub-species. This large number of forms has enabled the family to occupy the most diverse habitats. They are of modest dimensions but have a heavy, thickset body; the legs are powerful, the hind legs a little longer than the front, and the toes equipped with robust claws; the method of walking is plantigrade. The head is rounded, the ears of small or medium dimensions, the tail long and sometimes prehensile; the fur is very thick, and sometimes forms a ring of a different shade round the eyes. The forefeet take the form of hands capable of skilful manipulation of objects. Though fundamentally carnivorous, many species have abandoned this form of diet to become omnivorous, with a preference for fruit.

The genus *Bassariscus*, considered the most primitive of the family, lives in the western United States, Mexico and Panama. Two species are known, the North American cacomistle or ring-tailed cat (*Bassariscus astutus*, illustrated here) and the Central American cacomistle (*B. sumichrasti*). Both are of medium dimensions, with a slender body and elongated muzzle; nocturnal in habit, with large ears, well-developed eyes, rather short legs and partially retractile claws. The dense fur is chestnut to yellowish-grey on the back and cream on the underparts. The tail, as long as the head and body combined, is ringed with black and white, and the eyes also are outlined in white fur. They are most useful to agriculture, eating rodents and insects for preference, a diet supplemented by berries and fruit.

The olingos of the genus *Bassaricyon* (one is illustrated here) live from Peru and Bolivia to the tropical forests of southern Mexico. They have long legs, the soles of the hind feet being covered with fur, round head with large eyes, sometimes protruding, and a long but non-prehensile tail. Arboreal in habit, they move slowly, using the tail for balancing. They hunt at night, taking small rodents and birds, but their diet is mainly of fruit.

Of the seven species of the genus *Procyon* the North American raccoon (*P. lotor*, illustrated here) and the crab-eating raccoon (*P. cancrivorus*, illustrated here) are the best known. The body looks fairly thickset because of the thick fur, the head is large and the muzzle pointed, and the long legs are furnished with strong claws;

the characteristic rings round the eyes form a 'mask'. The fore-limbs have sensitive fingers making possible skilful manipulation and a delicate sense of touch. These raccoons are extremely nocturnal and are famed as intelligent opportunists that will always find a way into a chicken coop or fruit store if it is at all possible.

The coatis of the genus *Nasua* (the coati, *N. nasua*, is illustrated here) are characterized by their long noses, elongated into a snout. They live in the forests of Central and South America. They travel in groups of five to twelve, consisting only of females and their young. The solitary males, known as coatimundi, join the group only briefly during the breeding season. Otherwise they live and hunt on their own. The diet consists of fruit, insects, birds and large lizards such as iguanas. They grub up small soil-dwelling creatures with their sensitive snouts, and also climb easily after birds, eggs and lizards. In case of need coatis are strong swimmers, using their limbs as paddles and turning their snouts upwards like a snorkel.

The sole representative of the genus *Potos* is the kinkajou (*P. flavus*, illustrated here) which, with numerous sub-species, lives in the forests from Mexico to Brazil. Similar in many ways to the olingos, it is distinguished from them by its larger dimensions and its prehensile tail. The diet is mainly of fruit with the addition of some insects; the tongue is long and is used to extract grubs and other small creatures from below the bark.

Ailuridae

The Ailuridae, pandas (sometimes considered as a sub-family of the Procyonidae), comprise two species, both of which live in the bamboo forests of Asia: the red panda (*Ailurus fulgens*, illustrated here) in the forests of the Himalayas and the mountains of western China, and the giant panda (*Ailuropoda melanoleuca*, also illustrated here) in some fairly limited areas of cool, damp bamboo forests in the mountains of central China. Its diet consists almost entirely of young bamboo shoots, and for this reason its molars have become flattened and it has developed a kind of sixth claw on its forefeet, formed of an elongation of the wristbone, which enables it to manipulate the bamboo shoots. It is one of the rarest of large animals, yet it is recognized everywhere being an attractive creature and symbol of the World Wildlife Fund.

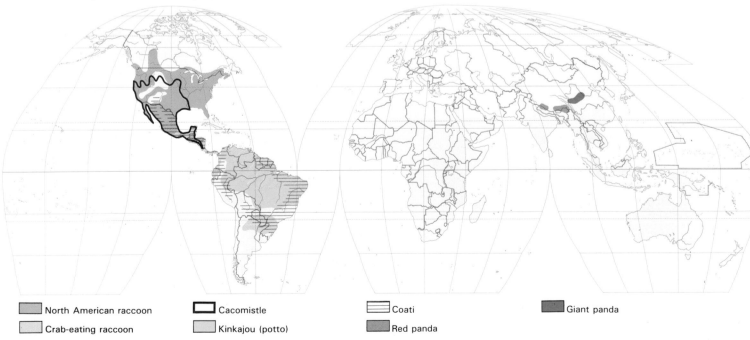

North American raccoon Cacomistle Coati Giant panda

Crab-eating raccoon Kinkajou (potto) Red panda

crab-eating raccoon

olingo

kinkajou (potto)

North American
cacomistle
(ring-tailed cat)

giant panda

red panda

coati

North American raccoon

Mustelidae

One of the principal families of carnivores is that of the Muste-
lidae, with twenty-eight genera and more than sixty-five species of
worldwide distribution except for Madagascar, Australia, New
Guinea and a few Oceanic islands. They are adapted to diverse
climates and occupy the most disparate habitats, from steppes to
marshes and to the sea. Their diet is carnivorous and they are
skilful predators; normally they kill by a powerful bite on the nape,
or in the case of larger prey the throat. The body is generally long
and slender in shape; the legs are short and they may be digitigrade
or plantigrade. The family is divided into the sub-families Mustelinae, Mellivorinae, Melinae, Mephitinae and Lutrinae.

Mustelinae. The Mustelinae – stoats, weasels, ferrets etc – comprise ten genera including *Mustela*, whose species are mostly of
small dimensions, with long bodies and short legs: familiar species
in Britain and Europe are the weasel (*M. nivalis*, illustrated here),
stoat (*M. erminea*) and polecat (*M. putorius*). The largest species is
the black-footed ferret (*M. nigripes*) of North America, while
another American species, perhaps the most famous, is the mink
(*M. vison*) which has now established free-living populations in
Britain, having escaped from fur farms. Mustelids are generally
animals of the woods, of cultivated lands or of the semi-arid
steppes; the mink is a waterside species. The genus *Martes* is
characterized by strong and well-developed hind legs which make
them very agile and good climbers. The stone marten (*M. foina*)
and pine marten (*M. martes*, illustrated here) are two species
present in Europe. Forest dwellers, they hunt amphibians, reptiles, birds and mammals, usually overtaking them in pursuit
through their superior speed. They also eat insects and fruit. With
their strong claws and supple bodies they are excellently adapted
for hunting arboreal prey. The Patagonian weasel (*Lyncodon
patagonicus*), the only representative of its genus, lives on the
pampas of Argentina and Chile, while the black and white zorilla
(*Ictonyx striatus*) lives in various African habitats. The white-
naped weasel (*Poecilogale albinucha*), of central and southern
Africa, attacks snakes in the same way as mangooses. The largest
member of the family is the wolverine or glutton (*Gulo gulo*,
illustrated here), a greedy and destructive predator that lives in
cold northern latitudes around the world.

Mellivorinae. The honey badger or ratel (*Mellivora capensis*, illustrated here) lives in Africa and southern Asia. It lives on ants,
beetles, reptiles and small mammals, but above all on honey,
which it finds sometimes with the help of the bird known as the
honey guide (*Indicator indicator*).

Melinae. The Melinae include the badger (*Meles meles*, illustrated
here), a large canivore which has survived in western Europe
largely because of its secretive habits. It lives also in much of Asia
including Japan. Earthworms are among its favourite food. The
ferret badgers, true badgers that look somewhat like ferrets, of the
genus *Melogale* (illustrated here) live in the forests and steppes of
Asia from China and Assam to Borneo.

Mephitinae. The Mephitinae, skunks, include the common or
striped skunk (*Mephitis mephitis*, illustrated here), also called the
polecat. When threatened it usually gives warning by stamping the
feet or standing on the forefeet, but if the threat continues it
discharges a spray of odoriferous liquid from glands in the anal
region. Other species are the hooded skunk (*Mephitis macroura*)
and spotted skunks of the genus *Spilogale*. All are American.

Lutrinae. The Lutrinae, otters, belong to several different genera;
all have elongated bodies, well-developed tails and a generally
aquatic habitat. The common Eurasian otter (*Lutra lutra*) lives in
the marshes, rivers and lakes of Europe and Asia, south-east to
Java and Sumatra, and also in North Africa. The smooth Indian
otter (*Lutra perspicillata*, illustrated here) lives in limited areas of
southern Asia. The giant otter (*Pteronura brasiliensis*) of the slow-
moving rivers of tropical South America is the largest representative, with a length of 2.20 m (7 ft) and weight of 24 kg (52 lb). It has
webbed feet and a flat tail. The sea otter (*Enhydra lutris*, illustrated
here), a rare species of the North Pacific coasts, floats on its back
with a stone on its chest and, catching molluscs on the seabed,
breaks them open by hitting with or on the stone.

The oriental small-clawed otter (*Amblonyx cinerea*) of southern
Asia lives along watercourses and feeds on molluscs, crustacea
and fish; the Cape clawless otter (*Aonyx capensis*) prefers the
coastal zones and the great forests between Liberia and Ethiopia.
The three species of *Paraonyx* live in rain forests and mountain
streams in Zaire, Cameroon and Uganda.

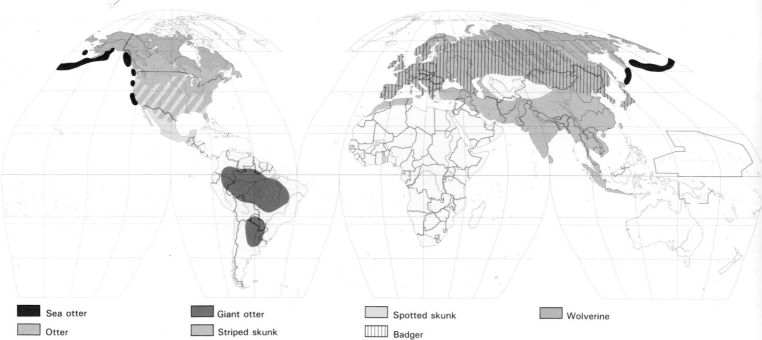

	Sea otter		Giant otter		Spotted skunk		Wolverine
	Otter		Striped skunk		Badger		

pine marten

badger

honey badger (ratel)

weasel

smooth Indian
otter

common or striped skunk

wolverine

Viverridae

Already present in the Miocene era (twenty-six million to seven million years ago), the Viverridae are one of the most ancient groups of carnivores and they also show a wide range of body forms, habitats occupied, and ways of life. The appearance resembles a combination of feline and canine; a sort of long-bodied, short-legged cat. The body is slender, the head small with an elongated muzzle, the ears usually small, the legs not greatly developed and the tail long, especially in the arboreal forms. The area of distribution comprises south-western Europe, Africa, Madagascar and southern Asia. Man has also introduced members of the family into other regions, sometimes causing irreparable ecological damage. The genet (*Genetta genetta*, illustrated here) widespread in Africa has been introduced into parts of southern Europe, occupying in part the niche left vacant by the wild cat, now rare or extinct in that area.

The family owes its success to the great capacity for adaptation to different environments. Some forms are able to live in very disparate habitats while others are limited to small specialized niches. Some species have adopted a curious method of breaking the shells of eggs or the casings of larger insects; they grasp the object between the forelegs and drag it along the ground, walking with the hind legs, until some roughness of the ground is encountered, which will break it. Another method is to seize the object between the jaws and batter it violently against a stone, or else to seize a stone between the forefeet and throw it down on the egg or insect, as is seen in the banded mongoose (*Mungos mungo*, illustrated on p. 273). All the senses are well developed, but eyesight and scent are predominant. Glands in the anal region secrete substances of a strong musky odour, used to mark out the territory or to squirt liquid against intruders; the secretion produced by the civets is used in perfumery. In the past, civets have been kept captive in 'farms' in order to harvest the scented secretions from the anal glands. This was done by pressing the glands with a small spoon-like spatula. Similar musk-like perfumes have been obtained from the tangalung (*Viverra tangalunga*) and the small Indian civet (*V. indica*).

Among the viverrids there are some solitary and some sociable species, with a broad range between the two extremes. The Cape grey mongoose (*Herpestes pulverentulus*), for instance, hunts

alone, but spends the night in communal refuges where several individuals live. Others, such as the dwarf mongoose (*Helogale parvula*, illustrated on p. 273) and the slender-tailed meerkat (*Suricata suricatta*), illustrated on pp. 272 and 273, are very social and live in groups containing large numbers. The pack keeps in touch with calls and cries, sometimes quite complex. Many viverrids live together with man, frequenting houses and making themselves useful in various ways such as catching rats and snakes, even though they sometimes take domestic animals such as rabbits and poultry. The mongoose has long been kept as a pet in Asian homes on account of its famous snake-killing abilities. In ancient times, among the Romans and the Egyptians, the genet played the role of a cat in the house and was reared for this purpose. The Vivirridae are sub-divided into various sub-families, the Viverrinae, Paradoxurinae, Cryptoproctinae, Galidiinae, Hemigalinae and Herpestinae.

Viverrinae. The Viverrinae are found from Western Europe across Africa and Asia to China. Their appearance resembles that of a cat but with a more elongated muzzle. Their habitat is very varied: some species occupy arid regions, others forests, while others are aquatic. The civets of the genus *Viverra* have a massive body supported by long, powerful legs terminating in feet provided with semi-retractile claws. The African civet (*V. civetta*, illustrated here) is found all over that continent, the large Indian civet (*V. zibetha*) in South-East Asia. The linsangs of the genus *Prionodon*, of southern and South-Eastern Asia, have a more slender body with a long tail, short legs and sharp claws, which make them perfectly adapted for an arboreal life. The spotted linsang (*Prionodon pardicolor*) of southern Asia, is an example of this, while the small Indian civet (*Viverricula indica*) prefers more open areas. The water civet of the Congo (*Osbornictis piscivora*) frequents watercourses, where it catches fish and other aquatic creatures. The small-spotted genet (*Genetta genetta*), previously mentioned, has nocturnal habits and hunts its prey – birds and mammals – either by using its speed in pursuit, by ambush, or by painstaking stalking. The victim is often trapped between the forelegs, unable to escape, and, before being eaten, is played with by the predator as a cat plays with a mouse.

Paradoxurinae. The Paradoxurinae comprise six genera with nine species, all found in Asia with the one exception, the two-spotted

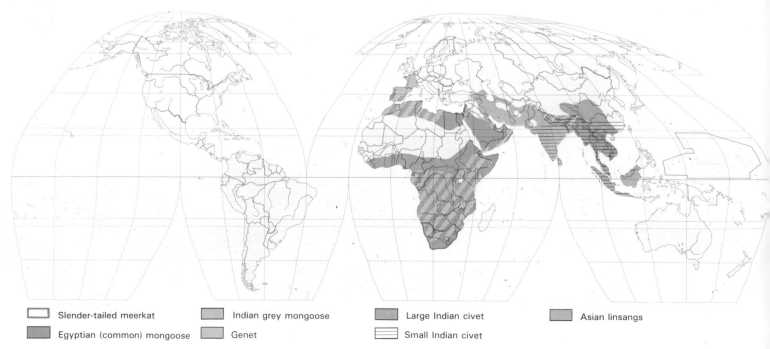

☐ Slender-tailed meerkat	▨ Indian grey mongoose	▨ Large Indian civet	▨ Asian linsangs
▨ Egyptian (common) mongoose	▨ Genet	▤ Small Indian civet	

spotted linsang

binturong

genet

ring-tailed mongoose

fossa

African civet

A slender-tailed meerkat with its young sits up and sniffs the air, ready to flee into its den at any sign of danger.

palm civet (*Nandinia nandinia*), found in Africa. The group comprises animals of medium dimensions, with a strong, massive body, short legs and rather long tail; the coat is often ornamented with stripes and spots, varying a great deal from species to species and in different sub-species. The masked palm civet (*Paguma larvata*) of south China, Taiwan and South-East Asia, has an unusual coloration on its head that forms a sort of mask. The stripes present on the coats of the arboreal palm civets are useful as camouflage. The most arboreal of the Paradoxurinae is the binturong (*Arctictis binturong*, illustrated on p. 271). It is larger than the palm civets and covered with long, shaggy black hair, which gives it a clumsy appearance, though it is in fact a skilful climber.

Nocturnal animals, the Paradoxurinae hunt birds, mammals and other small animals. Some forms, however, are vegetarian, with a preference for fruit; one such is the common palm civet (*Paradoxurus hermaphroditus*, illustrated here), found from south China and India to Indonesia.

Cryptoproctinae. The Cryptoproctinae have only one member, the fossa (*Cryptoprocta ferox*, illustrated on p. 271) of Madagascar. It is the largest carnivore of that island, and may be regarded as a living fossil, whose survival has been due to the complete isolation of Madagascar. It has a slender body, short legs, very long tail, and short fur, reddish-brown on the back and yellow ventrally. It lives in both the dry forests in the west and the rain-forests of the east, and hunts, either on the trees or on the ground, birds, mammals and the lemurs which are also inhabitants of Madagascar.

Galidiinae. The Galidiinae, Malagasy mongoose, are also found only on Madagascar. They are in general weasel-like in appearance, with a long, supple body, pointed muzzle, short and round ears; the claws are short and non-retractile, the tail is long and the fur very thick. The coat is usually striped, though there are exceptions such as the ring-tailed mongoose (*Galidia elegans*, illustrated here on p. 271) and the brown-tailed mongoose (*Salanoia unicolor*). They prey on various animals, both vertebrate and invertebrate, and take birds' eggs from the nests; to break these, they roll over on their back and throw them into the air with their feet to crack on the ground nearby.

Hemigalinae. One of the members of this small group is the falanouc (*Eupleres goudoti*, illustrated here) of Madagascar. Another is the fossa (*Cryptoprocta ferox*, mentioned above), also known as the Malagasy civet. The banded palm civet (*Hemigalus derbyanus*) lives in South-East Asia, Sumatra and Borneo; the otter civet (*Cynogale bennetti*, illustrated here) or mampalon, a true civet that has come to resemble an otter because of its similar way of life, lives in the rivers of Malaya, Sumatra, Borneo and also of Vietnam. Owston's banded civet (*Chrotogale owstoni*) is found in Vietnam and Laos; *Diplogale hosei* only in Borneo. Apart from the amphibious otter civet, the principal habitat of the Hemigalinae is the forests, and they are all skilled climbers.

Herpestinae. The Herpestinae, mongooses, are the most numerous and complex sub-family of the Viverridae. There are more than forty species belonging to about fifteen genera. They are small, short-legged animals with a long, slender body, sharp muzzle, moderately long tail, and well-developed but non-retractile claws. The fur is particularly thick and firm, and the colour varies from grey and brown to yellow. The original area of population was Europe, Asia and Africa, though some were introduced into Hawaii and the West Indies with disastrous results. They are generally earth-dwellers, but some species, such as the common or Egyptian mongoose or ichneumon (*Herpestes ichneumon*, illustrated here) of Africa, are capable climbers of trees. The ichneumon was sacred to the ancient Egyptians and mummified remains of this creature have been found in tombs. Like the modern domestic cat, it kept the household free of general vermin. There is a subspecies of *H. ichneumon*, called the Spanish mongoose, that lives on the Iberian peninsula. The brown mongoose (*Mungos obscurus*) of West Africa excavates deep burrows, though it will also take over for its own use the lairs of other animals. The marsh mongoose (*Herpestes paludinosus*) of sub-Saharan Africa, prefers marshy environments and is an excellent swimmer, living on young waterfowl, small mammals, fish and insects. It also digs up the eggs of crocodiles and is particularly fond of birds' eggs, which it breaks by picking them up in its forepaws and dashing them to the ground. The best-known member of the family is the Indian grey mongoose (*Herpestes edwardsi*) which featured in Kipling's *Jungle Book* as Rikki-tikki-tavi; they will attack, kill and eat the largest of cobras, using speed and agility to evade its bites (to which they are not immune), seizing it by the nape of the neck and cracking its skull with a powerful bite. Many legends have surrounded the snake-killing ability of this creature. There are reports of tame, hand-reared specimens that have unhesitatingly attacked real or toy snakes upon first encounter with any snake-like object. Several mongooses are known to have died from eating snakes; the teeth of the latter have punctured the mongoose's stomach wall and allowed the deadly venom into the blood.

falanouc

otter civet

common or
Egyptian mongoose

banded mongoose

dwarf mongoose

common palm civet

slender-tailed meerkat

Protelidae

The aardwolf (*Proteles cristatus*) of the plains of southern Africa is the sole representative of the Protelidae, living between Sudan and the Cape, six sub-species being known. It is a half-way species between the weasels and the hyenas (Hyaenidae). The body is typical of the hyaenas, but much smaller; the forefeet have five toes and the hind feet four. The muzzle is elongated and the ears large and sharply pointed; the coat varies in colour between the different sub-species but is often yellow-grey, and is ornamented with dark stripes on the back, sides and legs; the back and neck carry an erectile crest or mane of long, dense fur, slightly darker in colour than the body coat; the tail is bushy. Despite its appearance, the aardwolf is no great predator; its teeth are quite unlike the powerful teeth of the hyaenas, being small and simple and widely spaced, and the diet in fact consists mainly of insects, with a preference for termites, which it collects with its long tongue. Its principal period of activity is from shortly after sunset until dawn. The resemblance to a hyaena is puzzling but one suggestion is that it may be due to a kind of mimicry by which some completely harmless animals imitate other and genuinely dangerous animals in order to terrify possible adversaries and so protect itself without having to fight. Its sole defence, since it is a slow runner, is to emit an extremely offensive smell from its anal glands. The aardwolf lives in a burrow which has several exits, and which it digs itself.

Hyaenidae

The Hyaenidae, hyaenas, are very important to the ecosystem, being natural scavengers. There are two genera with three species, living in Africa and south-western Asia: the striped hyaena (*Hyaena hyaena*, illustrated here), the brown hyaena (*Hyaena brunnea*) and the spotted hyaena (*Crocuta crocuta*, illustrated here). Animals whose appearance recalls that of a dog, they may reach lengths of 1.5 m (5 ft) and heights of 90 cm (36 in); the weight varies from 40 to 85 kg (88 to 185 lb). The forelegs are longer than the hindlegs; all the feet have four toes provided with strong claws. The head is large with very strong jaws, broad ears – with rounded tips in the spotted hyaena, pointed in the striped hyaena – very strong neck, and short tail with a terminal tuft of hair. The teeth, adapted for breaking or cutting through bones with one crunch of the jaws, are capable of breaking the femur of a zebra. Despite their appearance of animals that would not be expected to run well, they can reach speeds in excess of 60 km per hour (37 mph) and their stamina is formidable.

They prefer an open habitat, savannah, steppe or semi-desert. The diet consists mainly of carrion but animals of large dimensions may be added to this; hyaenas have been known to kill and eat injured human beings and old and feeble lions. They hunt in groups and the technique is similar to that used by the Canidae: the prey is first followed and isolated from the herd, then attacked and killed by bites in the ventral region. Extremely combative in the defence of their food, hyaenas in packs are capable of scaring off lions or leopards; yet at other times they will seem fearful and cowardly to the extent of feigning death in order to dismiss an intruder, even if it is no more than a dog. They also act in a manner which reinforces our impressions of them as degenerate, lazy, cowardly and generally unattractive: they eat human dung, dig up freshly buried bodies from burial grounds, and attack old, sick or very young humans.

The most widely distributed species is the striped hyaena of North Africa and southern Asia. The colour varies from region to region from shades of yellowish brown to sandy; back, sides and legs have black stripes. From neck to tail there is a long erectile mane. Animals of the twilight and darkness, they live alone or in couples, rarely in small groups. The different individuals communicate with shrill cries that can be heard over a considerable distance. In the neighbourhood of villages they do not hesitate to attack domestic animals. The brown hyaena has become very rare and localized after extensive hunting by men aimed at exterminating them because they cause damage to livestock. It survives in the Kalahari and in a few other limited areas of south Africa and is known to search the shoreline for food.

The major representative of the family is the spotted hyaena, which is also the largest. In contrast to the other hyaenas it has a short tail and small ears. Mainly nocturnal in habit, it lives south of the Tropic of Cancer, in the African savannah and desert zones, and sometimes also in mountainous areas. A great scavenger, it feeds on abandoned carrion but also on prey newly killed by lions and other large predators. An effective hunter, it joins together with others into packs to attack larger animals such as zebras and gnus.

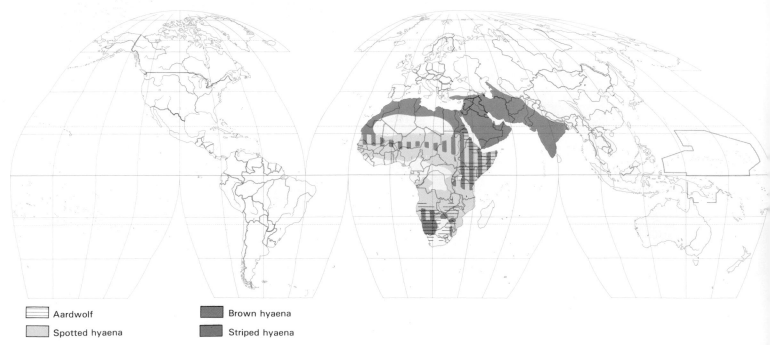

Aardwolf

Spotted hyaena

Brown hyaena

Striped hyaena

striped hyaena

aardwolf

spotted hyaena

Felidae

Of all the carnivores, those that have reached the greatest perfection as predators are undoubtedly the Felidae, the cats, found in Europe, Asia, Africa and America. The appearance shows certain general characteristics: a muscular and flexible body, massive head with short muzzle, well developed legs, feet with retractile claws, walking in the digitigrade fashion, canine teeth elongated into fangs; they are usually excellent climbers and runners, and most are also able swimmers. Except for a few rare cases, the great predators are solitary animals. The colour of the coat is brown, reddish brown or fawn, often ornamented with dark stripes or spots as an aid to mimetism. The dimensions are extremely variable, from the cat to the Siberian tiger, ranging from a couple of kilograms (4 lb) to 290 kg (640 lb). Apart from the lion, the Felidae occupy an individual territory which they defend against all invaders. At times the territory is formed of several areas joined by fixed paths, used by other individuals who are tolerated once a certain hierarchy has been established. The family is divided into two sub-families: Felinae and Acinonyxinae.

Acinonyxinae. The sole member of this sub-family is the cheetah (*Acinonyx jubatus*, illustrated here). Its height at the shoulders is about 70 cm (28 in). The legs are long with only partially retractile claws.

Either solitary or moving about in small packs, the cheetahs occupy territories in which they often tolerate the presence of intruders. Able predators, they hunt at night or in the freshest hours of the day. When they have identified the prey, they approach it stealthily, keeping concealed as far as possible, but since they live in open country they cannot get very close in this way. At the last possible moment they leap forward and pursue the prey at speeds of the order of 100 km per hour (60 mph) and, if they catch it, throw it to the ground and kill it; but they lack stamina, and if the prey is not overtaken within about half a kilometre (¼ mile) or less they slow down to wait for a more favourable occasion. With their slender body, long tail and well-developed legs, they are ideal sprinting machines.

Felinae. The sub-family Felinae comprises two tribes, the Felini and the Pantherini. There are sixteen genera of the Felini with

twenty-nine species and many sub-species. The genus *Felis* contains five species including the wild cat (*F. silvestris*, illustrated on p. 278) of Europe and western Asia. Each individual of this species has a well-delimited territory which no other individual is permitted to approach; it hunts birds and small mammals. Generally the wild cats prefer forest habitats, but some, such as the sand cat (*F. margarita*, illustrated on p. 278), are well adapted to the desert. In the rocky terrains of Central Asia lives the Pallas's cat (*Octocolobus manuel*, illustrated on p. 279), similar to the wild cat but more massive. The serval (*Leptailurus serval*, on p. 279) is a creature of elegant appearance; larger and lighter in physique than the common wild cat, it has a small head and rather large ears. It lives primnairly in arid and open areas in Africa, but also in forests, in the vicinity of rivers, and other humid zones. The lynxes, of the genus *Lynx*, live in both the Old and New Worlds, with two species, the common or northern lynx (*L. lynx*) of Europe, northern Asia and North America, and the bobcat (*L. rufus*) of North America, both illustrated on p. 279. The height at the shoulders is about 60 cm (24 in) and the weight about 20 kg (44 lb); the legs are long and the tail very short; there are characteristic tufts of hair on the ears and thick, pointed 'side-whiskers' at the sides of the muzzle. The thick, soft fur of these fine animals has been one of the causes of the destruction of many of the northern lynxes, so that they are now only found in limited areas. The southern population of the European lynx have spotted coats and are classified as a sub-species *L. Lynx pardellus*. Another sub-species, the Canadian lynx (*L. lynx canadensis*) lives in Canada and the northern part of the USA. The bobcat is still fairly abundant and is the commonest wild feline of America.

The caracal (*Caracal caracal*, illustrated on p. 279), of the warm savannahs and deserts of Africa and Asia, is distinguished from the lynxes by the absence of side-whiskers on the cheeks and by the longer tail. The genus *Profelis* comprise species geographically far removed from each other: the African golden cat (*P. aurata*, illustrated on p. 279), Temminck's golden cat (*P. temmincki*), found from the Himalayas to Sumatra, and the bay cat of Borneo (*P. badia*). The fishing cat (*Prionailurus viverrinus*, illustrated on p. 279) frequents forests and humid zones from India to Indonesia and hunts, besides fish, birds and mammals, sometimes of quite large dimensions. The leopard cat (*P. bengalensis*, illustrated on p. 278) has a similar distribution. The genus *Leopardus* unites five species, all of

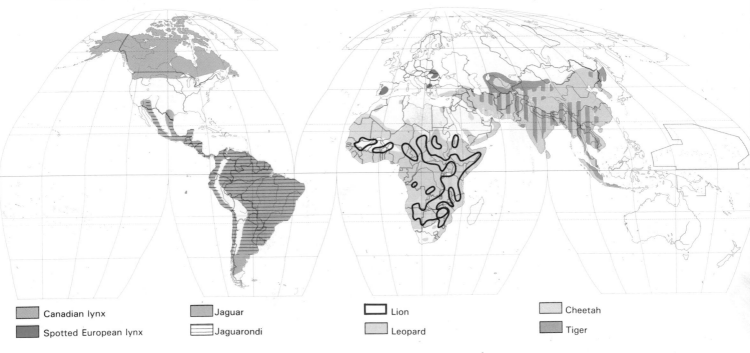

Canadian lynx	Jaguar	Lion	Cheetah
Spotted European lynx	Jaguarondi	Leopard	Tiger

snow leopard (ounce)

cheetah

puma

clouded leopard

leopard

lion

tiger

the New World: the ocelot (*L. pardalus*, illustrated here), the margay (*L. wiedi*, illustrated here), the tiger cat (*L. tigrinus*), Geoffroy's cat (*L. geoffroyi*) and the kodod (*L. guigna*), the first two being of Central and South America and the last three of South America only. Among the rarest feline is the mountain cat of the Andes (*Oreaihurus jacobita*, illustrated here). The jaguarondi (*Herpailurus yogouarundi*, illustrated here) whose appearance recalls that of a weasel rather than a feline, is found in South America. The largest of the Felinae is the puma (*Puma concolor*, illustrated on p. 277), which lives, with numerous sub-species, from Canada to Tierra del Fuego, in every kind of habitat. The clouded lepard (*Neofelis nebulosa*, illustrated on p. 277) of South-East Asia, Borneo, Sumatra and Java is about twice the size of a common cat, with short legs and a very long tail; the body is slender and it is perhaps the most strikingly marked of all the felines. Mostly nolcturnal, it inhabits densely wooded country and preys on birds and fairly small mammals.

The larger Felidae belong to two genera. Of the genus *Uncia* there is only one species, the snow leopard or ounce (*Uncia uncia*, illustrated on p. 277). It lives in the Altai mountains and the Himalaya, where it hunts wild goats, wild sheep, deer, wild boar and smaller mammals. Living up to 6000 m (19,000 ft) above sea level, it has very long, thick fur for protection from the cold.

The bigger genus is *Panthera*, with the four species. The leopard (*P. pardus*, illustrated on p. 277) is the smallest, weighing up to 70 kg (150 lb), and is an agile climber. The distribution stretches from the whole of Africa to southe Asia; for this reason there exist several sub-species among which is the famous black panther of the humid forests of South-East Asia. The jaguar (*P. onca*, illustrated here), a more massive species than the leopard, with a shorter tail, more thickset build and larger black spots with interior markings, lives in various different habitats in South America as far south as Patagonia, with a preference for humid environments.

The largest living feline is the tiger (*P. tigris*, illustrated on p. 277), which is present in Asia with various sub-species, among them the giant Siberian tiger, measuring as much as 4 m (13 ft) in length. The basic colour is variable from yellow orange or white, with a typical ornamentation of black stripes which provide a superb camouflage among canes or reeds, in the forest shadows. The habitats of the tiger are extremely varied, from marshes and the forests to the interminable expanses of the Siberian plains where the coat is much paler and less marked.

The most notable of the genus is however the lion (*P. leo*), with its exceptionally powerful body, large head adorned, in the males, with a thick mane, long tail terminating in a tuft of hair, and golden coat. Lions are the only truly social cats and live in prides made up of a mature male with several females and young. Hunting is carried on by groups; a few individuals isolate the prey and drive it towards the others who wait hidden in the grass. Once common throughout the Old World, the lion, though still preserved in Asia, is only at all flourishing in the grasslands and savannahs of Africa. The north African form is now extinct (though formerly was a frequent 'star' in the Roman circus arena) and the Indian lion is now rare and confined to a small area.

Andean mountain cat

sand cat

wild cat

leopard cat

margay

jaguarondi

common or northern lynx

serval

bobcat

jaguar

caracal

African
golden cat

ocelot

fishing cat

Pallas's cat

Carnivora: Pinnipedia

The Pinnipedia, seals, have changed their appearance completely in order to return to the water. The body is more or less spindle-shaped and free from protuberances, the head is rather small, the limbs are transformed into paddles for swimming. The body is covered with thick warm fur or blubber. The sense of smell has become highly developed so that a female can recognize her offspring among thousands; the sense of hearing is also good.

They are distributed in all the oceans, as well as in inland seas such as the Black Sea, the Caspian, and Lakes Ladoga, Onega and Baikal in the USSR. Some species are highly social and live in colonies containing great numbers of individuals, while others prefer a life either alone or in small family groups. The pinnipeds which live near the poles undertake migrations at the beginning of winter to escape from the extreme cold, and return at the beginning of the summer to their breeding-places.

There are three families in the Pinnipedia: Otariidae, Odobenidae and Phocidae.

Otariidae

The Otariidae are divided into two sub-families or tribes: Arctocephalinae (fur seals or eared seals) and Otariinae (sealions). The body is tapered and streamlined; the dimensions cover an extremely wide range from about 50 kg (110 lb) in weight to about 1000 kg (2200 lb). The fur is thick and soft, and even thicker around the neck; the tail, though it may be small, is always present, and the ears are small. They hunt fish and various marine invertebrates with a preference for some crustacea.

The northern fur seal (*Callorhinus ursinus*, illustrated here) belongs to the Arctocephalinae. It lives in the Pacific Ocean between Alaska and Japan, and breeds on the Pribilof Islands and Commande Islands in the Bering Sea. It is harvested especially on the Pribilof Islands where 20–60,000 are taken per year, mainly sub-adults. The males fight for possession of the females, harems of up to 100 may be defended, and the duels are sometimes violent. The genus *Arctocephalus* is widely distributed in the southern hemisphere, with seven species among which is the South American fur seal (*Arctocephalus australis*, illustrated here), another species that was formerly hunted extensively for its fur.

The Otariinae contain five genera and six species known as sealions, because of their powerful roaring. Steller's sealion (*Eumatopias jubatus*, illustrated here) lives in the northern Pacific Ocean, and the Californian sealion (*Zalophus californianus*, illustrated here) off the Californian coast and in the Sea of Japan. This is the species often seen in circuses where it quickly learns to perform tricks. The greatest concentration of Steller's sealions is certainly that on the Aleutian Islands, where about 100,000 individuals live. An adult male of this species may often exceed 1000 kg (2200 lb) in weight and 3.5 m ($11\frac{1}{2}$ ft) in length. The Galápagos sealion (*Zalophus wollebaeki*) lives on the Galápagos Islands, the South American sealion (*Otaria byronia*) along the South American coasts and those of the Falklands, while the Australian sealion (*Neophoca cinerea*) is found along southern Australian coasts and those of Japan. There is also a species limited to New Zealand waters, *Phocarctos hookeri*.

Odobenidae

The family Odobenidae contains the one species, the walrus (*Odobenus rosmarus*), with three sub-species, those of the Arctic, the Pacific and the Laptev Sea, north of Siberia. The Arctic and Pacific sub-species (*O. r. rosmarus* and *O. r. divergens*) are illustrated here. The walruses have a massive body that may attain a length of 3.5 m ($11\frac{1}{2}$ ft) and a weight of more than 1500 kg (3300 lb). The head is small in relation to the body, the upper lip is covered with a thick moustache and the canine teeth are transformed into long and powerful tusks. They feed on molluscs and crustacea which they gather by dredging the seabed with their tusks. They crunch up this hard-shelled food with their flat molar teeth. They live in the shallow waters at the edge of the polar ice, moving southwards in the winter as the ice moves southwards and returning north to the breeding-grounds in summer, the Pacific sub-species passing through the Bering Straits on their migrations.

Phocidae

The Phocidae, true seals, are the pinnipeds that have attained the greatest degree of adaptation to the marine environment. The shape is extremely streamlined; the head is small, with a pointed snout and spindle-shaped body; the forelimbs are much reduced

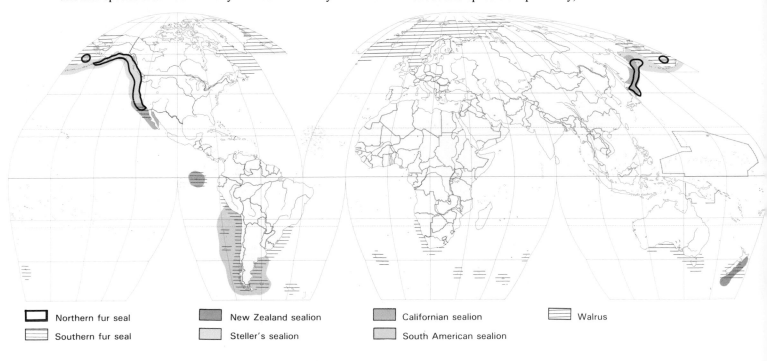

Northern fur seal	New Zealand sealion	Californian sealion	Walrus
Southern fur seal	Steller's sealion	South American sealion	

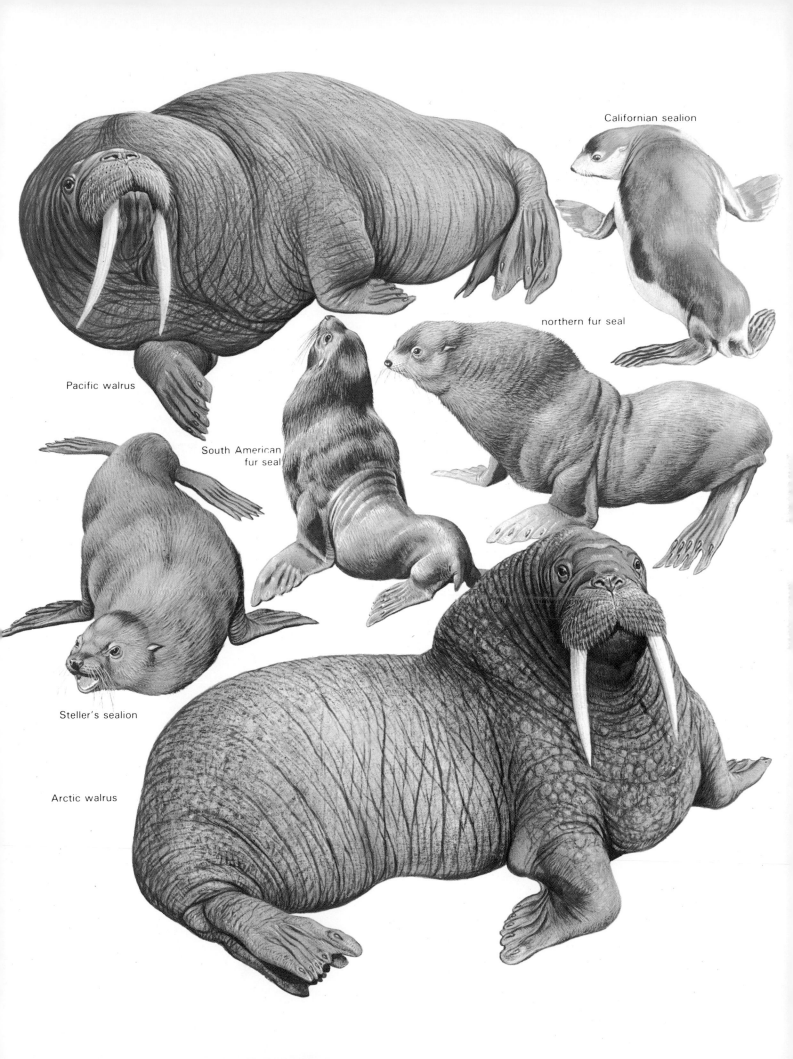

Californian sealion

northern fur seal

Pacific walrus

South American
fur seal

Steller's sealion

Arctic walrus

and not used on land, and the hind limbs, always turned backwards, are used as propulsive organs for swimming – compared to the Otarid seals where the front flippers are large and used for locomotion and the back flippers are big too and can be turned forwards and used as hind feet. The eyesight is very good thanks to the large eyes, and hearing is also excellent, despite the fact that external ears are almost invisible. They are fast swimmers and can descend to depths of 150 m (500 ft); can remain without breathing for twenty minutes. They prey on fish, seabirds and marine invertebrates, and are themselves the prey of sharks, killer whales and polar bears. They are intelligent, active and curious creatures. There are four sub-families.

Monachinae. The Monachinae, monk seals, comprise three species of the genus *Monachus* (illustrated here): the monk seals of the Caribbean (*M. tropicalis*), of Hawaii (*M. schauinslandi*) and of the Mediterranean, the Black Sea and the north-western African coasts (*M. monachus*). The Mediterranean monk seal is now found only in a few coastal areas that are particularly inaccessible, having been to a great extent exterminated by fishermen, who consider it to be a serious competitor. It has been a protected species for some years, but the measure may have been taken too late to prevent extinction.

Lobodontinae. The Lobodontinae contain four genera, each with only one species: the Weddell seal (*Leptonychotes weddelli*), leopard seal (*Hydrurga leptonyx*, illustrated here), Ross seal (*Ommatophoca rossi*) and crab-eater seal (*Lobodon carcinophagus*). The four species live together in cold Antarctic seas and extend northwards as far as Australia, New Zealand and the south coasts of South America without interfering with each other, since they have different diets: the Weddell seal is an exceptionally able catcher of fish, the leopard seal preys on penguins, the crab-eater seal hunts crustacea and the larger planktonic animals, which it strains from the water using its curious hooked teeth, while the Ross seal feeds mainly on squid, but also fish and crustaceans.

Cystophorinae. The Cystophorinae contain two genera with three species. The two species of *Mirounga* are the southern elephant seal or sea elephant (*M. leonina*) which lives along the coasts of

South Georgia, Argentina and Tierra del Fuego, and the northern sea elephant (*M. angustirostris*, illustrated here), found only in the Galápagos.

A male sea elephant can exceed 6.5 m (21 ft) in length and 3600 kg (8000 lb) in weight. The males are distinguished from the females by the remarkable proboscis that covers the lips. They fight for possession of a harem, uttering powerful cries and biting each other fiercely, sometimes causing deep wounds. The males also use their teeth to hold onto the cow during mating. The southern sea elephant is another species hunted close to extinction, for meat and blubber. The third genus, *Cystophora*, comprises only one species, the hooded seal (*C. cristata*, illustrated here) of the Arctic regions.

Phocinae. The last sub-family is that of the Phocinae, including the genus *Pusa*. The ringed seal (*P. hispida*, illustrated here) is found along the North American coasts, and those of Greenland and the North Sea, extending as far as the Baltic and some Scandinavian and Russian lakes. A completely aquatic animal, in order to breathe in the winter it digs holes in the ice from below towards the surface. *P. sibirica* and *P. caspica* live in Lake Baikal and the Caspian Sea respectively. The bearded seal (*Erignathus barbatus*), which measures more than 3.5 m (11½ ft) in length and weighs about 400 kg (880 lb), lives in small groups in Arctic waters. The harp seal (*Pagophilus groenlandicus*) lives in enormous colonies off Greenland, in Baffin Bay and in the North Atlantic off Iceland and in the Sea of Azov and as far as Novaya Zemlya and beyond. It undertakes long migrations, also en masse. This is the species that holds the unenviable record of being slaughtered en masse; every year thousands of harp seal pups are killed by hunters with blows of their cudgels. The ribbon seal (*Histriophoca fasciata*, illustrated here), characterized by bands of a lighter colour running along the body, is found in the North Pacific, north-west of North America and north-east of Asia. Finally the grey seal (*Halichoerus grypus*) is found in the North Atlantic, North Sea and Baltic, and the common seal (*Phoca vitulina*, illustrated here) is widely distributed in coastal waters of the Northern Hemisphere. In North America it is called the harbor seal. This is the species often seen off southern England. They normally stay underwater for a minute or two but can stay submerged for ten or fifteen times longer if circumstances dictate.

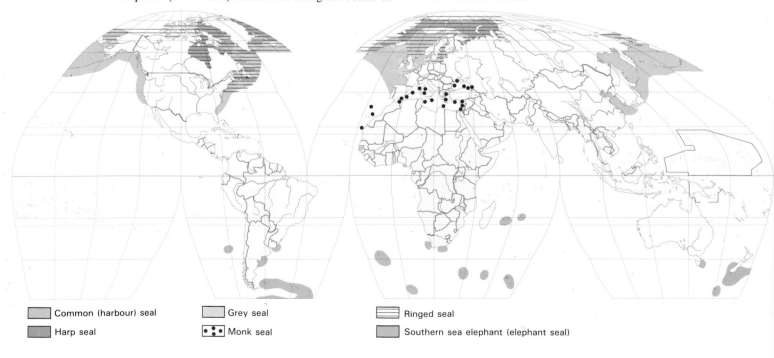

Common (harbour) seal　　　Grey seal　　　Ringed seal

Harp seal　　　Monk seal　　　Southern sea elephant (elephant seal)

leopard seal

ribbon seal

monk seal

common seal

southern sea elephant

ringed seal

hooded seal

Cetacea: Mysticeti

The cetaceans are mammals that have completely returned to the water, and have undergone a series of special evolutionary adaptations. The forelegs have been transformed into flippers, while the hindlegs have completely disappeared though a rudimentary pelvis remains. The tail has been horizontally flattened into flukes and functions as a propulsive organ. The skin, thick and elastic, is smooth and hairless, so diminishing friction with the water. The cetaceans come to the surface only to breathe, and the reserves of oxygen necessary for prolonged intervals between breathing, sometimes at great depths, are assured by highly efficient lungs and by the possibility of storing up large quantities of oxygen in the blood and muscles. On returning to the surface, they almost empty the lungs of air; this is made visible by the sudden condensation of the water it contains so that it appears as spray, a characteristic of all the larger species of cetaceans. This enabled the whale-hunters of old to follow the animals with the cry of 'There she blows!' as their quarry surfaced and breathed out a fountain of vapour.

The Cetacea are divided into the sub-orders Mysticeti and Odontoceti. The mysticetes (whalebone whales) include the largest known animals. The head is enormous and may be a third of the total length; the mouth, lacking teeth, has instead a row of whalebone (or baleen) plates, hanging down from each side of the palate, that serve to filter out the food, made up of plankton. There are three families of Mysticeti: Balaenidae, Eschrichtidae and Balaenopteridae.

Balaenidae and Eschrichtidae

Three genera belong to the Balaenidae. The Greenland right whale (*Balaena mysticetus*), which can exceed 18 m (58 ft) in length, is now very rare and is limited to the Bering Sea and some areas of the Canadian Atlantic. The genus *Eubalaena* contains the black right whale (*E. glacialis*), the Pacific right whale (*E. sieboldi*) and the southern right whale (*E. australis*); this last was also once widely distributed, but is now rare. The smallest whale, 6 m (19 ft) in length, is the pygmy right whale (*Caperea marginata*) of the cold seas of the Southern Hemisphere. The family Eschrichtidae contains only the Californian grey whale (*Eschrichtius glaucus*), 15 m (50 ft) long, which winters near the coasts of Southern California, where it also gives birth.

Balaenopteridae

The largest living animals belong to the Balaenopteridae. Despite their size they are fast swimmers, reaching 30 km per hour (18 mph) with a possible peak of 50 km per hour (30 mph). The blue whale (*Balaenoptera musculus*), of worldwide distribution, is the largest species with lengths of 30 m (100 ft) and more, and 130,000 kg (120 tons) in weight. The species (like many whales) is now protected, after the slaughter to which it was subjected in past years. The common roqual or fin whale, also worldwide (*B. physalus*), reaches lengths of 20 m (65 ft) and weights of 60,000 kg (55 tons). The sei whale (*B. borealis*) is also worldwide, while Bryde's whale (*B. brydei*) is found in South African seas. The lesser rorqual (*B. acutorostrata*), also worldwide, is some 10 m (32 ft) in length; its diet includes fish. The humpback whale (*Megaptera novaeangliae*), of coastal waters throughout the world, is extremely agile and will sometimes leap out of the water several times in succession. This may be to rid itself of skin parasites, or it may

simply be 'play'. This social species has a 'song', which is a method of communication thought to be audible to companions at distances up to 10,000 km (6000 miles) or more.

Cetacea: Odontoceti

The second group of the cetaceans is that of the Odontoceti, the toothed whales, which lack baleen. They are grouped into several superfamilies.

Physeteroidea

The Physeteroidea comprise the families Physeteridae (sperm whales) and Ziphiidae (beaked whales). Of the first, the sperm whale (*Physeter catodon*), of worldwide distribution, can reach 25 m (80 ft) in length and weights of 50,000 kg (45 tons). The males are solitary, while the females live in large groups with a number of young. Preferring temperate or warm seas, the sperm whale commonly dives to great depths, up to 900 m (4000 ft). It feeds primarily on cephalopods, including the giant squid (genus *Architeuthis*), and also on fish. Its teeth, in the lower jaw only, fit into sockets in the upper jaw when the mouth is closed. The pygmy sperm whale (*Kogia breviceps*) is a dolphin-like whale 4 m (13 ft) long, living in large groups in most of the oceans. The beaked whales of the Ziphiidae family number about eighteen species in five genera; some are little known. They exist in all the oceans, and are characterized by beak-like snouts. They include the bottle-nosed whales, *Hyperoodon ampullatus* and *H. planifrons*.

Platanistoidea

The Platanistoidea comprise three families of freshwater dolphins of Asia and South America. They have long, slender beaks and rather poor eyesight. The Gangetic dolphin of India (*Platanista gangeticus*) belongs to the Platanistidae; Geoffroy's dolphin, of the Orinoco and Amazon river systems (*Inia geoffrensis*), and the Chinese river dolphin (*Lipotes vexillifer*) to the Iniidae; and the La Plata dolphin (*Stenodelphis blainvillei*) to the Rio de la Plata and other South American rivers.

Monodontoidea

The superfamily contains only one family, the Monodontidae, with two species, both of Arctic northern waters, the white whale or beluga (*Delphinapterus leucas*) and the narwhal (*Monodon monoceros*). The beluga attains a length of about 5 m (16 ft); it has only eight to ten teeth. Usually it travels in bands numbering only a few individuals, but when food is plentiful these may unite into larger herds. The narwhal, about the same size, has only one tooth that grows as a long, straight tusk extending forwards from the snout. This can attain a length of 2.5 m (8 ft); its function is obscure.

Delphinoidea

The last superfamily is that of the Delphinoidea, divided into two families: Phocoenidae (porpoises) and Delphinidae (dolphins, killer whales and pilot whales). There are seven species of porpoises in three genera, the commonest being *Phocaena phocoena*, found throughout the Northern Hemisphere. They are primarily fish eaters and attain 2 m (6 ft 6 in) in length and weights of 50 kg

(110 lb). They are marine mammals except for one species that ascends the fresh waters of the Yangtze river.

The Delphinidae comprise thirteen genera with about twenty-five species. The common dolphin (*Delphinus delphis*) is widely distributed in warm and temperate seas. Dolphins are noted for their intelligence, playfulness and friendliness to man. They feed mostly on fish and are gregarious, appearing in groups numbering from a few individuals to several hundred. The bottle-nosed dolphin (*Tursiops truncatus*, illustrated here) is the species most often seen in aquaria, being more approachable than the common dolphin. Other well-known species are the bridled dolphin (*Stenella frontalis*) of the Atlantic and Indian Oceans, and the worldwide Risso's dolphin (*Grampus griseus*). The white-sided dolphin and white-beaked dolphin of the genus *Lagenorhynchus* are other Atlantic species. The rough-toothed dolphin (*Steno bredanensis*) is wide-spread in the warm waters of the Atlantic, Pacific and Indian Oceans, the Amazonian white dolphin (*Sotalia fluviatilis*) inhabit

A school of bottle-nosed dolphins leap clear of the water as they track an accompanying ship.

the rivers of northern South America, and the six species of the genus *Sousa* live in coastal and brackish waters of southern Asia, Australia and Africa. Pilot whales of the genus *Globicephala* are also highly intelligent and capable of being trained; they are gregarious, feed mainly on squid, and are often accompanied by bottle-nosed dolphins. The killer whale, *Orcinus orca*, is a predator living in all the oceans from the Arctic to the Antarctic. It travels in groups of a few to fifty individuals. Attaining lengths of up to 10 m (32 ft), it feeds on fish, penguins, and warm-blooded marine animals such as porpoises and dolphins. Many thousands of dolphins are accidentally killed each year in fishing nets, especially those of tuna fishermen in the Pacific Ocean. The dolphins seem to be drawn to the nets partly by curiosity but also to feed on the trapped fish.

Proboscidea

Only one family survives of the order Proboscidea, the Elephantidae, containing the largest terrestrial mammals, the elephants. There are only two species, the African elephant (*Loxodonta africana*) and the Indian elephant (*Elephas maximus*) (both illustrated here). Given the size of the areas they inhabit, and the consequent long isolation of groups of individuals in the various regions, it is not surprising that several sub-species have sprung up: for the Indian elephant, those of Bengal, Ceylon, Sumatra and Malaya, and for the African a western, an eastern and a southern form.

The origins of the order are rather obscure, and one theory is that they shared a common ancestor with the dugongs and manatees (Sirenia) and with the hyraxes (Hyracoidea). What is certain is that at one time the order was very rich in species; the best-known of the extinct forms is the mammoth (*Elephas primigenius*), which co-existed for a certain period with early man. Apart from their specialized nostrils and upper lips (the trunk), their unusual dentition, and their massive size, elephants retain many primitive mammalian characteristics and show a reasonable ancestral plan for other, more modified mammal groups.

The elephants are truly massive. The head, very large, possesses small eyes and broad ears; the upper lip and nose are fused and elongated to form the trunk, an extremely versatile organ used to carry food to the mouth, to suck up drinking water and to take a shower. They are vegetarians, and the large quantities of food necessary for their support makes it necessary for them to be constantly on the move. They are in fact nomads, or, rather, they were; since the occupation by man of vast tracts of territory has confined them in comparatively small areas where they have been forced to become sedentary, often causing considerable ecological damage and leading to the need to cull the herds.

The elephants are proverbial for their long memories. Their eyesight is not particularly good, but they have extremely acute hearing and a well-developed sense of smell. The soles of the feet are particularly sensitive, so that they can tread delicately despite their weight; the trunk, which does duty for a hand, is particularly sensitive. The great strength of these huge animals has been exploited by man to assist him in his labours, and from ancient times in Asia elephants were captured and domesticated. Because of the long pregnancy (twenty-one months) and slowness of growth, it is usual to capture individuals to be domesticated rather than rear them. This, besides hunting and the diminution of the areas available for them to live in, has greatly reduced the population of Indian elephants. (African elephants are more difficult, though not impossible, to train.)

Elephants have peculiar teeth. They are replaced from behind, instead of below; a succession of six teeth move through each jaw, with only four functional teeth in upper and lower jaws at any one time. Once the sixth tooth is about half worn away, the elephant is not able to chew its food properly, but is by then about eighty years old. Elephants are one of the few mammals that live like man, long enough to suffer from degenerative diseases.

Stories of 'elephant graveyards' with fantastic riches in ivory are probably the result of floodwaters drowning the animals and washing their remains into a valley; it seems unlikely the elephants collect in one place to die.

The Indian elephant, up to 3 m (10 ft) high at the shoulders and weighing about 5000 kg (nearly 5 tons), was at one time found from Persia and Mesopotamia to Java. Smaller than the African elephant, it lives for preference in forests; the female has no tusks and in the Sri Lanka sub-species the male lacks them also. Indian elephants live in groups of females with many young males; the young females who have not yet produced young may live in a separate group, while the adult males lead a solitary life and approach the herd solely for the purpose of reproduction.

The African elephant is the largest land mammal, more than 3 m (10 ft) tall at the shoulders and up to 7500 kg (7 tons) in weight. Its range once included the whole of Africa except the deserts. Now it is limited to the national parks, where it often lives in excessive numbers, to the detriment of other species such as rhinoceroses, whose food it takes. The head of the African species is more elongated than that of the Indian and it has much larger ears. It lives in the savannahs; during the day the temperatures can be very high, and this brings with it the necessity for the animals to disperse heat; the large ears act as cooling surfaces, and when excessively hot the elephants flap them vigorously.

Right A female Indian elephant takes a cooling dip with her offspring, a calf of four or five years.
Below A pair of African elephants show their affection for each other during one of the phases of courtship.

Sirenia

The Sirenia (dugongs and manatees), which closely resemble seals, Proboscidea (elephants, dealt with on p. 286) and Hyracoidea (hyraxes, see below), which resemble rodents, are three outwardly very different groups. However, evolutionary studies show that they are quite closely related and so these three orders are placed together in the superorder termed the Paenungulata. In turn there are two other superorders that are not at all similar to the Paenungulata but are considered to be closely related to them: these are the Protoungulata (the only extant representative being the aardvark) and the Ungulata, a vast and expanding group divided into two main orders, the Perissodactyla (odd-toed ungulates, including horses) and the Artiodactyla (even-toed ungulates, including pigs).

The Sirenia are the mammals most completely adapted to an aquatic life after the cetaceans. They live in fresh and brackish coastal waters, and survive only because the waters of their habitat are too shallow for predators like sharks and killer whales, and too salty for other hunters like crocodiles.

Trichechidae

The Trichechidae, manatees, consists of one genus *Trichecus*, living in tropical American and African coastal waters. The body is spindle-shaped with a massive head and small eyes. The forelimbs are flattened and the fingers joined together to form a simple flipper or paddle, the hind limbs are absent and the tail is flattened to form a wedge-shaped organ used for propulsion. Able swimmers, they can remain underwater without breathing for no more than about fifteen minutes. The length may be as much as 4 m (13 ft) and the weight may exceed 600 kg (1300 lb).

The North American manatee (*Trichechus manatus*, illustrated here) is distributed from Florida to the West Indies and the Caribbean coasts of South America, where they live in the brackish waters of lagoons and river mouths. They are important ecological agents in the control of waterweeds, which form the basis of their diet. They eat huge quantities of weed, preventing the canals and waterways from being clogged with vegetation. Exclusively aquatic, they risk death by suffocation if they get stranded, and their lives are in danger also if the temperature of the water falls below 20°C (64°F). They are often injured by the propellers of passing pleasure boats as they rest at the surface. The South American manatee (*Trichechus inunguis*) lives in the Amazon and Orinoco, and is the only one of the three species to live only in fresh water. The West African manatee (*Trichechus senegalensis*) lives in the rivers and coastal waters of West Africa and in Lake Chad.

Dugongidae

The dugong (*Dugong dugong*, illustrated here), the sole living species of the Dugongidae, is smaller than the manatees, being 3 m (10 ft) long and weighing 400 kg (880 lb). The body ends in a flipper that broadens out into two symmetrical wings and so resembles the horizontal tail flukes of cetaceans. The habitat is exclusively marine and the area of distribution runs from the Red Sea down the east coast of Africa to Madagascar, the waters around Sri Lanka and from China to the Philippines, and those around New Guinea and the north of Australia. Like the manatees, the dugongs live in family groups and are herbivorous, browsing on seaweed, and remaining submerged for about ten minutes as they do so. During the day they browse at greater depths, coming to the surface only to breathe. A species that became extinct in comparatively recent times was Steller's sea cow (*Hydrodamalis gigas*) discovered in the Bering Sea in 1741. It was 8 m (26 ft) long and weighed 1000 kg (2200 lb); the entire population of about 5000 animals was wiped out by sealers and whalers by 1768.

The name of Sirenia was given to this strange group of creatures because they are said to have reminded seamen who first became acquainted with them of the mermaids and singing sirens of marine legend, through their habit of rising out of the water till half their bodies were exposed, and nursing their young in a human fashion. The call of a young dugong supposedly resembles a human baby crying, and is said to have inspired the Australian aboriginal 'bunyip', a wailing mythical beast that inhabits watercourses, estuaries and coastal shallows.

Hyracoidea

The Hyracoidea comprise the hyraxes, small animals with strange characteristics. Resembling rodents in appearance, they are in fact

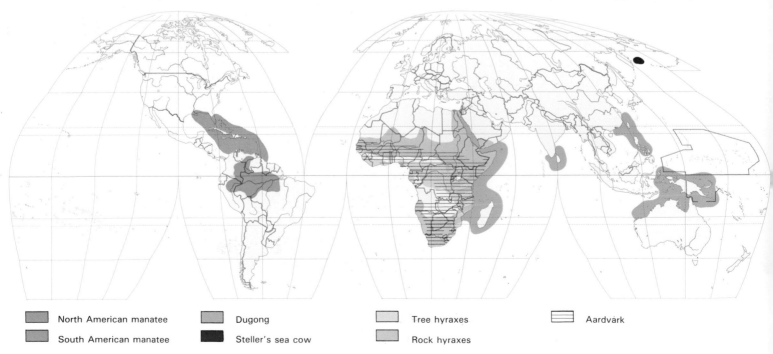

North American manatee

South American manatee

Dugong

Steller's sea cow

Tree hyraxes

Rock hyraxes

Aardvark

related to the ungulates and their nearest relatives are the elephants and the sirenians. They have four hoof-like toes on the front feet and three on the hind feet, the middle toes being longer than those at the sides. The incisors are long and grow continuously; the feet are provided with elastically cushioned soles, perfectly adapted for animals dwelling among rocks. They are skilled climbers and are sometimes seen climbing rock chimneys in the fashion of mountaineers, with the back against one side and the feet 'walking' up the other. Most species live in Africa, only one being found in south-western Asia; their habitats are steppes, savannahs and forests. They are also known as dassies.

The arboreal hyraxes are of the genus *Dendrohyrax*. They include the most primitive species, Beecroft's hyrax (*D. dorsalis*) and the tree hyrax (*D. arboreus*). Both are often solitary and nocturnal. The rock-dwelling hyraxes, mostly living on low rocky hills rising only a few score of metres above the plain, are of the genus *Procavia*, including the rock hyrax (*P. capensis*) with many subspecies. They are social animals and live in colonies containing considerable numbers. Primarily vegetarian, they graze on the herbage during the day; while they do so, members of the group keep watch as sentinels for possible predators, which include pythons, eagles and large cats. They are prolific breeders and have several young per litter; in one species the females have six teats each. The young are born fully furred after a gestation period of seven or eight months.

Besides the tree and rock hyraxes there exists a species of steppe hyrax, *Heterohyrax syriacus*, the only member of the group to live in south-western Asia. They are partly arboreal and partly rock-dwellers in habit.

Tubulidentata

The aardvark (*Orycteropus afer*) is the sole member of its order. It is also called the African ant bear. A living fossil, weighing about 100 kg (220 lb), it is much the same in appearance and behaviour as its ancestors twenty million years ago. At first sight it looks like an extravagant mixture of half a dozen different animals. The front feet have four toes, the hind feet five; the claws are powerful and capable of digging deep holes in the earth. The den consists of a tunnel up to 4 m (13 ft) long, terminating in a circular chamber which serves as its permanent abode. The few teeth are peg-shaped, consisting of molars and premolars that grow continuously. The teeth have a unique structure, with the pulp cavity in the form of numerous parallel tubules; hence the name of the order – Tubulidentata. Canines and incisors are absent; the snout is long and pig-like, the tongue long and extensible and covered with a sticky secretion. It has long, donkey-like ears that aid it in detecting the movements of termites inside their mounds. The aardvark lives in central and south Africa, where termites' nests are to be found outside the forest areas. It is solitary and nocturnal, and is not an aggressive animal but will defend itself against lions and leopards by rolling over on its back and lashing out at them with its strong claws.

The female bears one young at a time, although twins have been reported. The birth is in midsummer and the young aardvark stays in the burrow for about two weeks; after this it accompanies the mother on feeding trips. At the age of six months, it is able to feed for itself and dig its own burrow, and becomes independent of its parent.

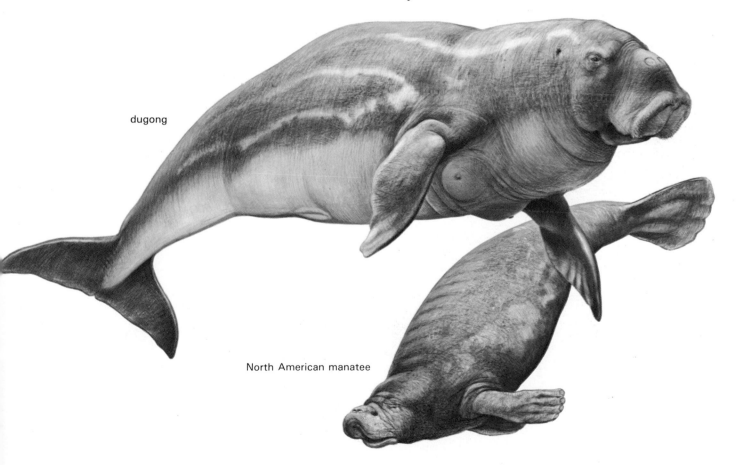

dugong

North American manatee

Artiodactyla

The ungulates – hoofed, herbivorous placental mammals (though the pigs are omnivorous) – comprise two orders known as Artiodactyla (even-toed ungulates) and Perissodactyla (odd-toed ungulates). Both have the last joint of the toes flattened and covered with horny tissue to form a hoof, but in the Artiodactyla the weight-bearing axis passes between the third and fourth toes, and in the Perissodactyla through the centre toe. The two groups have in fact arrived at their hooved condition through different evolutionary routes and differ in other respects including the digestive system, which in the even-toed ungulates involves a multiple-chambered stomach. There are three sub-orders, Suiformes (pigs and hippopotamuses), Tylopoda (camels) and Ruminantia, a large group containing deer, giraffes and cattle of all kinds. Thus Periosodactyls stand on a single finger or toe which terminates in a single hoof, whereas Artiodactyls stand on two toes of each foot and the hoof is of two parts, giving them the common name of 'cloven-hoofed'.

Suidae

The most primitive members of the order are the pigs (Suidae) and peccaries (Tayassuidae). Being non-specialized, omnivorous animals, the Suidae have successfully occupied many habitats. The genus *Sus*, originally present in Europe, Asia and Africa, has been introduced to the American and Australasian continents. The Javan pig (*S. verrucosus*) is found in Java, Sulawesi and the Philippines. Weighing 150 kg (330 lb), it is represented by several sub-species, as is the Bornean pig (*S. barbatus*) of Borneo, Sumatra and Malaysia.

The smallest species of the genus is the pygmy hog (*S. salvanius*) of Nepal, now rare; it measures only 30 cm (12 in) high at the shoulders. The wild boar (*S. scrofa*) is a Euroasiatic species found from the Atlantic coasts to the Pacific. The wide distribution of this species has given rise to innumerable sub-species, and from it the domestic pig is derived. The wild boar was once present in great numbers in Europe, but after centuries of hunting it has now largely disappeared except for a few forested areas, though it is still common in parts of France and Germany. It is also still plentiful in parts of Asia. It will eat virtually anything, includ-

ing carrion, any small animals that come its way, grasses, bushes, fruit, berries and fungi of various kinds. It will root for truffles and tubers, and in doing so will dig up the soil which is excellent for the health of wild woodlands but disastrous for agriculture. In many areas it has no natural enemies – wolves and feral dogs being all it has to fear except man and rinderpest – and its uncontrolled proliferation can be excessive; 35 per cent of the females are capable of reproduction by the time they are one year old, and breeding can bring about a three-fold increase in the population in a single season. The males usually live alone, while the females and young form groups; mating takes place during the winter.

The babirus (*Babyrousa babyrussa*, illustrated here) is a very rare suid, found only on Sulawesi. It has highly developed canine teeth transformed into tusks, the upper ones growing in a loop through the skin of the upper jaw.

Three species live in Africa, one of which is the bush pig (*Potamochoerus porcus*, illustrated here), weighing hardly 80 kg (175 lb), which is found in tropical areas south of the Sahara. The giant forest hog (*Hylochoerus meinertzhageni*, illustrated here) lives in densely forested areas of Kenya and the Congo; it may stand nearly 1 m (3 ft 3 in) high, and weigh over 150 kg (330 lb). It was discovered only in 1904. The warthog (*Phacochoerus aethiopicus*) is usually about 75 cm (30 in) high and weighs about 100 kg (220 lb); it lives in the open woodlands of South and East Africa and has particularly well-developed upper tusks. Both these last two species are illustrated here.

Tayassuidae

The American Suiformes belong to the family Tayassuidae which has only one genus (*Tayassu*) and two species, the collared peccary (*Tayassu tajacu*) and white-lipped peccary (*T. albirostris*), both illustrated here.

The collared peccary lives in an area ranging from the southern United States to Argentina, in groups of ten to fifteen, sometimes up to fifty. The leader of the group is usually a female; the various members of the band often seek physical contact with each other, apparently to reinforce their sense of security, and may travel leaning on each other. They eat plants, small animals and carrion, and when confronted with an aggressor group together, gnashing and rattling their teeth.

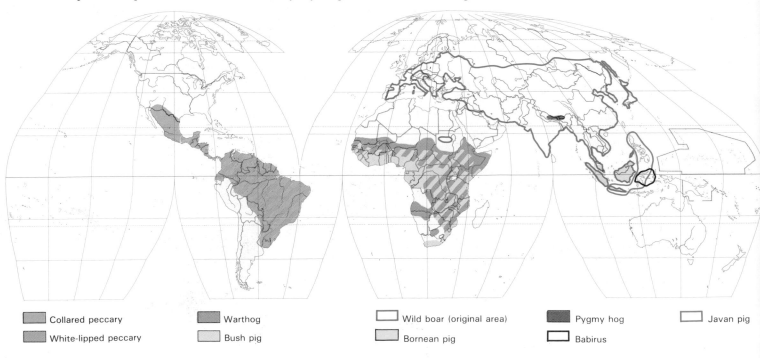

Collared peccary	Warthog	Wild boar (original area)
White-lipped peccary	Bush pig	Bornean pig

Pygmy hog	Javan pig
Babirus	

white-lipped peccary

babirus

bush pig

collared peccary

warthog

giant forest hog

Hippopotamidae

Another family with primitive characteristics and very closely related to the Suidae is that of the hippopotamuses, represented today by only two genera, each with only one species, living in Africa. The pygmy hippopotamus (*Choeropsis liberiensis*, illustrated here) was at first taken to be a dwarf sub-species of the common hippopotamus, about one-tenth the latter's size, but further examination revealed more extensive differences. Its distribution is limited to the coastal regions of Liberia and neighbouring states of West Africa, and its population is much decreased, with considerable danger of its becoming extinct. It is more solitary than the common hippopotamus and less aquatic, spending much of the night in the forests but lying concealed in the vegetation near the river banks during the day. Its habits are closer to those of the pig, and like the pig it suckles its young while lying down.

The common hippopotamus (*Hippopotamus amphibius*, illustrated here) is much better known. 4.5 m (15 ft) long and weighing 2-3000 kg (up to 3 tons), it has a heavy cylindrical body supported on sturdy legs; the tail is small and used for spraying dung about to leave 'scent markers' along the pathways made by the animal on shore, and its head is enormous. The eyes are small and so are the ears, which the animal shakes when it emerges from the water. Both are set high on the head so the animals can see and hear while the rest of its head and body are underwater. The mouth has an impressively wide opening and the lower canine teeth are transformed into powerful tusks which can reach 60 cm (24 in) in length and weigh 2.5 kilos. The other teeth are often hidden by the lips but are also massive, the molars especially so. The skin is very thick, so that the leather made from it has a thickness of 4 cm (1½ in); there is no hair on the body (though there is some on the tail and the muzzle) but it has numerous glands secreting a pink substance that protects the skin when an excessive time is spent in the water. A complete skin, deeply lined with fat, can weigh 500 kg (1100 lb).

At the present time hippopotamuses are found only in restricted areas, mostly protected, as in the national parks. In earlier times they lived in a much wider area, spreading as far as the delta of the Nile and even Israel. Land 'improvements' – drainage and reclamation for agriculture – and uncontrolled hunting have greatly reduced the population and in many areas exterminated it completely.

They move heavily on land but can show an agility unexpected in view of their great mass, but it is in the water that they are really at ease, and spend much of the day there remaining half submerged. Adjustment to an amphibian life can be shown in many adaptations, such as the nostrils which are provided with a valve which closes them perfectly during immersion. They are no great swimmers, but manage well enough, as is proved by the fact that they succeeded in colonizing Zanzibar, which could only be reached by swimming. Normally however they prefer waters about a metre or more (3 ft) deep so that they can walk on the bottom without undertaking the burdensome task of carrying their own weight. In deeper courses they have been filmed walking or even galloping along the river bed, completely submerged. Their greyish-blue skin helps to conceal their bulk in the steely African river waters. Water is very important for the regulation of their body temperature; in fact, with immersion, the hippopotamus

Above left Two hippopotamuses indulge in play in a quiet African river.
Left A pygmy hippopotamus mother tends her calf; this species is now extremely rare.

succeeds in keeping itself cool in otherwise very hot places. Continual bathing of the skin is also a means of defence against external parasites.

After spending the day in the water, sometimes in deep pools, rising to the surface to breathe every five minutes or so, they go ashore in the evening and make their way along well-marked paths to their feeding-places. The males leave the groups, to feed alone, but the females remain together to defend the young against possible predators. The routes to the feeding-places can easily be identified, since the hippopotamuses are creatures of habit and return every evening to the same place. The paths may even ascend quite steep slopes. If danger threatens the hippopotamus ceases to feed and sets off towards the water at a gallop; this is one of the occasions when they can be dangerous, though they are normally fairly placid animals. The weight of food consumed per night by each individual ranges from 25 to 40 kg (55 to 88 lb), according to its size. Sometimes the feeding areas chosen are situated among cultivated fields, and it is natural that the farmers in these circumstances may look on the hippopotamus as an enemy rather than an interesting animal to be preserved at all costs.

A Zambian river churns with hippoptamuses; many of the females have young. Hippo society is matriarchal and males treat senior females with deference.

In the ecology of rivers the hippopotamuses play an extremely useful part; in walking along the river beds they stir up the mud, which is carried away by the flow, and so renew and cleanse the bed. In addition their faeces still contain a quantity of nutritious material which is used as a source of food by fish, thus making the rivers more productive for fishermen. The animal's habit of spraying its faeces around with its tail helps the nutrients in them to be recycled very quickly.

The adult animals have very few natural enemies except, as always, man, though the young may be attacked by crocodiles, lions or leopards. Mating takes place in the water, and the young are born there too; after a brief emergence into the air, they return to the water to suckle. Sexual maturity is attained at about eight years of age and mating usually takes place at the end of the dry season, so that after the seven to eight months of gestation the young are born in October or April, the most favourable seasons.

Camelidae

The members of the Tylopoda are different from all the other ungulates in that they stand on the last and next-to-last joints of the toes; and, having no third stomach (omasum), they are separate from the ruminants. The only existing family is that of the Camelidae, with two genera: *Camelus* in the Old World and *Lama* in the New. Two species of camel are known: the Bactrian (or wild) camel (*Camelus ferus*, illustrated here) and the Arabian camel (*C. dromedarius*). Towards the end of the last century it was not known whether there still existed populations of wild bactrian camels, since this animal was only known in the domesticated state. Przewalski, the Russian explorer who discovered and named the wild horse, found surviving wild camels in the Gobi desert.

The camel is tall, with long legs, the tail ending in a tuft of hair, an elongated neck, the head with the muzzle stretched out forwards, with large nostrils and small ears. It possesses two humps on the back, each surmounted by a crest of hair; the coat is of the characteristic 'camel' colour and is shaggier and thicker in the Bactrian than in the Arabian camel, enabling it to resist the intense cold of the Central Asian winter. There are, however, in the domestic races great differences in the colour and length of the hair. They are somewhat heavier in appearance than the wild form.

The Arabian camel differs from the Bactrian in having only one hump; its dimensions are much the same (500 to 600 kg – 1100 to 1300 lb – in weight) but it has longer, thinner legs and a lighter build. No truly wild populations exist today and it is difficult to establish what was the original area of distribution, though it may be supposed that it was North Africa and the Near East. Today, many free-running herds exist in North Africa and also in Australia, where camels were introduced as beasts of burden for outback explorers. The camel is the ideal desert animal, resisting heat and with an outstanding ability to endure long periods without drinking. During the torrid summer, if it can find a little fresh food in the way of a few leaves or tussocks of grass, it can go without water for as much as five days. If the temperature is not excessively high its periods without drinking can rise to two weeks, but if it can graze on green grass this period may be extended to twenty days or more.

During the period of going without water a camel may lose up to 30 per cent of its weight without diminishing its vital functions; humans need hospital treatment following loss of only 10 per cent body weight from dehydration. To lessen the loss of water these animals are capable of varying their internal temperature by 6 to 7°C (9 to 11°F) between night and day. The rare pools of the desert are an instant remedy; the camel will drink 100 litres of water (22 gallons) at the rate of 15 litres (25 pints) a minute.

The dromedary is an Arabian camel bred for racing and riding, with longer legs and a lighter body.

The four American species of Camelidae all live in South America. The llama (*Lama glama*) has been domesticated since the time of the Incas and none exist in the wild state. The males over three and a half years old are used as pack animals, the females as a source of wool and for breeding. The fur supplies rugs and rope, the hides footwear, the fat is made into candles and the droppings used as fuel; the flesh is eaten. The llama was sometimes in the past regarded as a domesticated version of the guanaco, but the two are now regarded as separate species.

The guanaco (*Lama guanicoe*, illustrated here) is found along the chain of the Andes from Peru and Bolivia southward to Tierra del Fuego, between sea level and the snow line. The females move about in small groups of four to ten, led by a male; the young males form herds of twelve to fifty individuals. The males are aggressive during courtship, fighting for the possession of females by biting and pushing, and guarding their group of females while they graze. The alpaca (*Lama pacos*) is smaller and lighter than the llama, standing about 90 cm (35 in) high at the shoulder, though it looks much bulkier because of its thick wool. Like the llama, it has been domesticated for centuries and no longer exists in the wild. It is bred and reared for its wool, highly valued for outdoor clothing since it is very resistant to rain and snow.

The vicuña (*Vicugna vicugna*, illustrated here) is the smallest of the group, standing only 75 cm (30 in) high. It lives on the high plateaux of the Andes in Peru, Bolivia, Argentina and Chile. Its fine, silky fur is much prized and was reserved for the use of royalty by the Incas. The species has been much hunted and is now protected. The females live in small herds of eight to twelve, dominated by a male. Young males are expelled from the herd by their mothers when they are eight to ten months old. The males not attached to herds live in groups up to one hundred strong. The dominant male defends the territory of his herd, repelling intruders by biting or spitting.

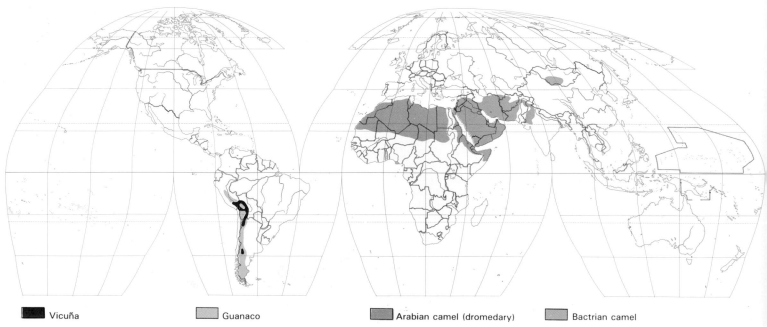

Vicuña   Guanaco   Arabian camel (dromedary)   Bactrian camel

vicuna

guanaco

young guanaco

Bactrian camel

Tragulidae

The most primitive family of the ruminants is that of the Tragulidae, chevrotains, which comprises animals of small dimensions, weighing between 2 and 10 kg (4½ to 22 lb). They do not possess horns, but have tusks derived from the elongation of the canine teeth of the upper jaw. The characteristics of some forms have remained unchanged from the Eocene period to the present day. The largest species is the water chevrotain (*Hyemoschus aquaticus*), found in western equatorial Africa. The genus *Tragulus* comprises three Asiatic species. The larger Malay chevrotain (*T. napu*) lives in Borneo, Sumatra, Cambodia, Vietnam and the Malay peninsula. The lesser Malay chevrotain (*T. javanicus*, illustrated here) lives in the same area and in Java. The third species is the Indian chevrotain (*T. meminna*) of India and Sri Lanka. The chevrotains are timid forest-dwellers, also known as mouse-deer.

Cervidae

The Cervidae family by contrast is rich in species, some of them having achieved a considerable evolutionary success. The most visible characteristic of the family is the possession of branched antlers, which are made of a bony material. They are shed after the breeding season and a new set is grown, of a more complex pattern. The new antlers are at first skin-covered, but the skin wears off leaving the naked bone. Antlers are usually present only in the males. There are several sub-families.

Moschinae. The only living representative of the Moschinae is the musk deer (*Moschus moschiferus*, illustrated here), which lives from Siberia to South-East Asia, and at one time probably extended as far as the Caspian. The musk deer was valued in ancient times for its musk-secreting glands, which were much sought after for the manufacture of perfumery. Like the chevrotains they have highly developed upper canines which emerge as tusks.

Muntiacinae. A higher stage in the evolution of the Cervidae is seen in the muntjacs (*Muntiacinae*), whose appearance is intermediate between that of the Moschinae and the other sub-families. Though still preserving the archaic characteristic of canines transformed into tusks they also possess a pair of antlers, even though

these are clearly of an archaic kind. The Indian muntjac (*Muntiacus muntjak*, illustrated here) has antlers about 13 cm (5 in) long with only one branch, set on long hairy bases from which ridges of bone extend down each side of the face. They are found all over South-East Asia and have become established as wild animals in parts of England and France, having escaped from parks. Their habitat is dense forest with impenetrable undergrowth, which has resulted in a solitary way of life and a structural adaptation making possible sudden swift movements and rapid penetration of bush and thicket. They stand 50 to 55 cm high (20 to 22 in) at the shoulder and weigh less than 25 kg (55 lb). The hind legs are better developed than the forelegs, and the neck is short. The two sexes usually only meet during the breeding season and gestation takes seven to eight months. Communication between members of the species is effected principally by scent signals deposited on branches or other supports by rubbing them with the glands found on the forehead and the region round the eye. There is also a vocal system of communication used mostly for signalling danger, and audible from a great distance. Their call sounds very like the barking of dogs; this has given them the alternative name of barking deer, another name being ridge-faced deer. There are several other species of *Muntiacus* present in the same region, and another genus of the Muntiacinae sub-family is the tufted deer (*Elaphodus cephalophus*) found in China and Burma.

Cervinae. The Cervinae, deer nearly all living in Eurasia, comprise four genera with some eighteen species. One of the best known is the fallow deer (*Dama dama*) which probably originated in the Mediterranean region and western Asia but is now widely distributed in Europe, western Asia and North Africa, where it lives in parks, forests and open woodland. A social animal, it lives in large herds, but in the summer these consist almost entirely of females and immature males, the adult males remaining apart until the Autumn rut. The coat is typically bright fawn with white spots on the back and sides, but there is also a dark grey-brown colour form which is commonly seen. Domesticated animals have sometimes been bred to produce coats of other colours from white to black and even 'blue' varieties. The fallow deer communicates by a variety of calls including the male's rutting cry, a deep grunt; the white pattern surrounding the anal region, prominently visible in flight, may also be regarded as a visual signal. There is a rare

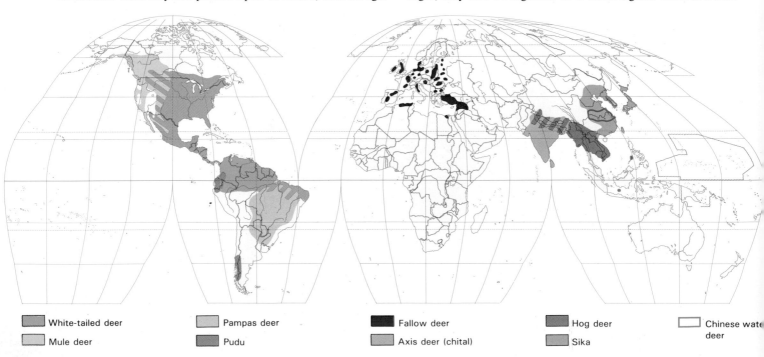

White-tailed deer	Pampas deer	Fallow deer	Hog deer
Mule deer	Pudu	Axis deer (chital)	Sika

Chinese water deer

Chinese water deer

musk deer

lesser
Malay
chevrotain

Indian muntjac

pudu

pampas deer

species of western Asia, the Persian fallow deer (*Dama meso-potamica*), which now survives only in a few small areas of Iran.

The axis deer (*Axis axis*, illustrated here) or chital lives in grasslands and forests in India and Sri Lanka, and has also been introduced into other parts of the world including Europe. It has a white-spotted reddish coat, with white underparts. The hog deer (*Axis porcinus*) is the same size as roe deer but clumsier in appearance. It prefers humid habitats such as marshes, but in proximity to rivers and forests. They lead solitary lives or else form herds of three to four individuals, in contrast to the chitals which form much larger groups, up to 200 individuals. In the mating season, however, they will gather into groups of about fifty, within which the males fight among themselves to establish their superiority. They live in the same area as the chital.

The sambar (*Cervus unicolor*, illustrated on p. 301) is a large, long-tailed deer, standing 1.2 to 1.4 m (47 to 55 in) at the shoulder, and living from India to Nepal to South-East Asia. There are several races in different parts of the species range including one on Timor, Java, Sulawesi and neighbouring islands, characterized by a thick ruff round the neck, and the Philippine sambar, the smallest race of the species, weighing only 50 kg (110 lb). It is nocturnal in habit, and lives in groups of five or six individuals, and is a forest-dweller, feeding on leaves.

The barasingha (*Cervus duvauceli*, illustrated here), or swamp deer, is found in India, Nepal and Assam. A tall and graceful animal, it lives in open forests and grasslands; it was formerly widespread but is now regarded as a rare animal. The tameng or Eld's deer (*C. eldi*, illustrated here) of southern Asia prefers marshy clearings in the forests where it finds rich and nutritious vegetation; it is also in danger of extinction resulting from improvements in agriculture. The sika (*C. nippon*, illustrated here), a forest-dwelling deer of Japan, China and Taiwan, has been bred from ancient times in the Far East for its antlers, used in traditional medicine. It has been introduced into various regions of the world including Great Britain where it is now common in parts of the south. The Japanese sika stands only 80 to 86 cm (31 to 34 in) at the shoulder.

One of the best-known members of the family is the red deer (*Cervus elaphus*), present in Europe and Asia. It stands sometimes more than 120 cm (4 ft) high at the shoulders and its antlers may measure 120 cm (4 ft) in length. It is reddish-brown in colour in the summer, darkening to greyish brown in winter. Its favourite habitat is forests with broad grassy clearings where it can pasture at night. The males and females live in separate herds except during the mating season, when the males (stags) fight each other for the possession of harems of females (hinds). These duels are preceded by the roaring cries typical of the males in the rutting season. When two males confront each other the antlers are first displayed as a symbol of potency; they are then lowered and the animals rush upon each other, interlocking their antlers and pushing each other until one admits the other's superiority and retires from the field. Red deer have been introduced to New Zealand where they have caused considerable ecological damage, but may soon become an important source of meat.

The red deer is closely related to the wapiti (*Cervus canadensis*, illustrated here) of North America where it is sometimes called the elk, a massive animal standing more than 30 cm (12 in) higher than the red deer. Once widespread, it is now confined to the Rockies, Wyoming and southern Canada. It is the second largest living deer, exceeded in size only by the moose.

Hydropotinae. The Hydropotinae contains only one species, the Chinese water deer (*Hydropotes inermis*, illustrated on p.297). It is a solitary and territorial species, living in marshes, fields and mountainsides in north-east China and Korea. It is most common in the reedbeds and low-lying marshy country along the shores of the Yangtze river. It is only 50 cm (20 in) high at the shoulder and has no antlers, but the upper canine teeth have grown into long tusks that protrude from the mouth. It has established a wild population in Britain, derived from escaped animals earlier this century.

Odocoileinae. The sub-family of Odocoileinae is present in both Eurasia and America and is divided into two groups, the roe deer and American deer. The roe (*Capreolus capreolus*), despite extensive hunting, is still widely distributed in Europe and Asia. It is small, standing 66 to 86 cm (26 to 34 in) at the shoulder, almost tailless, and has small, three-tined antlers with a rough surface. It is an inhabitant of lightly wooded country. Its presence can often be detected by the circular or figure-of-eight tracks made during the mating season, when the male sometimes chases the female repeatedly round the same route, circling one or more bushes. The roe deer is not gregarious, but lives in pairs or small family groups.

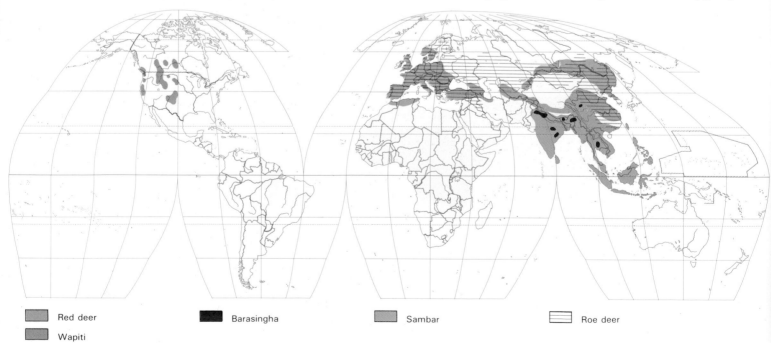

Red deer	Barasingha	Sambar	Roe deer
Wapiti			

axis deer

white-tailed deer

barasingha

sika

Eld's deer

The males mark their territory and patrol its borders regularly, watching out for intruders. In the rutting season, in July, the males fight each other fiercely according to a set ritual. The two males confront each other, advancing slowly with the head held high and slightly turned to one side. One of the two may even at this stage signal its inferior status, but otherwise the two both lower their heads to display the set of antlers, then charge and interlock them. The females bear one or two spotted young after about nine months, of which four are spent in a delayed implanting of the embryo in the wall of the uterus, and the other five in actual gestation.

The American species include the white-tailed deer or Virginia deer (*Odocoileus virginianus*, illustrated on p. 299), found from southern Canada to Brazil. A common woodland species, it is distinguished by the white underside of the tail, which is held upright like a signalling flag when the animal us running. The other American species of the genus is the mule deer (*O. hemionus*) which lives in western North America from Alaska to Mexico; it is shorter and more thickset than the white tailed deer, and lives in rough mountainous country and in deserts. The marsh deer (*Blastocerus dichotomus*) and pampas deer (*Ozotoceros bezoarticus*, illustrated on p. 297) are both South American species, the latter a small deer weighing little more than 30 kg (66 lb) and at the present time in danger of extinction. The genus *Hippocamelus* has two species living in the Andes, the Peruvian animal (*H. antisiensis*) and the Chilean guemal (*H. bisulcus*). The four species of the genus *Mazama* are the brocket deer of Central and South America.

The pudu (*Pudu pudu*, illustrated on p. 297) have very reduced antlers and lack canines; they are the smallest representatives of the Cervidae, with weights between 7 and 12 kg (15 and 26 lb). They live in Chile and Argentina. There is a second species found further north in Peru and Colombia, the Northern pudu (*P. mephistophiles*).

Alcinae. The only species of the Alcinae is the moose or elk (*Alces alces*, illustrated here). This is the largest of the Cervidae with its height of 2 m (6 ft 6 in) at the shoulders and 800 kg (1700 lb) in weight. The moose is the American name, the elk the European name, for the same animal; the American race is slightly larger than the Eurasian. It is an able swimmer and likes to stand half submerged in the water of marshes and streams; its habitat is the taiga or tundra of the north. The head is large, with an extended, fleshy nose; the huge antlers, which are grown only by the male, are flattened to a spoon-shaped form, and may reach a width of 2 m (6 ft 6 in). The legs are long and the hooves can be spread apart, allowing the animal to walk without difficulty on marshy terrain. Elks are not well designed for grazing but mostly browse from trees or bushes, or enter the water to feed on aquatic plants growing on the surface. They are not gregarious, mostly living alone except for temporary unions during the mating season or mothers with infant males until weaning; but small groups may be formed during summer and larger ones in winter.

Rangiferinae. The sole species of Rangiferinae is the reindeer (*Rangifer tarandus*, illustrated here), the caribou of North America, regarded by some authorities as the same species, but since there are marked differences others regard them as separate species. Certainly there are as many as twenty sub-species with weights varying from 60 to 300 kg (132 to 660 lb); this is not surprising in view of the vast area they cover, across the whole of the northernmost regions of America, Europe and Asia. They are the only species of deer in which both males and females have antlers. Reindeer have been domesticated for centuries by the Lapps, who use them as draught and pack animals, and as a source of meat and milk, of hides for boots and clothing, tents and bedcoverings, and of horn for various implements. They vary in height from 0.7 to 1.4 m (2 ft 4 in–4 ft 8 in) at the shoulder, and have long legs terminating in broad hooves that can be splayed out so that they are admirably suited for travelling over marshy or snow-covered terrain. The coat, usually greyish or brownish, lightening in colour in winter, is thick, with hard, brittle outer hairs covering a dense under-fur. In winter the diet is mostly a lichen (*Cladonia rangiferina*) commonly called reindeer-moss, which they can obtain by scraping away the snow with their forefeet; in summer they also eat grasses and young saplings. Wild reindeer are now rare, and none are found in Europe, but North American caribou are still abundant in the wild state. They are highly gregarious, travelling in herds of many thousands of animals, and undertake long migrations between their winter quarters and summer pastures in the far northern tundra. In summer they split up into smaller groups that scatter over the tundra, reuniting again in the autumn for the long migration.

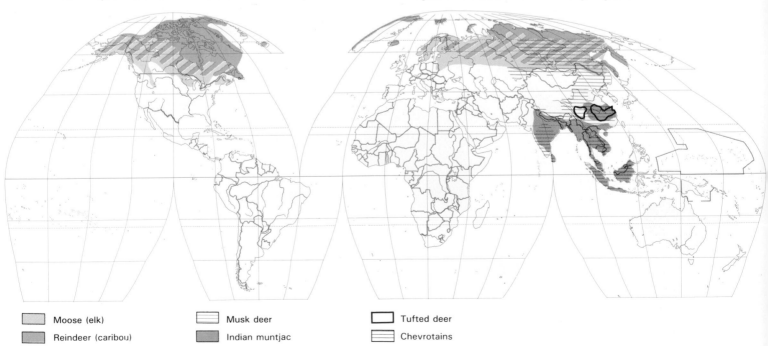

Moose (elk)

Reindeer (caribou)

Musk deer

Indian muntjac

Tufted deer

Chevrotains

moose (elk)

sambar

wapiti

reindeer (caribou)

Giraffidae

The giraffe family appeared more than twenty-five million years ago and has had some measure of evolutionary success; now there remain only two genera, each with one species.

One species is the okapi, an animal which looks to us like a hybrid between a giraffe and a zebra (though doubtless if we had discovered the okapi first, then the giraffe or zebra would be the odd-looking creature).

In 1900 Dr P. L. Schlater, secretary of the Zoological Society of London, gave the name *Equus johnstoni* to an animal he identified from pieces of skin sent to him by Sir Harry Johnston, Governor of Uganda. Shortly afterwards two skulls and a complete skin were obtained from the pigmy natives by a Belgian named Eriksson. It was immediately apparent that the creature was not odd-toed like a horse, but even-toed and possibly a member of the giraffe family. Schlater realized the mistake and in June 1901 the newly discovered species was officially named *Okapia johnstoni* after its discoverer.

The discovery of the okapi provoked a rivalry between museums and zoological gardens, both of which wished to acquire examples of the species. Large hunting expeditions were sent out which, however, had no success, owing to the difficulties of the dense forest terrain occupied by the animal. Its appearance recalls in some ways that of a horse and at the same time that of a giraffe. The body is rather heavy, supported on long legs; the shoulders are higher than the rump; the long neck ends in a large head with big eyes, and the tail is short. The upper parts of the forelegs are partly, and the hindlegs wholly, ornamented with zebra-stripes in dark chocolate brown and white, while the lower parts of the legs are white except for black rings just above the hooves. The body is a deep reddish-brown. Male okapis have a pair of pointed horns naked at the tips. The height is 1.5 m (5 ft) at the shoulders and the weight is up to 250 kg (550 lb). The okapi is regarded as a living fossil, its appearance having remained virtually unchanged for twenty million years. The area of distribution is restricted to the dense equatorial forests of Zaire. The diet is mostly leaves, which it

A giraffe mother allows her calf to suckle. The young will continue to take milk for up to a month after birth though it will start to browse on leaves at three weeks or so.

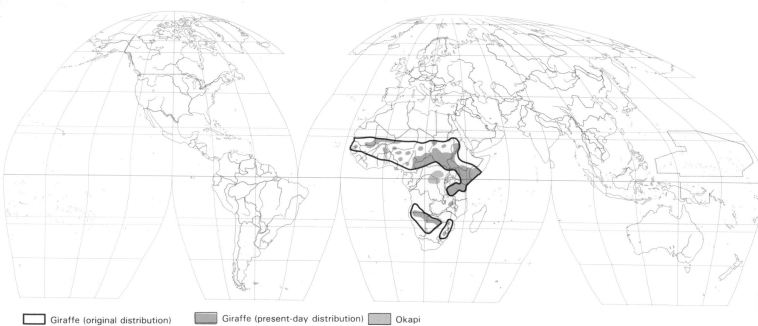

☐ Giraffe (original distribution)   ▨ Giraffe (present-day distribution)   ☐ Okapi

can gather from the trees up to 3 m (10 ft) from the ground; in this it is aided by the long, prehensile tongue that grasps the boughs and strips them. Solitary animals, each one occupies a considerable area; they come together temporarily in couples during the mating season. After the birth of the young the mother remains with her offspring, but this often is left alone, crouching among the vegetation, and sees its mother only when suckling. In courtship the female – slightly larger than the male – is bold, inviting the male with gurgling and coughing sounds.

The other genus of the family is also monospecific, comprising the giraffe (*Giraffa camelopardalis*, illustrated here) with its several sub-species. Its present area of distribution is much reduced compared with its original area which extended from the Sahara to South Africa except for a few desert areas. The form of the giraffe, known to all, is somewhat strange: at the shoulder it stands up to 3 m (10 ft) high and at the head 6 m (19 ft). The shoulders are much higher than the rump, the legs very long, the neck inordinately so, and adorned throughout its whole length with a mane. Despite the length of the neck it is supported by the same number of vertebrae (seven) as the neck of humans and most other mammals. The long head, with its flattened nose, recalls that of a camel; it has two short horns. The tail is fairly long and terminates in a tuft of long hair. The body is typically marked with large irregular polygonal spots forming a pattern varying from one sub-species to another. The most important of the senses is eyesight, owing to the height at which the eyes are situated. The diet is basically of leaves, especially of various species of acacia, gathered at heights from 2 to 6 m (6 to 19 ft). As with the okapi, the tongue is prehensile and is used to strip the boughs of their foliage. Drinking is made difficult owing to the length of the forelegs; which have to be splayed to allow the head to descend down to the ground. The even circulation of blood to various parts of the body has necessitated special adaptations of the heart, arterial and venous systems. Giraffes live typically in

A small group of pronghorn antelope graze warily in the dry grassland. This animal is the fastest New World mammal, cruising easily at 50 km/hr (30 mph).

savannah country, where the trees are high enough to browse from, but spaced out enough to permit a good range of vision. They spend their lives in herds either of females with offspring or of young adults, adult males being isolated or in small groups.

Antilocapridae

The family Antilocapridae has one representative, the pronghorn (*Antilocapra americana*, illustrated here). The male has forked hollow horns, renewed every year; the female's horns are more rudimentary. Pronghorns were once found throughout the short grass prairies from Alberta to northern Mexico, but the range and numbers are now much reduced due to both hunting and loss of habitat. It is now a protected species. The typical habitat is open unconfined grassland, sagebrush, and even high plateaux up to 2000 m (6500 ft). The reproductive season (rut) begins in the autumn when the males spar for possession of three or four does. In spring the herds disband and the females give birth to usually two young in May or June.

Bovidae

The bovids – wild cattle in their various forms – comprise the largest family of ungulates and include well over fifty genera. Bovidae encompasses deer, bison, antelope, gazelle and mountain goat plus the various domesticated forms familiar over most of the world.

According to some authorities the bovids represent an evolutionary summit, and they share with the primates a pinnacle of mammalian development. All members of the family possess horns termed 'true horns', that is, they consist of a bony core covered with a layer of permanent horny sheath which is derived from hardened skin tissue. The horns are unbranched, though in many species they are twisted or curved into a variety of interesting shapes. Also, the horns are usually borne by both sexes, though they are usually larger in the males. The bovids are generally organized into large herds that graze on open plains, as opposed to small family groups under the charge of a dominant stag, as in the Cervidae.

The family is almost worldwide in distribution, though having been introduced to South America and Australia by man. The evolutionary adaptations of the various sub-families are enormously varied and have allowed them to occupy the most diverse habitats and climates. The most 'typical' representative of the Bovidae is probably the antelope in its various guises, but the family includes such diversities as the ox, the cow and the sheep.

Cephalophinae. The Cephalophinae, duikers, are the most primitive sub-family of the Bovidae, with two genera, *Cephalophus* and *Sylvicapra*. They are forest-dwellers, which explains their shape: a squat body, the hindlegs longer than the forelegs, a short neck and short horns turned backwards. They are called 'duiker', Afrikaans for 'diver', because when alarmed they dive for cover. The dimensions vary widely: the blue duiker (*Cephalophus monticola*) weighs barely 5 kg (11 lb) while the yellow-backed duiker (*C. silvicultor*, illustrated here) and Jentink's duiker (*C. Jentinki*) may attain a weight of 80 kg (176 lb).

The duikers are territorial animals and mark their borders by scent signals; the face glands (visible as black slits below the eyes) produce a strong-smelling substance which is deposited on twigs and branches. This secretion is used also as a social marking between a male and female by rubbing each other muzzle to muzzle, or between two males as a part of the grooming process which cements social bonds and confirms the ranking of seniority between members of a group.

In contrast to the duikers of the genus *Cephalophus*, the grey duiker (*Sylvicapra grimmia*, illustrated here) is a resident of savannah country. It often lives near streams and rivers, and browses on leaves, twigs and berries; it will also sometimes eat small animals, snails, insects and even carrion.

Neotraginae. The sub-family Neotraginae comprises small and medium-sized animals all living in Africa. The royal antelope (*Neotragus pygmaeus*), Bates's dwarf antelope (*Neotragus batesi*) and the suni of East Africa (*N. moschatus*) all live in dense bush or forest where they can move about with great speed and agility.

The dik-diks are members of the genus *Madoqua* (including Salt's dik-dik, *M. saltiana*, illustrated here). They are found in dry bushy scrub and semi-desert areas in East and South Africa. They live in couples in territories that are marked out by the scent glands of both males and females, and which they defend against invasion by others of the same species. Their name comes from the alarm call of the female, sometimes written 'zik-zik'. Dik-diks are well known for disturbing other game with their calls, and also shrill whistles, when danger presents. In the days of big game hunting they were slaughtered not for their trophy value (since they have none) but so that they could not alert larger species.

One of the most agile of the ungulates is the klipspringer (*Oreotragus oreotragus*, illustrated here), whose most characteristic feature is the possession of unusually tall hooves assuring perfect support even on the steepest of rocks. Klipspringers can make great leaps of over 6 m (20 ft) from one rocky outcrop to another. They are extremely fast and agile, but can 'freeze' in a characteristic position with all four feet close together. They are found in all the rocky regions of Africa south of the equator.

The genera *Raphicerus* and *Ourebia* comprise about twenty-four species with short, straight horns, well-proportioned bodies, and hindlegs longer than the forelegs. The steinbok (*Raphicerus campestris*) inhabits the semi-arid plains of central to west Africa. The grysbok (*R. melanotis*) lives in similar arid areas in southern Africa. The oribi (*Ourebia ourebi*, illustrated here) is a swift runner, capable of leaping high in the air with its legs together. Finally the Beira antelope (*Dorcatragus megalotis*, illustrated here) is an inhabitant of the most arid and rocky regions.

Tragelaphinae. The sub-family Tragelaphinae comprises ten species grouped in four genera, *Tragelaphus*, *Taurotragus*, *Boselaphus* and *Tetracerus*. The first two of these are large-headed antelopes with spiral horns and long and slender legs carrying a large, agile body. One of the best known of the genus *Tragelaphus* is the greater kudu (*T. strepsiceros*), with its imposing dimensions: up to 1.5 m (5 ft) at the shoulders and 350 kg (770 lb) in weight. It

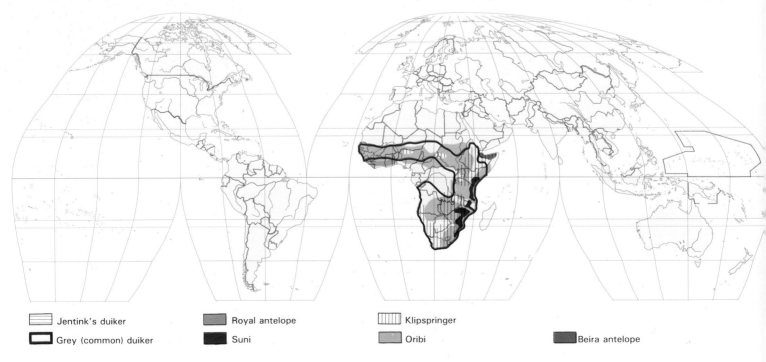

Jentink's duiker	Royal antelope	Klipspringer
Grey (common) duiker	Suni	Oribi
		Beira antelope

Beira antelope

klipspringer

oribi

grey duiker

Salt's dik-dik

yellow-backed duiker

lives in forests will provided with bushy clearings, in east, central and southern Africa. Its coat is grey with white stripes on the flanks; the lower part of the neck is adorned with a long, thick mane; the spiral horns are long and diverge strongly so that the tips may be 1.25 m (4 ft) apart. They travel alone or in small parties of cows and immature bulls, the adult bulls only joining the herd during the mating season. Members of a group are dispersed when feeding but when they rest they lie down close together. They often take part in mutual grooming, licking each other's head and foreparts often to a quite frantic degree.

The lesser kudu (*T. imberbis*) lives in the dry bushy areas of central and east Africa. The females differ from the males in being smaller and lacking horns. The mountain nyala (*T. buxtoni*) is an antelope of 200 kg (440 lb) in weight living in the mountains of southern Ethiopia; the population is much decreased and the animal seems to be on the way to extinction. Its present habitat is either forested zones or high plateaux covered with giant heather bushes, about 2500 m (8000 ft) above sea-level. The nyala of the plains (*T. angasi*, illustrated here) resembles the greater kudu in general appearance but is much lighter, weighing 120 kg (260 lb). The female, lacking horns, is patterned and maned in the same way as the male, but its coat is brownish-red rather than grey. The habitat is fairly wet, bushy, more or less open country, either flat or hilly, in Natal, Transvaal, Mozambique and Zimbabwe. The diet consists of leaves, shoots and fruit.

The sitatunga (*T. spekei*, illustrated here) is a large antelope whose weight may exceed 100 kg (220 lb). It has long hooves, broadly splayed out; between them is an interdigital membrane which permits the animal to walk with ease on soft surfaces such as the mud of marshes. The sitatunga spends much time in water and is a good swimmer. It is found in central Africa from Senegal to Kenya and as far southward as the tropic of Capricorn.

The bushbuck (*T. scriptus*, illustrated here), the smallest of the genus, weighing only 75 kg (165 lb), lives in mountain forests and bushy areas over most of tropical Africa, up to 4000 m (13,000 ft) above sea level. The bushbuck tends to be solitary but it is not unusual to encounter a couple together, either of the same sex or mixed. The habitat is rather varied, including, besides forest, cultivated land and arid areas.

The largest living antelopes are the bongo (*Taurotragus eurycerus*), the eland (*T. oryx*, illustrated here) and the giant eland (*T. derbianus*). The bongo is the largest forest antelope, weighing up to 230 kg (500 lb); it lives in the humid African forests between Kenya and Sierra Leone. The largest of the savannah antelopes, however, are the elands, with a height of 1.5 m (5 ft) at the shoulders and up to 1000 kg (2200 lb) in weight. These large and heavily built animals live from central east Africa to the Cape. They lead a gregarious life, gathering together in large herds, and are notably agile considering their size. The horns, which are possessed by both males and females, are their best form of defence, and even large predators such as lions may suffer grave wounds from the horns, as well as from kicks of the hooves. Elands have a hump on the shoulders and a prominent dewlap; most have a series of white stripes on the body, fading away towards the rump. The bongo's horns have only one twist, and possess peculiar yellow tips. Its colouring of bright hues broken with white stripes is excellent camouflage for breaking up its outline in the dappled forests where it lives.

The nilgai (*Boselaphus tragocamelus*, illustrated here), weighing 200 kg (440 lb), has a massive body and rather small horns, absent in the female. The forelegs are longer than the hind legs, giving it a rather ungainly gait when running. It is the largest of the Indian antelopes, standing 135 cm (54 in) high at the shoulder. It lives in India and Pakistan, in arid, bushy areas. The males have a typical bluish colour but the cows are brownish. The composition of the herds is very varied: isolated bulls, herds of bulls, herds of cows, single cows with one or more calves, or groups of cows with calves; the cow-and-calf herds tend to grow in size after the calves are one year old.

Finally, the four-horned antelope (*Tetracerus quadricornis*, illustrated here), with its two pairs of horns of which the front ones are the shorter, lives in the humid forests of central India.

Bovinae. The sub-family Bovinae is one of the best known of the family Bovidae, containing buffaloes and bison. It is of relatively recent origin, its original area of distribution is in the Old World, with the American bison the only New World species. One of the most primitive species is the anoa (*Anoa depressicornis*, illustrated on p. 309), found only on the island of Sulawesi in Indonesia. Two sub-species are known, one of the plains and one of the mountains. The massive body is supported on slender legs, the horns are straight and turned backwards; the weight can be up to 300 kg (660 lb). Its

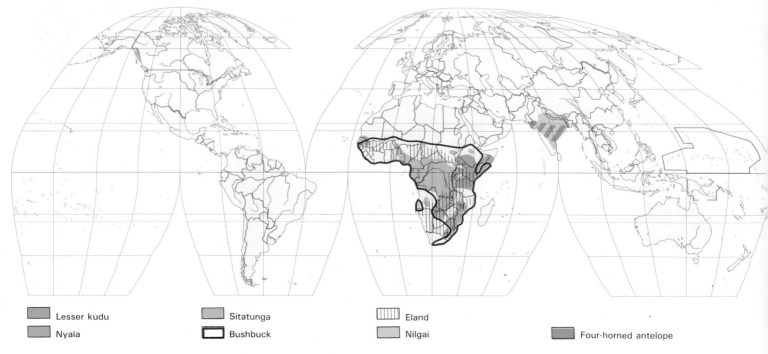

Lesser kudu   Sitatunga   Eland

Nyala   Bushbuck   Nilgai   Four-horned antelope

bushbuck

nyala

nilgai

eland

sitatunga

four-horned
antelope

straight horns sweep backwards rather like those of an antelope.

The Indian or water buffaloes are gigantic creatures weighing more than 1000 kg (2200 lb) and standing 1.8 m (nearly 6 ft) high at the shoulder. They have large horns, flattened and curving backwards. The water buffalo (*Bubalus arnee*) once roamed widely over Asia and Africa and perhaps Europe, but today is found only in Asia. Its habitat is marshes and ponds, where the animal stands immersed up to the shoulders for the greater part of the day. It lives in herds of about twenty individuals, made up of females and young with a few adult males, but older males are solitary. It is the wild ancestor of the domestic buffalo (*Bubalus bubalis*) which has been domesticated from remote times and is still today of immense importance in agriculture, with an estimated population of seventy million head throughout the world, mostly in east, south and South-East Asia. It is used as a draught animal, as a pack animal, and as a source of milk and meat.

The African buffalo (*Syncerus caffer*, illustrated here) is similar in size to the Indian buffalo but lives in swamps and arid savannah country. The dwarf forest buffalo, a sub-species of the African buffalo (*S. c. nanus*) is a much smaller animal, weighing only 35 kg 77 lb) and living in the forests and mountains of central and west Africa. It lives alone or in pairs, but the other sub-species, often called the Cape buffalo (*S. c. caffer*) to distinguish it from the dwarf buffalo, lives in herds usually of up to fifty individuals, but sometimes in immense herds of 2000 head. The herds are however composed of females and young, with only a few males, most of the males being either solitary or living in groups of five or six individuals.

All domestic cattle (*Bos taurus*) are descended from wild members of the genus *Bos*. Among wild oxen, the gaur (*B. gaurus*) of southern Asia survives in reduced numbers in a few scattered localities. The gaur is the ancestor of the domestic breed, the gayal (*Bos frontalis*, illustrated here). The banteng of southern Asia, Java and Borneo (*Bos javanicus*, illustrated here) is of smaller dimensions than the gaur, reaching 1.7 m (5 ft 6 in) in height at the shoulder and 900 kg (2000 lb). There are three sub-species corresponding to the three major areas of distribution. The species is endangered due to the transformation of its forest habitat to agricultural land.

A new species was described in 1936, the kouprey (*B. sauveli*), which lives in small numbers in Indo-China. The aurochs (*Bos*

primigenius), the wild ox of Europe, from which modern domestic cattle are probably descended, survived in Poland till 1627. It was a large black animal, standing 1.8 m (6 ft) high, with spreading, forward-curved horns. The bulls of the Camargue and those reared for bullfighting in Spain may be among the most primitive descendants of the aurochs.

The yak (*Bos grunniens*, illustrated here) may attain a height of 1.8 m (6 ft) at the shoulder hump and weigh 1000 kg (2200 lb). The body is covered with long, thick hair, which hangs down on the sides in a long fringe reaching the ankles. It lives on the most elevated plateaux of Tibet and Szechwan (China) at heights above 4000 m (13,000 ft), as high as any mammal anywhere. It has been domesticated for centuries, but some wild specimens still exist in the most remote localities. Herdsmen occasionally search out and introduce wild specimens into their herds to improve the domestic stock; although the body sizes of the domesticated and the wild strains are substantially different, being of the same species they have no trouble interbreeding. Domesticated yaks are used for riding, as pack animals and as a source of milk and meat, besides cords and ropes (from the long hairs), fuel (the dried dung), leather (the hides) and fly whisks (the tails).

There are two species of bison, one European and one American. The American bison (*Bison bison*, illustrated here) is an impressive animal with its heavy head and immense shoulders and hump, looking larger than it is because of its thick wool coat. It can weigh well over a ton (1000 kg). The horns are well developed. At the beginning of the nineteenth century there were sixty million bison (often wrongly called 'buffalo') roaming the plains; by 1889 there were less than 600 left. Protective measures were taken in time to preserve the species and there are now over 20,000, living in parks and reserves.

The European bison (*Bison bonasus*) has not existed in the truly wild state since 1927, but the species still exists, descended from three wild survivors in Upper Silesia and other specimens kept in zoos. From these the present wild-living European bisons, numbering many hundred, were derived.

Alcelaphinae. The sub-family Alcelaphinae comprises large animals with long horns, long heads and long ears. The coat of the two sexes is similar or identical. Facial and hoof scent glands serve for the marking out of territory. The hartebeest (*Alcelaphus*

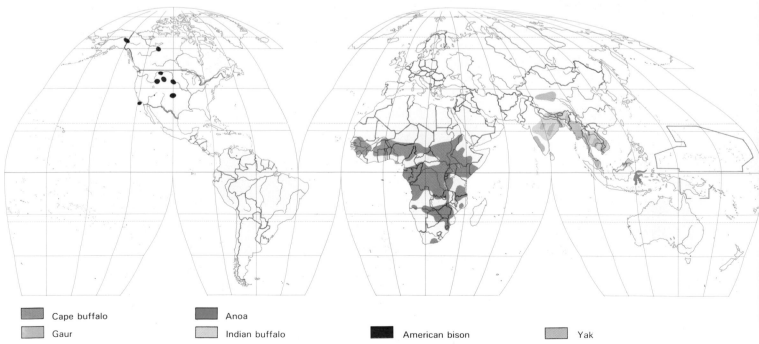

▦ Cape buffalo	▦ Anoa	■ American bison
▦ Gaur	▦ Indian buffalo	▦ Yak

gayal

African or Cape
buffalo

American bison

yak

anoa

banteng

buselaphus) has many sub-species, surviving today in semi-arid parts of Africa. The bubal hartebeest (*A. b. buselaphus*) of North Africa, known in Roman times, is however extinct. Swayne's hartebeest (*A. b. swaynei*) was discovered at the end of the last century; it was then very numerous and lived in herds containing thousands of individuals. Today there are about 500 in Ethiopia and a lesser number in Somalia. Other sub-species such as the tora (*A. b. tora*) and the Cape hartebeest (*A. b. caama*) survive in small numbers in, respectively, the region of the Blue Nile in the Sudan and in the Kalahari Gemsbok National Park on the northern borders of Namibia and South Africa. Lichtenstein's hartebeest (*A. b. lichtensteini*, illustrated here), found in eastern southern Africa, prefers forested and bushy areas but is also, like the other hartebeests, found in savannah country. Coke's hartebeest (*A. b. cokii*) is fairly common in Kenya and Tanzania, where it frequents the grasslands up to 2000 m (6500 ft) above sea level. The females give birth in March and September, that is, before the rainy season.

Antelopes of the genus *Damaliscus* are known as hartebeests. They live mostly in dry grasslands and woods. *D. dorcas*, living in southern Africa, has two sub-species, the blesbok and bontebok, standing slightly over 1 m (3 ft 3 in) high at the shoulder and weighing 80 to 100 kg (170 to 220 lb). The blesbok is slightly the smaller of the two. The coat is reddish brown, the face, legs, stomach and rump being marked with broad white patches. The horns, of medium length, are slightly curved in an S-shape. The blesbok (*D. d. philippsi*) is abundant, being protected and semi-domesticated. The bontebok (*D. d. dorcas*, illustrated here) was hunted almost to extinction, but is now protected and survives in much reduced numbers. The sassaby (*D. lunatus*) lives in small family groups but it sometimes happens that several of these small groups meet and form herds of up to 200 head. They are found on fairly humid grasslands from the Zambezi to Botswana, Transvaal and Natal. The topi (*D. korrigum*) of the African savannahs is particularly gregarious and has been observed in herds of 12,000 head during its migrations; usually the groups number thirty to forty head. Hunter's hartebeest (*D. hunteri*) is about the size of a bontebok and is reddish brown with white face markings; it is found from the Tana River in Kenya to the Juba River in Somalia.

The gnu, or wildebeest, belongs to the genus *Connochaetes*. There are two species. The brindled gnu, or blue wildebeest (*C.* *taurinus*), is fairly abundant over the grasslands of much of central and south-eastern Africa. It is dark silvery-grey with a black mane, tail and face. The white-tailed gnu (*C. gnou*, illustrated here) is now nearly extinct in the wild but is well protected on a number of ranches. Gnu live in herds of considerable size and undertake long seasonal migrations in search of pasture and pools of water.

Hippotraginae. Among the most elegant and imposing of the Bovidae are the sub-family Hippotraginae, long-horned antelopes of weights varying from 150 to 300 kg (330 to 660 lb). Species of the genus *Hippotragus* have massive bodies carried on slender legs. The neck is thick and muscular with a large head and imposing backward-curving horns. The roan antelope (*H. equinus*) lives on the grassy plains in the vicinity of water, in equatorial Africa. There are numerous sub-species. The muzzle is ornamented with a characteristic black and white mask, and it has an erect mane darker than the rest of the coat, which is reddish-brown. The sable antelope (*H. niger*, illustrated here) lives in the forests of south-eastern Africa; both sexes bear horns, those of the male are particularly impressive, reaching lengths of 170 cm (68 in). The neck of the sable antelope bears a mane, and the stomach and anal region are white.

The other Hippotraginae belong to the genera *Oryx* and *Addax*. *Oryx gazella* has two sub-species, the Cape oryx or gemsbok (*O. g. gazella*) and the beisa oryx (*O. g. beisa*). They live in the arid or semi-desert regions of southern and eastern Africa, stocky animals taller at the shoulder than at the rump, both sexes having long, sharp horns. The coat is greyish-brown, with dark patches on the face and forehead and on either side of the eye, and dark markings on the legs. The Arabian oryx (*O. leucoryx*, illustrated here) is the most imposing species, with a yellowish white coat, dark markings on the face and underparts, and dark legs. It formerly lived in the Arabian desert, but is now probably extinct in the wild through indiscriminate hunting, though it survives in protected areas and zoos. Captive breeding has increased numbers sufficiently to permit the release of animals back into their former haunts in an attempt to re-establish wild populations in Jordan and Oman. The addax (*Addax nasomaculatus*, illustrated here), once found in considerable numbers in the deserts between the Nile and Senegal, is now restricted to a much more limited area of the southern Sahara. It has long, spirally twisted horns, present in both sexes.

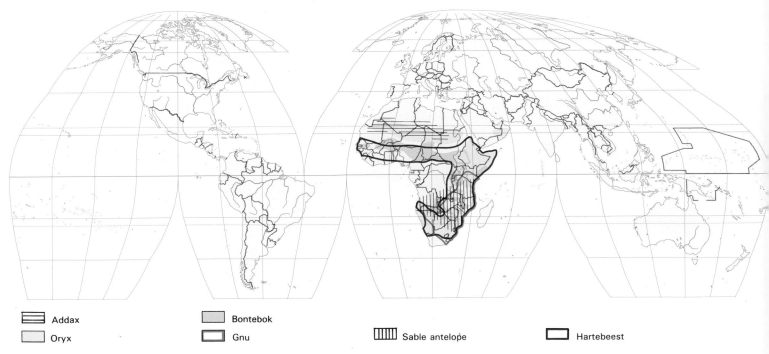

Addax	Bontebok		
Oryx	Gnu	Sable antelope	Hartebeest

sable antelope

white-tailed gnu

bontebok

addax

Lichtenstein's
hartebeest

Arabian oryx

Reduncinae. The Reduncinae are antelopes of medium dimensions, among which are two groups of animals with very diverse habitats: the Vaal rhebok (*Pelea capreolus*) has a similar appearance to a roe deer; the horns are short and straight, and the height at the shoulders is less than that at the rump. It is found in southern Africa, in bushy and rocky upland areas. It is still quite numerous. The waterbucks are similar in appearance but bigger. They are always found near water in such places as marshes, woodlands, and swamps. The horns are long and turned forwards, and are present only in the males. The species most attached to marshy environments are those of the genus *Kobus*. The common waterbuck (*K. ellipsiprymnus*, illustrated here), weighing 300 kg (660 lb), is found widely in Africa south of the Sahara, with some 13 sub-species. The coat is long and rough and is particularly long round the neck, sufficiently so as to form a mane. Sebaceous (fatty) glands lubricate the coat, rendering it impermeable to water and so suitable for a wet environment. The waterbucks are very territorial; the adult males defend their own territories against others, while the younger males live in herds of one sex while they await sexual maturity.

The kob (*K. kob*) is smaller than the common waterbuck, weighing only 120 kg (270 lb); the horns are more curved, the hair is shorter and there is no mane round the neck. There are many sub-species of kob, including the famous Ugandan kob (*K. kob thomasi*), which is well known for its characteristic social organization and mating behaviour patterns.

The complex social order of the kob was unravelled by Dr Hal Buechner, of the Smithsonian Institution in Washington, in the 1950s and 1960s. When the untrained observer looks across the African plains he sees scattered concentrations of kob, wandering and grazing apparently at will in a random pattern. But the herds are actually very highly organized. Each herd is enormous, and is divided into sub-herds that may still be a thousand strong. Here and there, on ridges or rises in the ground, are special places called arenas. Each arena is a generally close-cropped and trampled piece of ground, and it is always occupied by about ten to fifteen males. Each male kob has a small circular patch of ground called a territory. The possession of a territory is the key to mating success, for females will only join the harem of a male and breed with him if he occupies a territory. To capture a territory, the kob males carry out ritualized duels with each other; there is rarely any serious injury, though the bucks lower their heads and interlock their horns, tussling to and fro with forefeet wide apart. Superior males defend their territories while homeless bucks weave in and out of the arena, on the lookout for a vacant plot or an older, weaker buck that may be successfully challenged.

When a female enters the arena she chooses her male, and he approaches her stiffly and touches her quite firmly with the forefoot; this is common among antelopes and is called the 'love kick'. Mating follows, and afterwards he continues to show affection for her. Only males holding territories are selected by the greatest number of females, and so breed most successfully. Since the females are on heat at all times of the year, and the males must be ready to fight at all times for the possession of their territory, from time to time the males begin to feel the strain and leave the territory for a brief period of vacation and rest, during which time they join up with the herd of young and single males.

The lechwe (*K. leche*, illustrated here) is similar in size to the kob, with long, slender horns, long hair and hooves which can be widely splayed, to support the animal on marshy ground; they can even run and jump over this difficult terrain. They live in central southern Africa as far south as the Tropic of Capricorn. The Nile lechwe (*K. megaceros*, illustrated here), also called Maria Gray's antelope, lives in small areas in the Sudan and in the vicinity of the White Nile. Its horns are very long, curving and divergent; it lives in herds of about fifty individuals in semiaquatic environments.

The reedbucks of the genus *Redunca* live in open, lightly wooded country in much of Africa south of the Sahara. The bohor reedbuck (*R. redunca*, illustrated here) lives along river banks in small groups containing one female with her young and, occasionally, a female offspring up to a year old. The group may be defended by a neighbouring male. The mountain reedbuck (*R. fulvorufula*) is more gregarious and unites in quite large herds, while the common or southern reedbuck (*R. arundinum*) occupies a territory during the mating season.

Antilopinae. The Antilopinae are a sub-family distributed in Africa and Asia and divided into six groups of which the most important is that of the gazelles with two genera, *Gazella* and *Procapra*; both males and females of these genera possess horns. Their habitat is arid and semi-arid regions. The damas gazelle (*Gazella dama*, illustrated on page 315) lives in northern Africa including

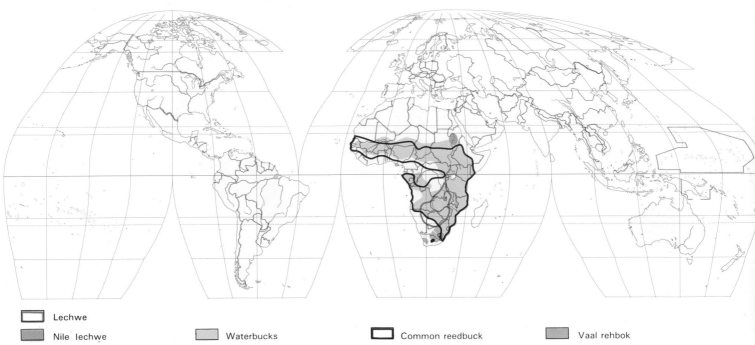

	Lechwe
	Nile lechwe		Waterbucks		Common reedbuck		Vaal rehbok

bohor reedbuck

common waterbuck

lechwe

Nile lechwe

parts of the Sahara, generally in small groups of a few dozen head, or sometimes alone. They feed on the sparse desert vegetation, do not need to drink.

Soemmering's gazelle (*G. soemmeringi*) is still common in Ethiopia. It lives in the savannahs and bushy hill country. As with Grant's gazelle (*G. granti*), mating takes place after a brief courtship and while the animals are on the move. Grant's gazelle lives in Ethiopia, Uganda, Kenya and Somalia; many sub-species are known, differing from each other by the colour of the coat and the shape of the horns. In the sub-species *granti* the horns have a characteristic lyre-shape, in *robertsi* their ends diverge widely, and in *rainey* they are parallel – but there is much individual variation and it may not be valid to distinguish these forms as separate sub-species. The habitat consists of grassy plains with low bushes, and also semi-deserts.

The mountain gazelle (*G. gazella*, illustrated here) was at one time distributed from Arabia to India but is now much reduced and survives only in limited areas where, fortunately, it is protected. Thomson's gazelle (*G. thomsoni*) lives in Kenya, Somalia, Sudan and Ethiopia. The smallest of the plains gazelles of East Africa, it stands less than a metre (3 ft 3 in) high at the shoulder, while the horns can reach 50 cm (20 in) in length. It is a gregarious animal; parties of females are collected by an adult male, while males over eight months old are expelled from these groups and form herds with other single males. Old males sometimes have their own territories where they live alone. In the dry season Thomson's gazelles migrate in herds of thousands, to areas with more water. At the beginning of the rainy season, however, they leave these before they become too wet, and return to their former haunts. These migrations sometimes involve distances of over 160 km (100 miles). Their principal enemies are the large carnivores such as lions, leopards and jackals, and in particular the spotted hyaena (*Crocuta crocuta*) and the cheetah (*Acinonyx jubatus*).

The dorcas gazelle (*G. dorcas*) has a widespread distribution from North Africa to south-west Asia, but has become very rare. The adult males are solitary while the young ones form herds of up to fifty individuals. Dorcas gazelles have a marked resistance to the harsh heat of the desert sun and lack of water. The slender-horned gazelle (*Gazella leptoceros*) is even better adapted to a desert life, but is even more seriously endangered. Spekes gazelle (*G. spekei*), living in a few areas of Somalia, is another species that

has become rarer. The same applies to the red-fronted gazelle (*G. rufifrons*) of the sub-Saharan belt from Senegambia to Ethiopia. An Asian species is the Persian gazelle (*G. subgutturosa*), which lives from Iran to Mongolia.

The genus *Procapra* is found in central Asia and comprises two species, the Tibetan gazelle (*P. picticaudata*) and the Mongolian gazelle (*P. gutturosa*, illustrated here). The two sexes remain separate during the major part of the year and only come together for mating and for the migration to winter quarters.

The blackbuck (*Antilope cervicapra*) is found widely in the grasslands of India, up to the foothills of the Himalayas. It has a slender body with large spiral horns (present only in the males) which can measure 75 cm (30 in) in length. It forms large herds, within which the dominant male stands out from the rest in having a black and white coat, instead of the normal brown. The genus contains only one species, as does the genus *Litocranius*, containing only the gerenuk (*L. walleri*, illustrated here). The name means 'giraffe-necked' in Somali. It feeds on the leaves of trees and tall bushes which it reaches by standing on its hind legs with its forelegs against the trunk, and reaching upwards with its long neck. It is found in Somalia, and the drier parts of Kenya and Ethiopia where it lives either alone or in small groups.

The dibatag (*Ammodorcas clarkei*, illustrated here) resembles the gerenuk, but is smaller. It lives in open bushy country in Somalia. Finally, two antelopes that are remarkably agile leapers are the springbok (*Antidorcas marsupialis*, illustrated here), the South African national emblem, that lives in the grasslands of south-western Africa, and the impala (*Aepyceros melampus*), typical of the savannahs and forest margins of south-eastern Africa. These extremely agile animals can leap 3 m (10 ft) high and 10 m (30 ft) in distance.

Saginae. The sub-family Saiginae contains two genera which occupy a halfway position between the gazelles and the goats. The Tibetan antelope (*Pantholops hodgsoni*, illustrated on p. 317) lives in Tibet between 4000 and 6000 m (13,000 and 19,000 ft) above sea level. It looks like a rather clumsy antelope; and nose bears a prolongation in the form of a proboscis, and the lyre-shaped horns may measure 70 cm (28 in). The saiga antelope (*Saiga tatarica*) is best known, and is also provided with a large inflated snout and proboscis. It was very common in earlier times and occupied a

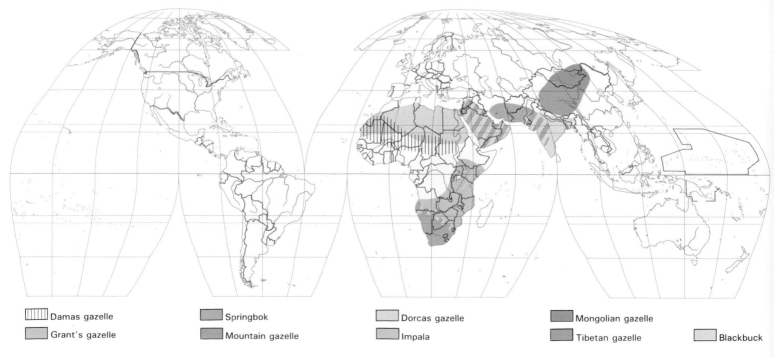

Damas gazelle	Springbok	Dorcas gazelle	Mongolian gazelle
Grant's gazelle	Mountain gazelle	Impala	Tibetan gazelle	Blackbuck

gerenuk

mountain gazelle

damas gazelle

dibatag

Mongolian gazelle

springbok

great area from Russia to Alaska; but became very rare due to overexploitation. It is now protected and is out of danger of becoming extinct. It lives in groups of a few dozen individuals, continually moving over the dry, cold grasslands.

Caprinae. The distribution of the sub-family Caprinae is widespread over the northern hemisphere. Apart from a few exceptions, the species are medium-sized. The smallest and most primitive is the goral (*Nemorhaedus goral*), which lives in the Himalayas at altitudes up to 4000 m (13,000 ft). The serow (*Capricornis sumatraensis*, illustrated here) and the Japanese serow (*C. crispus*), which are very shy, live in the moist, warm forests of the Far East, the former also on the large islands of South-East Asia. The Rocky Mountain goat (*Oreamnos americanus*) is found in western Canada and the north-west USA. Its coat is white the whole year round; the horns are small, sharp, straight and black. An extremely skilful climber, it lives mostly alone or in small groups and is active from twilight till dawn. The chamois (*Rupicapra rupicapra*) is the typical mountain ungulate of the Alps, Pyrenees, Apennines, Carpathians and the mountains of southeastern Europe and south-west Asia. Both sexes have pointed, vertical horns that hook backwards at the ends. They ascend to the snowline in summer but in the winter descend to forest areas, developing a darker coat for improved camouflage.

The takin (*Budorcas taxicolor*, illustrated here) resembles the gnu in appearance but is closely related to the musk-ox, and lives in the mountains of central Asia; it is a large animal weighing 350 kg (770 lb) and standing 130 cm (52 in) high at the shoulders. The heavy body is covered with dense fur and both sexes have large horns. The musk ox (*Ovibos moschatus*) is a massive animal of a similar height and weight, found in Alaska, northern Canada and Greenland. In the presence of a predator, the musk oxen form a hollow circle with the females and young at the centre and the males with their massive heads and horns facing outwards; their principal enemy, apart from man, is the wolf.

The most primitive of the Caprinae is the tahr of the Himalayas (*Hemitragus jemlahicus*, illustrated here), which, like the Nilgiri tahr (*H. hylocrius*, also illustrated here), of the Nilgiri Hills of southern India, and the Arabian tahr (*H. jayakari*) lives in small herds on steep, wooded slopes in mountainous districts. Tahr have been introduced to New Zealand.

The ibex (*Capra ibex*) is the best-known species of the genus *Capra*. The strong body is provided with enormous backward-curved horns, that can reach 130 cm (52 in) in length. They live in Europe, North Africa and Asia, in mountainous regions. The Walia ibex (*C. i. walie*, illustrated here) is one of the rarest of several sub-species. A similar species, the Spanish ibex (*C. pyrenaica*) lives in the Pyrenees; it is distinguished by the triangular section of its horns. Also of the genus *Capra* are the markhor (*C. falconeri*, illustrated here) of the Himalayas from Kashmir to Afghanistan and the Siberian and Nubian ibexes (*C. ibex sibirica* and *C. i. nubiana*). The Barbary sheep or aoudad (*Ammotragus lervia*, illustrated here) lives on the mountains of North Africa and has been introduced to the USA. It has large horns and the adult males have a long fringe of hair hanging from the throat and chest reaching nearly to the ground. It is also known as the maned sheep. The bharal (*Pseudois nayaur*, illustrated here) is also known as the blue sheep of the Himalayas.

The genus *Ovis* contains the wild and domestic sheep. The mouflon (*Ovis musimon*) of Sardinia and Corsica has been introduced into other regions of Europe with some success. The red sheep or urial (*O. orientalis*) is found from Asia Minor to the Himalayas. The argali (*O. ammon*) of the semi-deserts of Central Asia is the largest living sheep; the sub-species include Marco Polo's sheep (*O. a. polii*) of the Pamirs.

The bighorn or mountain sheep of North America live among the crags and cliffs of remote mountainous areas. There are two species, the Canadian bighorn (*O. canadensis*), which once ranged from Canada to northern Mexico but now survives only in small inaccessible or protected areas, and the Dall sheep or white bighorn (*O. dalli*) ranging from Alaska to British Columbia. Originally from the mountains of south-west Asia, domestic sheep and goats have long been important partners of man. They have been introduced to most regions and have been responsible for changes in habitat, notably the deforestation of the Mediterranean area and the maintenance of huge areas of grassland in Australia and New Zealand.

All domesticated sheep belong to the same species (*O. aries*). The Merino is a breed well known for its fine wool; it originated in Spain but is now distributed worldwide and played the central role in the rise of Australia to become the greatest wool-producing country in the world.

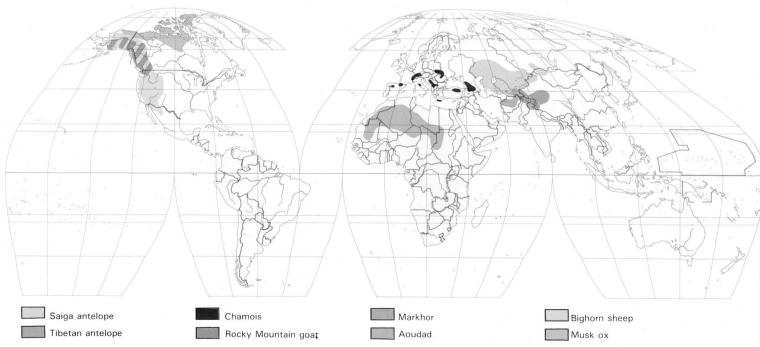

Saiga antelope	Chamois	Markhor	Bighorn sheep
Tibetan antelope	Rocky Mountain goat	Aoudad	Musk ox

walia ibex

takin

bharal

barbary sheep
(aoudad)

markhor

Tibetan
antelope

nilgiri tahr

Himalayan tahr

serow

Perissodactyla

The Perissodactyla, odd-toed ungulates, in which the axis of the foot passes through the middle digit, reach their maximum degree of specialization in the family Equidae, horses. In the horse only one toe of the original five remains, the third. This is developed into a large, blunt, solid hoof, supremely adapted for running. The hoof is strong and firm, yet light in weight, which reduces its momentum and therefore the energy required to move it to and fro when galloping.

Equidae

In the course of evolution the family Equidae has undergone profound modifications which are well known from the existence of numerous well preserved fossils. The earliest form, *Eohippus*, appeared in the Eocene period, fifty-four to thirty-eight million years ago. It was the size of a cat, with four toes on the forefeet and three on the hind feet. There followed the forms known as *Miohippus* and *Mesohippus*. The shape of the horse was more closely approached with the later appearance of *Merychippus* and *Pliohippus*, in which the side toes were much reduced.

The evolutionary process led to a form which was adapted to life on the great spaces of the grasslands, where it was necessary to have long legs and strong hooves for swift running, together with a slender but powerful body to give the necessary strength to the legs. The diet had to be of grass, so the teeth (previously suitable for eating leaves in the forest) had to be adapted for cropping the grass and chewing it. Good eyesight and hearing completed the animal's equipment. The first of the Equidae to possess these characteristics was *Hyracotherium*, which can justifiably be considered as the first founder of the family. In the evolutionary line there followed *Hipparion* and *Anchitherium*, and finally *Equus*. While *Equus* was perfected in Eurasia and Africa, the line became extinct in America. There are at present six living species of *Equus*, which can be grouped roughly as zebras, asses and horses.

The mountain zebra (*Equus zebra*) lives in the southern parts of Africa that are most harsh and arid. In 1913 the population of the typical mountain zebra *E. zebra zebra* consisted of only twenty-seven individuals. The cause of this dramatic fall in numbers was due to the transformation of their natural habitat into agricultural

land. As an attempt to save the sub-species, a park was set up in Cape Province; it contains at present 150 head of these animals. The quagga, a partially striped zebra, also from South Africa, became extinct, through being overhunted during the nineteenth century.

Other sub-species, as for instance *E. zebra hartmannae*, are a little more numerous. The common zebra (*E. burchelli*, illustrated here) is on the other hand fairly numerous, occupying an area which extends from East Africa south of Somalia to the south-west in Namibia. It forms large herds, often mixed in with antelope, ranging over savannah and open grassland. The zebra eat coarse grasses which the antelope cannot manage.

The largest zebra is Grévy's zebra (*E. grevvyi*), which reaches 300 to 400 kg (660 to 880 lb) in weight and a height of 150 cm (5 ft) at the shoulder; it lives in Sudan, Kenya, Eritrea and Somalia, with a population at most of 20,000 head; probably far fewer, but its habitat is inhospitable and surveys are difficult to undertake. Unlike the other two species, Grévy's zebra is highly territorial; the mares with young may form separate groups from the stallions, which are sometimes but not always solitary. The three species can be distinguished from each other by the different patterns of stripes.

The African asses belong to the species *Equus asinus*, with three sub-species, the Nubian (*africanus*), North African (*atlanticus*) and Somalian (*somalicus*). The North African sub-species is certainly extinct, and the other two are seriously endangered. They are of medium dimensions, of semi-desert areas reaching weights of 300 kg (660 lb); the colour is nearly always yellowish grey with a dark line along the back and, in the Somalian variety, zebra-stripes on the legs. The males are territorial and the areas they defend are immense.

The Asiatic asses belong to the species *Equus hemionus*, which is also in grave danger of extinction in the wild, though captive herds breed well. The original area extended from the Near East to Tibet and Mongolia, and northwards to a great part of Russia. Several sub-species are known to have existed in recent times, but some are now extinct, such as *anatoliensis*, of Anatolia, and others are on the verge of it, such as *hemippus* which may still exist in a few small areas of Syria or northern Arabia. Others survive in much reduced numbers, such as the onager (*E. h. onager*) of northern Iran and Turkmenistan, the kulan (*E. h. hemionus*) of Central

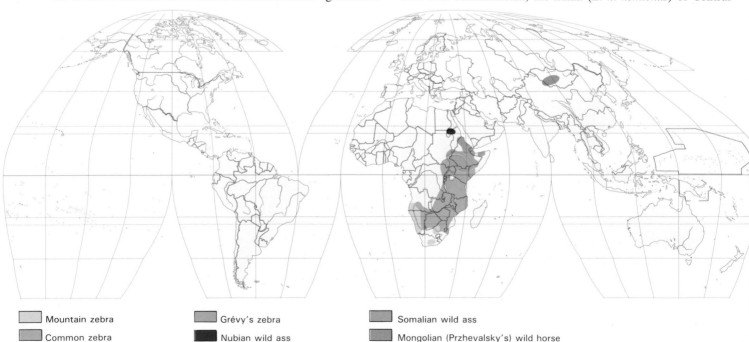

Mountain zebra

Common zebra

Grévy's zebra

Nubian wild ass

Somalian wild ass

Mongolian (Przhevalsky's) wild horse

Above A small herd of common zebra are joined by an oryx at a watering hole.
Right An adult Malayan tapir. This is the only species of tapir living in Asia; the other three species come from Central and South America. Despite this discontinuous distribution all four species are very similar.

Asia, the kiang (*E. h. kiang*) of Tibet and the ghorkhar or khur (*E. h. khur*) of India and Pakistan.

The horse, as we know it today, was descended from a wild horse whose nature cannot be exactly determined, and which once roamed the forests and grasslands of Europe. It probably resembled the tarpan, a wild horse which lived in southern Russia; it became extinct in the wild state in 1870, though some specimens lingered on in captivity until the twentieth century. Another of its close relatives was certainly the Mongolian wild horse (*Equus przewalskii*), which was discovered in 1879 by the Russian explorer N. M. Przhevalsky in western Mongolia. Specimens breed well in zoos – it is reddish-brown, with a short, stiff, erect mane, white muzzle and black mane and tail – but expeditions in recent years have failed to find any pure-bred specimens, and it may be that if any do still survive in the wild, they are diluted by inter-breeding with domestic horses running wild in the area. Typically they have a pale muzzle, a feature also seen in the wild Exmoor ponies of Britain.

The horse was one of the earliest domestic mammals, used over 6000 years ago for dragging tents and heavy equipment by the people of Central Asia. Riding horses only came later. No domestic horses were known in North America until Europeans brought them there in the sixteenth century.

Tapiridae

The most primitive family of the Perissodactyla is that of the Tapiridae, whose four species, all of the genus *Tapirus*, are looked on as authentic living fossils since thirty-five to forty million years ago their form was very similar to the present one. The forest habitat has determined the appearance of this animal, whose robust body is reminiscent of that of a wild boar; when confronted by danger the tapir dashes into the densest vegetation for conceal-ment or escape. The nose is prolonged forwards to form a proboscis, mobile and retractile, which is used both for smelling out and for grasping edible materials. The Malayan tapir (*Tapirus indicus*, illustrated here) of South-East Asia shares it ecological niche in the forest with the rhinoceros and the elephant. In America the family is represented by the Central American tapir (*T. bairdi*), 120 cm (48 in) high at the shoulders and weighing 400 kg (880 lb), which is found from Mexico to Central America; the mountain tapir (*T. roulini*), only half the weight of the former, which lives in the Andes between 2000 and 4000 m (6500 and 13,000 ft) above sea level; and the Brazilian tapir (*T. terrestris*), the most widely distributed, which lives in the Amazon basin and attains heights of 1 m (3 ft 3 in) at the shoulder and a weight of 250 kg (550 lb). The diet of the tapirs consists of leaves, shoots and small branches, and their ideal habitat is the very humid tropical forests. It likes to spend long periods immersed in water, and is an excellent swimmer. In moving about, the tapir always uses the same paths, and so produces well-marked routes, often tunnels, exactly matching its width, through the dense vegetation.

Rhinocerotidae

The last family of the Perissodactyla is that of the Rhinocerotidae, comprising animals of large dimensions characterized by the possession of either one or two horns on the muzzle. These are not true horns as in the Bovidae for there is no bony core, only a dense mass of compacted fibres. They are very heavy in appearance; the massive body is supported by sturdy legs, the feet having three toes; the head is very large with small eyes and large ears. The teeth are reduced, only three molars and three to four premolars remaining on each side of each jaw.

The Sumatran rhinoceros (*Dicerorhinus sumatrensis*, illustrated here) is also called the hairy rhinoceros and may be descended directly from the extinct woolly rhinoceros (*Rhinoceros ticho-rhinus*). Two horns are present on the muzzle, the first about 25 cm (10 in) long and the second, set further back, hardly noticeable. The weight is about 600 to 700 kg (1300 to 1500 lb) with a height at the shoulder of 1.5 m (5 ft). The Sumatran rhinoceros is probably still present in Borneo, Burma, Thailand, Sumatra and the Malay peninsula, but it is the only rhinoceros to live in deep forest and is difficult to observe.

Two Asiatic species belong to the genus *Rhinoceros*, both having a very thick skin with heavy folds on the neck, shoulders, flanks and thighs. It hangs loosely in large sections, almost like plates of armour. This appearance of metal covering is enhanced in the Indian species by numerous tubercles (round knob-like projections) in the skin that look like rivets. The Javan species has an irregular plate-like scaly pattern apparently embossed into the skin. The Indian rhinoceros (*R. unicornis*, illustrated here), with one horn, is inoffensive but extremely large, up to 2 m (6 ft 6 in) at the shoulder and weighs up to 2000 kg (2 tons). The species survives now in national parks and protected areas, the number of survivors being about 800. It spends most of its time in long grass and areas of marsh and swamp. It often wallows and remains in water for long periods. It is an excellent swimmer. It is a solitary animal and, like other ungulates, has its established tracks which may be its own or communal. The Javan rhinoceros (*R. sondaicus*), is smaller and is now very rare and probably close to extinction.

The best-known and most numerous of the African rhinoceroses is the black rhinoceros (*Diceros bicornis*), standing 1.5 m (5 ft) high at the shoulder and weighing up to 2000 kg (2 tons). It formerly ranged from Egypt to the Cape but it is now found mostly in Tanzania, Mozambique and South Africa, with small surviving populations in Somalia, Sudan, Chad and Uganda. It is probable however that its only secure future lies in game reserves and National Parks. The preferred habitat is open grassland, savannah, scrub forest or marsh, but it avoids dense forest and can adapt itself to life at altitudes of up to 2000 m (6500 ft). The muzzle bears two horns the first of which is about 50 cm (20 in) long and the second (rearward) one about 18 cm (7 in). The upper lip is long and prehensile, for browsing on the leaves and shoots of shrubs and bushes. It is much less dangerous than its reputation asserts, but is unpredictable and sufficiently large that even a half hearted charge can have serious consequences.

The giant of the family is the white rhinoceros (*Ceratotherium simum*, illustrated here). It measures 2 m (6 ft 6 in) tall at the shoulder and 4 m (13 ft) in length, and may weigh more than 3000 kg (3 tons). It is the largest land animal after the elephants. Apart from its size it differs from the black rhinoceros in having a more squared-off muzzle and lacks the proboscis. These are adaptations to grazing rather than browsing habits seen in the black rhinoceros. Two subspecies are known: *simum*, which at the time of its discovery was distributed south of the Zambezi and north of the Orange River, and *cottoni*, living in Zaires, the Central African Republic, Sudan and Uganda. Their habitat is thorny savannah, where they graze on grass, using the trees only for cover; water is necessary for both drinking and bathing. The mother stays with the young for at least three years; the young one, who by then weighs about 1000 kg (1 ton) then seeks for adolescent companions. Females who are not yet mothers may also join with others and with adolescent females to form groups of five or six individuals. The adult males remain solitary.

The white rhinoceros was first discovered in 1817 and seventy years later it was already getting quite rare as a result of hunting. All rhinoceros have in fact become much rarer due to hunting, despite the fact that their meat is too tough to be attractive. It is their horn that the hunters want. Powdered rhino horn is much in demand for traditional medicines owing to the erroneous belief that it is an aphrodisiac. In fact it is completely indigestible, but nevertheless can be sold for almost its own weight in gold. Lately there has been demand for horn to make fancy dagger handles. All trade is officially banned but poaching continues.

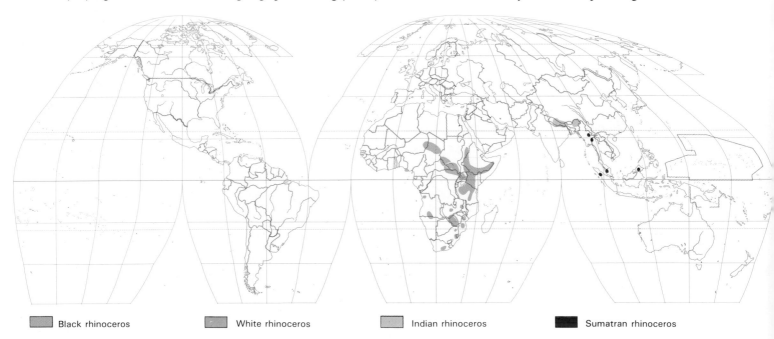

Black rhinoceros   White rhinoceros   Indian rhinoceros   Sumatran rhinoceros

Sumatran rhinoceros

Indian rhinoceros

black rhinoceros

white rhinoceros

Prosimii

The primates, to which man biologically belongs, are, according to most authorities, the most highly evolved order of all the mammals. Exactly why we regard the primates and relations as the most evolutionarily advanced order has never been clearly stated; some contemporary experts have suggested that it is simply because they resemble ourselves most closely. A more detached approach reveals that the primate plan, with its ancestral five-fingered limb and lack of any really notable adaptations, is in fact a fairly primitive body form. Mammals such as the Cetacea might perhaps be regarded as far more highly modified.

Primates are placental, plantigrade, five-fingered, and fundamentally adapted to an arboreal way of life. Their hands, and often also their feet are prehensile; the thumb is set opposite to the other fingers; the eyes are on the front of the face, looking forward, and the brain is remarkably well developed. They are divided into the sub-orders Prosimii (prosimians) and Anthropoidea (anthropoids).

The prosimians, which first appeared sixty million years ago, represent the most primitive group of the primates, and one which, like other groups of mammals, is evolved from the insectivores. The modification of the extremities and the transformation of the claws into flat nails made it possible for them to perfect their grasp and hence their ability to manoeuvre more actively in the trees. In this way the group conquered the arboreal environment and became its rulers for millions of years. As the fossil evidence shows, the prosimians were cosmopolitan, being absent only from Australia. Today their distribution is limited to Africa, Madagascar and South-East Asia. Their dimensions range from the 13 cm (5 in) of the microcebids or mouse lemurs of Madagascar to the 95 cm (38 in) of the indriids. They are primarily nocturnal and for this reason possess large eyes, capable of distinguishing minute variations in light intensity.

Tupaiidae

The Tupaiidae contain species whose appearance recalls that of squirrels, so much so that the natives of Malaysia call by the name of *tupai* both the true tupaiids and the various species of squirrels that live there. Creatures of small dimensions – they measure about 20 cm (8 in) – they have elongated muzzles, large eyes and ears, bodies covered with soft fur and fairly bushy tails. Another characteristic is the presence of claws on the fingers, which permit them to clamber about the trees like squirrels; they are also the only prosimians capable of perceiving colours. The teeth are similar to those of the insectivores; because of this and their appearance zoologists for long included them among the insectivores. Today, many zoologists believe that these animals are neither insectivores nor Primates and the group is classified as a separate order, the Scandentia. They are diurnal animals and may be either carnivorous, feeding primarily on insects, or herbivorous. They are distributed throughout southern and south-eastern Asia. The family is divided into two sub-families which can be recognized by the form of the tail.

Tupainae. The first sub-family is that of the Tupaiinae (tree-shrews), whose species are characterized by having a tail completely covered with thick fur. To this family belong the genera *Anathana*, *Urogale* and *Dendrogale*, which are found from Kampuchea to Borneo and Sumatra, and include the well-known common tree-shrew (*Tupaia glis*, illustrated on p. 325) which lives in Indo-China and southern China.

Ptilocercinae. The sub-family Ptilocercinae contains the single species *Ptilocercus lowii* (illustrated on p. 325), the pen-tailed tree-shrew of Borneo and Malaysia. The tail carries only a tuft of hair on the terminal part, the rest being covered with scales. Like the other tree-shrews, they are day-active, nest in tree hollows and feed on insects, fruit and some small animals.

Lemuridae

The families Lemuridae, Indriidae and Daubentoniidae contain the prosimians found only in Madagascar, including the lemurs. The Lemuridae are divided into Cheirogaleinae and Lemurinae.

Cheirogaleinae. The Cheirogaleinae – dwarf lemurs and mouse lemurs – are creatures of small dimensions and nocturnal habits, living primarily on insects. During the dry seasons, which coincide with the coolest periods, they become torpid, a process known as estivation which corresponds to the hibernation of animals living

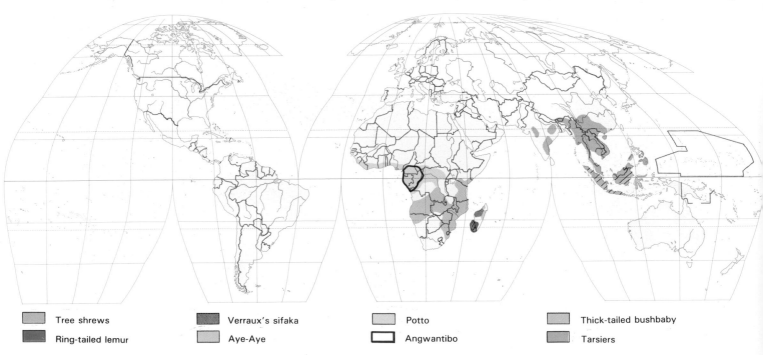

Tree shrews

Ring-tailed lemur

Verraux's sifaka

Aye-Aye

Potto

Angwantibo

Thick-tailed bushbaby

Tarsiers

weasel lemur

fork-marked
mouse lemur

Verraux's sifaka

ring-tailed
lemur

lesser mouse lemur

black lemur

aye-aye

in cold climates. The animal rolls itself into a ball and sleeps in a nest of grass or leaves, or in a tree hollow. It survives by using up the reserves of fat stored up in the hind legs and the tail. Six species are included in this sub-family, among which is the smallest of the primates, the lesser mouse lemur (*Microcebus murinus*, illustrated on p. 323), which is hardly 13 cm (5 in) in length. Other species are Coquerel's mouse lemur (*M. coquerli*), the fork marked mouse lemur (*Phaner furcifer*, illustrated on p. 323) and the two dwarf lemurs of the genus *Cheirogaleus*, the hairy-eared dwarf lemur, greater dwarf lemur and fat-tailed lemur.

Lemurinae. The proper lemurs, so called, are those of the sub-family Lemurinae. They attain 50 cm (20 in) in length and the tail may be longer than the body, up to 70 cm (28 in). They are closer in appearance to primates than the preceding species.

The weasel lemurs of the genus *Lepilemur* live a nocturnal life in the forests and feed exclusively on the foliage of particular plants. The have pointed and rather short muzzles; their bodies attain 30 cm (12 in) in length with a tail of similar length. The weasel lemur (*L. mustelinus*, illustrated on p. 323) and the sportive lemur (*L. ruficaudatus*) belong to this genus.

The true lemurs belong to the genus *Lemur*. There are six species: the ring-tailed lemur (*L. catta*, illustrated on p. 323), the ruffed lemur (*L. variegatus*), which is the largest species, the brown lemur (*L. fulvus*), the mongoose lemur (*L. mongoz*), the red-bellied lemur (*L. rubriventer*) and the black lemur (*L. macaco*, illustrated on p. 323) with its characteristic sexual dimorphism of the coat, black in the males and reddish-brown in the females. Active during the day, those prosiminians can best be observed in the morning while, sitting with arms outstretched, they are intent on warming themselves in the first rays of the sun. The ring-tailed lemur, with its striking tail ringed with black and white, is unlike the other lemurs in not being arboreal, but lives in the south of Madagascar in rocky areas where there are no trees. It feeds largely on fruit, but also eats insects and birds' eggs. Although they belong to the most primitive primates, the ring-tailed lemurs live in fairly large groups and show a considerable degree of social organization.

The two species of the genus *Hapalemur* live on the flatlands of Madagascar: the grey gentle lemur (*H. griseus*) in the forests and plantations of the west coast, and the broad-nosed gentle lemur (*H. simus*) in the marshy zones of the east coast.

Indriidae

The second family of the Lemurs is that of the Indriidae. It is made up of four species, all having a vegetarian diet. The sifakas – Verreaux's sifaka (*Propithecus verreauxi*, illustrated on p. 323) and the diadema sifaka (*P. diadema*) – are about 1 m (3 ft) long, of which about half is tail, with a small head and large eyes. A characteristic feature is the presence of patagium, a membrane which connects the forelimbs to the base of the neck and the trunk, and permits a gliding flight from one branch to another. The coloration of the coat varies according to the surroundigs in which the animal lives: dark in sifakas of the hot humid zone, light in those of drier and cooler localities.

The largest living prosimian belongs to this family. It is the indri (*Indri indri*), which measures 95 cm (38 in) including the short tail, 5 cm (2 in) long. These animals live in couples or in small groups in the forests, where in recent times they have become rare due to loss of habitat. It is difficult to observe them, but easy to hear their typical chorus at dawn and sunset. The fourth species of the family is the avahi or woolly indri (*Avahi laniger*). It has enormous eyes

and very fat big toes and thumbs. This species has also become very rare, and little is known of its habits. It is greyish-brown and about 35 cm (14 in) long, with a slightly longer, furry tail.

Daubentoniidae

The only member of the Daubentoniidae is the Aye-aye (*Daubentonia madagascariensis*, illustrated on p. 323). It is one of the rarest of all mammals. It has large eyes with yellow-orange irises, which confirm its nocturnal habits, and reaches 1 m (3 ft) in length, of which more than half is the tail. Its principal diet is wood-boring beetles and their larvae, which it discovers by tapping the wood with its long fingers and listening with its acute sense of hearing to the faint sounds produced. It then tears open the wood with its sharp incisors, or digs the insects out with the long, strong claw of its middle finger, which is even longer than the others. Unlike other primates the aye-aye has two big incisor teeth in each jaw.

Lorisidae

The Lorisidae, lorises and bushbabies, are both arboreal and nocturnal. The lorises are slow-moving creatures living in the tropical forests of Asia and Africa. Equipped with prehensile hands and feet, they have flat nails on all the fingers except the second toe of the hind foot which is provided with a long claw, used for cleaning the fur in the complicated cleaning ritual it engages in when it wakes at sundown. The slender loris (*Loris tardigradus*, illustrated here) and the slow lorises of the genus *Nycticebus* (*N. coucang* and *N. pygmaeus*) live in the forests of southern Asia. The two African species are the angwantibo (*Arctocebus calabarensis*), found only in the Camerouns area and very rare, and the potto (*Perodicticus potto*, illustrated here), widely distributed in the forest belt of west, central and east Africa.

The galagos, or bushbabies, live in the African forests south of the Sahara. Unlike the lorises and pottos they are swift-moving and make spectacular leaps from branch to branch. They are nocturnal and mostly insectivorous and, like the lorises, regularly urinate on their hands and feet, either to improve their grip or to mark out their territories. They have enormous eyes outlined in black. There are six species; the lesser bushbaby (*Galago senegalensis*, illustrated here) is extremely active and lively. The thick-tailed bushbaby (*G. crassicaudatus*) solitary and rather aggressive, is the largest species, about 70 cm (28 in) long including the tail. The smallest species is Demidoff's dwarf bushbaby (*G. demidovi*), 14 cm (5½ in) long with 18 cm (7 in) of tail. Others are Allen's bushbaby (*G. alleni*), and the two needle-clawed bushbabies of the genus *Euoticus*, *E. elegantulus* and *E. inustus*.

Tarsiidae

The last family of the prosimians is that of the tarsiers (Tarsiidae). Very small (9 to 16 cm – 3.5 to 6 in – long) nocturnal primates, with a globular skull, enormous eyes and batlike ears constantly in motion, they are found on several islands of South-East Asia, including the Philippines, Sulawesi, Borneo and Sumatra. The fingers and toes end in disc-like adhesive pads that enable them to adhere to the surfaces of vertical treetrunks. Swifter at jumping than even the bushbabies, they live in dense jungles where they feed on insects and small animals. The spectral tarsier (*Tarsius spectrum*) of Sulawesi is the best known; other species are the western tarsier (*T. bancanus*, illustrated here) of Sumatra and Borneo, and the Philippine tarsier (*T. syrichta*).

pen-tailed
tree-shrew

potto

ender loris

lesser
bushbaby

western tarsier

common tree-shrew

Anthropoidea

The anthropoids are the second sub-order of primates and comprise the monkeys, apes and man. It is sometimes divided into the New World anthropoids, platyrrhines, and those of the Old World, catarrhines, both of whom may have been derived from the Omomyidae, an extinct family of prosimians of primitive characteristics, similar to the tree-shrews. Characteristics common to all the anthropoids are: a rounded skull, eyes facing forwards, complex ears of medium dimensions. The muzzle is generally lacking in hair, with a proper nose. Not only is the face smooth, but often the buttocks are too and also the areas near the external sexual organs. They possess twenty-eight to thirty-six teeth, and the canines may be transformed into tusks used for defensive purposes. Except for the hominids, the anthropoids have prehensile hands and feet, with the thumb and the big toe opposable to the other digits. In some New World species the tail is also prehensile.

In the anthropoids there is continuous development of the brain, which becomes progressively more complicated, and an enlargement of its surface due to the increasing number of cerebral convolutions – wrinkles in the cerebrum increasing the amount of 'grey matter' that forms a layer over the rest of the brain and is associated with intelligence and mental ability. While the eyesight becomes more efficient, thanks to the frontal position of the eyes that permits binocular vision and to the perception of colours, the sense of smell has become less important and has led to the relative reduction of the area of the brain that governs it.

The development of face muscles permits the monkeys to communicate with each other by a series of facial expressions so subtle as to constitute a form of language. They are also capable of emitting a range of highly variable sounds produced by the larynx and modulated by the vocal chords.

Cebidae

The monkeys of the family Cebidae, together with those of the family Callithricidae (marmosets and tamarins), comprise all the monkeys of the New World. Members of these two families are often grouped together and called 'platyrrhine' monkeys; the name derives from the presence of nostrils set wide apart on the face and opening forwards. The Cebidae live primarily in South America. The family is divided into five sub-families plus one aberrant species, Goeldi's monkey, whose classification is disputed.

Aotinae. The douroucouli (*Aotus trivirgatus*, illustrated here), also called the owl monkey, is the typical species of the Aotinae and is the only true monkey that is active at night. It lives in the forests of Central and South America, where it catches insects and birds. It also eats fruit and leaves. It sleeps in trees by day and is very loud-voiced. The other species of Aotinae are all called titi monkeys, of the genus *Callicebus*. They include the collared titi (*C. torquatus*, illustrated here), so called from its characteristic white collar, the dusky titi (*C. moloch*) and the masked titi (*C. personatus*). They can reach a metre (3 ft) in length of which half is tail. Their faces have beards and folds resembling side-whiskers that stand out from the rest of the face because of their different colour. They rarely leave the tree-tops.

Pitheciinae. The Pitheciinae – uakaris and sakis – also live in South American forests and usually move about in small family groups. The uakaris live in the tops of high trees. Their bodies are covered with very long chestnut-coloured hair, which protects them from the frequent rains which are characteristic of the area where they live, in eastern Peru and western Brazil. The head is hairless, and the face is bright scarlet; unlike all the other New World monkeys, they have a short tail, useless in balancing. Their diet consists of fruit, nuts and leaves. The species include the red uakari (*Cacajao rubicundus*), bald uakari (*C. calvus*) and black-headed uakari (*C. melanocephalus*). The sakis live along the river banks and the borders between forest and savannah, in the Guianas and the Amazon basin. They feed mostly on berries but also on fruit, leaves, birds, bats and mice. Their foreheads and shoulders are covered with long hair, otherwise they are shorter-haired than the uakaris. The species include the monk saki (*Pithecia monachus*), the white-faced saki (*P. pithecia*), the black-bearded saki (*Chiropotes satanas*) and the white-nosed saki (*C. albinasus*).

Cebinae. The Cebinae contain two genera, *Cebus* (the capuchin monkeys) and *Saimiri* (the squirrel monkeys). The squirrel monkeys are of small dimensions, as befits species that are highly adapted to an arboreal environment, measuring 25 to 40 cm (10 to

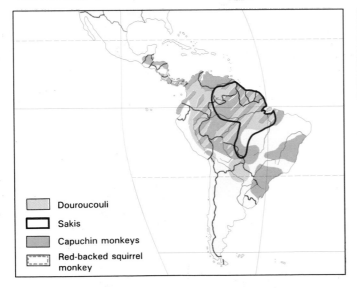

Douroucouli

Sakis

Capuchin monkeys

Red-backed squirrel monkey

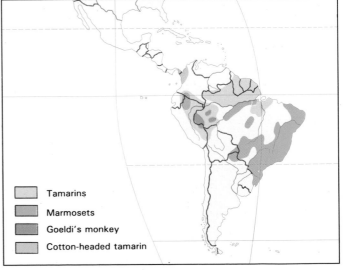

Tamarins

Marmosets

Goeldi's monkey

Cotton-headed tamarin

douroucouli

collared titi

brown capuchin

red-backed
squirrel monkey

common
woolly monkey

black spider monkey

rufous-handed
howler

16 in) long with non-prehensile tails about 40 cm (16 in) long. They are the commonest primates of the riverside forests of the southern parts of Central America, the Guianas and the Amazon basin. Their diet is omnivorous; climbing and jumping from one branch to another with the agility of squirrels, they search for fruit and berries, and also for insects, small vertebrates (among which they prefer tree-frogs), eggs and birds. A characteristic of the squirrel monkeys is the notable dimensions of the brain, which, despite the smaller number of cerebral convolutions, is the largest among the primates in relation to body size. Along with the great development of the brain there is an increasing complex social behaviour. They live in large groups containing upwards of 500 individuals. At the same time they are inquisitive, noisy and quarrelsome, contending among themselves for the warmer central positions in the troop at night. The species include the common squirrel monkey (*Saimiri sciureus*) and the red-backed squirrel monkey (*S. oerstedi*, illustrated on p. 327).

The capuchin monkeys comprise the white-throated capuchin (*Cebus capucinus*), pale-fronted capuchin (*C. albifrons*), weeper capuchin (*C. nigrivittatus*) and brown capuchin (*C. apella*, illustrated on p. 327). Their name arises from the tuft of hair on the head, supposed to resemble a monk's hood. They have many characteristics in common with the squirrel monkeys, but in addition they are provided with a partially prehensile tail. They also have a large brain relative to the size of the body, and are perhaps the most intelligent of the platyrrhines. Like the squirrel monkeys, they habitually urinate on the palms of the hands and the soles of the feet. Living as they do in large groups, it is probable that the traces of their odour serve to mark out the routes they have taken, and facilitate their recognition by other members of the group. They have a very extended range, from the warm humid forest of Honduras in the north along the slopes of the Andes to Argentina in the south.

Alouattinae. Ther Alouattinae (howler monkeys) are the first of the monkey to possess a really prehensile tail. They are good climbers and rarely perform long leaps but run steadily through the trees. They mostly eat fruit, leaves and young shoots, and will sometimes let go of the branches with all four limbs and swing supported by their long tails to reach some particular item of food. They have very loud voices, the sound produced being amplified by the enlargement of the hyoid bone – the bone at the base of the tongue – into a kind of box, their lower jaws and throats being enlarged to contain it. Sometimes it is only the dominant male who howls, with the aim of indicating the extent of his territory and defying would-be intruders, but the howl may be taken up not only by his fellow-males but by those of neighbouring troops, when the chorus may be continued for some hours. The howler monkeys live in various parts of Central and tropical South America. The Guatemalan howler (*Alouatta villosa*) lives from Central America to Colombia and Ecuador; the mantled howler (*A. palliata*) has a more limited area. Other species are the red howler (*A. seniculus*), the rufous-handed howler (*A. fusca*) and the black howler (*A. caraya*), this last having a more southerly distribution, as far as Argentina.

Atelinae. The Atelinae are the last subfamily of the Cebidae. A characteristic of the group is the prehensile tail, which is used in gathering food as well as in climbing. The woolly monkeys of the genus *Lagothrix* are so called from their thick, short, woolly fur. They live in small family groups and feed on fruit, leaves and nuts. The commonest woolly monkey (*L. lagothrica*, illustrated on p.

327) lives in the warm, humid forests of the Amazon basin. The spider monkeys that form the rest of the Atelinae are so called from the agility with which they move about in the trees and from their long, thin limbs. The woolly spider monkey (*Brachyteles arachnoides*) of the south-eastern forests of Brazil is now rare. The other species belong to the genus *Ateles* and are the Central American black-handed spider monkey (*A. geoffroyi*), the black spider monkey (*A. paniscus*, illustrated on p. 327) of the Amazon basin, the brown-headed spider monkey (*A. fusciceps*) and the long-haired spider monkey (*A. belzebuth*).

Goeldi's monkey (*Callimico goeldii*) was discovered in the forests of the upper Amazon only in 1904. It is a small, long-tailed monkey that represents an intermediate stage between the Cebidae and the Callithricidae. It is the only species of the genus.

Callithricidae

The other family of the platyrrhines is that of the Callithricidae, the marmosets and tamarins. They are small monkeys, often with vivid colouring, active during the day; tree-dwellers, they live in small groups, are quick-moving, with claws on all the digits except the big toes, which help them in scampering along the branches in a squirrel-like fashion. They are mostly located in the Amazon region. They fall into two groups, the marmosets with short lower canines and the tamarins with longer lower canines or tusks. They have shrill, twittering voices and live on insects, fruit, berries, shoots and small birds.

The marmosets of the genus *Callithrix* include the common marmoset (*C. jacchus*, illustrated here) notable for the white plumes on either side of its head. The pygmy marmoset (*Cebuuella pygmaea*, illustrated here), is the smallest of all living monkeys, with a body length of only 10 cm (4 in), the tail being about the same length. It has been found in areas far distant from the usual range of these creatures and it may be that its secretive nature has concealed a much wider distribution than was suspected. Species of the genus *Leontideus*, who owe their Latin name to the possession of thick, lion-like manes, form a halfway stage between the marmosets and tamarins. They include the golden lion marmoset (*Leontideus rosalia*), which is a bright golden-yellow in colour, the golden-headed tamarin (*L. chrysomelas*) and the golden-rumped tamarin (*L. chrysopygus*). The true tamarins are of the genus *Saguinus*, including the red-handed tamarin (*S. midas*) and the white tamarin (*S. melanoleucus*, illustrated here), all occurring round about the mouth of the Amazon. The emperor tamarin (*S. imperator*, illustrated here) is one of the species that have notable moustaches; the bare-faced tamarin (*S. bicolor*) has a hairless nose and ears like those of a bat. The cotton-headed tamarin (*O. oedipus*, illustrated here), with its characteristic shock of white hair, is sometimes called the nightingale monkey from its extraordinary voice. It comes from Colombia and Panama. The white-footed tamarin (*O. leucopus*) is a native of northern Colombia.

Cercopithecidae

The catarrhines, with the two super-families Cercopithecoidea and Hominoidea, comprise all the monkeys and apes of the Old World and also man. The name 'catarrhine' derives from the presence of nostrils turned downwards and separated by a narrow nasal septum; in these respects they differ from the platyrrhines. Like man, they are equipped with broad ear-laps, a long auditory duct and thirty-two teeth. The tail may or may not be present, but

emperor tamarin

cotton-headed tamarin

white tamarin

pygmy marmoset

common marmoset

usually it is not prehensile; the digits of the hands and feet are provided with flat nails. The Cercopithecoidea, divided into the two families of Cercopithecidae and Colobidae, are monkeys of dimensions varying from 30 to 110 cm (12 to 44 in) and weights from a few kilograms to 50 kg (110 lb) in the species of the genus *Mandrillus*. They nearly always give birth to a single offspring after a period of gestation of between 165 and 240 days. They live mostly in groups, and generally have a fairly high degree of social organization.

The various species of macaque belong to the family Cercopithecidae and are included in the genus *Macaca*. Among them is the Barbary ape (*M. sylvana*), the only macaque to be found outside Asia. It lives in the forests of north-west Africa. There is a small colony living wild on the Rock of Gibraltar (the only non-human primate in Europe), but this is probably descended from ancestors brought by man from Africa rather than the relic of a European population. They are large and tail-less with a dense coat. The Japanese macaque (*M. fuscata*), which is almost tail-less, has aroused scientific interest by its ability to develop patterns of behaviour of different kinds in different groups. Another well-known macaque is the rhesus macaque (*M. mulatta*), in which the rhesus blood factor or Rh-factor was discovered, and whose presence or absence is important in human blood transfusion and in certain diseases. It is used extensively in research; in the wild it lives from Afghanistan over most of southern Asia. Closely related species are the Assamese macaque (*M. assamensis*) and the Taiwan macaque (*M. cyclopis*). The lion-tailed macaque (*M. silenus*, illustrated here) lives in dense forests in the mountains of south-west India, and is distinguished by the stiff ruff of hair surrounding its face. The pig-tailed macaque (*M. nemestrina*, illustrated here) is found in South-East Asia and the islands of Sumatra and Borneo, and is often trained to go up palm trees and pick coconuts for its owner. The crab-eating macaque (*M. irus*, illustrated here) lives in forest regions near rivers and seacoasts in Malaysia, Sumatra, Java, Borneo and the Philippines. The moor macaque (*M. maura*) lives on the island of Sulawesi, as does the

A yellow baboon cradles its young. This species is widely distributed in Africa, ranging from Angola to Tanzania and Mozambique.

black ape (*Cynopithecus niger*, illustrated here), a tail-less or almost tail-less species with some affinities with the African baboons, though it spends much of its time in the trees.

Another genus is *Papio*, the African baboons and the hamadryad baboon of Ethiopia and south-west Arabia. They are larger than the macaques, provided with robust limbs and powerful teeth, with canines which grow to forbidding fangs in the males. They live in rocky areas, or in savannah country or lightly wooded country, but rarely in dense forest. Their social life is fairly well organized. The communities of African baboons, besides females and young, include adult male, every one of which occupies a precise place in the hierarchical order, but the hamadryas baboons form groups which are more of the harem type. One of the largest of the African species is the black-faced, dark-furred chacma baboon (*P. ursinus*), found in southern Zimbabwe and South Africa, while the most widespread species is the yellow baboon (*P. cynocephalus*, illustrated here) found further north in East Africa. The olive or anubis baboon (*P. anubis*, illustrated here) lives in the savannah country between Lake Chad and Ethipia, while the Guinea baboon (*P. papio*), the smallest species, lives in the western part of the savannah country south of the Sahara. The sacred or hamadryas baboon (*P. hamadryas*, illustrated here) is the most imposing, with a large mane or cape of hair surrounding the shoulders; it lives in eastern Sudan, Ethiopia and south-western Arabia. The baboons live on stems and roots, and insects and honey.

The strangest of all the monkeys in appearance are perhaps those of the genus *Mandrillus*, the mandrill (*M. sphinx*) and the drill (*M. leucophaeus*, illustrated here). They live in the Camerouns, the mandrills in the south and the drills in the north. Though they are forest-dwellers they spend most of their lives on the ground, feeding on plants and insects which they find beneath bark and under stones. They live in fairly small groups. The mandrill has a highly coloured face; the drills are smaller and their faces are black. The gelada baboon (*Theropithecus gelada*, illustrated here) lives on the hillsides in Ethiopia, at altitudes of up to 2400 m (8000 ft) above sea level.

Species of the genera *Cercocebus* (mangabeys) and *Cercopithecus* (gueonons) are mostly arboreal. The mangabeys, with slender bodies and long tails, live in the forests of West Africa. Four species are known: the white-cheeked mangebey (*Cercocebus albigena*), the sooty mangabey (*C. torquatus*), the black mangabey (*C. atterrimus*, illustrated on p. 333) and the agile mangabey (*C. galeritus*). There are at least ten species and numerous sub-species of the guenons, the classification being based mainly on the colour of the coat; they are in fact the most variably colourd of any of the Old World monkeys. They are widely distributed, living in both savannah and forest countries south of the Sahara. The most widely distributed species is the grass monkey (*Cercopithecus aethiops*), which is one of the commonest of African primates, living from Sierra Leone across to the Red Sea and down to the Cape. It lives on plants, insects and lizards. Among other species are the diana monkey (*C. diana*) of the rain forests of West Africa, known for its variegated colouring, de Brazza's monkey (*C. neglectus*), of the Congo basin, Uganda and Kenya, and the white-nosed monkey (*C. petaurista*) of the West African forests. All these last four species are illustrated on p. 333. The mona monkey (*C. mona*) is found from Guinea to the Congo basin, and the moustached monkey (*C. cephus*) near watercourses in the forests from the Camerouns to the Congo.

Another genus of the Cercopithecidae is *Erythrocebus*, with one species, the Patas monkey (*E. patas*, illustrated on p. 333). It is a ground-dweller, inhabiting the stretch of dry grassland and semi-

pig-tailed macaque

crab-eating macaque

drill

sacred or
baboon
hamadryas

olive or anubis
baboon

black ape

lion-tailed macaque

gelada baboon

desert south of the Sahara and north of the tropical rain-forests. Patas monkeys are swift runners and live in small, silent, rather orderly bands.

Colobidae

The Colobidae, langurs and colobus monkeys, are mostly vegetarian, as is evidenced by the volume of their stomach, which is three times as great as that of the other monkeys'. There are six genera, of which five are Asian and one African. The species of the genus *Presbytis* are found in southern Asia. They include the entellus langur (*P. entellus*, illustrated on p. 335), the sacred monkey or Hanuman langur of India, which roams at will, helping itself to crops and the stocks of merchants; the purple-faced langur (*P. senex*, illustrated on p. 335) of Sri Lanka; and John's langur (*P. johni*) of the Nilgiris. All these have many sub-species. Others are the silvered leaf monkey (*P. cristatus*) of South-East Asia, Sumatra, Java and Borneo and the white-fronted leaf moneky, *P. frontata*, of Borneo.

The genus *Pygathrix* contains the douc langur (P. nemaeus, illustrated on p. 335), of the forests of Vietnam. It differs from the other Colobidae in having arms and legs of equal length, whereas in the other species the hind legs are longer than the forelegs.

The other Asiatic members of the Colobidae are three genera of monkeys characterized by their unusual noses. Those of the genus *Rhinopithecus*, with upturned noses, live in mountainous regions: the snub-nosed monkey (*R. roxellanae*, illustrated on p. 335), with long golden hair and a blue face, lives from South China to Burma, *R. brelichi* in south-western China, and the Tonkin snub-nosed monkey (*R. avunculus*) in Vietnam. The snub-nosed monkey has one of the most northerly distributions of all monkeys, and in a large part of its range there is now snow cover virtually all year long. A nose of most singular appearance is characteristic of the proboscis monkey (*Nasalis larvatus*, illustrated on p. 335) of Borneo; the adult males have a drooping nose that may be 10 cm (4 in) long, while in the females and the young the nose is much smaller and is turned upwards. The pig-tailed langur (*N. concolor*) is another snub-nosed, macaque-like monkey found in three islands of the Mentawi group west of Sumatra.

The only African genus of the Colobidae is *Colobus*, the colobus monkeys or guerezas. It appears that they originated in Asia and

only appeared in Africa during the Upper Tertiary period (about sixty-five million years ago). The name *Colobus*, which means mutilated, has been attributed to early zoologists who believed that the much reduced – or, in some species, completely absent – thumb was due to a mutilation. They are found in equatorial African forests: the green colobus (*C. verus*) in West Africa, the red colobus (*C. badius*, illustrated on p. 335) in West Africa and the Congo basin, and the black-and-white colobuses, northern (*C. abyssinicus*, illustrated on p. 335) and southern (*C. polykomos*) in a broad area from the Cameroons in the west to Ethopia in the east.

Hylobatidae

The second super-family of the catarrhines, that of the Hominoidea, contains three families: the tail-less monkeys of the Hylobatidae (gibbons), Pongidae (great apes) and Hominidae (man). They are known broadly as the anthropoid apes.

The smallest forms of the Hominoidea are the gibbons of the family Hylobatidae. They lead an arboreal life, swinging from one branch to another with great agility, suspended by their long, strong arms. They live in family groups usually consisting of a male and a female and their young, and defend their own territories with aggressive attitudes, powerful cries, and violence if necessary. There are two genera, one (*Symphalangus*) containing only the siamang (*S. syndactylus*, illustrated on p. 336), the largest of the gibbon group, standing about 90cm (36 in) high and weighing more than 20 kg (44 lb). It has very long arms which at full stretch, from one set of fingers to the other, may measure 180 cm (76 in). It has a typical vocal sac below the throat that is inflated just before it starts calling. It is found in the Malay peninsula and in Sumatra, where it inhabits forests up to altitudes exceeding 1500 m (5000 ft).

The other gibbons, of the genus *Hylobates*, are smaller, lack the vocal sac and on the ground walk more or less erect, with the arms held upwards above the head. They are found in South-East Asia and in the islands of the Sunda group from Sumatra to Timor. The species include the black gibbon (*H. concolor*) of South-East Asia, which has a tuft on the head of the males, the females possessing two smaller tufts, one on each side of the head; the males are the only ones of the genus to possess a vocal sac. Other species are the hoolock gibbon (*H. hoolock*), characterized by a white stripe on the forehead and a very long, thick coat that hides the rough

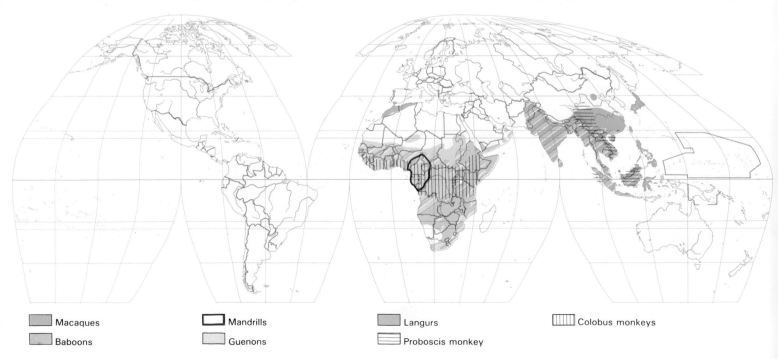

Macaques Mandrills Langurs Colobus monkeys

Baboons Guenons Proboscis monkey

black mangabey

white-nosed monkey

Patas monkey

Diana monkey

grass monkey

de Brazza's monkey

patches of skin – the ischial callosities – on their hindquarters; and the lar or white-handed gibbon (*H. lar*, illustrated on p. 336), with a coat of varying colours and a smooth, black face surrounded by a white beard. The different colour forms are sometimes regarded as separate species.

Pongidae

The Pongidae comprise the orang-utan, the gorilla and the two species of chimpanzees.

The orang-utan (*Pongo pygmaeus*, illustrated on p. 336) is the only one of the great apes to be found outside Africa, living exclusively in the low-lying forests of Borneo and Sumatra. It is a large animal which, if were to stand erect, would be 1.4 m (4½ ft) tall. Its arms may stretch to a span of over 2 m (6½ ft). The body is covered with long, shaggy, reddish-born hair. Orang-utans are normally placid, slow-moving animals and move through the forest in small groups searching for the fruit – particularly the durian – which is their principal food. At nightfall each animal builds its own sleeping platform of twigs in the forth of a tree. It is an endangered species, through hunting and the destruction of its habitat.

The chimpanzees and gorillas are nearer to man. Among the characteristics they have in common are the long period of gestation and the long dependence of the young on the parents, with its consequent advantage of a greater possibility of learning behavioural traits from the adults.

The gorilla (*Gorilla gorilla*, illustrated on p. 336), the largest of all the primates, has two sub-species: the lowland gorilla (*G. g. gorilla*) of the western regions of equatorial Africa, to the north and west of the river Congo, and the eastern or mountain gorilla (*G. g. beringei*) of the mountains in the region of Lake Kivu, on the borders of Rwanda and Zaire. It lives in groups composed of females, the young of both sexes and young adult males, led by an older adult male. It is primarily a ground-dweller and walks on all four limbs, supporting part of its weight on the knuckles of the hands. The diet consists of leaves, stalks roots and young shoots. At dusk each gorilla builds a sleeping nest of branches either in the fork of a tree or on the ground.

The chimpanzees are undoubtedly the nearest of the anthropoids to man in many respects, including their remarkable intelligence, their behaviour patterns and their ability to use tools. In this last regard they show a particular ability, using sticks both for offence and defence; smaller sticks, after being moistened with saliva, are pushed into termites' nests and withdrawn, in order to eat the termites adhering to them; banana skins are used to clean the fur and also to clean wounds; leaves are used to collect rainwater for drinking. In captivity chimpanzees show an ability to draw and to paint abstract pictures. They are, however, unable to concentrate on these tasks for any length of time, and their attention soon wanders.

They are found in central Africa, in the western regions up to the great lakes of the Rift Valley. They live in various environments from the humid forests to savannah country. There are two species, the common chimpanzee (*Pan troglodytes*) and the pygmy chimpanzee or bonobo (Pan paniscus), which is smaller and black faced, and lives south of the Congo river. Both species are illustrated on p. 336).

Hominidae

The last family of the Hominoidea is that of the Hominidae, who developed from a primitive stock of ape-men existing towards the end of the Miocene epoch or during the Pliocene epoch, up to twelve million years ago. The path of human evolution has always been, and still is, the subject of much controversy. Currently it is generally agreed that our own evolutionary line diverged from that of the gorillas and chimpanzees about fourteen to eight million years ago, as shown by fossil remains of the extinct ape *Ramapithecus*. About five to one-and-a-half million years ago lived the first of the hominids (*Australopithecus* genus). They walked upright and possibly used tools. The first members of our genus (*Homo*) appeared two to one million years ago in East Africa and are called *H. habilis* ('handy man') from their extensive use of stone tools; fossils show that their brain size in relation to body size was close to that of modern man.

Another species (*H. erectus*) appeared over one million years ago with the most recent remains being dated at a few hundred thousand years. However for technical reasons it is not considered as our direct ancestor but, like the 'cave man' of Neanderthal (100,000 to 40,000 years ago), as an evolutionary side line that became extinct. Today the sole representative of the family *Hominidae* is man (*H. sapiens*), worldwide in distribution.

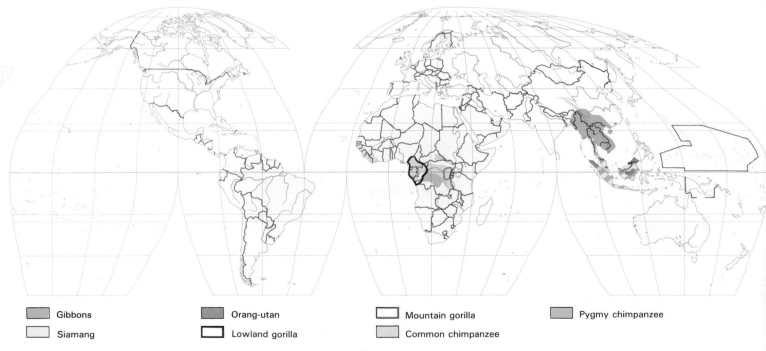

	Gibbons		Orang-utan		Mountain gorilla		Pygmy chimpanzee
	Siamang		Lowland gorilla		Common chimpanzee		

snub-nosed monkey

red colobus

entellus langur

northern black-and-white colobus

proboscis monkey

purple-faced langur

douc langur

lar (white-handed gibbon)

pygmy chimpanzee

common chimpanzee

orang-utan

siamang

gorilla

INDEX

Figures in italics indicate illustrations; (m) indicates a distribution map.